I0819625

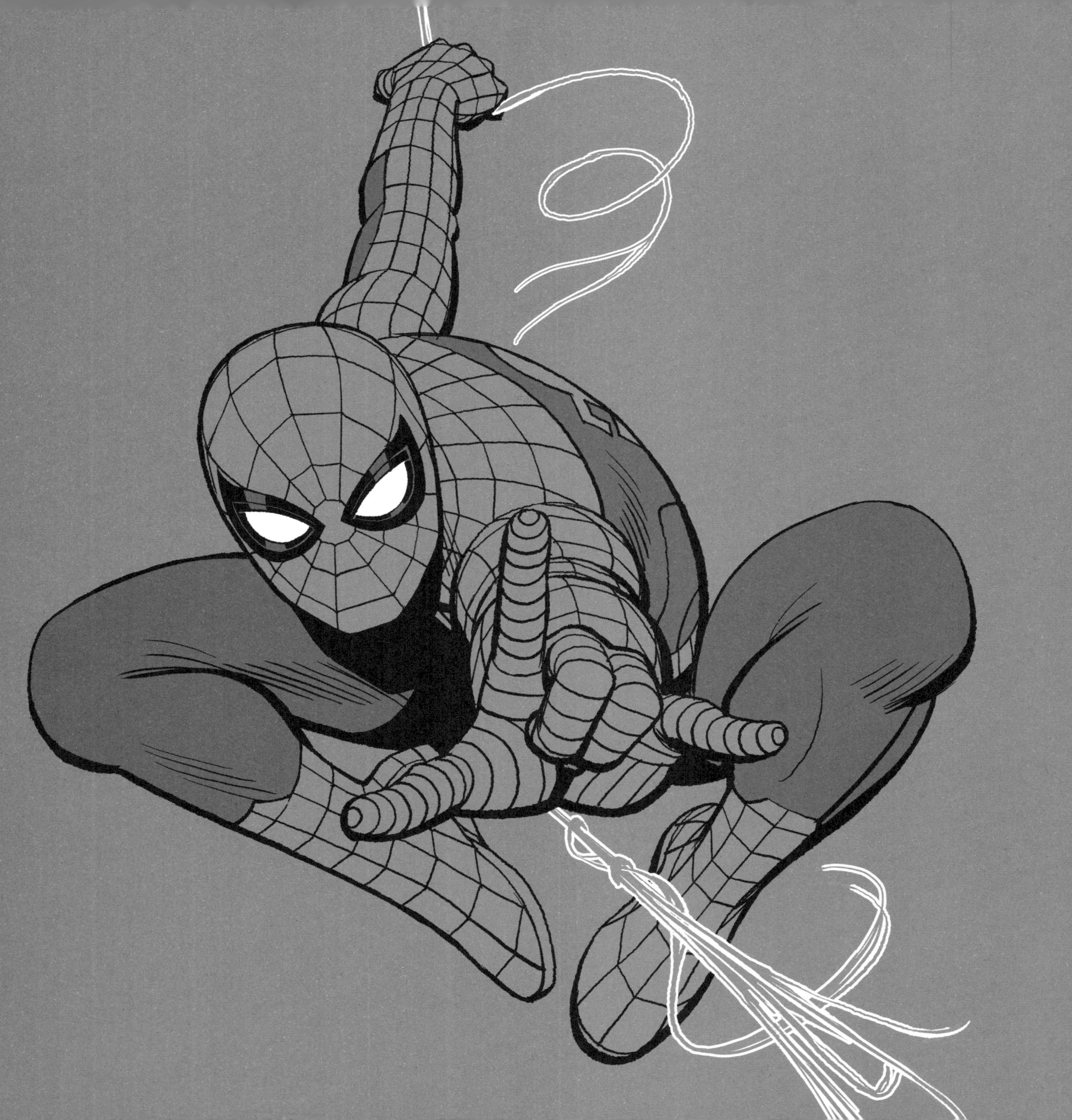

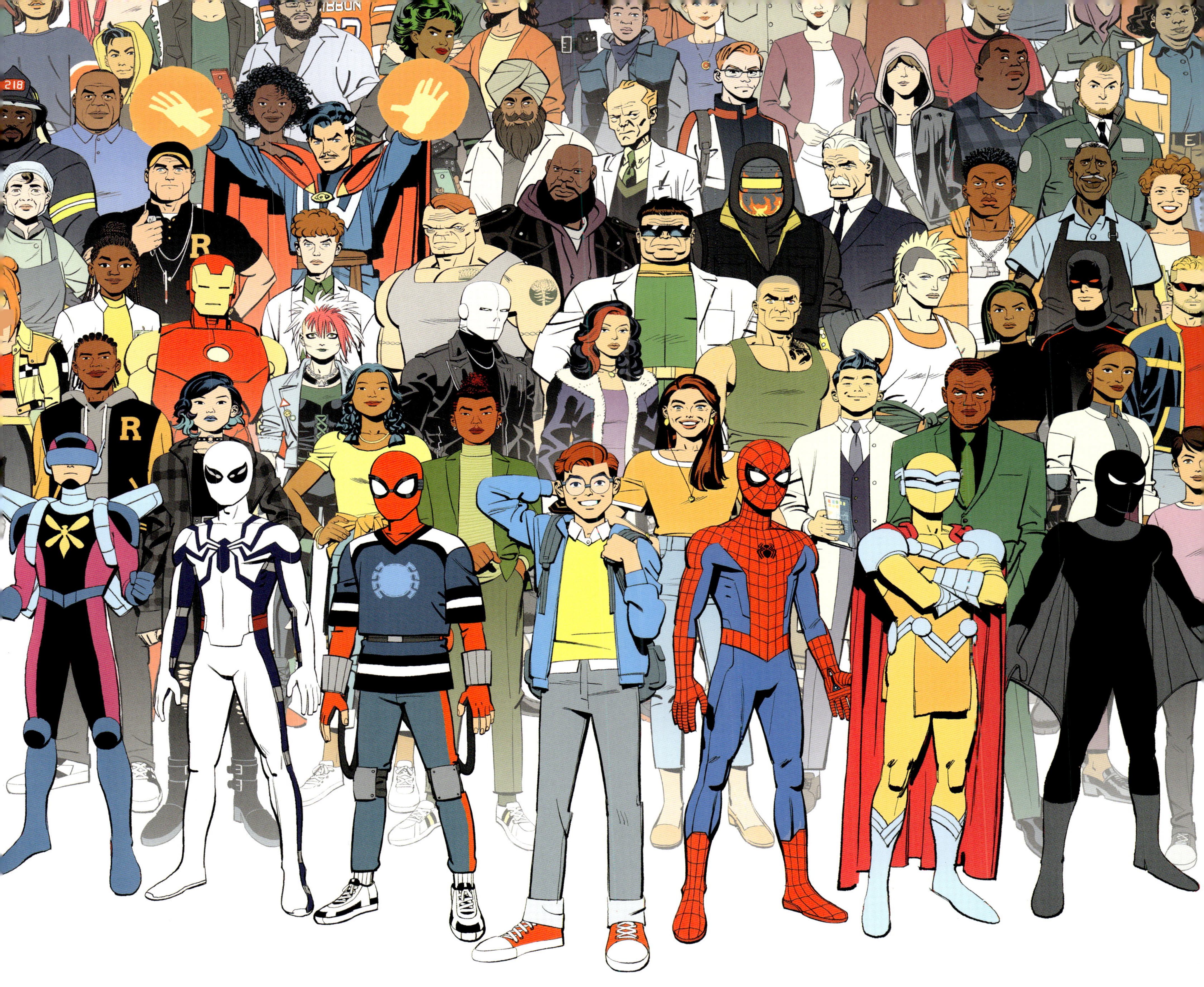
218

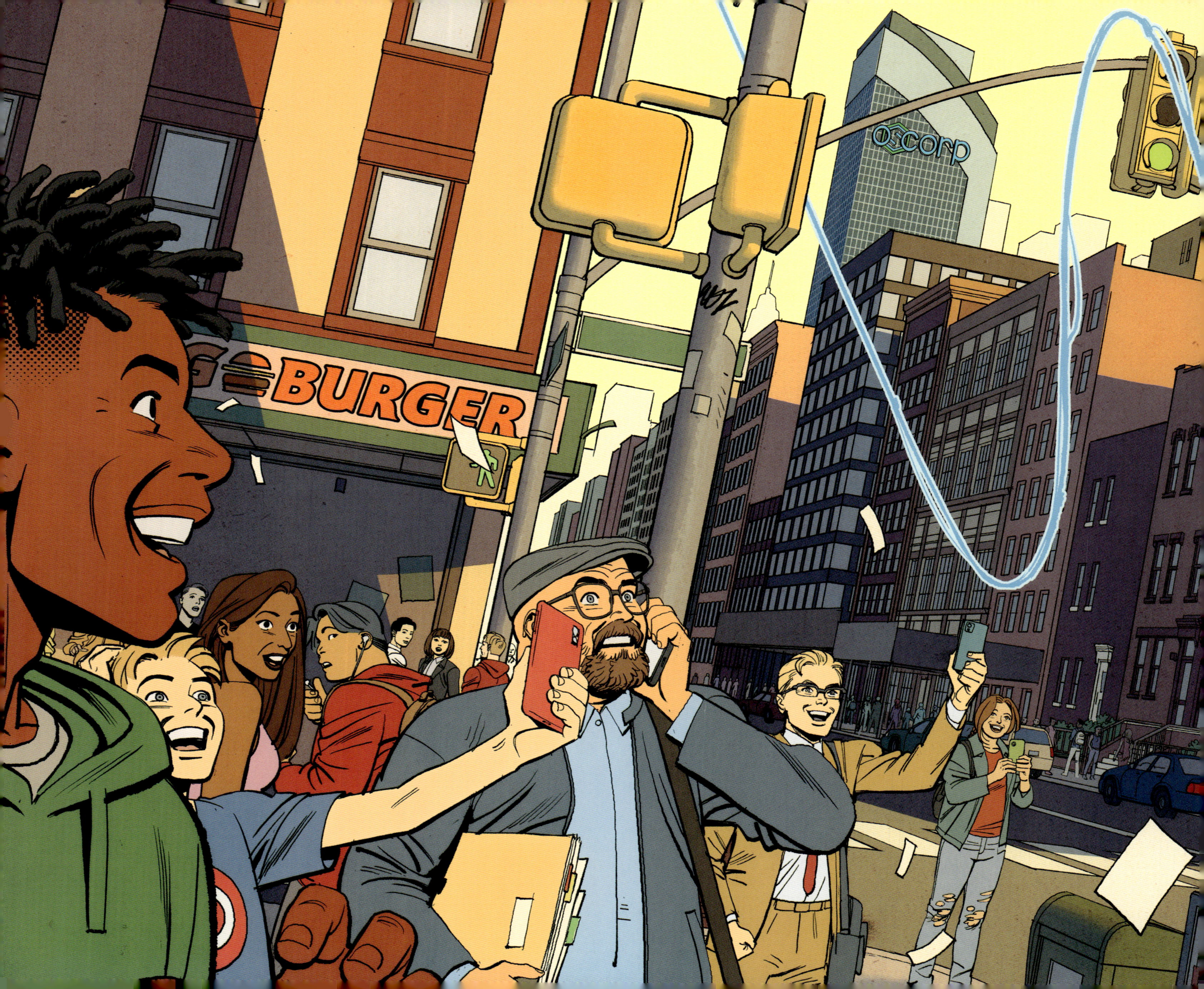
BURGER
OSCORP

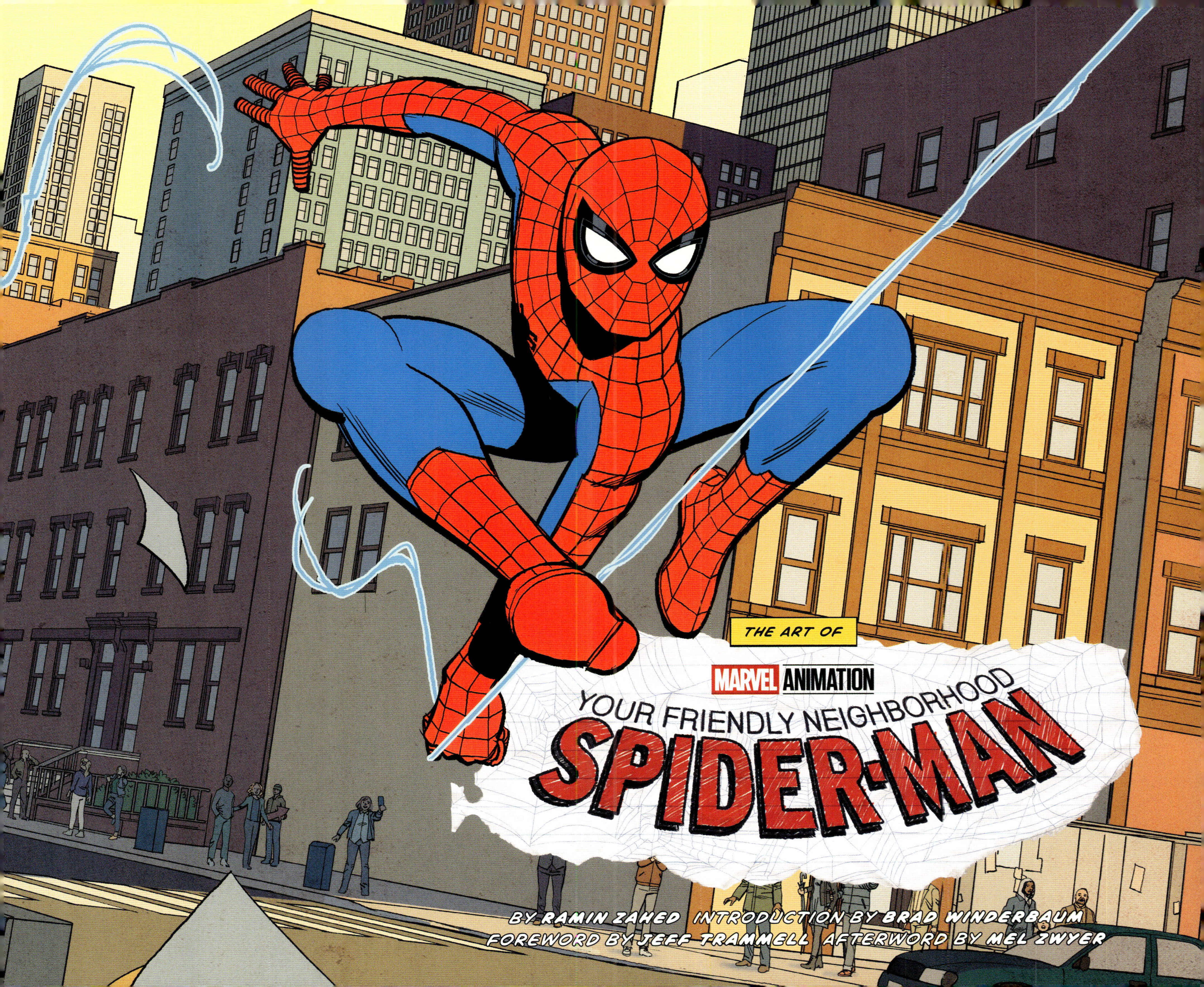
THE ART OF
MARVEL ANIMATION
YOUR FRIENDLY NEIGHBORHOOD
SPIDER-MAN
BY RAMIN ZAHED INTRODUCTION BY BRAD WINDERBAUM
FOREWORD BY JEFF TRAMMELL AFTERWORD BY MEL ZWYER

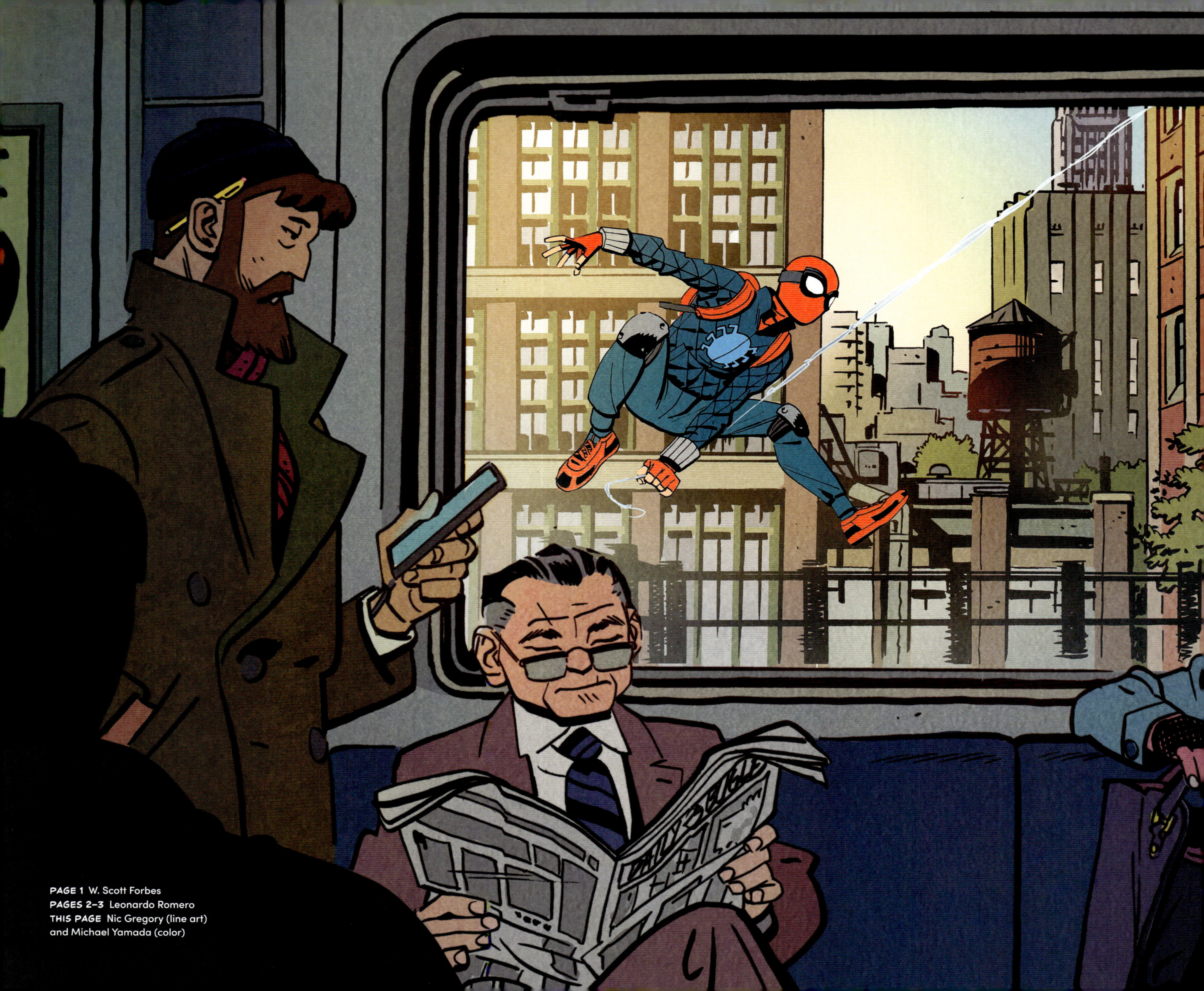

PAGE 1 W. Scott Forbes
PAGES 2–3 Leonardo Romero
THIS PAGE Nic Gregory (line art) and Michael Yamada (color)

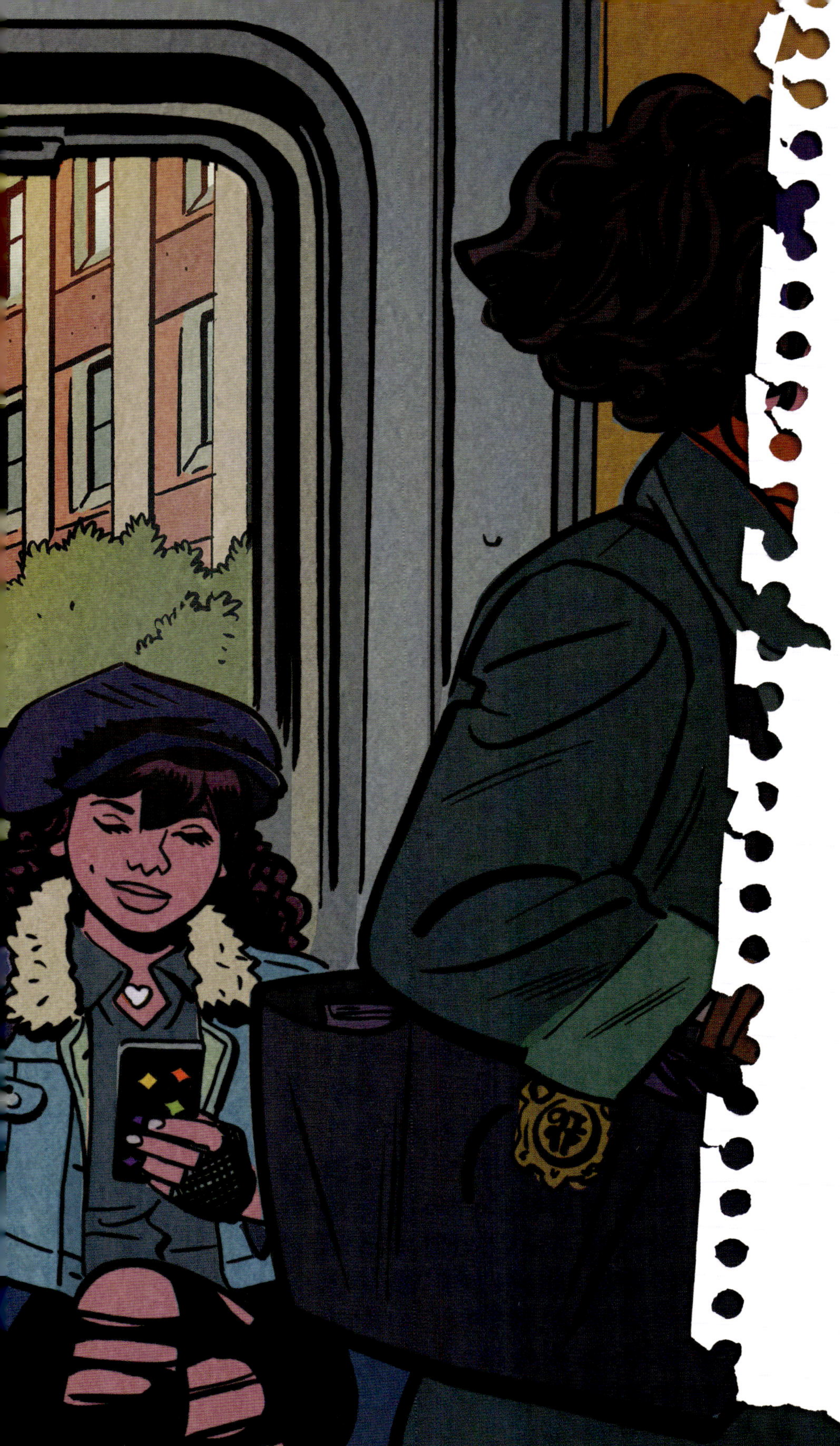

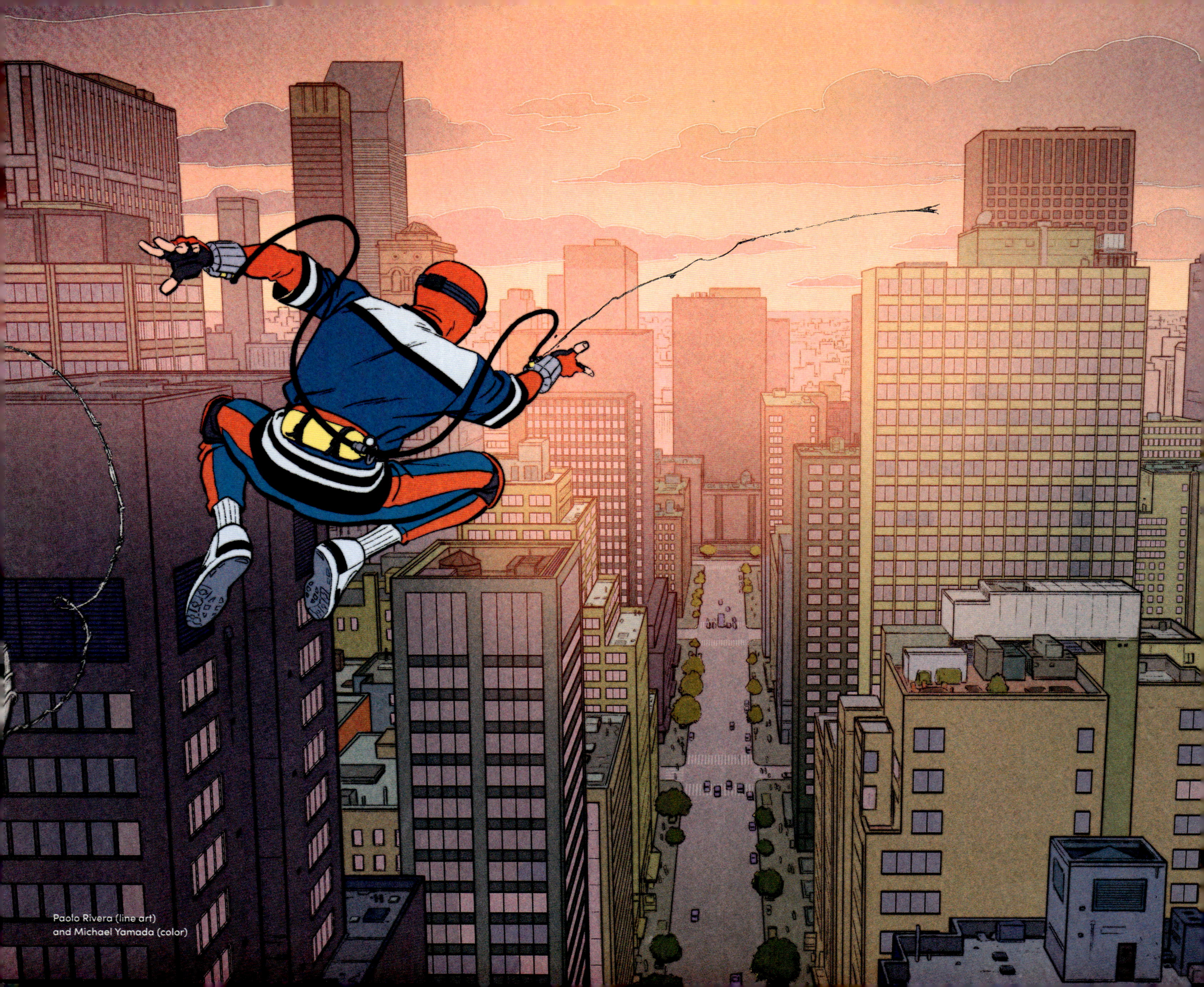

Paolo Rivera (line art)
and Michael Yamada (color)

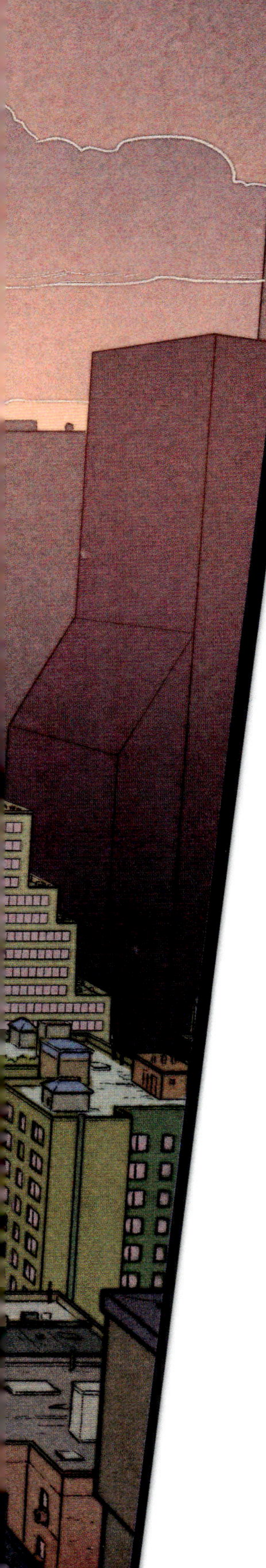

INTRODUCTION BY

BRAD WINDERBAUM

WHEN I WAS A KID, walking into my local comic shop was like stepping through a magic portal. I'd grab the latest issue, crack it open, and I was gone. Whole new world. Different rules. Wild colors. Voices in my head from the page. And every single book felt different because Marvel has always been a gateway to countless realms of storytelling. That variety is the trick. That's the thing I fell in love with, and it's why we wanted to give people at home a new take on Spider-Man that still felt like it belonged in that glorious, unpredictable Marvel universe.

Now, here's the thing, telling a new Spider-Man story in 2025 for audiences who have seen it all is a tall order. Spidey's been on TV, in movies, in video games, on lunchboxes, you name it. There's a lot to live up to. But there's one version that we were eager to explore in animation: Steve Ditko's 1960s New York. That world popped off the page. It was brash, colorful, a little weird, and full of big personalities on both sides of the mask. We wanted to bottle that energy in a way that would feel fresh while reaching all the way back to Spidey's comic origin.

And that's when destiny took the wheel and I was introduced to one of the smartest storytellers I've ever worked with, our Showrunner/Executive Producer, Jeff Trammell. If you know *Craig of the Creek*, you know the guy can build worlds that feel much grander than the sum of their parts. He thinks in arcs, he thinks in details, and he builds these characters brick by brick, moment by moment, until they feel like real friends. Jeff is a huge fan of Spidey, the comics, the movies, and every single animated incarnation of the character through the decades. He has true love for those shows. He and his team crafted a multi-season story where Peter actually grows up. Just like Stan Lee always wanted. Year by year, issue by issue, season by season, you're going to see him go from freshman to sophomore to hopefully senior and beyond, making new mistakes, new enemies, and new friends along the way.

Season one was a blast: Peter figuring out his powers, juggling homework with alien invasions, facing down muggers one minute and monsters the next. And because Marvel history is a shared neighborhood, we brought in some surprise guest stars you might not expect to see walking down the street. That's one of my favorite things about the show; it feels like you're watching a real city in the Marvel Universe where any Super Hero might be waiting just around the corner.

Massive shout-out to Ryan Meinerding, our visual wizard; Dana Vasquez-Eberhardt, the glue that keeps the whole thing together; Mel Zwyer, our fearless Supervising Director; Leo Romero, whose designs made us all giddy; and honestly, everyone on this incredible crew. You made a show that I would binge on my couch even if I didn't work here.

This book is your backstage pass. It's proof of how much love, sweat, and pure bullpen energy went into this series. And just like we were inspired by every bold Spider-Man interpretation that came before us, we hope this one lights a spark for the next generation. If one kid flips through these pages, gets bitten by the bug, and decides to tell their own Spidey stories one day, then we've done our job. Because that's what Spider-Man does: He inspires you to swing a little higher.

BRAD WINDERBAUM,
Head of Marvel Television and Marvel Animation

FOREWORD BY

JEFF TRAMMELL

SPIDER-MAN HAS ALWAYS BEEN a major facet of my life. As a kid, I watched *Spider-Man: The Animated Series* and dressed as him for Halloween. As a teenager, I played the video games. (Shout-out to *Ultimate Spider-Man* on the PS2!) And throughout it all, I read the comics and watched the movies . . . In fact, I can remember the exact seat I sat in at the Burbank AMC 16 the moment Spider-Man appeared on screen in Marvel Studios' *Captain America: Civil War* and joined the Marvel Cinematic Universe. That's one of the many reasons that it's never stopped being incredibly cool to me that we got the chance to replicate some of those moments in *Your Friendly Neighborhood Spider-Man.*

From the moment I started working on this show, I wanted *Your Friendly Neighborhood Spider-Man* to be a love letter to Spider-Man, not just as a character but to everything else he represents. I wanted to pay homage to the creative roots of legends like Stan Lee, Steve Ditko, John Romita Sr., and everyone that has added to this rich legacy in the form of comic books, television shows, films, and video games.

Fortunately, our team felt the exact same way: excited and honored to add to the Spider-Man mythos by introducing new supporting characters and fresh takes on the classics. From the second we got the go-ahead from our executive team of Brad Winderbaum and Dana Vasquez-Eberhardt, we hit the ground running by starting to figure out a season arc that could encompass everything we thought *Your Friendly Neighborhood Spider-Man* could be. Alongside our writers Charlie Neuner and Raven Kone and our writer's assistant Dan Park, we crafted our own "freshman year" of television and started something special. It would only become more special through the help of our amazing story team, led by our Co-Executive Producer/Supervising Director Mel Zwyer, our Episodic Directors Stu Livingston and Liza Singer, and our animation lead Rick Glenn, who helped us bring these characters to life, each with their own unique movements and idiosyncrasies, as well as our spectacular team of character designers, led by Leonardo Romero, who I am forever grateful that we managed to bring on. Leo never ceases to amaze me with how he manages to bring a modern take to characters while retaining the classic look that we all know and love. When it comes to this series, Leo's style is exactly what we needed to allow us to both stand out amongst the rest of the Spider-Verse but also honor our roots. And ultimately, [there was also] our sensational background & prop designers, pre-vis department, editorial department, production team, and our vendor studios, Polygon Pictures and CGCG Inc. Each and every person within these departments came together to help this show become a reality and for that I will never be able to say thank you enough.

Throughout this book, you will see the work of the many talented artists and creatives who added something special to this series. In addition to their breathtaking designs, various Easter eggs to classic moments in Spidey history, and a glimpse into all the work that goes into creating a television show like this, you'll also see just how evident their love is for the wall-crawler. This show is our love letter to Spider-Man, and this book is our love letter to the crew behind *Your Friendly Neighborhood Spider-Man.*

JEFF TRAMMELL,
Executive Producer, Head Writer

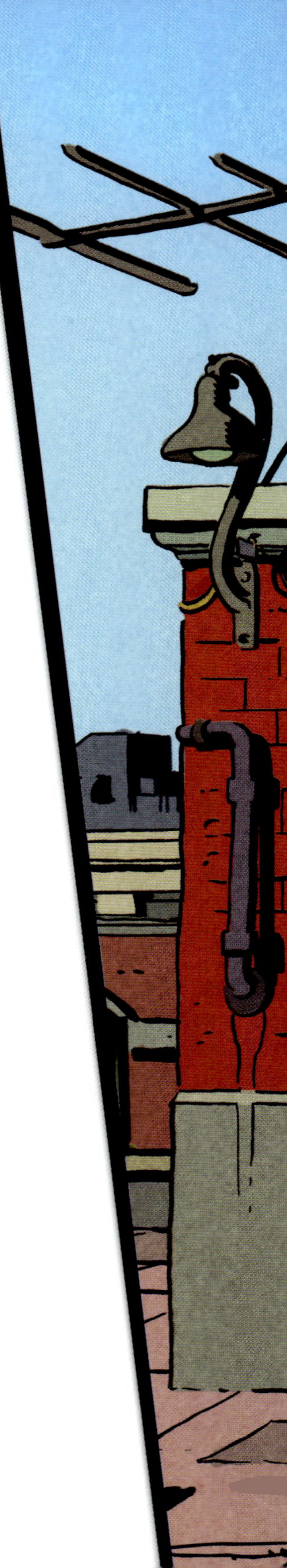

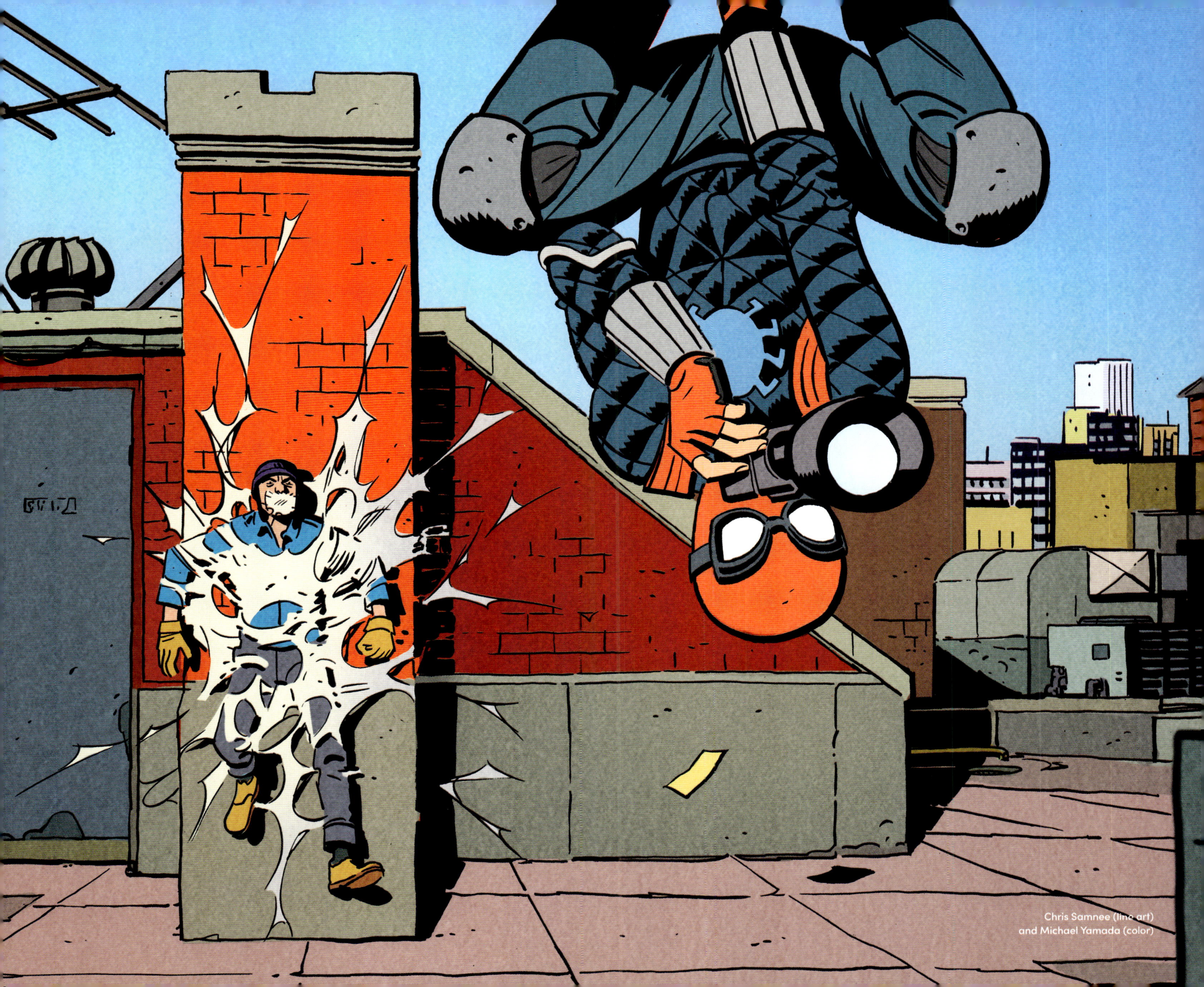

Chris Samnee (line art)
and Michael Yamada (color)

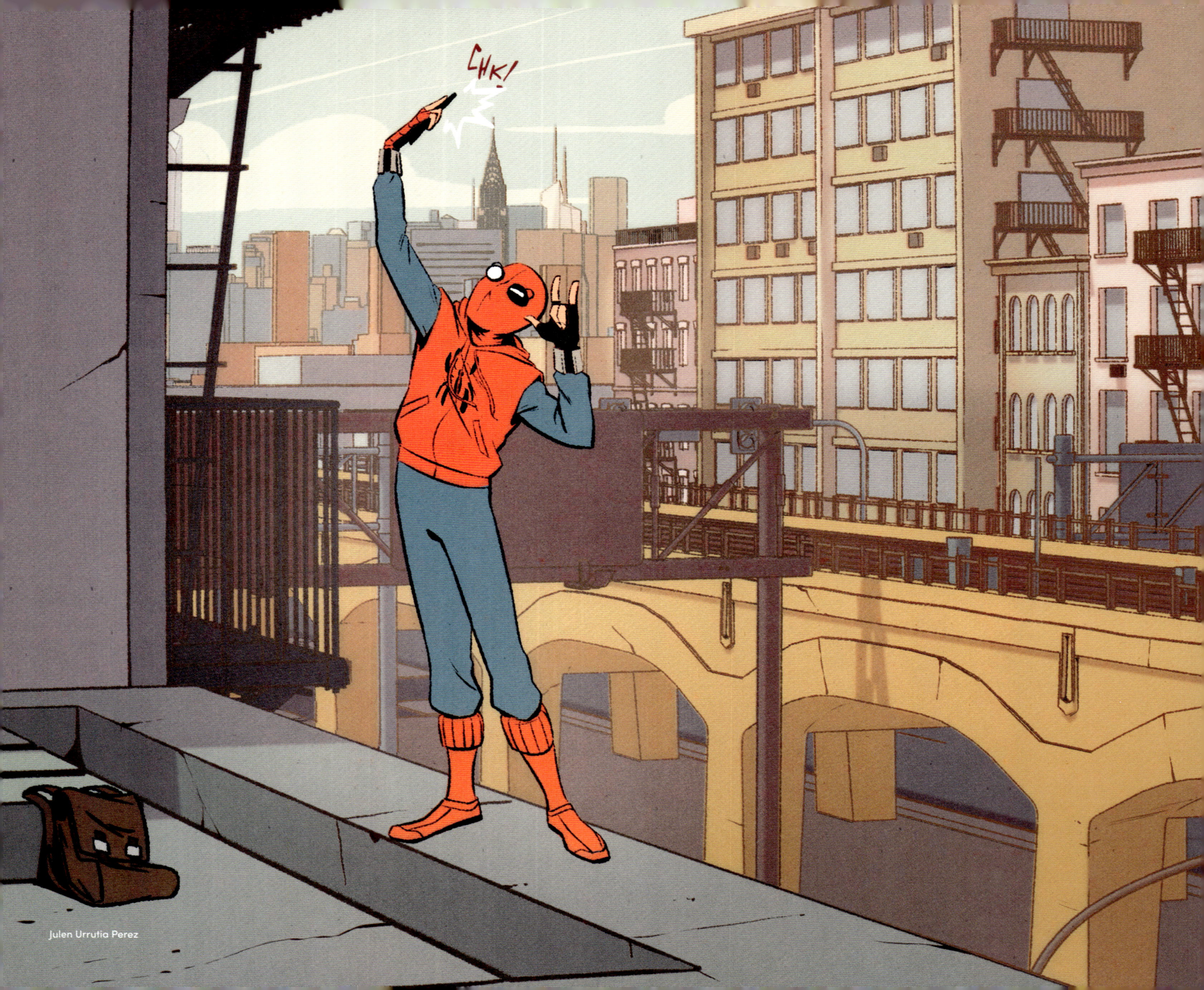

Julen Urrutia Perez

PROLOGUE

A RETRO HERO FOR A MODERN WORLD

THERE'S SOMETHING both very contemporary and inherently retro about Marvel Animation's *Your Friendly Neighborhood Spider-Man*. From the first minutes of the opening episode, as a young Peter Parker rushes to get ready for his first day of high school, there's a sense that the show's creative forces knew exactly how to breathe new life into the classic property. The spirit and soul of the webslinger, first introduced by Stan Lee and Steve Ditko in *Amazing Fantasy* issue #15. (Aug. 1962), is kept alive while using the latest animation tools to create eye-popping visuals for the home screen.

The series, which premiered on Disney+ on January 29, 2025, is executive produced by the expert team of Kevin Feige, Louis D'Esposito, Brad Winderbaum, Dana Vasquez-Eberhardt, and Showrunner and Head Writer Jeff Trammell. Winderbaum, Marvel Studios' Head of Television, Streaming, and Animation, first pitched the show as part of a block of animated projects that included *I Am Groot*, *X-Men '97*, *Marvel Zombies*, and *Eyes of Wakanda*. "It was that time during the pandemic where everyone was stuck inside and time seemed to stop. That's when I pitched our big slate to my bosses at Disney and Marvel—at the time, over Zoom," he recalls.

During that time, Winderbaum was watching a lot of cartoons with his kids, and they turned him on to a Cartoon Network show called *Craig of the Creek*. "I loved the way the series took a relatively small idea of interconnected backyards and a creek that was between them all and created a universe out of it with characters that you really got to know episode after episode," he notes. "So, that's why the show's head writer, Jeff Trammell, was on my mind. When I started looking for showrunners for *X-Men '97*, he had a great pitch for that series, but honestly, all I could think of was that he would be great for Spider-Man. It was something about the way he approached the story and the characters that made me realize he'd be the perfect fit. So, I called him and asked him whether he wanted to work on the show, and thankfully, he said, 'Yes!'"

Trammell says he couldn't have said "yes" faster. "I made sure he knew that I was super interested," he remembers. "Early on, we wanted the new show to be very reminiscent of the Marvel Cinematic Universe with Tom Holland's version of Spider-Man (from *Captain America: Civil War* and his standalone adventures in *Spider-Man: Homecoming*, *Spider-Man: Far from Home*, and *Spider-Man: No Way Home*) in mind. The goal was to fill in the gaps and answer some of the questions that one might have in this universe while offering something that felt new and fresh, with a different direction."

Then there was the big commitment to the legacy of the Silver Age of Comic Books (1956–1970). "We wanted to really tap into a Steve Ditko and John Romita Sr. [original Spider-Man artists] kind of vibe for Peter, as well as making sure that it still has the kind of action and comedy that we've come to expect from the MCU [Marvel Cinematic Universe]," adds Trammell. "I do think that our Peter Parker intrinsically goes back to basics. His life may be based in his high school and his corner of Queens and New York City, but bigger problems come his way as well."

Winderbaum points out that this latest account of Peter Parker's adventures does take place in the modern world, but it's a world viewed through the lens of the 1960s. "If you go back to the earliest cartoons that Marvel put on the air, they were attempts to animate that 1960s Marvel Comics aesthetic. Now, with all this new technology, we're able to do it in a way that's very fluid and cinematic, but it still has that quintessential linework and color palette of those Steve Ditko comics."

The show allows viewers to return to the beginnings of Peter Parker's story, when he first acquires his powers, thanks to that famous spider bite. "We are exploring aspects of his young life that we haven't seen in the Marvel Cinematic Universe," says Winderbaum. "In Marvel Studios' *Spider-Man: Homecoming*, he's already got his powers, but in our show, we look at a more insecure, earlier version of Peter. He's new to his powers and figuring out how to balance the world of taking care of Aunt May, making sure you have enough money, and doing your schoolwork, while balancing everything else."

Winderbaum also emphasizes that the show works as a character ensemble piece overall. "The way Jeff tells stories, he's always thinking about the long-term picture. As a storyteller, he takes his time. That doesn't mean the series isn't without conflict, big action, or excitement—all the things that you want out of a Spider-Man show. But, from a character point of view, he lets these characters collide and simmer in a gradual way. So, when everything begins to pay off, it feels really cathartic since you've spent so much time investing in these relationships."

Trammell mentions that when he was a young boy, one of the first things that drew him to Spider-Man was the colors of the character and his world. "When you're a kid, you're immediately attracted to the bright colors," he says. "But I also loved the fact that he was funny. That's a big part of what makes him stand out. There are many other heroes that embody some of the other characteristics that Spider-Man does, but he is always funny. There's always heart there too. He's never a 'punch first, ask questions later' kind of a guy. If there's a way he can help someone—even if they're a villain—he'll do what he can to try to come to their aid. That level of compassion was something that I thought was really interesting as a kid, and that still resonates with me."

For Executive Producer Dana Vasquez-Eberhardt, one of the most impressive aspects of the show is the fact that the creative team shares a sense of reverence and responsibility for the Spider-Man legacy. "There's a joy and sophistication that this crew brings to the show, and that joy is rooted in legacy," she says. "It's really an ensemble piece, and as a viewer, you are invested in all the characters in this community. There are a lot of stories within that neighborhood, brought about by Jeff Trammell's amazing clarity of vision. We're not telling a galactic-sized MCU story. Instead, we're embracing this "friendly neighborhood" Spider-Man's neighborhood. It's been this Super Hero's moniker for generations, so it felt natural to make that the heart of this show. That has been clear from the get-go."

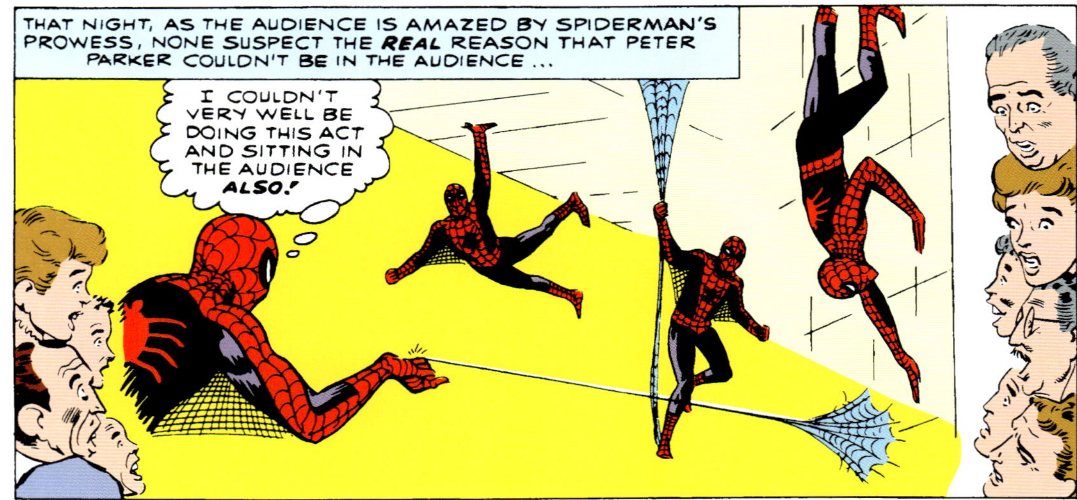

1

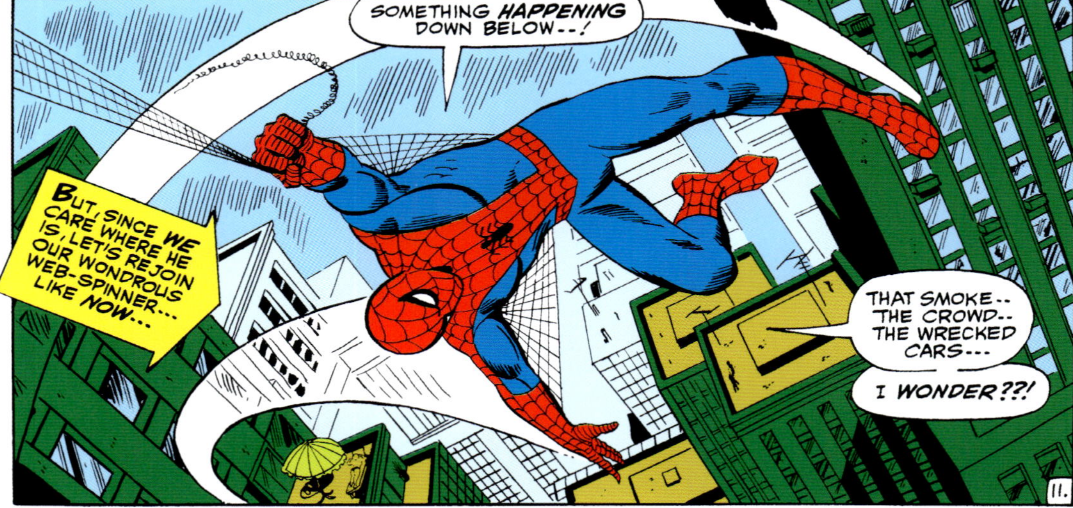

2

What Marvel's Head of Visual Development, Ryan Meinerding, finds unique about the show is the ability to see a teenage Peter Parker face the challenges of becoming a hero for the first time. "The idea of Marvel Animation creating a Spider-Man that is a freshman is a lot of fun," he notes. "Part of the uniqueness in what we're striving for is in the style of the show. We've found a look that is evocative of Spider-Man's rich traditions in the comics and comic strips, as well, and finding a way to translate that into a modern animation style is one of the best parts of the show. We found ways of representing these characters that are iconically, unabashedly direct from the comics."

Associate Producer Alex Scharf (Marvel Animation's *What If...?*, Marvel Animation's *X-Men '97*) says he fell in love with Trammell's vision for the show right from the beginning. "I remember when he came back with his pitch like a day after we had the first conversation with him," he says. "Jeff said this is going to be about Spider-Man's unseen freshman year, and here are all the adventures that he had, which we didn't see in the movies—kind of our version of *Star Wars Rebels*. So, this was a lot of fun but also challenging and constrictive at the same time—because we know that he couldn't fight Thanos in his freshman year. He's just getting his powers. In a way, that street-level, high school version of Peter Parker is in the show's DNA."

Trammell is proud of the final results. "There are so many talented people on our team. We worked with two amazing vendor studios—Polygon Pictures in Tokyo and CGCG in Taipei—to create an interesting mixture of 3D CG [computer generated] with a 2D look," he says. "It gave us the opportunity to bring the comic books to life. They've been truly innovative, and we've been able to work together to make something really special. I think it stands out amongst sixty-plus years of different Spider-Man incarnations."

He concludes, "I'm glad that this show was able to resonate with so many people but also that it could showcase the talents of so many incredible people that came together to make it happen. Our incredible cast, who lend their voices to the series, are so intertwined with the characters, but so are our composers, designers, storyboard artists, editors, everyone on the technical side. It's so easy to forget that behind the scenes, there are hundreds of people who truly love and care about these characters so much, and they're putting all that love into the show. Ultimately, our show is a love letter to Spider-Man in every sense of the word."

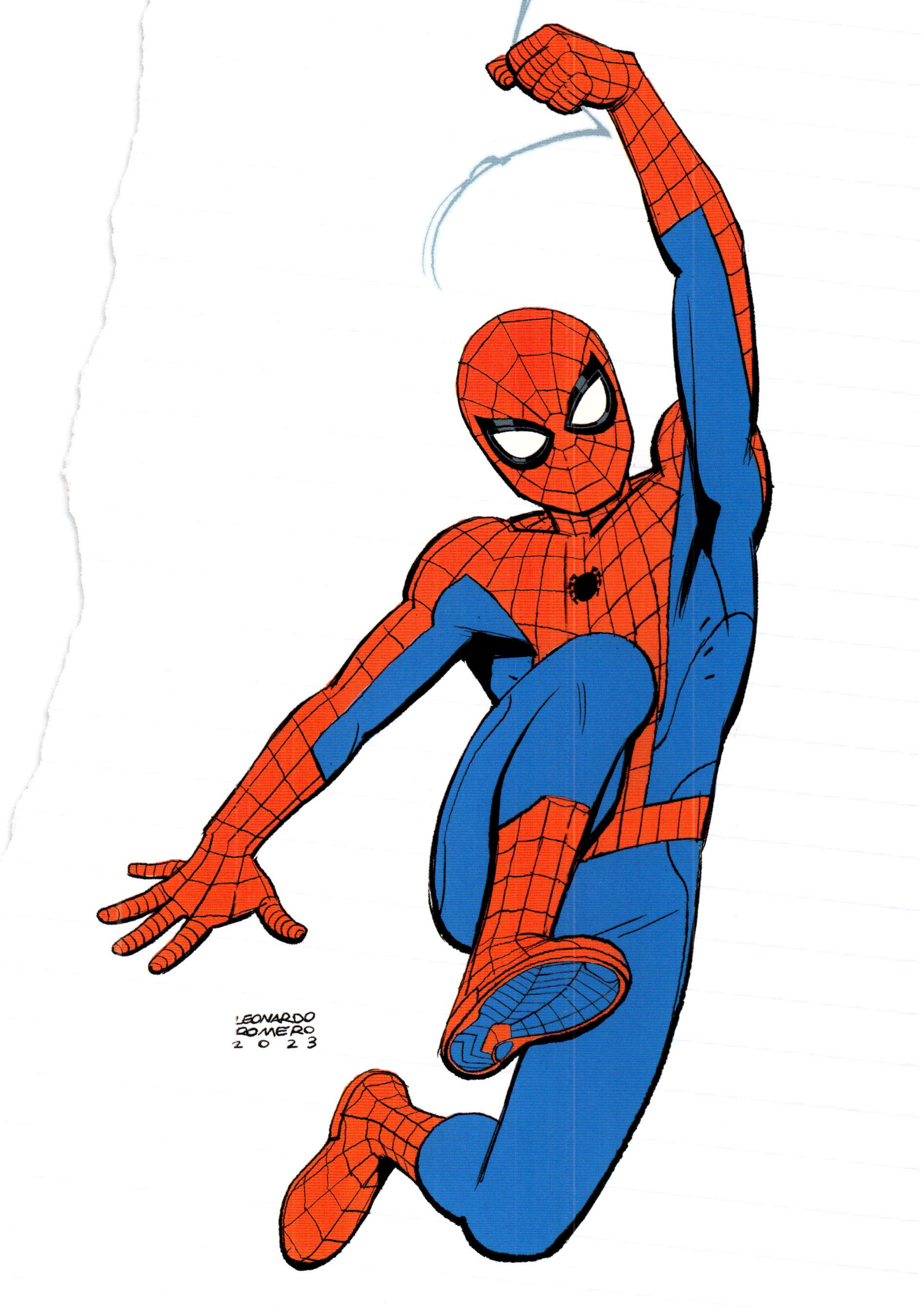

1 *The Amazing Spider-Man* (1963) #1.
Steve Ditko and Sol Brodsky (pencils and inks) and Stan Goldberg (colors)
2 *The Amazing Spider-Man* (1963) #55.
John Romita Sr. (pencils) and Mike Esposito (inks)
RIGHT Leonardo Romero

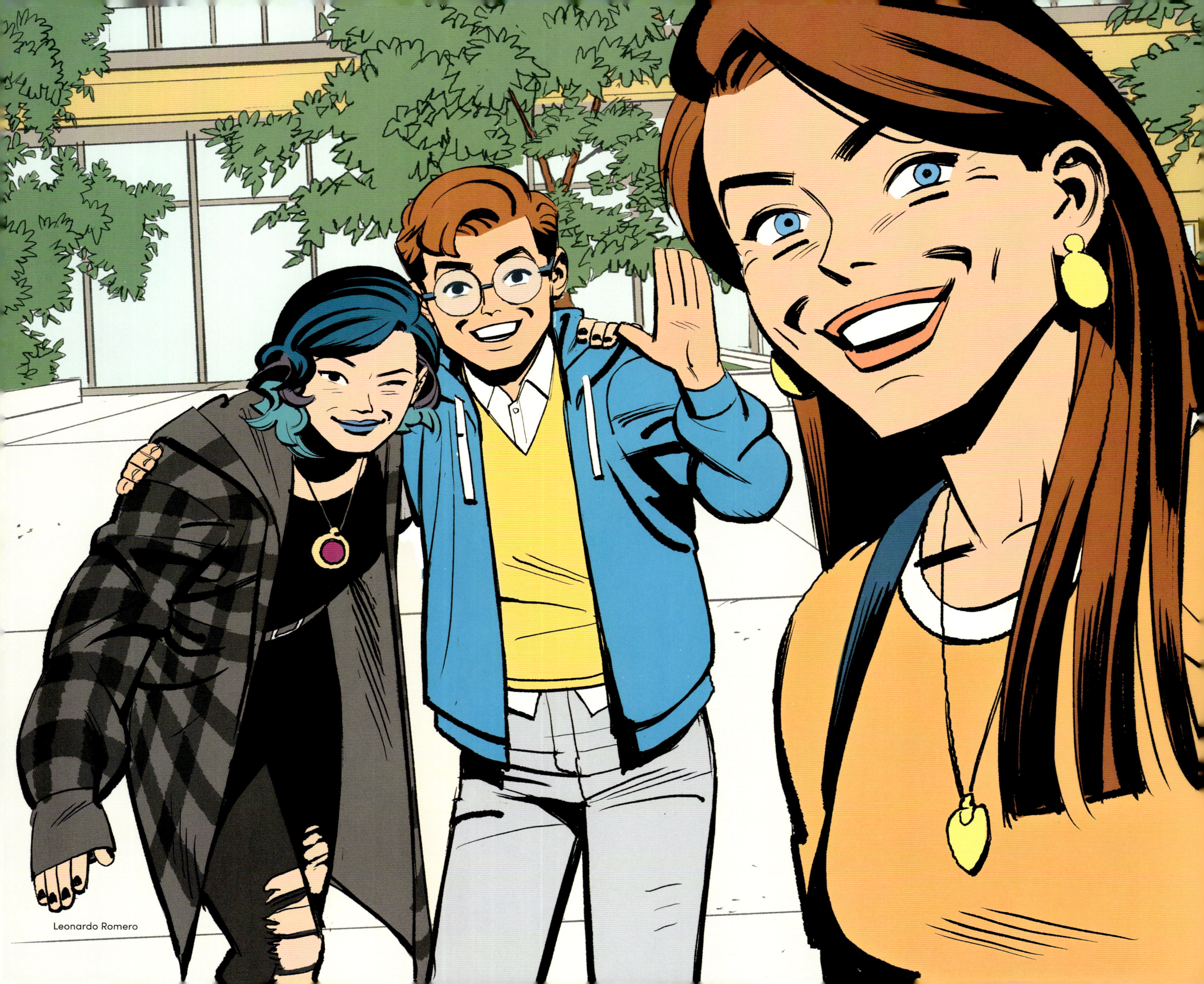
Leonardo Romero

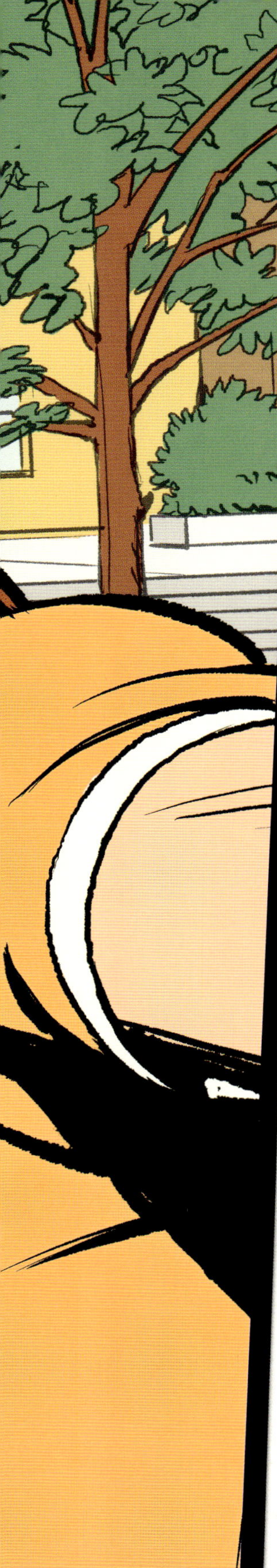

DEVELOPMENT

SPINNING A WEB OF POP VISUALS

WITHOUT A DOUBT, the biggest calling cards of *Your Friendly Neighborhood Spider-Man* are the eye-popping, 3D cel-shaded animation and the single-toned colors and comic book frames that pay homage to the franchise's source material. Leonardo Romero's cool but classic character designs, Ryan Meinerding's world-building visual design, and Michael Yamada's slick production design raise the bar in the highly competitive world of TV animation. The well-choreographed 3D animation work of the fight sequences and the iconic images of the hero swinging from the rooftops leave lasting impressions.

"Once we had our Co-Executive Producer/Supervising Director, Mel Zwyer, on board, Jeff Trammell and our head of visual development, Ryan Meinerding, designed the visuals and really tried to reference Steve Ditko and some of the other classic Spider-Man artists in a modern setting," says Executive Producer Brad Winderbaum. "That's why we have the bright colors and the comic book panel designs, and Peter's glasses [just like the Ditko comics], and the costumes as well. Even with Peter's classic Spider-Man suit, we knew we had to earn it. We see a lot of homemade suits throughout the show. He changes his costume multiple times throughout the season, which is really fun. Just like the storytelling and the building of the characters, the design work is incremental. Everything has to be earned over time, and it's not just handed to you on a silver platter."

Meinerding points out that because Spider-Man has gone through many incarnations, one of the initial challenges was to zero in on some unexplored territory people love and feel nostalgia for but haven't seen in a while. "We revisited some of the earliest Ditko and John Romita Sr. drawings and found inspiration from the general way Peter Parker, Norman Osborn, Scorpion, or Doc Ock were drawn, also borrowing from that whole era of comics," he recalls. "We tried to find hallmarks from an older generation of comics and animation. We looked at the hallmarks of the first *Spider-Man* TV show [1967–70, executive produced by Robert L. Lawrence, Ray Patterson, and Ralph Bakshi] and tried to pull things like the simplicity of the big color blocks into the show as well."

He adds, "Another big influence was Alex Toth, an amazing comic book artist and animator/designer, who worked on some of the popular animated shows of the 1960s and 1970s [such as *Space Ghost*, *Birdman*, and *The Fantastic Four*]. These shows were done before my time, but they were still in syndication when I was a kid. A lot of the solutions that he came up with in those shows were simple, clean, and brilliant."

Meinerding believes that the Super Hero imagined by Romita Sr. is just as iconic and unique, but he's a bit older. "We set out to design a Peter Parker that evokes those classic designs but also feels timeless. The best designs are often the ones that readers and TV and movie audiences remember most."

A big push was made not only to replicate those classic designs but also to modernize them. As Trammell explains, "Our North Star was to create a show that felt like you were watching a moving comic book. We were lucky to be able to work with a team that included many talented comic book artists, who were also brilliant at interpreting these characters and modernizing them." He continues, "In addition, thanks to our animation production vendors, Polygon Pictures and CGCG, we were able to make that happen on screen in a way that feels very fluid and visually immersive."

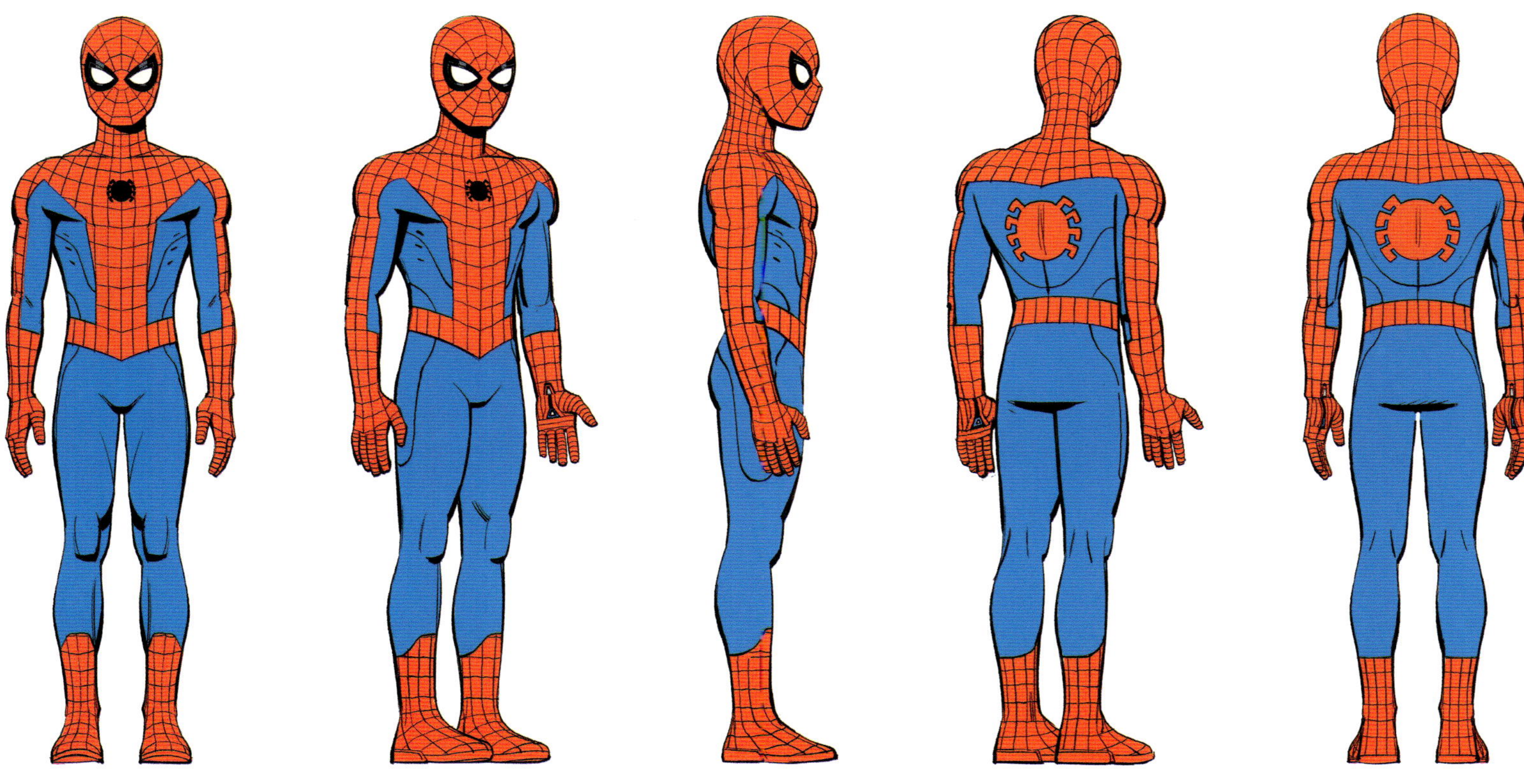

One of the show's major artistic weapons is Leonardo Romero, a Lisbon-based artist who became the project's lead character designer. "We were very lucky when we found Leo, who has almost made his life's goal to draw like Alex Toth," notes Meinerding. "He's such an amazing and hardworking talent, and everything that comes out of his pen looks like it's from a bygone era of animation. Leo can truly capture the spirit of a character through simple linework."

Romero's love for Spider-Man goes back to his childhood. "Like everyone else, I've always been passionate about this character and his world," he recalls. "But to be able to bring these characters to animated life with my artistic point of view has been an amazing dream come true. My biggest artistic influence is Alex Toth, and his work is one of the main things I love about comic books. John Romita Sr. has been an influence on me since I started drawing as a teenager. Spanish comic book artist Marcos Martín Milanés and Paolo Rivera and Chris Pianka, who were also part of the creative team on the show, were big inspirations as well."

The young artist says because he came from the world of comic books, working in the world of CG animation was a new experience for him. "In comics, we can cheat a lot more, so a character can look a bit different from one panel to the next," he explains. "But in CG animation, every image has to work from every angle, so I learned quickly how to adapt to what was required."

As Character Design Supervisor Joshua Shaw, who also worked on *What If...?* and *X-Men '97*, explains, "Leo has taken this retro aesthetic and elevated it so that there's an interesting balance of flat and graphic visuals. He can draw very volumetric shapes, and he understands all the underlying forms, structures, and anatomy of the characters very well. Then he sort of crunches all of that into these flat, vibrant, and bold shapes and designs. Then our technical artist Julen Urrutia Pérez did an amazing job of really cracking the code to take Leo's designs and use them as a blueprint for the 3D models."

Meinerding agrees. "Our biggest challenge boiled down to trying to do looks that still have that '60s animation aesthetic but feel relevant to a modern world because if this show had completely felt like it was out of the past, it would exist as a pure piece of nostalgia," he explains. "Trying to do these very simple—but sophisticated and elegantly designed—characters and making them work in 3D was quite a big task. Leo's drawings had to be translated into 3D, and they needed to be animatable and renderable so that they would feel flat like a 3D animation cel. Julen Urrutia Pérez was really good at 3D and was able to take Leo's drawings and turn them almost immediately into 3D."

ABOVE Leonardo Romero
OPPOSITE CGCG Inc.

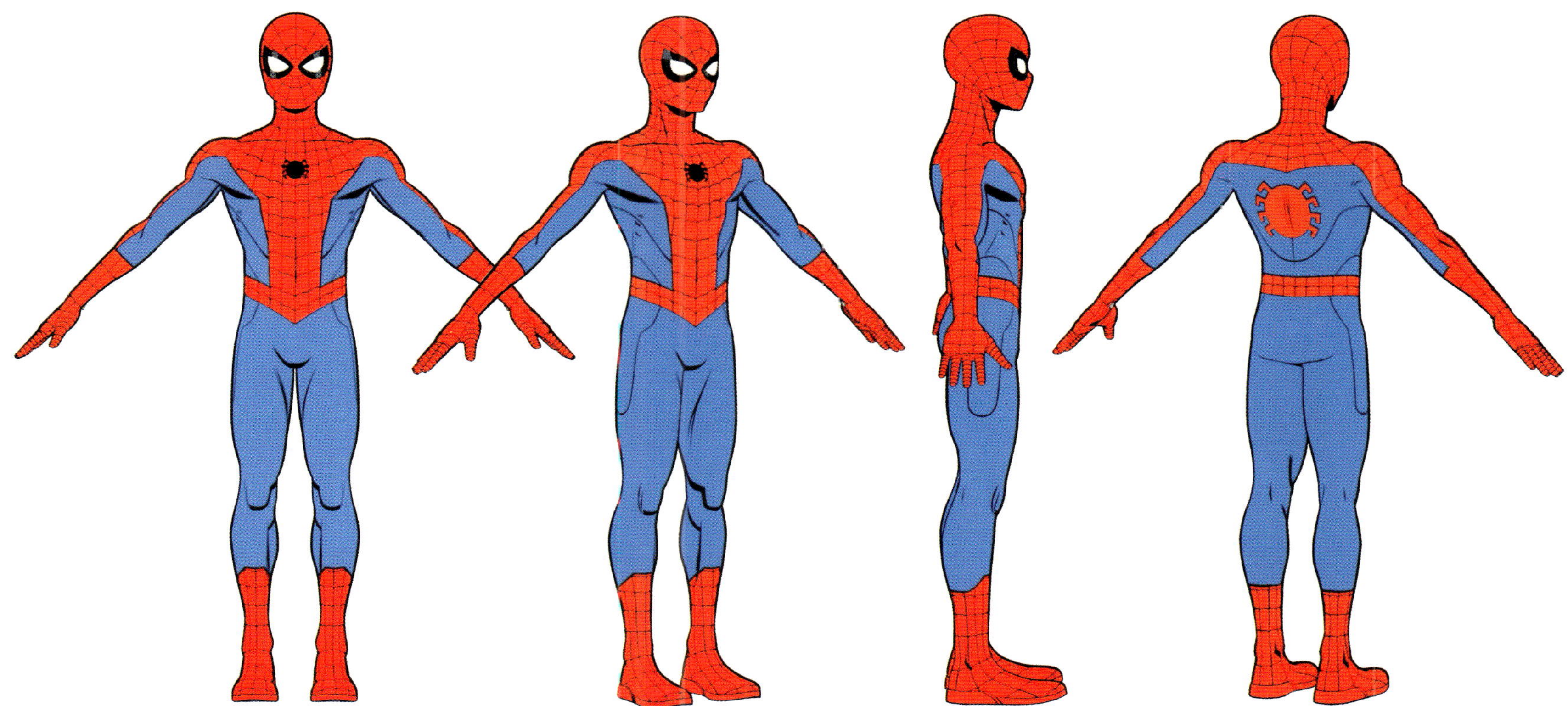

According to Joshua Shaw, the show's character design supervisor, the production relied on the usual animation and visual effects tools of the trade to create the project's highly original visuals. The special ingredients were lots of beautifully crafted designs and hours of painstaking reviews. "There was no fancy tech involved, but most of the work came down to lots of attention to detail and placing the best lines on the models," he explains. "Once we got the initial character designs down, we skipped the orthographic stage and just took it straight to 3D. Every piece of linework was actually a flat piece of geometry created in ZBrush [a digital sculpting tool that combines 3D/2.5D modeling, texturing, and painting]. Mostly, what we used were hand-drawn lines and generated lines so that each piece of geometry would produce its own silhouette. During the reviews, we were trying to art direct as we went through the three-quarter, or side view, of the top and bottom views. Hopefully in the near future, there will be some sort of a 3D system where you can actually rotate objects and characters in real time with all the textures."

During the daily design reviews, the lead 3D artist or 3D character artist would present the various angles of everyone's models in three-quarter side and back view, as well as a full turnaround of the head, body, and hands or specialty item. Then the coordinator would take a screen capture of the views and send them to the production studios for animation. "Once it would come back from the studios, we would have to do the process again, because they would have to get the characters through their pipeline as well," explains Shaw. "If there was any magic involved, it was the persistence to police every pixel until the producer takes them out of your hands! There's a lot of love and pain involved because the animation has to look like 2D illustration. Sometimes when you're working with technical people, you have to make sure that illustration-like quality is retained through all the angles. It is really the process of providing the best care for designs with the amount of notes and time that you have."

Julen worked with Creative Director Adam Liepins, who was able to make the linework change so you can spin the characters in 3D. The core team of Leo, Julen, and Adam really helped bring these characters to life at a very early stage.

"I hope the show's retro quality and its original style find the same kind of love that I had for Spider-Man when I was growing up," Shaw concludes. "I think the show's earnestness and wholesome quality go hand in hand with the visuals that we were shooting for, and that style allows the audience to understand the character and his world even better."

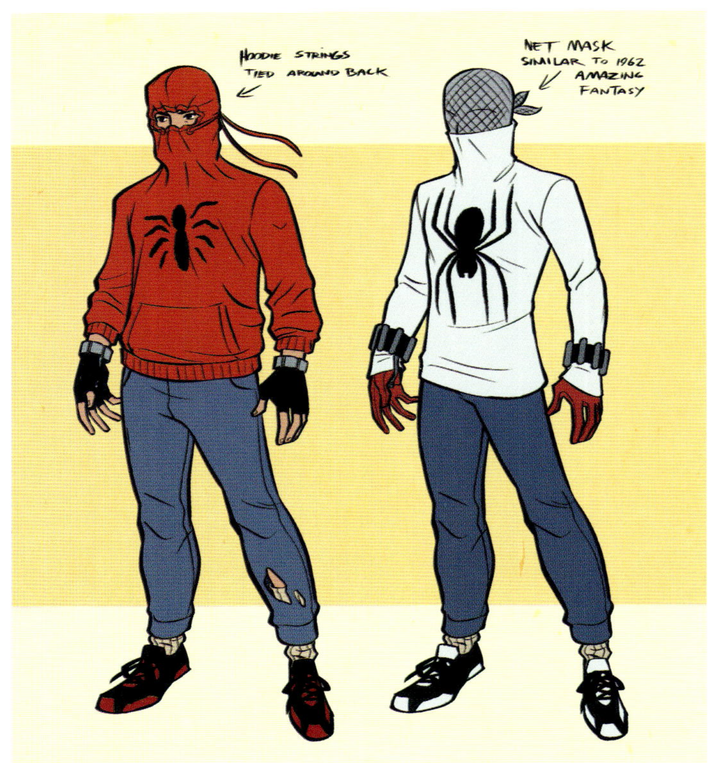

1

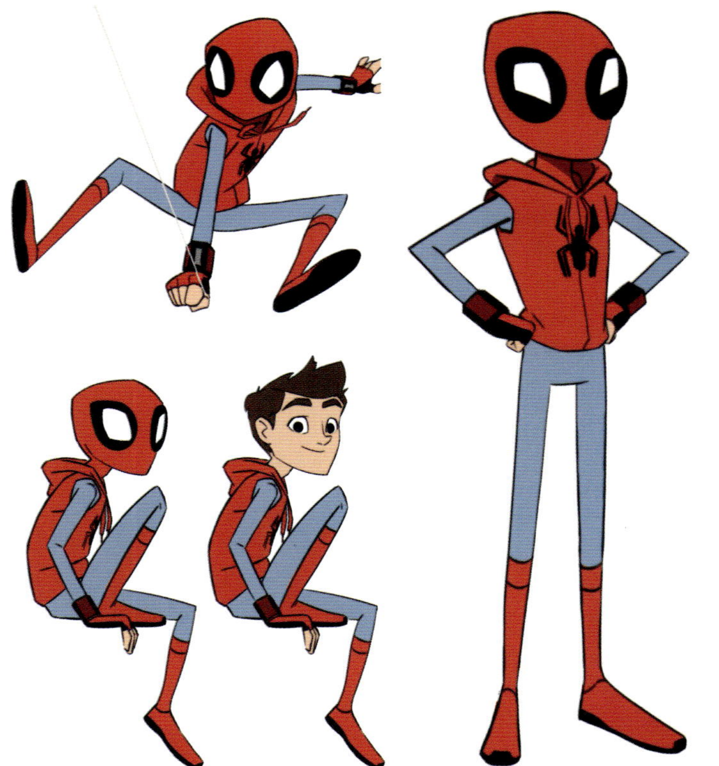

2

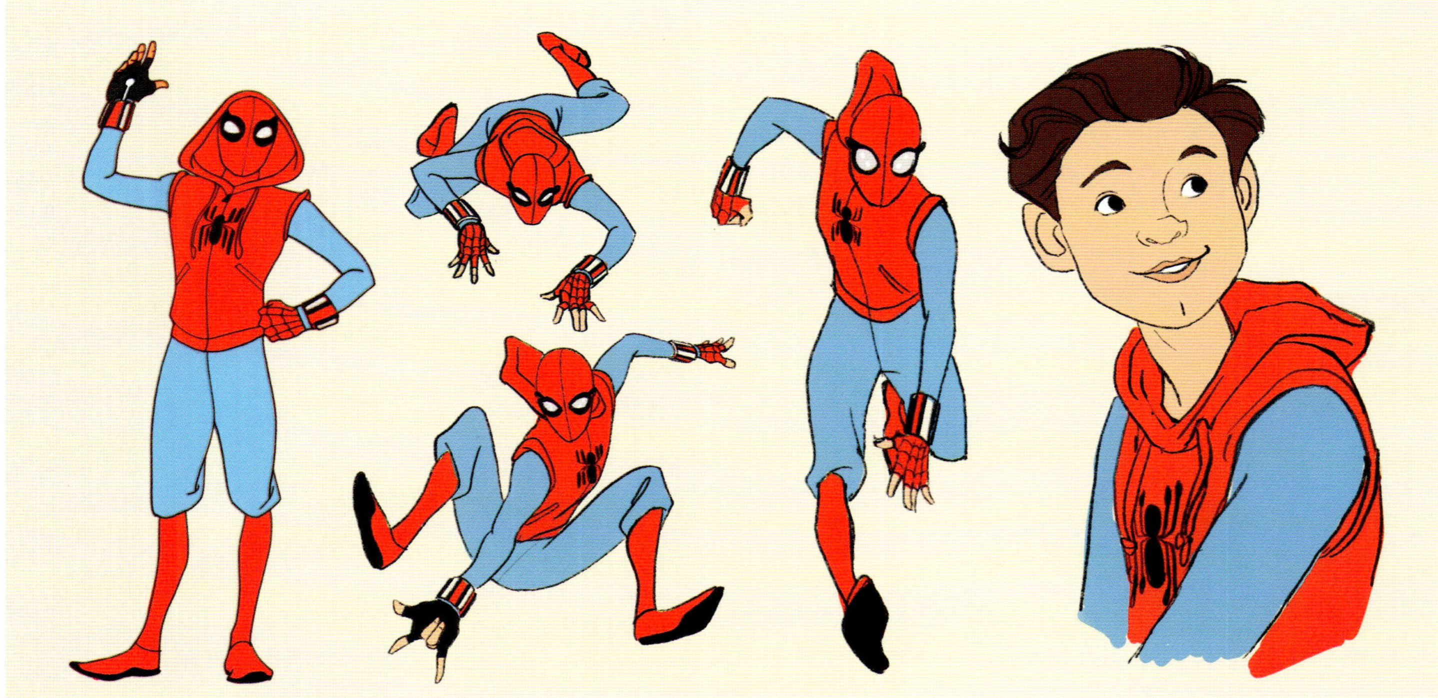

3

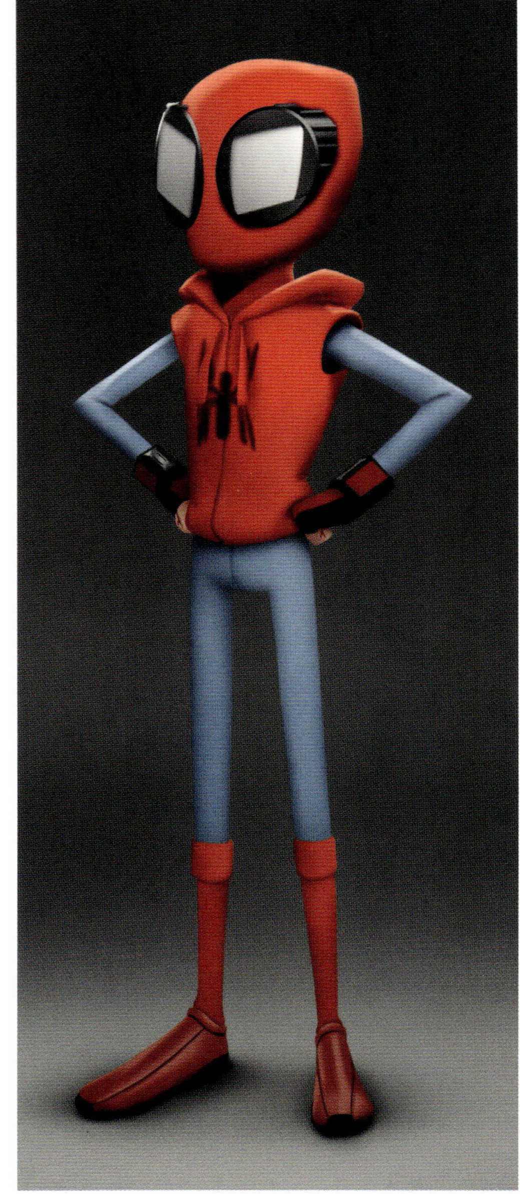

4

1 Joey Vazquez **2** Ryan Lang **3** Ryan Meinerding
4 Ryan Lang **5–6** Michael Yamada
7 Julen Urrutia Perez **8** Paolo Rivera

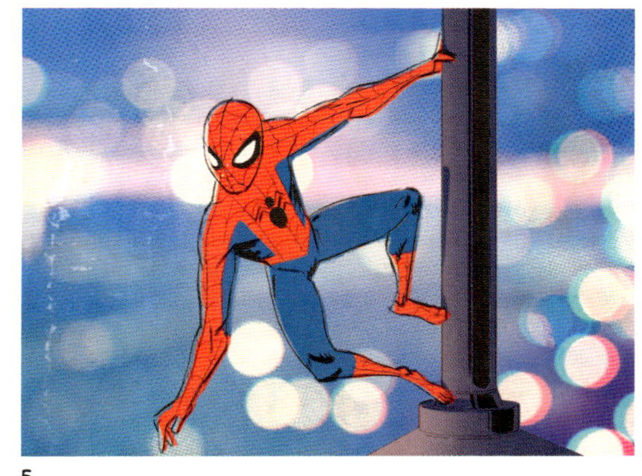

5

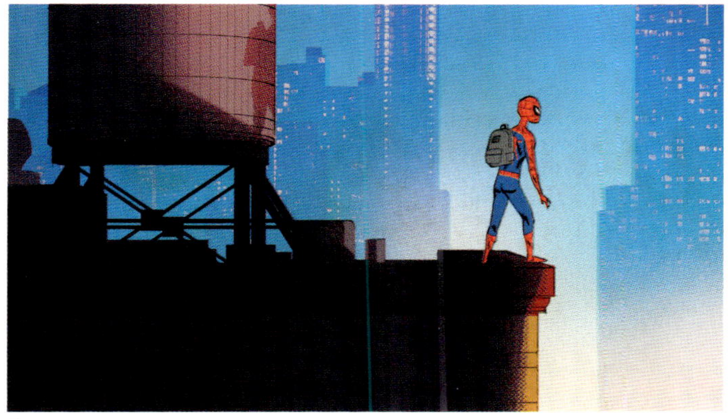

6

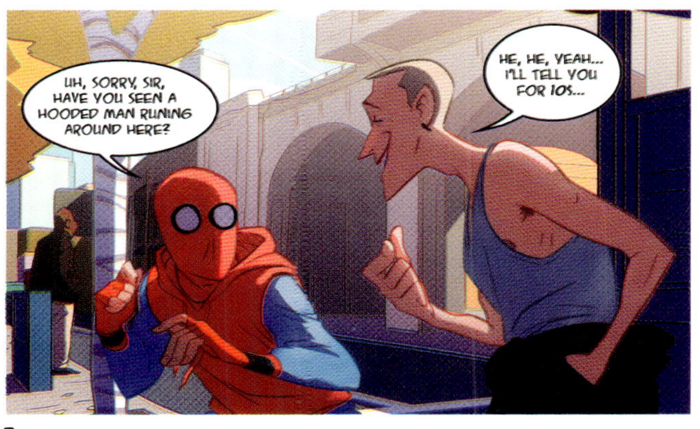
UH, SORRY, SIR, HAVE YOU SEEN A HOODED MAN RUNING AROUND HERE?
HE, HE, YEAH... I'LL TELL YOU FOR 10$...

7

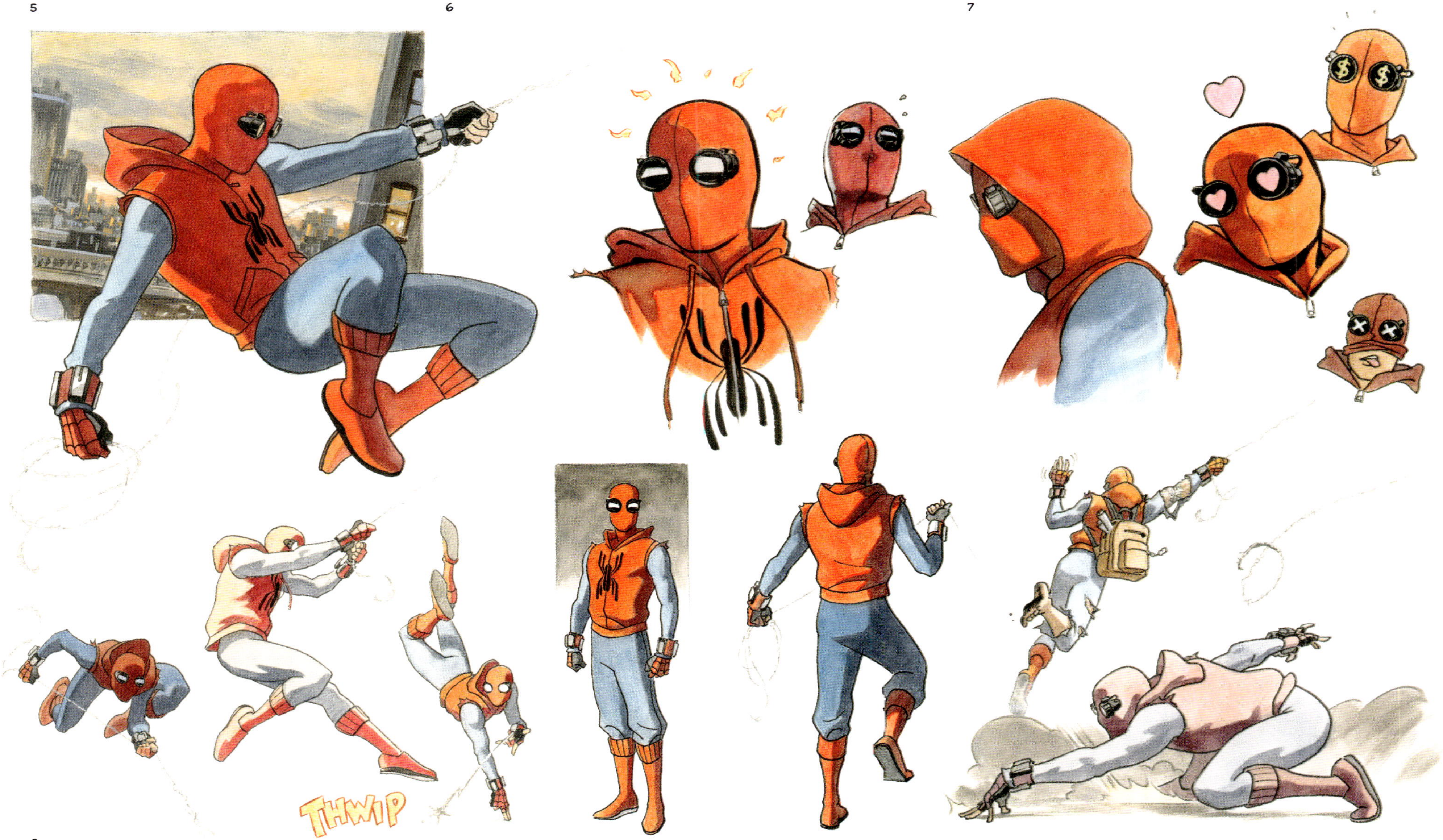

THWIP

8

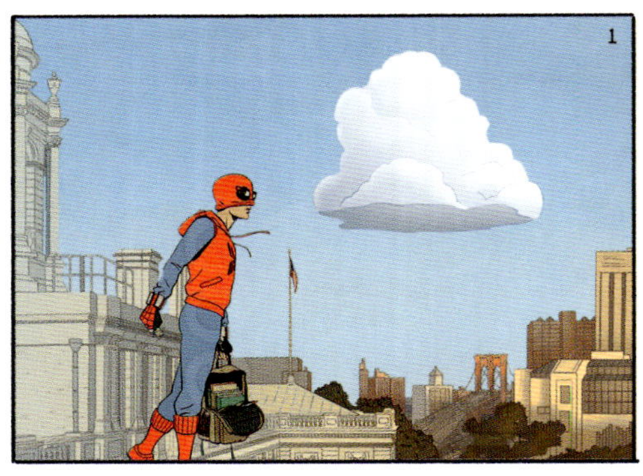
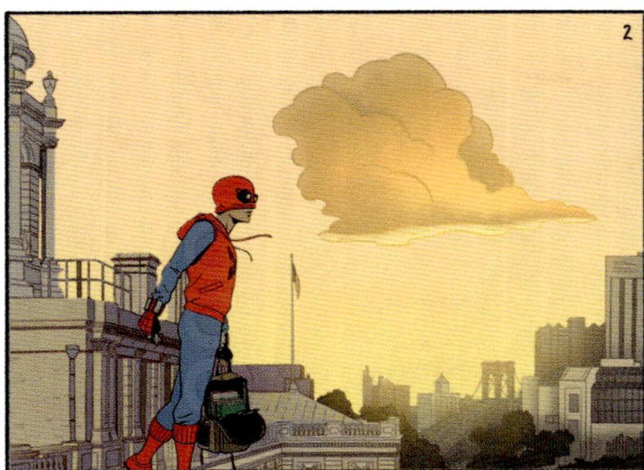
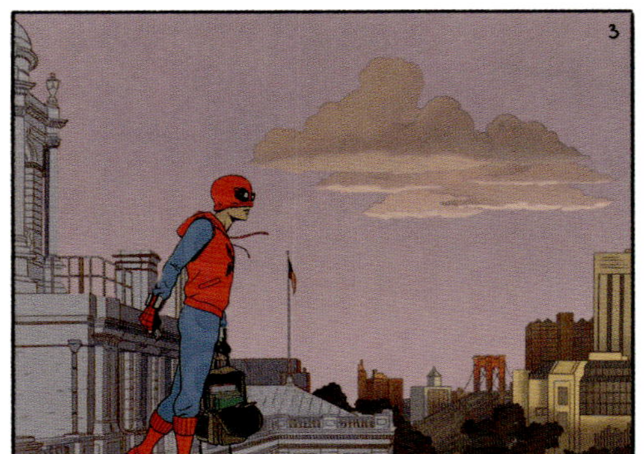
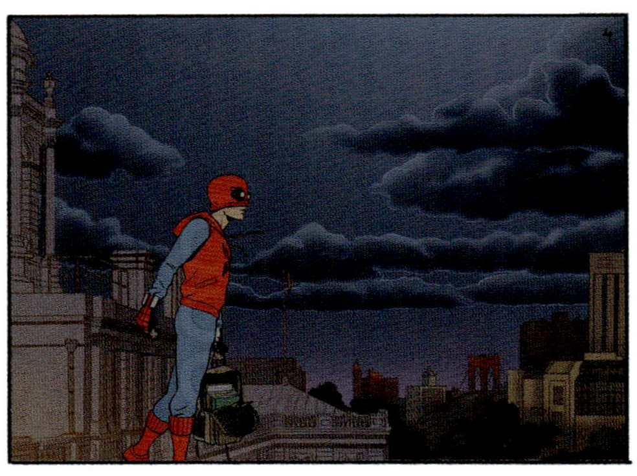

1

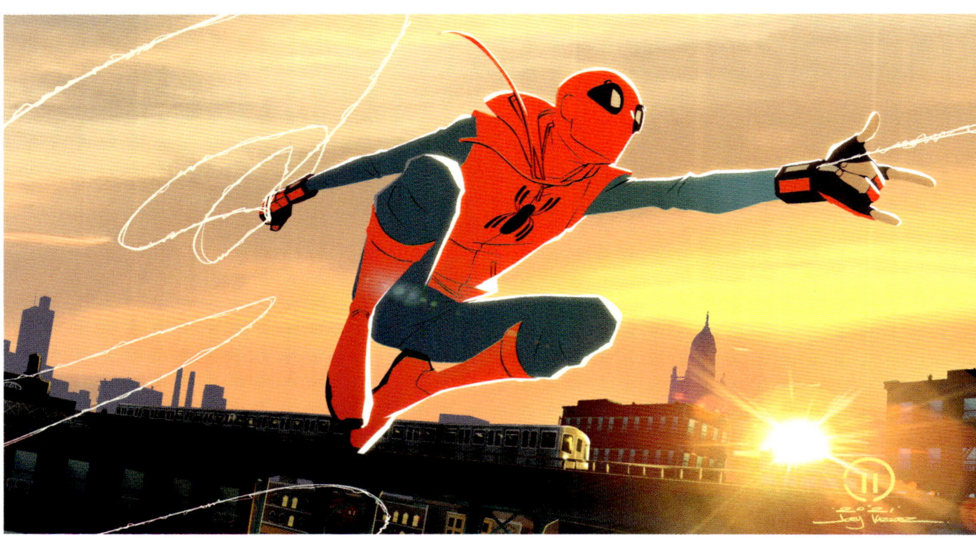
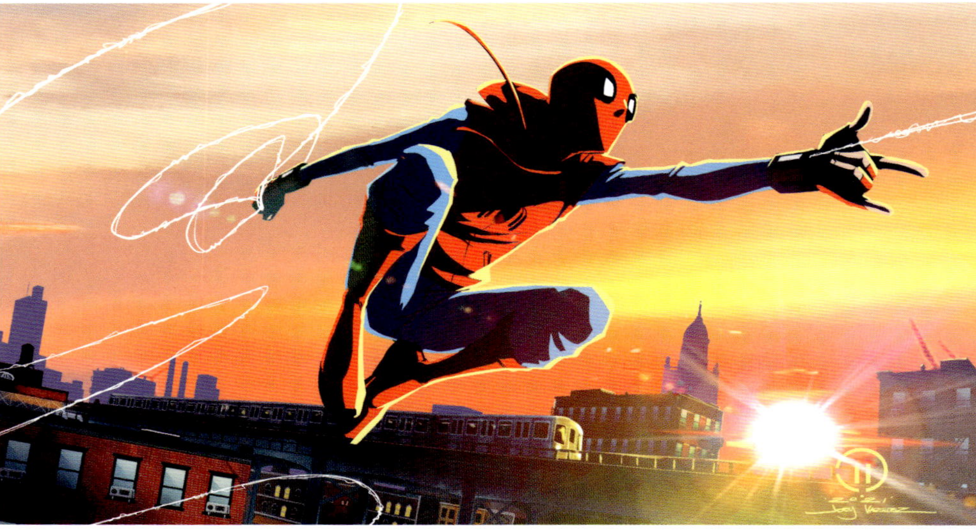

2

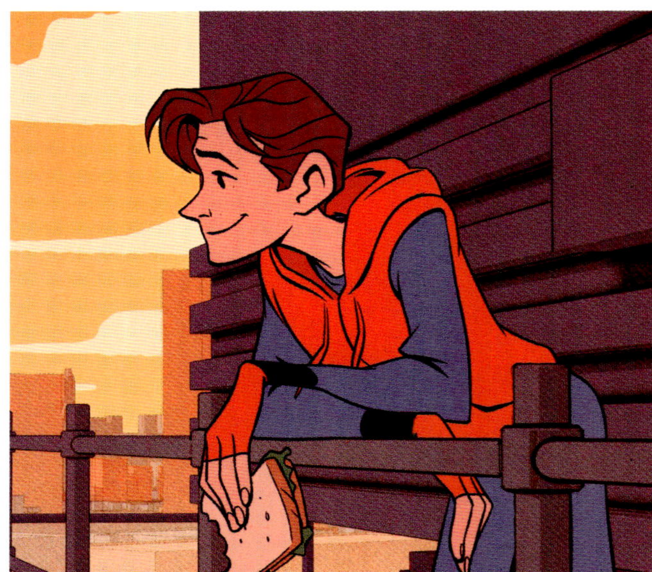
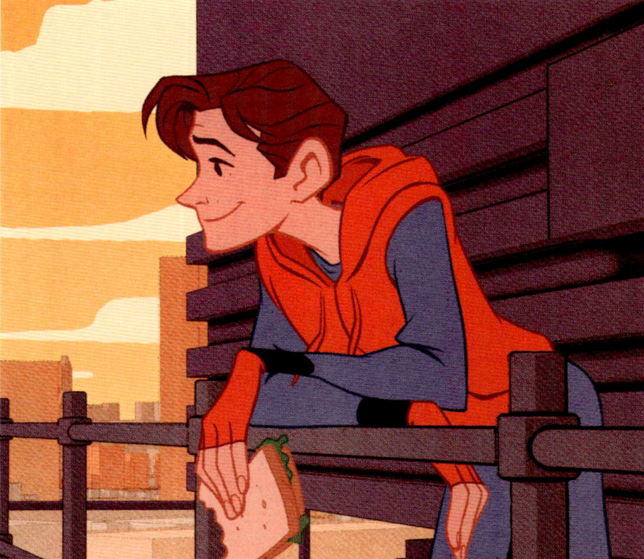
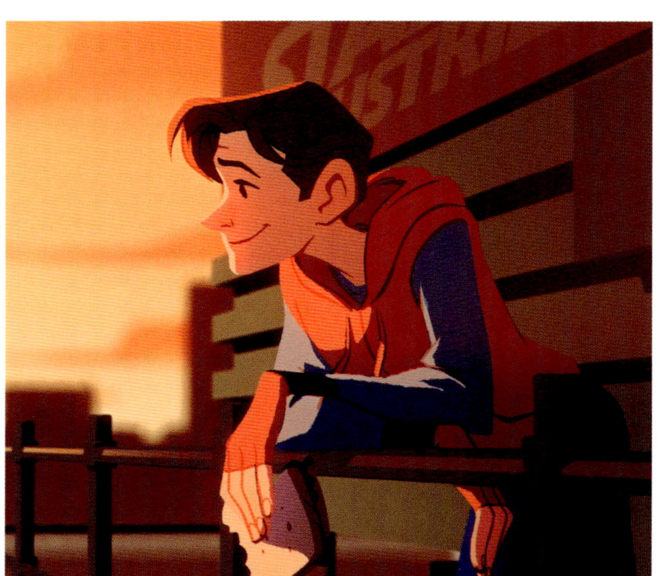

3

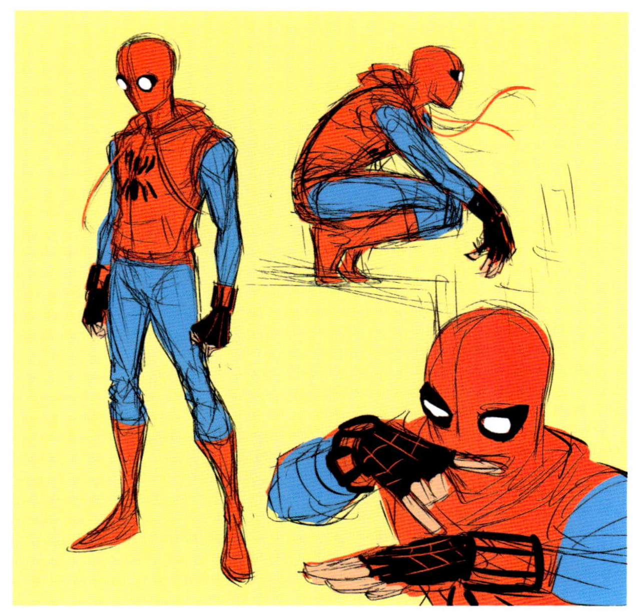

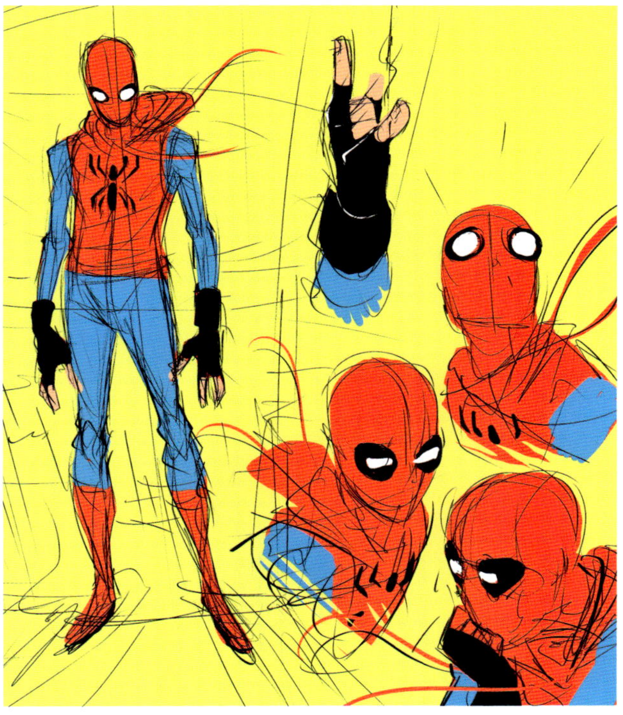

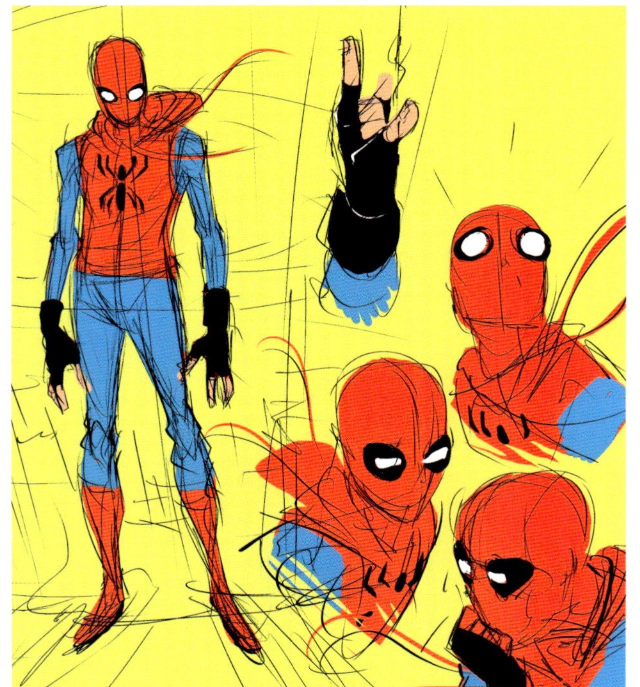

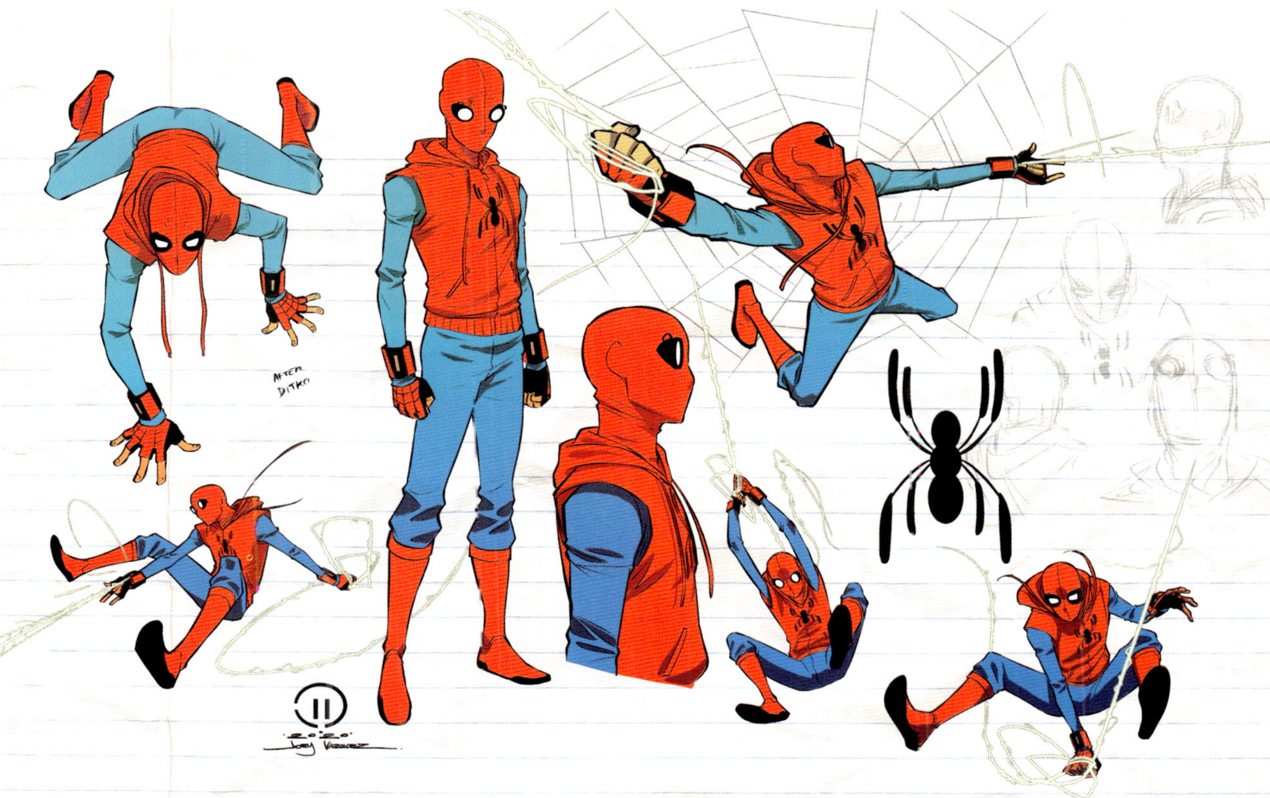

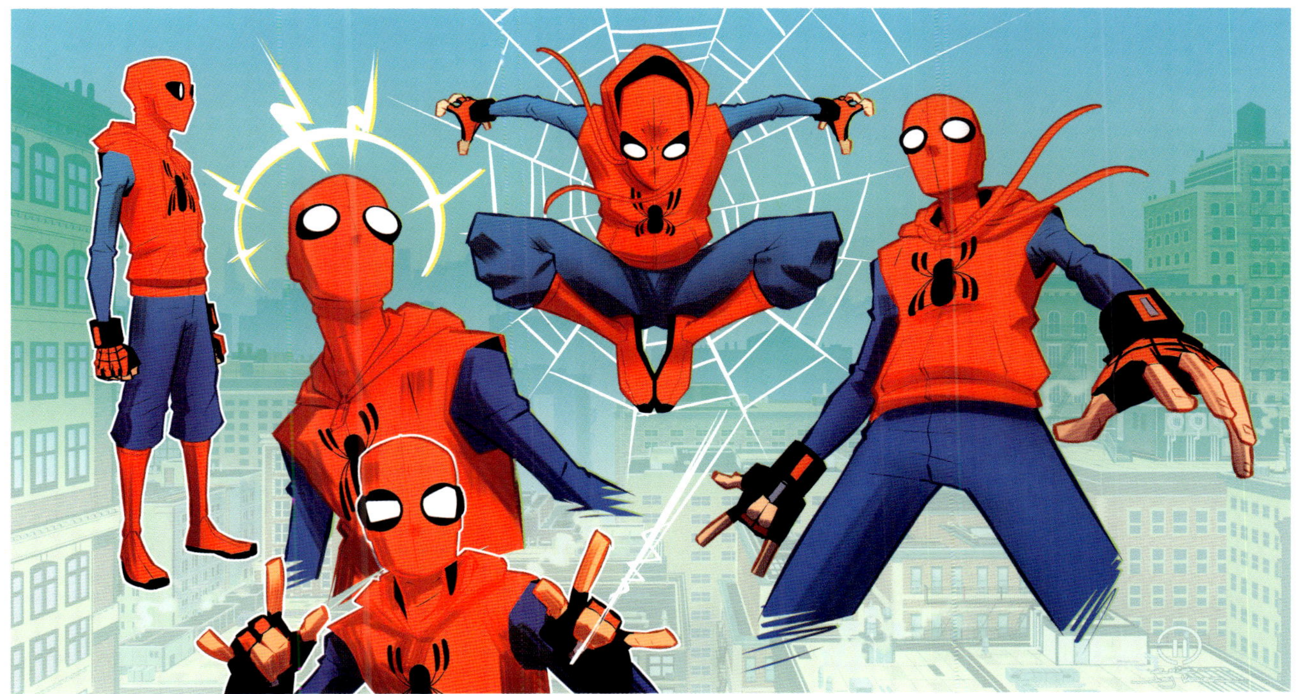

1 Nic Gregory **2–3** Joey Vazquez
THIS PAGE Joey Vazquez

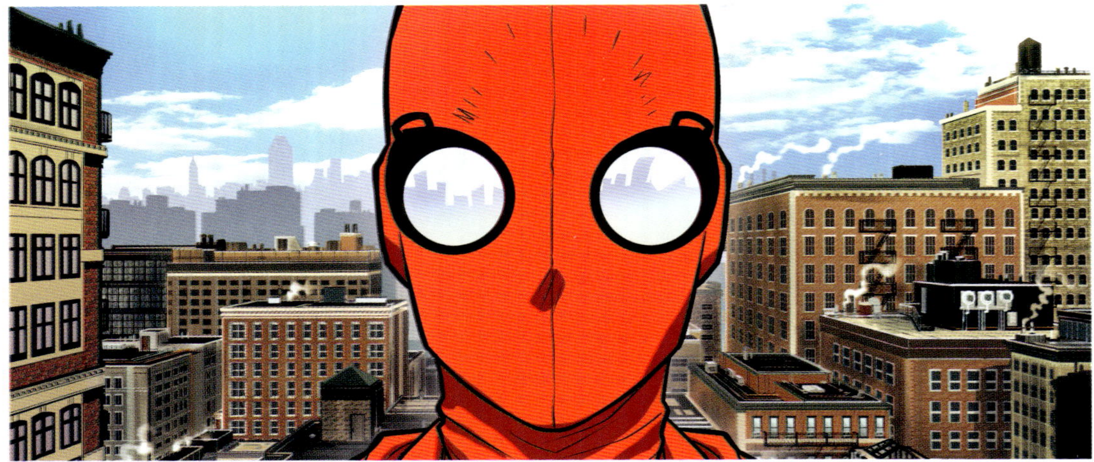

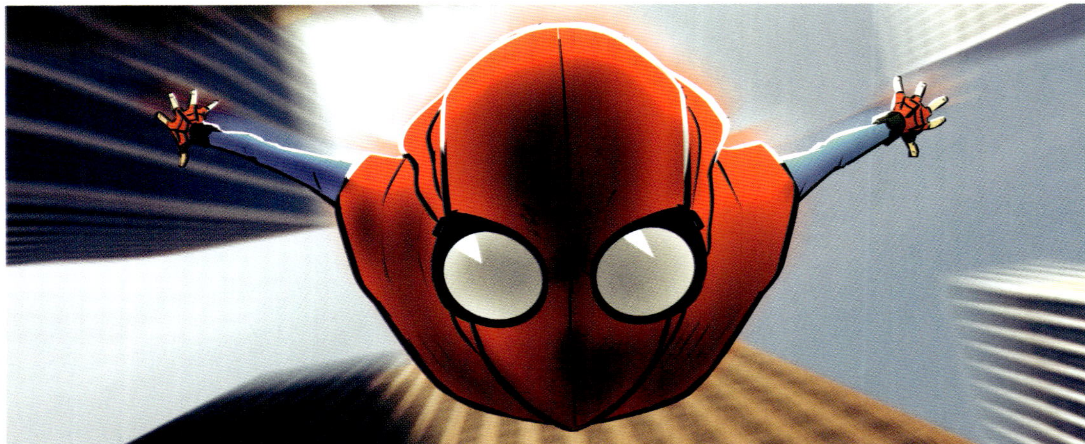

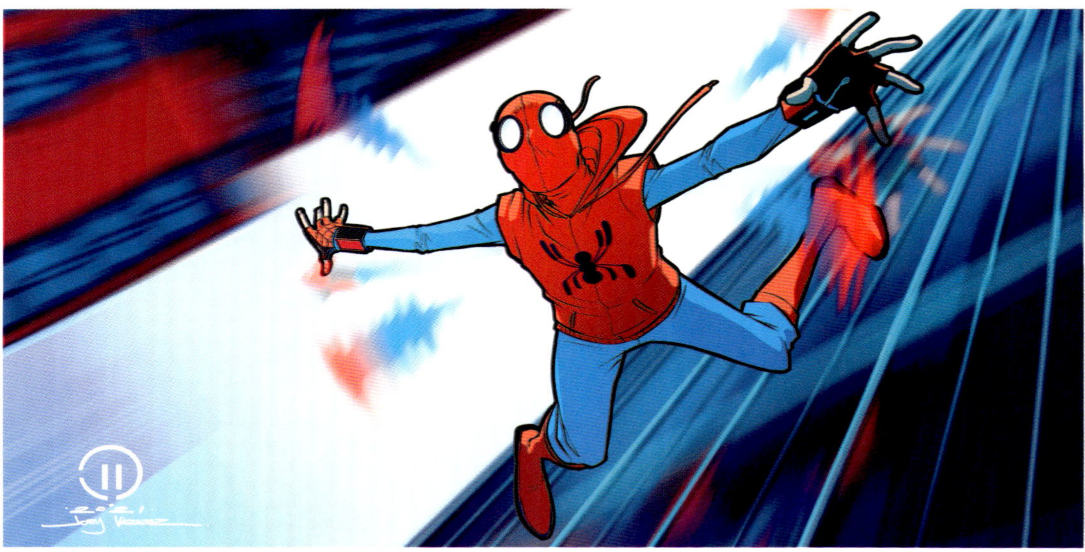

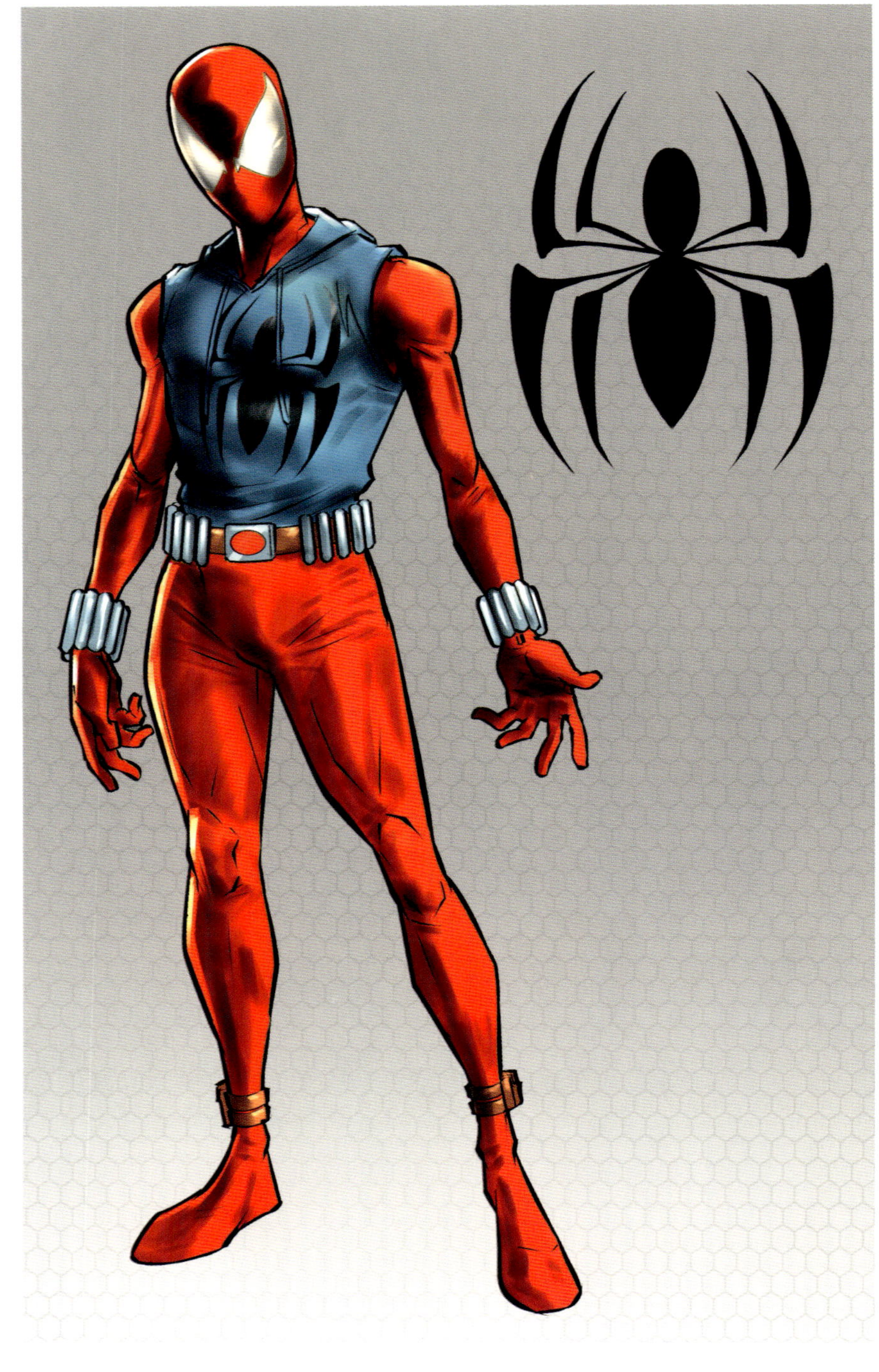

THIS PAGE Joey Vazquez **1** Ryan Meinerding
2 Leonardo Romero **3–6** Joey Vazquez

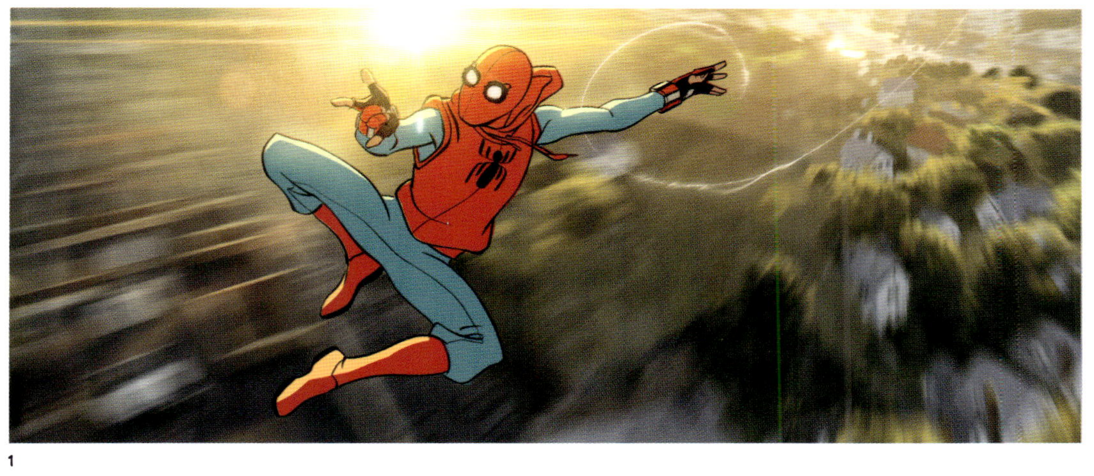

1

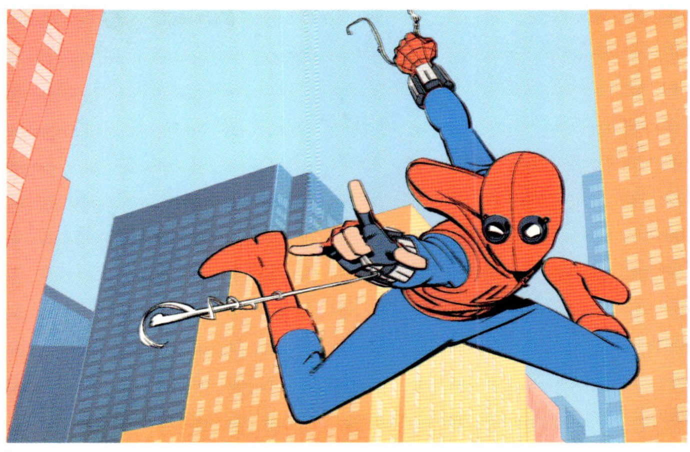

2

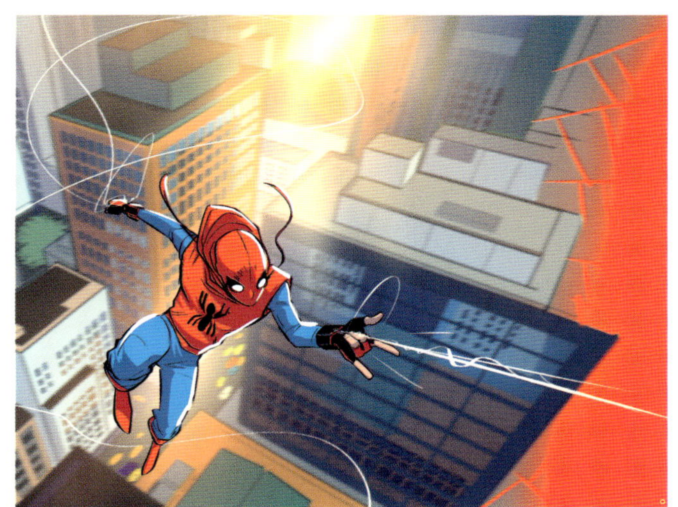

3

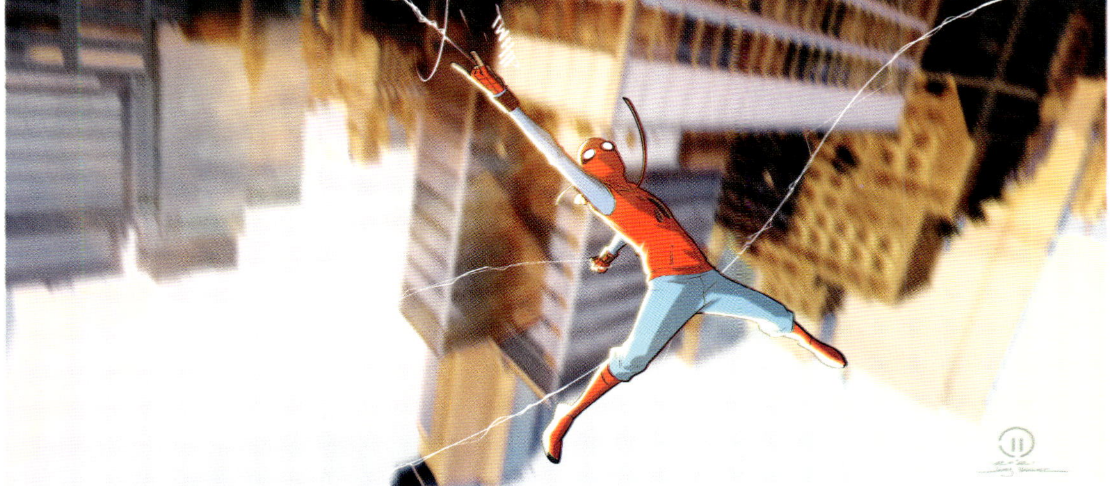

4

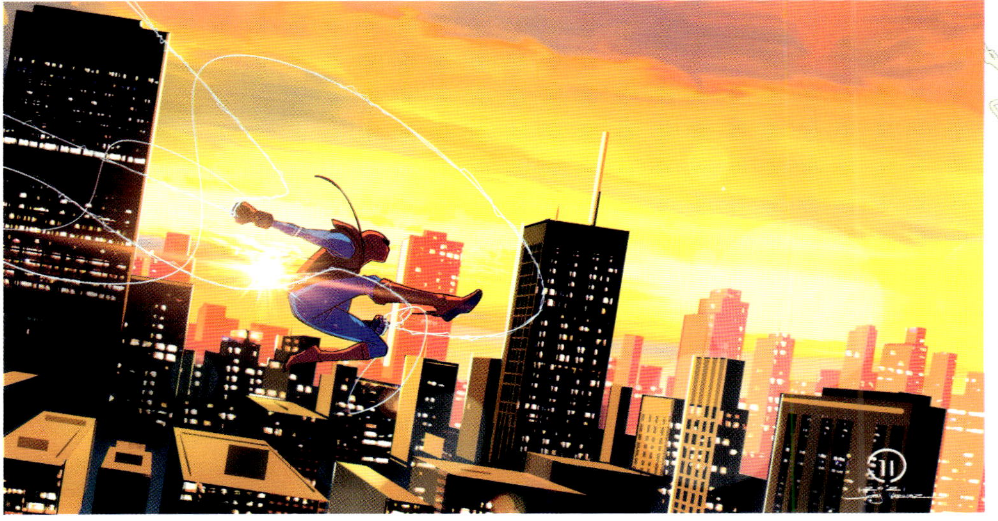

5

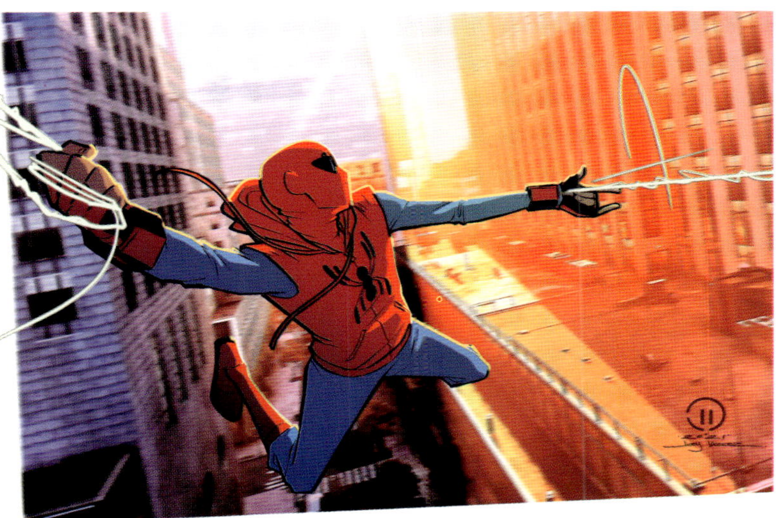

6

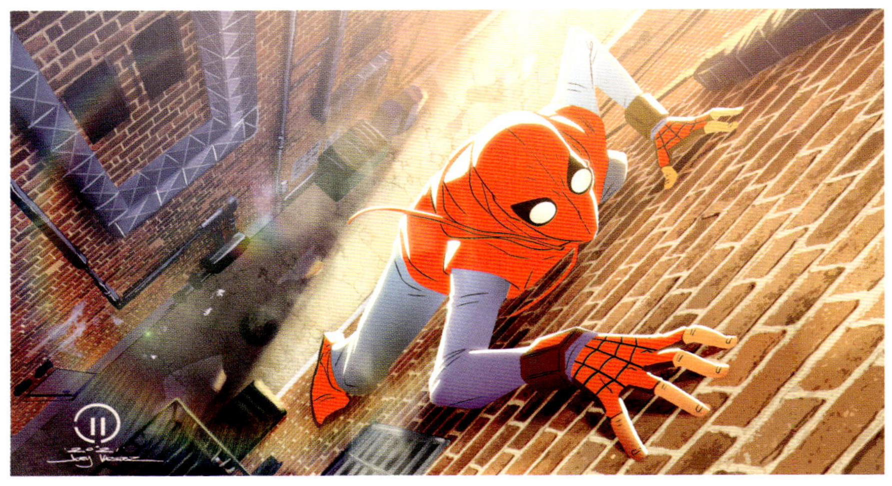

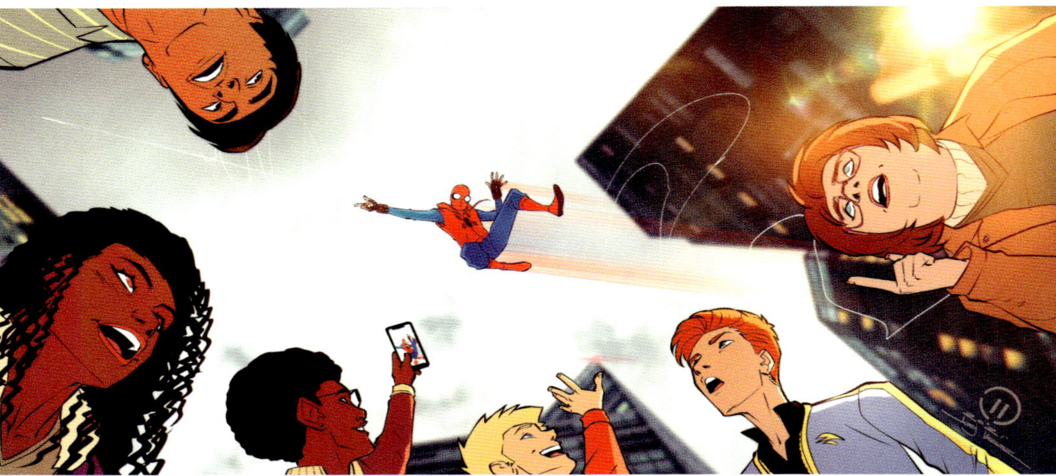

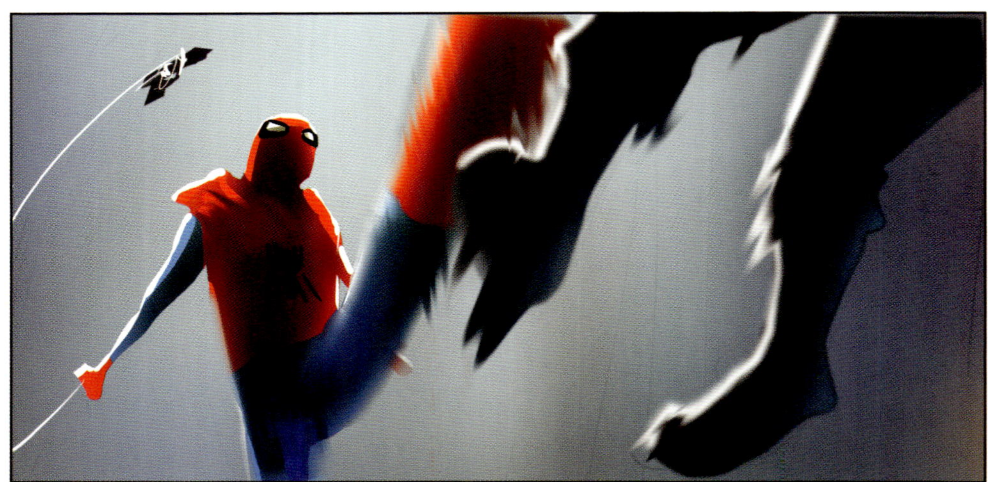

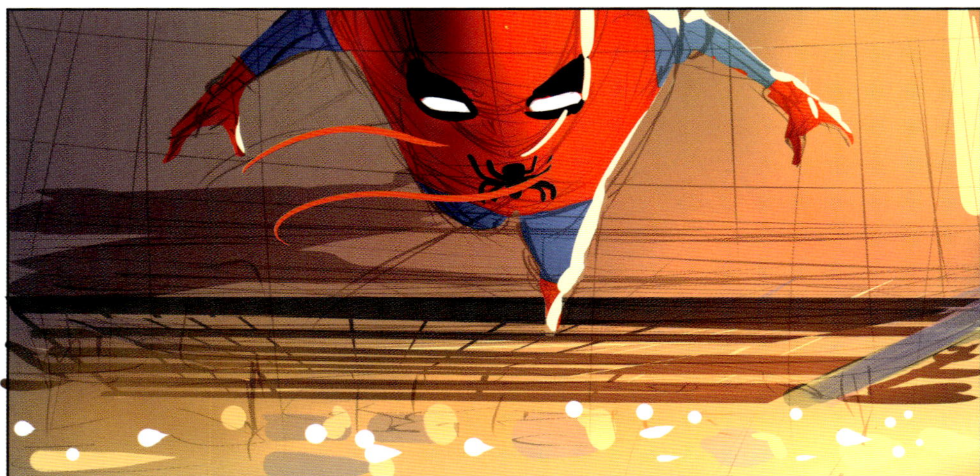

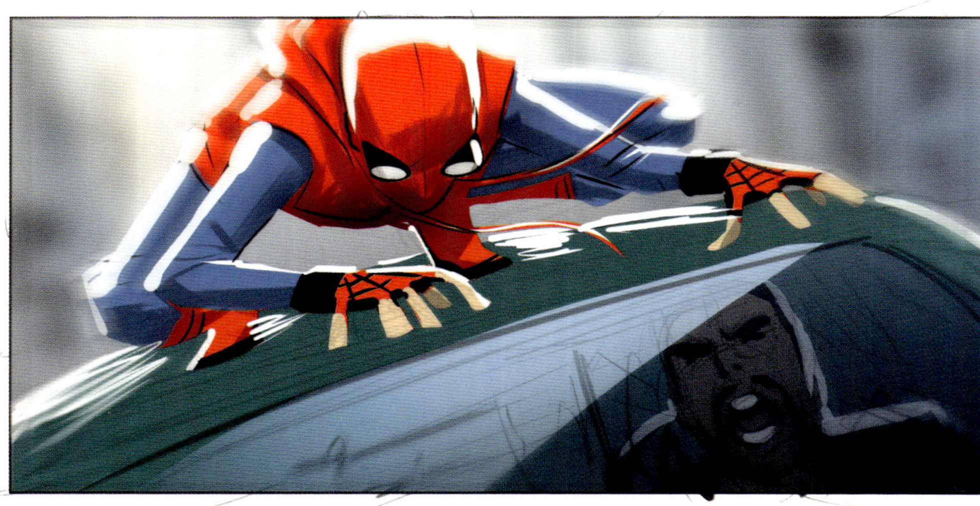

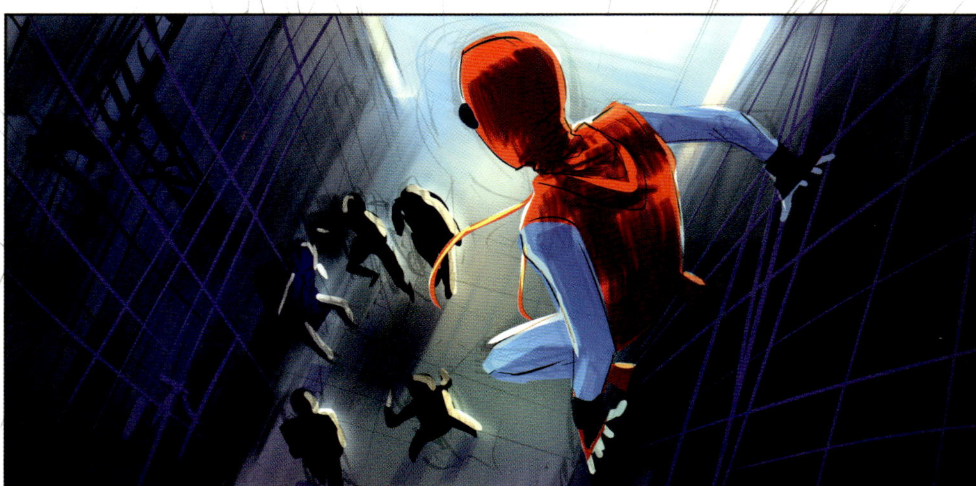

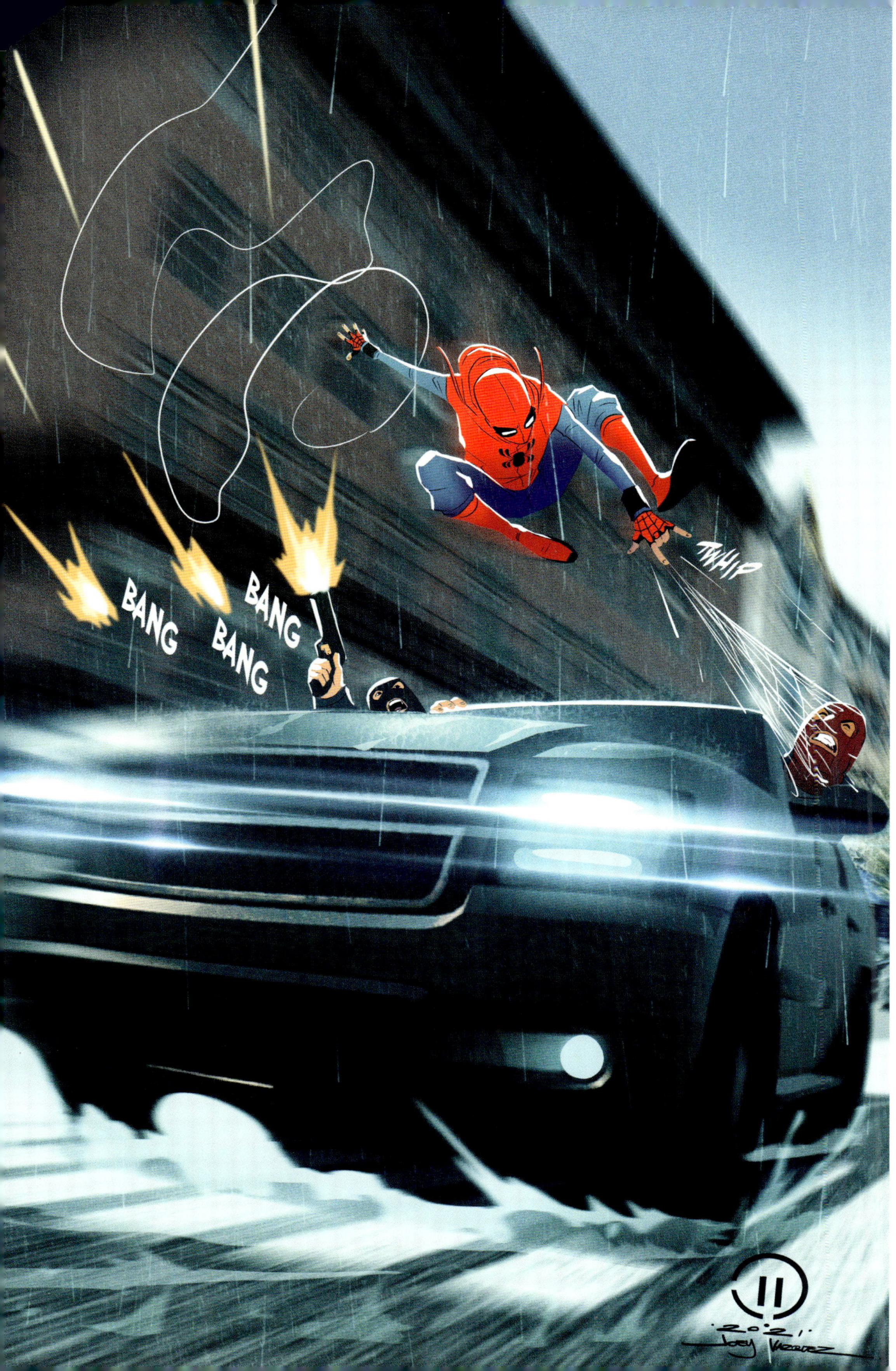

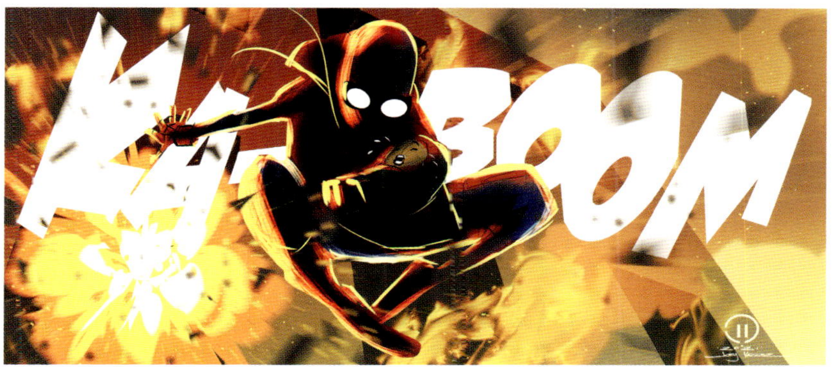

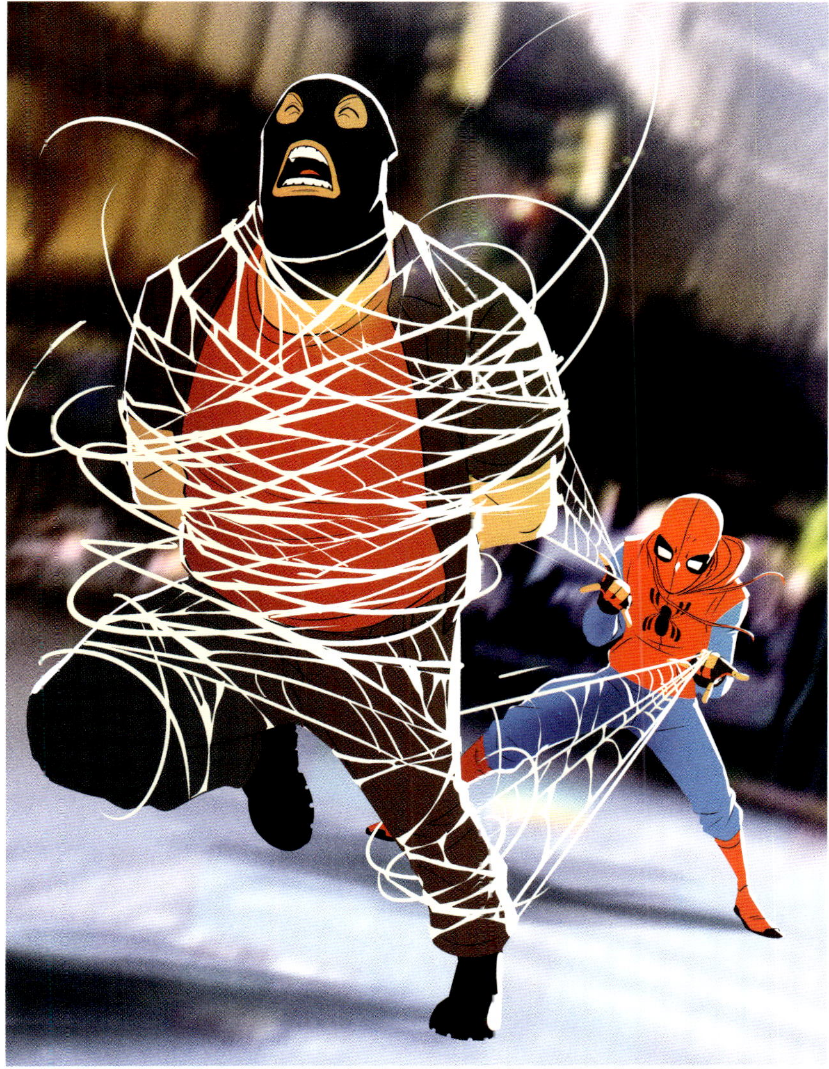

THIS SPREAD Joey Vazquez

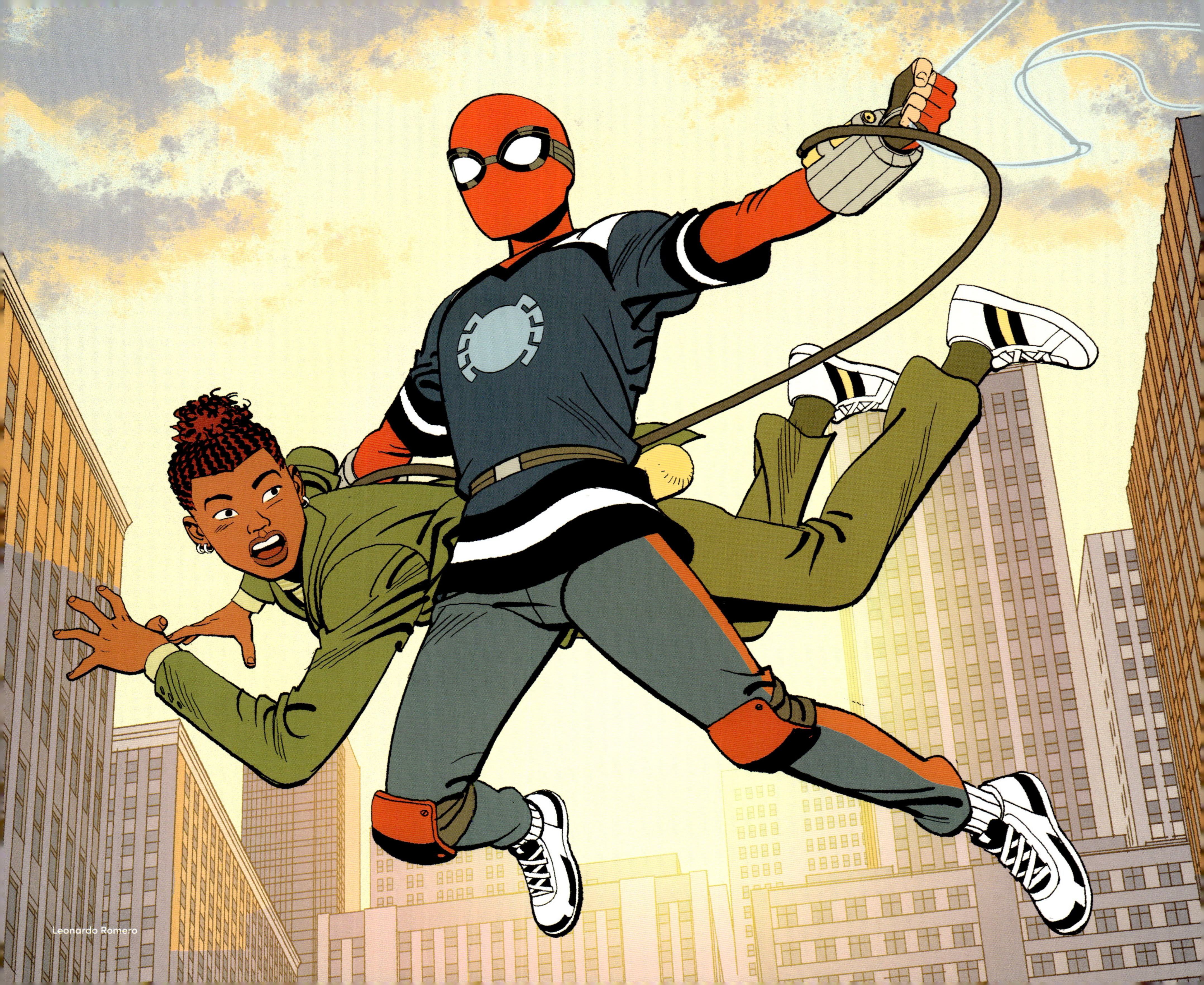
Leonardo Romero

EPISODE ONE

AMAZING FANTASY

THE SERIES KICKS OFF ON AN ELECTRIC, HIGH-ENERGY NOTE AS IT INTRODUCES VIEWERS TO A NEW VERSION OF PETER PARKER—VOICED BY HUDSON THAMES (MARVEL ANIMATION'S *WHAT IF...?*, MARVEL ANIMATION'S *MARVEL ZOMBIES*). ON HIS FIRST DAY AT MIDTOWN HIGH SCHOOL, PETER RESCUES HIS NEW FRIEND NICO MINORU (GRACE SONG) FROM A SYMBIOTIC ALIEN BEING PURSUED BY DOCTOR STRANGE THROUGH A PORTAL. THE PORTAL ALSO BRINGS A SPIDER INTO THIS WORLD, WHICH ENDS UP BITING PETER AND GIVING HIM HIS SPIDEY SUPER-POWERS. WE FLASH FORWARD A FEW MONTHS AND FIND PETER GOING THROUGH THE TRIALS AND TRIBULATIONS OF HIGH SCHOOL LIFE. AN OPPORTUNE MEETING WITH NORMAN OSBORN (COLMAN DOMINGO) LEADS TO AN INTERNSHIP AT HIS PREEMINENT TECH COMPANY, OSCORP. THE EPISODE ALSO INTRODUCES VIEWERS TO PETER'S CHILDHOOD CRUSH AND FORMER BABYSITTER, PEARL PANGAN (CATHY ANG), AND HER NEW BOYFRIEND, FOOTBALL TEAM CAPTAIN LONNIE LINCOLN (EUGENE BYRD). PETER ALSO CROSSES PATHS WITH NORMAN'S SON, HARRY OSBORN (ZENO ROBINSON), WHEN HE SAVES HIM FROM A GROUP OF THUGS.

"IT'S VERY HARD to set up this colorful world and introduce all these characters even if you feel like you know them in the pilot," says Executive Producer/Showrunner Jeff Trammell. "The challenge with the first episode was that we had to get a lot across in a very short time. Just seeing Peter get ready and immediately go with the big fake out of 'Oh, he missed the train . . . is he going to swing to school?' and 'Wait, he doesn't even have the powers yet?' Then we immediately thrust you into the conversation where we find out that Ben has passed, so already a lot of this world is different from what we're expecting."

"We put a spin on his origin story in this opening episode," says Executive Producer Brad Winderbaum. "If you remember that moment in *Captain America: Civil War* where he [Peter Paker] finds the DVD player in the trash and walks home to his apartment, you follow him down the hallway, and who's sitting on his couch? It's Tony Stark. Well, in this universe, there's someone very different sitting on that couch, and it's Norman Osborn, who recruits him into an elite internship for high-school-age geniuses. In future episodes, we learn that every character Norman's recruited is a suspect: They're all people that he thinks might be Spider-Man."

Of course, the twists keep coming, and viewers discover things are different from the Peter Parker storyline known from the live-action movies. "For me, it was important to lean on a lot of the really classic moments and very relatable instances," adds Trammell. "We were building a world by introducing people and places

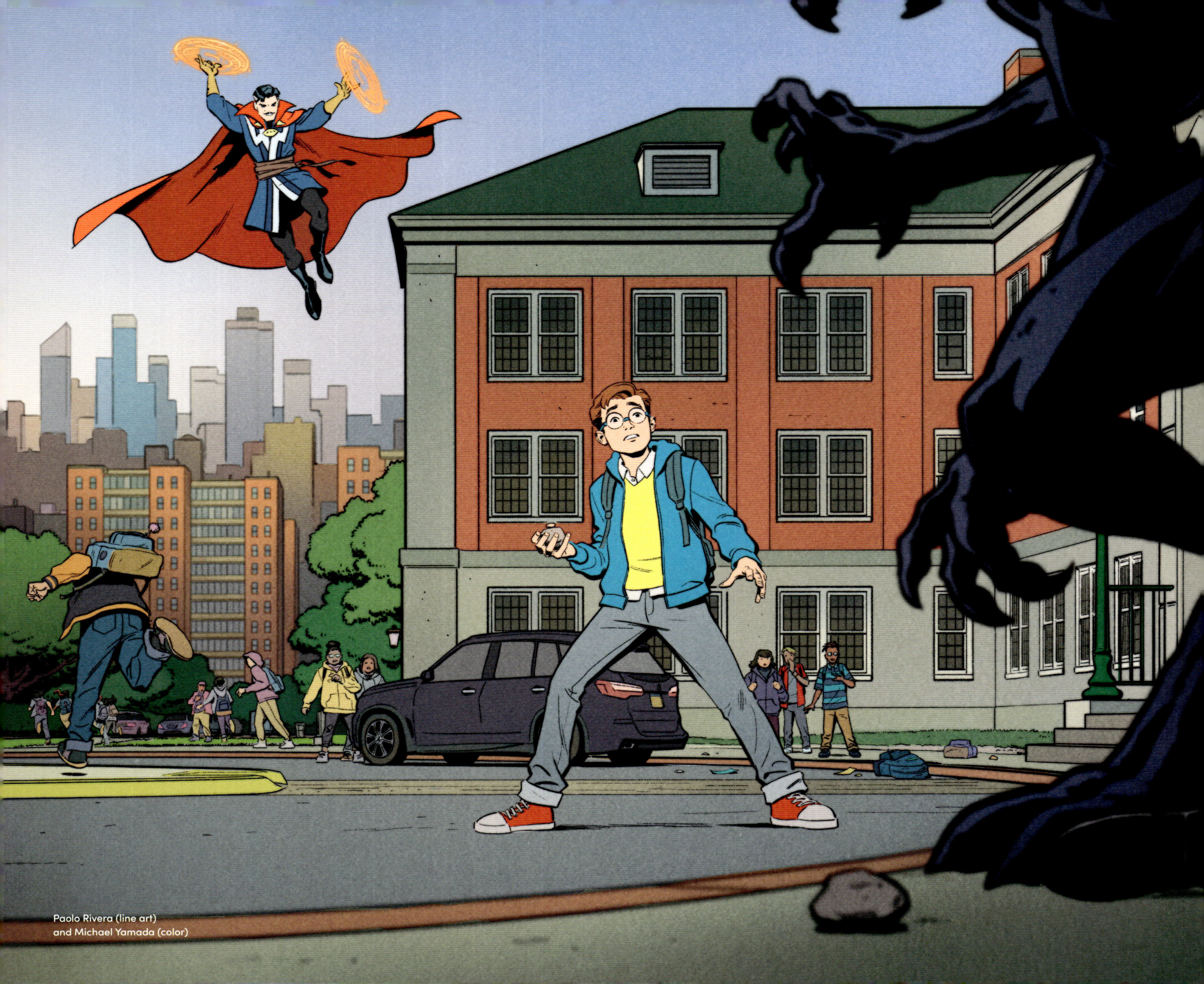

Paolo Rivera (line art)
and Michael Yamada (color)

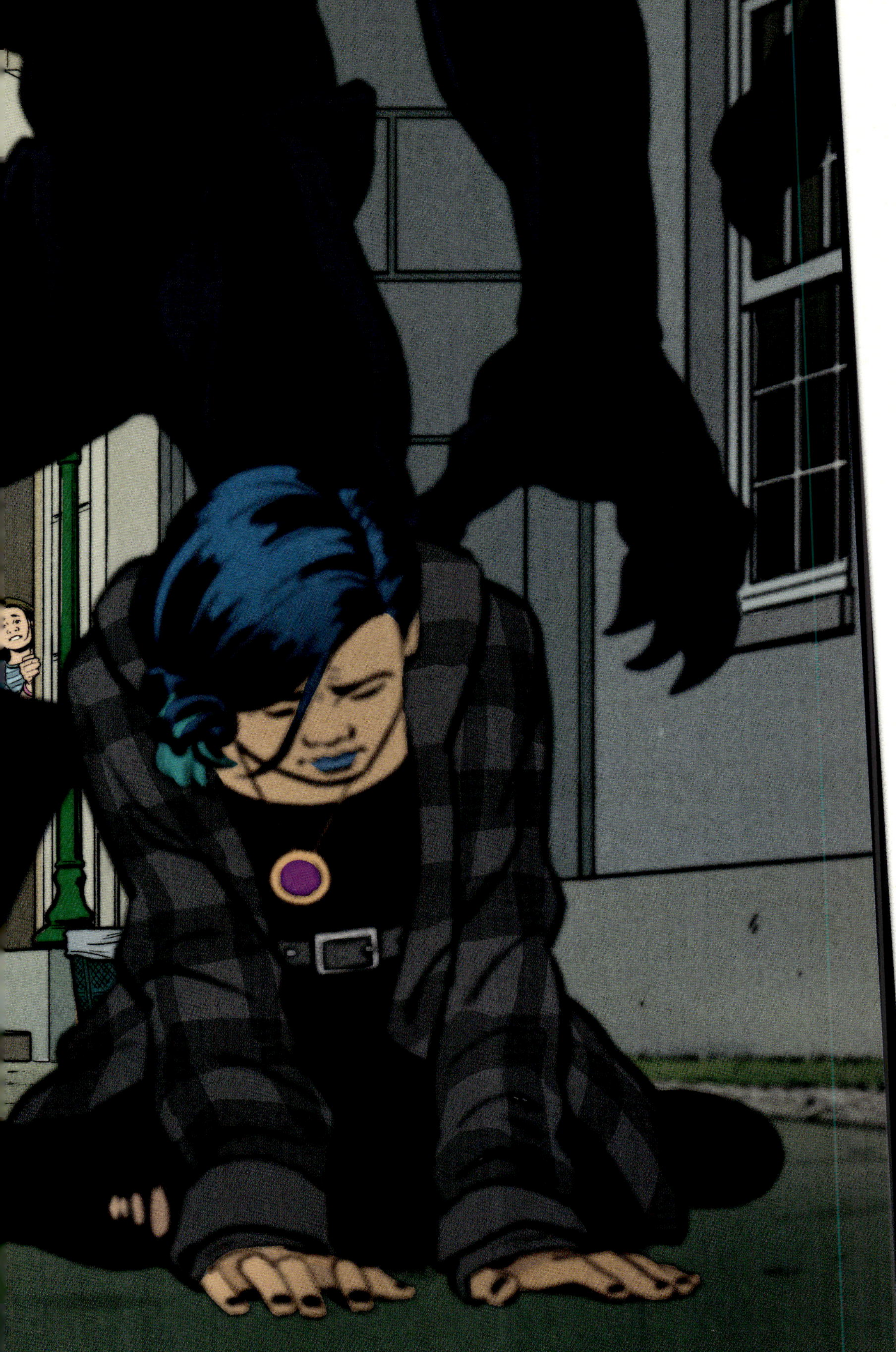

that might be familiar, but then changing those things just to keep the audience on their toes—just like the way we introduced Norman Osborn into the show."

Co-Executive Producer/Supervising Director Mel Zwyer says he also enjoys the playful twists featured in the first episode. "After we introduce how Peter gets bitten by the spider, we jump a few months into the future, and we skip the parts where he begins to realize he has these powers," he says. "We introduce Norman Osborn, which, according to the MCU, should have been the Robert Downey Jr. version of Tony Stark, but we switched it up—almost like a big *What If...?* episode. We filmed it exactly like *Captain America: Civil War*. I also loved how Peter's homemade suit works compared to all the other Spider-Man outfits. We gave him this little pressurized tank with the connecting tube on the lower hip. It looked totally homemade and realistic—it just felt right!"

Trammell and his team made sure to hide fun Easter eggs throughout the show. Eagle-eyed fans may notice a "Pizza Time" sign in the pilot (in the scene where Peter is picking up a pizza)—an homage to Sam Raimi's 2004 movie *Spider-Man 2*. And when we see Peter waking up, there's an *Amazing Fantasy* issue 14 on his head, which is the issue right before Spider-Man was introduced in 1962. Additionally, in the opening credits of each episode, there are different comic book covers. "I remember thinking that it would be cool if we could feature a different cover for every episode," says Trammell. "So, once we got the approval to do that, I went through and picked a different cover based on every single episode. I compiled them all and sent them to our lead character designer, Leo Romero, who then drew them in his style for the opening credit sequence."

Winderbaum also points out that the first episode of the series had to be in sync with the finale because of the complexity of the time loop. "The only way something like that can work is if you do all the math ahead of time," he notes. "When you go back and watch the first episode after you watch the finale, everything lines up perfectly."

He shares another interesting tidbit about Nico's role in the events of the episode. "She introduces herself right before the spider bite takes place, and as the season goes on, you might notice that her medallion has protective powers. In the drag race episode, it protects her from the vehicle that's going to smash into her. So, I like to think that Peter's involvement in the Symbiote battle at the school had something to do with her amulet too! Maybe the whole thing is the result of some magic spell that puts Peter in Nico's life to protect her from harm."

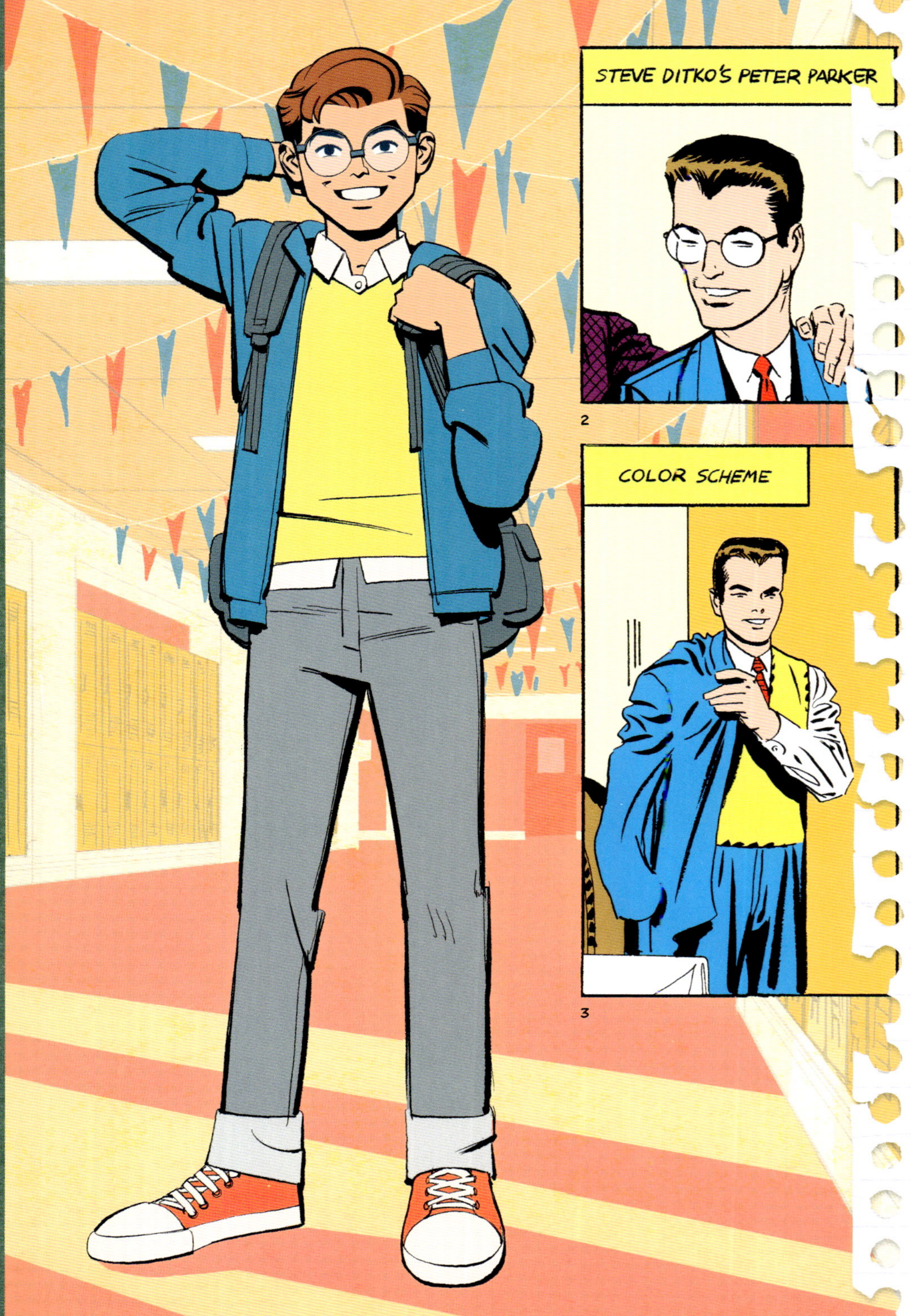

1 2 3

PETER PARKER/ SPIDER-MAN

Stan Lee and Steve Ditko's beloved high school student was first introduced in the August 1962 issue of the anthology comic book *Amazing Fantasy* (#15). Stan Lee once told the *Chicago Tribune* he liked Spider-Man because he was the character most like himself. "Nothing ever turns out 100 percent for him. OK . . . he's got a lot of problems—and he does things wrong. I can relate to that," said Lee.

The creators behind this latest incarnation of the optimistic character wanted him to follow in the footsteps of all his predecessors, while being a good reflection of who a young hero should be in our modern world. In the series, Peter is voiced by actor Hudson Thames, who also plays the character in Marvel's *What If...?* and *Marvel Zombies*.

"There is such a great history with this character and so many different reasons fans identify with him," says Executive Producer Dana Vasquez-Eberhardt. "There is huge love for all his iterations in the many comics, animated shows and movies, and live-action features. A lot of the older fans are parents, and they love sharing their version of Peter Parker and Spider-Man with their own kids. They're sharing the values that they learned from Spidey, so that's why it's very personal to audiences."

Executive Producer/Showrunner Jeff Trammell says he loves Peter's good and trusting nature. "He's very driven to help people. One of my favorite things about him is that although he's got all this power, he's a diamond in the rough. So, there's a lot of influence from the outside world that is constantly coming at him—that includes how he's perceived by his friends or his aunt or the lessons that he learned before we even begin with him in the series. I'm looking forward to tackling that more in future seasons, but at the core of everything, we have a hero who is a very good person that wants to help people, and we get to see him tested. But at the end of the day, he always has that main hero component."

Lead Character Designer Leonardo Romero says he has a folder on his computer with something close to 300 different designs for Peter Parker. "Naturally, designing the main character took the most effort, but it was also the most fun," says the artist. "In my head, I imagined Peter as a modern, teenage version of the character imagined by John Romita Sr. I tried to draw based on that image. There were ones that had different hairstyles that echoed Ditko's version too. We also had ones that looked a bit more like Tom Holland in the movies."

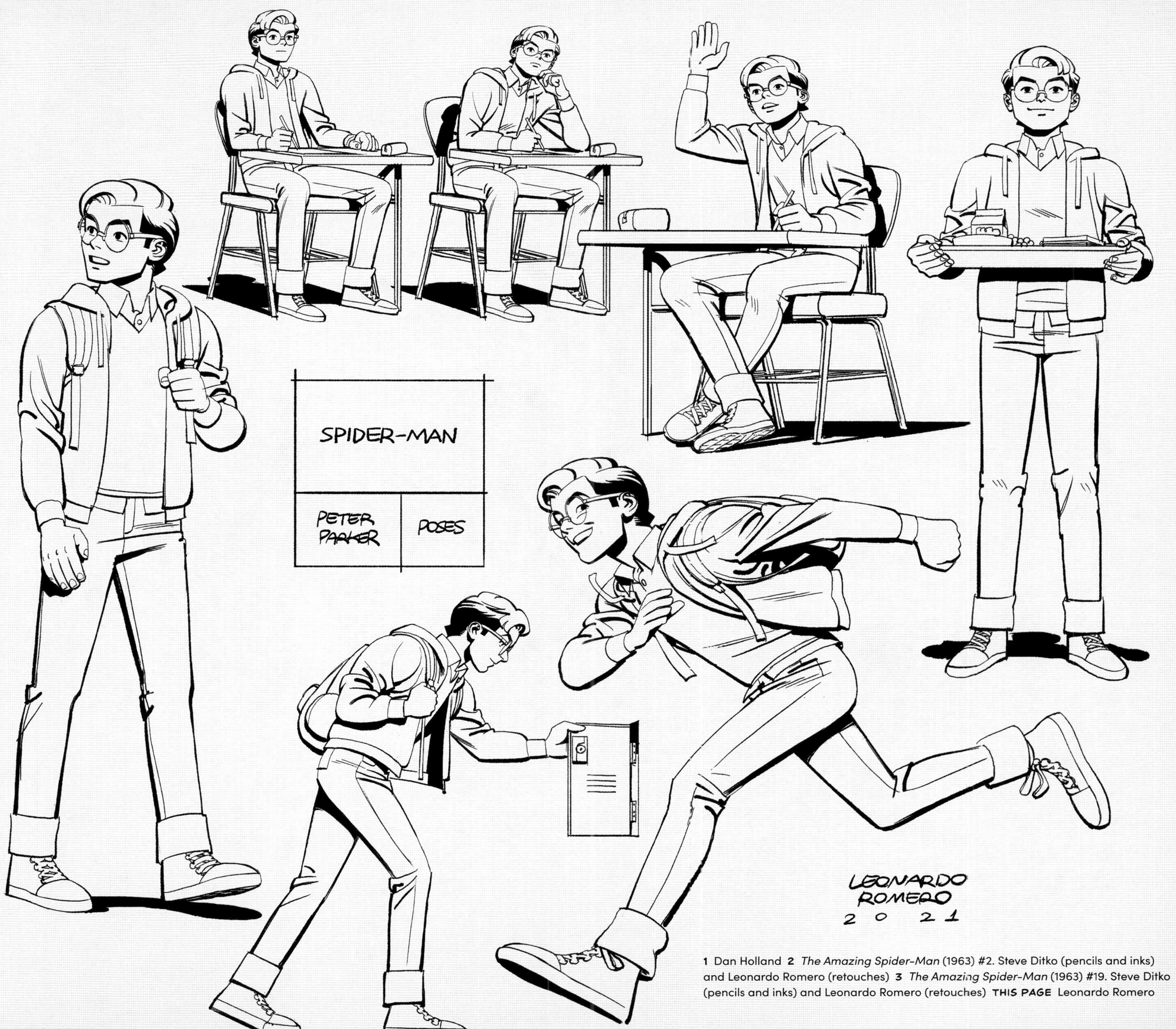

1 Dan Holland **2** *The Amazing Spider-Man* (1963) #2. Steve Ditko (pencils and inks) and Leonardo Romero (retouches) **3** *The Amazing Spider-Man* (1963) #19. Steve Ditko (pencils and inks) and Leonardo Romero (retouches) **THIS PAGE** Leonardo Romero

Of course, no discussion of Spider-Man would be complete without the evolution of his Spidey suit throughout the first season. Romero says the first drawings he did for the suit were inspired by the homemade suit seen in the MCU projects. "[Showrunner] Jeff Trammell and [Co-Executive Producer/Supervising Director] Mel Zwyer wanted our costume to be a bit different. So, it started to evolve into its own thing. First, it's more of a hoodie, then a shirt, then you have the Oscorp suit that becomes the foundation for the final payoff. We were aiming to take that classic Spider-Man and put our own stamp on it. That was the toughest part because Ditko did such a great job from the get-go. So, the question was, how do we offer something that is different but doesn't move away too much from that? It had to be unique and classic at the same time."

Executive Producer Brad Winderbaum adds, "Jeff [Trammell], Ryan [Meinerding], and the rest of our design team really tried to reference what Steve Ditko did in a modern setting. We also knew that we had to earn the final version of the classic suit. We designed a new homemade suit and several others throughout the show, and he changes his costume multiple times, which was really fun. Again, it was one of those instances of the design work being incremental: Everything had to be earned over time."

Associate Producer Alex Scharf mentions that the show's executive producer, Ryan Meinerding, who is also Head of Visual Development at Marvel Studios, is a huge Spider-Man aficionado. "He had designed all the suits for the Spider-Man MCU movies," says Scharf. "He just knows all the details, including what makes it iconic, as well as the tech lines and different colorings. It's a very tricky thing because you don't want to go too extreme or out there, and everyone will say, 'Hey, that's not the Spider-Man we're used to.' He brought this extreme eye to detail and knowledge to the table."

THIS PAGE Julen Urrutia Perez
OPPOSITE Joey Vazquez

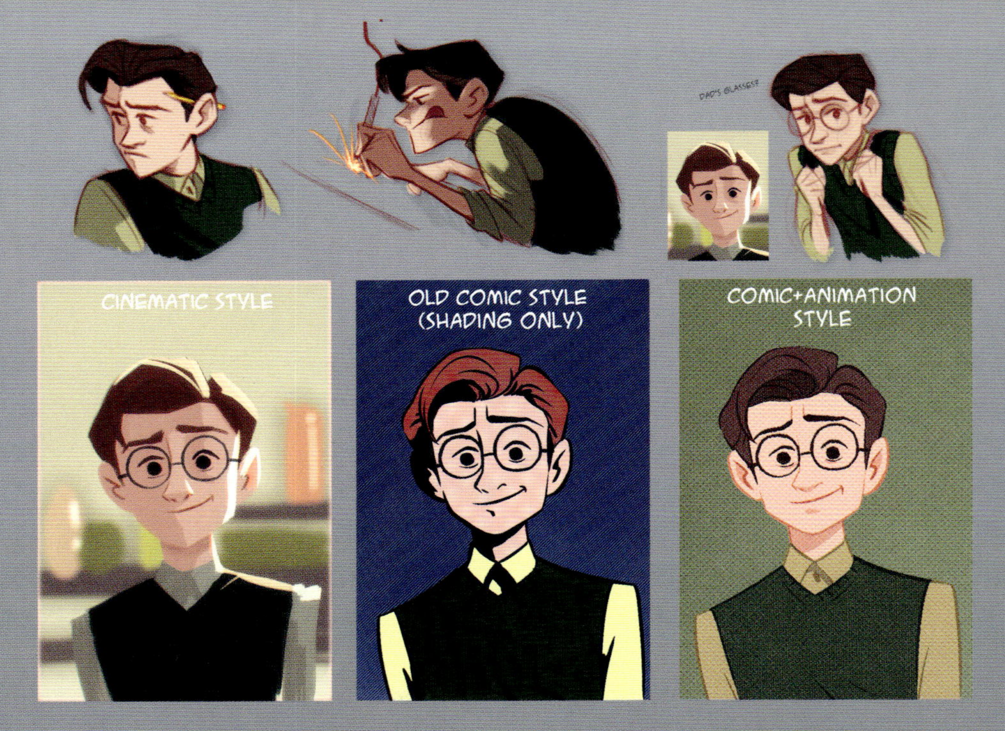

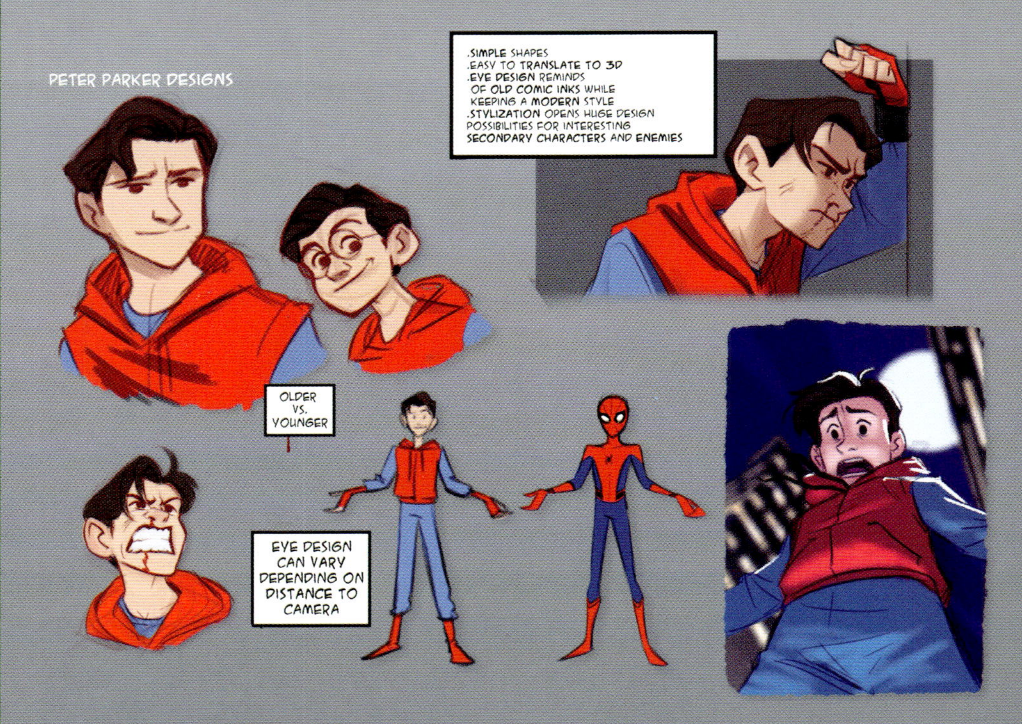

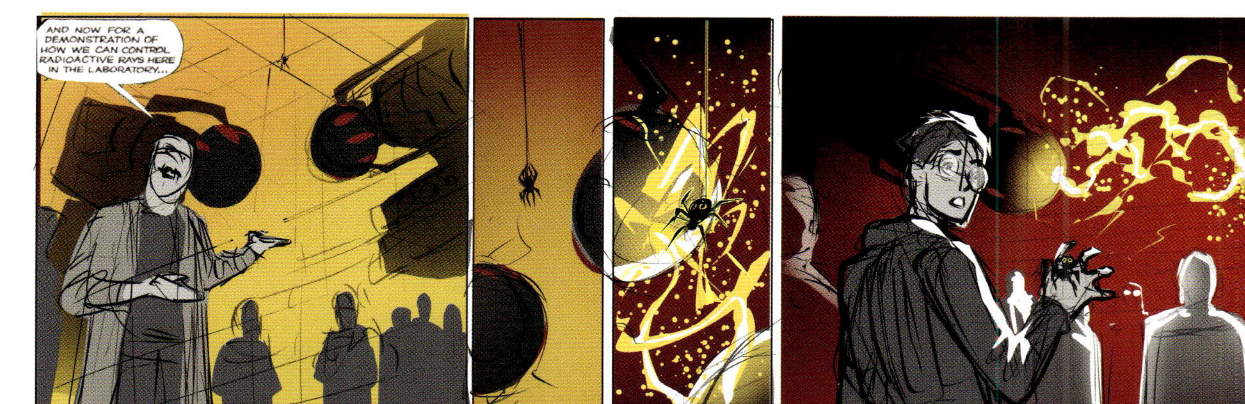
AND NOW FOR A DEMONSTRATION OF HOW WE CAN CONTROL RADIOACTIVE RAYS HERE IN THE LABORATORY...
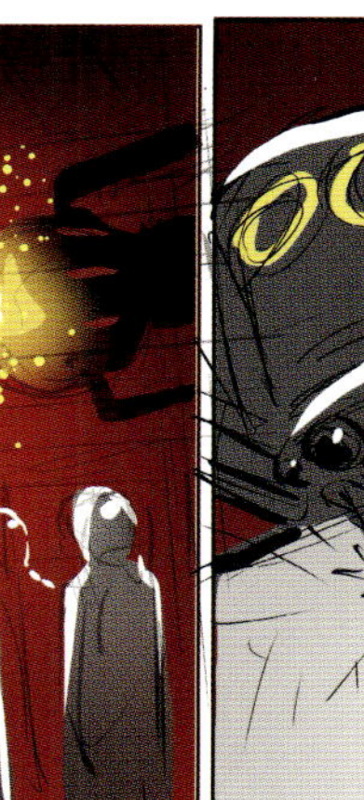
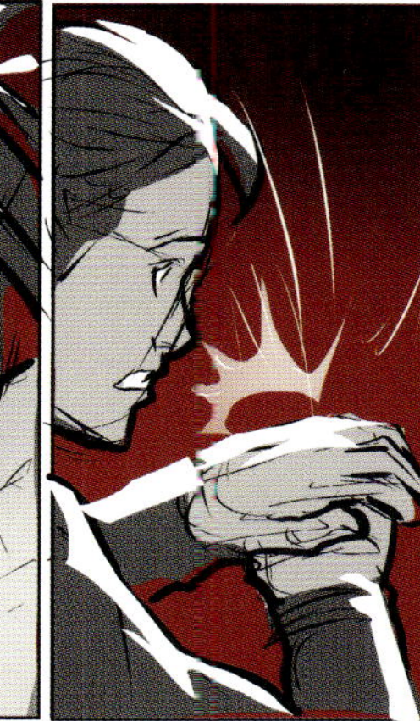
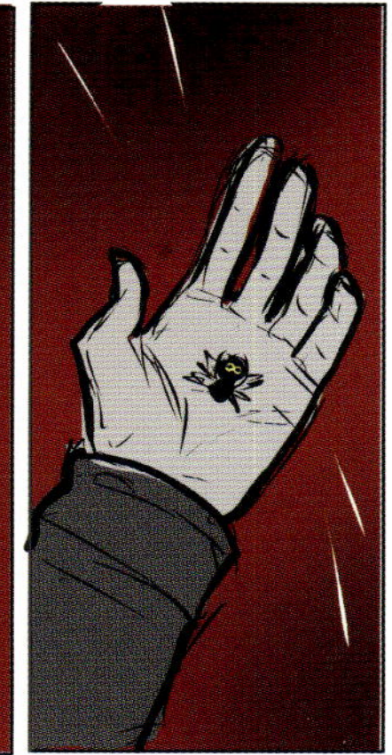
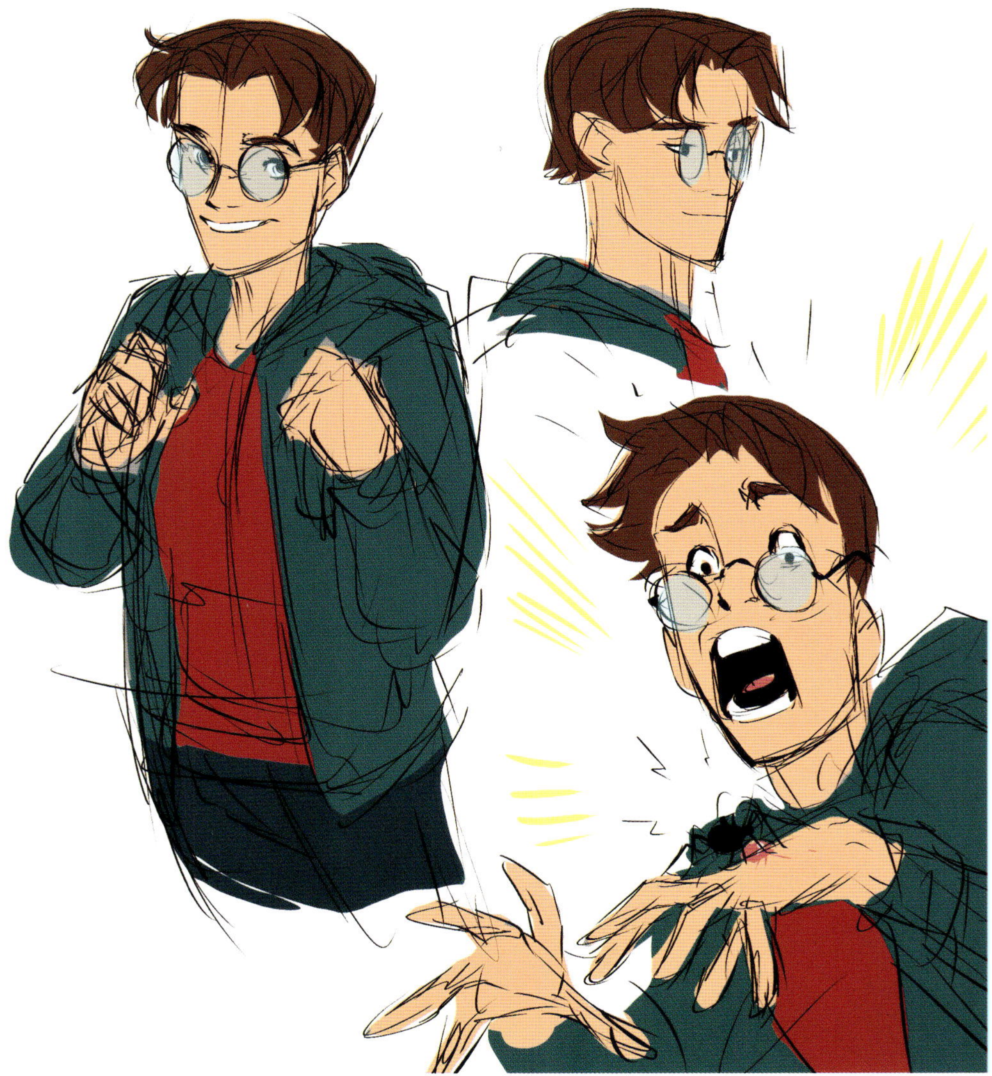
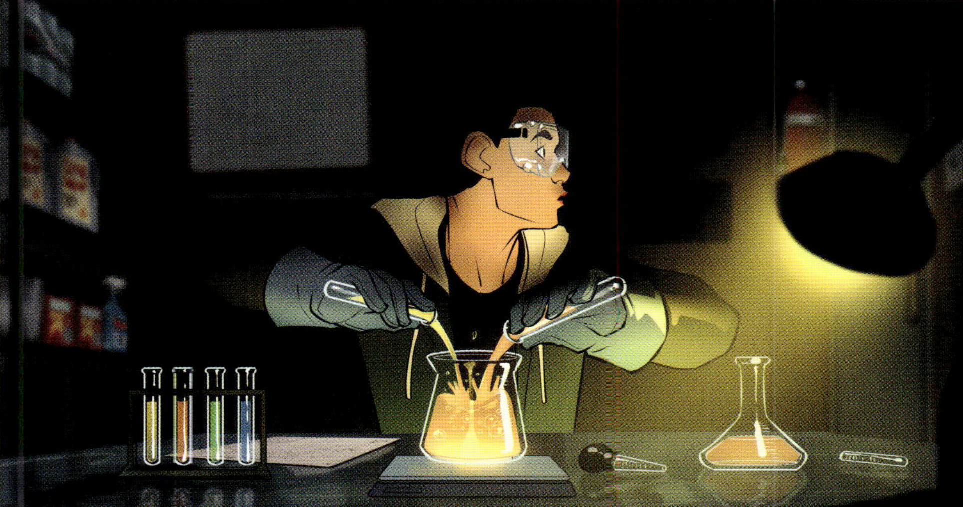
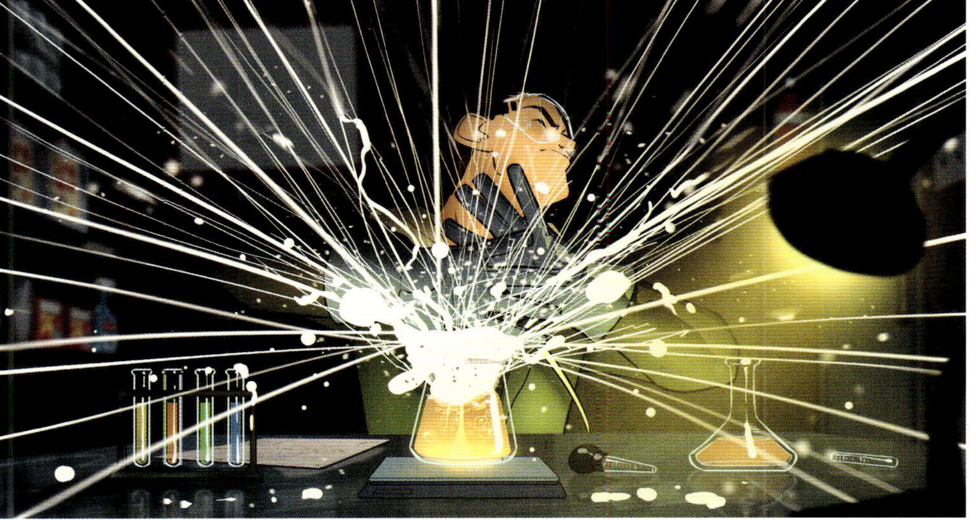

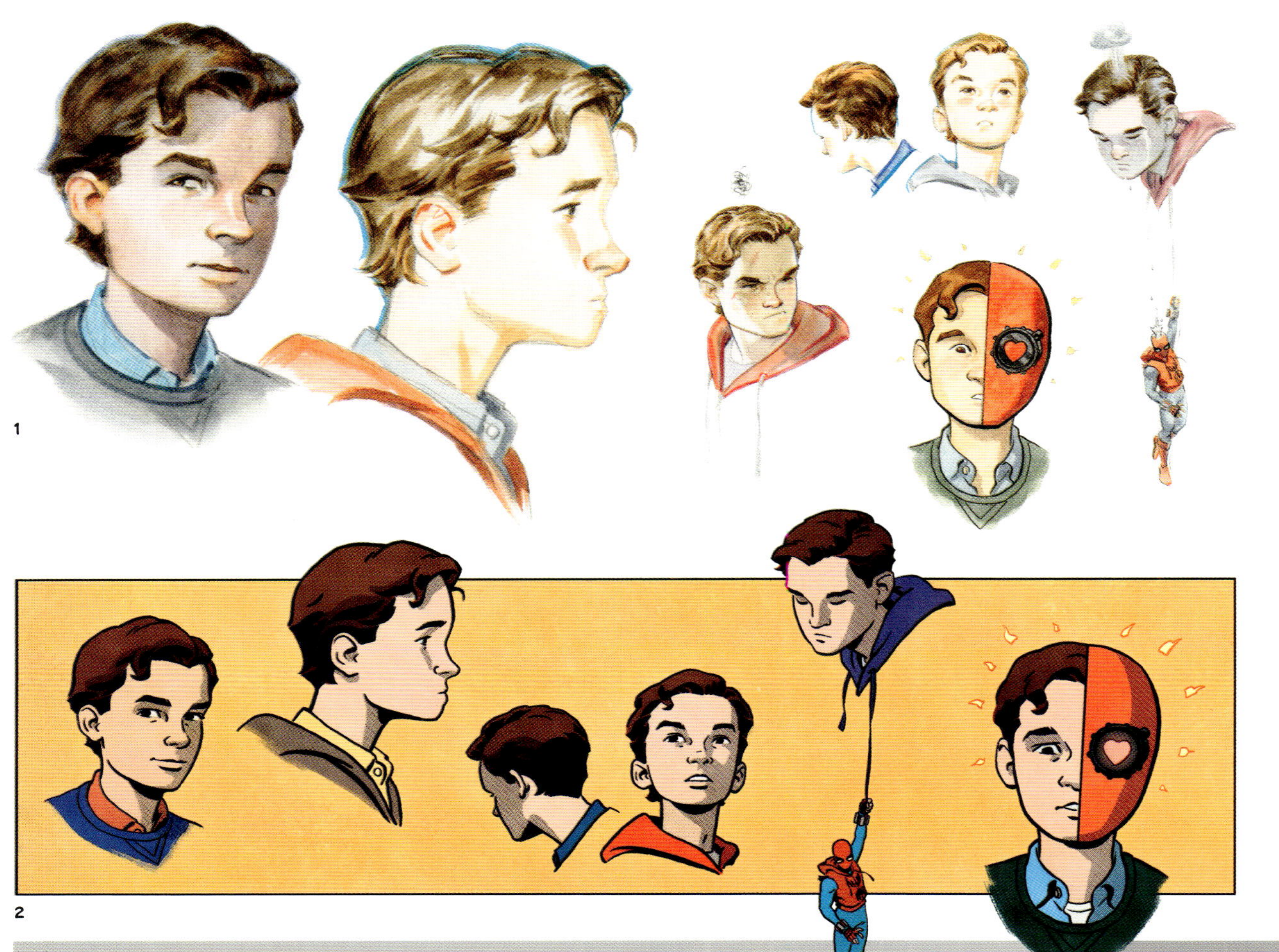

1

2

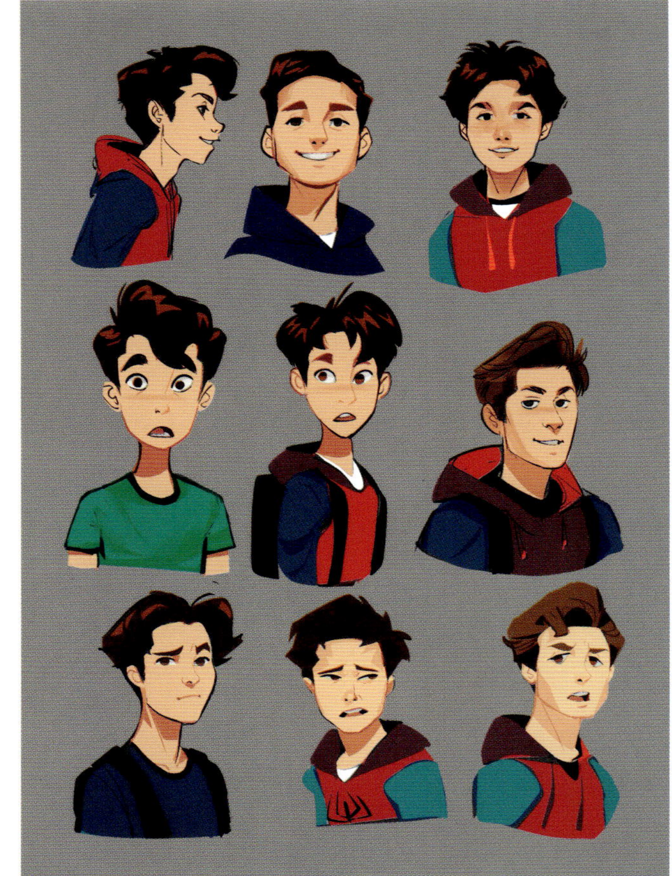

3

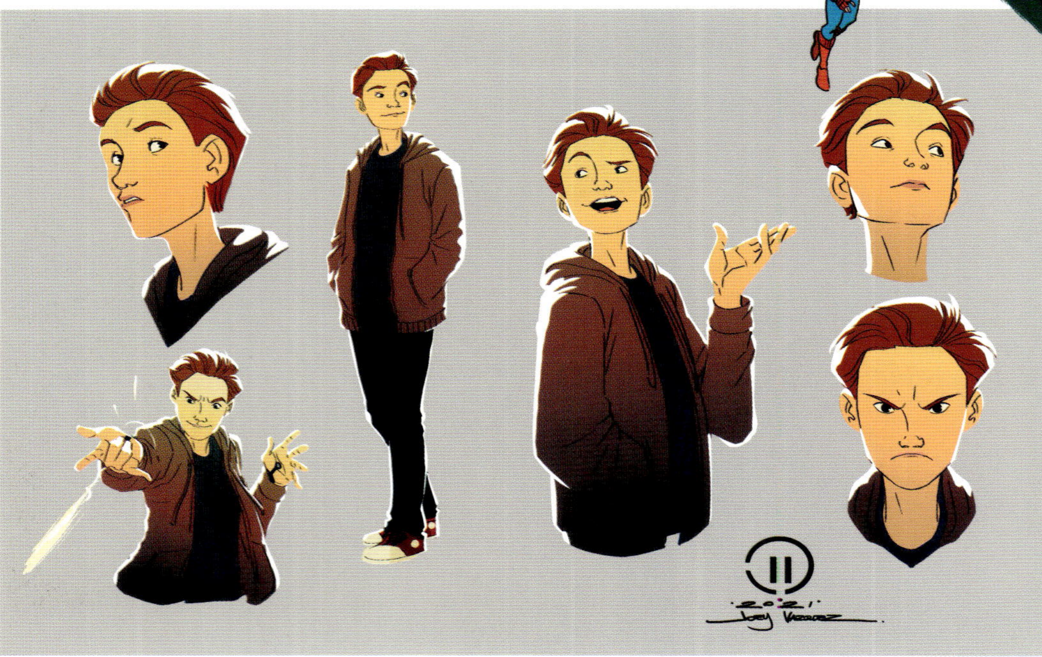

4

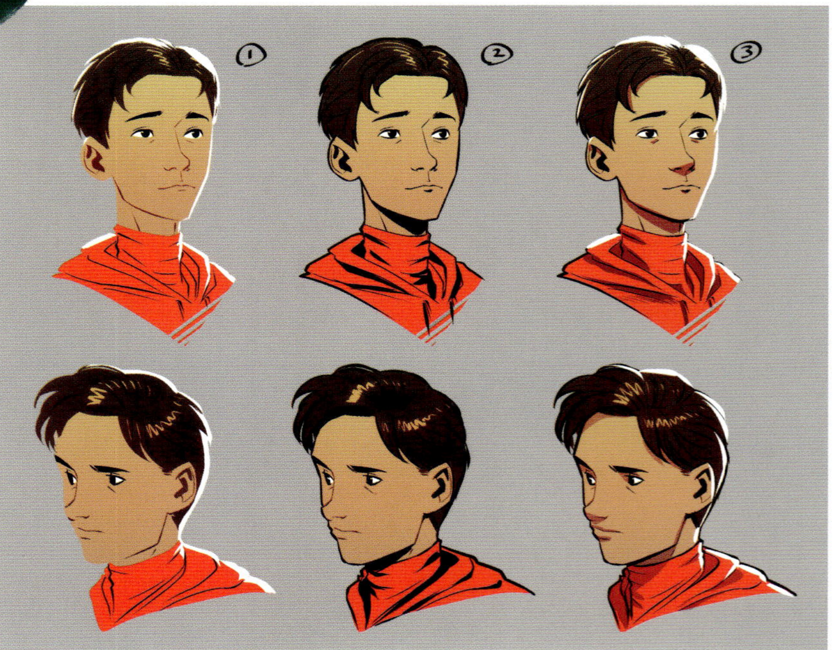

5

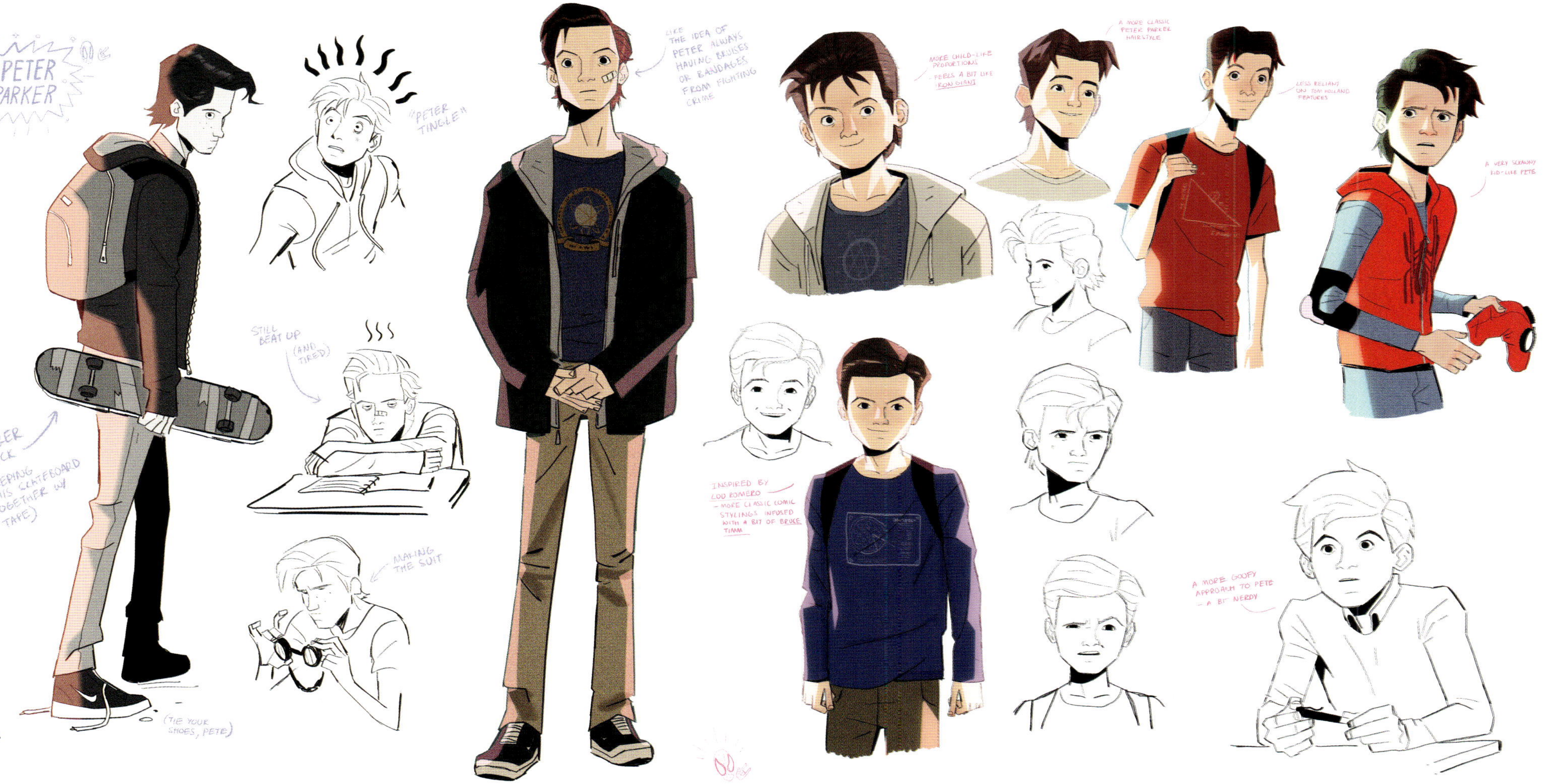

PETER PARKER

"PETER TINGLE"

PARKER LUCK (KEEPING HIS SKATEBOARD TOGETHER W/ TAPE)

STILL BEAT UP (AND TIRED)

MAKING THE SUIT

(TIE YOUR SHOES, PETE)

LIKE THE IDEA OF PETER ALWAYS HAVING BRUISES OR BANDAGES FROM FIGHTING CRIME

MORE CHILD-LIKE PROPORTIONS
- FEELS A BIT LIKE IRON GIANT

A MORE CLASSIC PETER PARKER HAIRSTYLE

LESS RELIANT ON TOM HOLLAND FEATURES

A VERY SCRAWNY KID-LIKE PETE

INSPIRED BY LOU ROMERO
- MORE CLASSIC COMIC STYLINGS INFUSED WITH A BIT OF BRUCE TIMM

A MORE GOOFY APPROACH TO PETE
- A BIT NERDY

6

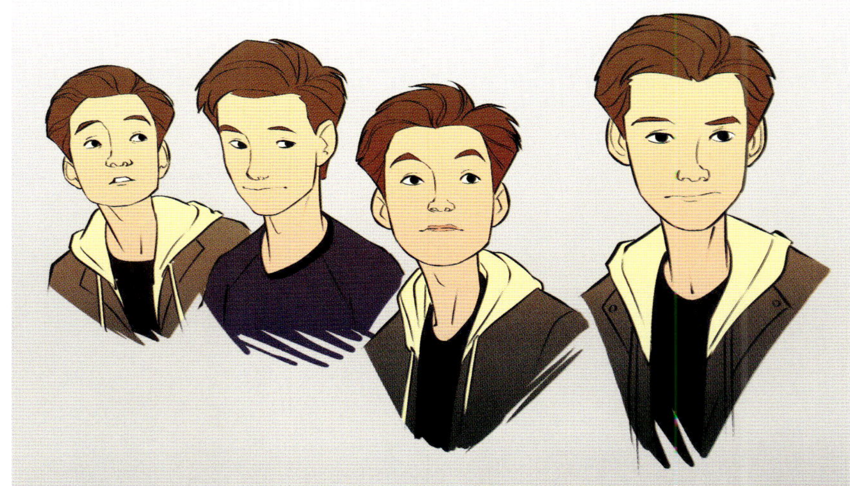

7

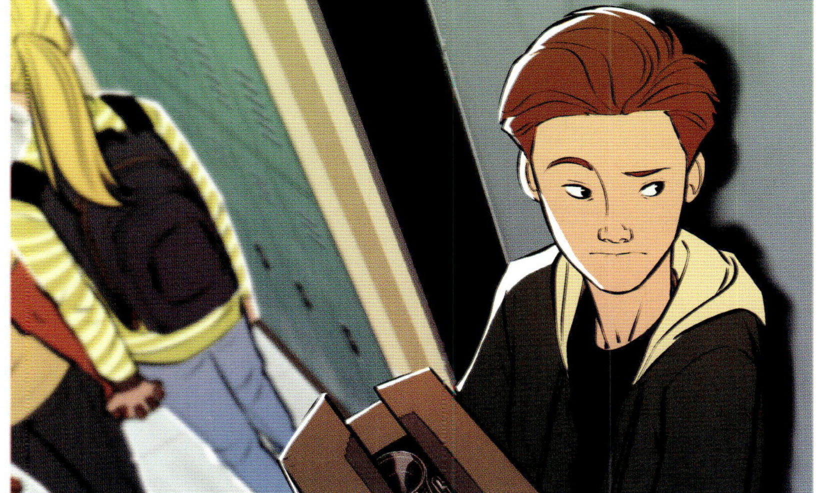

8

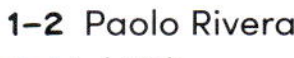

1–2 Paolo Rivera
3 Mel Milton
4–5 Joey Vazquez
6 Kal Athannassov
7–8 Joey Vazquez

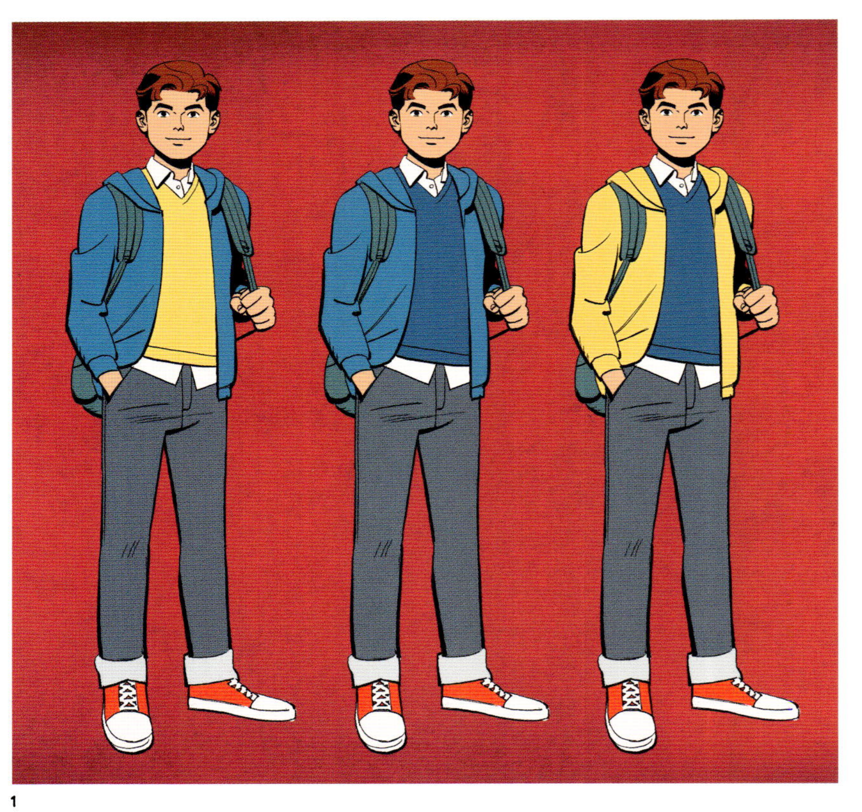

1

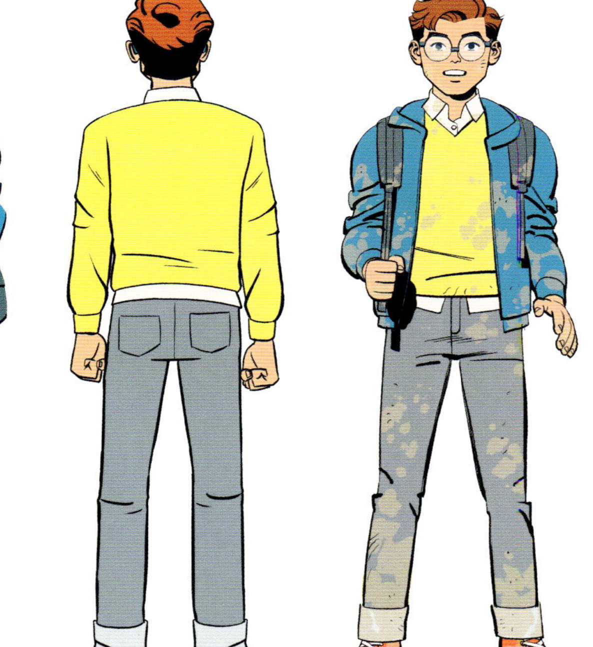

2

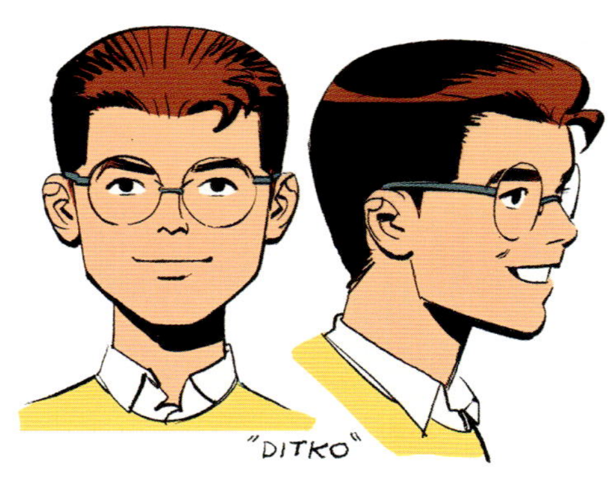

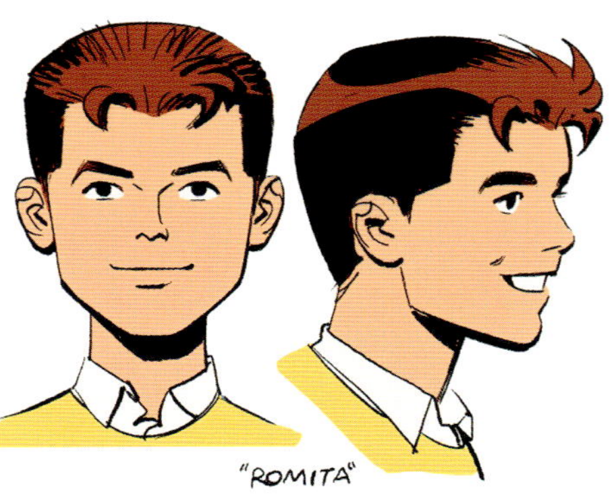

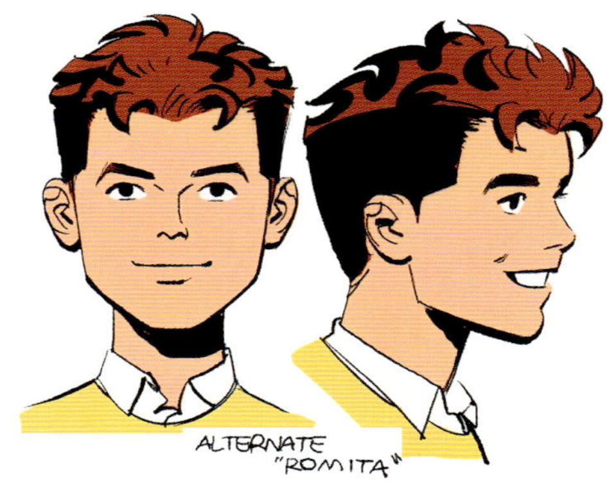

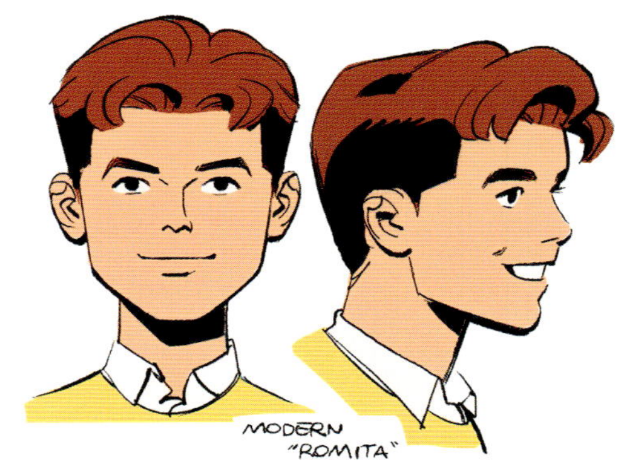

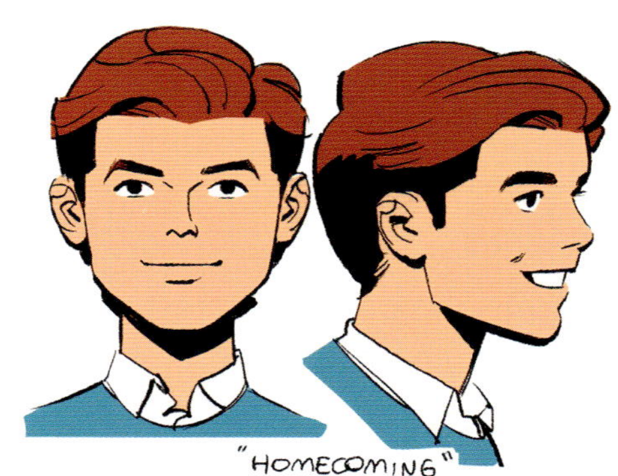

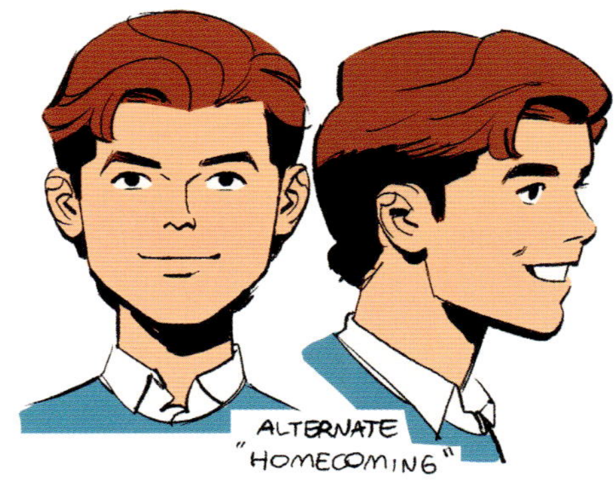

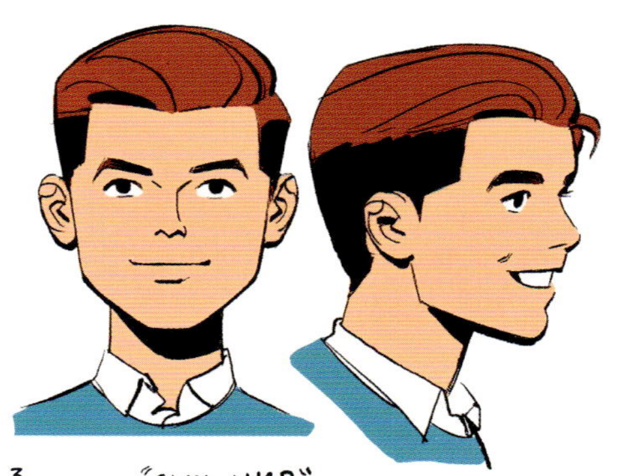

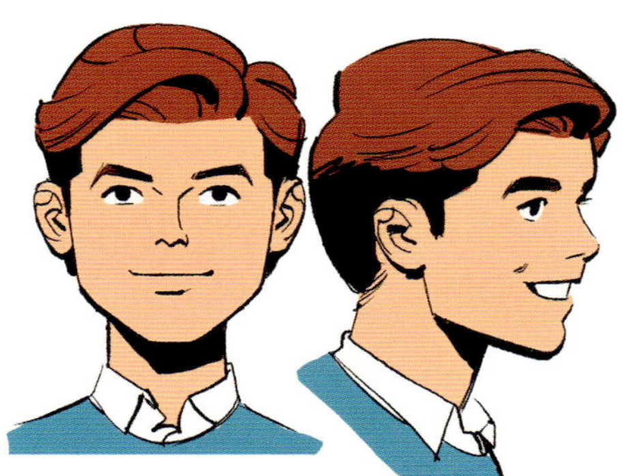

3

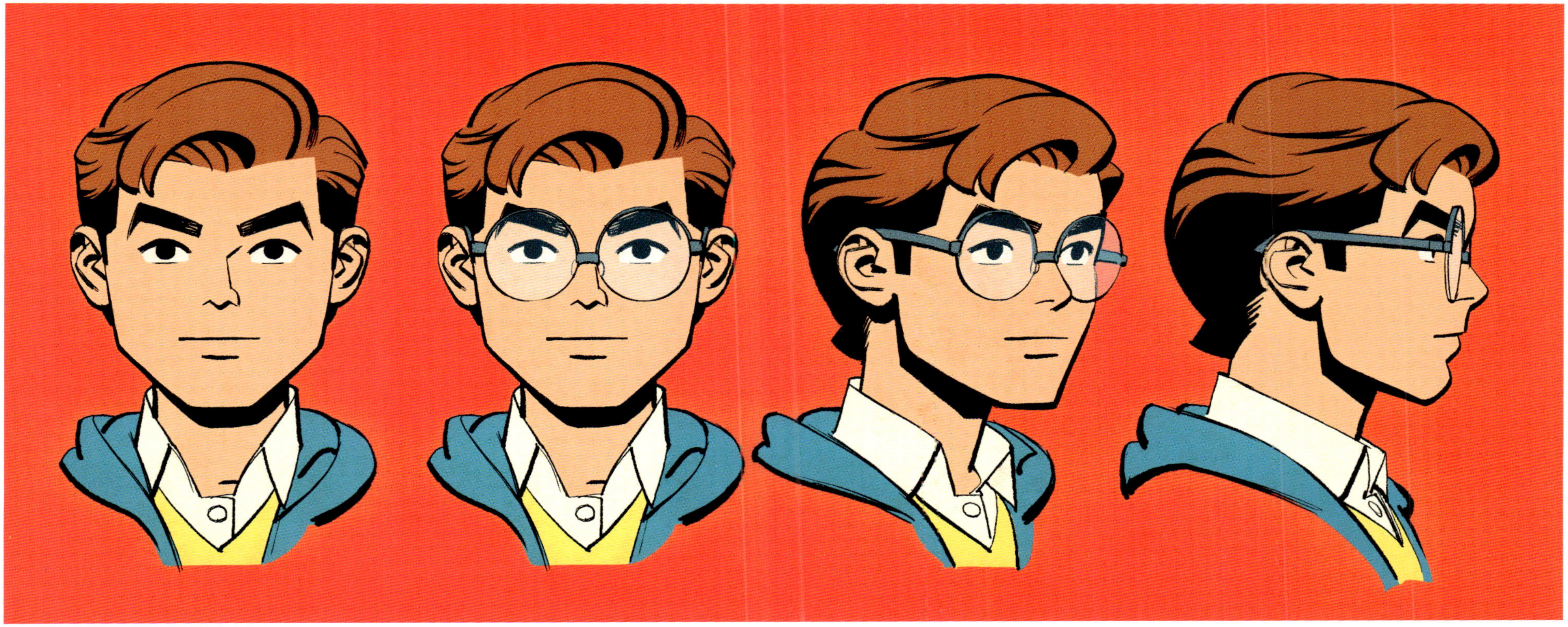

4

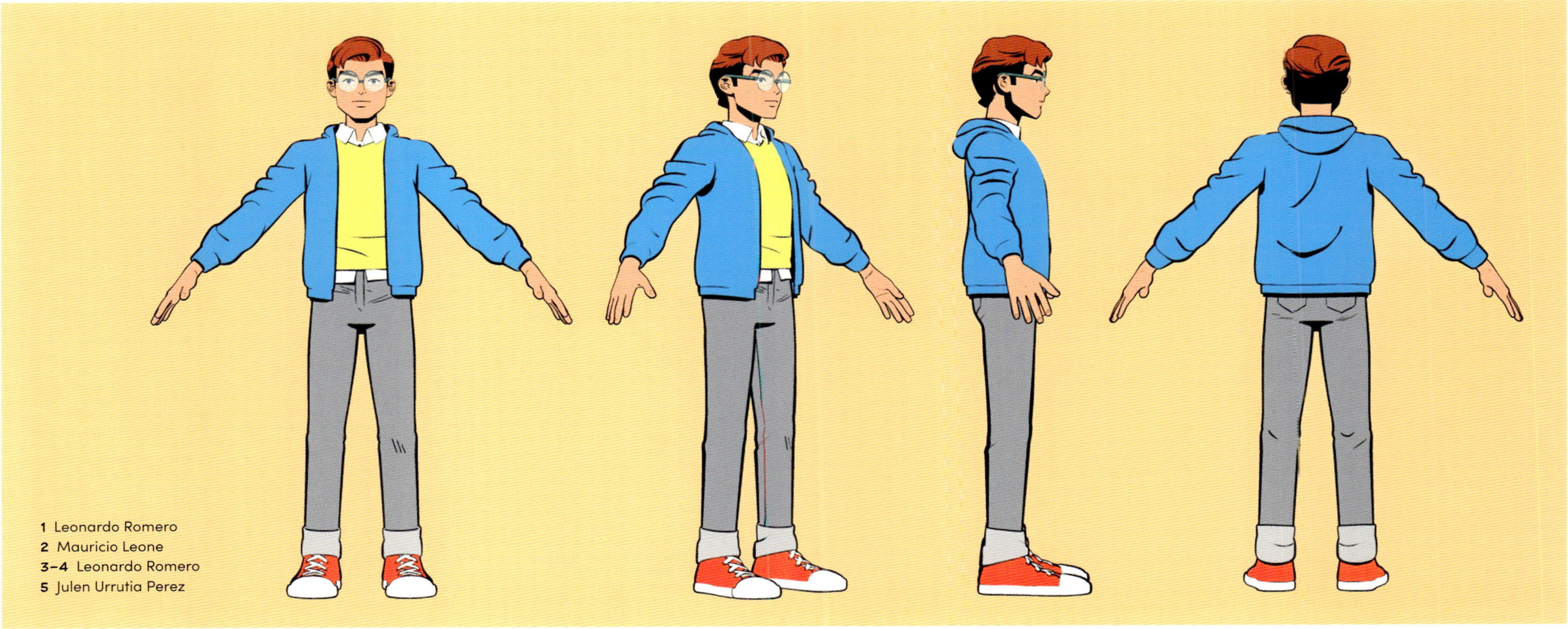

5

1 Leonardo Romero
2 Mauricio Leone
3–4 Leonardo Romero
5 Julen Urrutia Perez

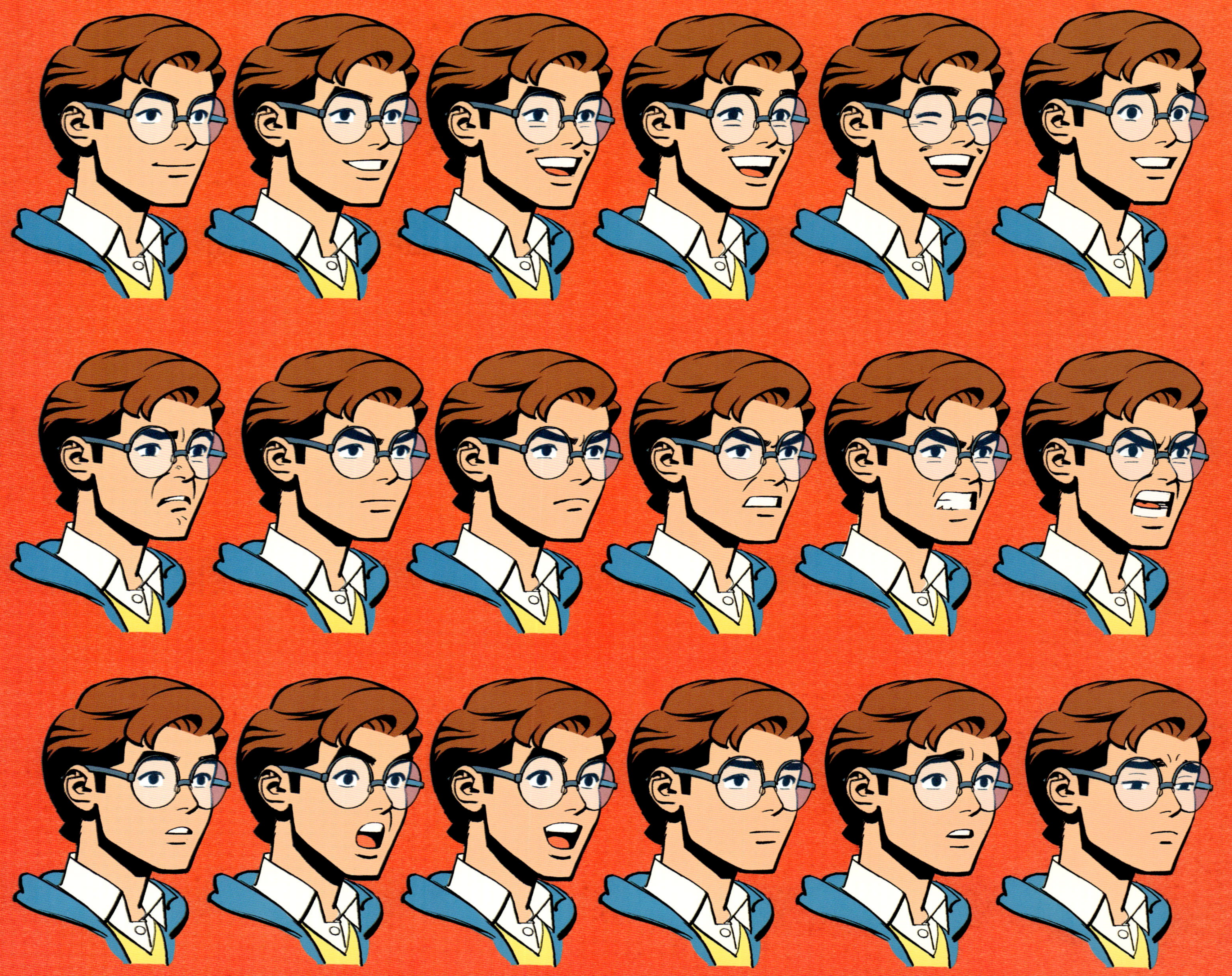

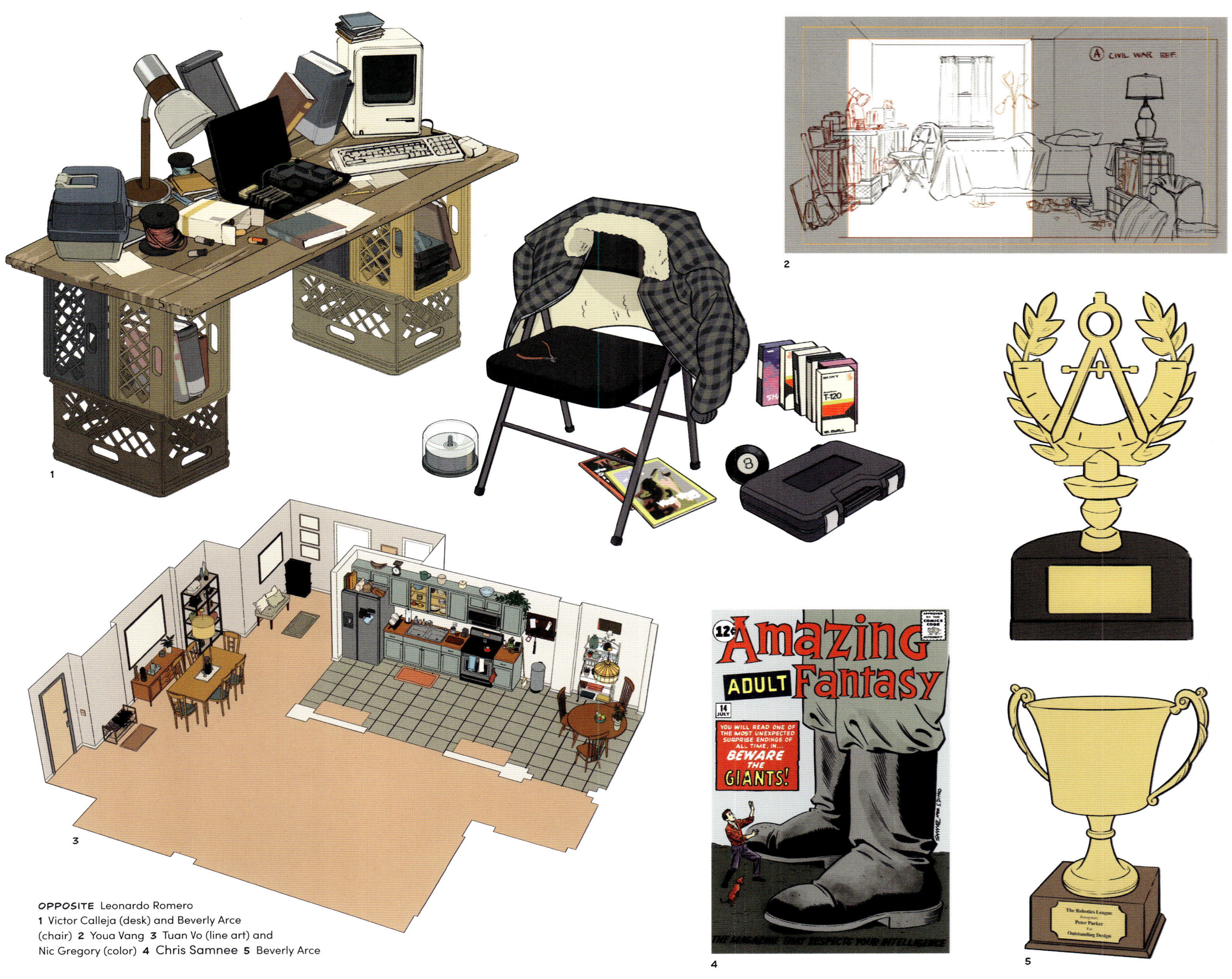

OPPOSITE Leonardo Romero
1 Victor Calleja (desk) and Beverly Arce (chair) **2** Youa Vang **3** Tuan Vo (line art) and Nic Gregory (color) **4** Chris Samnee **5** Beverly Arce

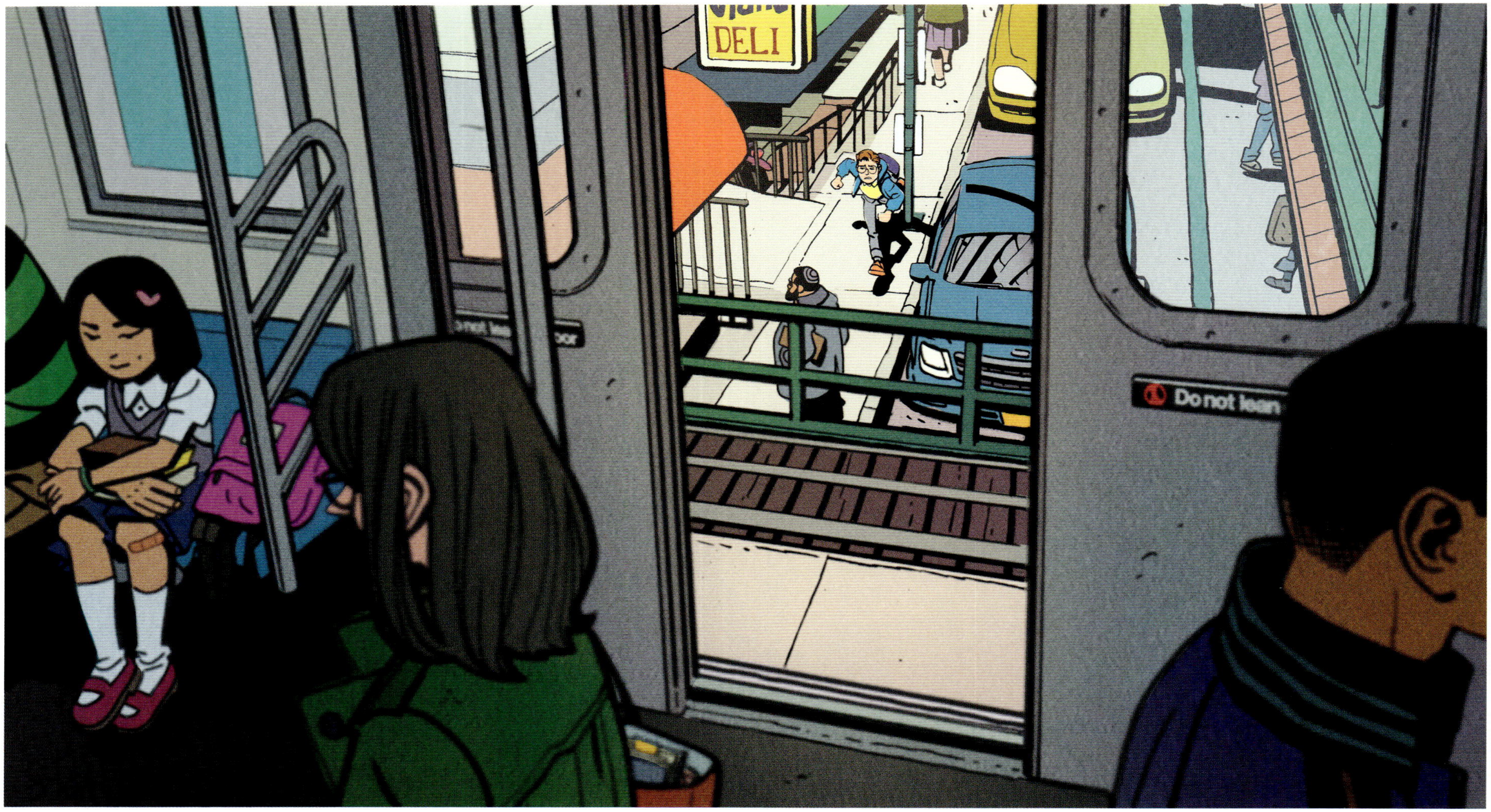

1

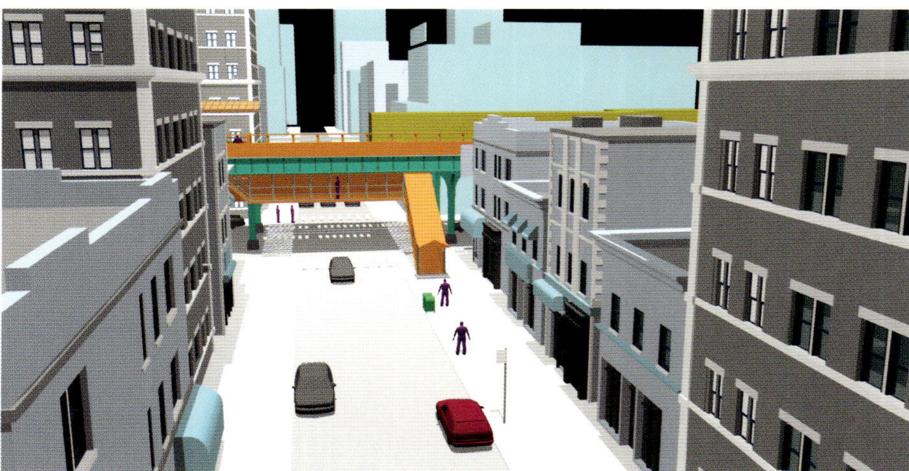

2

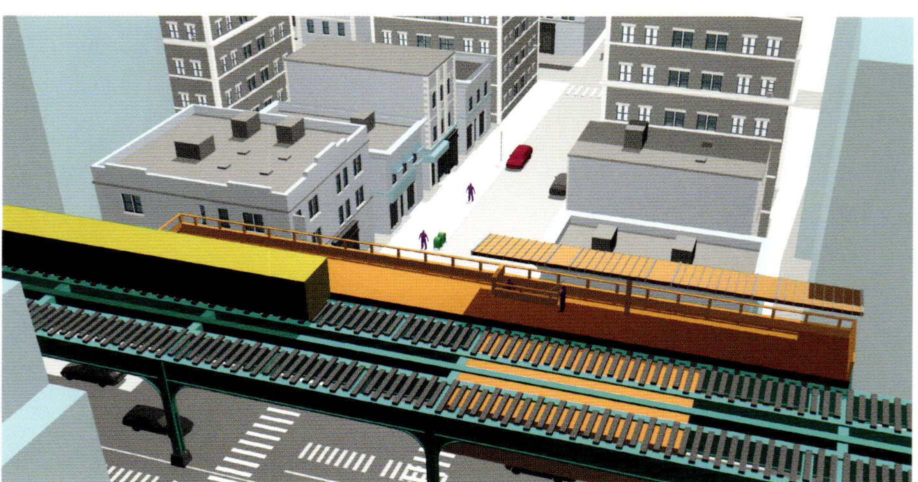

3

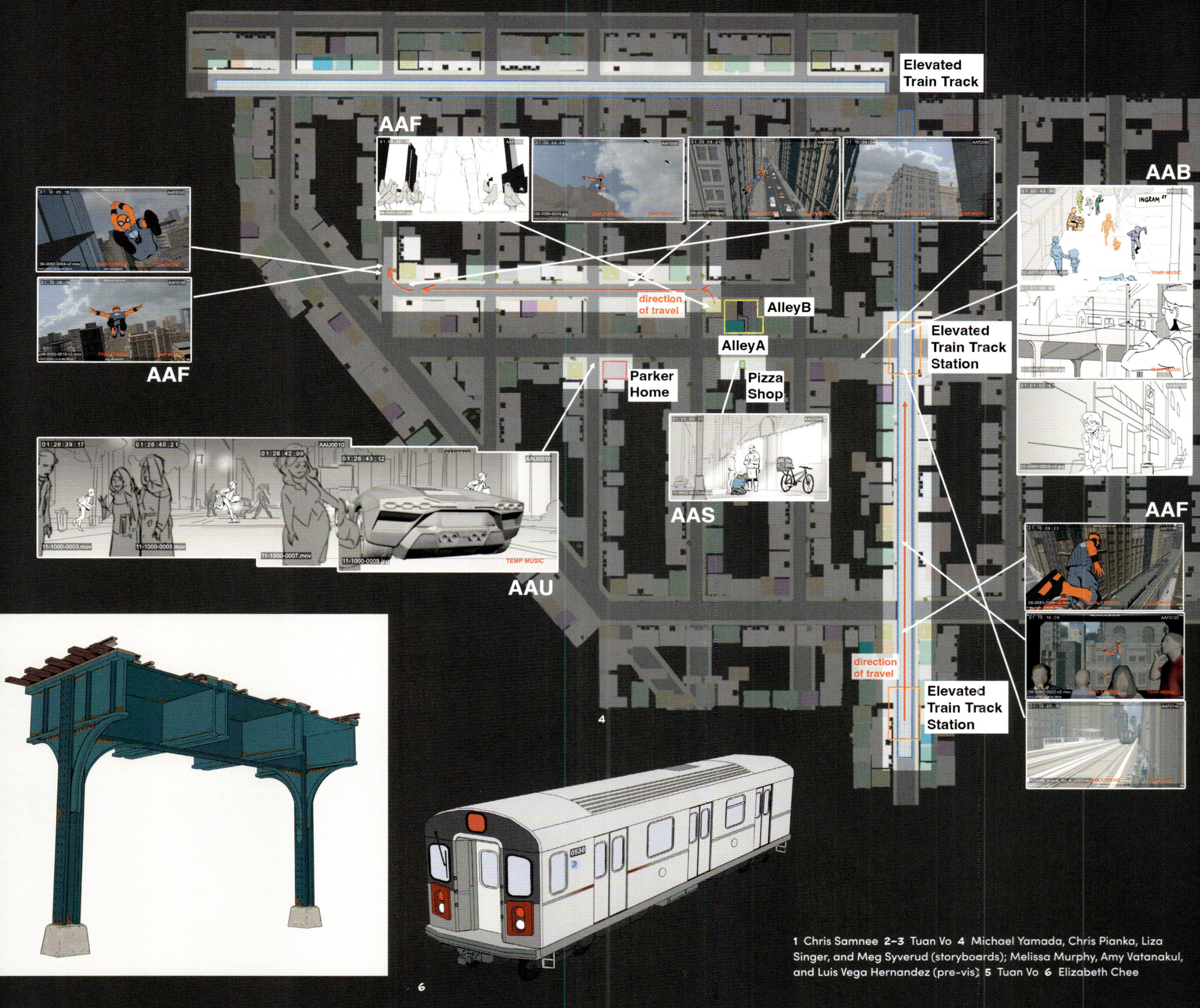

1 Chris Samnee 2–3 Tuan Vo 4 Michael Yamada, Chris Pianka, Liza Singer, and Meg Syverud (storyboards); Melissa Murphy, Amy Vatanakul, and Luis Vega Hernandez (pre-vis) 5 Tuan Vo 6 Elizabeth Chee

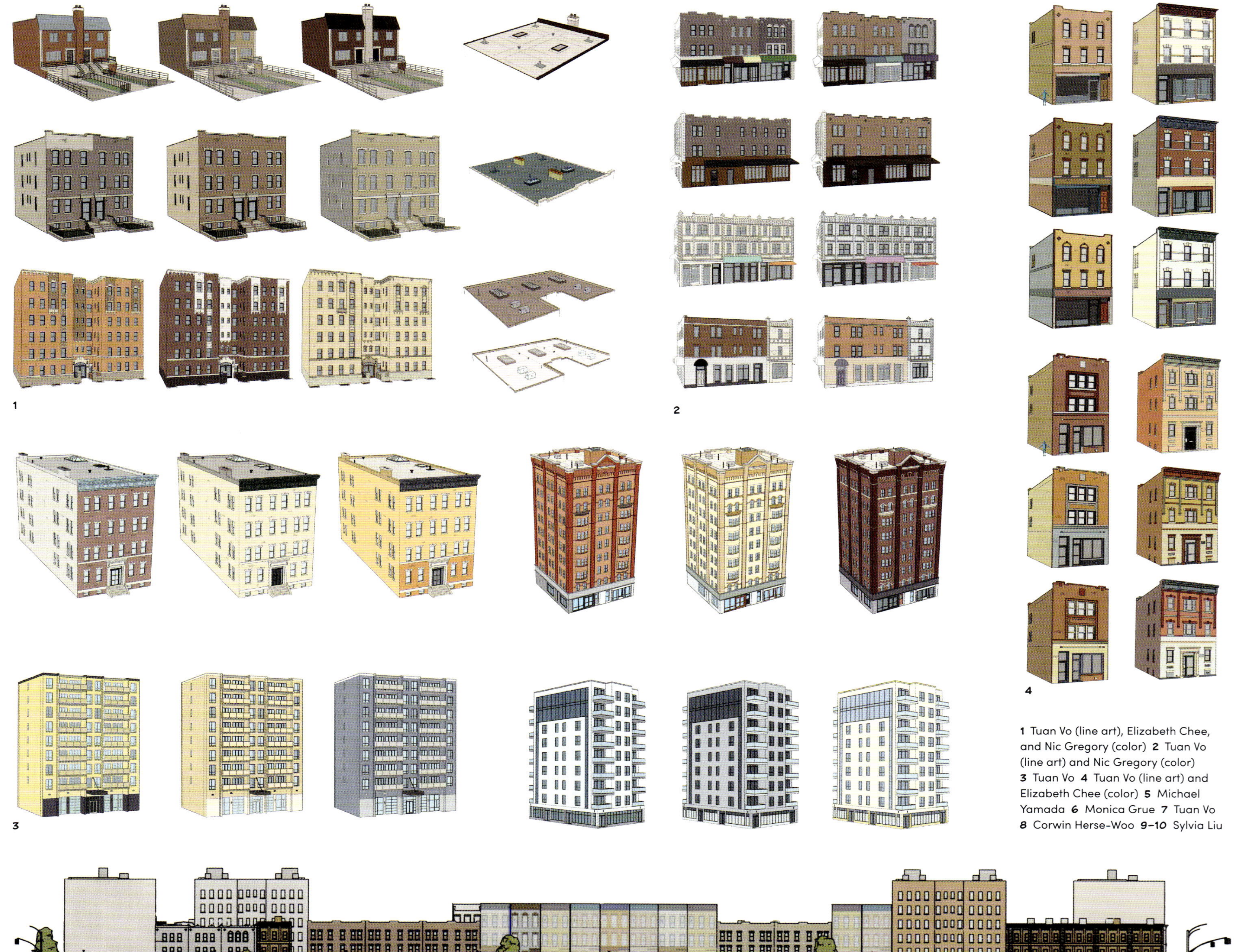

1 Tuan Vo (line art), Elizabeth Chee, and Nic Gregory (color) 2 Tuan Vo (line art) and Nic Gregory (color) 3 Tuan Vo 4 Tuan Vo (line art) and Elizabeth Chee (color) 5 Michael Yamada 6 Monica Grue 7 Tuan Vo 8 Corwin Herse-Woo 9–10 Sylvia Liu

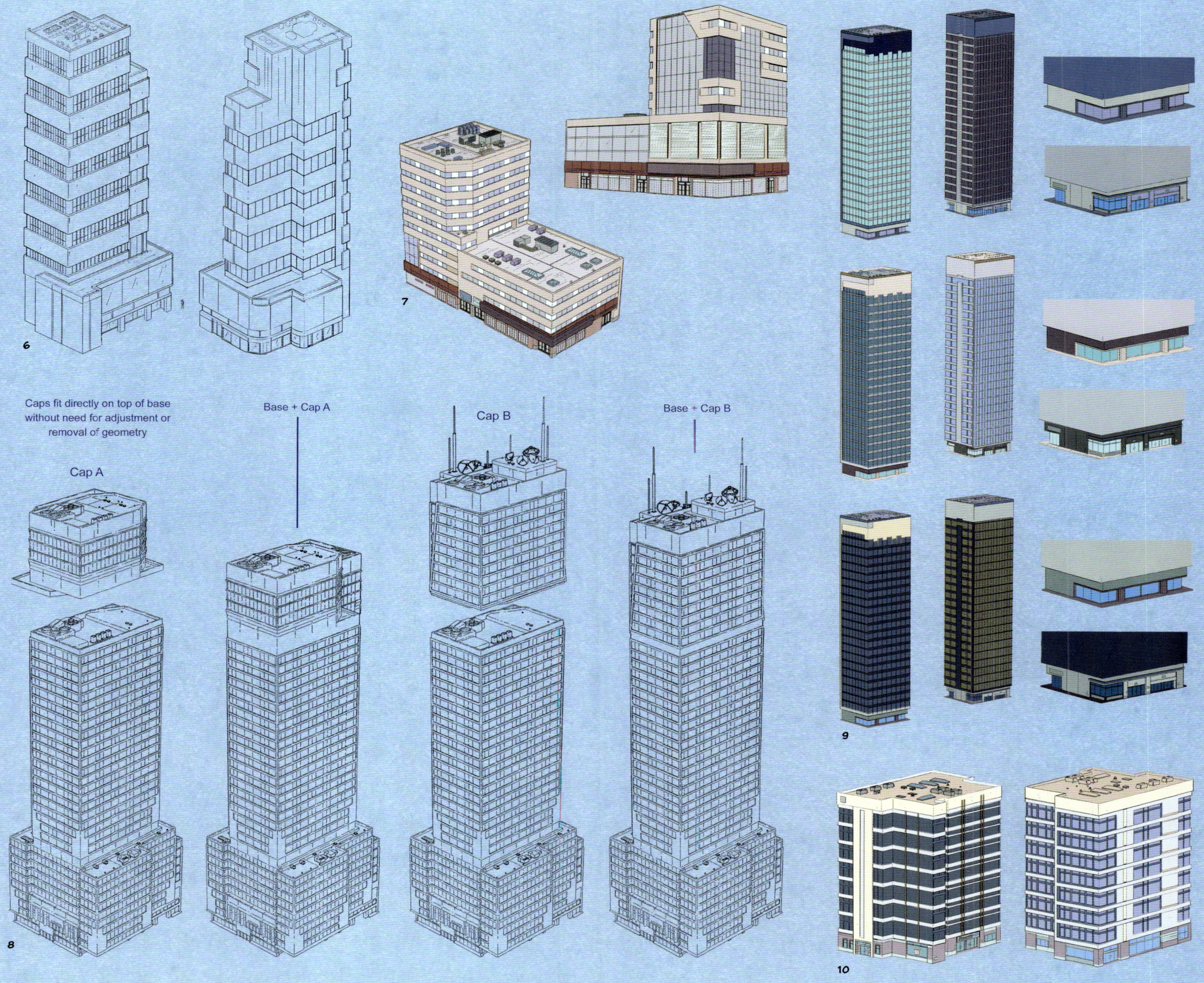
6
7
Caps fit directly on top of base without need for adjustment or removal of geometry
Cap A
Base + Cap A
Cap B
Base + Cap B
8
9
10

Small blocks use three base layouts which are rearranged and rotated to make up the right half of the set
A
C
C
B
B
C
C
C
A
B

1

2

3

JEWELRY STORE
HERE
A
B
C
D + 2x HATS
E
F

2x BUILDING "HATS"

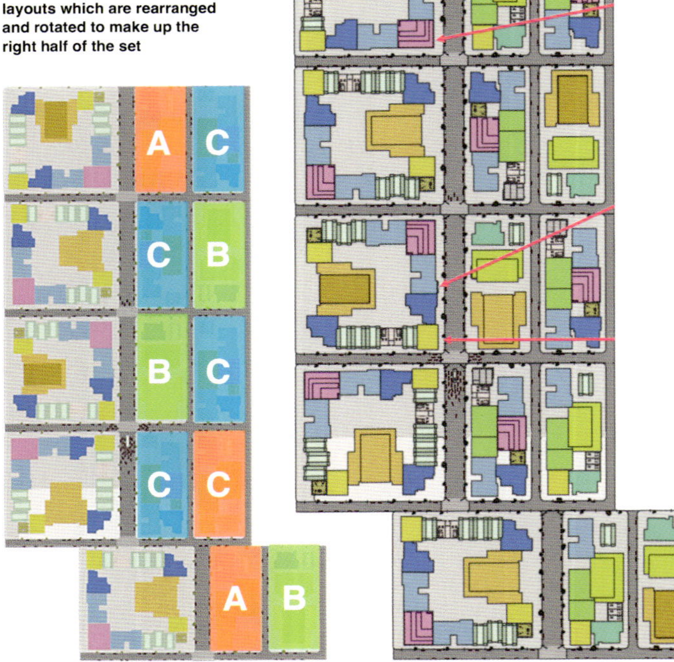

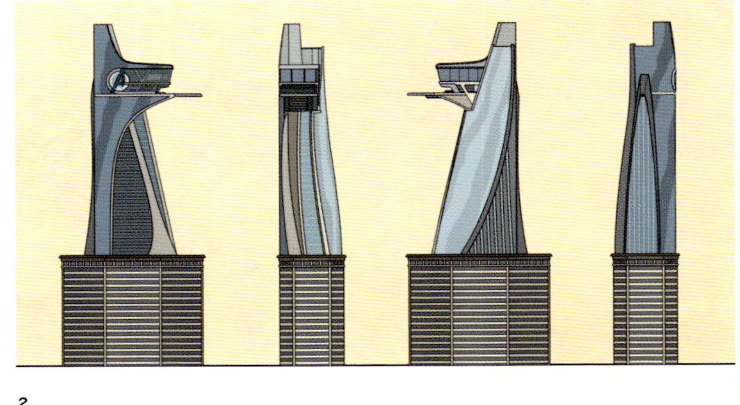

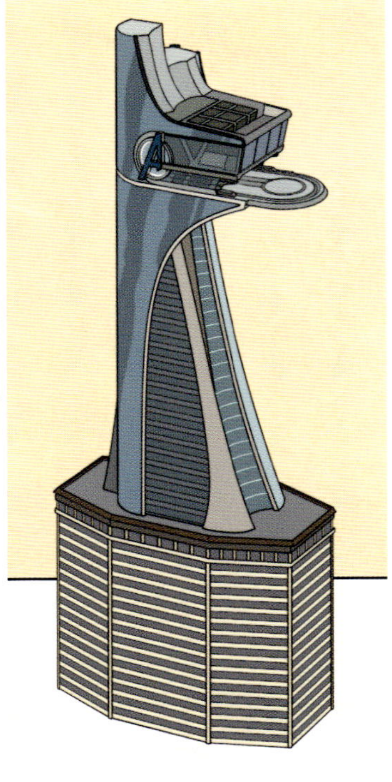

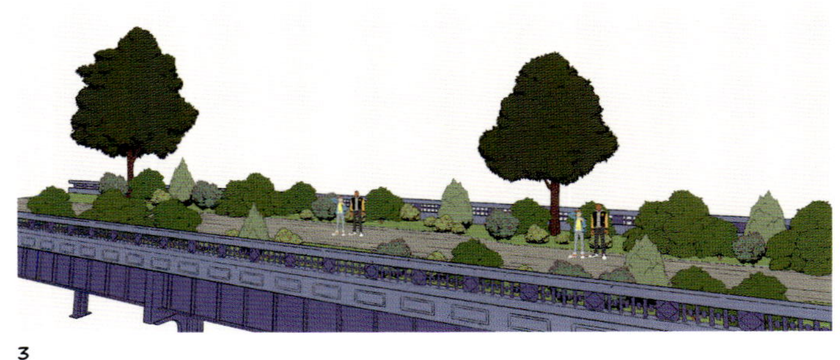

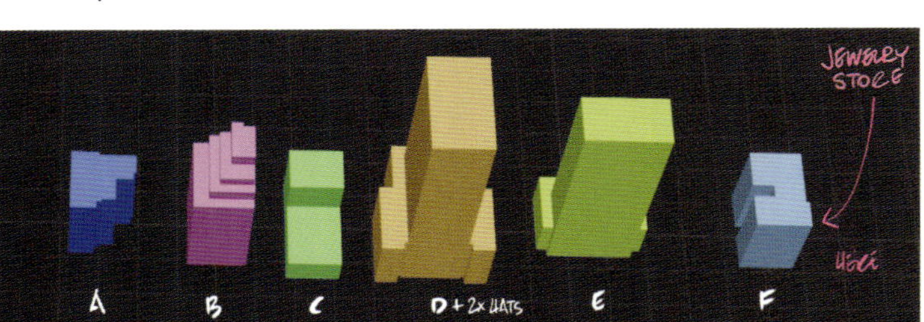

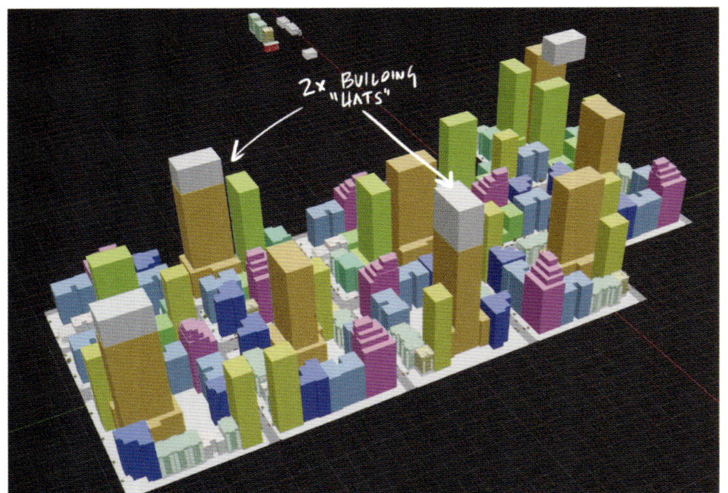

4

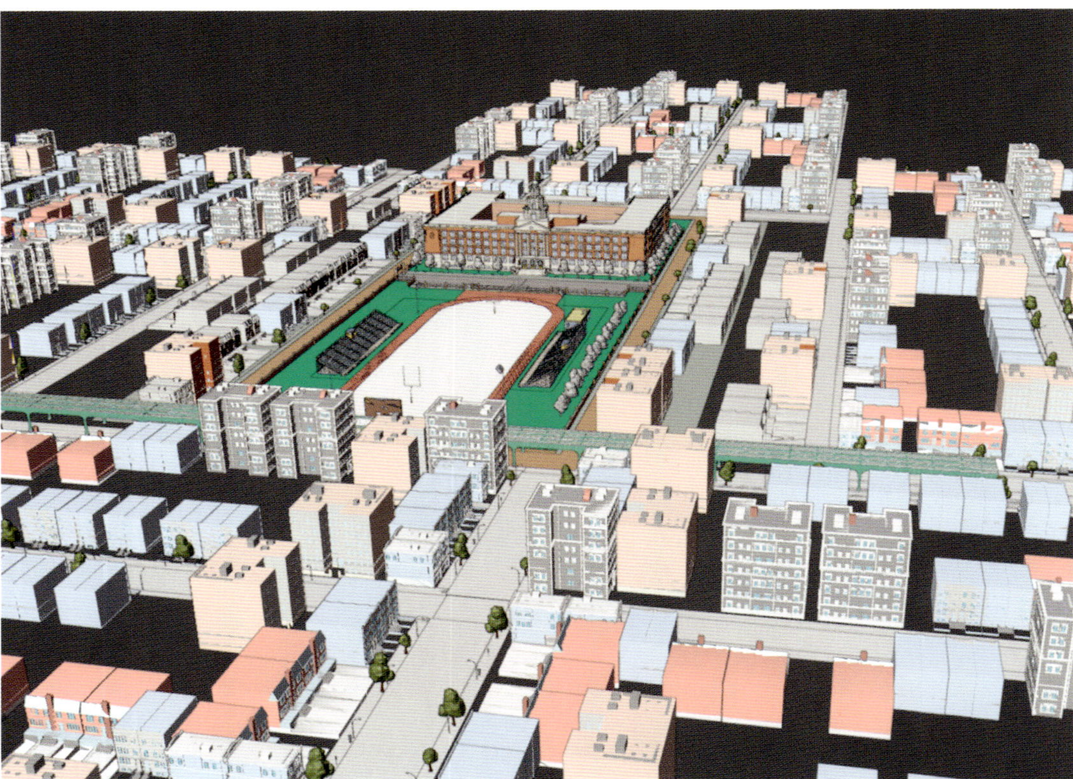

5

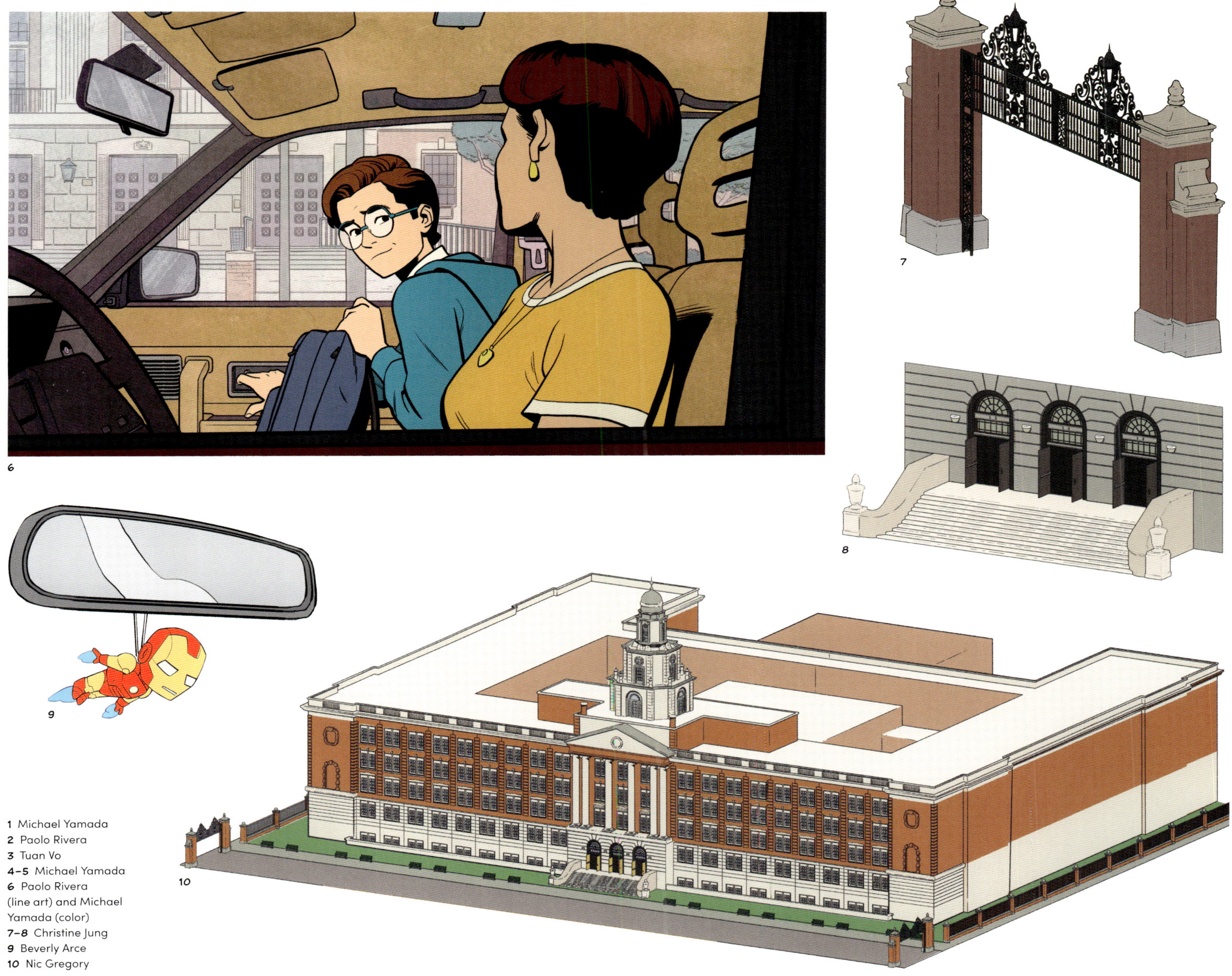
6

7

8

9

10

1 Michael Yamada
2 Paolo Rivera
3 Tuan Vo
4–5 Michael Yamada
6 Paolo Rivera (line art) and Michael Yamada (color)
7–8 Christine Jung
9 Beverly Arce
10 Nic Gregory

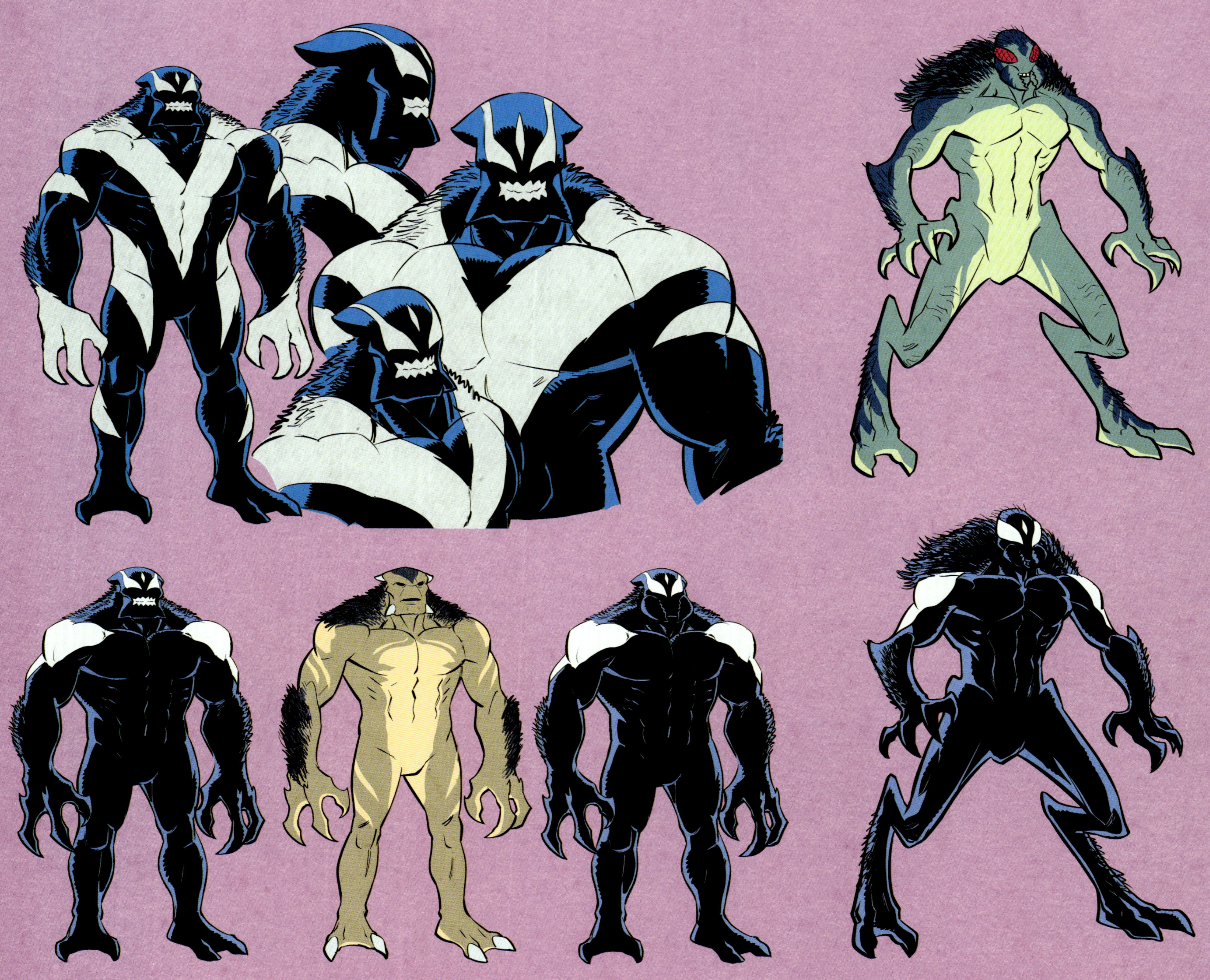

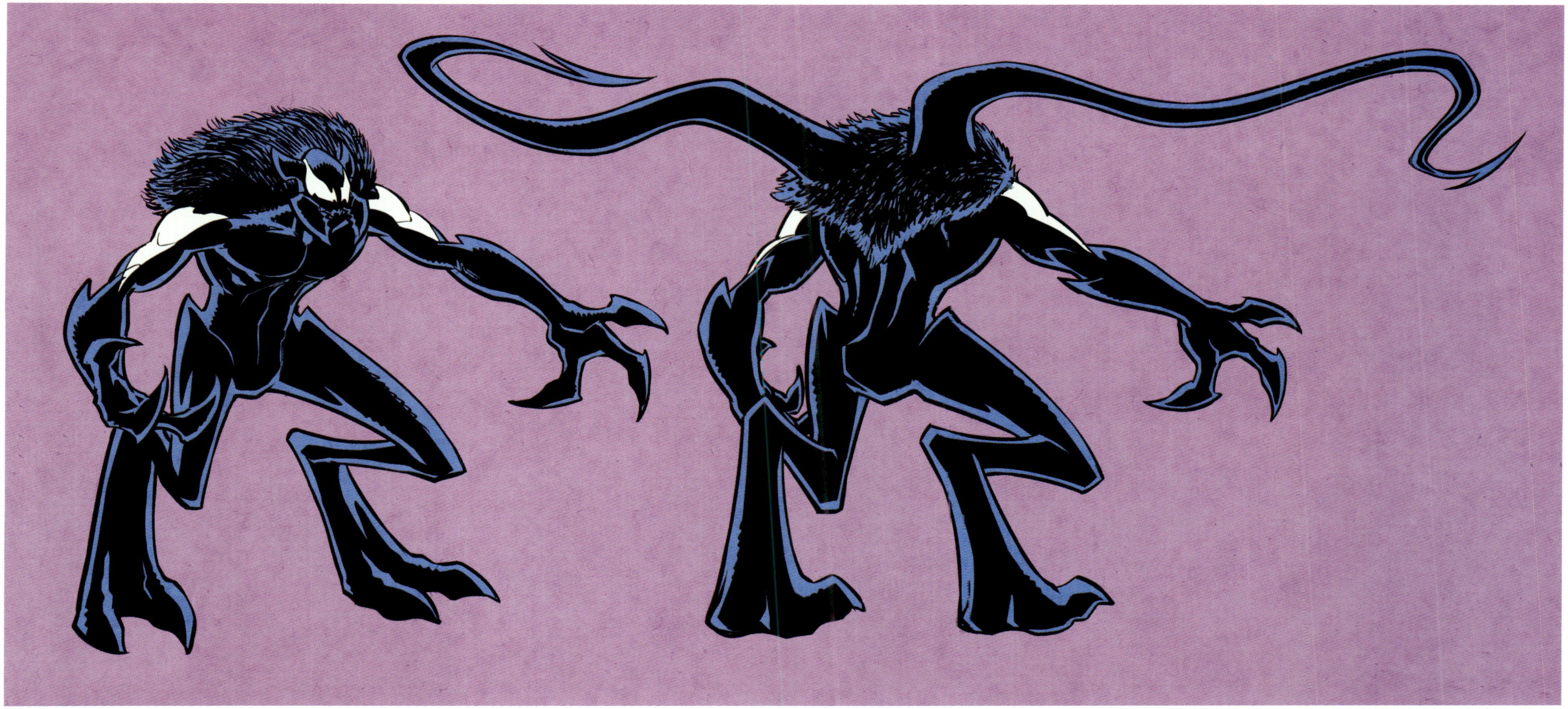

1

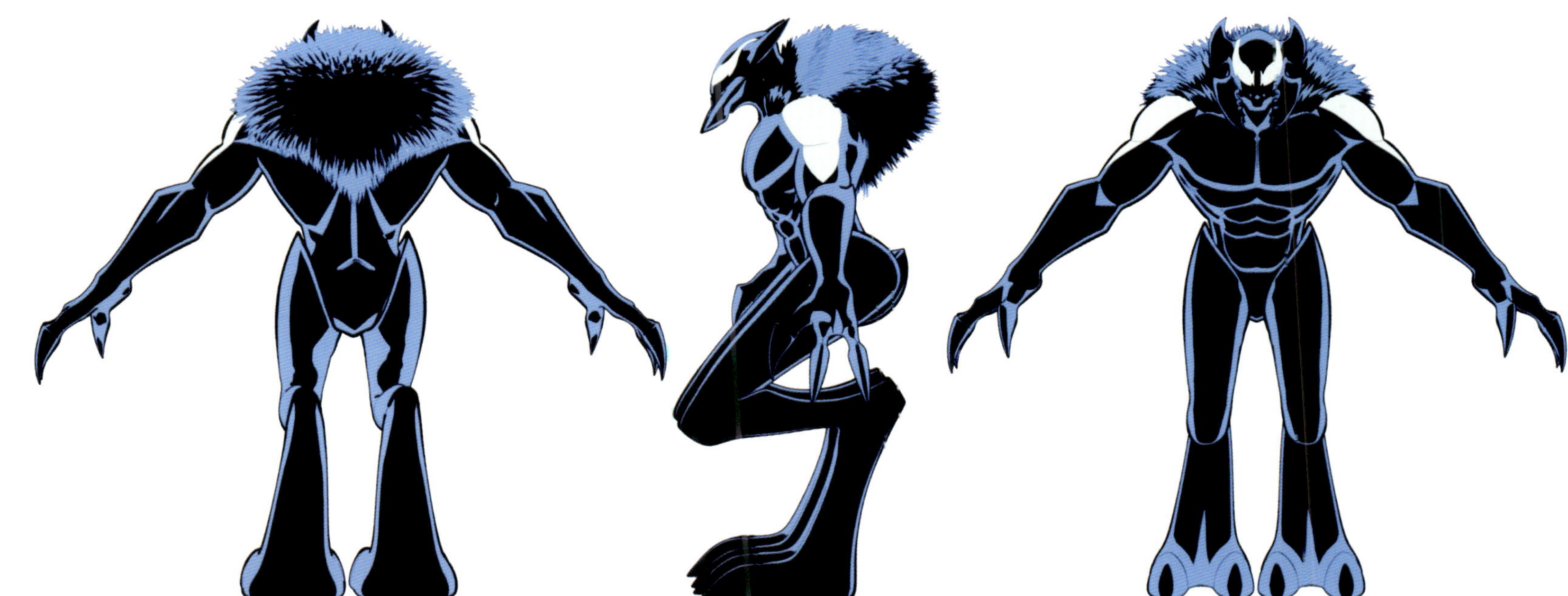

2

OPPOSITE Joey Vazquez
1 Joey Vazquez
2 Polygon Pictures

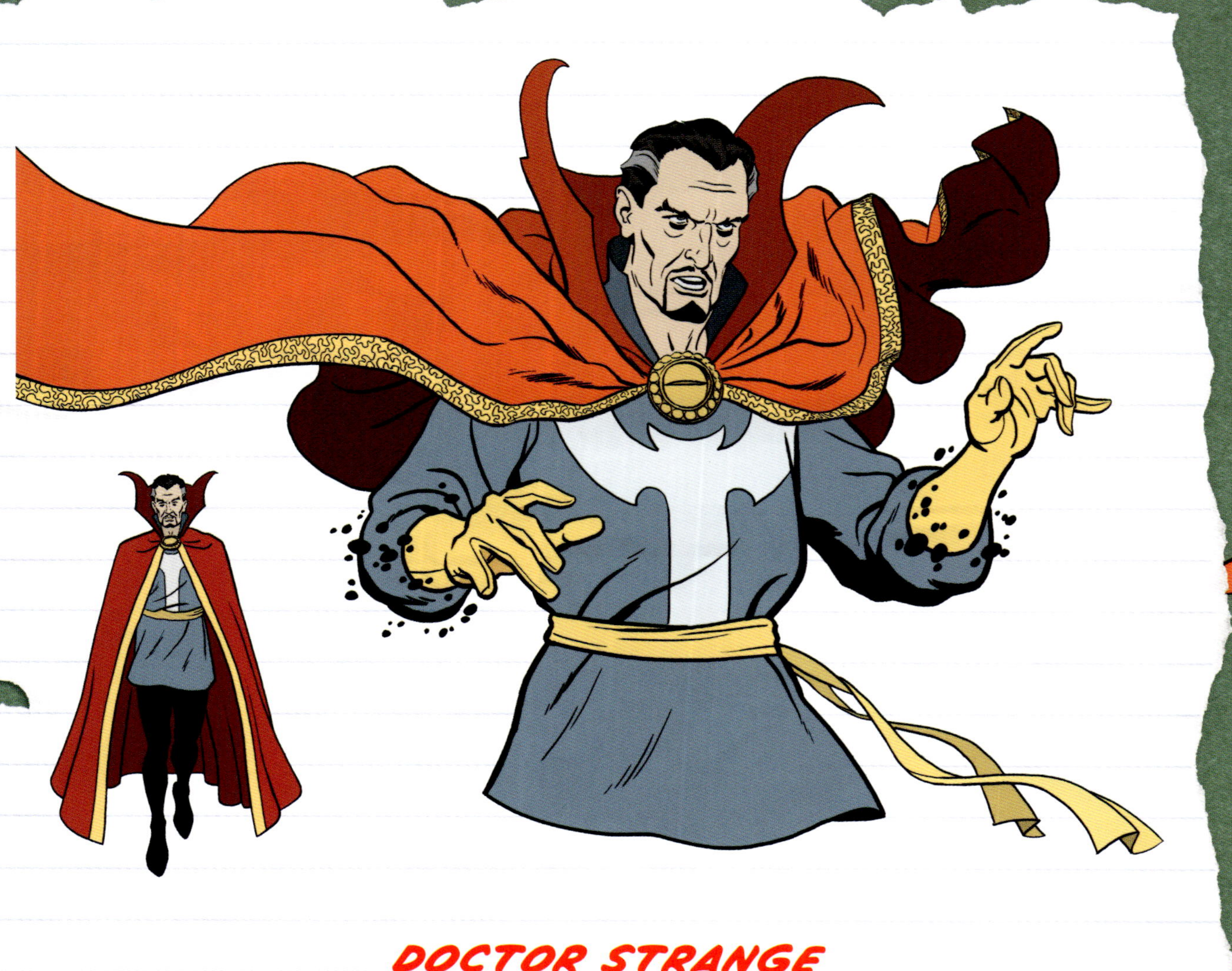

DOCTOR STRANGE

The first well-known visitor to Peter Parker's world in the show is none other than the Master of the Mystic Arts, Doctor Strange, who kick-starts Peter's transformation into Spider-Man when he chases the alien Symbiote through the portal.

"We knew from very early on that Doctor Strange would play a huge part in the show," says Executive Producer/Showrunner Jeff Trammell. "I love that we exist in the MCU, so we can use all those amazing characters. I remember watching the 1990s-era *Spider-Man: The Animated Series*, and some of my favorite memories are seeing Spider-Man, Doctor Strange, Daredevil, and War Machine. Stephen Strange is not someone Peter is familiar with, so when he first pops up, we're seeing this new era of heroes, at least to Peter. Strange affects Peter's journey without even knowing it, and in fact, this could only happen in this universe. On the show, you wouldn't have Spider-Man without Strange!"

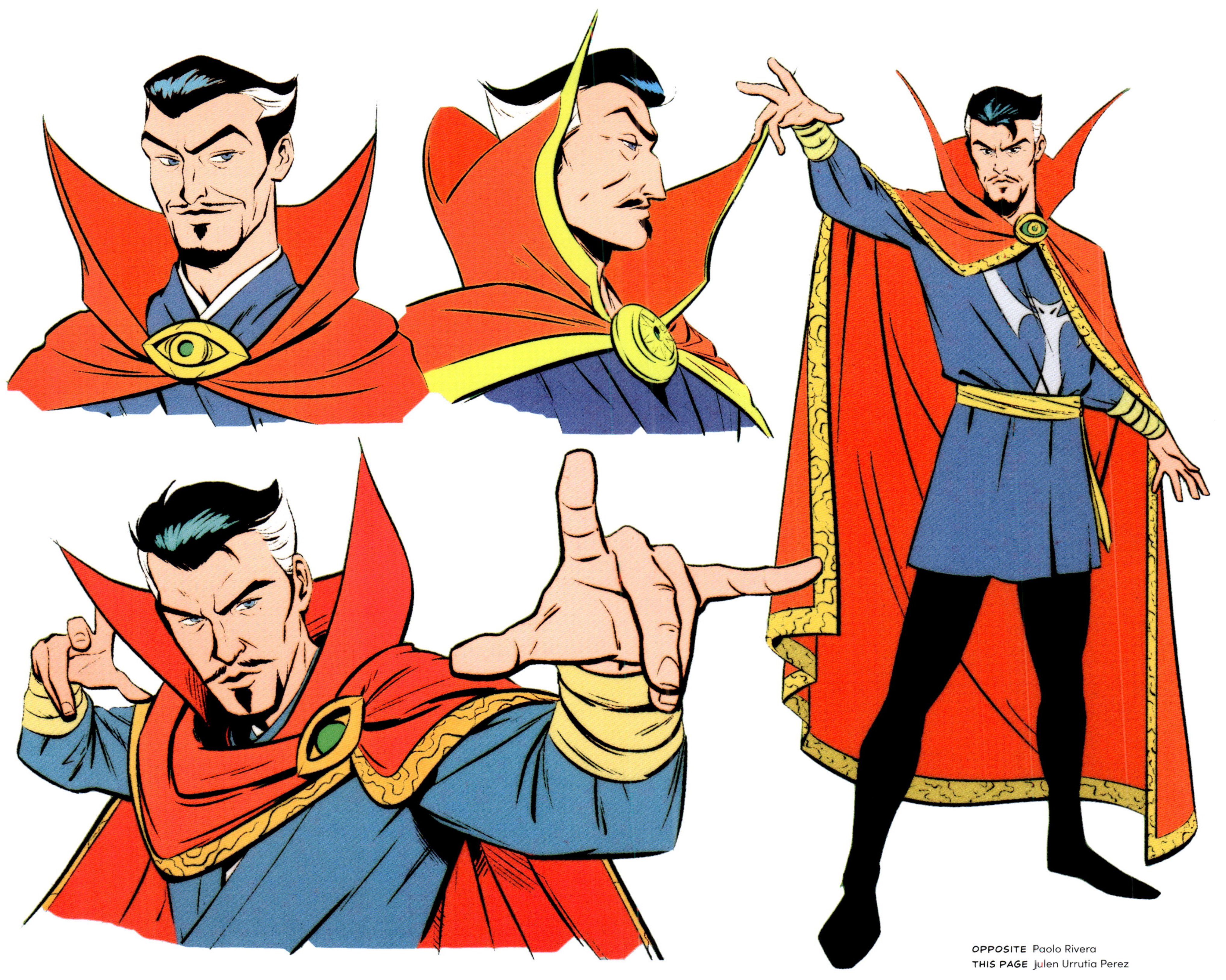

OPPOSITE Paolo Rivera
THIS PAGE Julen Urrutia Perez

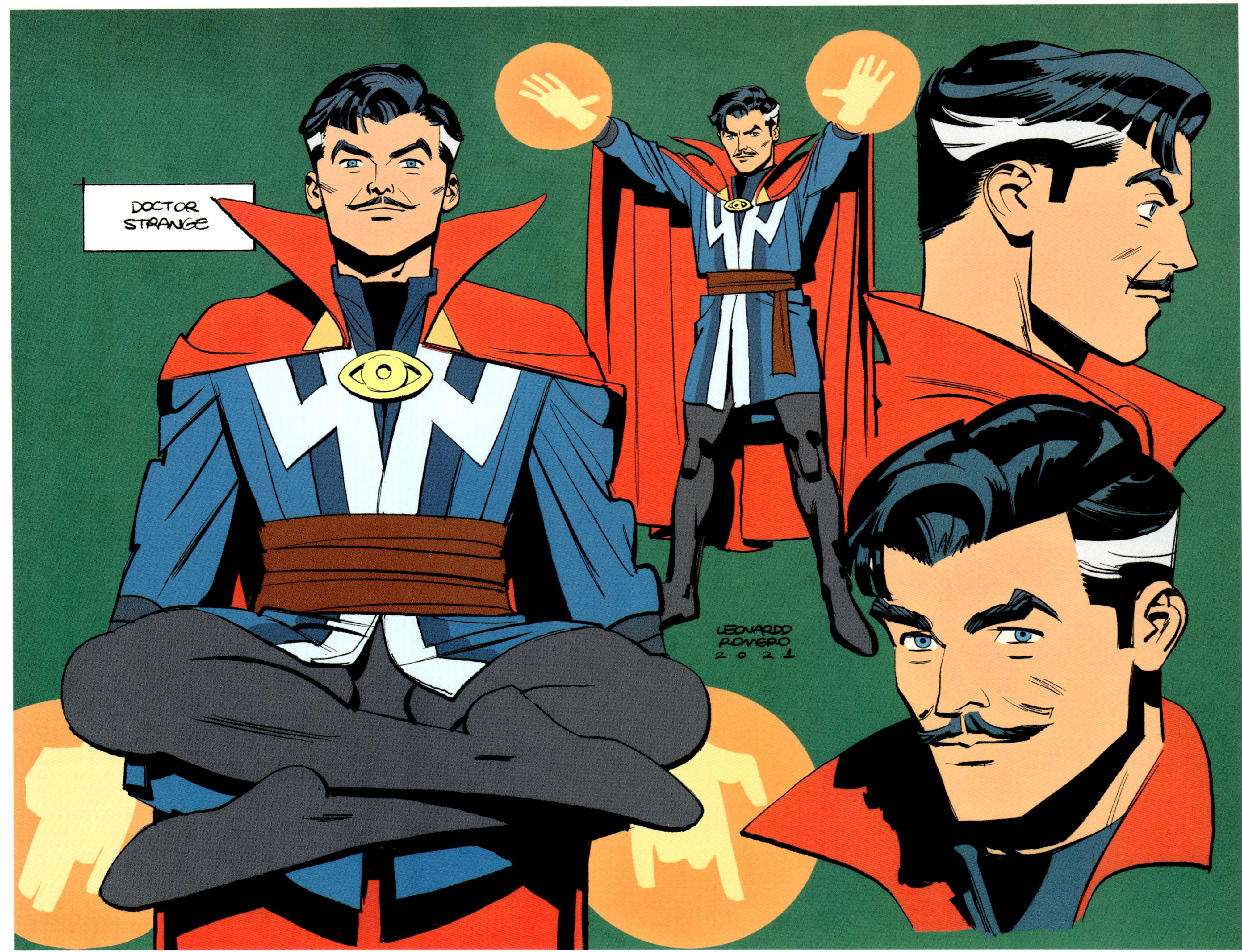
DOCTOR
STRANGE
LEONARDO
ROMERO
2021

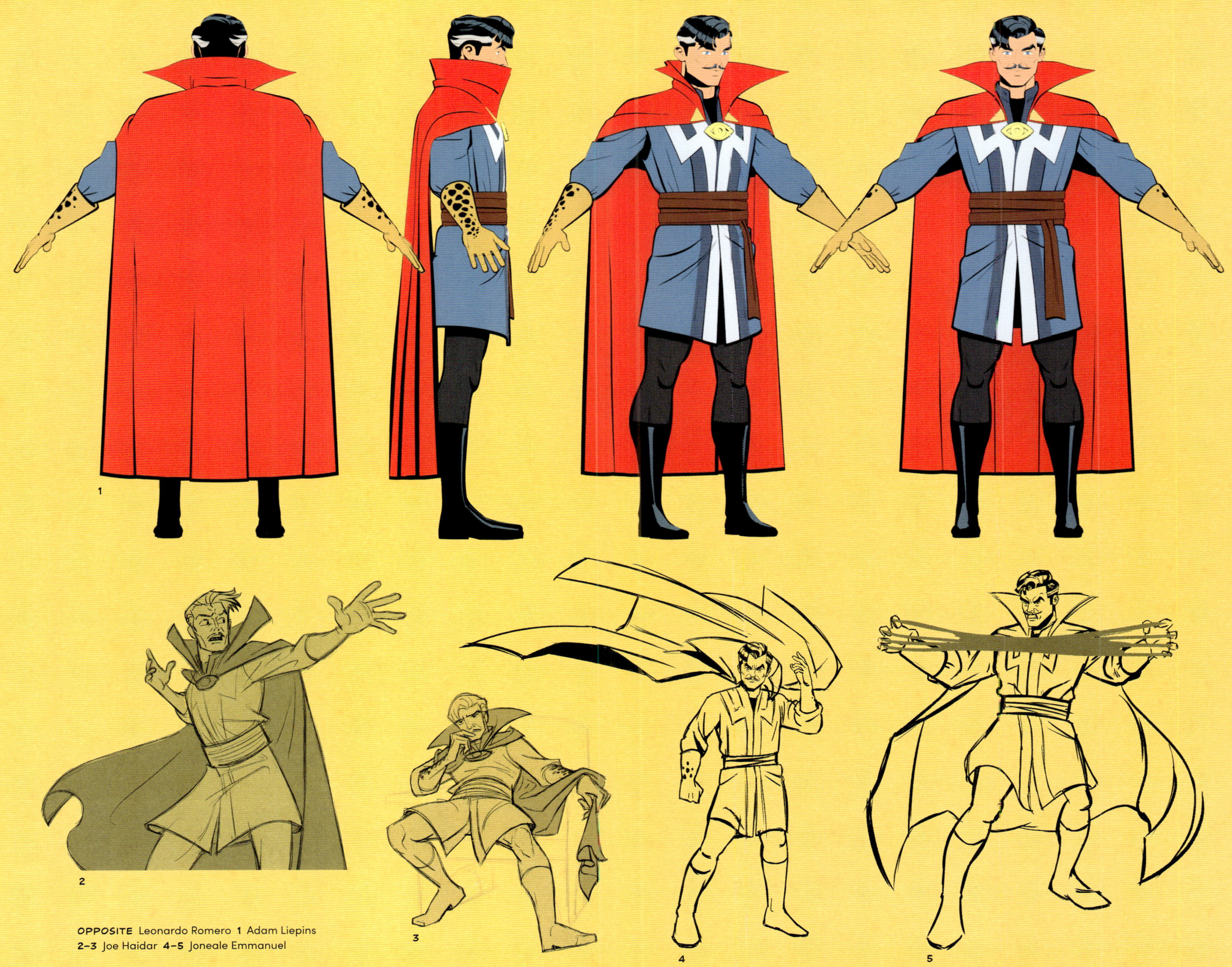

1

2

3

4

5

OPPOSITE Leonardo Romero **1** Adam Liepins
2–3 Joe Haidar **4–5** Joneale Emmanuel

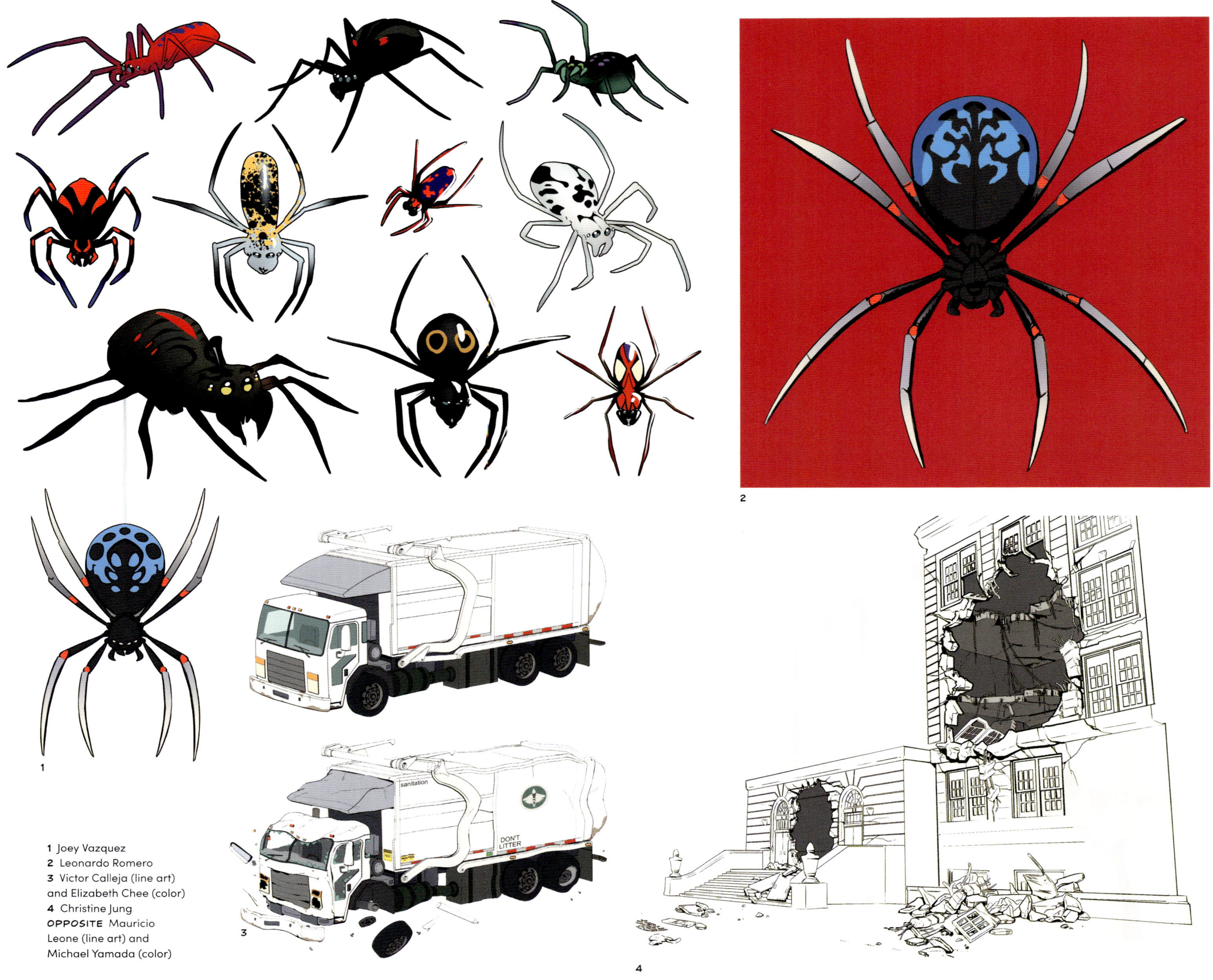

1 Joey Vazquez
2 Leonardo Romero
3 Victor Calleja (line art) and Elizabeth Chee (color)
4 Christine Jung
OPPOSITE Mauricio Leone (line art) and Michael Yamada (color)

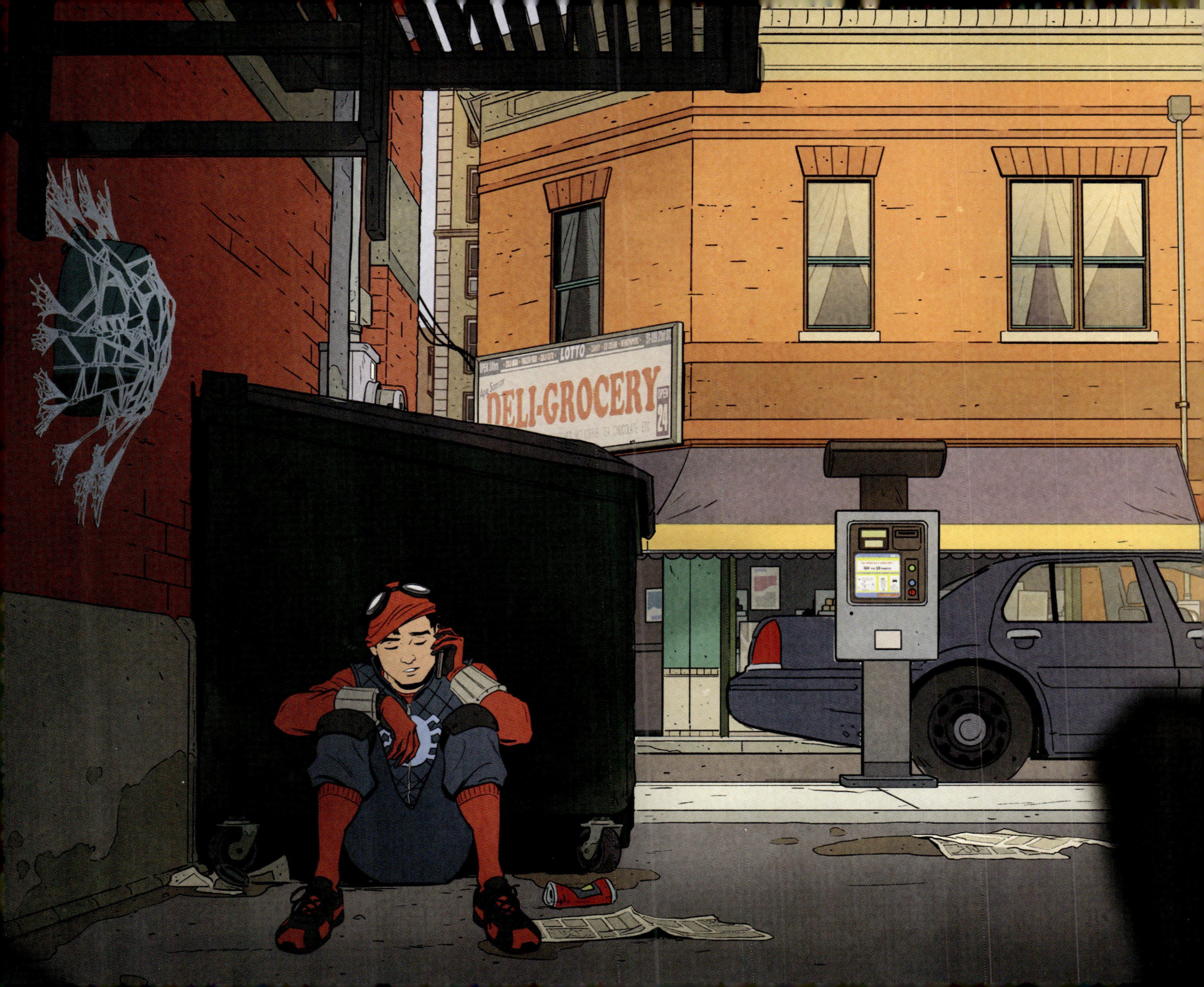
LOTTO
DELI-GROCERY
OPEN 24

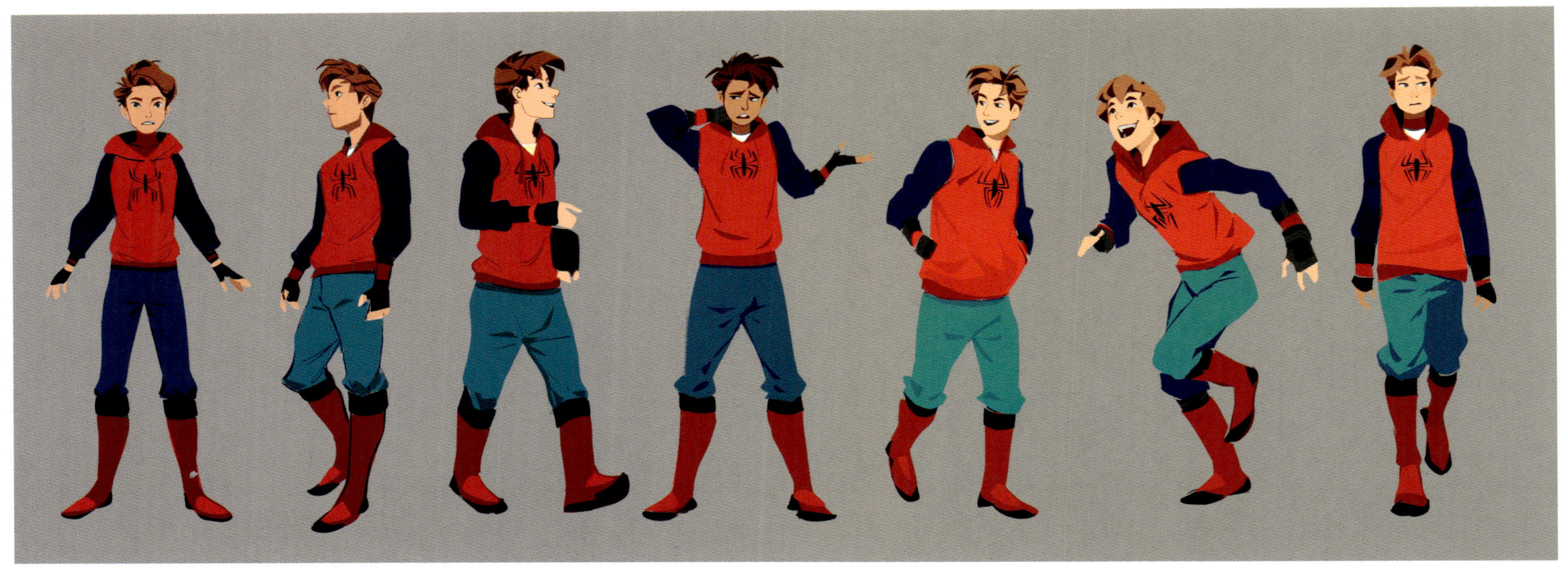

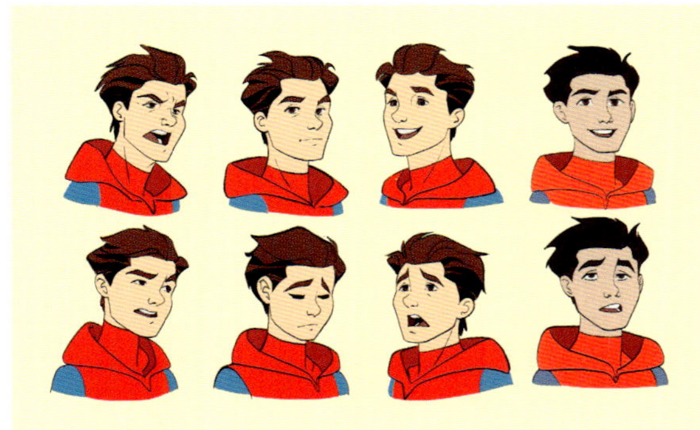

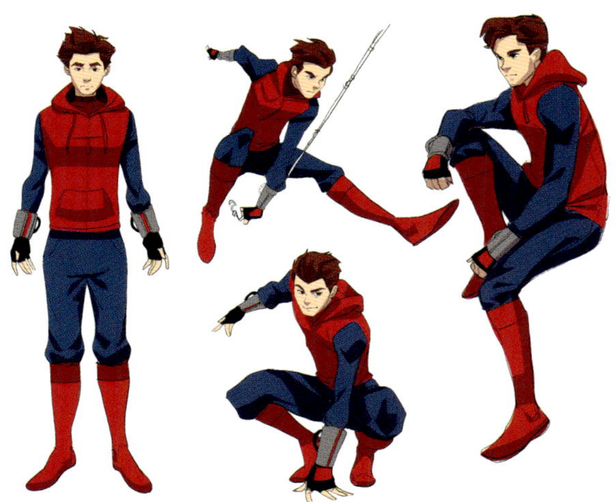

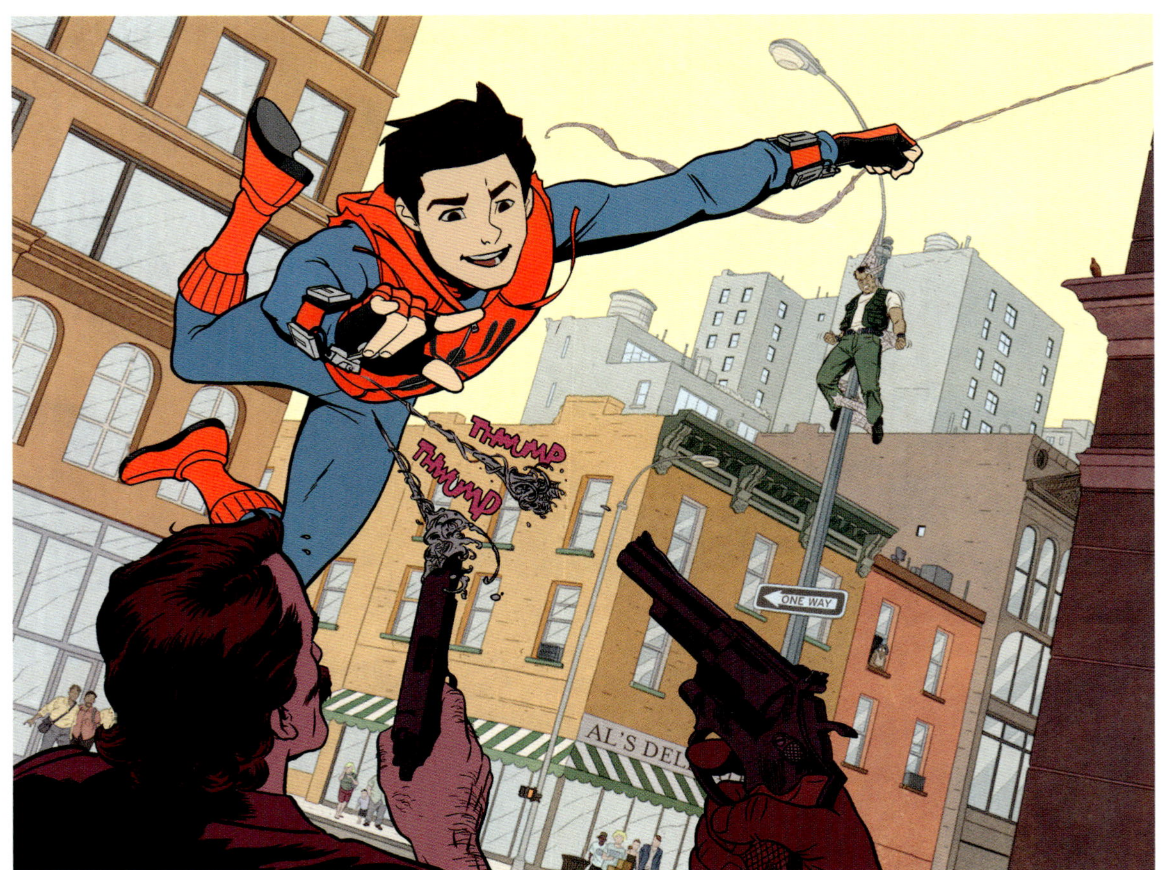
THWUMP
THWUMP
ONE WAY
AL'S DEL

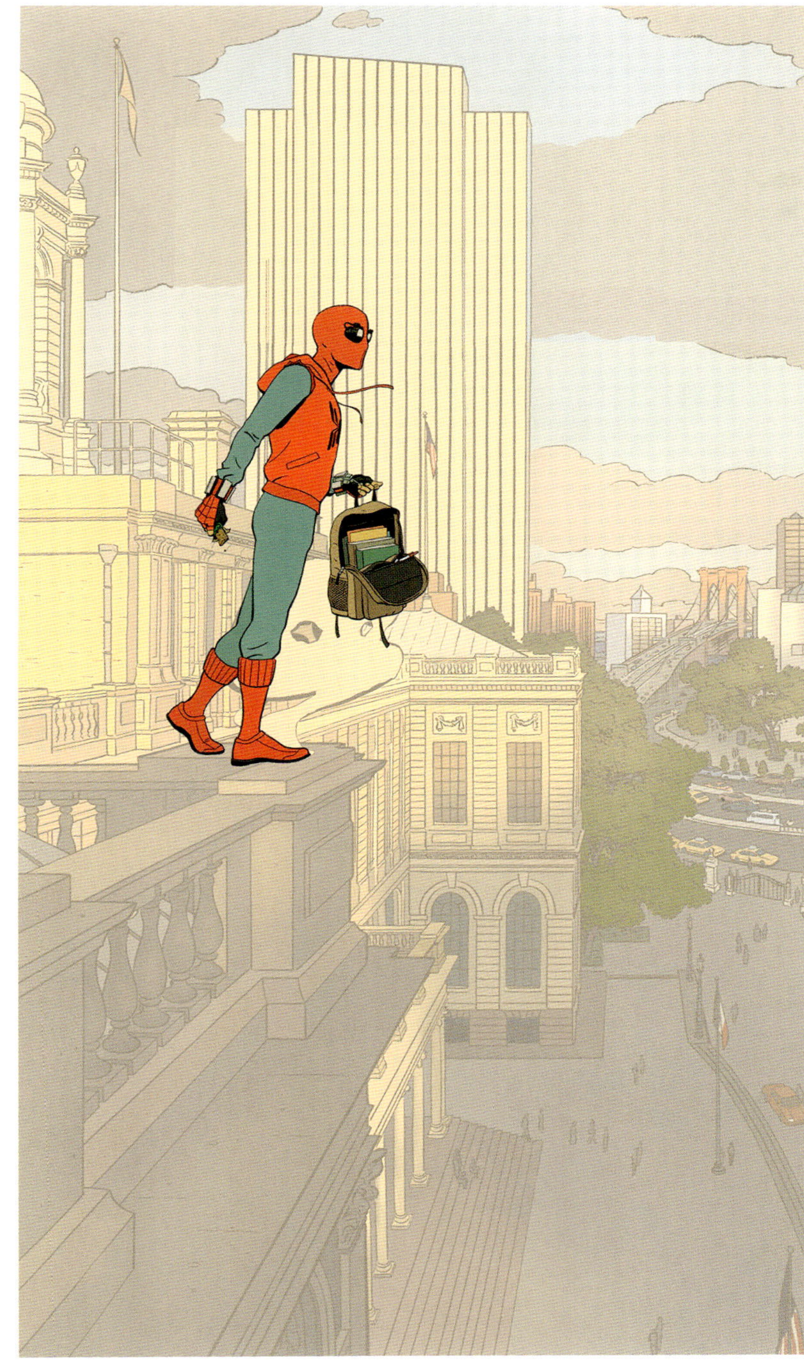

1

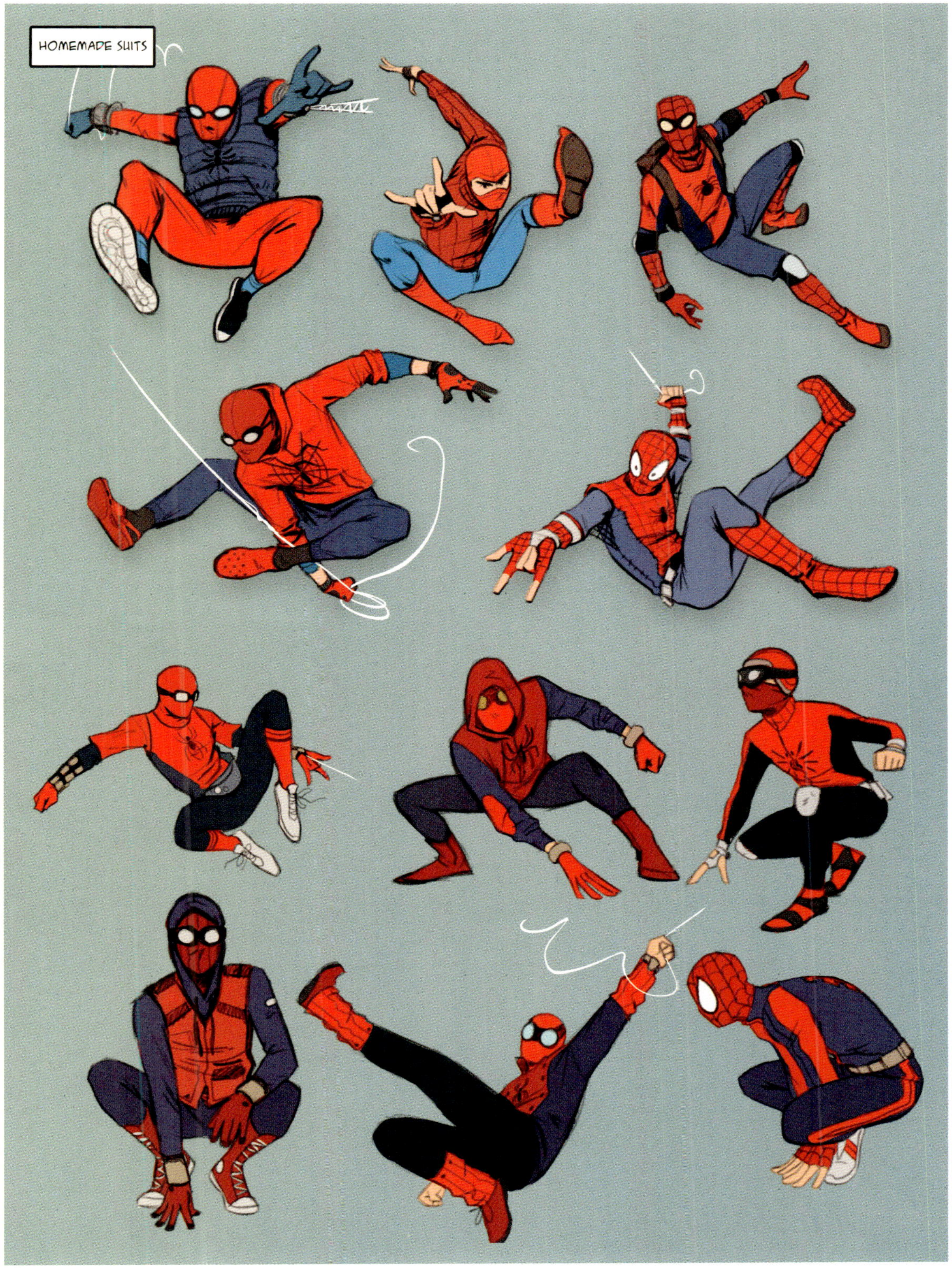

HOMEMADE SUITS

2

OPPOSITE Mel Milton **1** Paolo Rivera **2** Julen Urrutia Perez

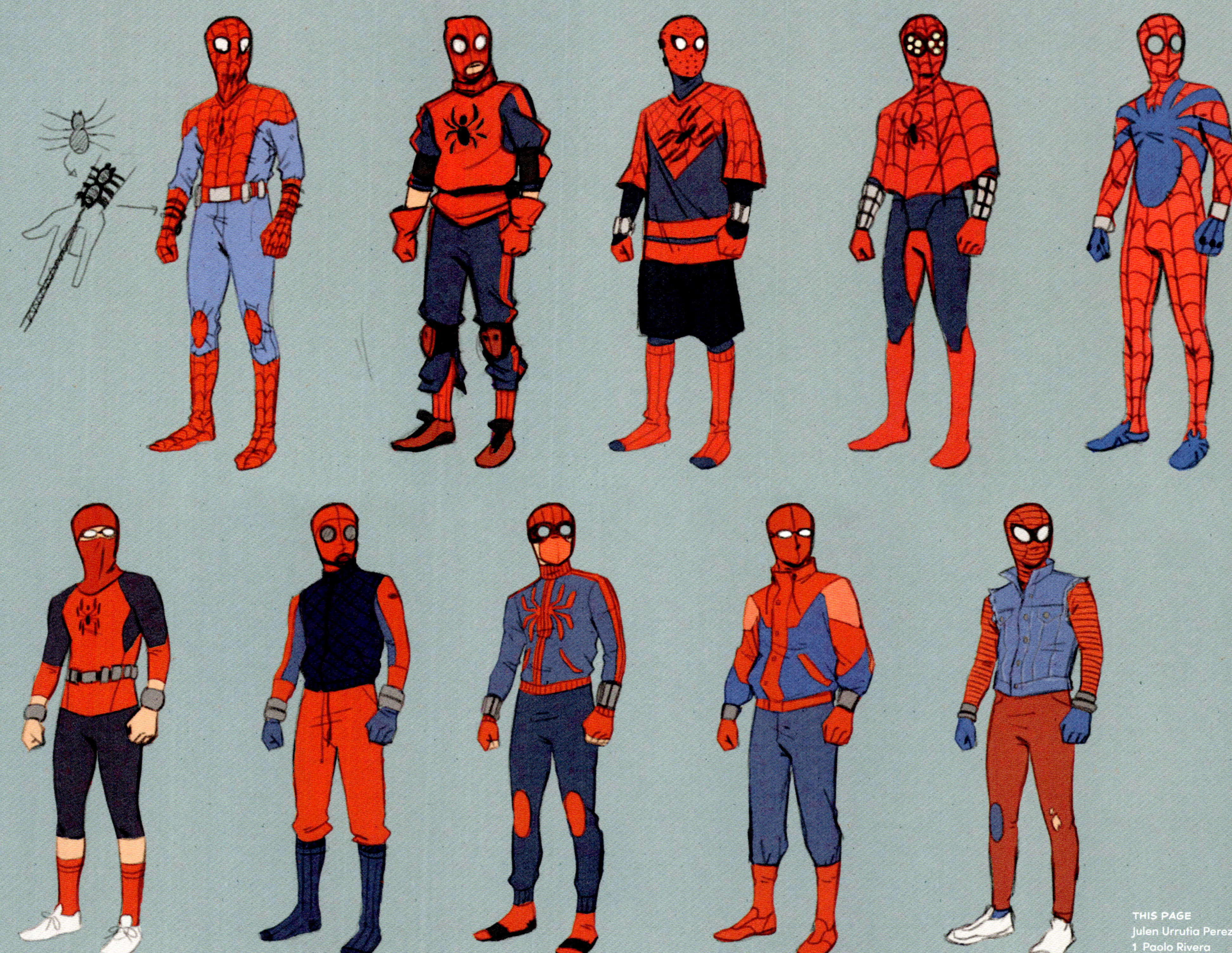

THIS PAGE
Julen Urrutia Perez
1 Paolo Rivera
2 Leonardo Romero

Ditko Blue
Ditko Navy
Ditko Black
P.E. Shorts
P.E. Shorts 2
Track Suit
Homecoming Navy Tweak
Homecoming Black Tweak
Scarlet Spider
Scarlet Spider 2

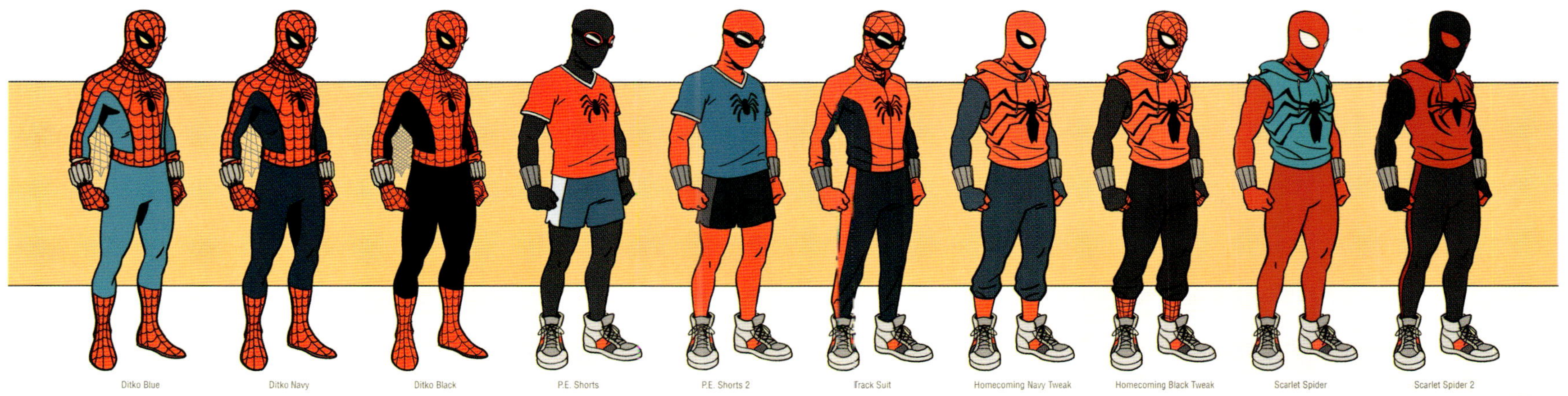

1

2

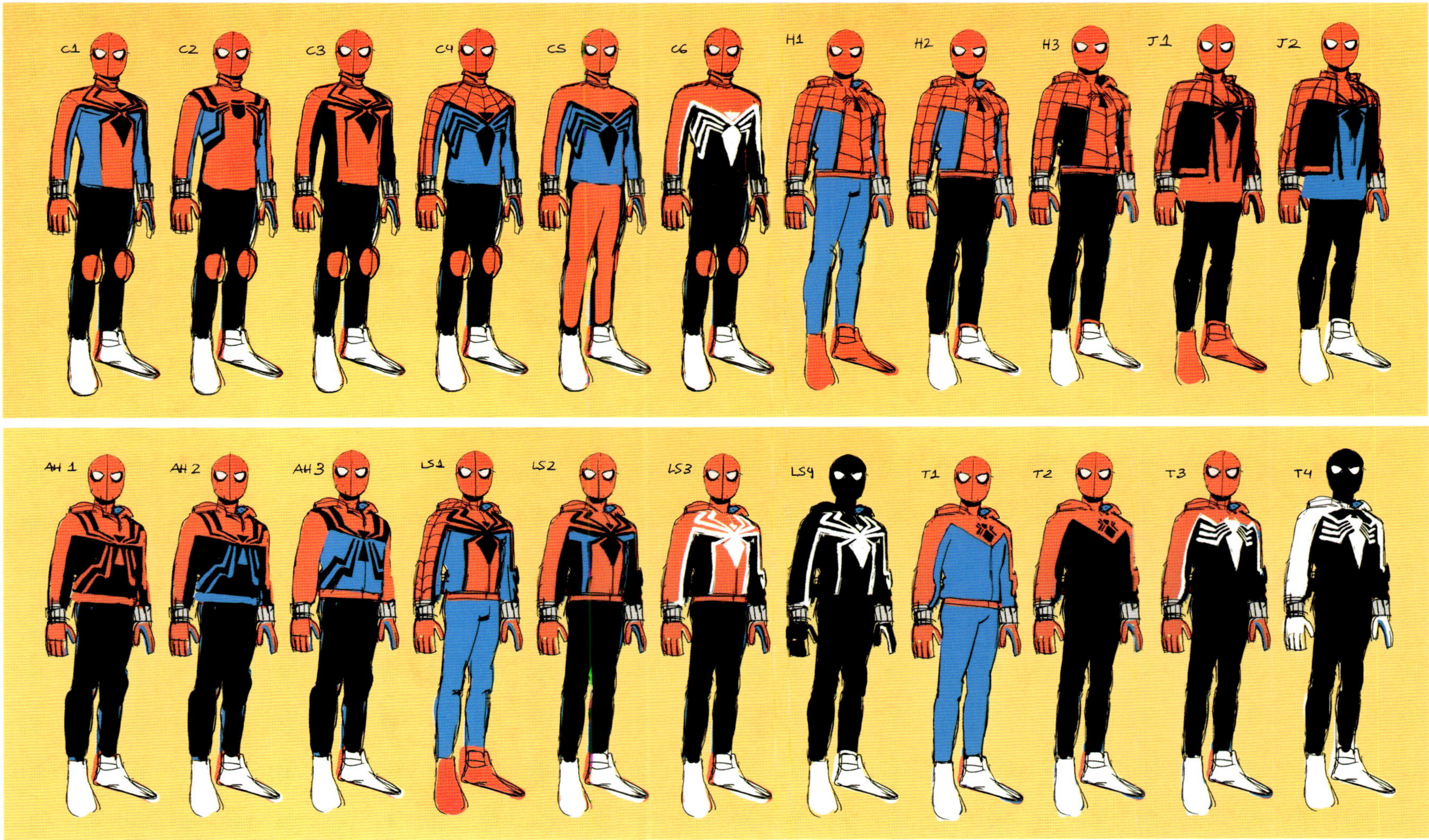

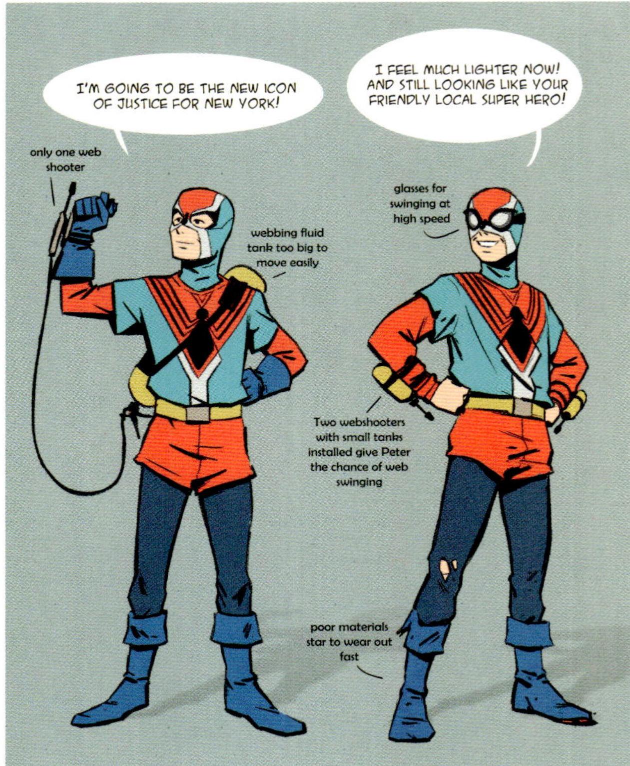

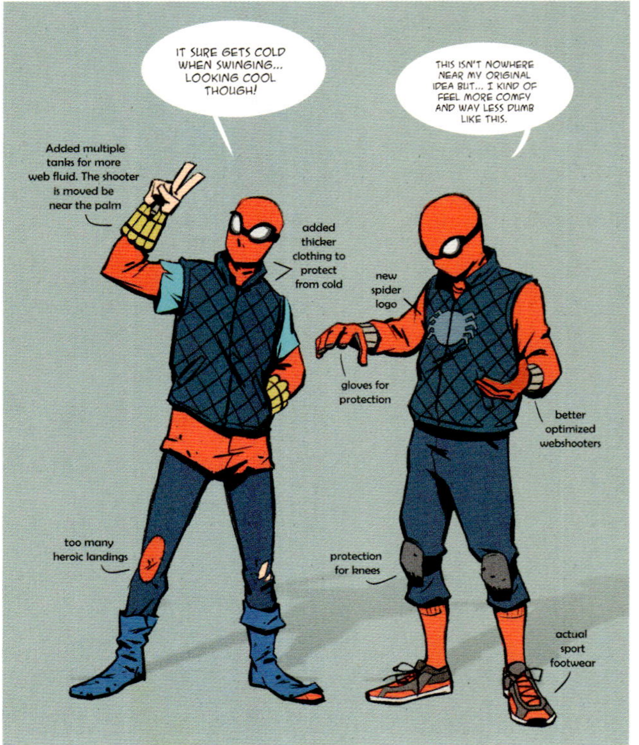

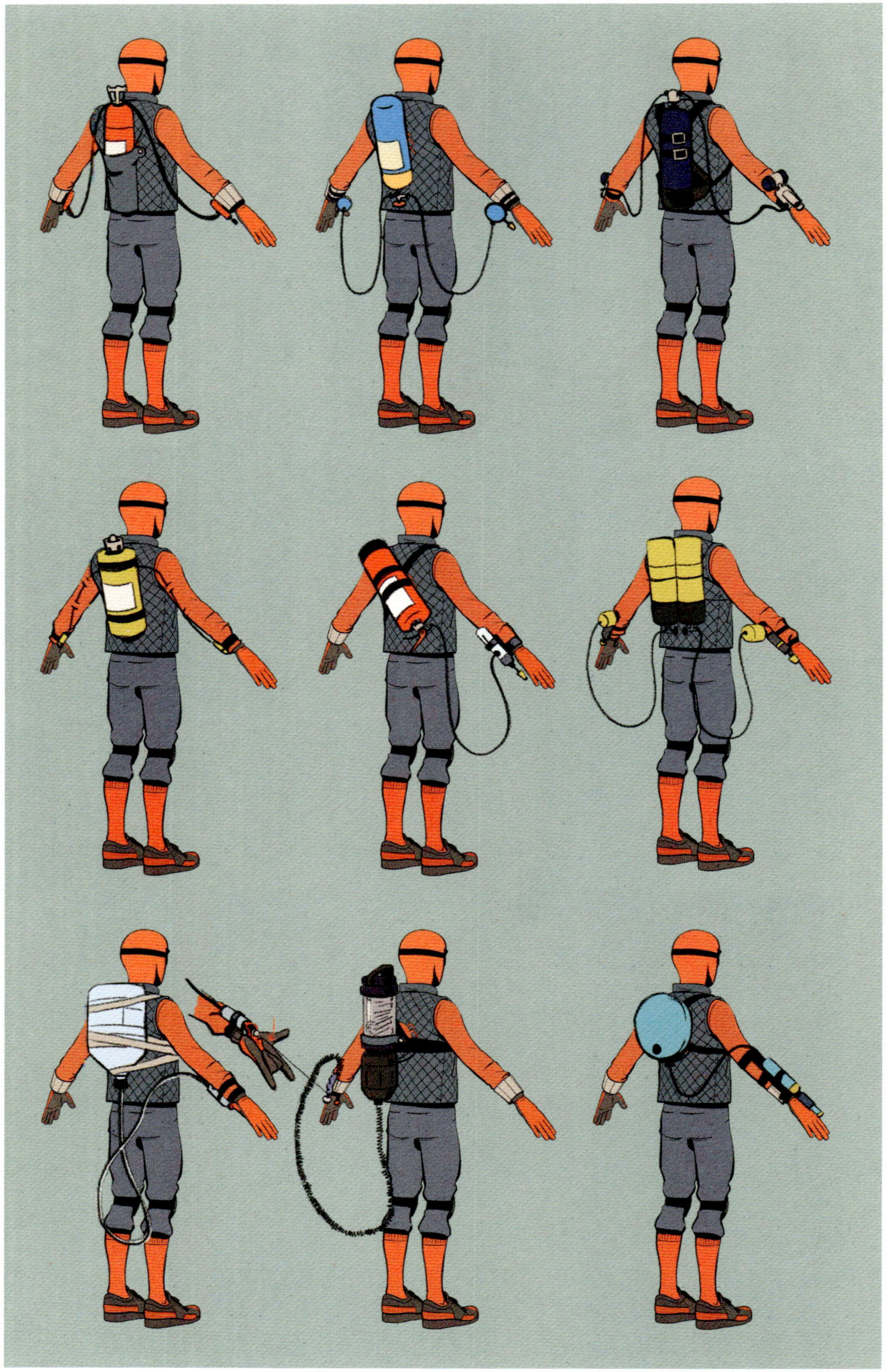

THIS PAGE
Julen Urrutia Perez
1 Julen Urrutia Perez
2 Paolo Rivera

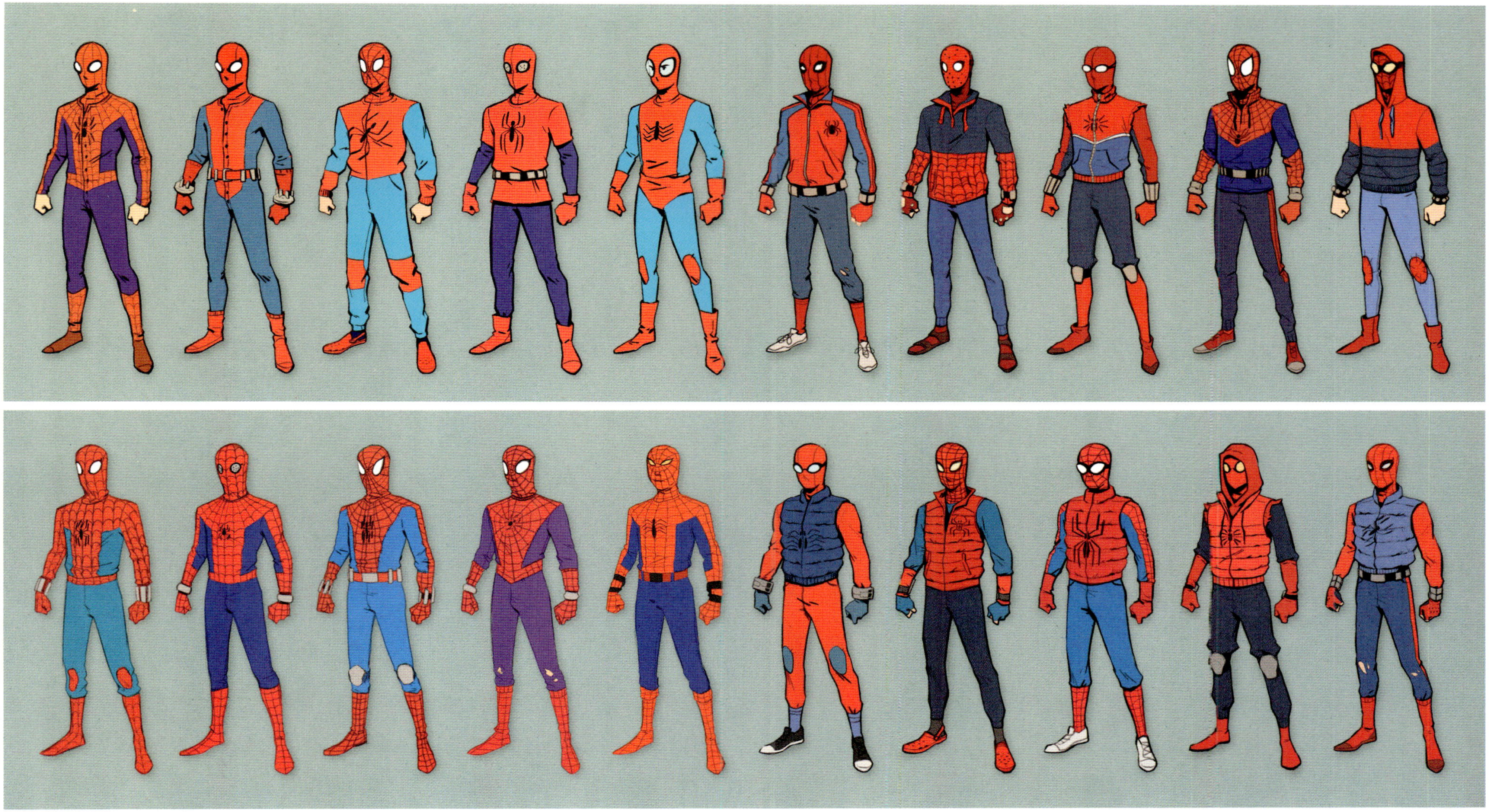

1

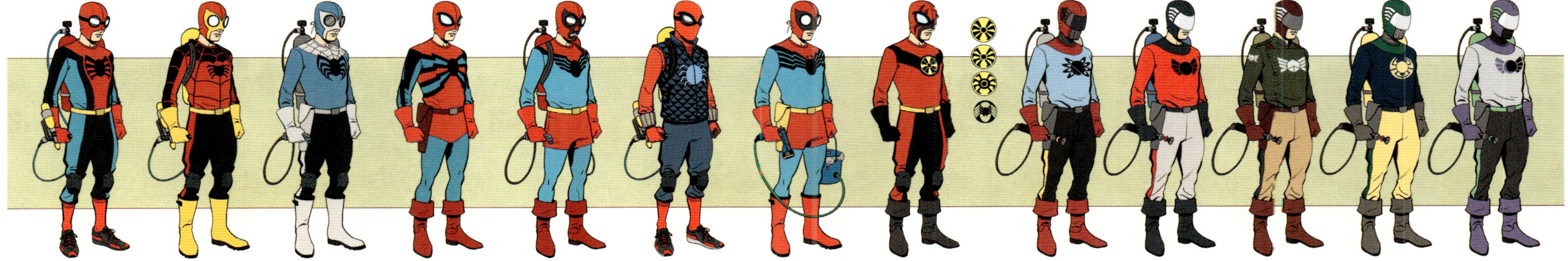

2

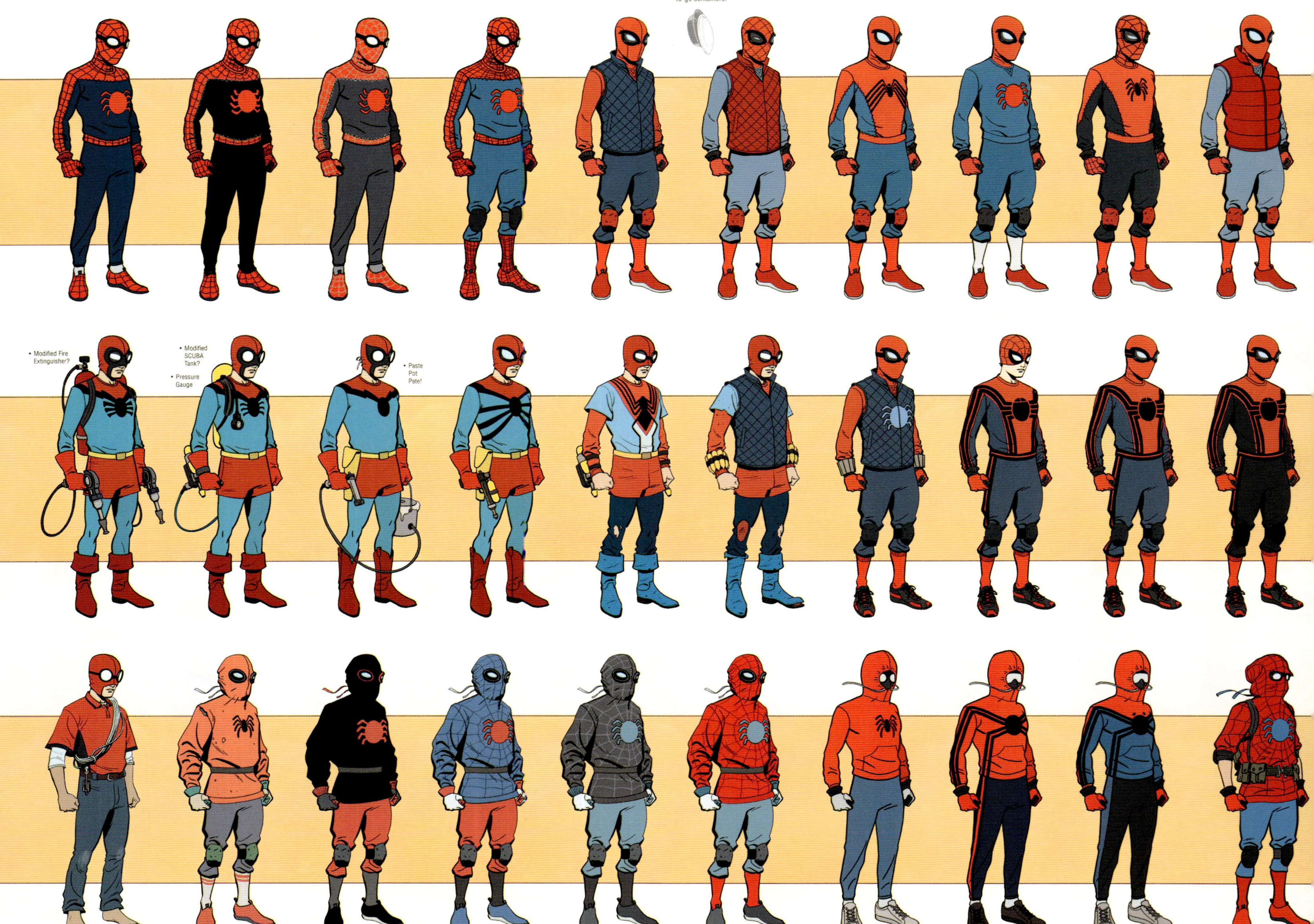

THIS SPREAD Paolo Rivera

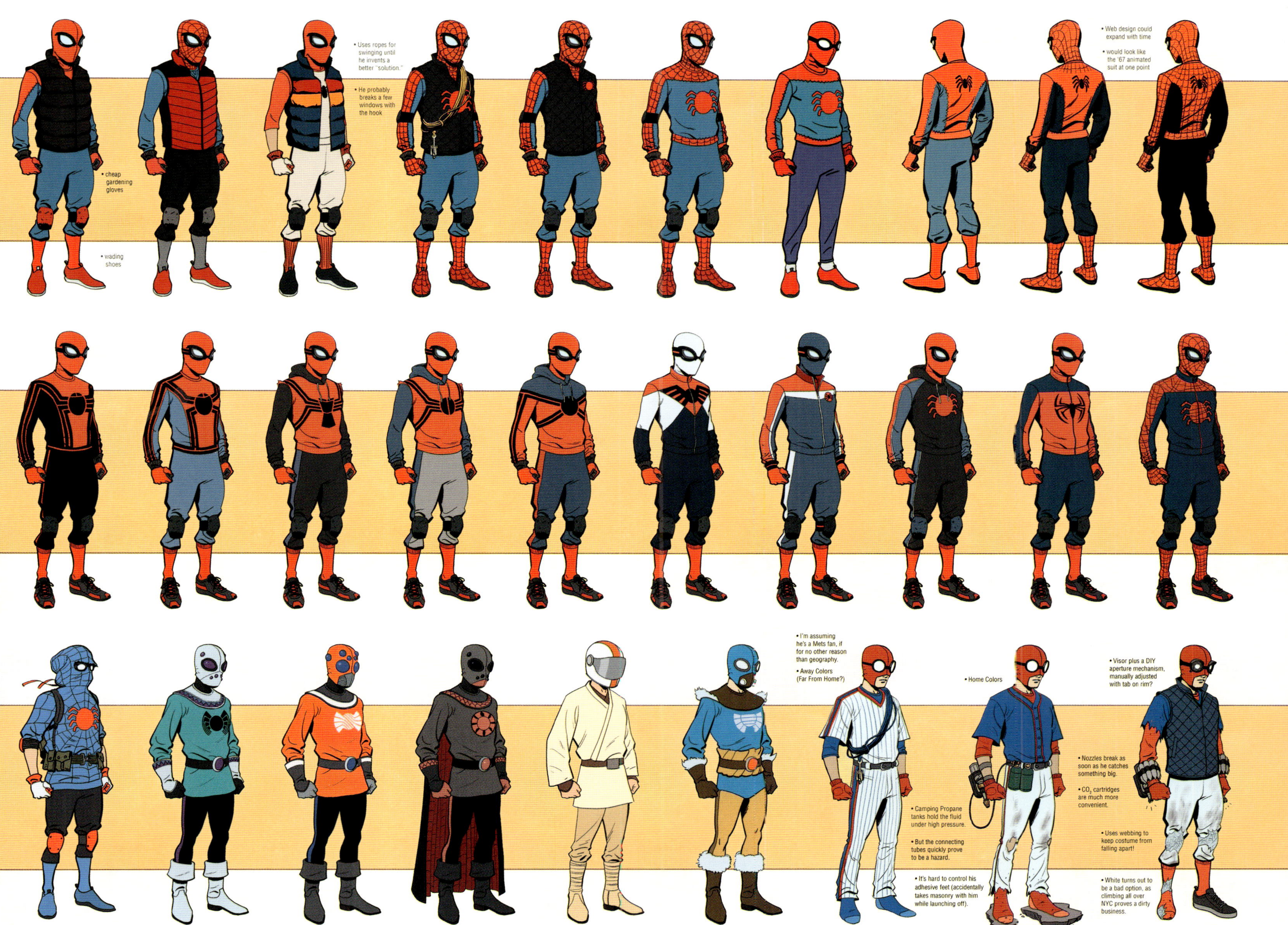
• cheap gardening gloves
• wading shoes
• Uses ropes for swinging until he invents a better "solution."
• He probably breaks a few windows with the hook
• Web design could expand with time
• would look like the '67 animated suit at one point
• I'm assuming he's a Mets fan, if for no other reason than geography.
• Away Colors (Far From Home?)
• Home Colors
• Visor plus a DIY aperture mechanism, manually adjusted with tab on rim?
• Nozzles break as soon as he catches something big.
• CO_2 cartridges are much more convenient.
• Camping Propane tanks hold the fluid under high pressure.
• But the connecting tubes quickly prove to be a hazard.
• Uses webbing to keep costume from falling apart!
• It's hard to control his adhesive feet (accidentally takes masonry with him while launching off).
• White turns out to be a bad option, as climbing all over NYC proves a dirty business.

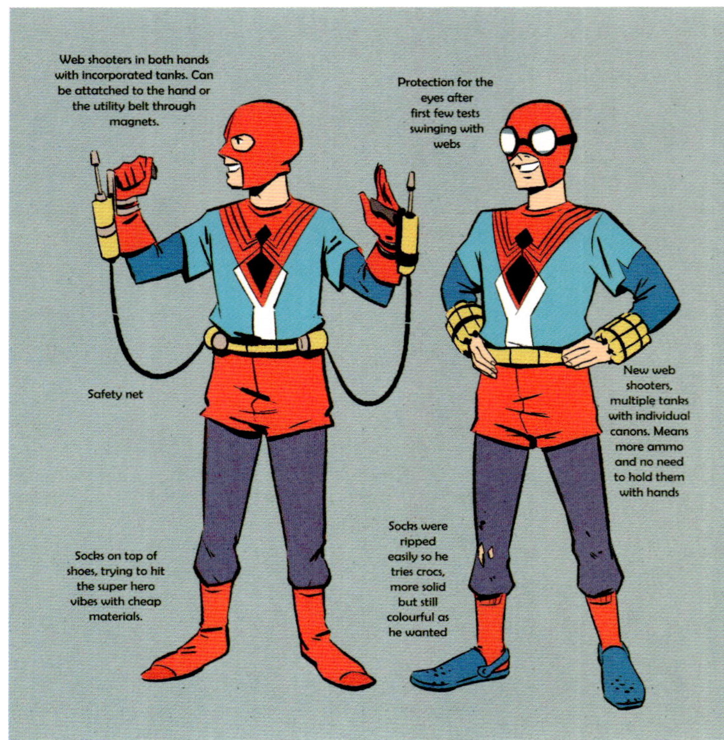
Web shooters in both hands with incorporated tanks. Can be attached to the hand or the utility belt through magnets.
Protection for the eyes after first few tests swinging with webs
Safety net
New web shooters, multiple tanks with individual canons. Means more ammo and no need to hold them with hands
Socks on top of shoes, trying to hit the super hero vibes with cheap materials.
Socks were ripped easily so he tries crocs, more solid but still colourful as he wanted

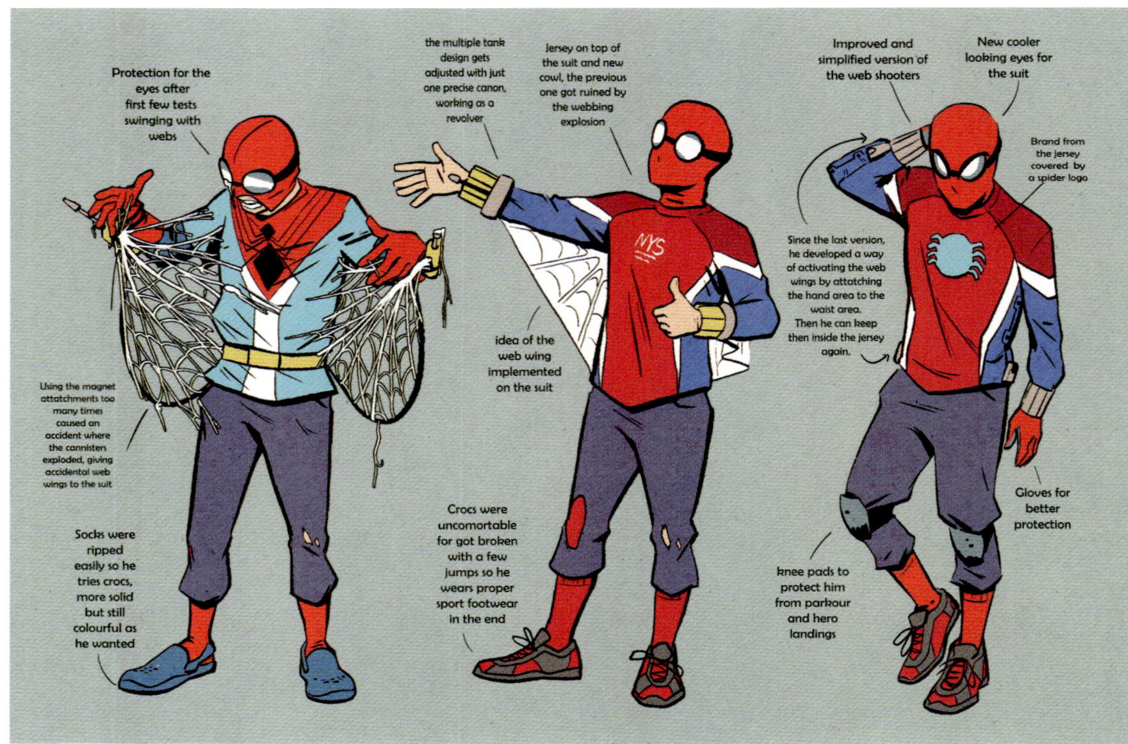
Protection for the eyes after first few tests swinging with webs
the multiple tank design gets adjusted with just one precise canon, working as a revolver
Jersey on top of the suit and new cowl, the previous one got ruined by the webbing explosion
Improved and simplified version of the web shooters
New cooler looking eyes for the suit
Brand from the jersey covered by a spider logo
Since the last version, he developed a way of activating the web wings by attatching the hand area to the waist area. Then he can keep then inside the jersey again.
idea of the web wing implemented on the suit
Using the magnet attatchments too many times caused an accident where the cannisters exploded, giving accidental web wings to the suit
Gloves for better protection
Socks were ripped easily so he tries crocs, more solid but still colourful as he wanted
Crocs were uncomortable for got broken with a few jumps so he wears proper sport footwear in the end
knee pads to protect him from parkour and hero landings

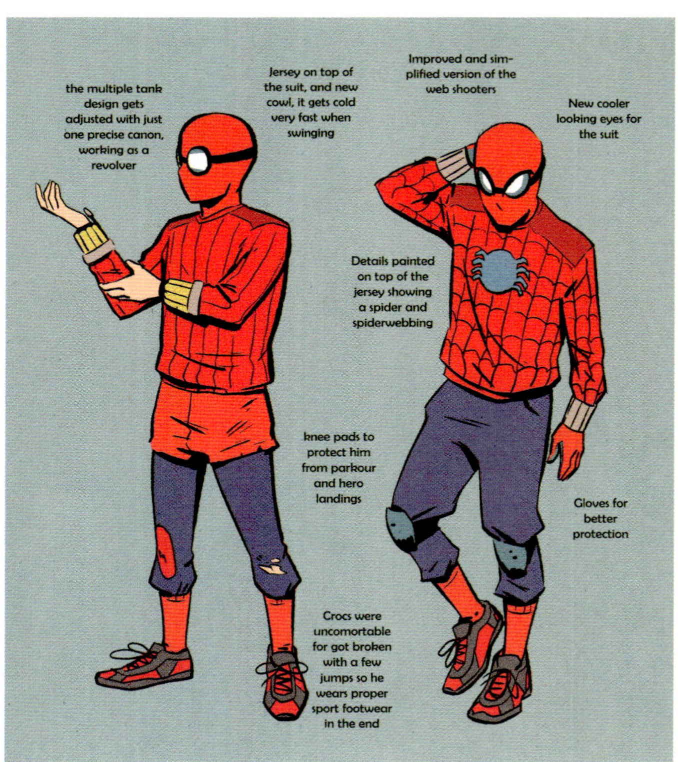
the multiple tank design gets adjusted with just one precise canon, working as a revolver
Jersey on top of the suit, and new cowl, it gets cold very fast when swinging
Improved and simplified version of the web shooters
New cooler looking eyes for the suit
Details painted on top of the jersey showing a spider and spiderwebbing
knee pads to protect him from parkour and hero landings
Gloves for better protection
Crocs were uncomortable for got broken with a few jumps so he wears proper sport footwear in the end

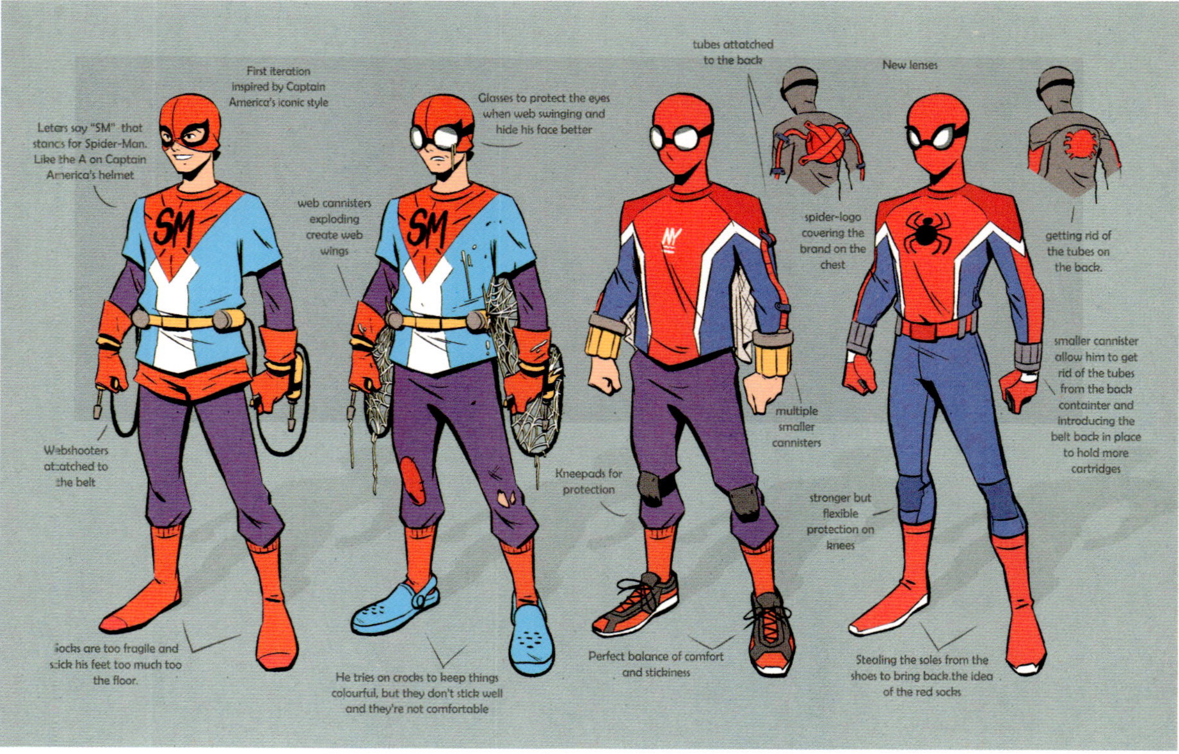
First iteration inspired by Captain America's iconic style
Leters say "SM" that stancs for Spider-Man. Like the A on Captain America's helmet
Glasses to protect the eyes when web swinging and hide his face better
web cannisters exploding create web wings
tubes attatched to the back
New lenses
spider-logo covering the brand on the chest
getting rid of the tubes on the back.
smaller cannister allow him to get rid of the tubes from the back containter and introducing the belt back in place to hold more cartridges
Webshooters attatched to the belt
multiple smaller cannisters
Kneepads for protection
stronger but flexible protection on knees
Socks are too fragile and stick his feet too much too the floor.
He tries on crocks to keep things colourful, but they don't stick well and they're not comfortable
Perfect balance of comfort and stickiness
Stealing the soles from the shoes to bring back the idea of the red socks

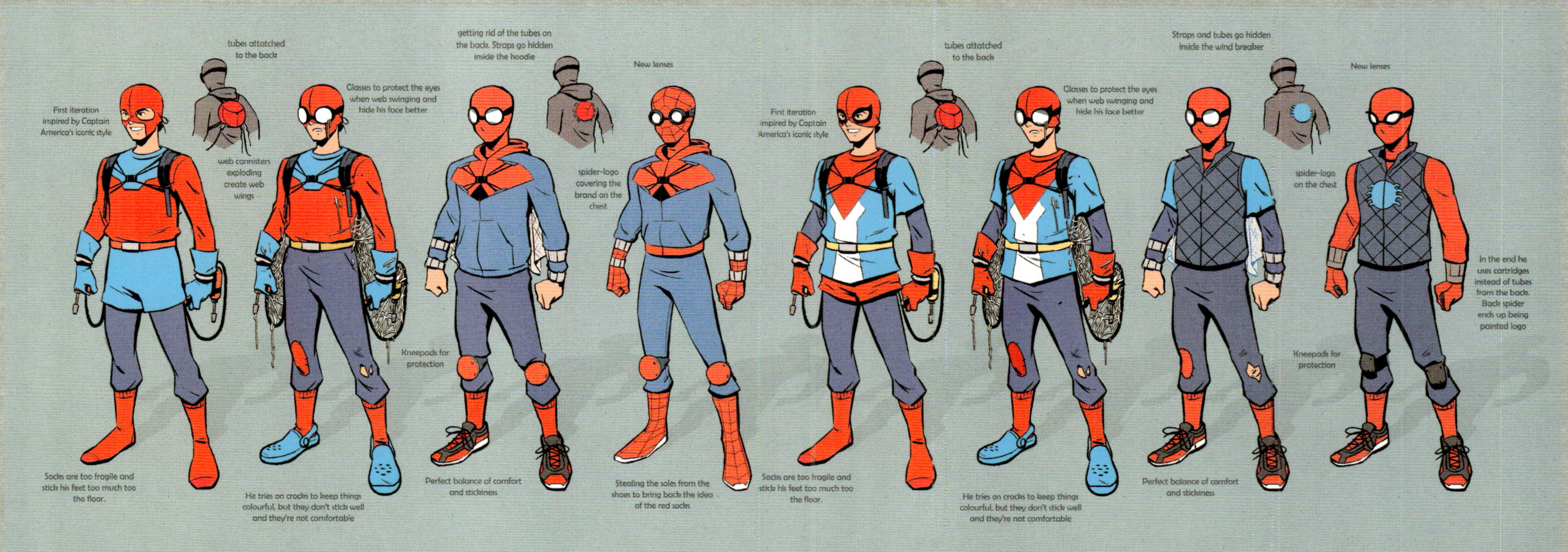

First iteration inspired by Captain America's iconic style

tubes attatched to the back

web cannisters exploding create web wings

Glasses to protect the eyes when web swinging and hide his face better

getting rid of the tubes on the back. Straps go hidden inside the hoodie

spider-logo covering the brand on the chest

New lenses

Socks are too fragile and stick his feet too much too the floor.

He tries on crocks to keep things colourful, but they don't stick well and they're not comfortable

Kneepads for protection

Perfect balance of comfort and stickiness

Stealing the soles from the shoes to bring back the idea of the red socks

First iteration inspired by Captain America's iconic style

tubes attatched to the back

Glasses to protect the eyes when web swinging and hide his face better

Straps and tubes go hidden inside the wind breaker

spider-logo on the chest

New lenses

In the end he uses cartridges instead of tubes from the back. Back spider ends up being painted logo

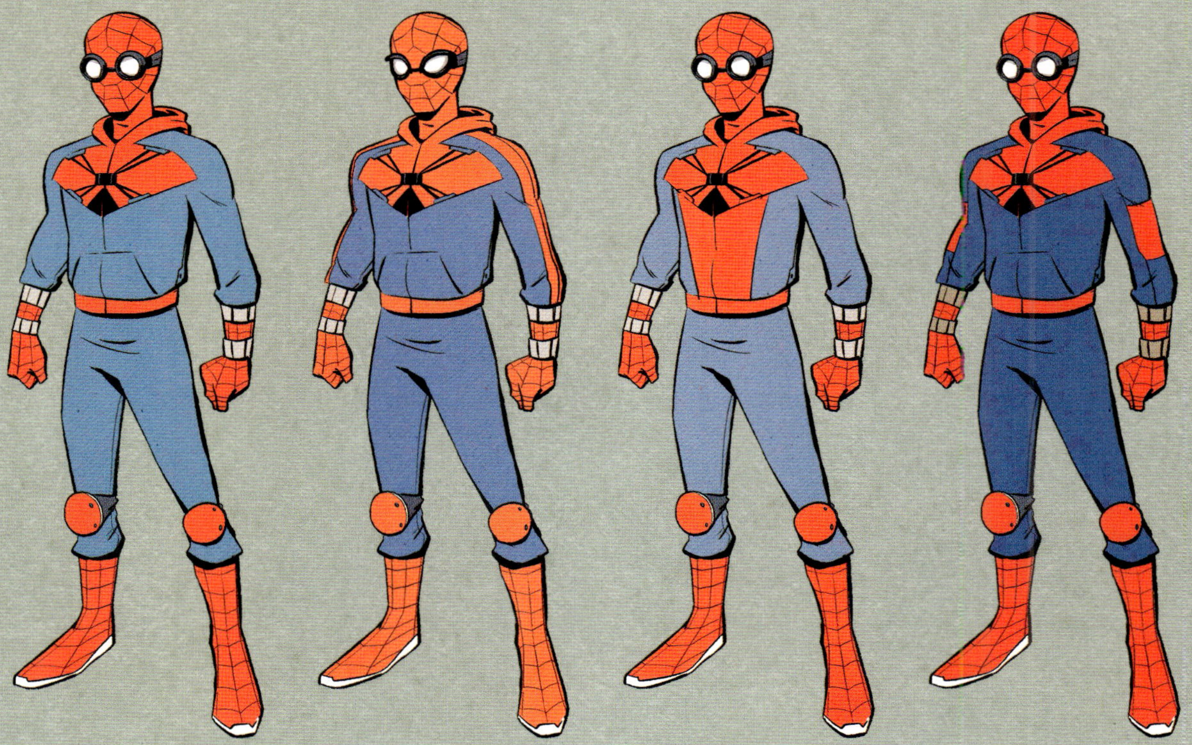

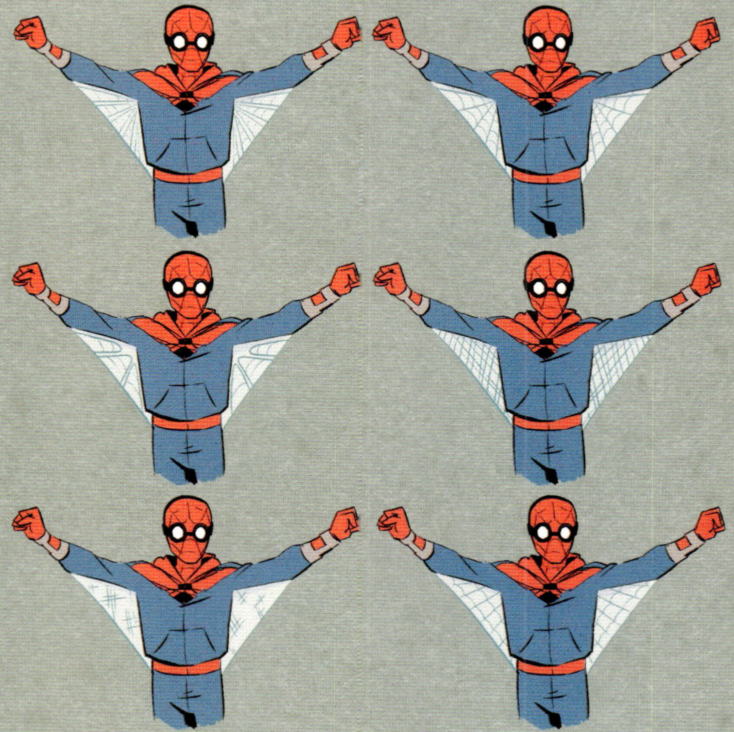

Kneepads for protection

Socks are too fragile and stick his feet too much too the floor.

He tries on crocks to keep things colourful, but they don't stick well and they're not comfortable

Perfect balance of comfort and stickiness

THIS SPREAD Julen Urrutia Perez

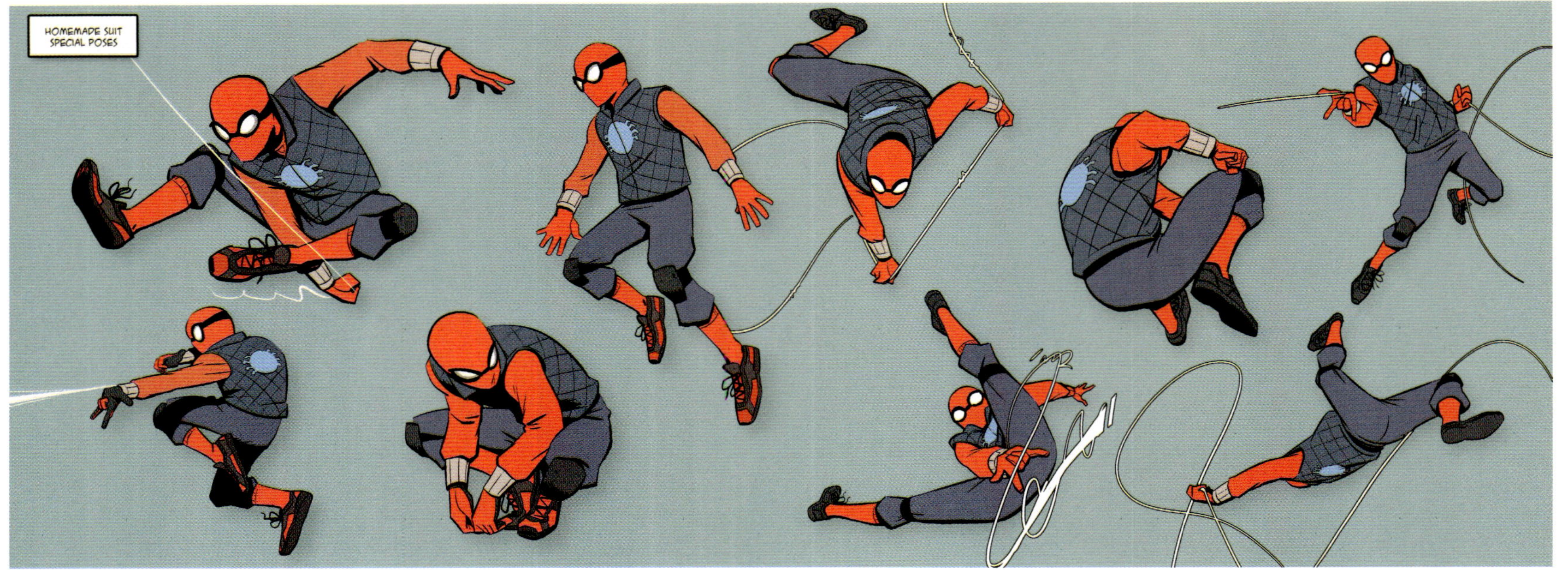

1

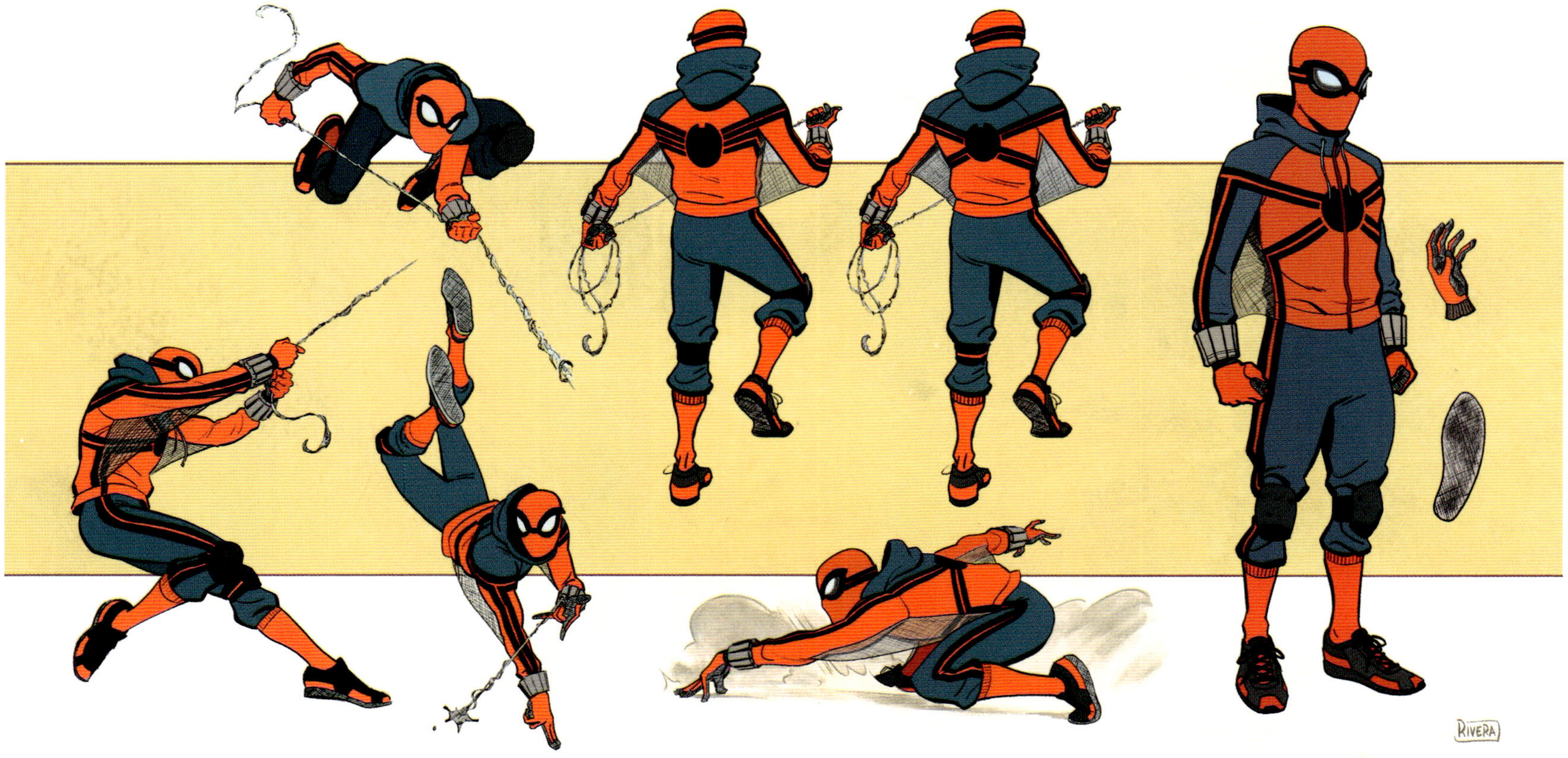

2

1 Julen Urrutia Perez
2 Paolo Rivera
3 Leonardo Romero
4 Paolo Rivera

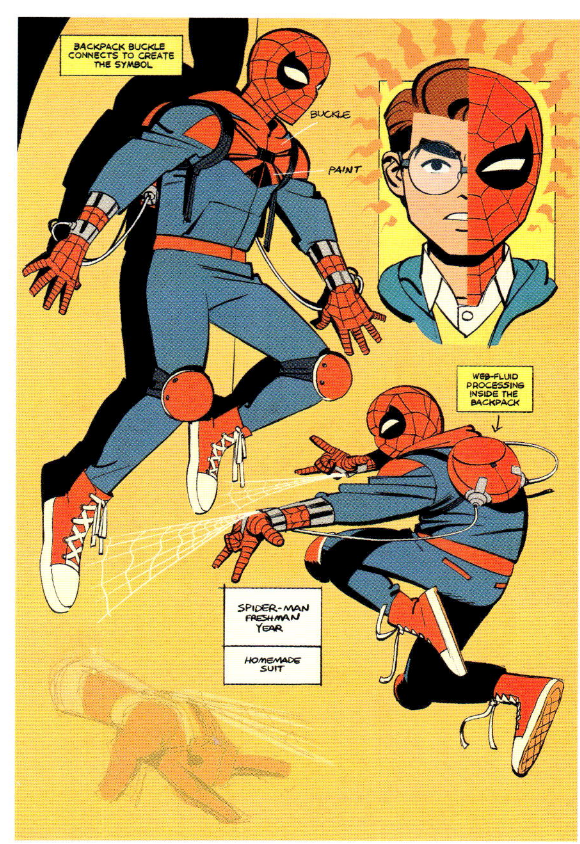

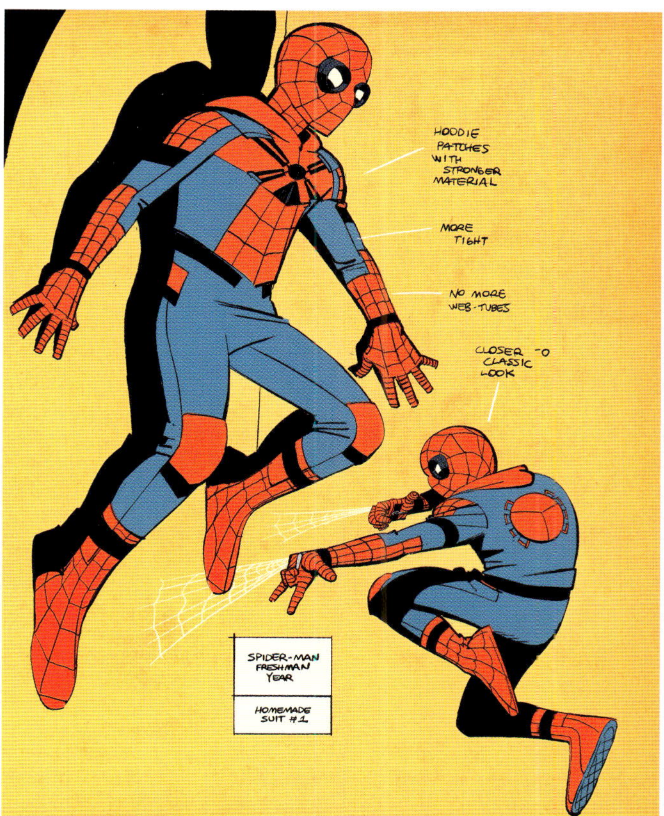

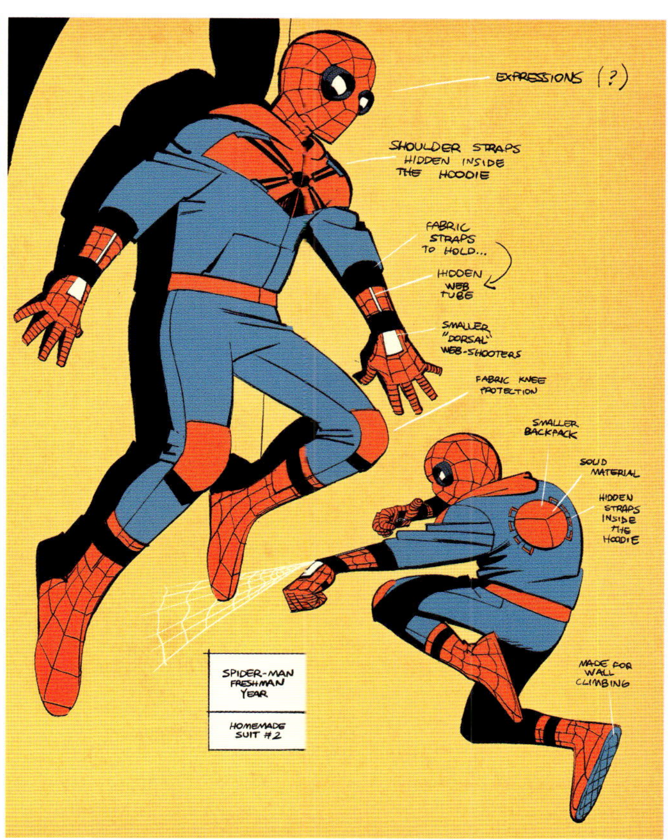

BACKPACK BUCKLE CONNECTS TO CREATE THE SYMBOL
BUCKLE
PAINT
WEB-FLUID PROCESSING INSIDE THE BACKPACK
SPIDER-MAN FRESHMAN YEAR
HOMEMADE SUIT

HOODIE PATCHES WITH STRONGER MATERIAL
MORE TIGHT
NO MORE WEB-TUBES
CLOSER TO CLASSIC LOOK
SPIDER-MAN FRESHMAN YEAR
HOMEMADE SUIT #1

EXPRESSIONS (?)
SHOULDER STRAPS HIDDEN INSIDE THE HOODIE
FABRIC STRAPS TO HOLD...
HIDDEN WEB TUBE
SMALLER "DORSAL" WEB-SHOOTERS
FABRIC KNEE PROTECTION
SMALLER BACKPACK
SOLID MATERIAL
HIDDEN STRAPS INSIDE THE HOODIE
MADE FOR WALL CLIMBING
SPIDER-MAN FRESHMAN YEAR
HOMEMADE SUIT #2

3

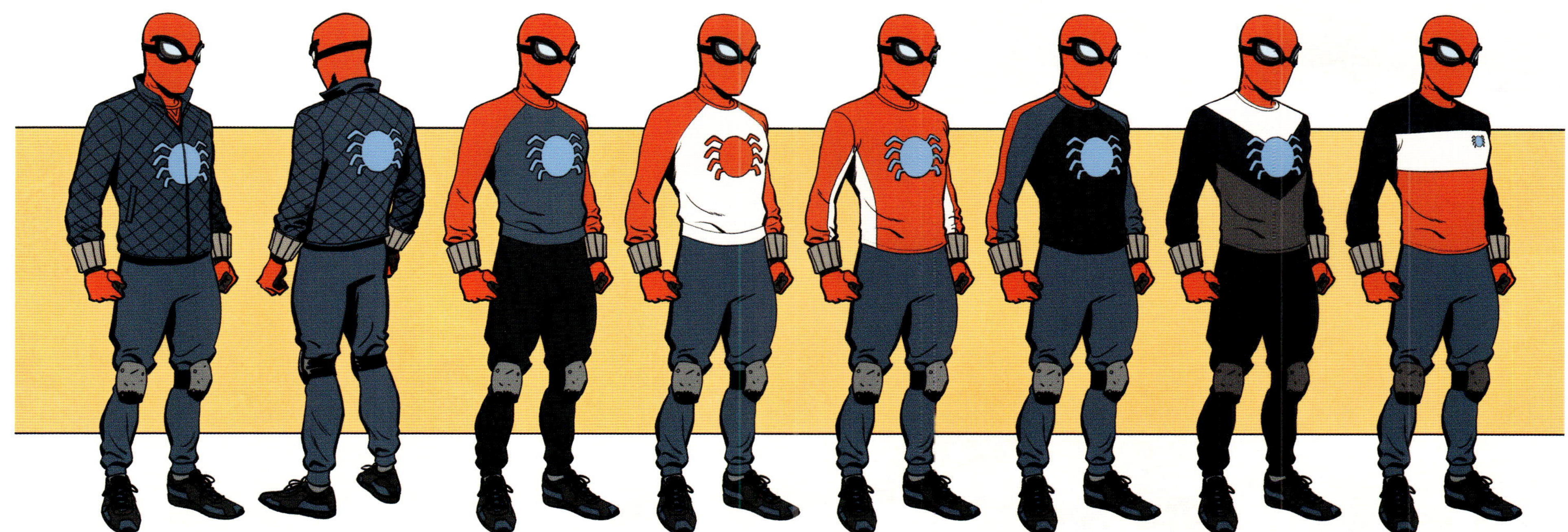
4

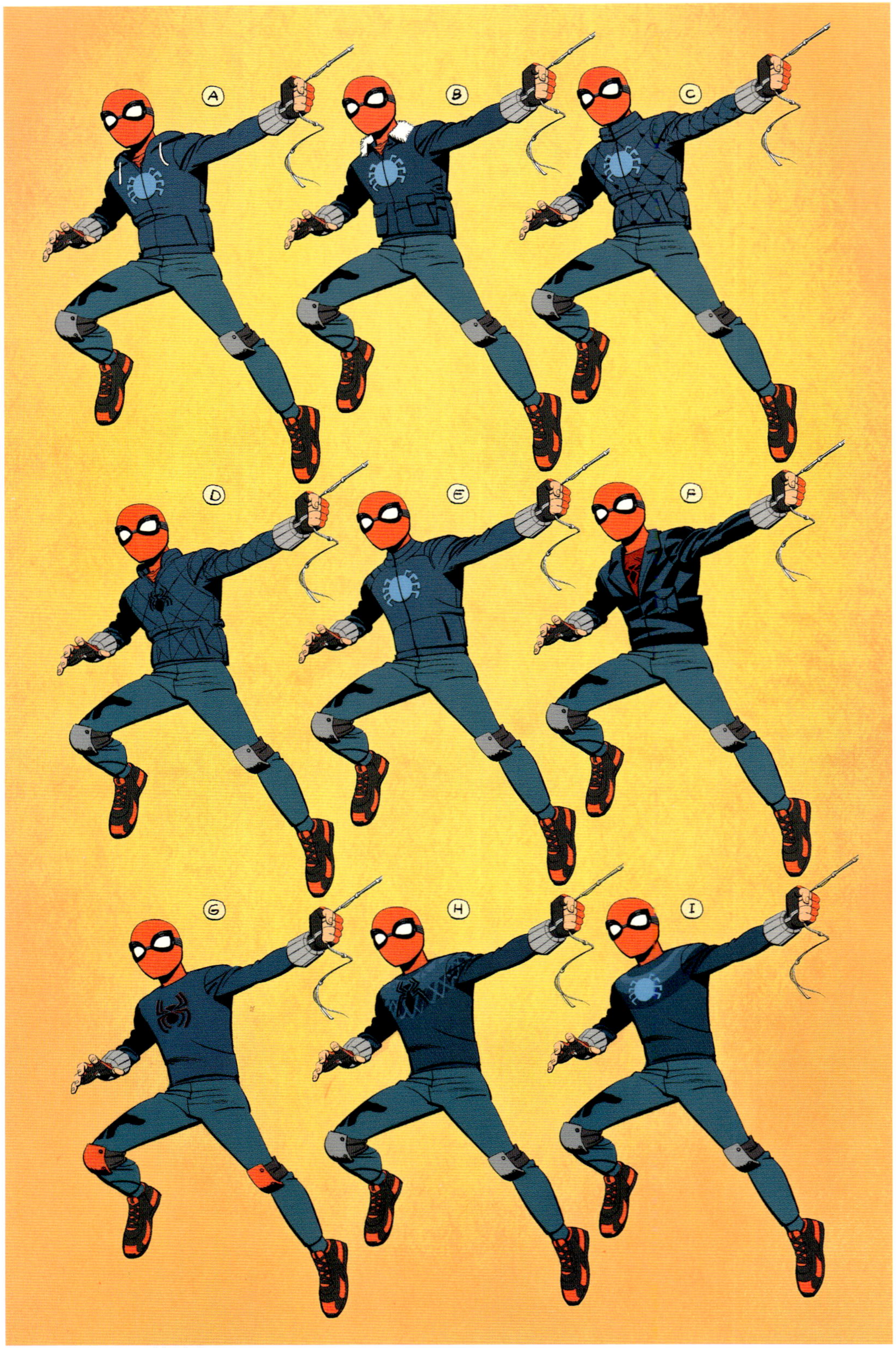

A
B
C
D
E
F
G
H
I

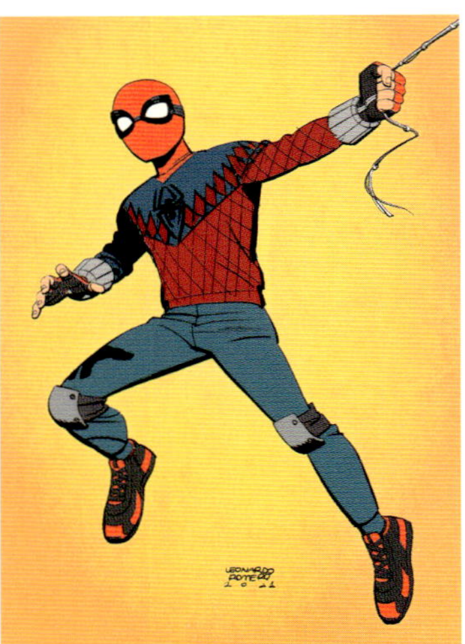

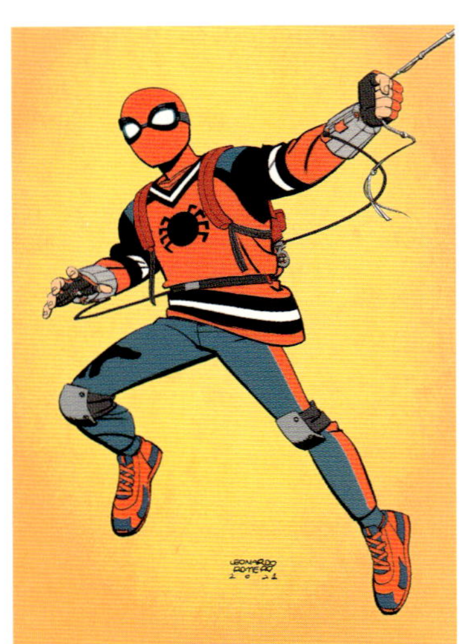

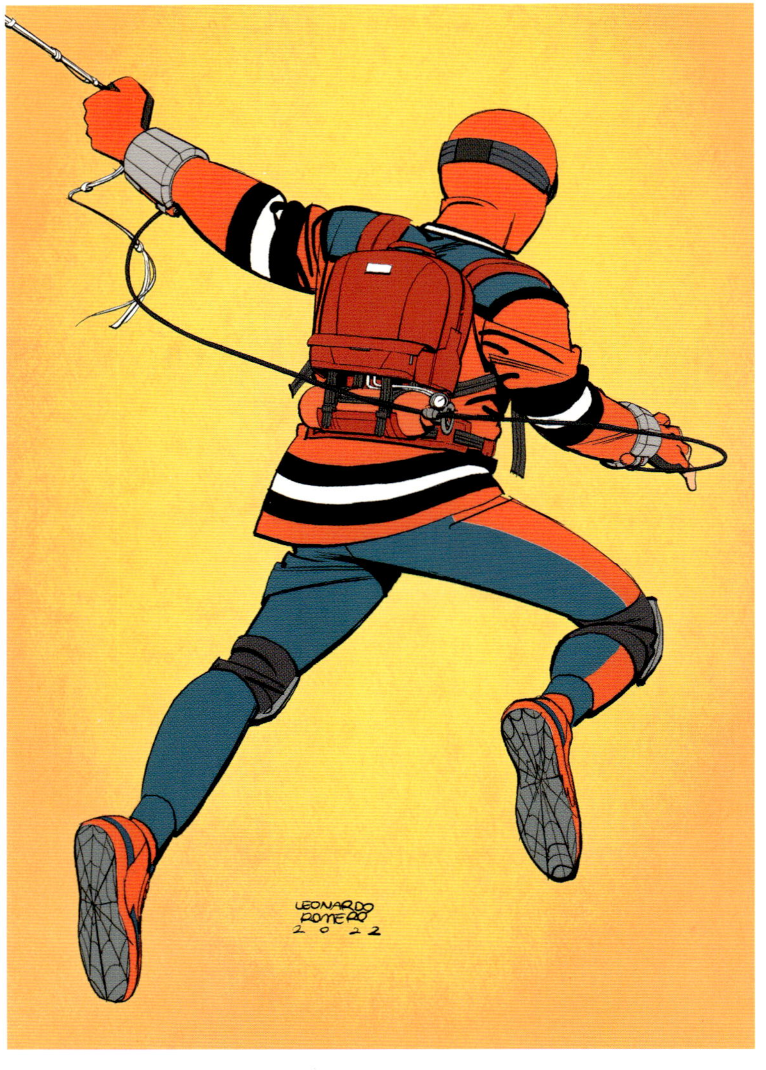
LEONARDO
ROMERO
2022

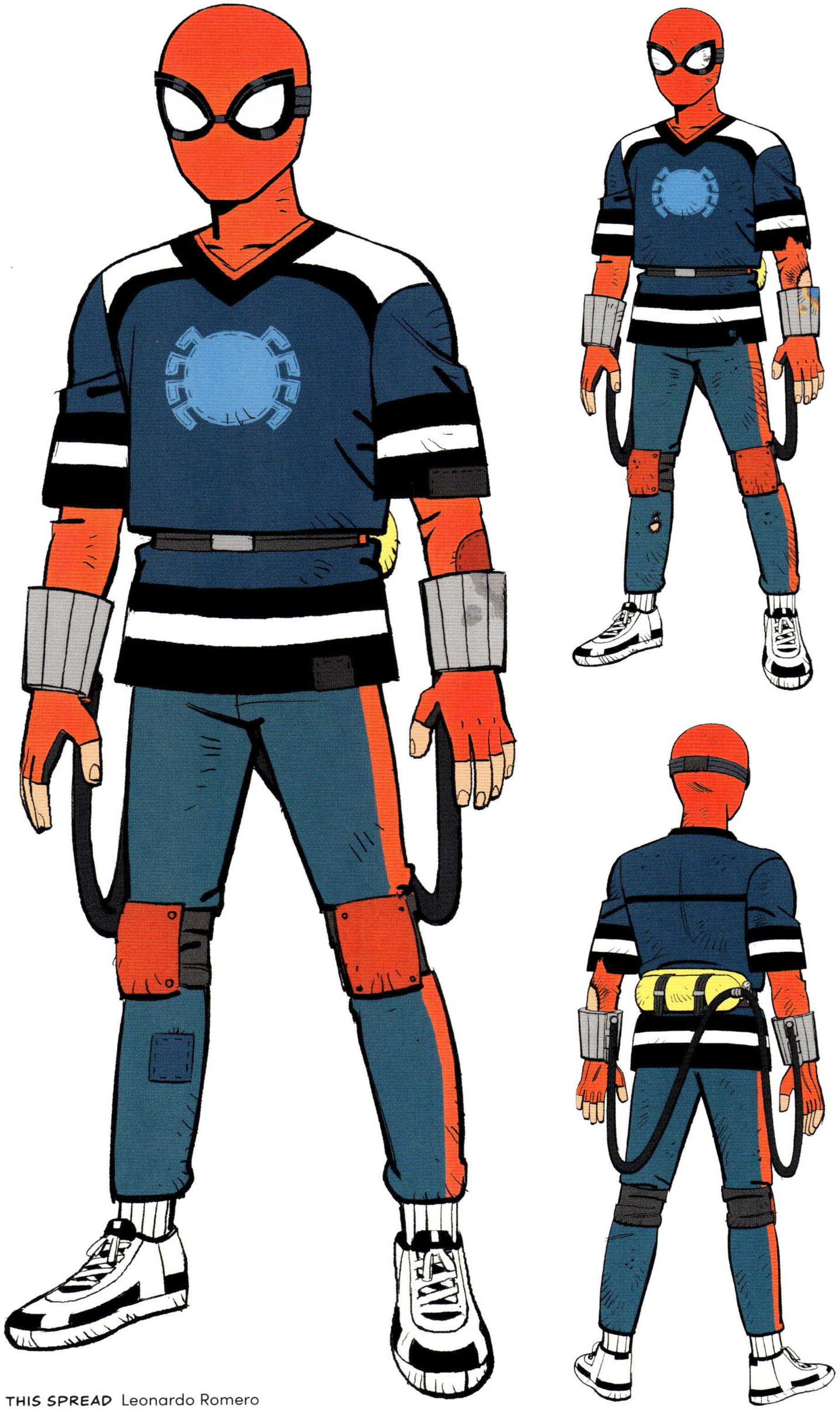

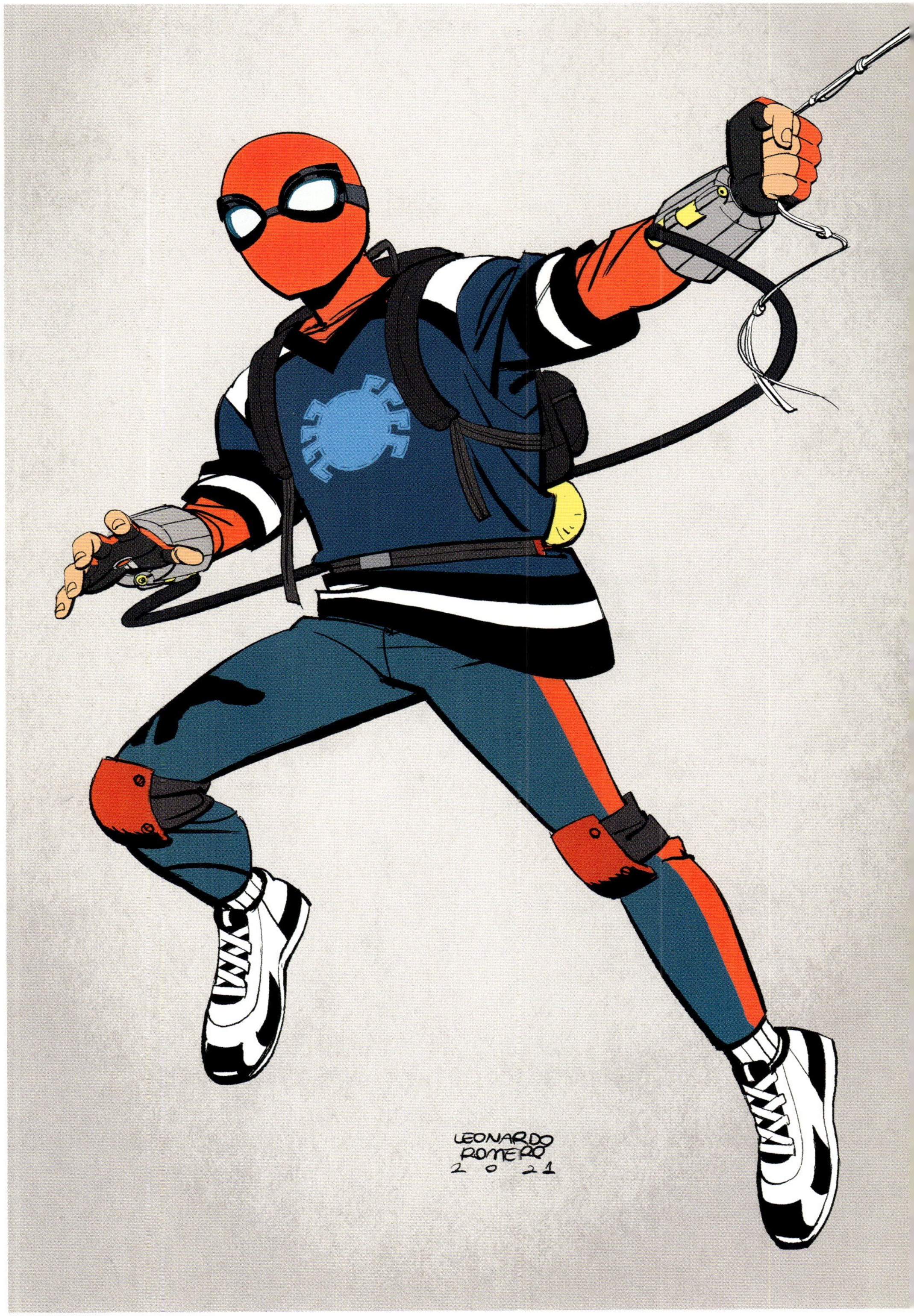

THIS SPREAD Leonardo Romero

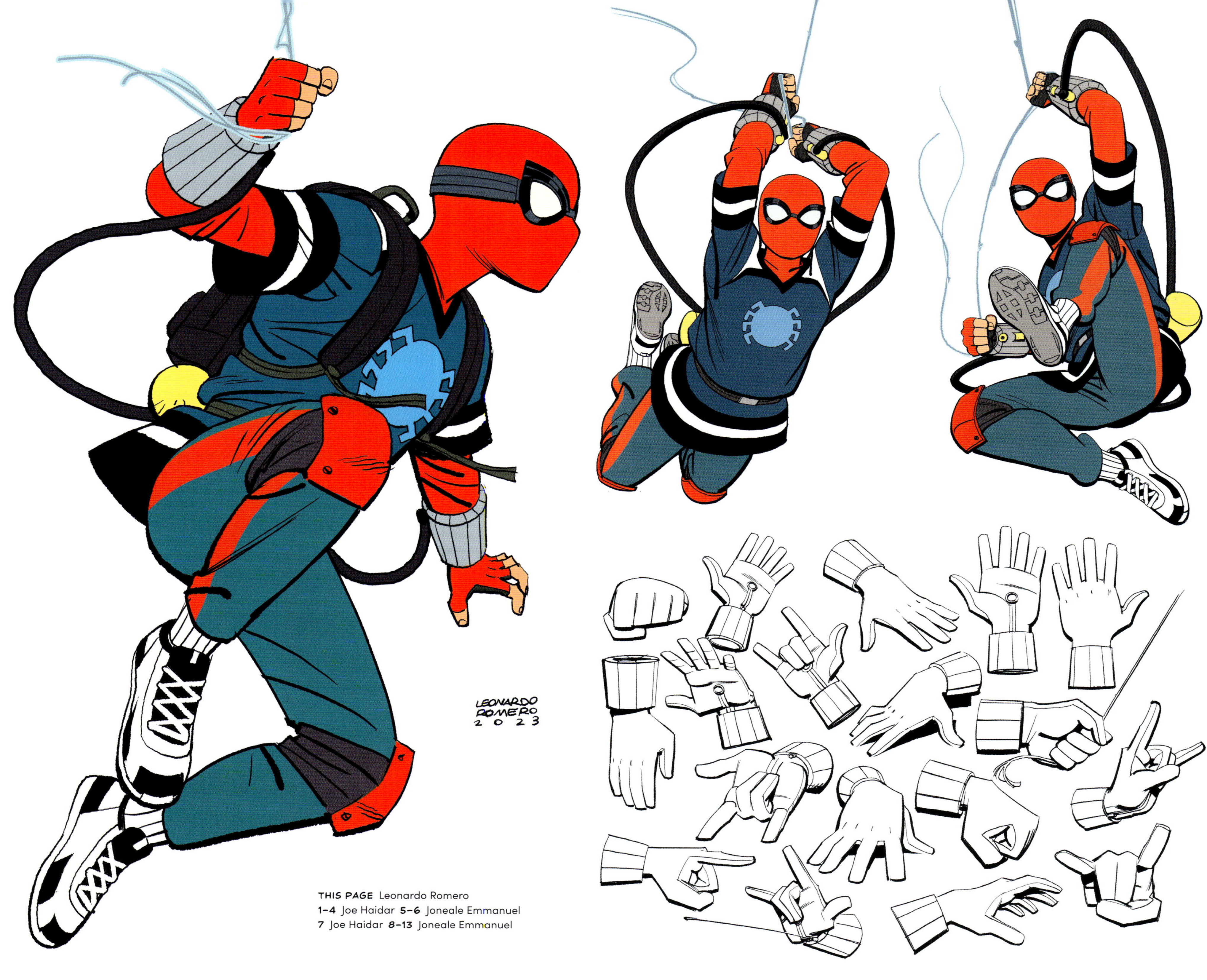

THIS PAGE Leonardo Romero
1–4 Joe Haidar **5–6** Joneale Emmanuel
7 Joe Haidar **8–13** Joneale Emmanuel

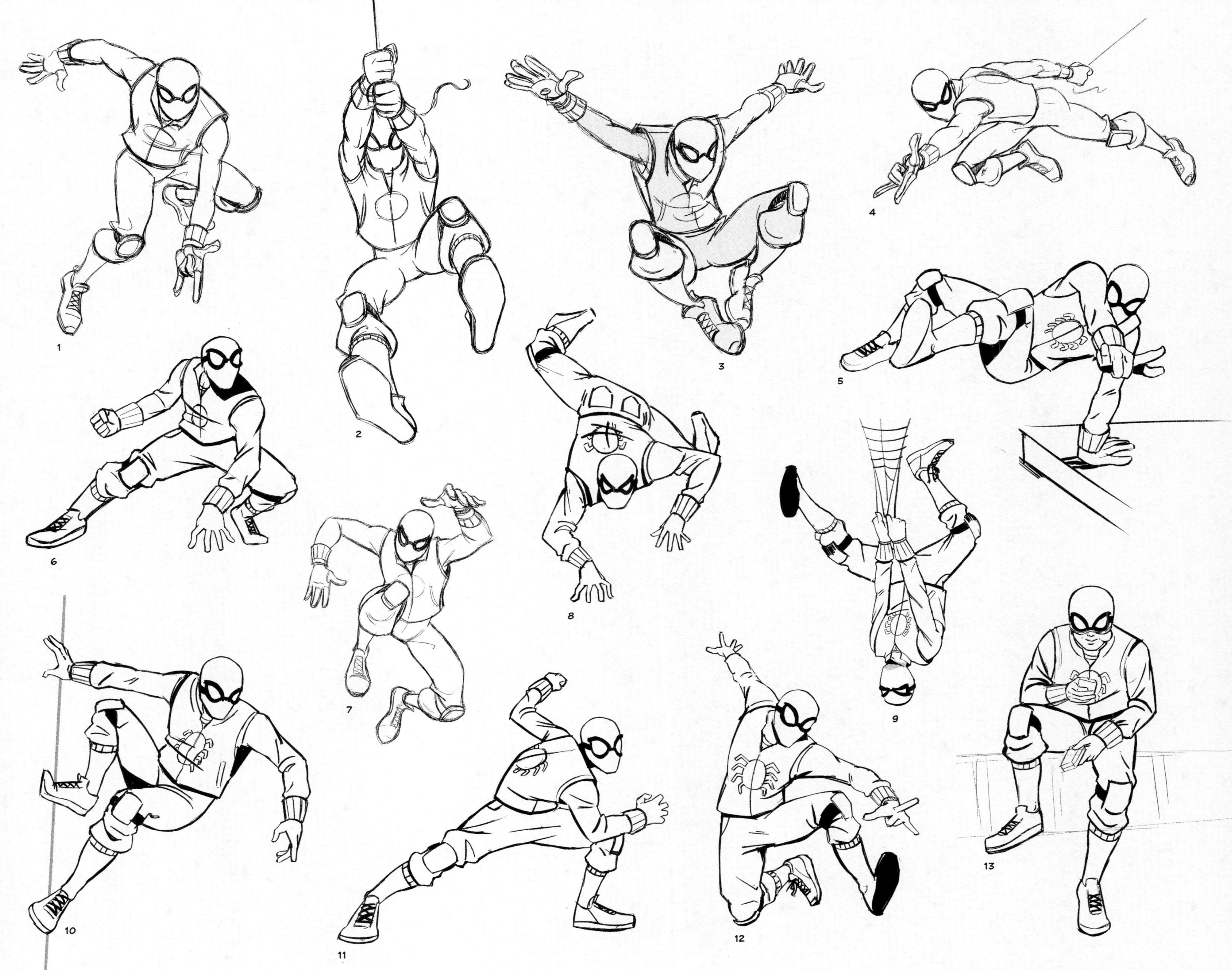
1
2
3
4
5
6
7
8
9
10
11
12
13

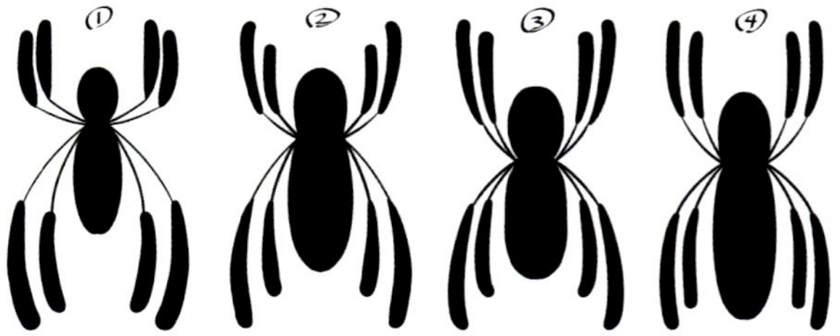

1

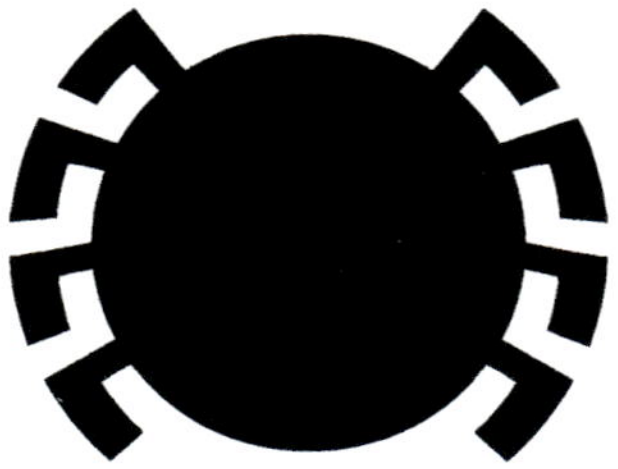

2

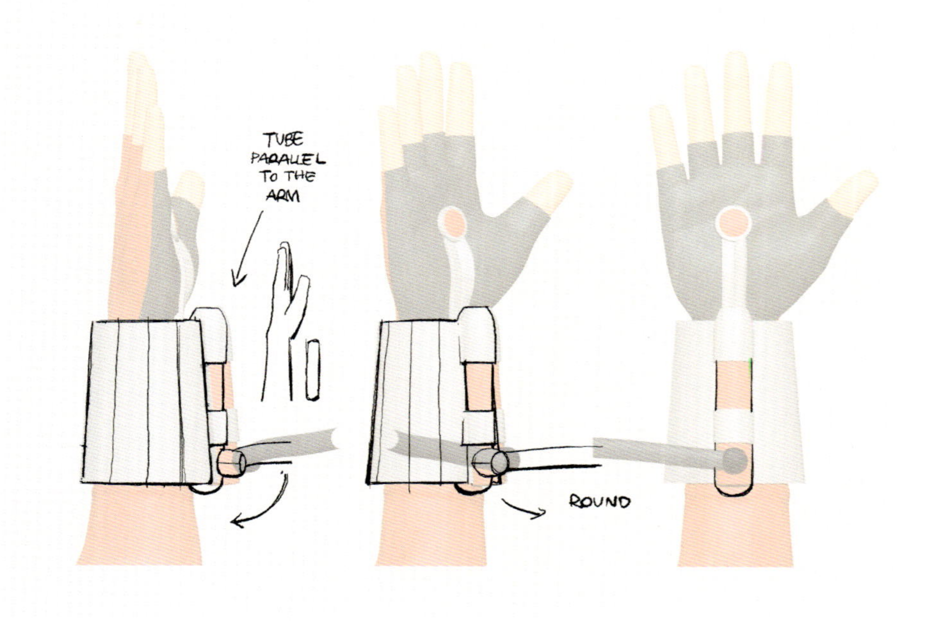

TUBE PARALLEL TO THE ARM

ROUND

3

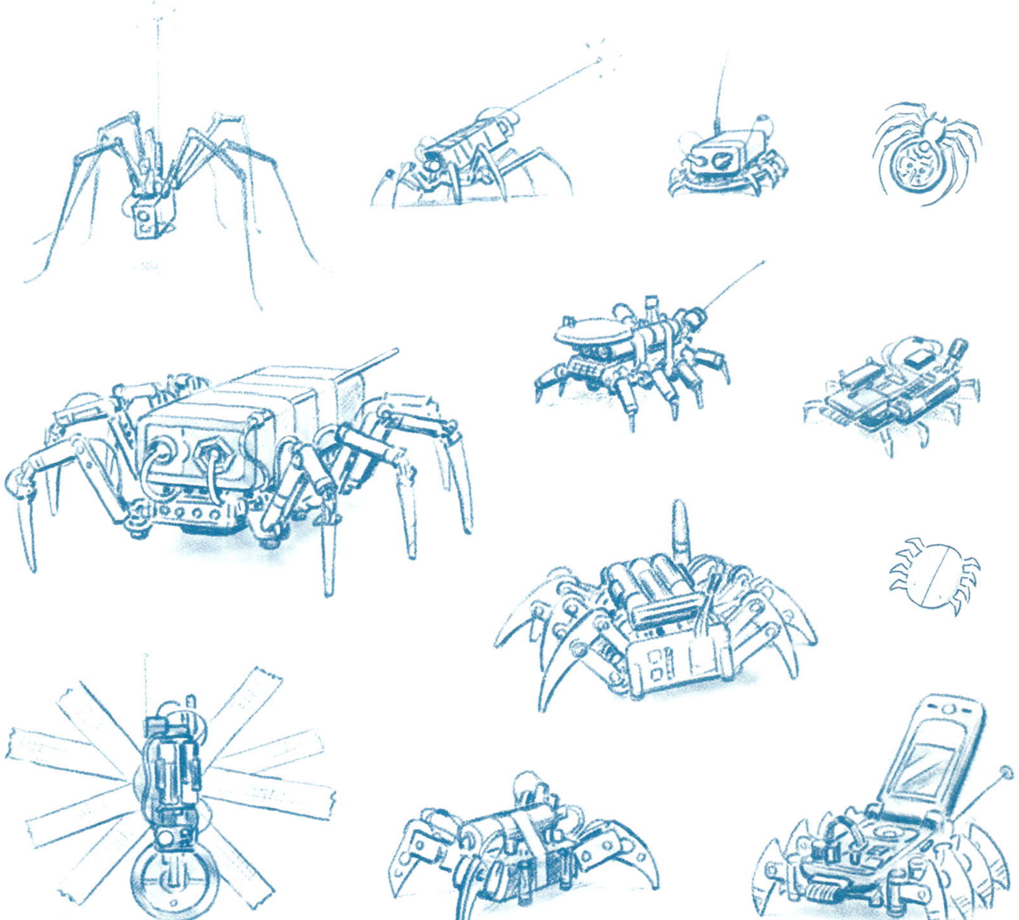

4

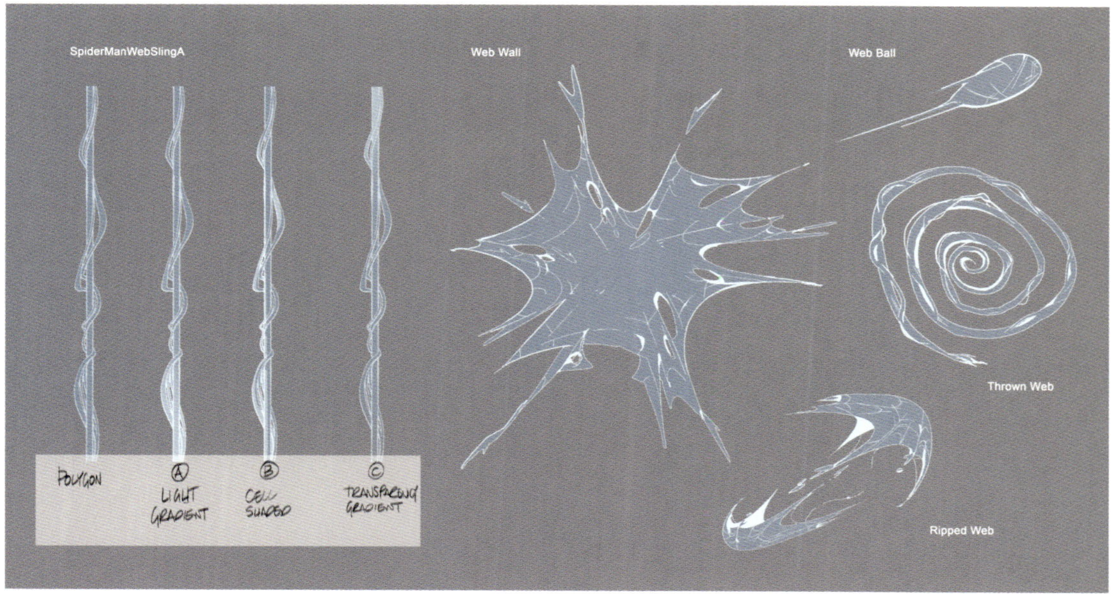

5

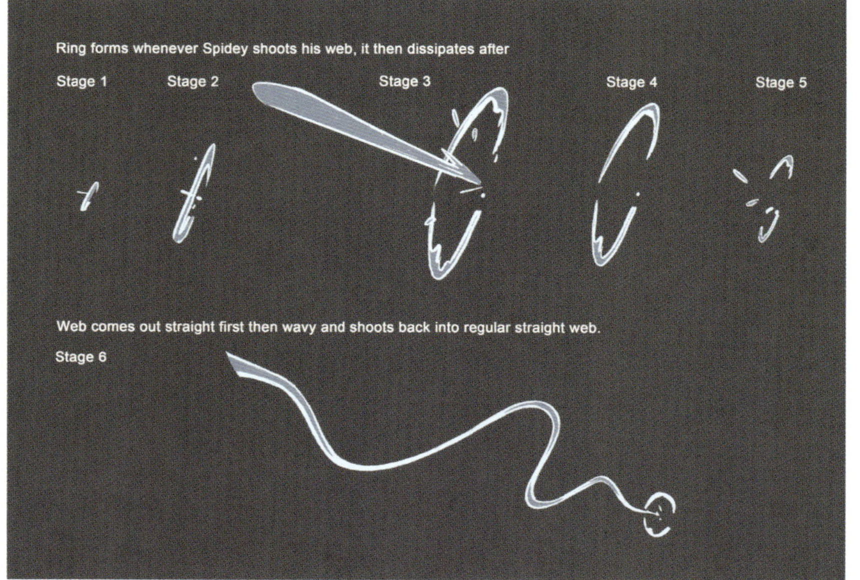

6

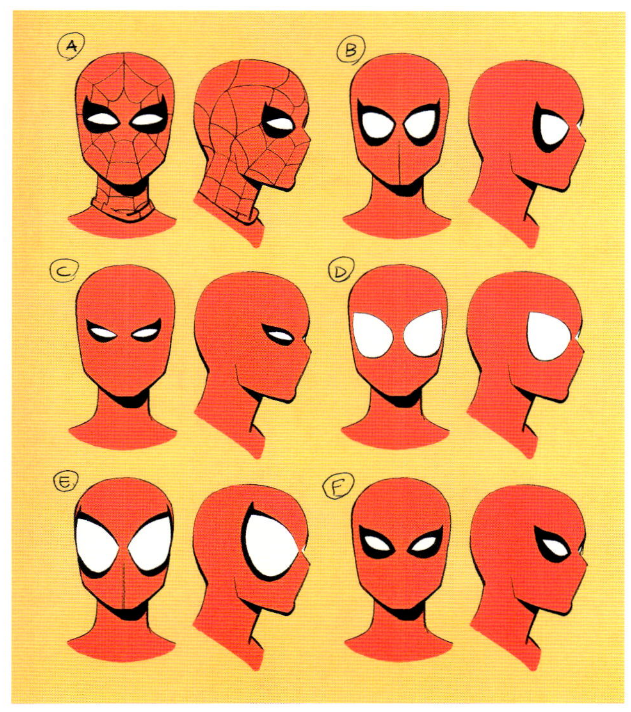

7

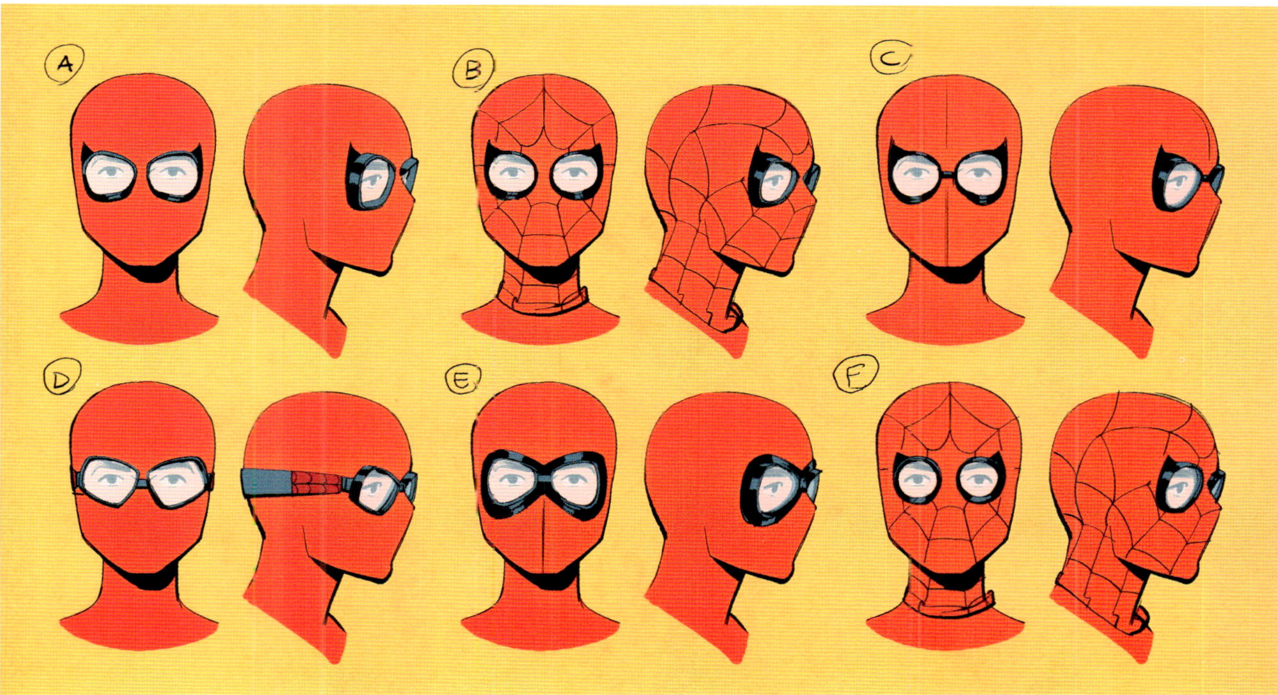

8

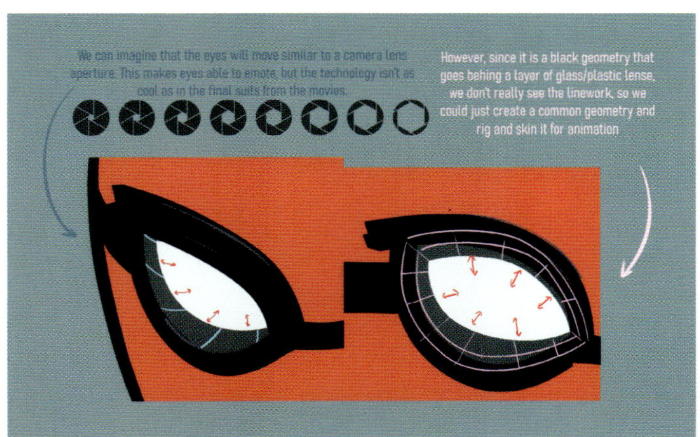

9

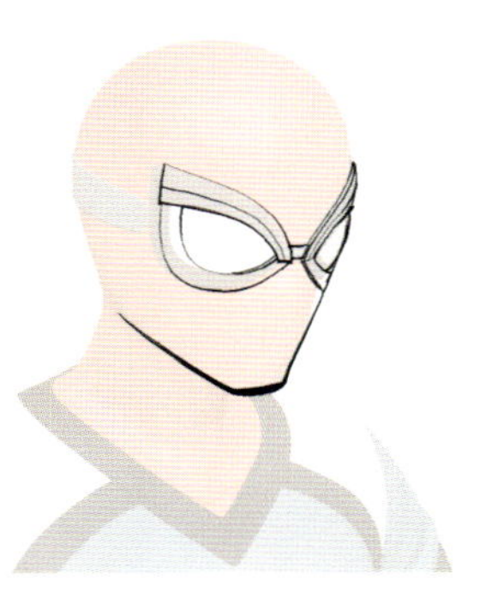

10

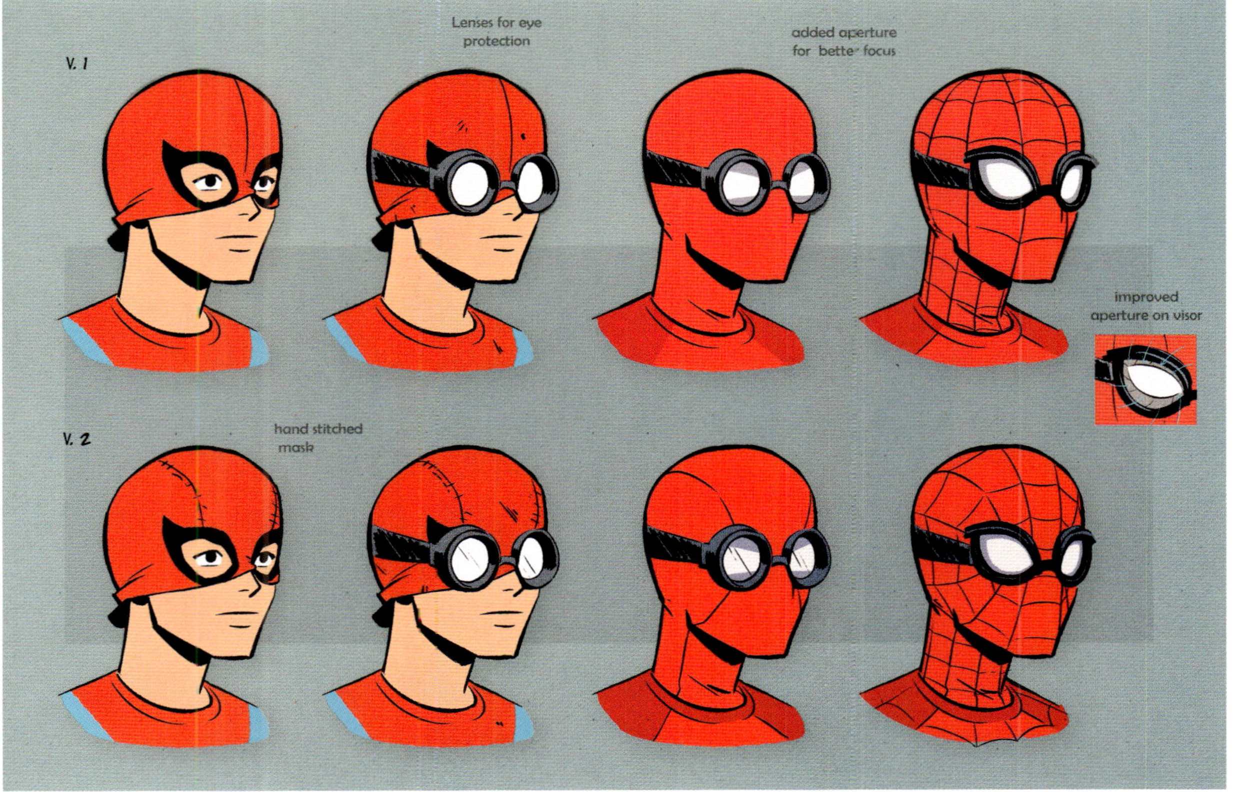

11

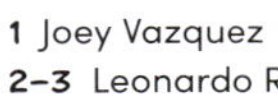

1 Joey Vazquez
2–3 Leonardo Romero
4 Paolo Rivera
5–6 Victor Calleja
7–8 Leonardo Romero
9 Julen Urrutia Perez
10 Leonardo Romero
11 Julen Urrutia Perez

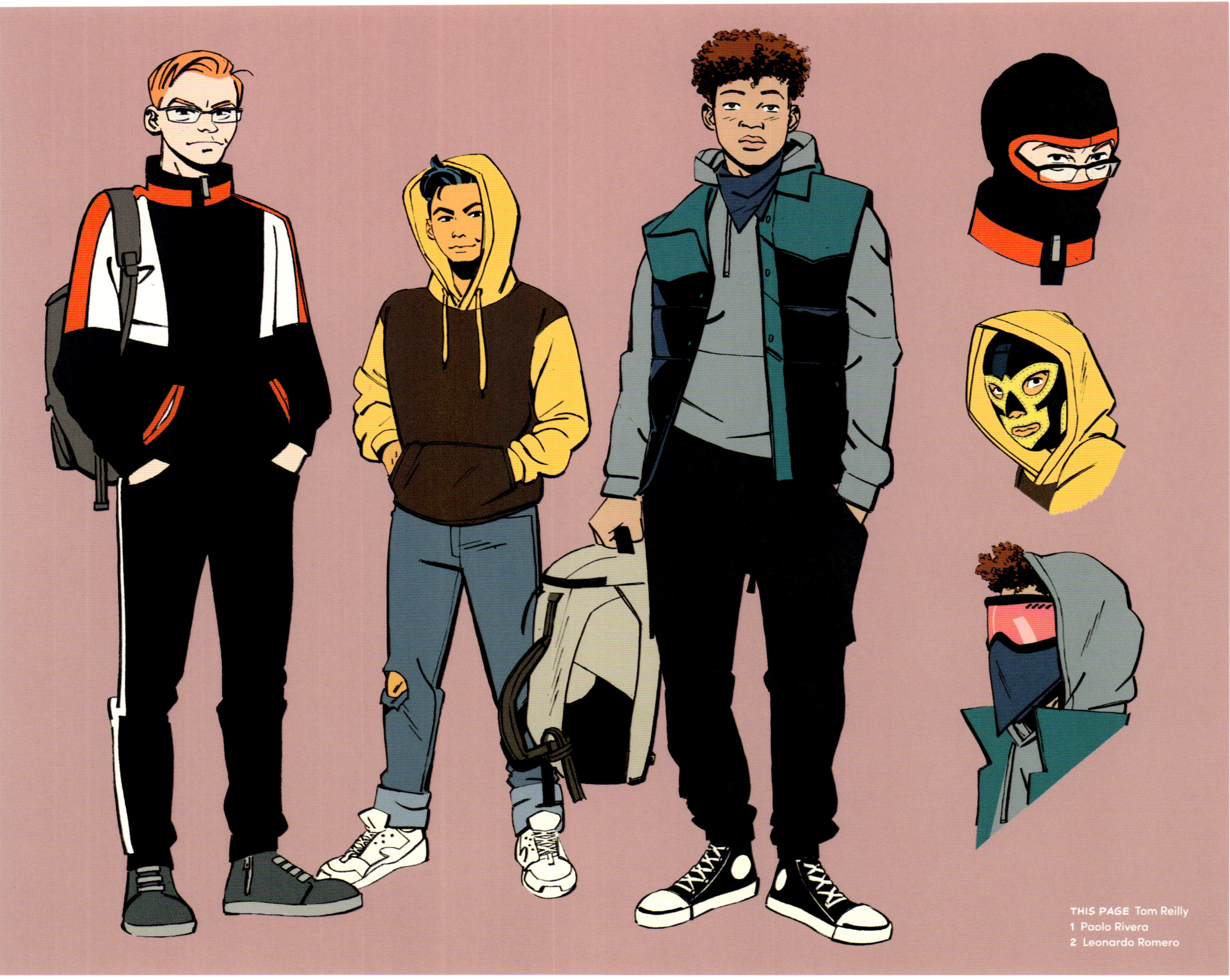

THIS PAGE Tom Reilly
1 Paolo Rivera
2 Leonardo Romero

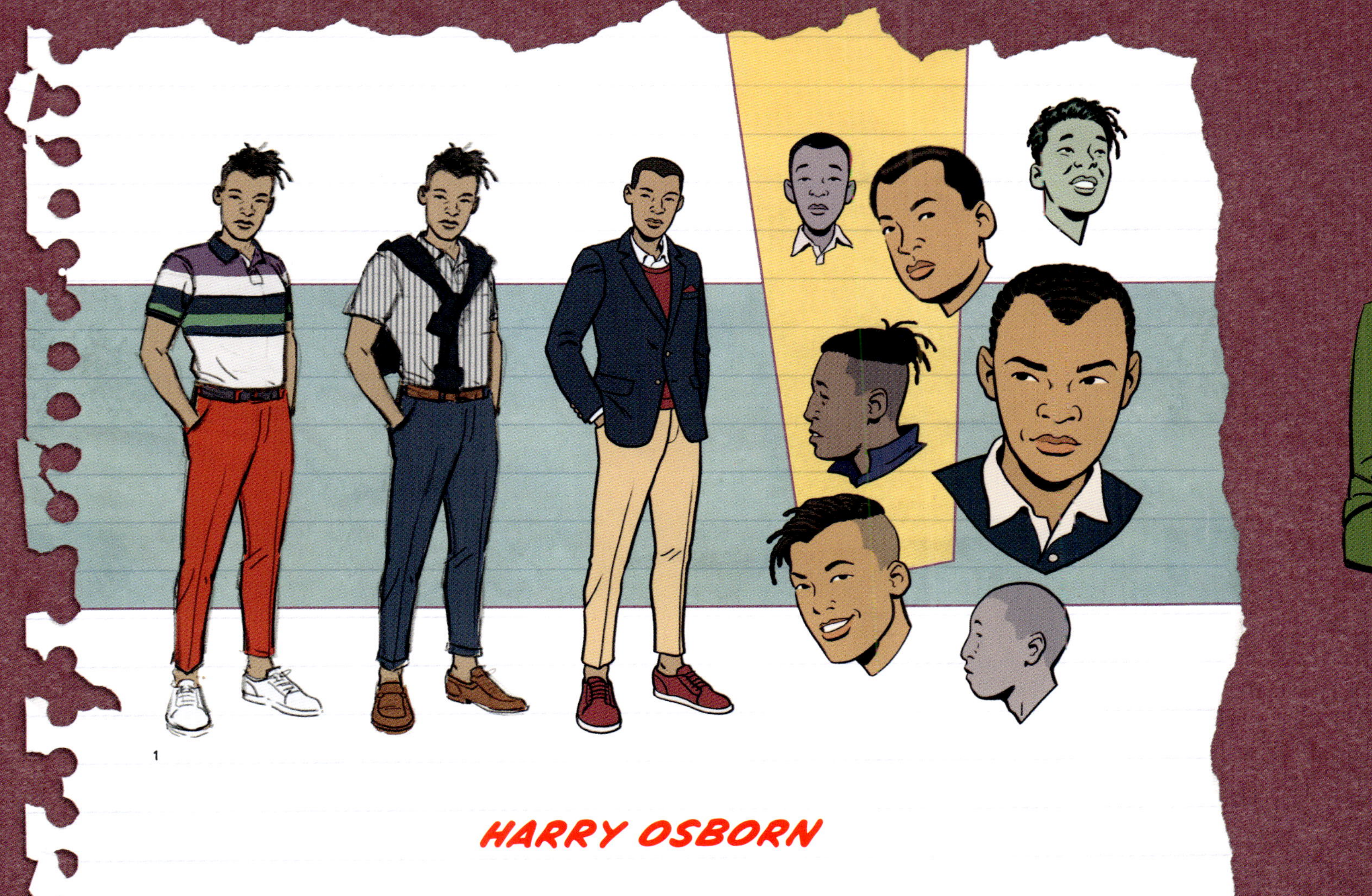

1

HARRY OSBORN

In the series, Norman Osborn's son is reimagined as a stylish and wealthy modern-day influencer always looking out for Peter's best interests.

"Figuring out this version of Harry was fun because I wanted to modernize the character, and I felt that if his dad is a huge business mogul, then Harry would definitely be in the public eye: someone who is trying to do his own thing and is trying to get attention. Although he's very popular, I think he can also be guarded like Nico, but for different reasons. Harry doesn't know if someone wants to befriend him because they really want to be his friend or if they are after his fame or money. I think his friendship with Peter and Nico makes them a really nice trifecta—three friends who come from very different backgrounds with very different views on life. We see how they affect each other and, hopefully, learn from each other."

"I got to reinvent a wavy hairstyle for Harry as well as his father," says Lead Character Designer Leonardo Romero. "They had similar wavy hair in the original comic books, but we wanted to put a nice, modern spin to it. I am not a big fashion follower myself, but I did a lot of research on Pinterest and Google to look for what kind of outfits a young, hip teenager with money would be wearing. For example, his shoes and suits were inspired by famous brands like Gucci and Dior."

2

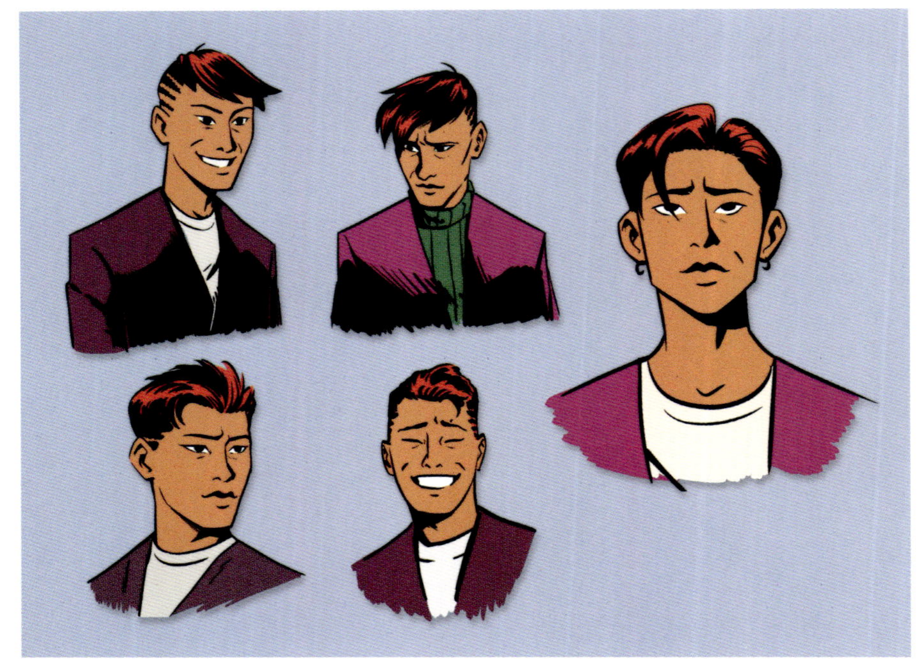
1

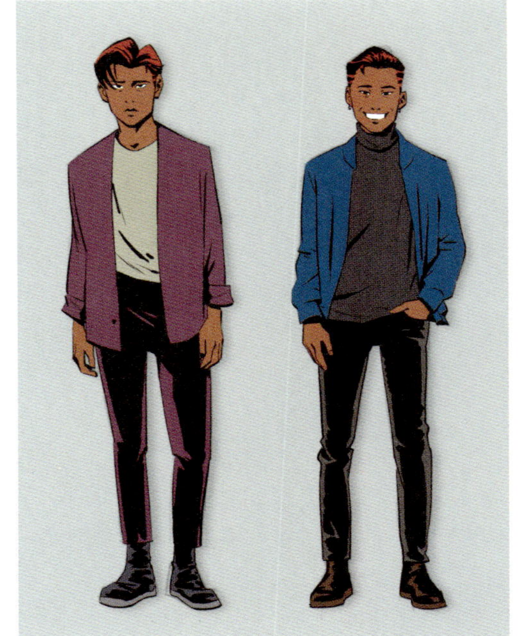
2

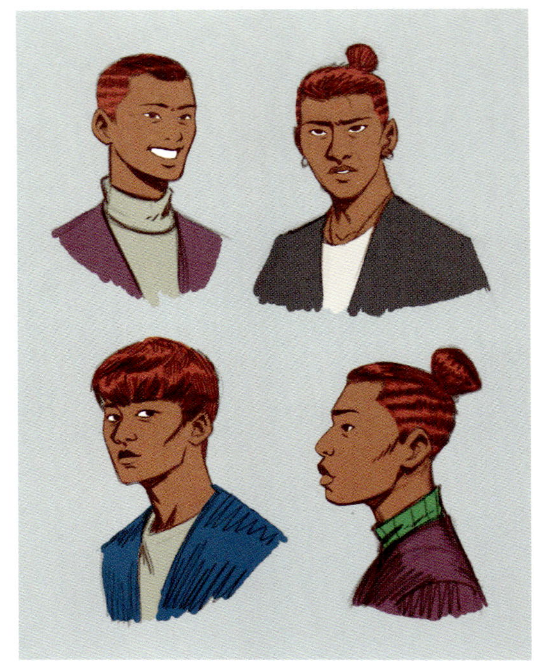
3

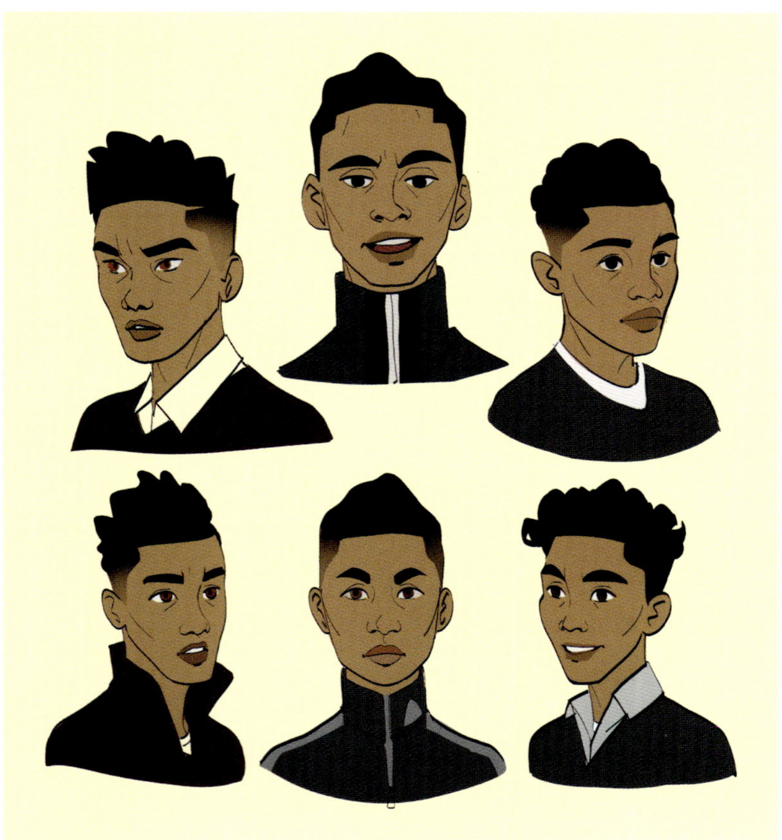
4

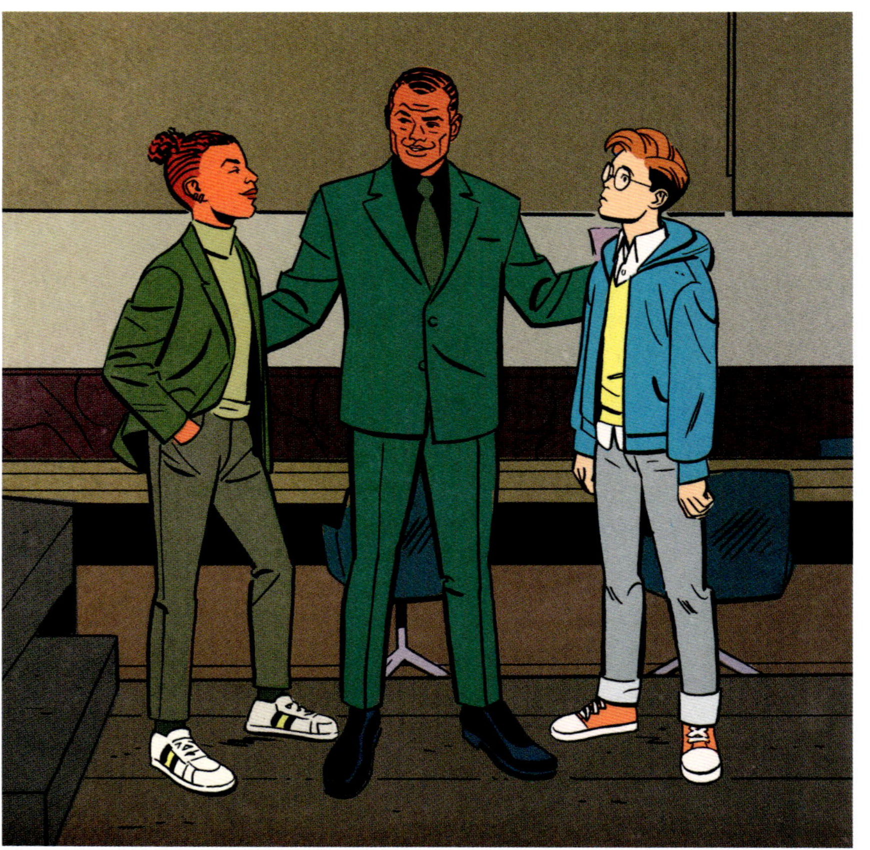
5

1–3 Julen Urrutia Perez
4 Mel Milton
5 Chris Samnee
6–7 Leonardo Romero
8–10 Beverly Arce
11–13 Ethan Young (line art) and Elizabeth Chee (color)
14 Leonardo Romero

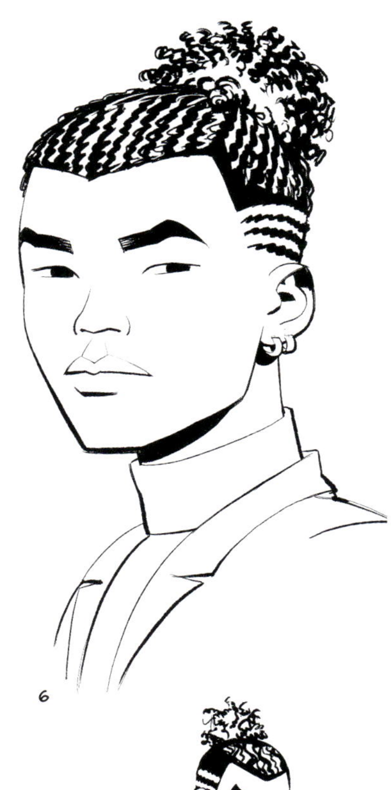

6

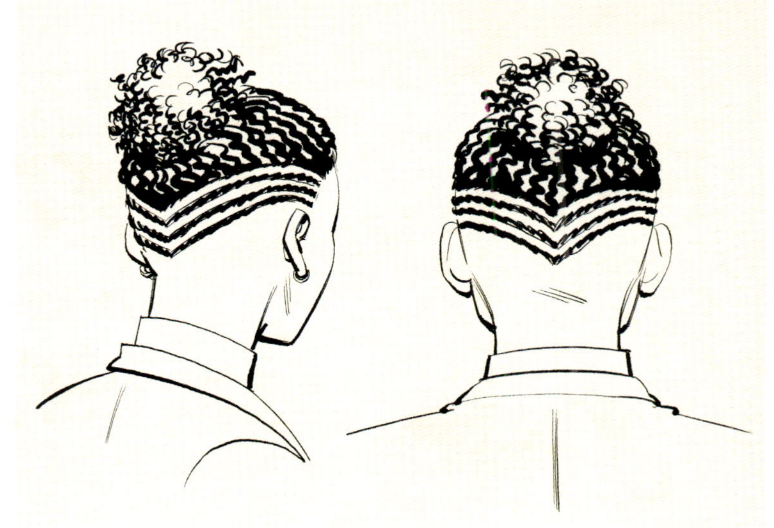

7

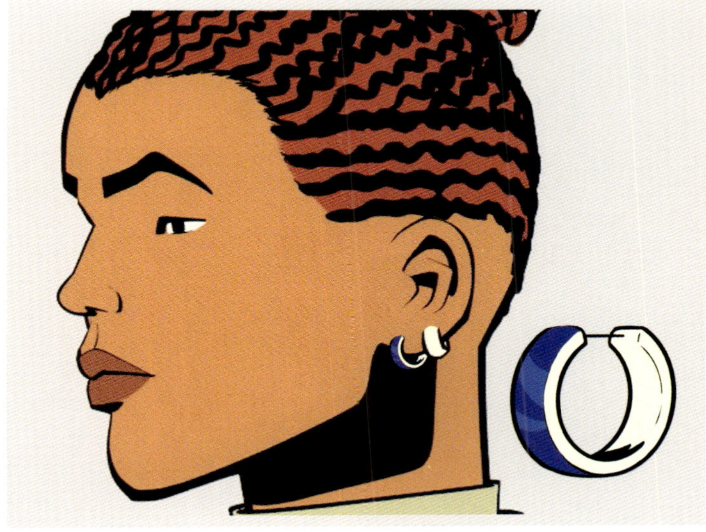

8

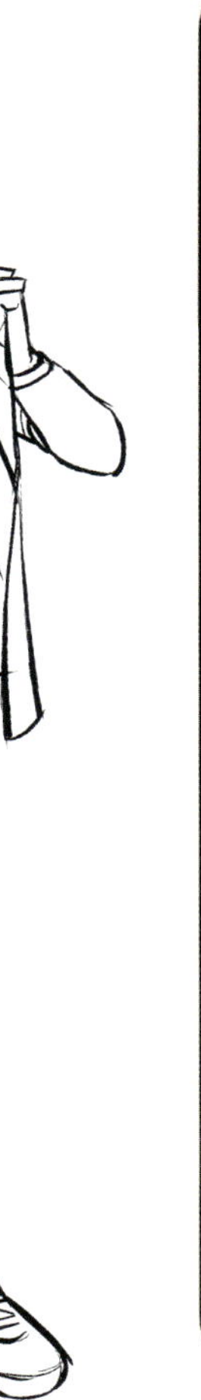

9

10

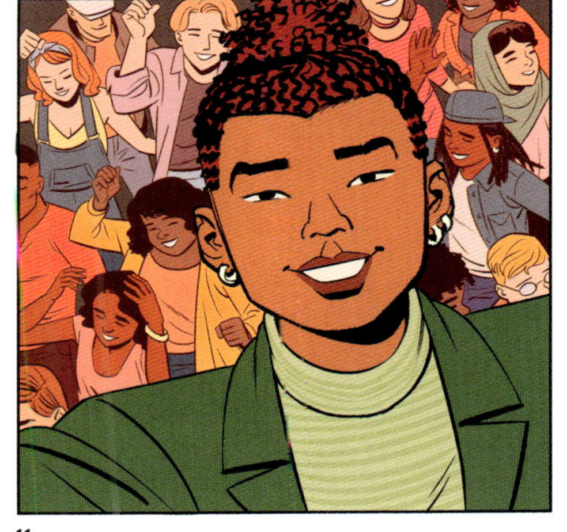

11

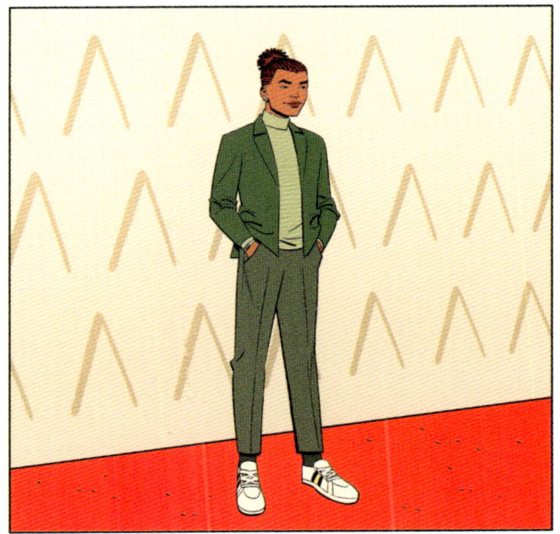

12

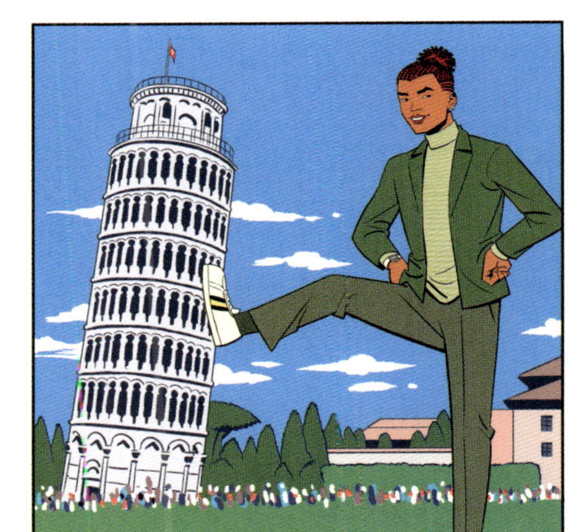

13

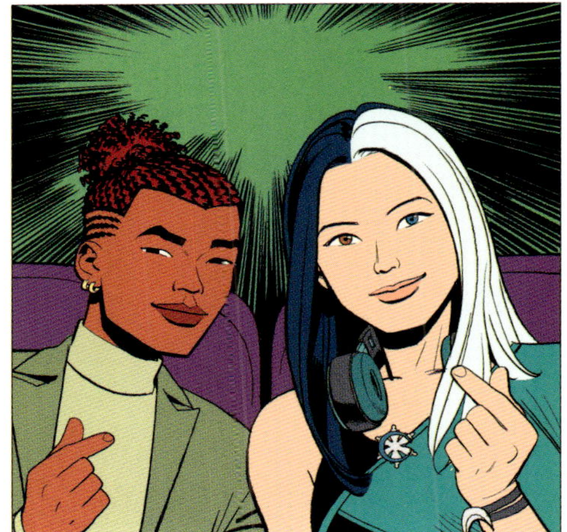

14

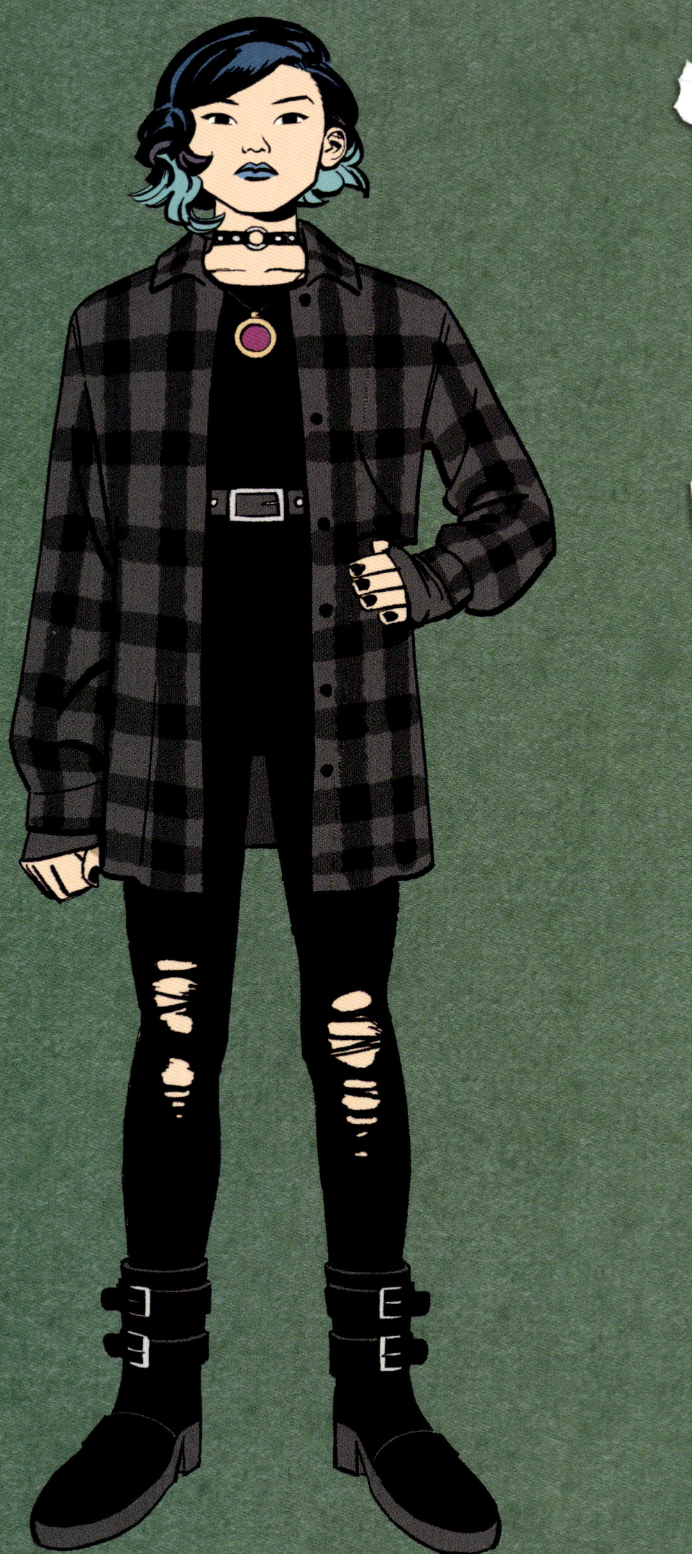

NICO MINORU

Peter Parker's smart, offbeat, and insightful best friend, Nico Minoru, is inspired by a character introduced in Marvel's *Runaways* comic (July 2003) created by Brian K. Vaughan and Adrian Alphona.

"Nico is Peter's best friend, and she is able to offer him a completely different worldview," says Executive Producer/Showrunner Jeff Trammell. "She's fiercely protective and loyal, and she comes into the season looking to hold on tight to those who are close to her. She has a lot of walls because she has lost a lot, but we'll learn more about that as the series goes on. She's not someone who sits back quietly and takes things in. She's opinionated and will always speak her mind, which is something Peter could learn from her."

Trammell mentions that he is a huge fan of Nico and *Runaways* and *Avengers Academy* (which features Jeanne Foucault/Finesse, another character seen in *Your Friendly Neighborhood Spider-Man*). "I think it was so cool that I could take characters and pour them into the world. I don't know that we could have done this had we just stuck with a straight MCU canon or if we were doing a show outside of Marvel Studios. We wouldn't have access to all these wonderful characters, so I'm very grateful that we were able to take advantage of Marvel's huge lineage of characters, and we were allowed to mix and match as it befitted the story."

Lead Character Designer Leonardo Romero says he hadn't read any of the *Runaways* comics, so he had to do his research to prepare for the assignment. "I found out that she [Nico] was a great character," he says. "I love the way we did her hair, with three different colors. One of the things that we were aiming for from the beginning was to make sure our teenage characters were wearing clothes that were simple enough to animate, but their clothes needed to be appealing to modern teens as well."

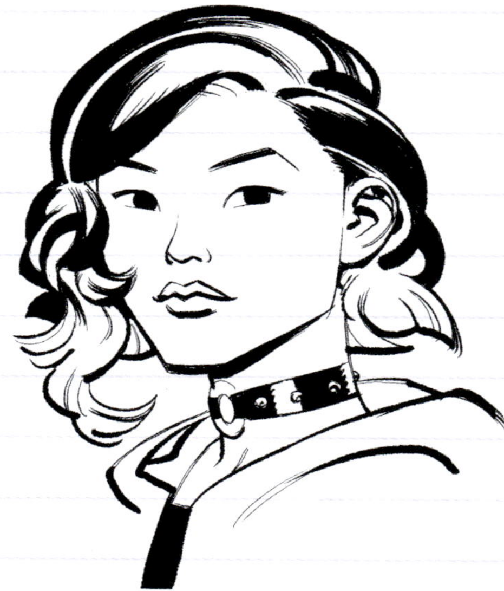

THIS PAGE Leonardo Romero
1 Leonardo Romero **2–3** Junyi Wu

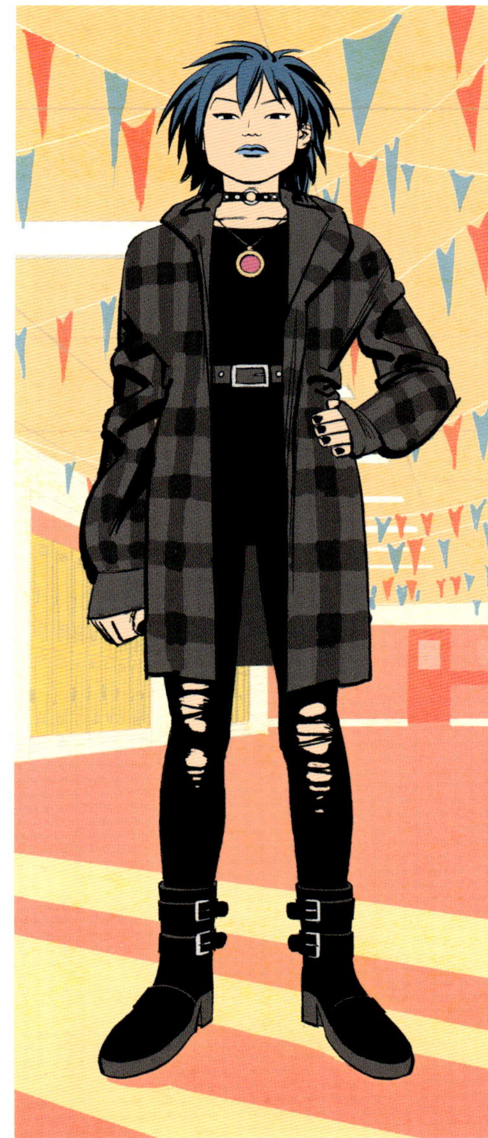
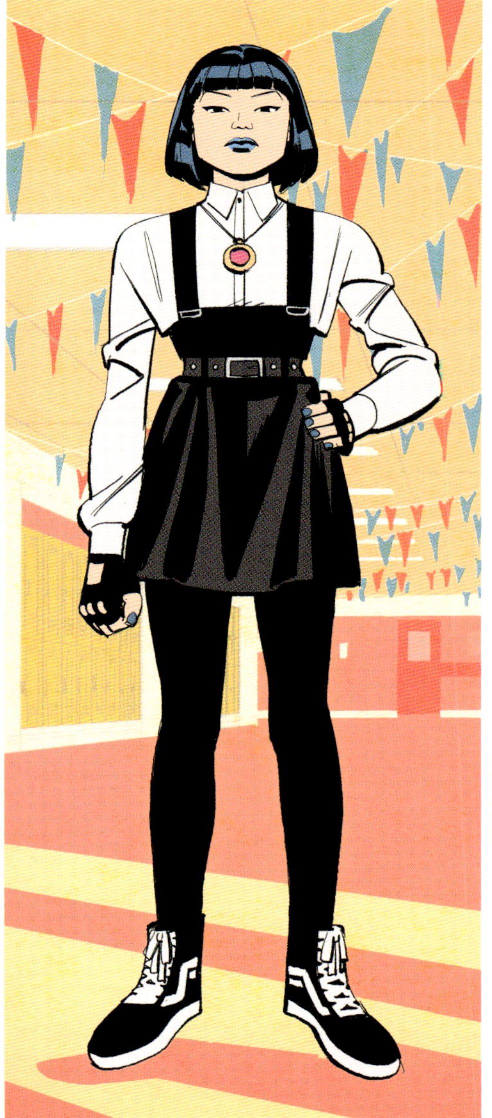
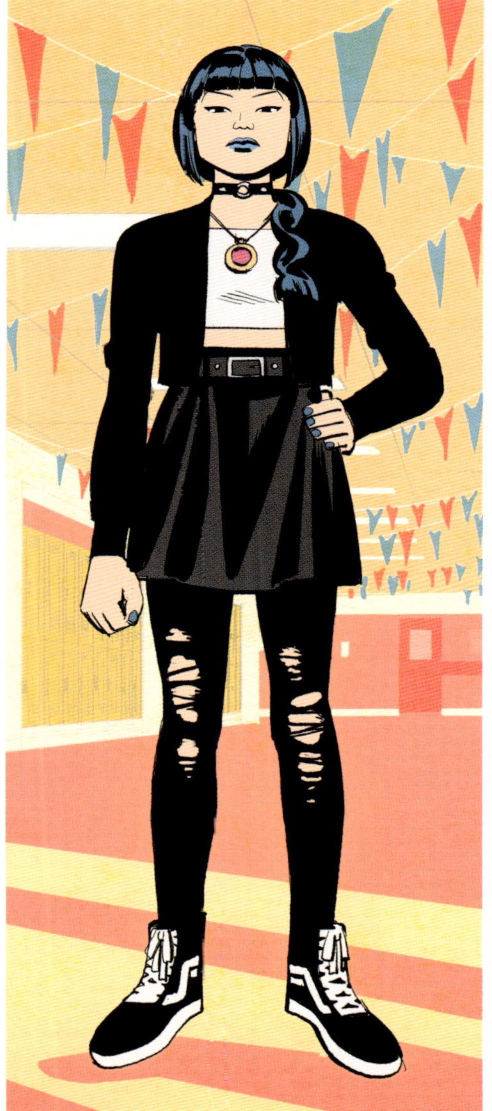
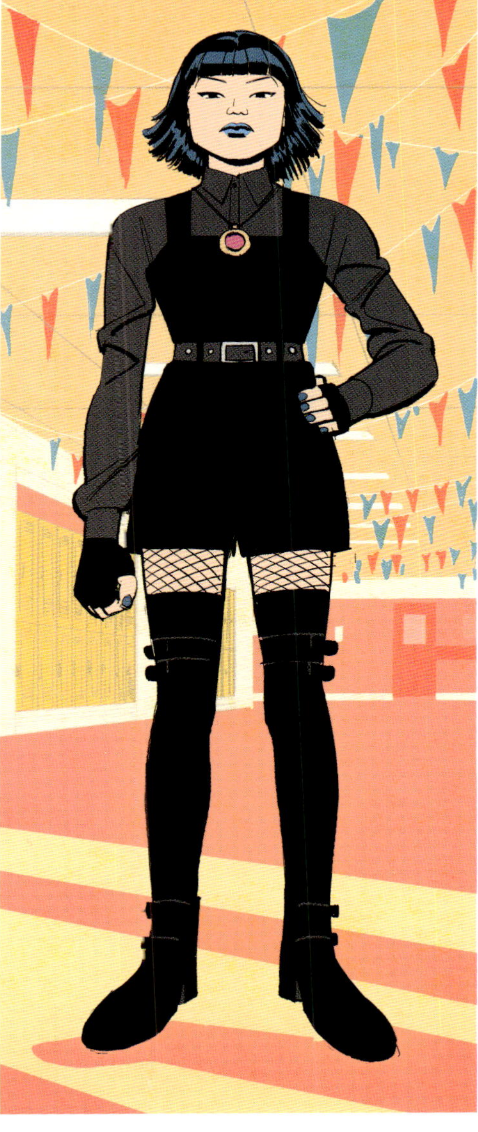

1

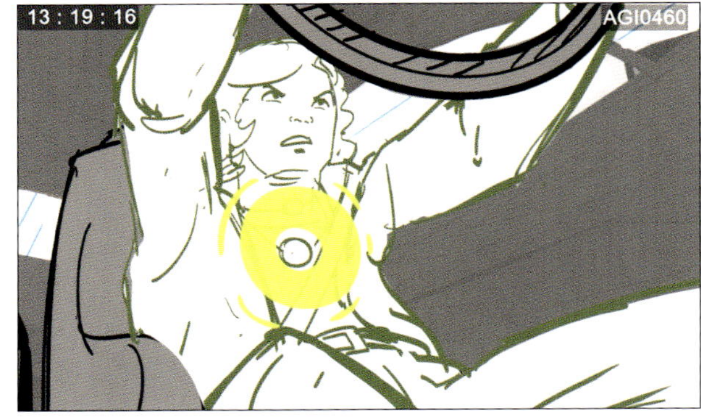

2

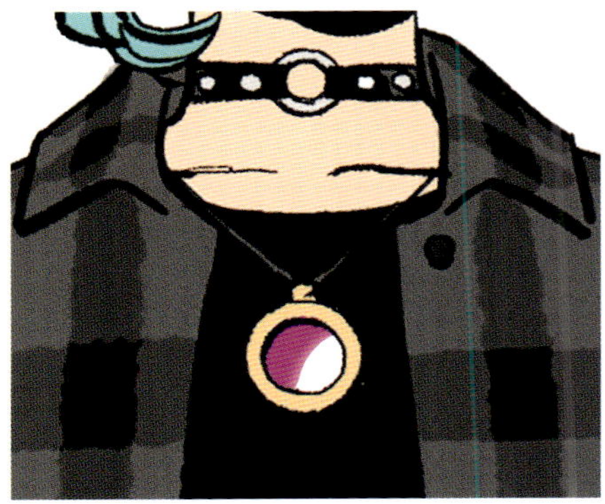
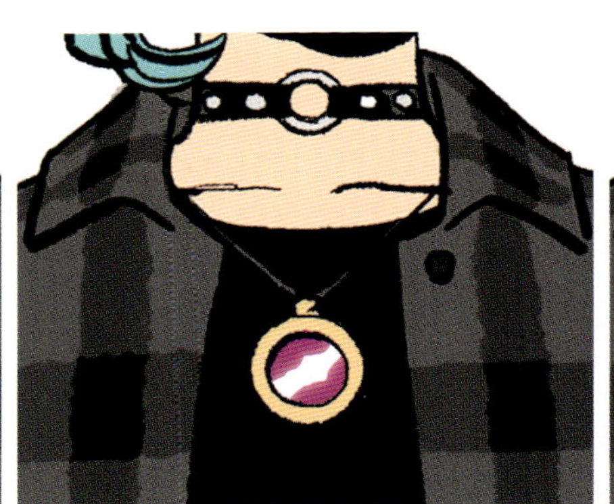
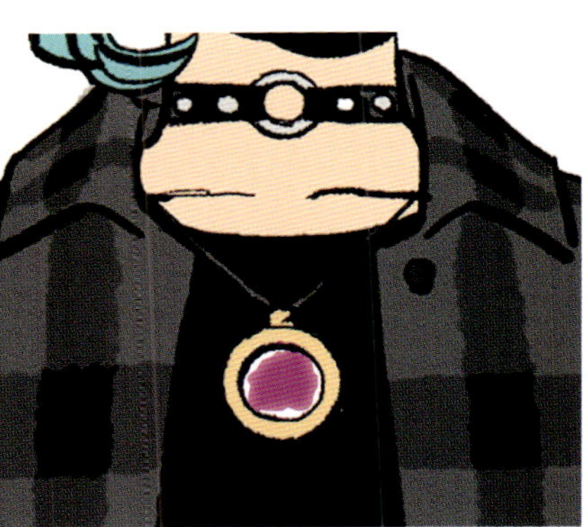

3

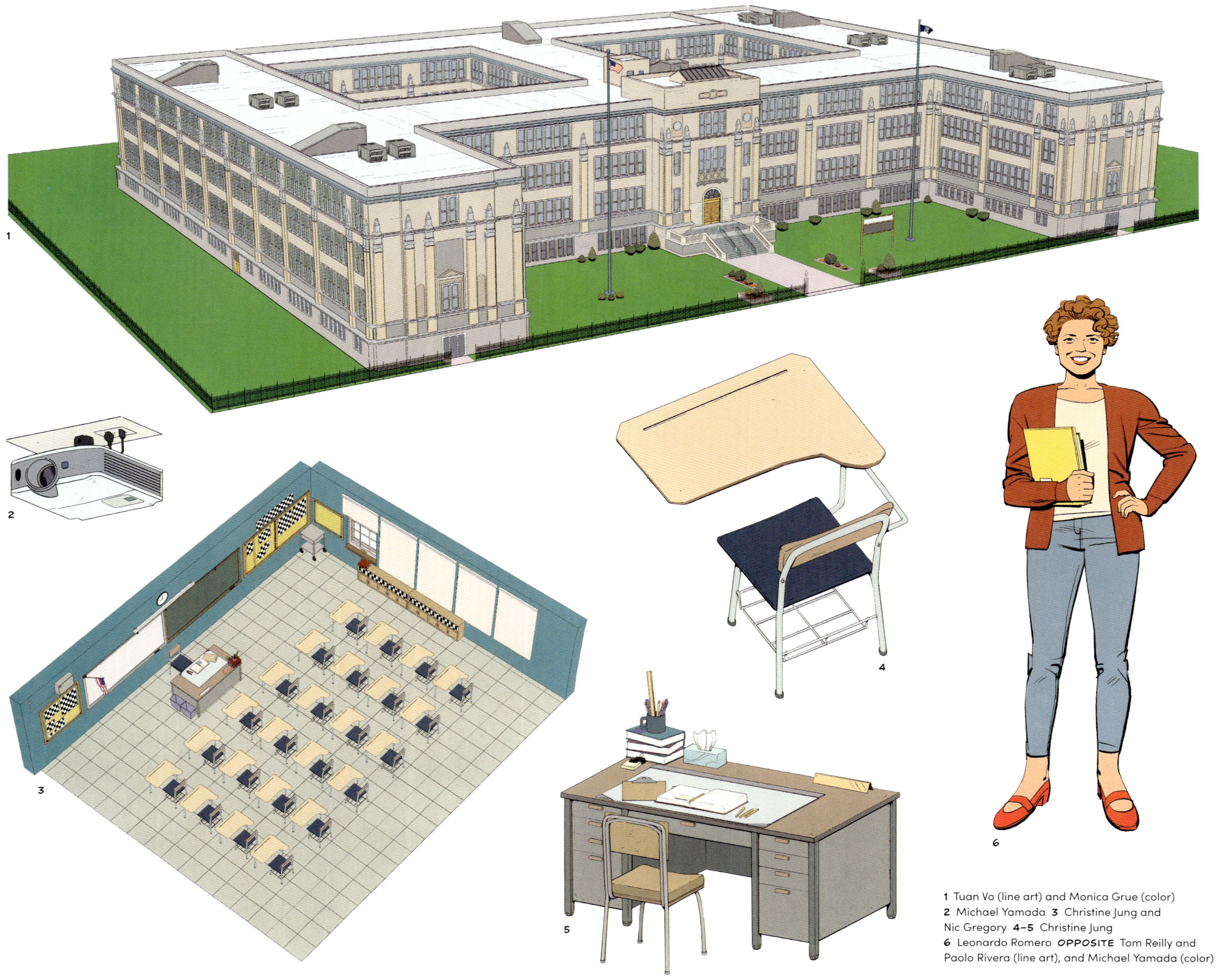

1 Tuan Vo (line art) and Monica Grue (color)
2 Michael Yamada **3** Christine Jung and Nic Gregory **4–5** Christine Jung
6 Leonardo Romero **OPPOSITE** Tom Reilly and Paolo Rivera (line art), and Michael Yamada (color)

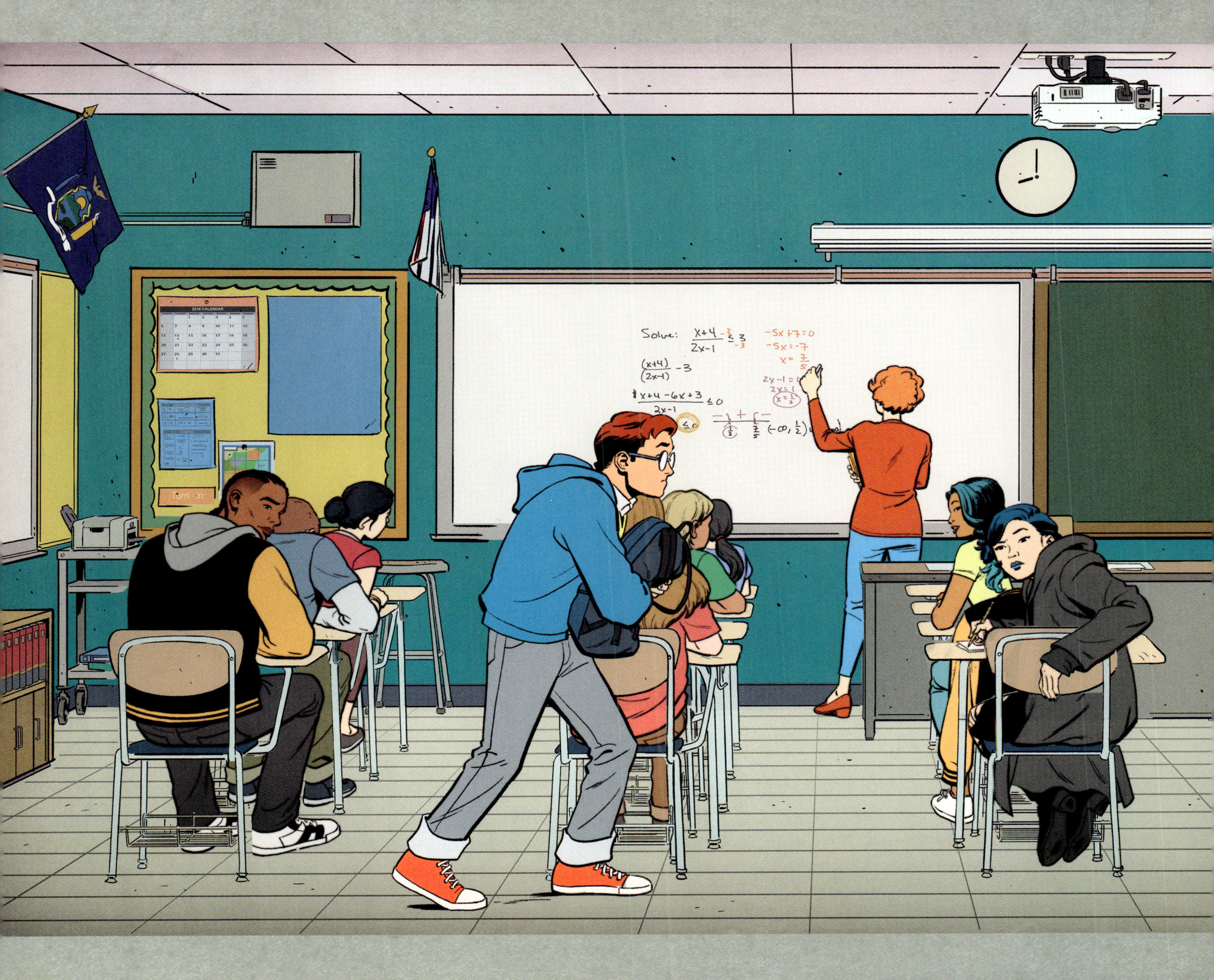

Solve: $\frac{x+4}{2x-1} \le 3$
$\frac{(x+4)}{(2x-1)} - 3$
$\frac{x+4-6x+3}{2x-1} \le 0$
$-5x+7=0$
$-5x=-7$
$x=\frac{7}{5}$
$2x=1$
$x=\frac{1}{2}$
$(-\infty, \frac{1}{2})$
2016 CALENDAR
Turn-in

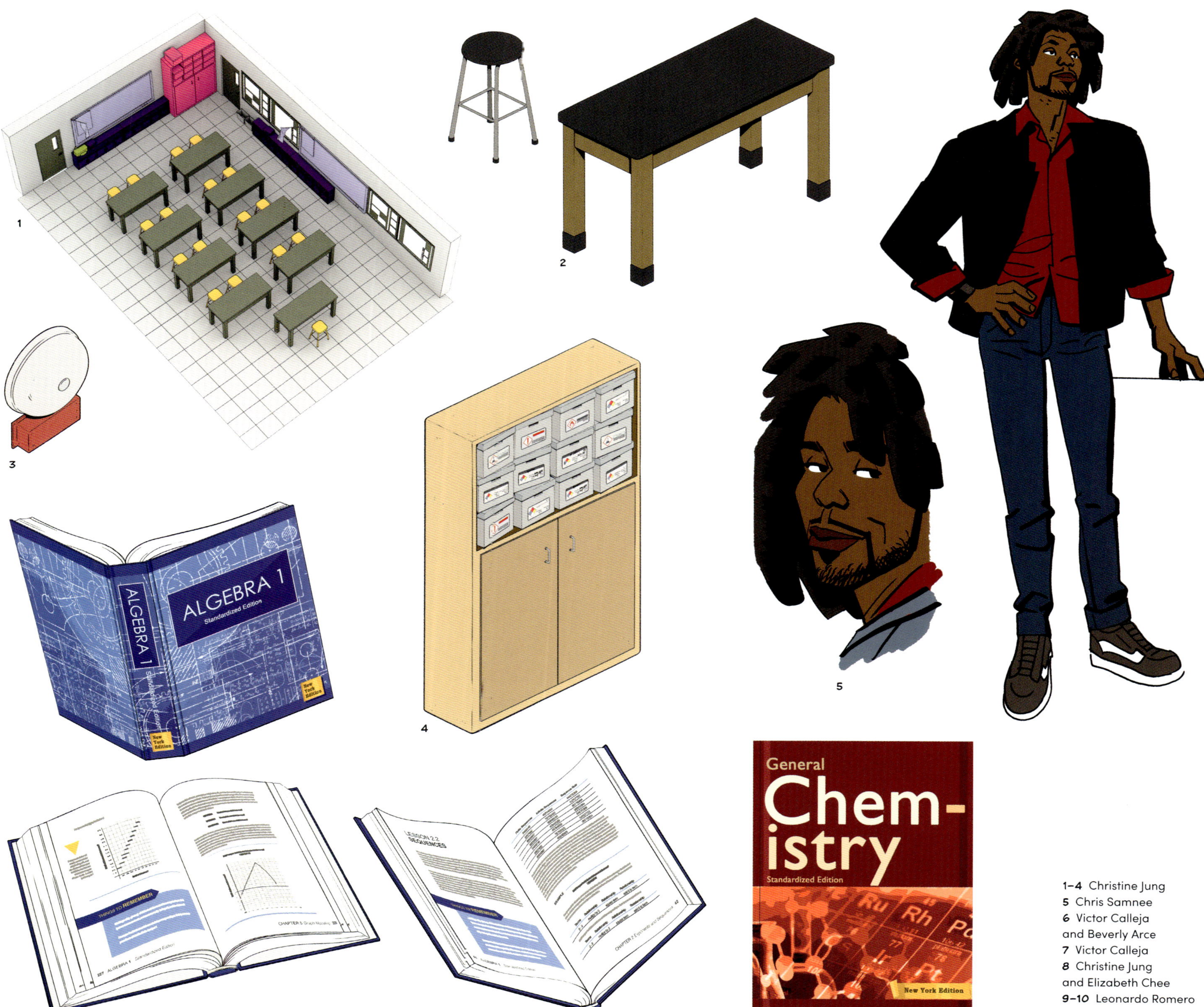

1–4 Christine Jung
5 Chris Samnee
6 Victor Calleja
and Beverly Arce
7 Victor Calleja
8 Christine Jung
and Elizabeth Chee
9–10 Leonardo Romero
11–12 Elizabeth Chee

8

9

10

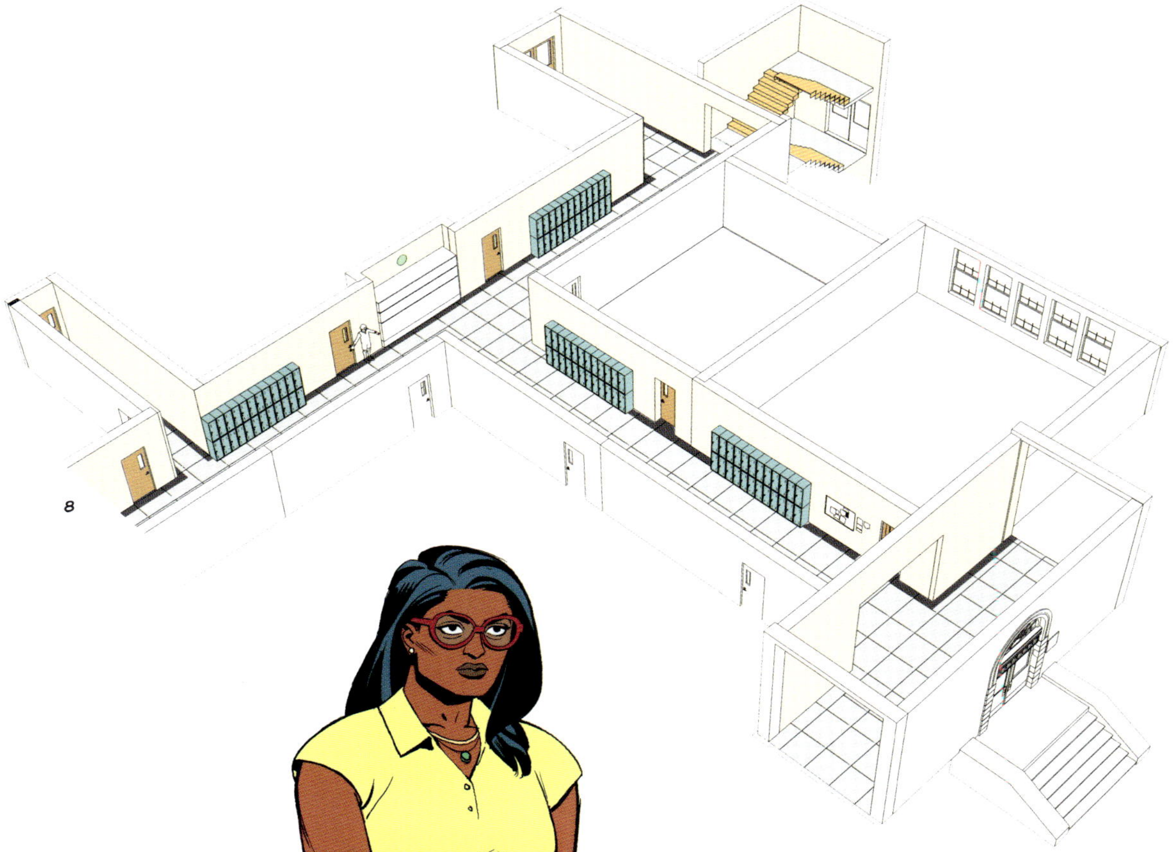

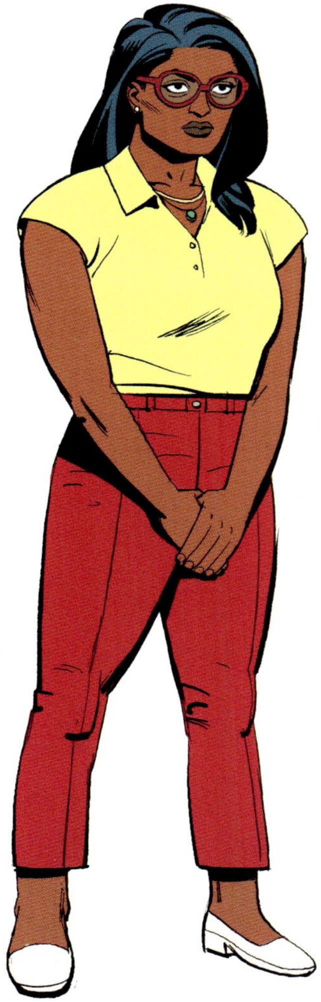

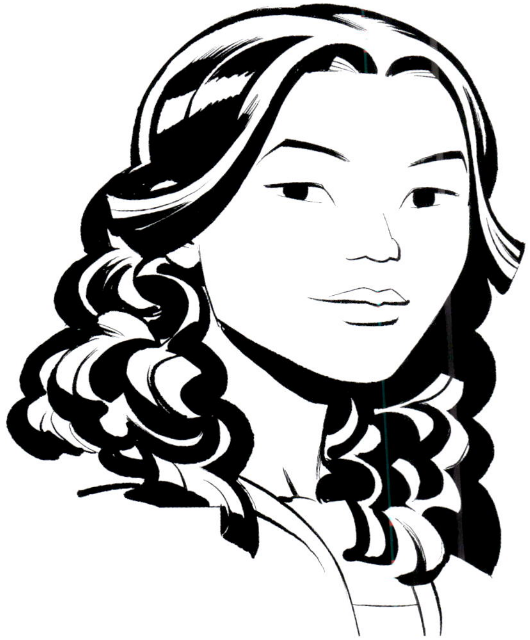

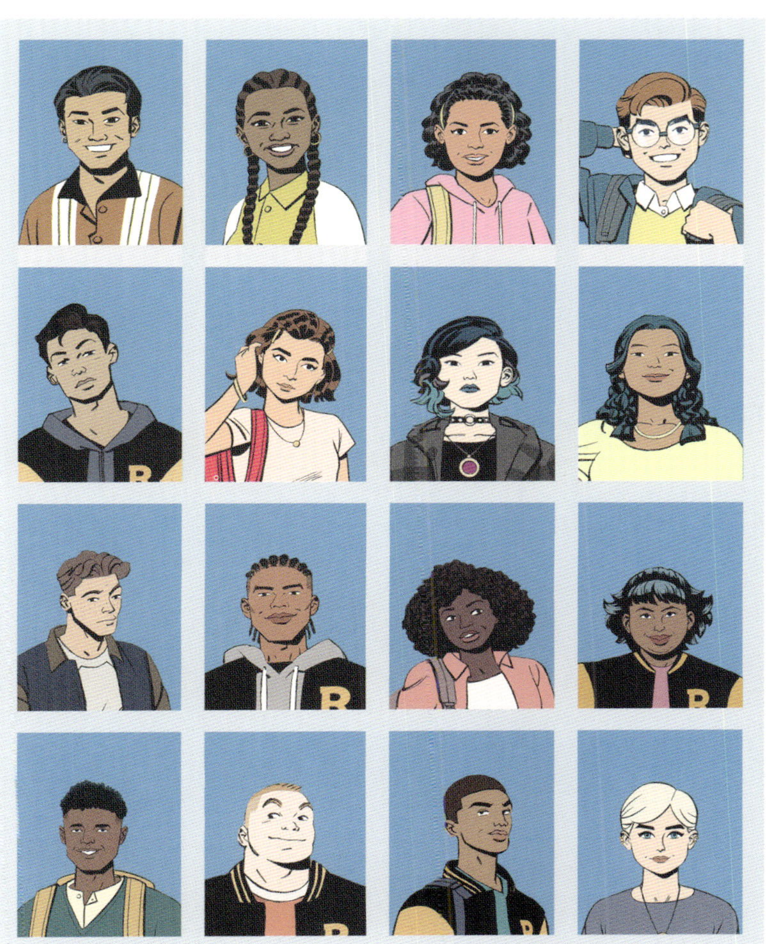

11

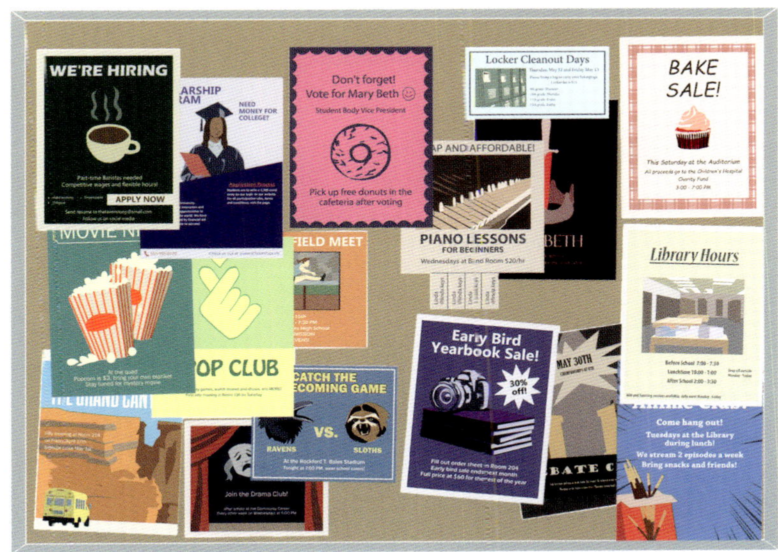
WE'RE HIRING
Part-time Baristas needed
Competitive wages and flexible hours!
APPLY NOW
NEED MONEY FOR COLLEGE?
Don't forget!
Vote for Mary Beth
Student Body Vice President
Pick up free donuts in the cafeteria after voting
Locker Cleanout Days
BAKE SALE!
This Saturday at the Auditorium
All proceeds go to the Children's Hospital Charity Fund
3:00 - 7:00 PM
PIANO LESSONS
FOR BEGINNERS
FIELD MEET
Library Hours
Before School 7:00 - 7:30
Lunchtime 10:00 - 1:00
After School 2:00 - 3:30
Early Bird
Yearbook Sale!
30% off!
Fill out order sheet in Room 204
MAY 30TH
CATCH THE
VS.
RAVENS
SLOTHS
Join the Drama Club!
Come hang out!
Tuesdays at the Library during lunch!
We stream 2 episodes a week
Bring snacks and friends!

12

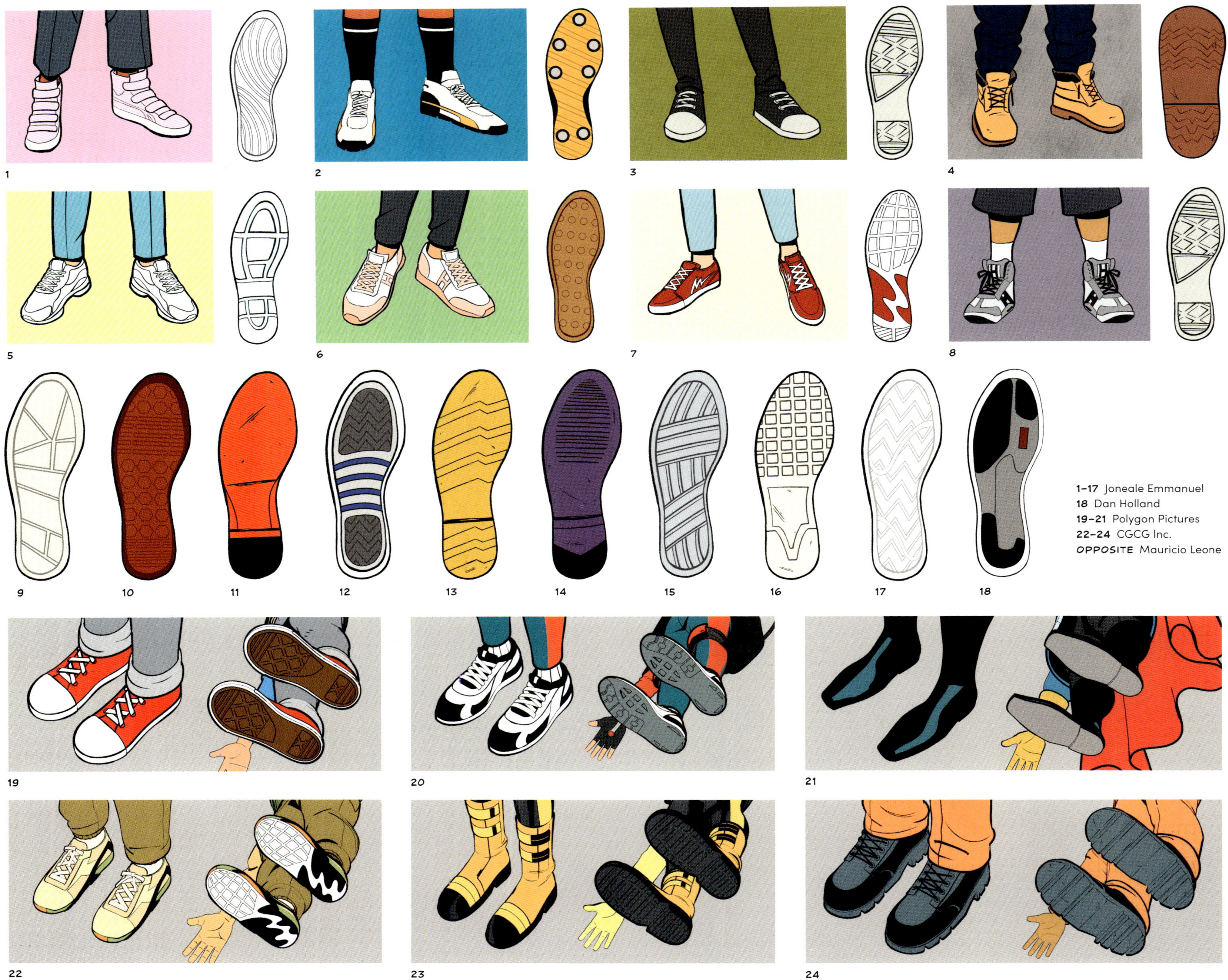

1–17 Joneale Emmanuel
18 Dan Holland
19–21 Polygon Pictures
22–24 CGCG Inc.
OPPOSITE Mauricio Leone

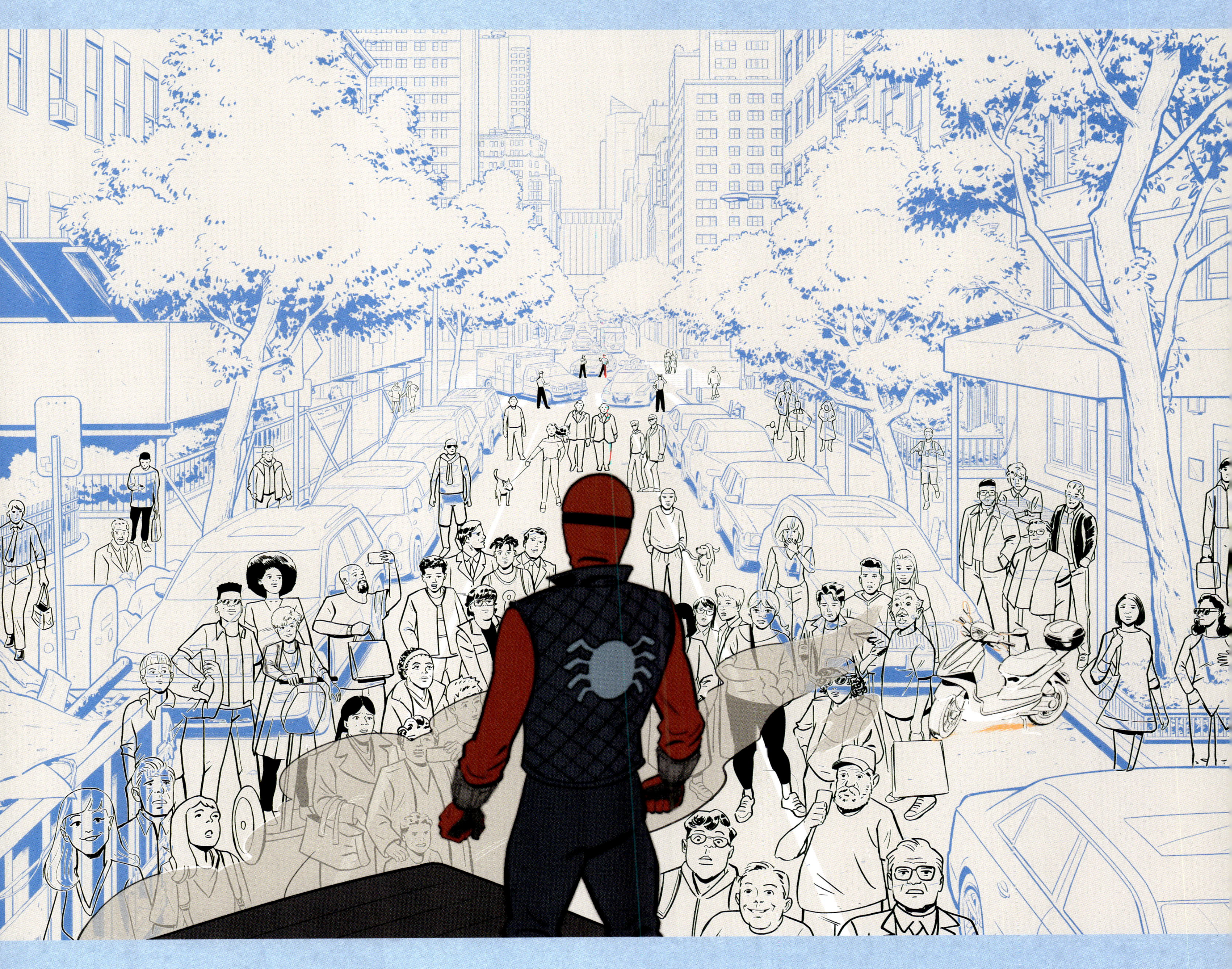

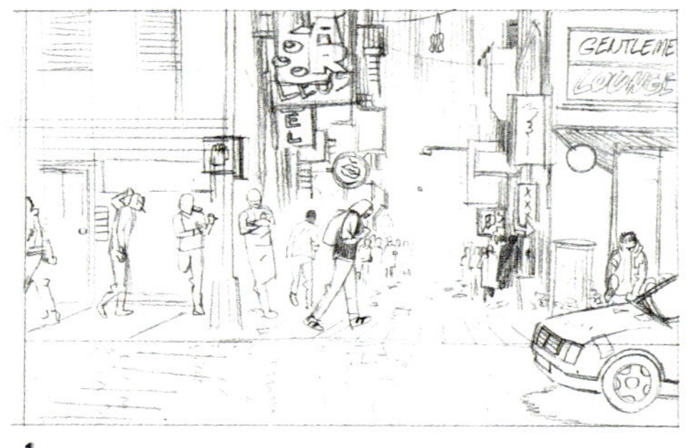

1

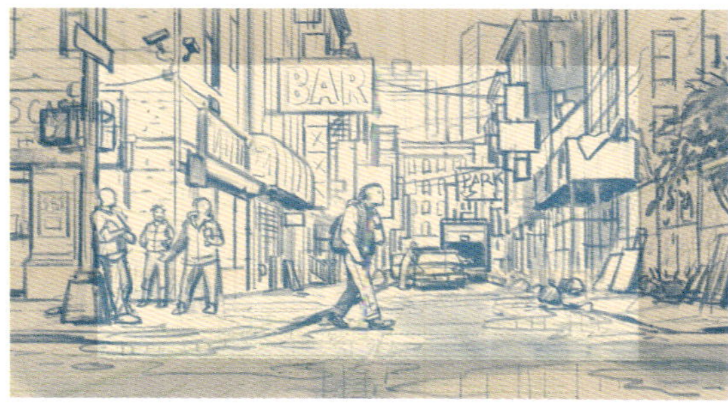

2

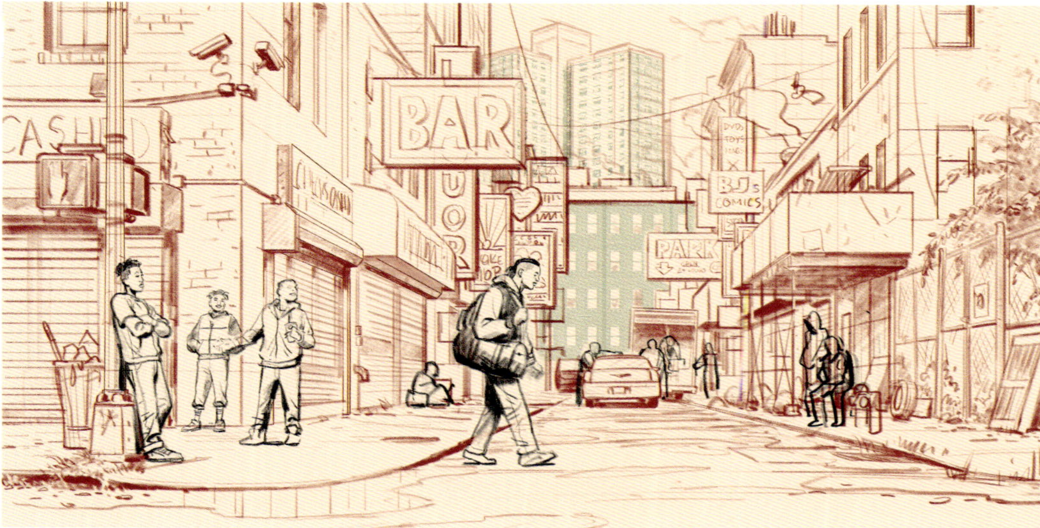

3

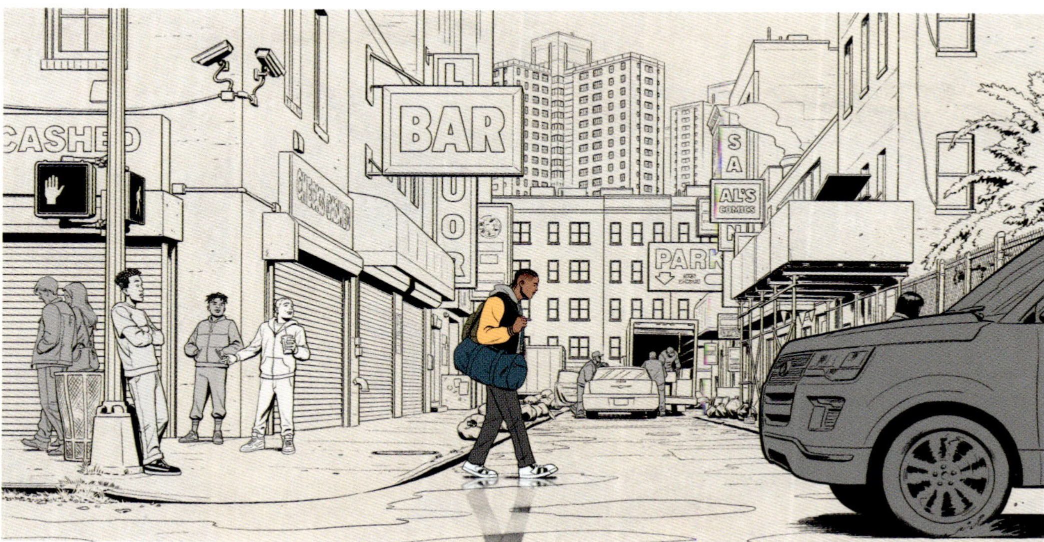

4

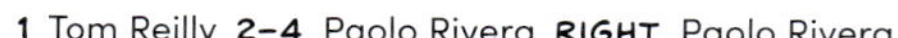

1 Tom Reilly **2–4** Paolo Rivera **RIGHT** Paolo Rivera

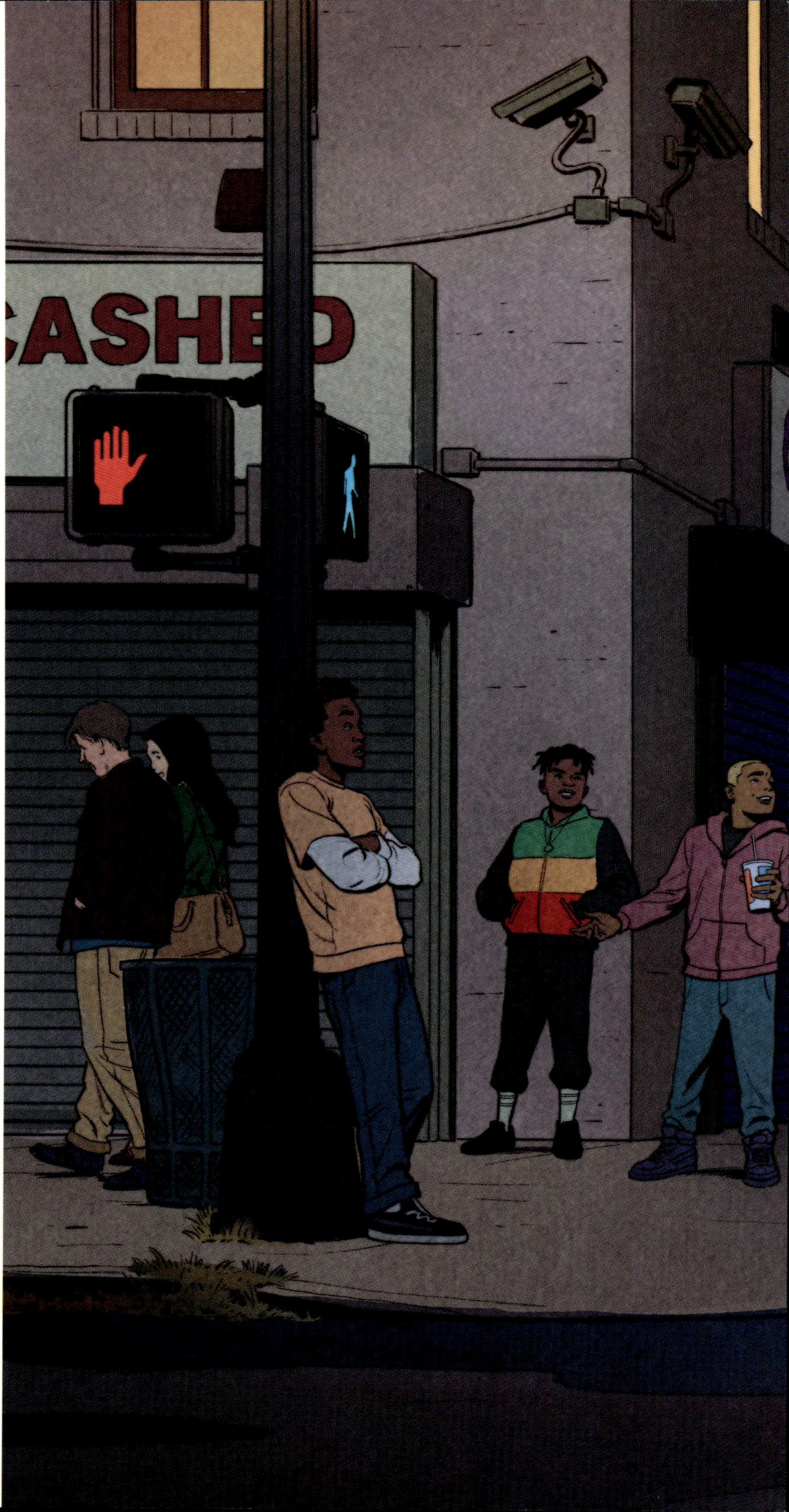

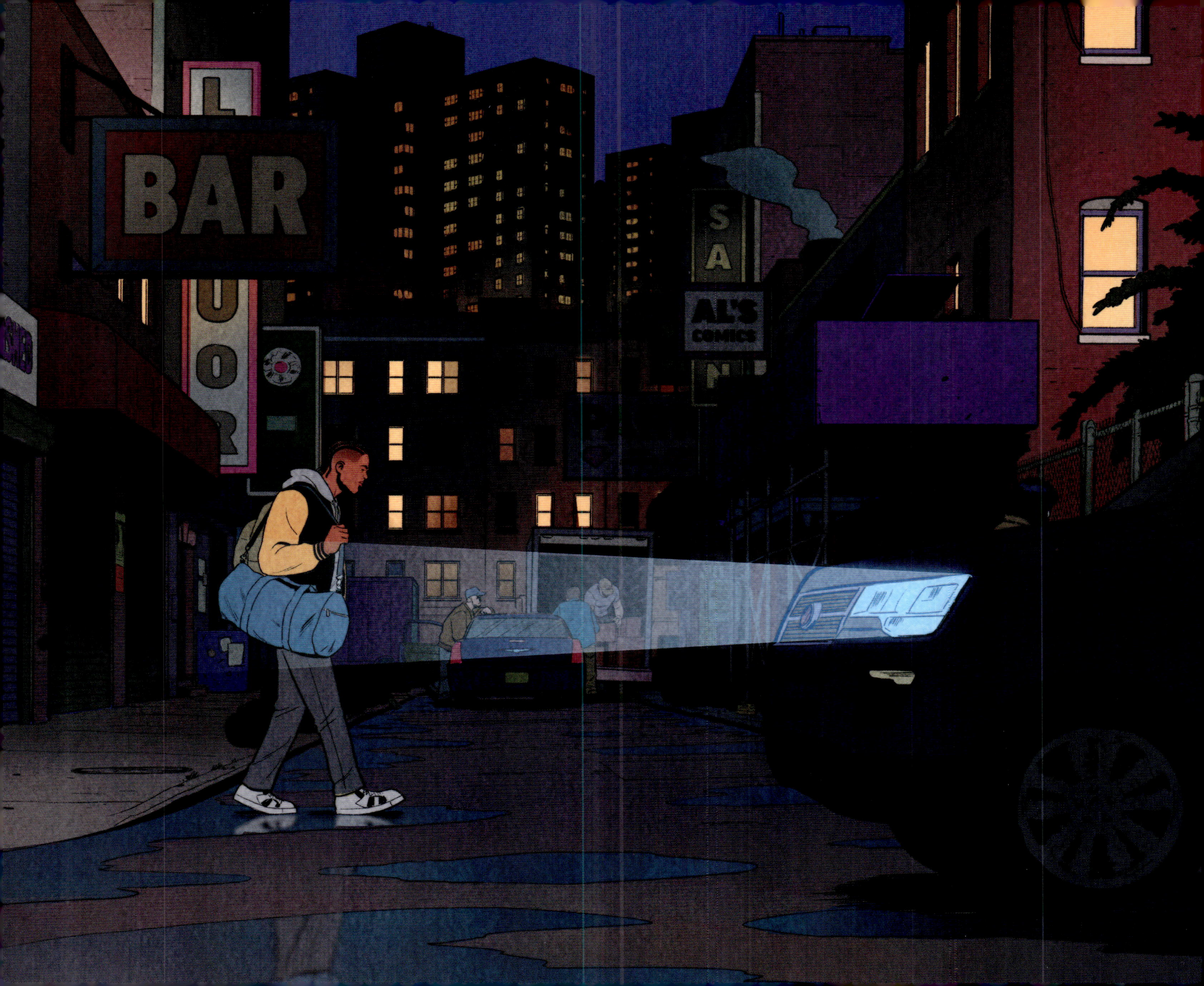
BAR
AL'S COMICS

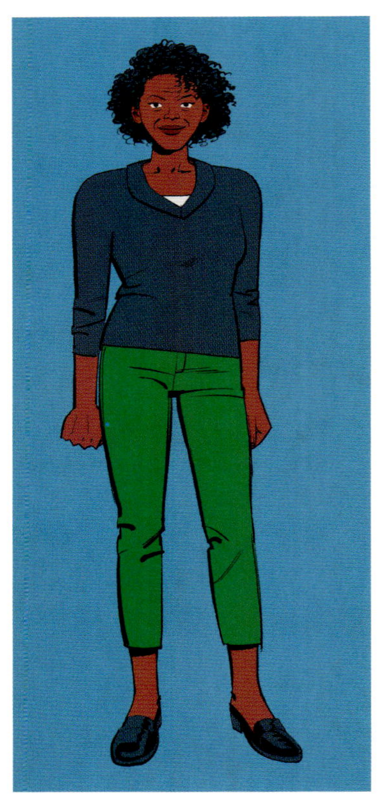

1

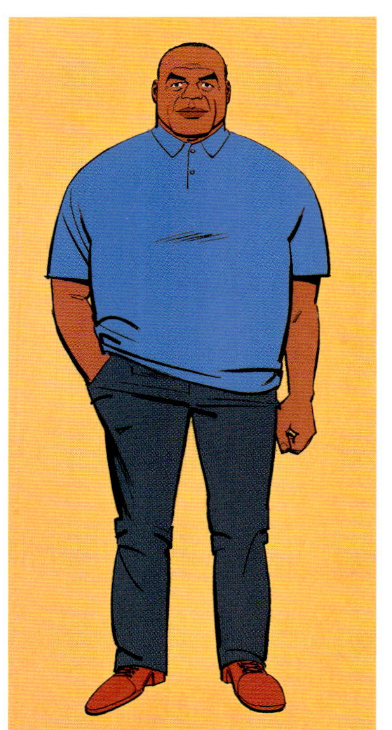

2

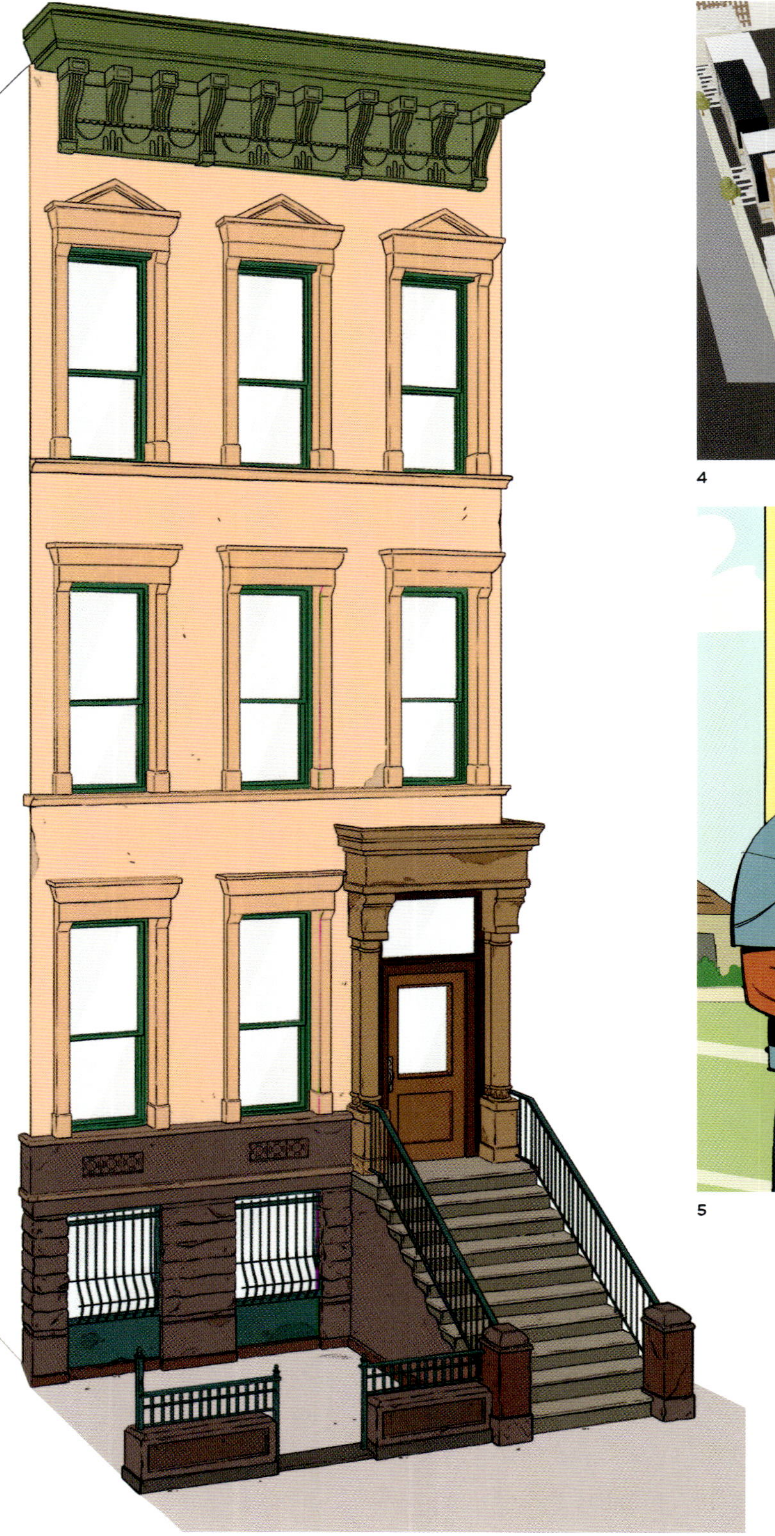

3

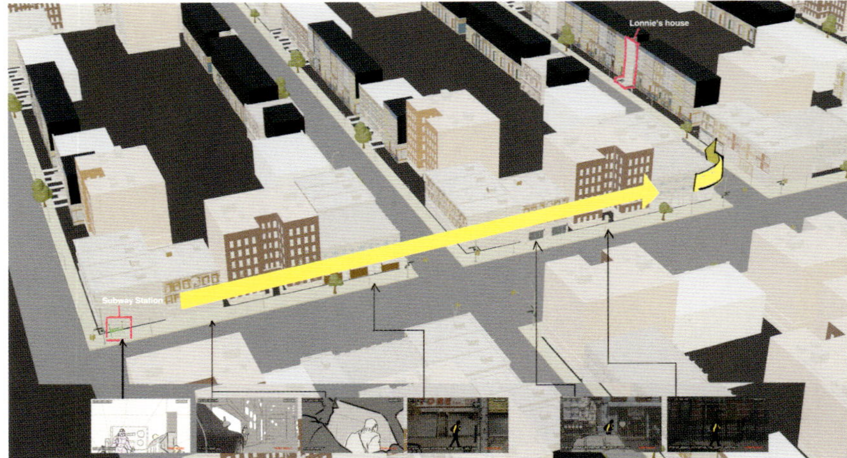

4

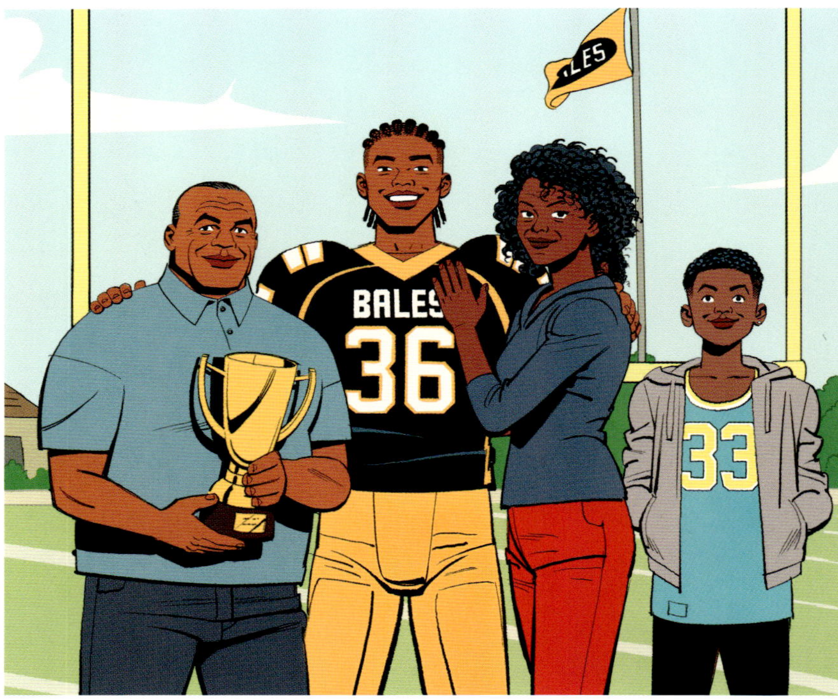

5

1–2 Leonardo Romero **3** Kelsey Roland **4** Michael Yamada **5** Leonardo Romero **6** Kelsey Roland (line art) and Elizabeth Chee (color) **7–8** Kelsey Roland **9** Paolo Rivera (line art) and Michael Yamada (color)

125 Street Station
A C B
Subway

6

Kelcheese's PIZZA
PIZZA TIME
HELP WANTED
OPEN

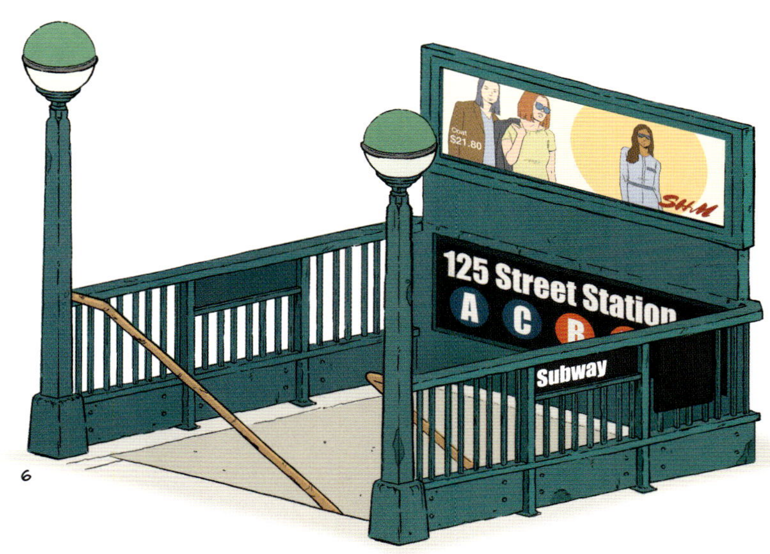

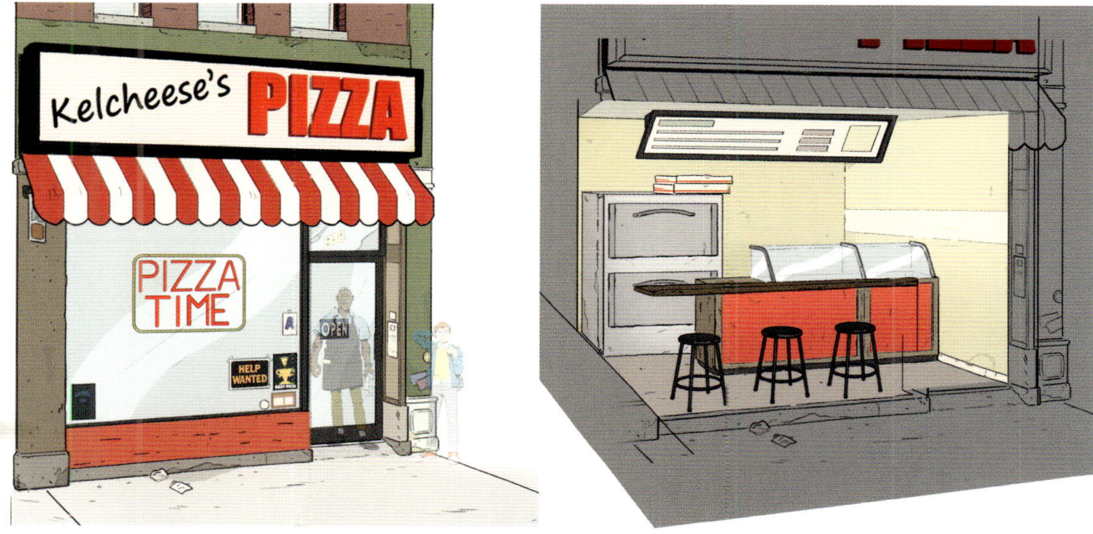

7

8

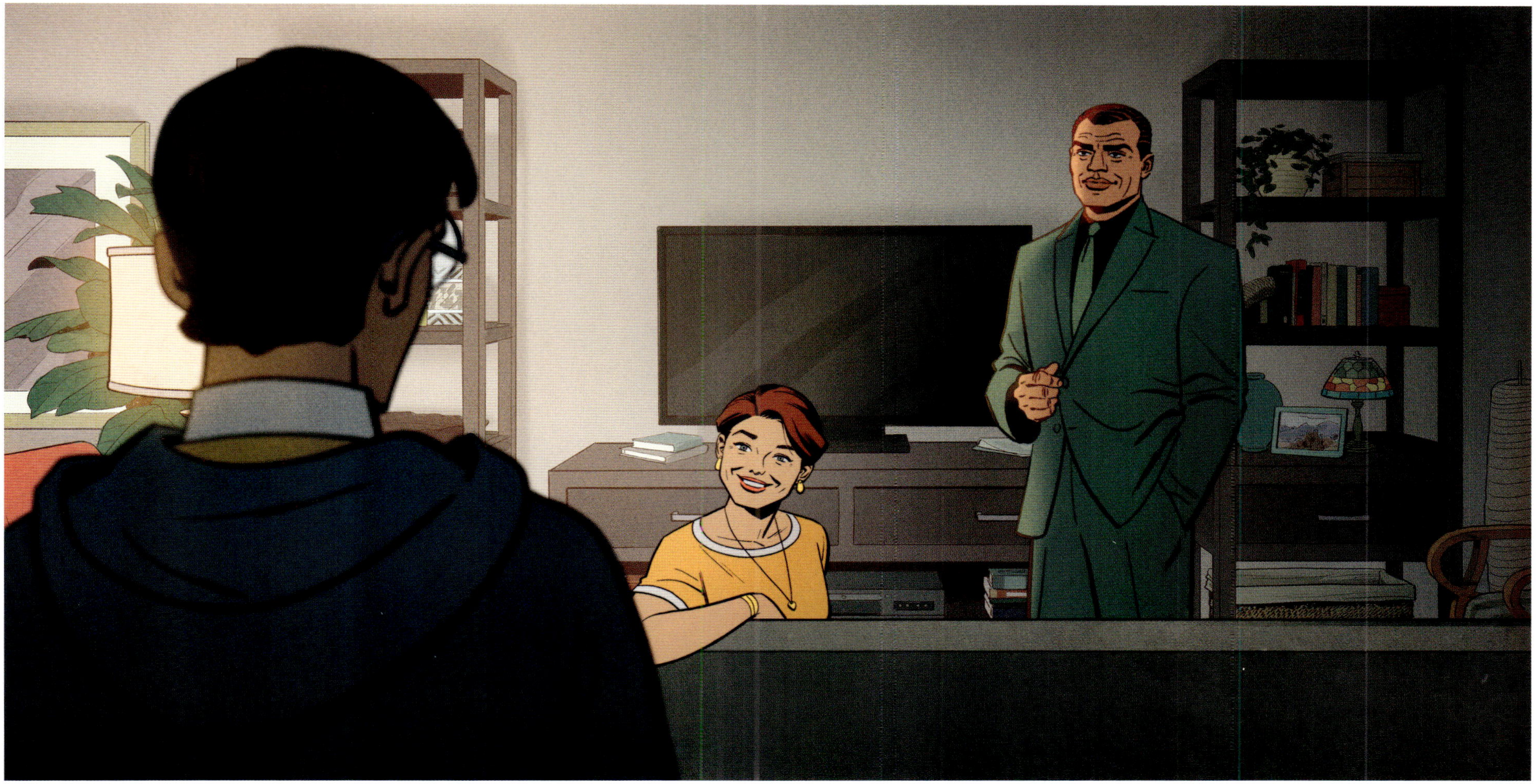

9

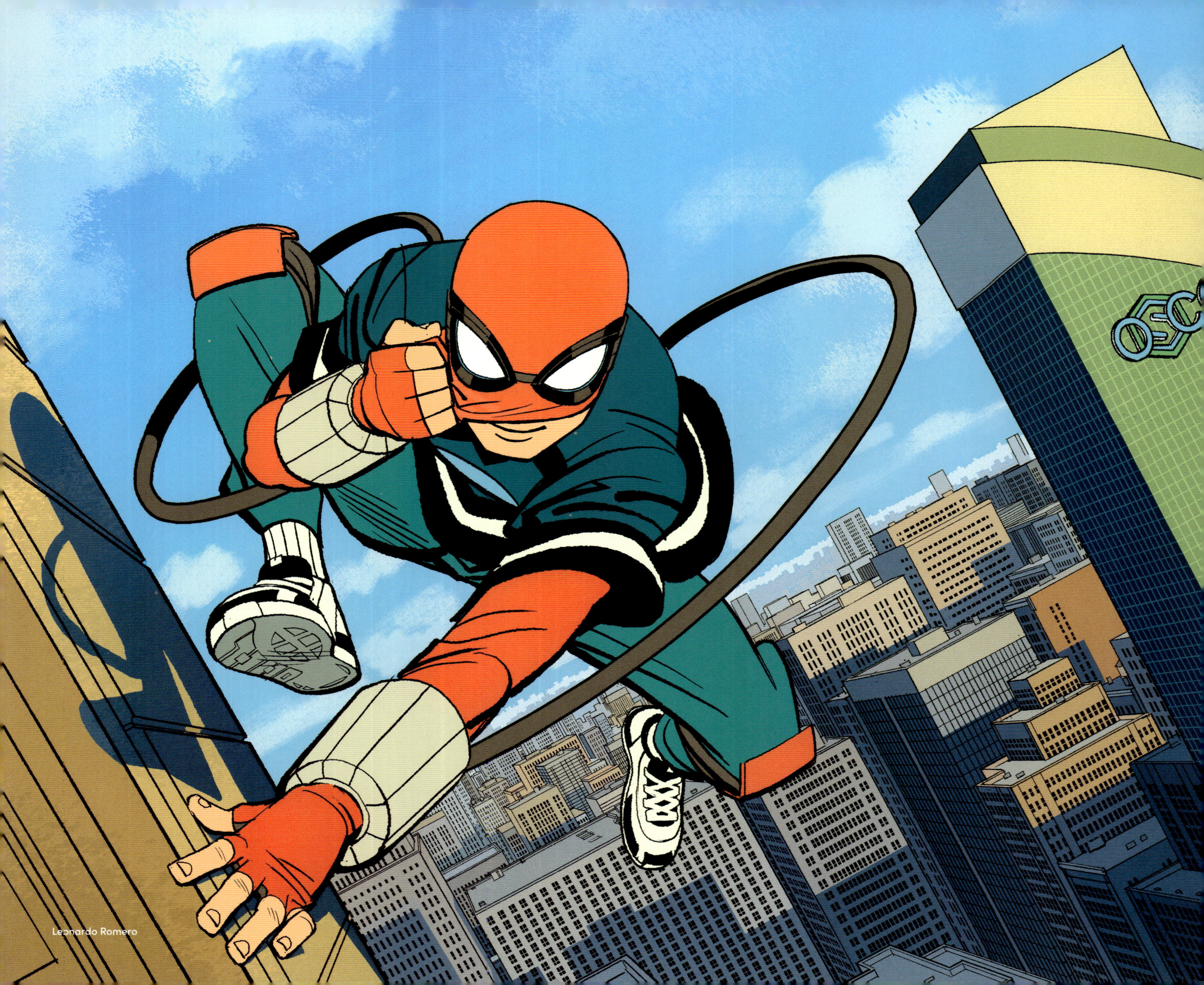

Leonardo Romero

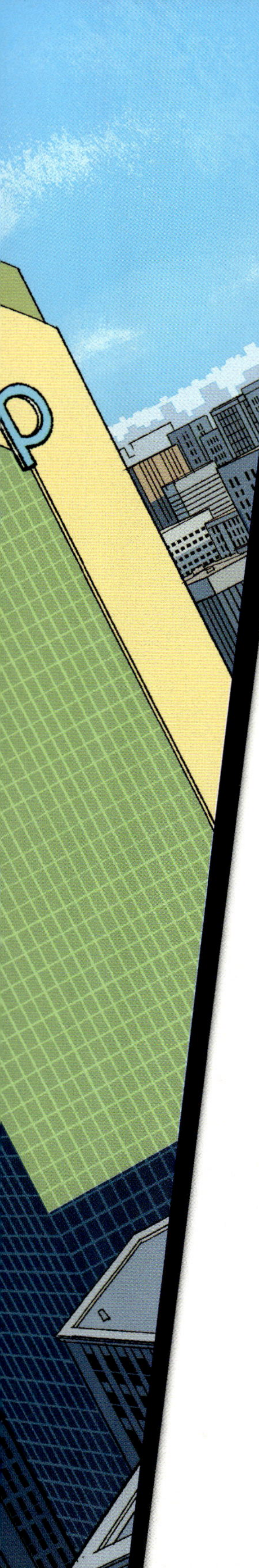

EPISODE TWO

THE PARKER LUCK

THE SECOND EPISODE OF THE SERIES INTRODUCES VIEWERS TO PETER'S FELLOW OSCORP INTERNS JEANNE FOUCAULT (ANJALI KUNAPANENI), ASHA (ERICA LUTTRELL), AND AMADEUS CHO (ALEKS LE). THE EPISODE ALSO FEATURES ODDBALL SCIENTIST BENTLEY WITTMAN (PAUL F. TOMPKINS) AS WELL AS CARLA CONNORS (ZEHRA FAZAL), WHO PETER PARTNERS WITH TO BUILD A RENEWABLE BATTERY (A PARALLEL TO THE STARK ARC REACTOR IN THE MCU). THIS INSTALLMENT INCLUDES AN INCIDENT INVOLVING ARSONIST BUTANE (JAKE GREEN), WHO HAS BEEN HIRED TO DESTROY A BUILDING WITH HIS FLAMETHROWERS AS PART OF AN INSURANCE SCAM. WHEN PETER COMES TO THE RESCUE AS SPIDER-MAN, HE DOESN'T REALIZE THAT HIS IDENTITY IS REVEALED ON SECURITY CAMERA FOOTAGE RETRIEVED BY NONE OTHER THAN NORMAN OSBORN.

"THIS EPISODE was a lot of fun for me because we get to visit Oscorp for the first time [in the MCU]," says Executive Producer/ Showrunner Jeff Trammell. "We get to meet these interns who are all really fun. I was a fan of having these characters there, and much of this episode is about introducing bigger Marvel Universe characters or fun, fresh takes on them. It's also the first time we see Spider-Man fight a villain on the show, and we wanted to make sure Butane felt like a threat. But we are definitely going to level up because he is kind of an idiot, as shown by his inability to burn down the correct building. However, he's also not someone that Spider-Man can take lightly. So, I wanted to start our threats kind of low and be able to scale up as we go forward."

"The Parker Luck" also introduces our Super Hero's classic dilemma. "Peter realizes that he can't have it all," notes Trammell. "This is the beginning of 'I got this job. I got school. I got friends. I also got to be Spider-Man. Something's gotta give!' This is also the first time Nico is the victim of Peter's secret identity crisis. So, in many ways, the show really gets started at this point."

Supervising Director Liza Singer mentions that this particular episode allowed her and the rest of the team to establish some of the key players in Peter's world. "After we get the writers' take on these characters, we have to find all their idiosyncrasies and nuances," she explains. "The second episode might look more simplistic because we are just getting to know them a little, but it was really allowing us to find our footing. This half hour helped keep the main character grounded and introduced Peter's dilemmas with the characters he meets. As the show expanded, we got more confident working with each of the characters."

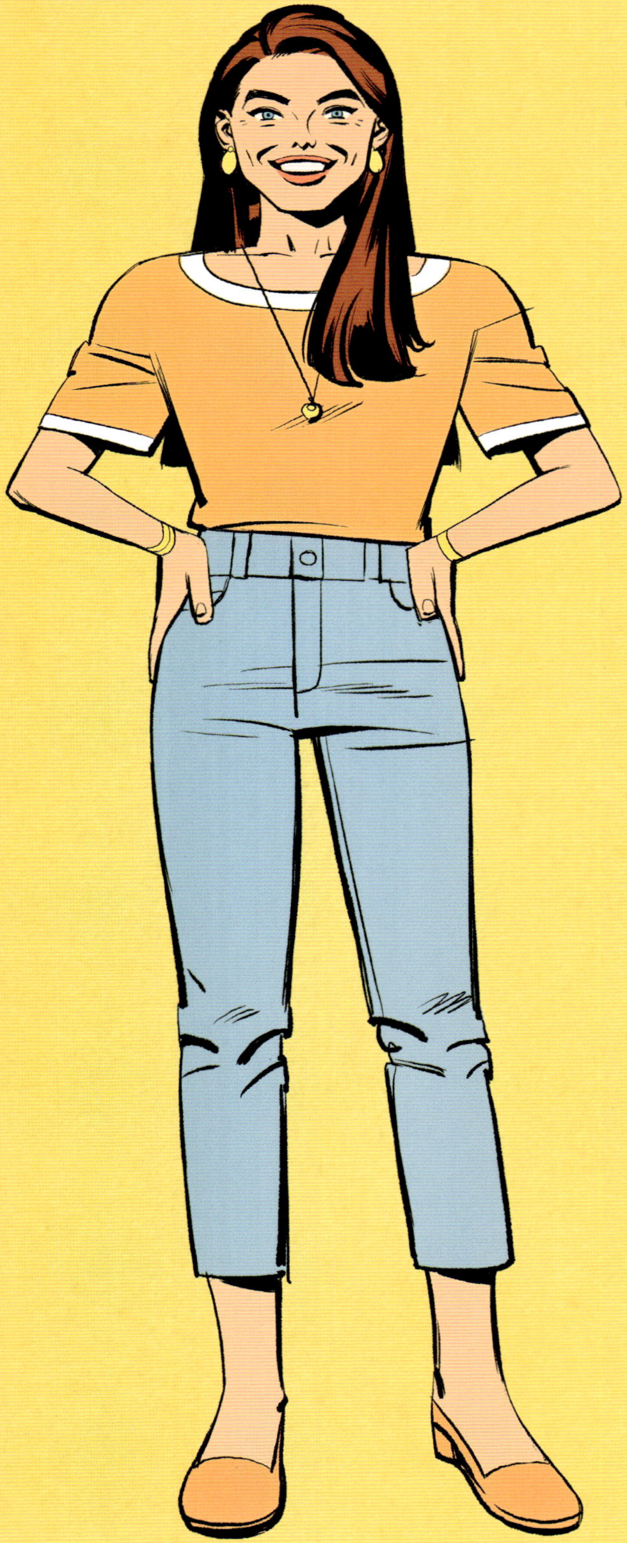

1

2

MAY PARKER

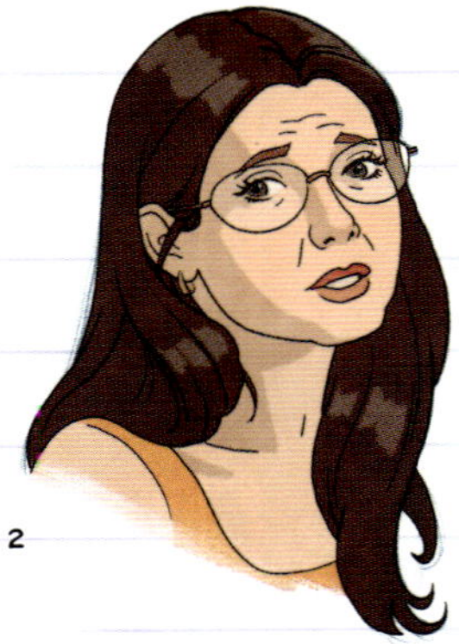

Peter's kind and nurturing aunt, May, has been a constant fixture in the world of Spider-Man from his very first appearance in the comics up through the many franchise adaptations. In the show, we see her portrayed as a young mother figure. "She is the sweetest, kindest, and most patient woman on the planet," says Executive Producer/Showrunner Jeff Trammell. "I think she is the only character in my recollection who's pretty much in every single version of Spider-Man because she is the moral compass—even more so than Ben. She's able to set Peter on the right path and give him the kind of love and support he needs to get back out there. I wanted to make sure that her presence is felt throughout the show, and although she's not in every episode, when she and Peter have their big moments, it feels all-encompassing. You realize how much he's learned from this extremely patient person who has been through so much, continues to find positivity in life, and supports this young boy during very challenging times."

Lead Character Designer Leonardo Romero says he also went back to the older versions of May in the classic comics and tried to imagine what she would have looked like as a younger woman. "Another source of inspiration was May as she was portrayed by actress Marisa Tomei [in *Captain America: Civil War*, *Spider-Man: Homecoming*, *Avengers: Endgame*, *Spider-Man: Far from Home*, and *Spider-Man: No Way Home*]," adds Romero. "So, she is a mix of the classic version and the new, modern May we know from the movies."

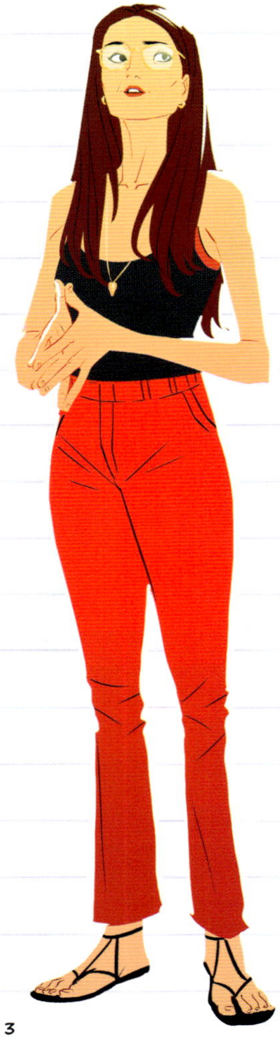

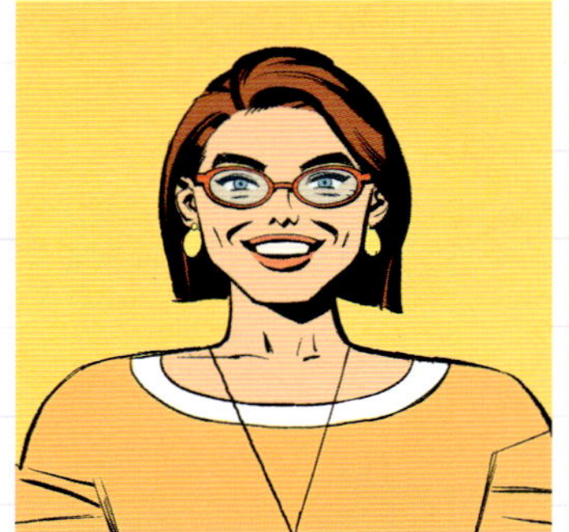

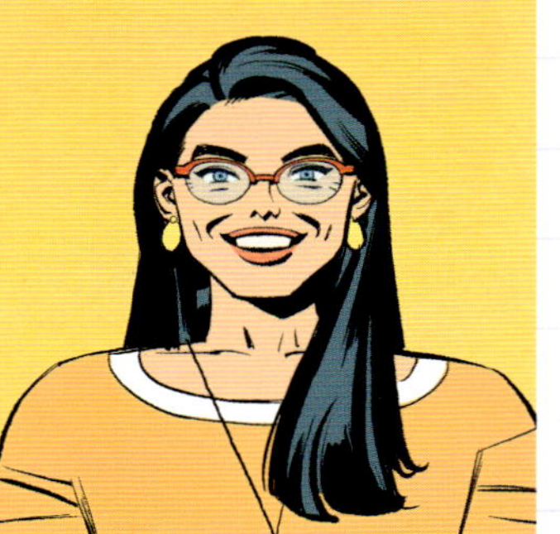

3

4

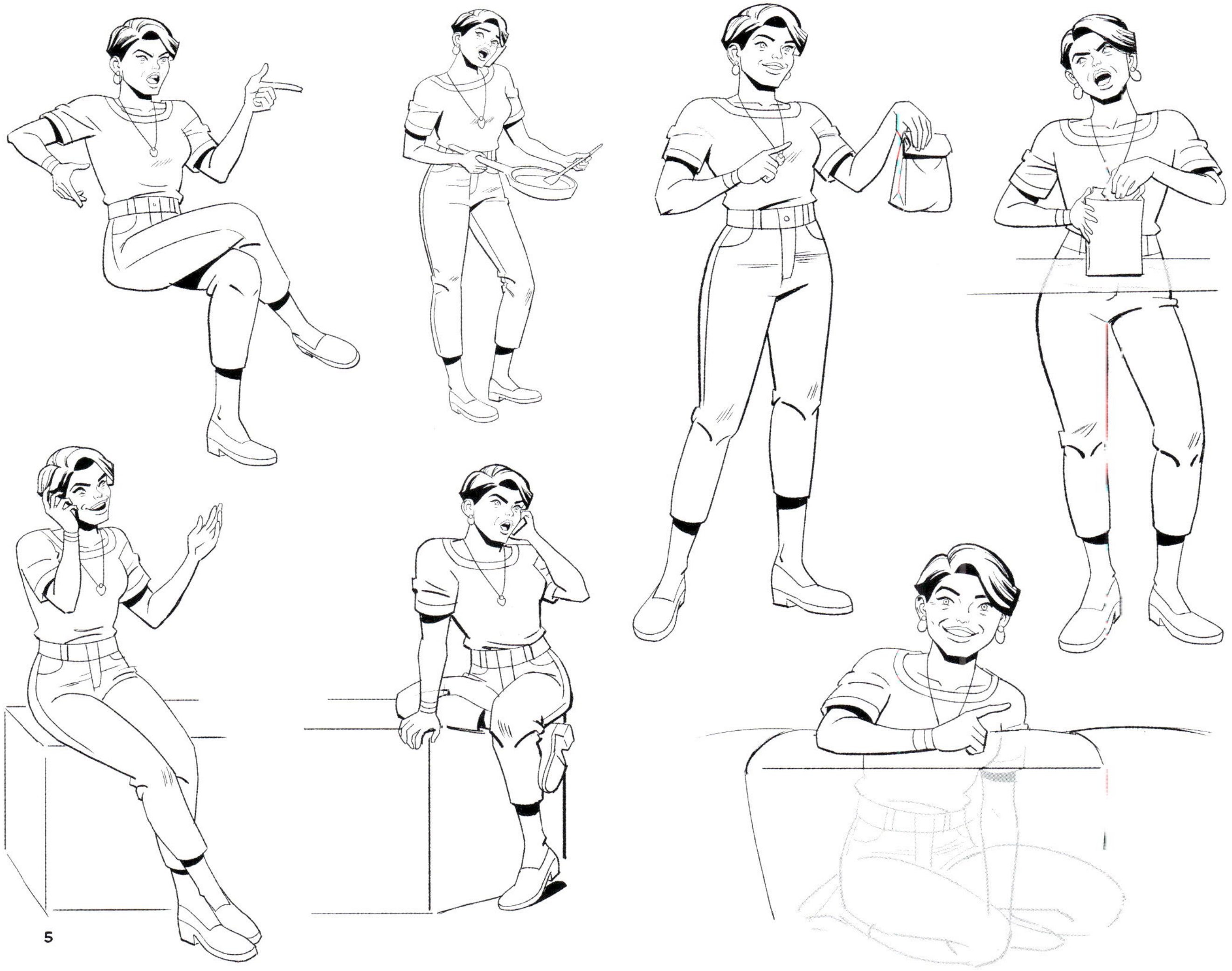

5

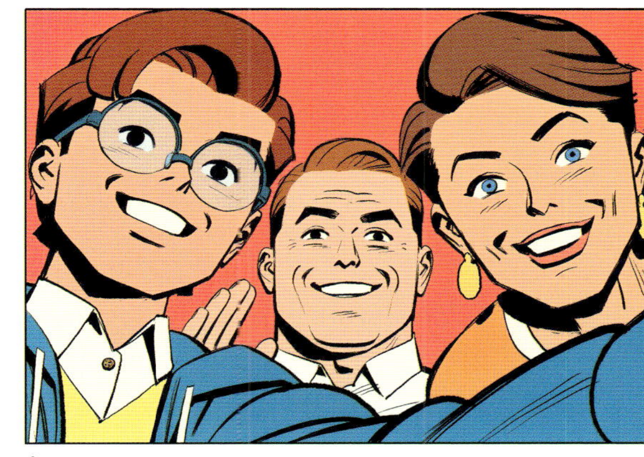

6

1 Leonardo Romero
2 Paolo Rivera
3 Joey Vazquez
4 Leonardo Romero
5 Dan Holland
6 Leonardo Romero
7 Ethan Young
8 Leonardo Romero

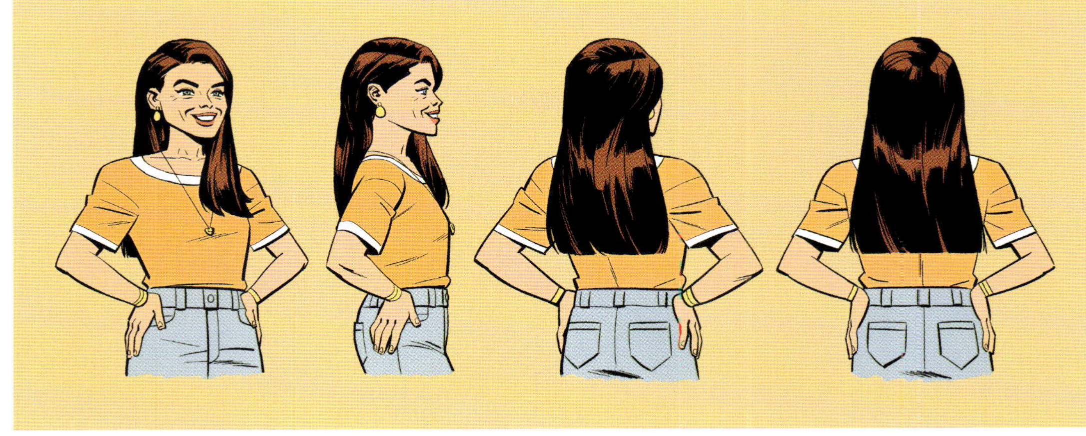

7

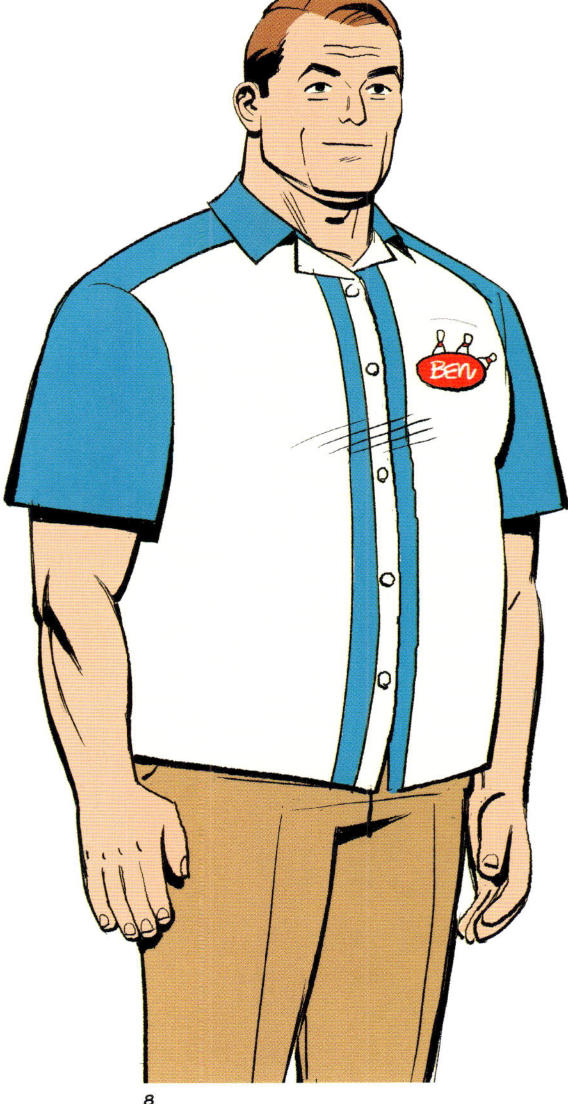

8

ROCKFORD
36
1

2

3

ROCKFORD T.
SENIOR HIGH SCHOOL
BALES
4

SENIOR HIGH SCHOOL
ROCKFORD T.
BALES
5

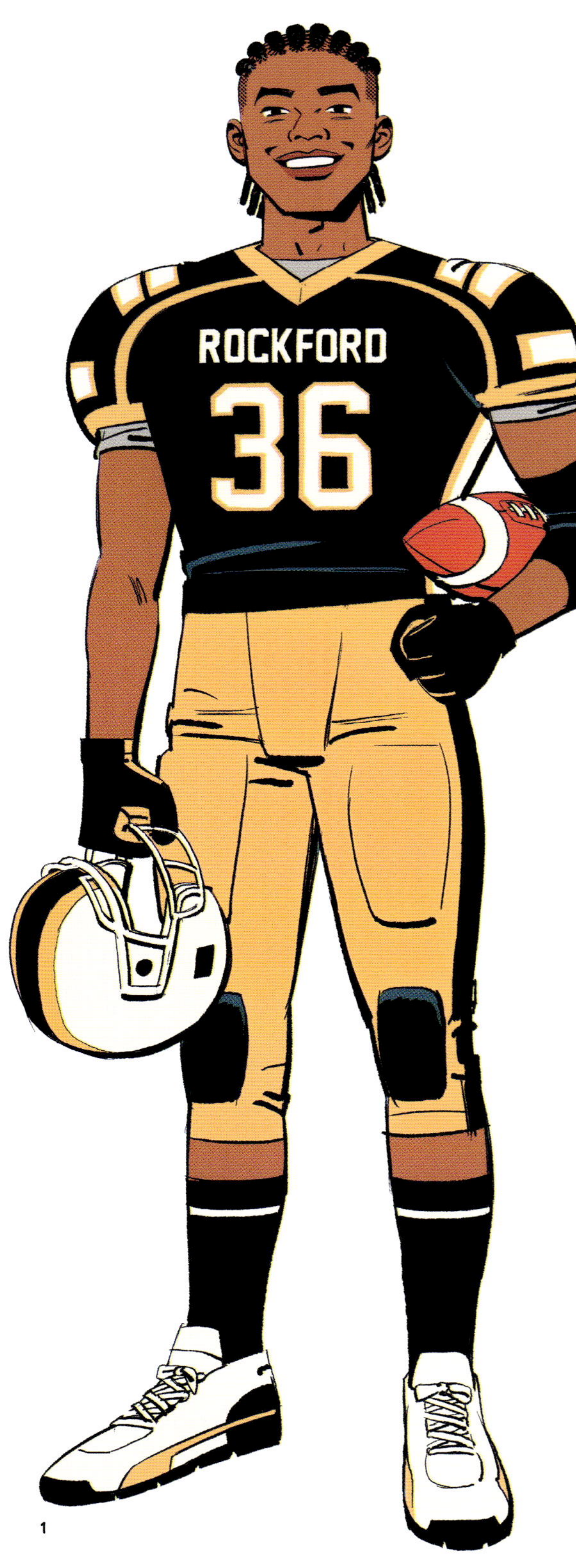

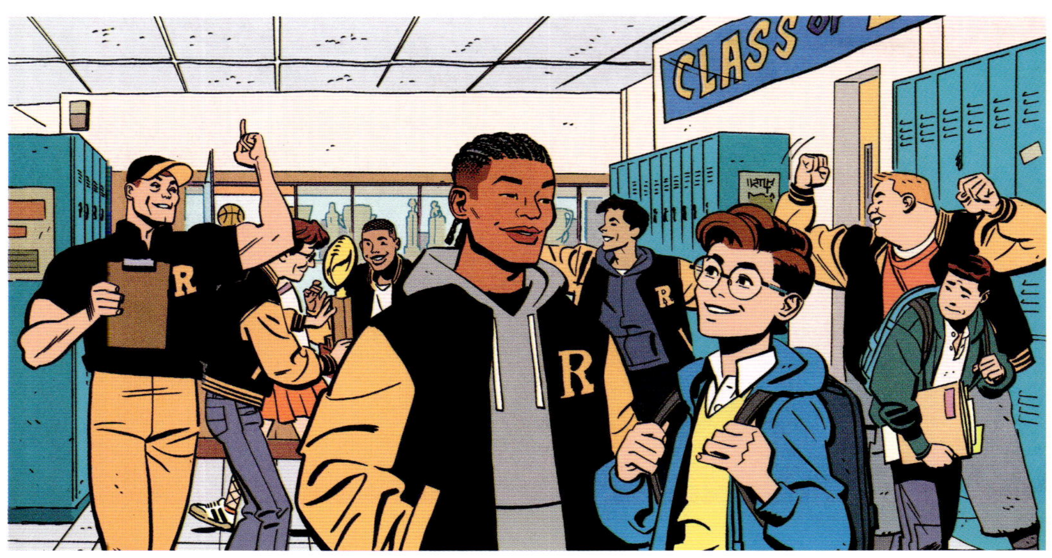

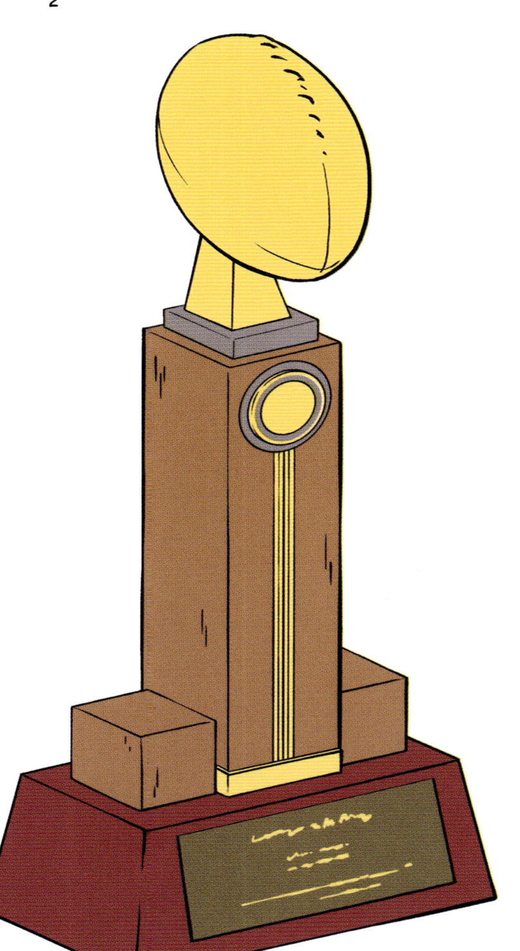

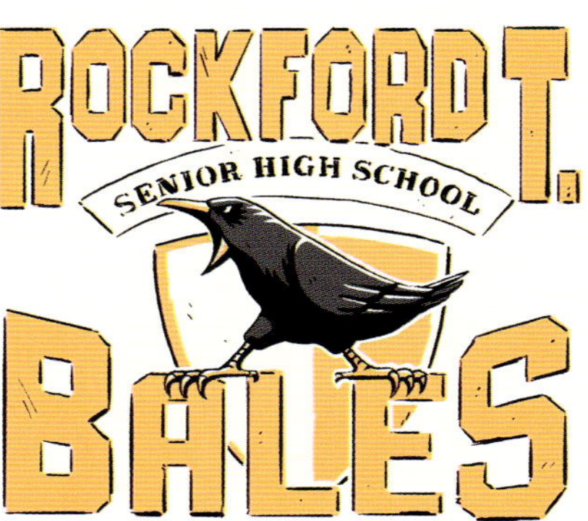

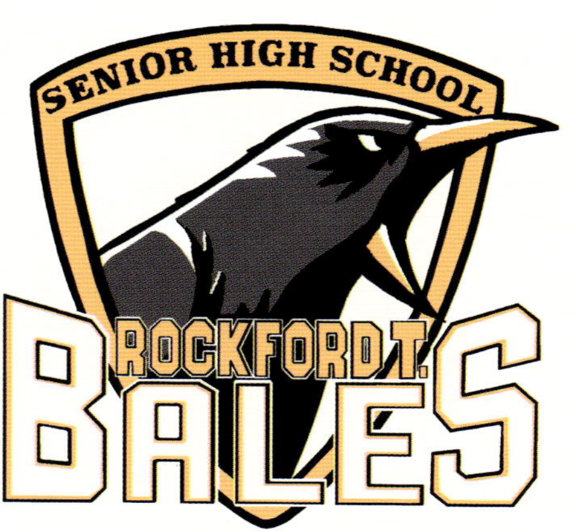

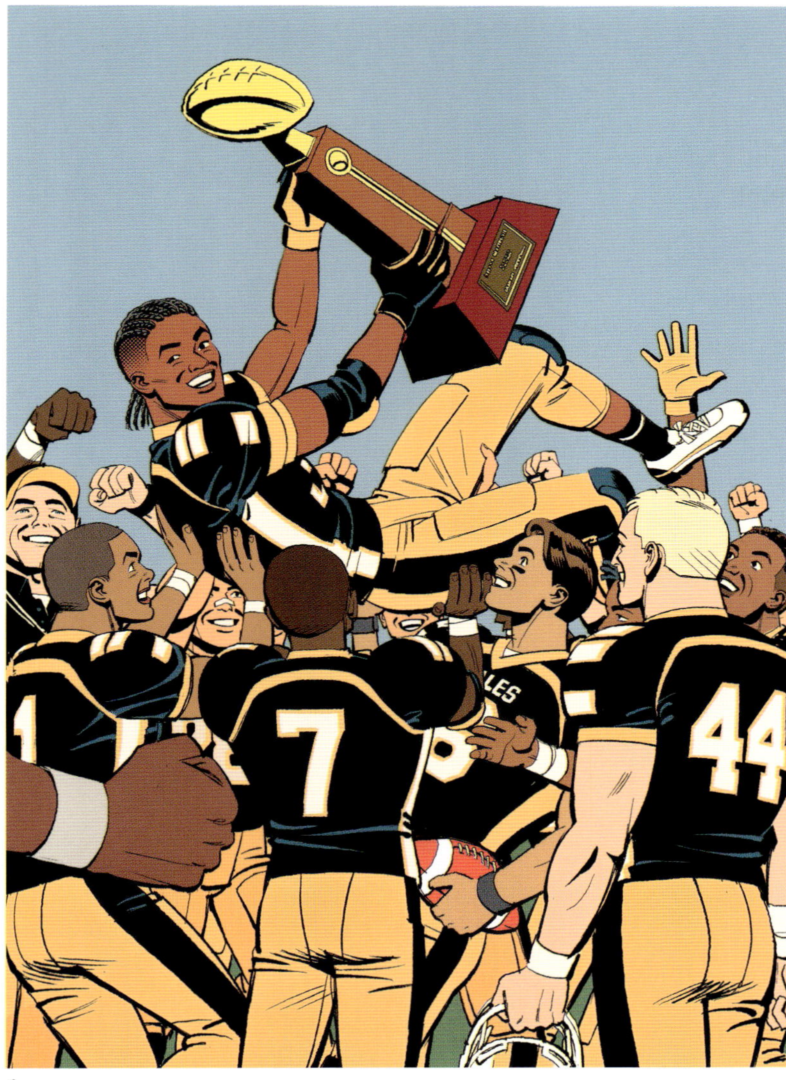

6

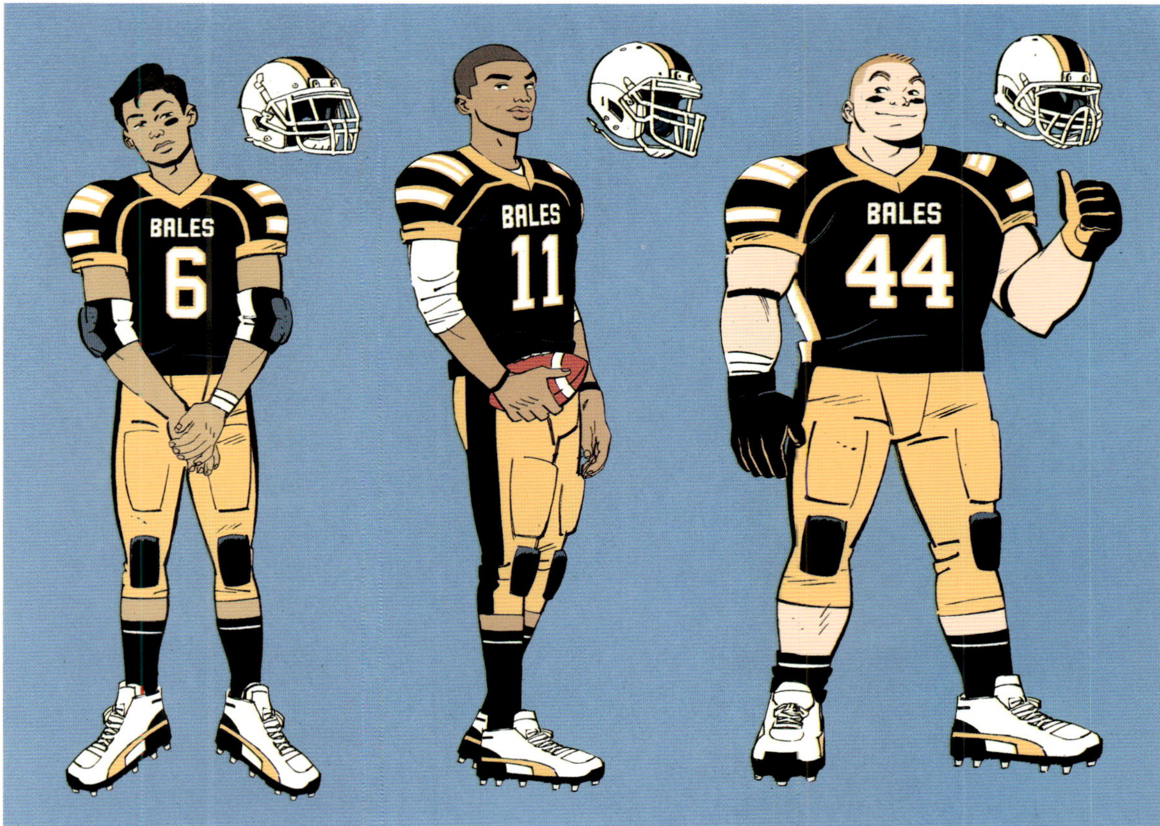

7

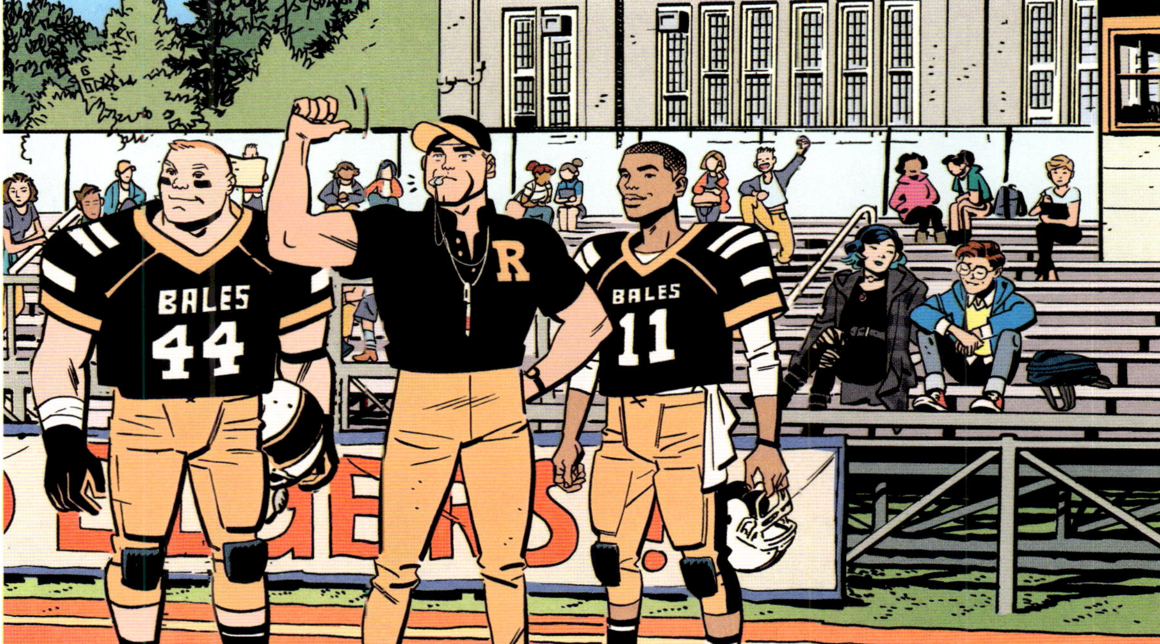

8

1 Leonardo Romero **2** Chris Samnee
3 Beverly Arce **4–5** Mauricio Leone and
Sylvia Liu **6** Leonardo Romero **7** Tom Reilly
8 Chris Samnee and Michael Yamada

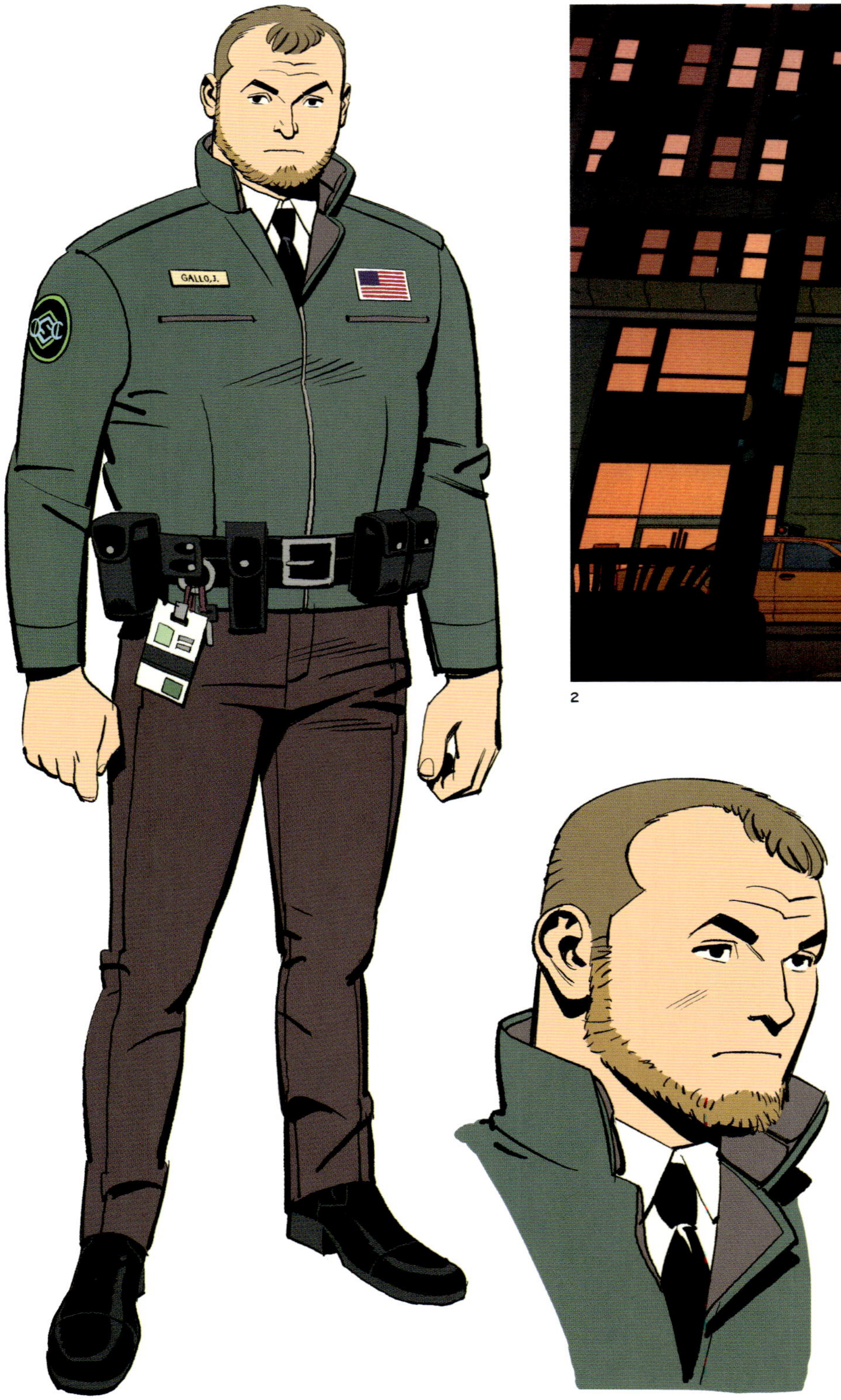

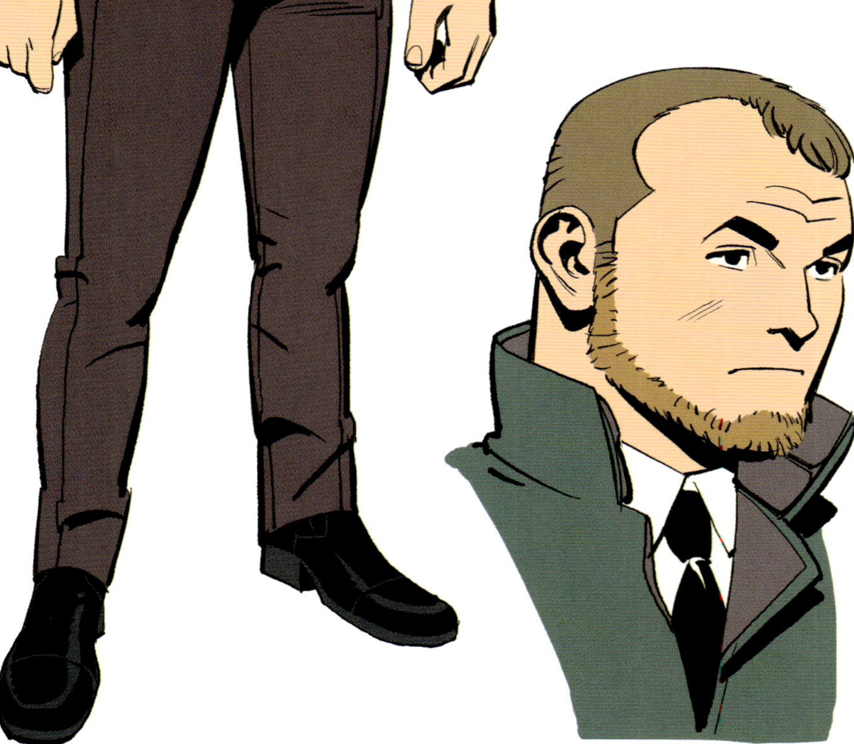

1

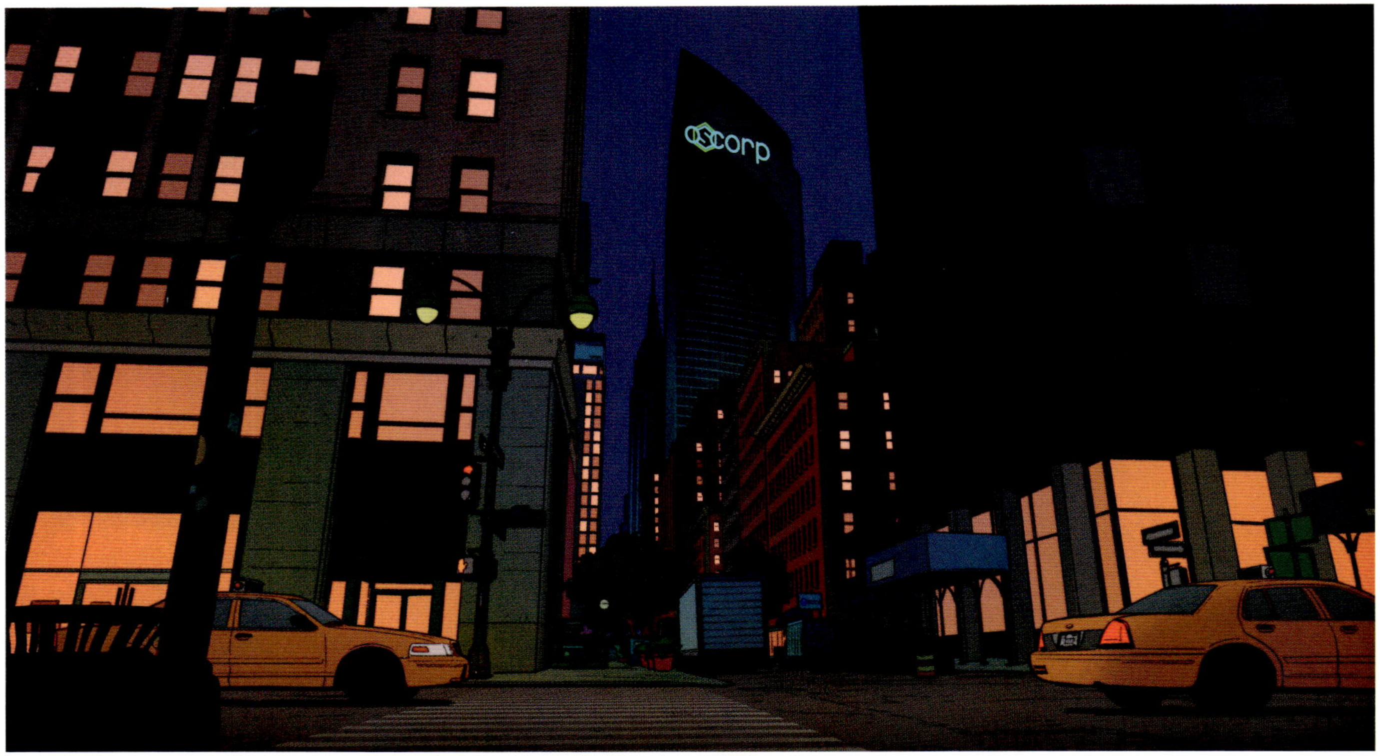

2

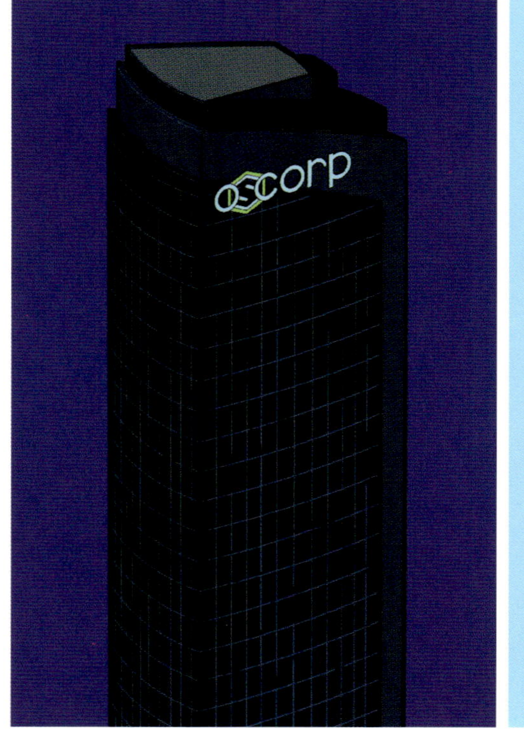

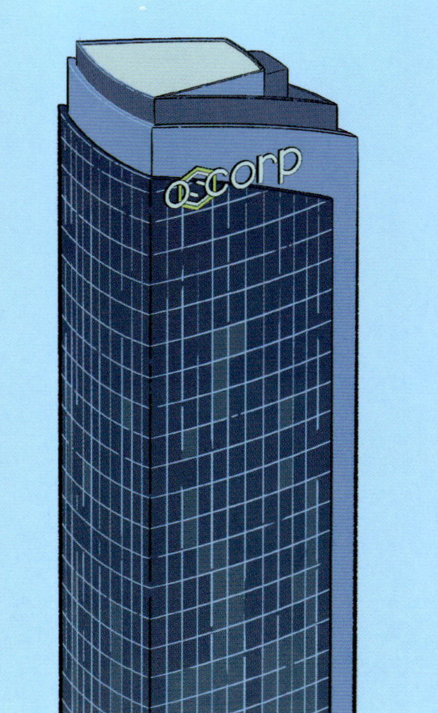

3

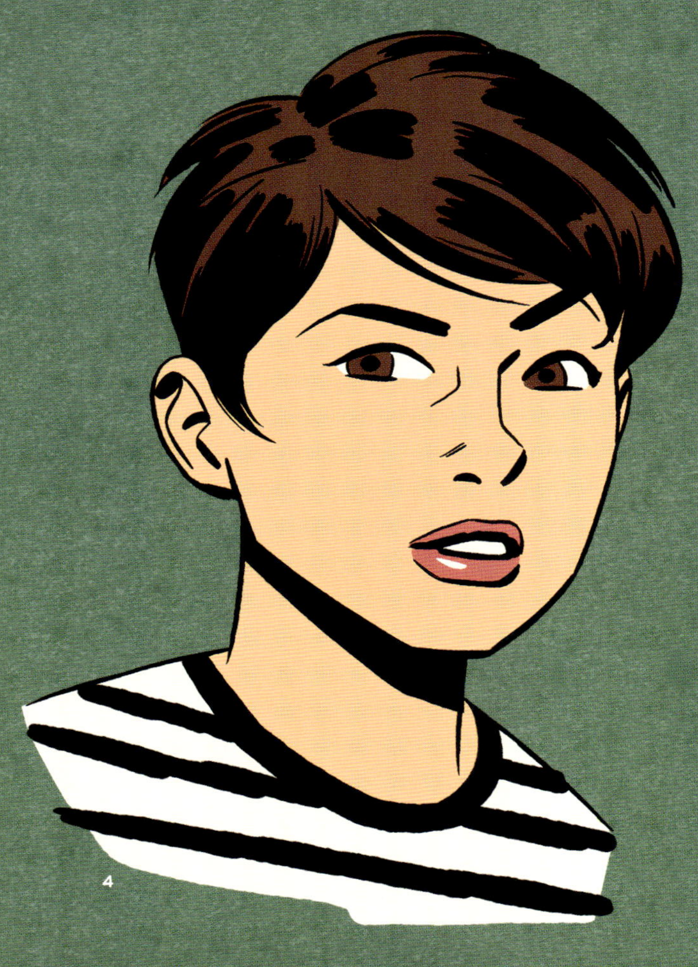

4

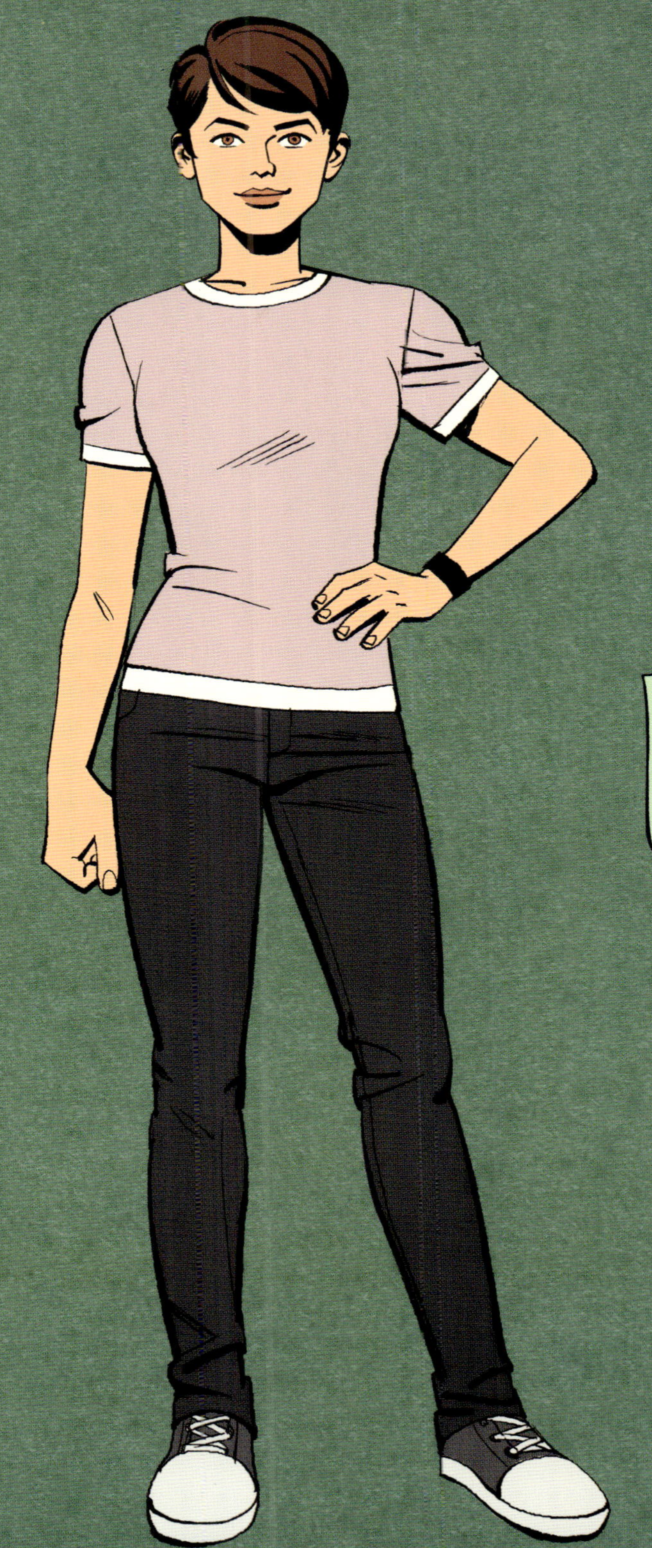

5

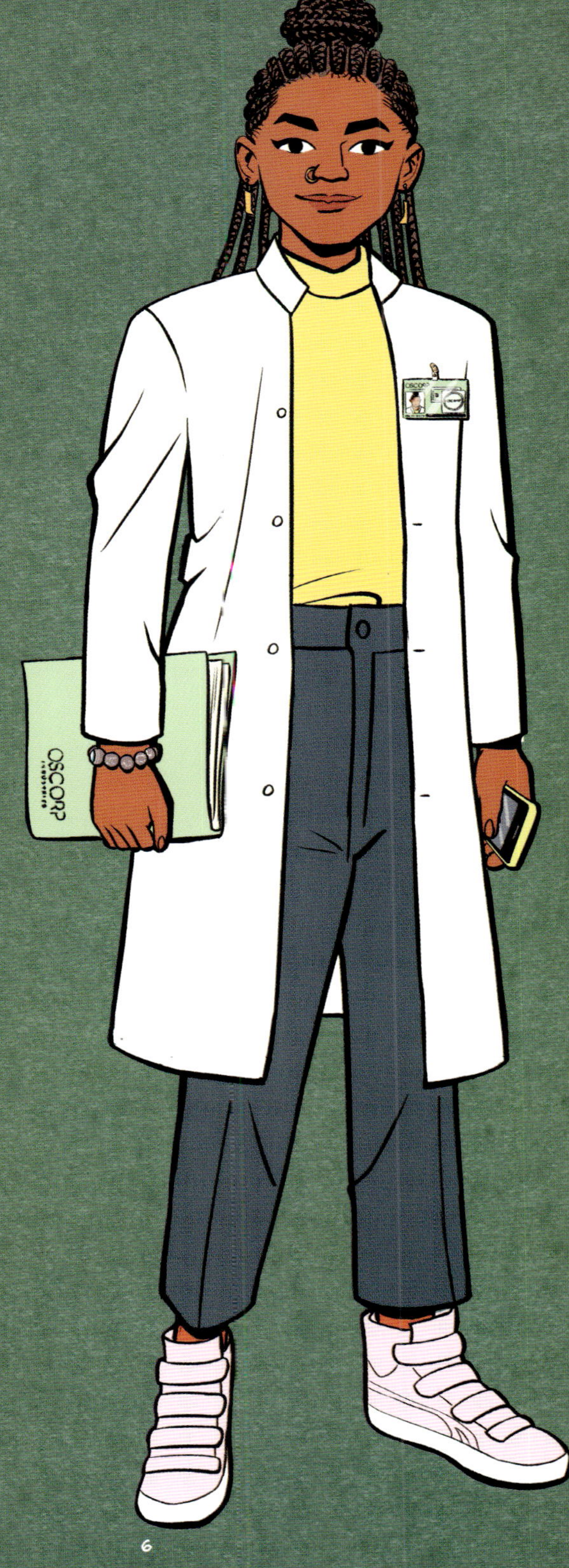

6

1 Leonardo Romero
2 Paolo Rivera (line art) and Michael Yamada (color) 3 Tuan Vo
4 Michael "Mike" Cho
5 Leonardo Romero
6 Mauricio Leone

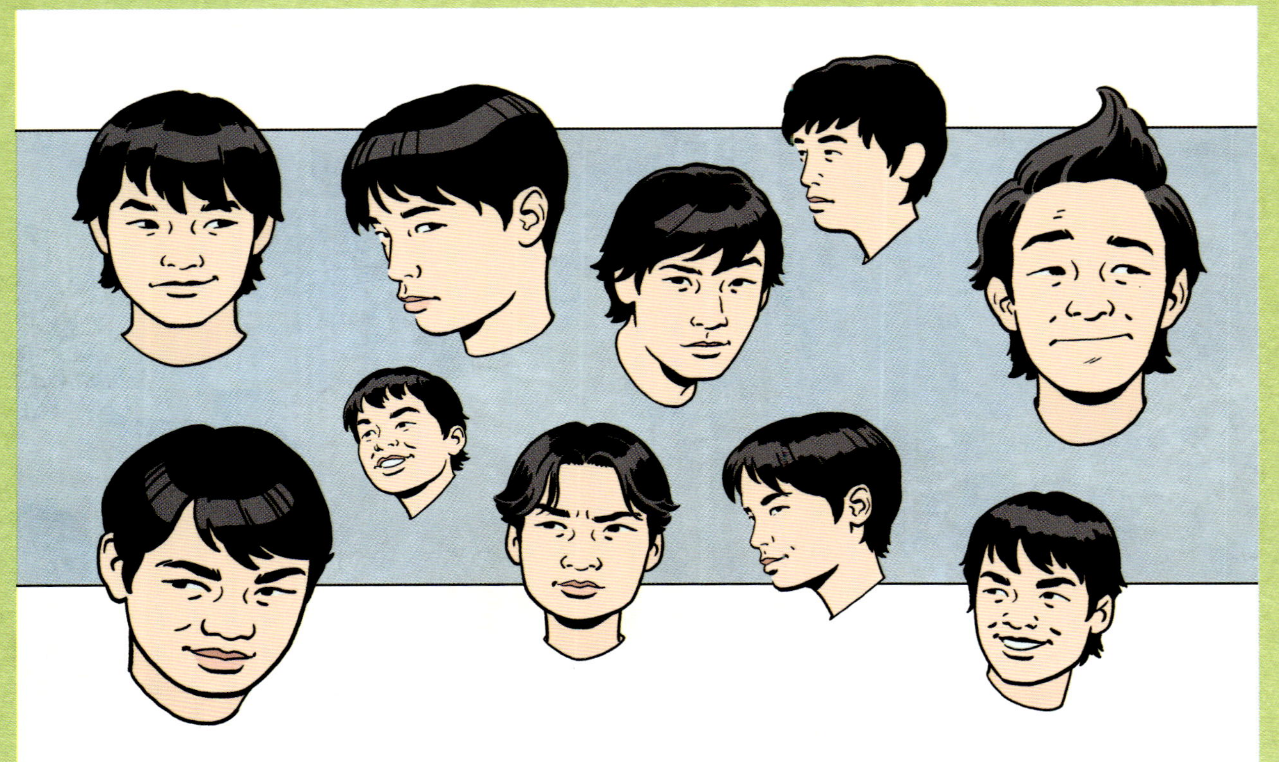

1

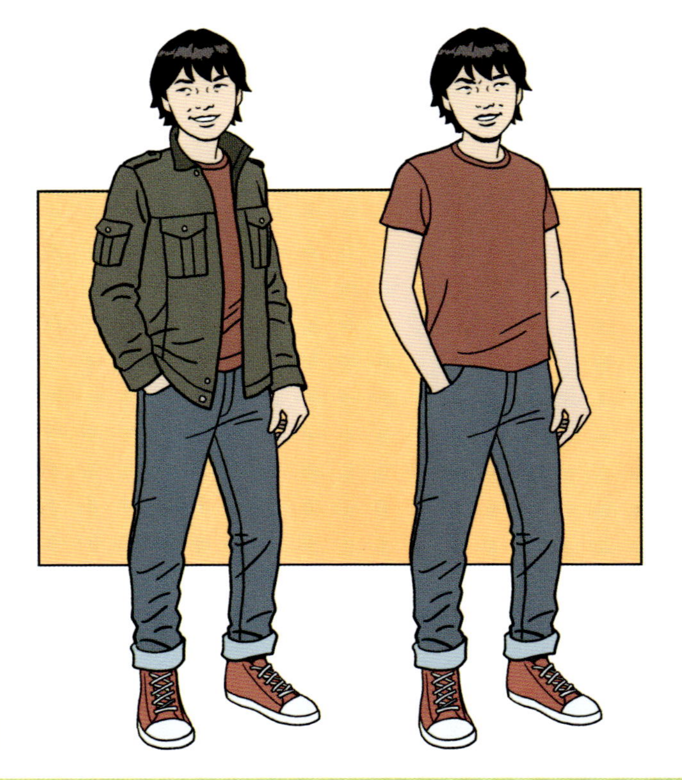

2

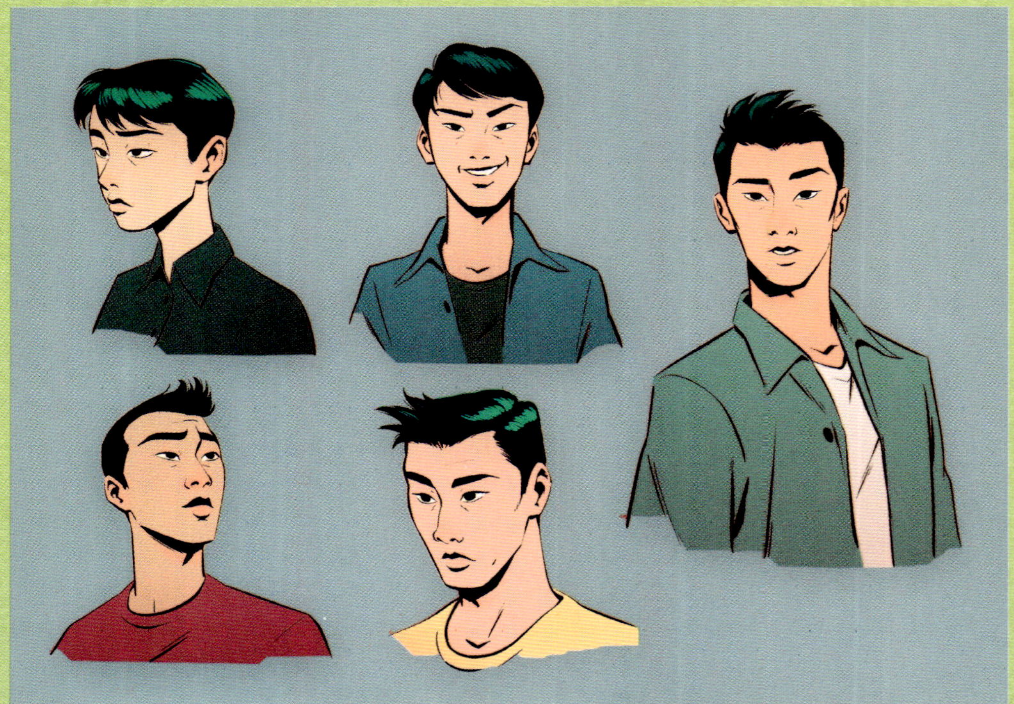

3

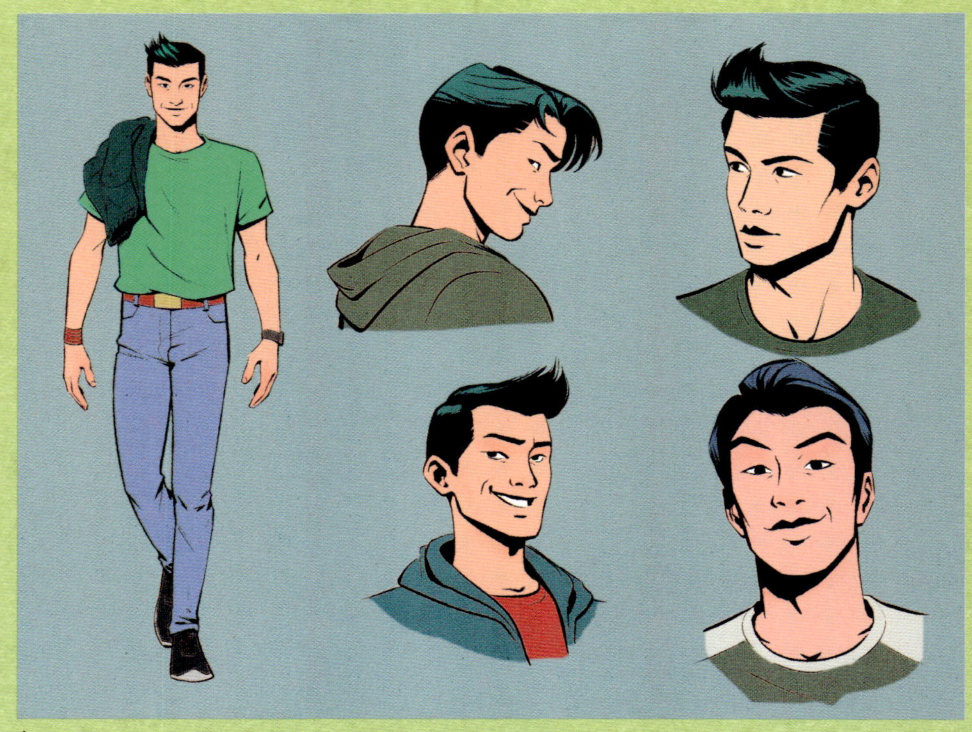

4

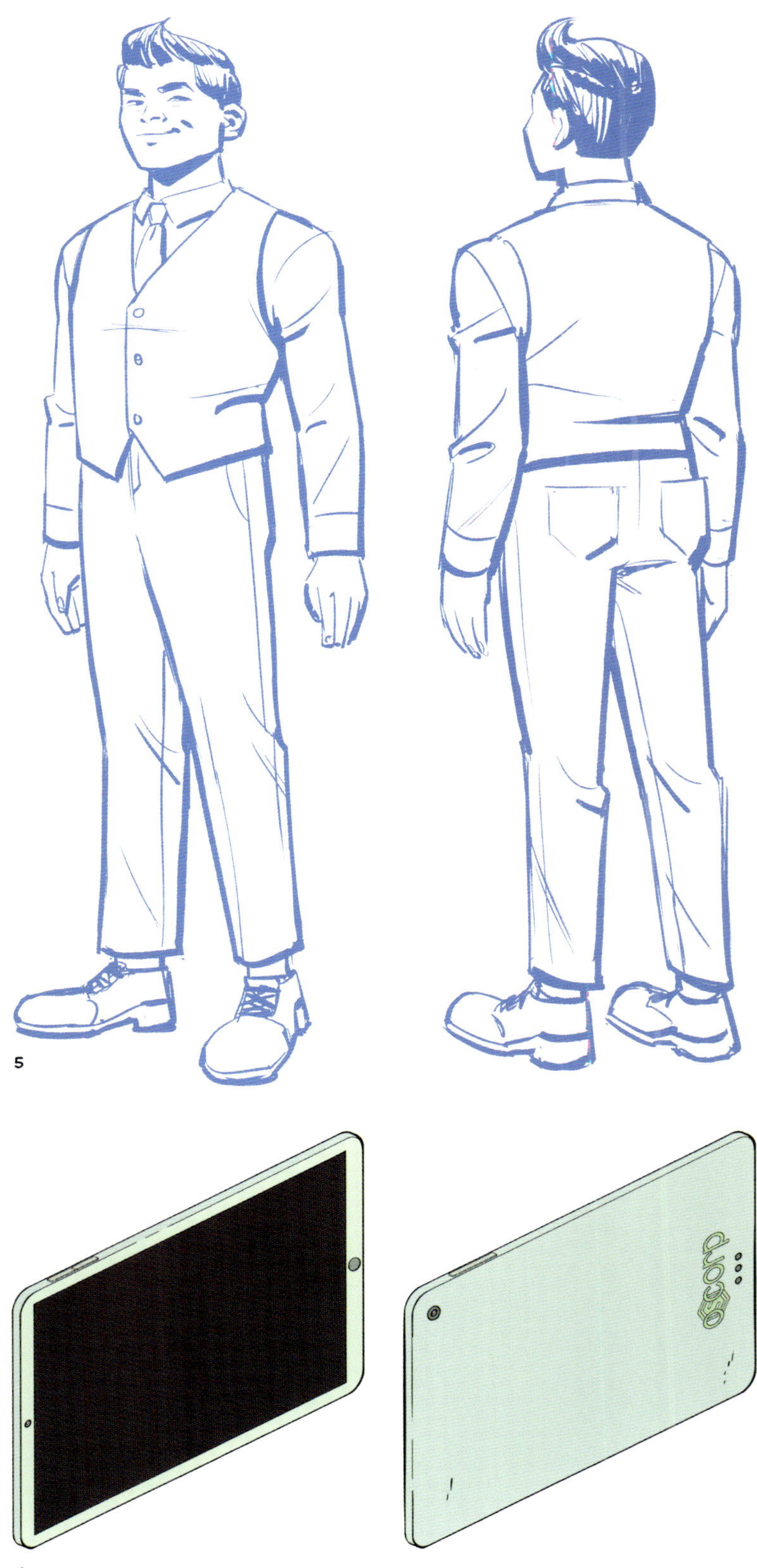

5

6

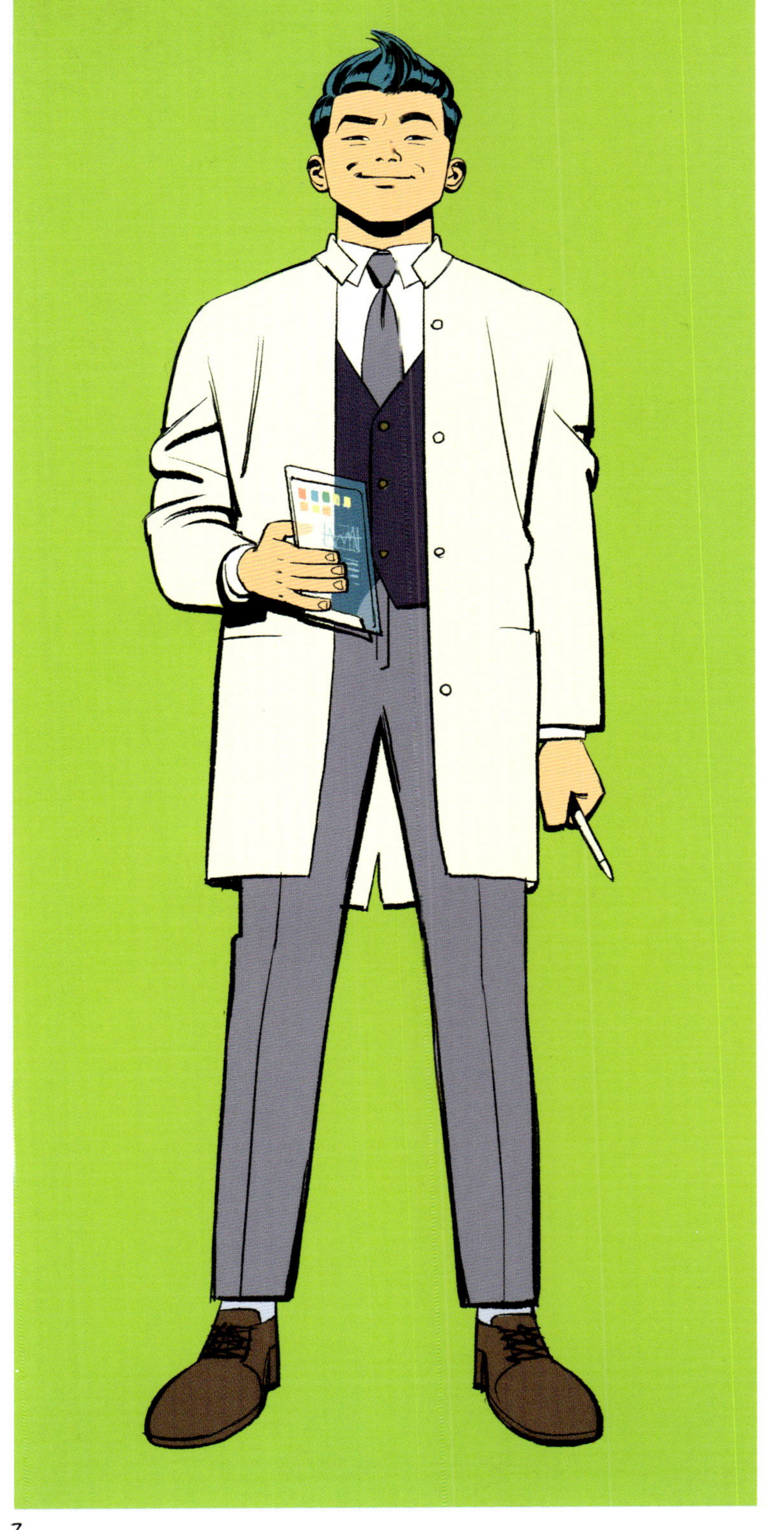

7

1 Leonardo Romero
2 Paolo Rivera
3–4 Julen Urrutia Perez
5 Ethan Young
6 Beverly Arce
7 Leonardo Romero

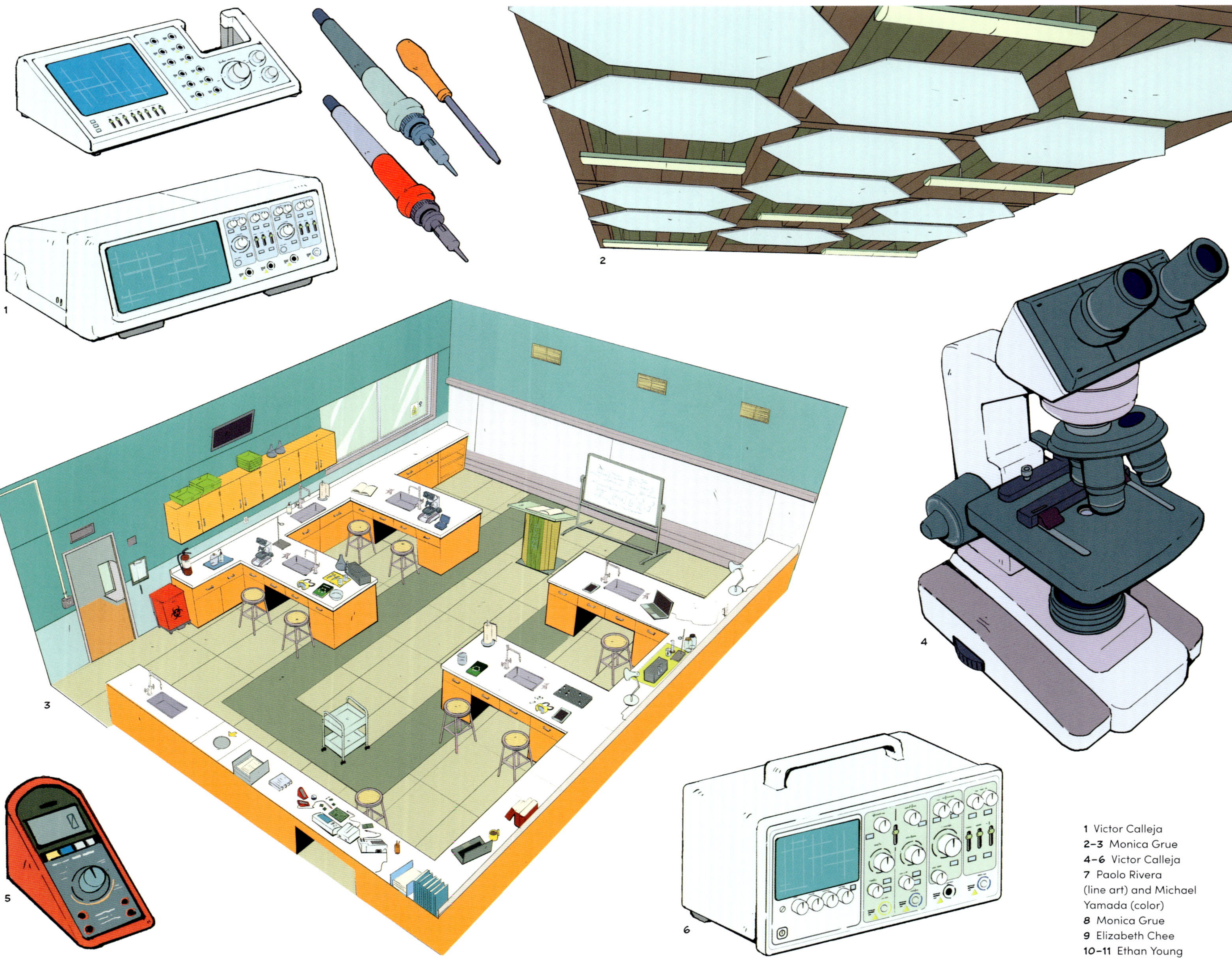

1 Victor Calleja
2–3 Monica Grue
4–6 Victor Calleja
7 Paolo Rivera (line art) and Michael Yamada (color)
8 Monica Grue
9 Elizabeth Chee
10–11 Ethan Young

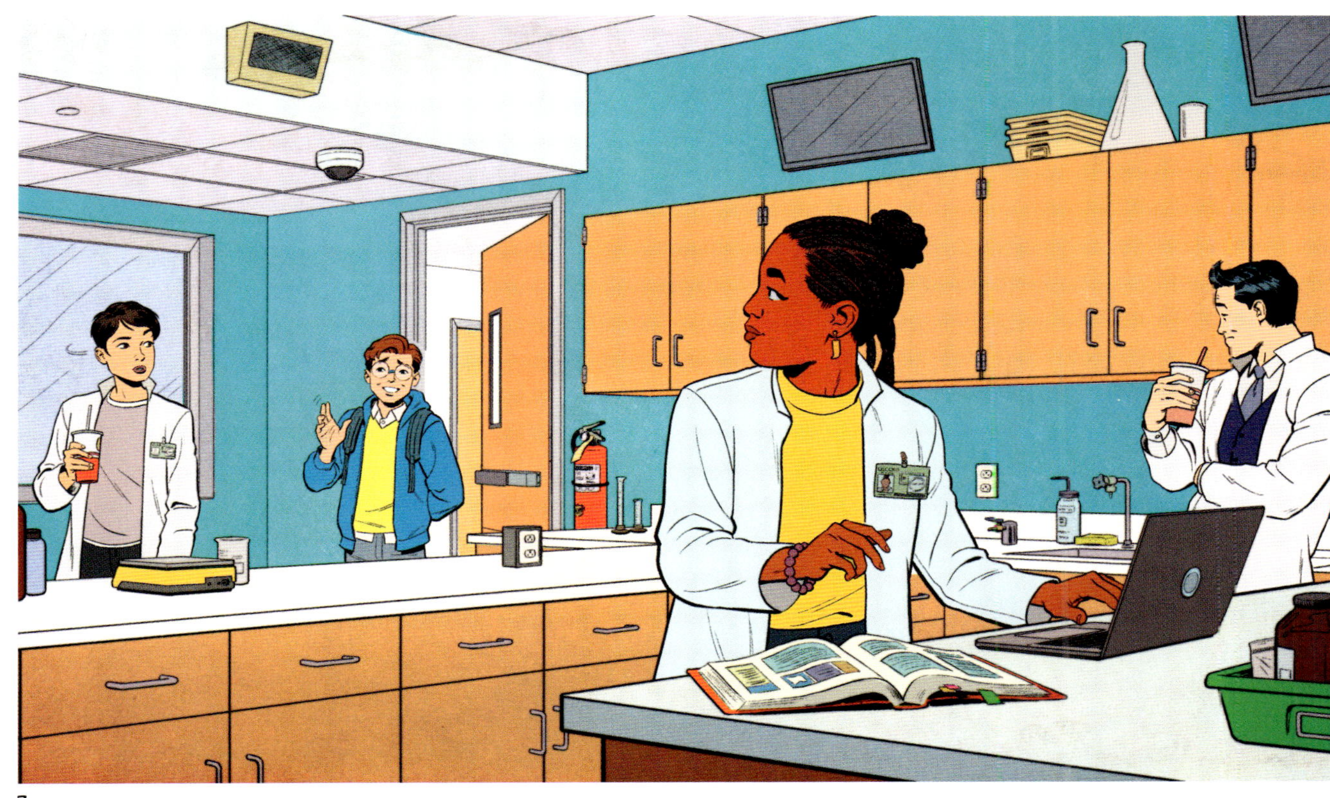

7

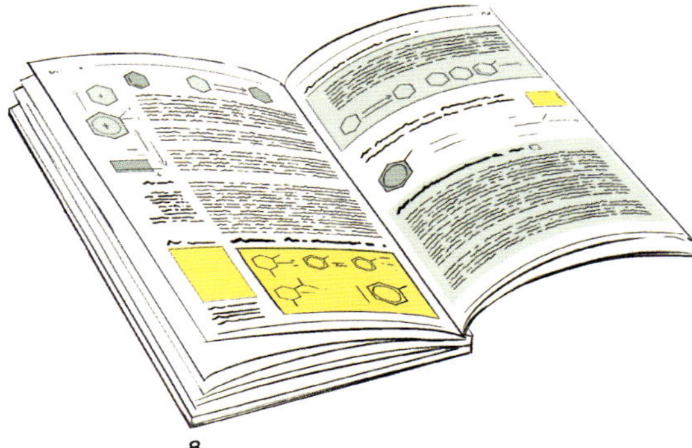

8

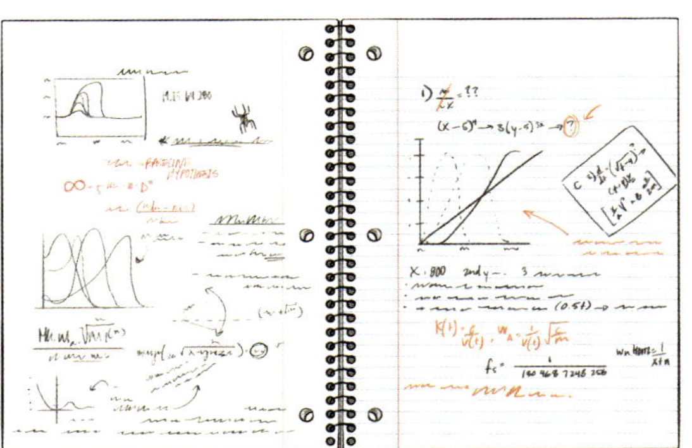

9

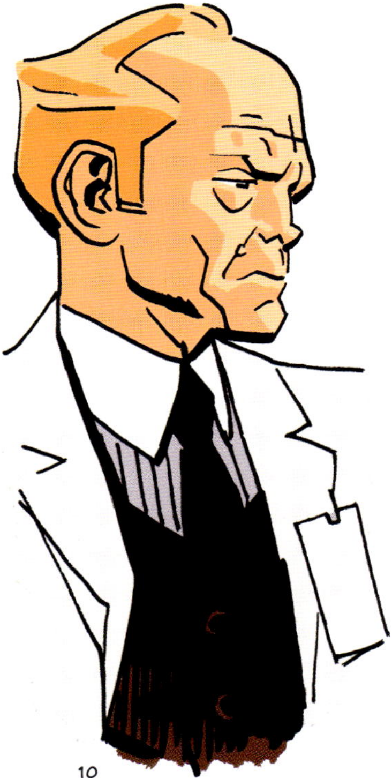

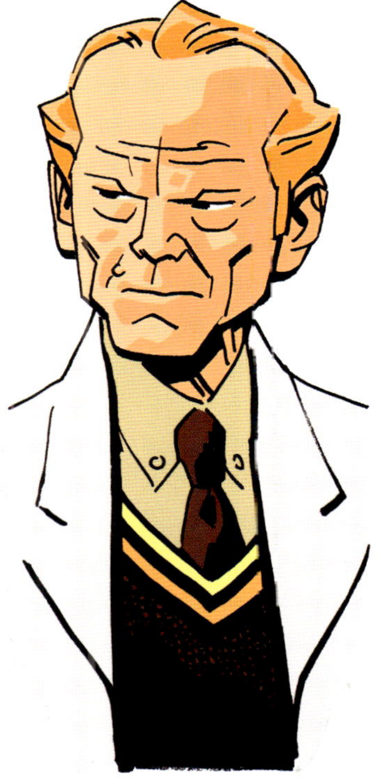

10

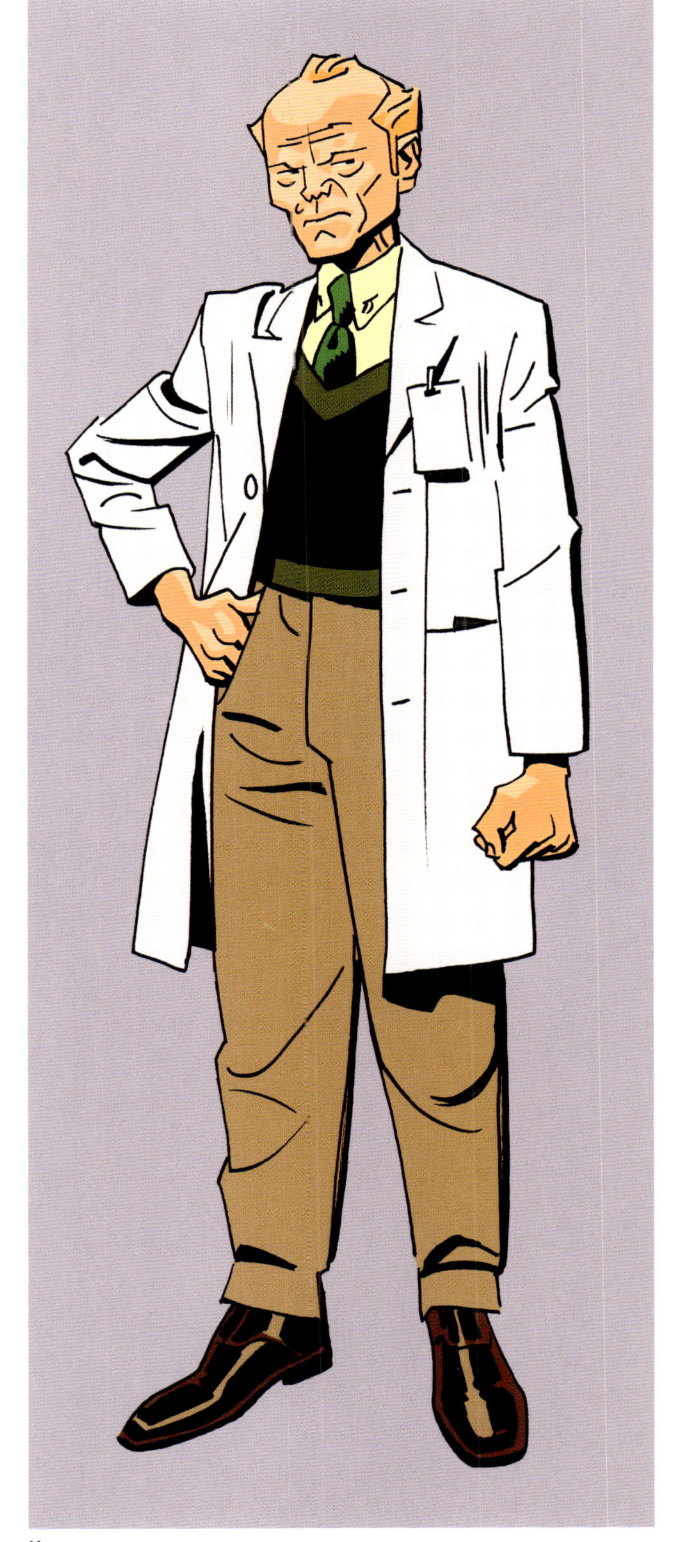

11

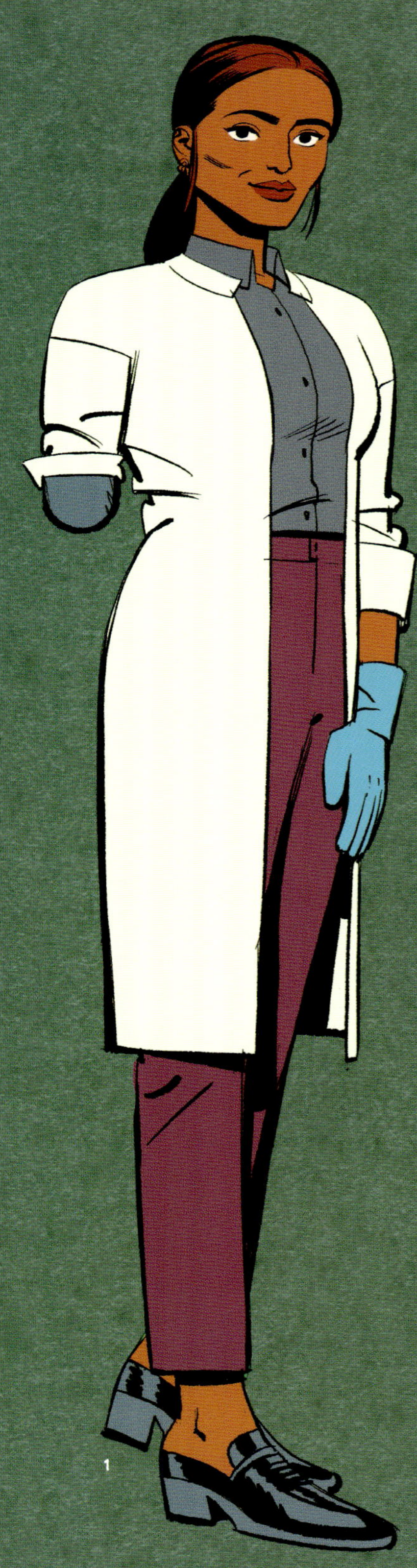

1

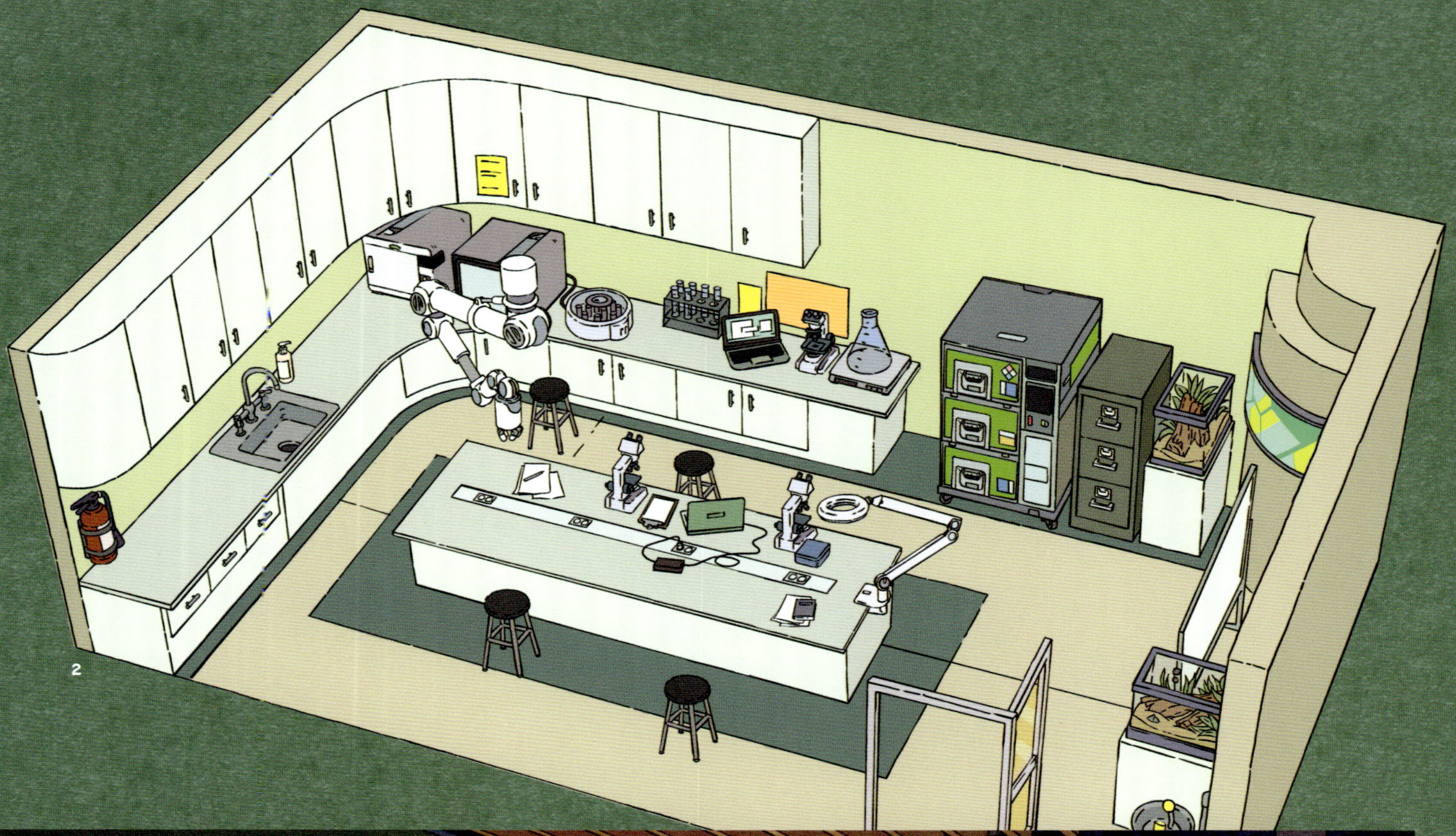

2

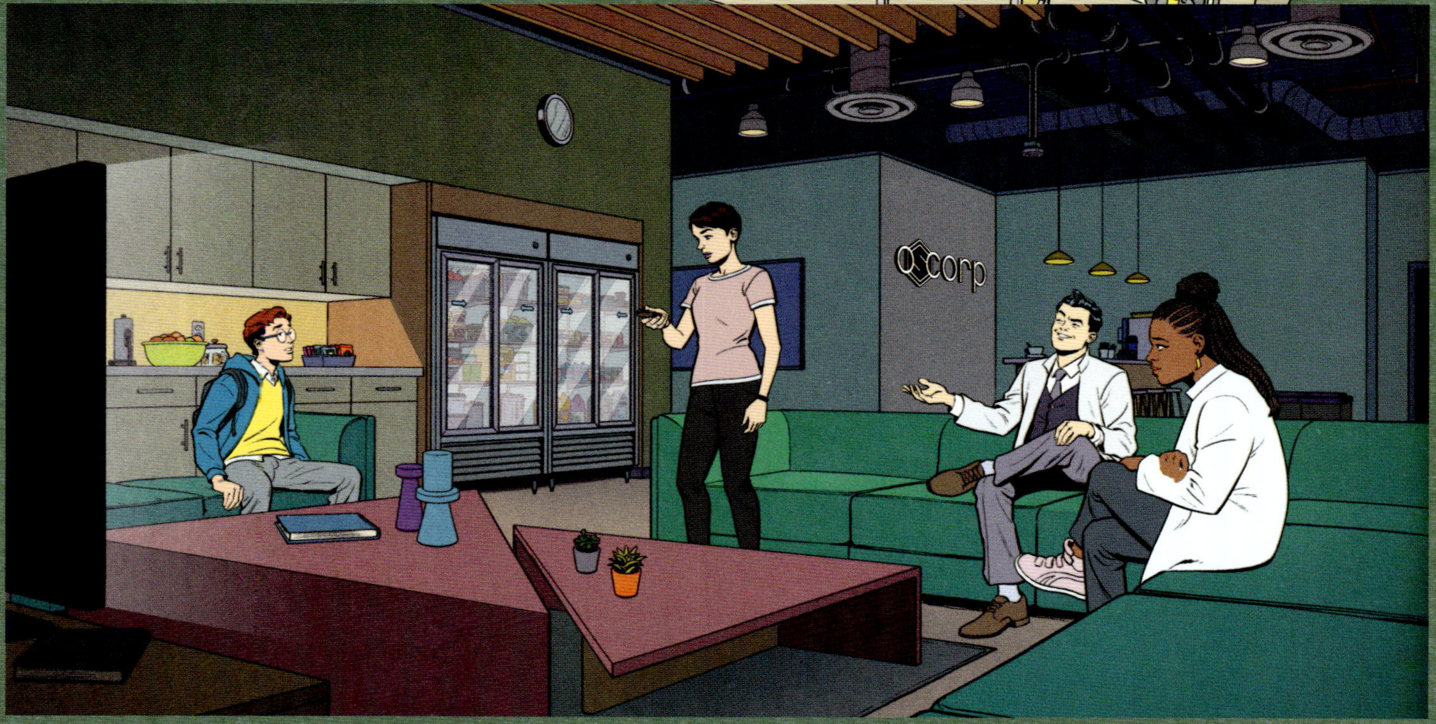

3

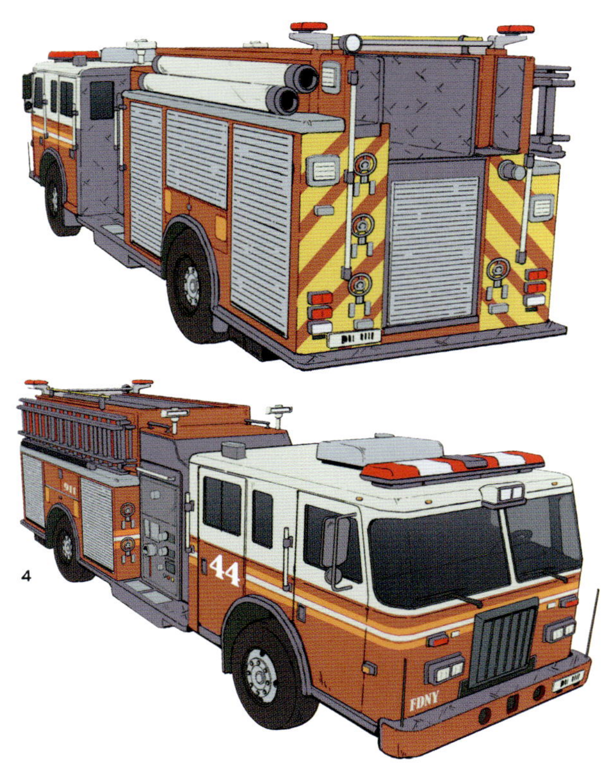

4

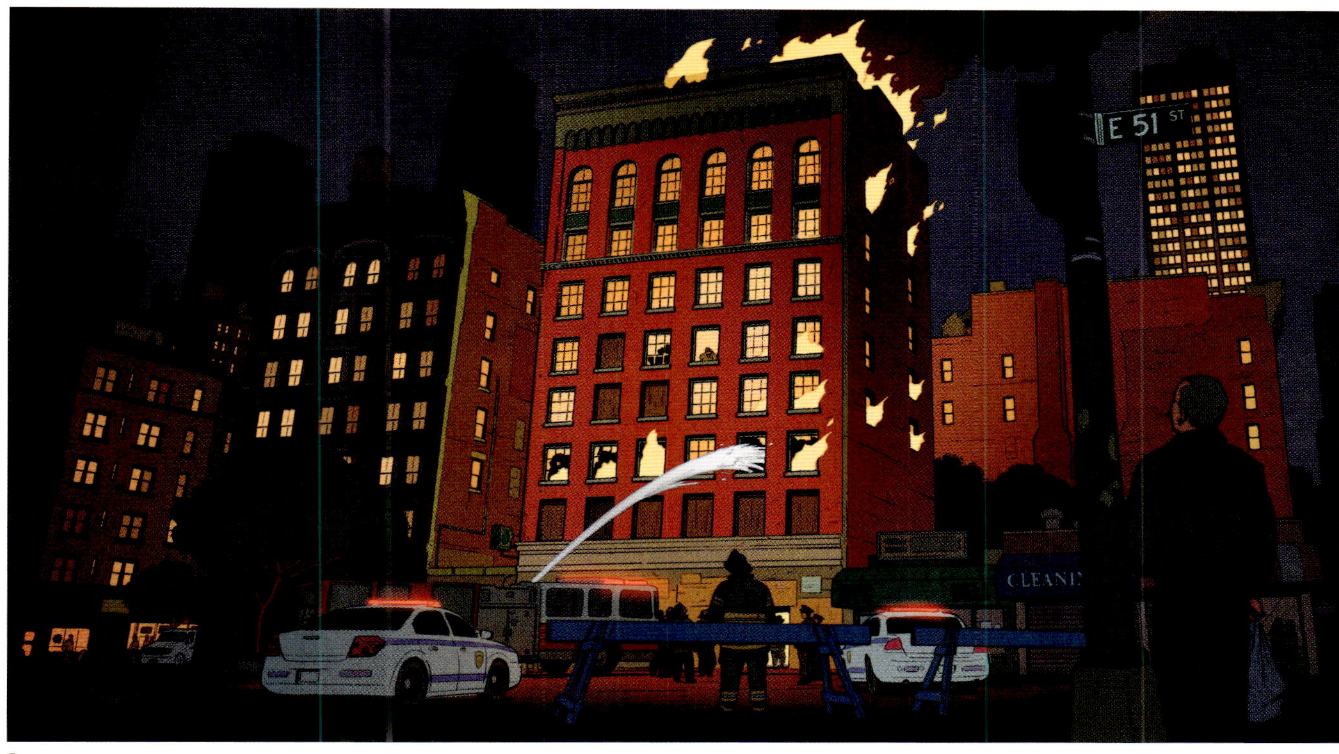

5

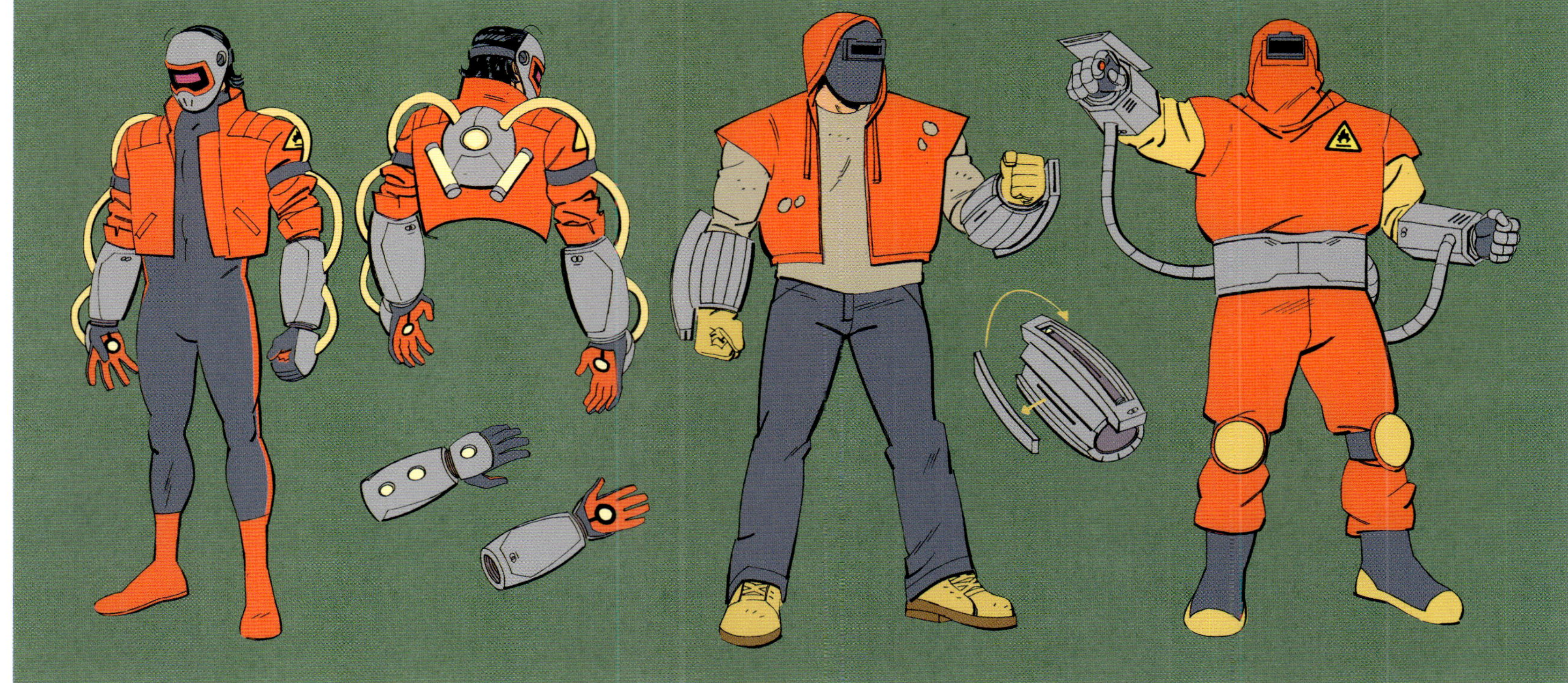

6

1 Leonardo Romero
2 Corwin Herse-Woo
3 Paolo Rivera (line art) and Michael Yamada (color) 4 Victor Calleja
5 Paolo Rivera (line art) and Michael Yamada (color) 6 Tom Reilly

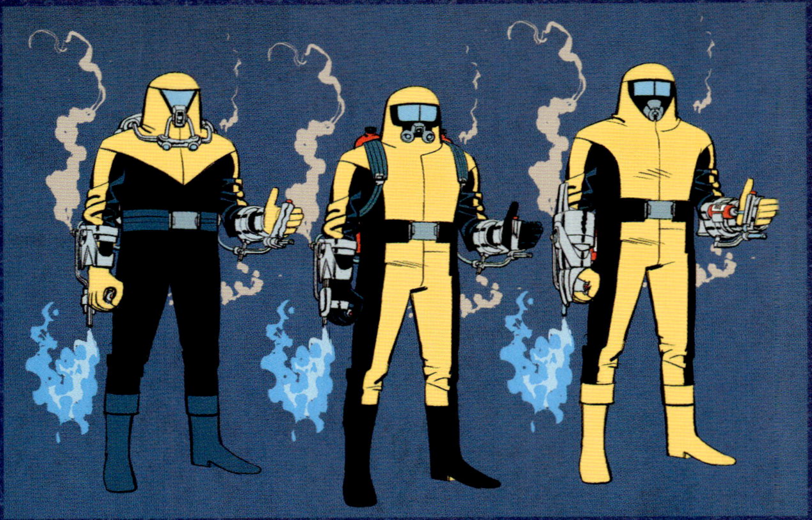

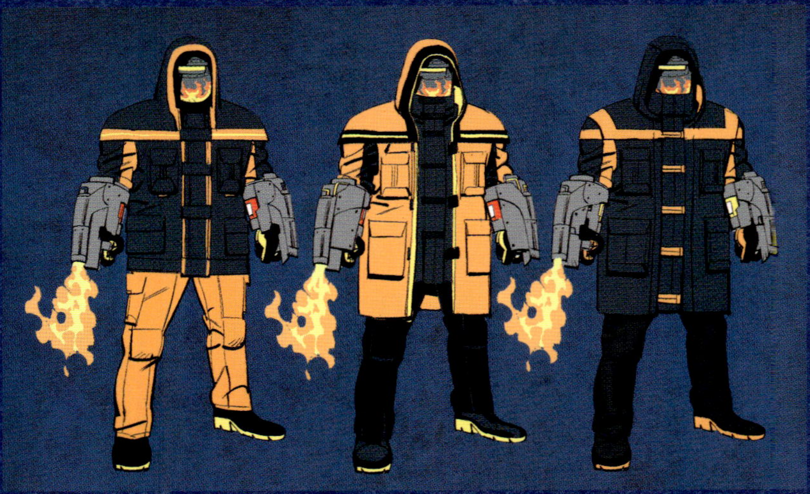

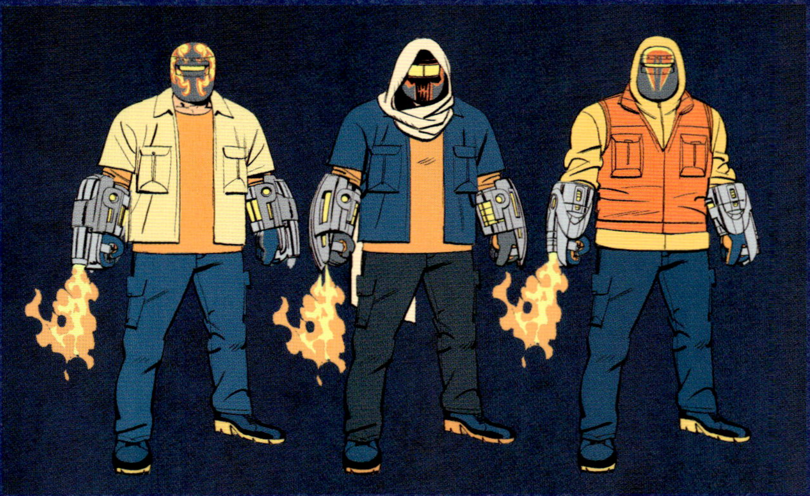

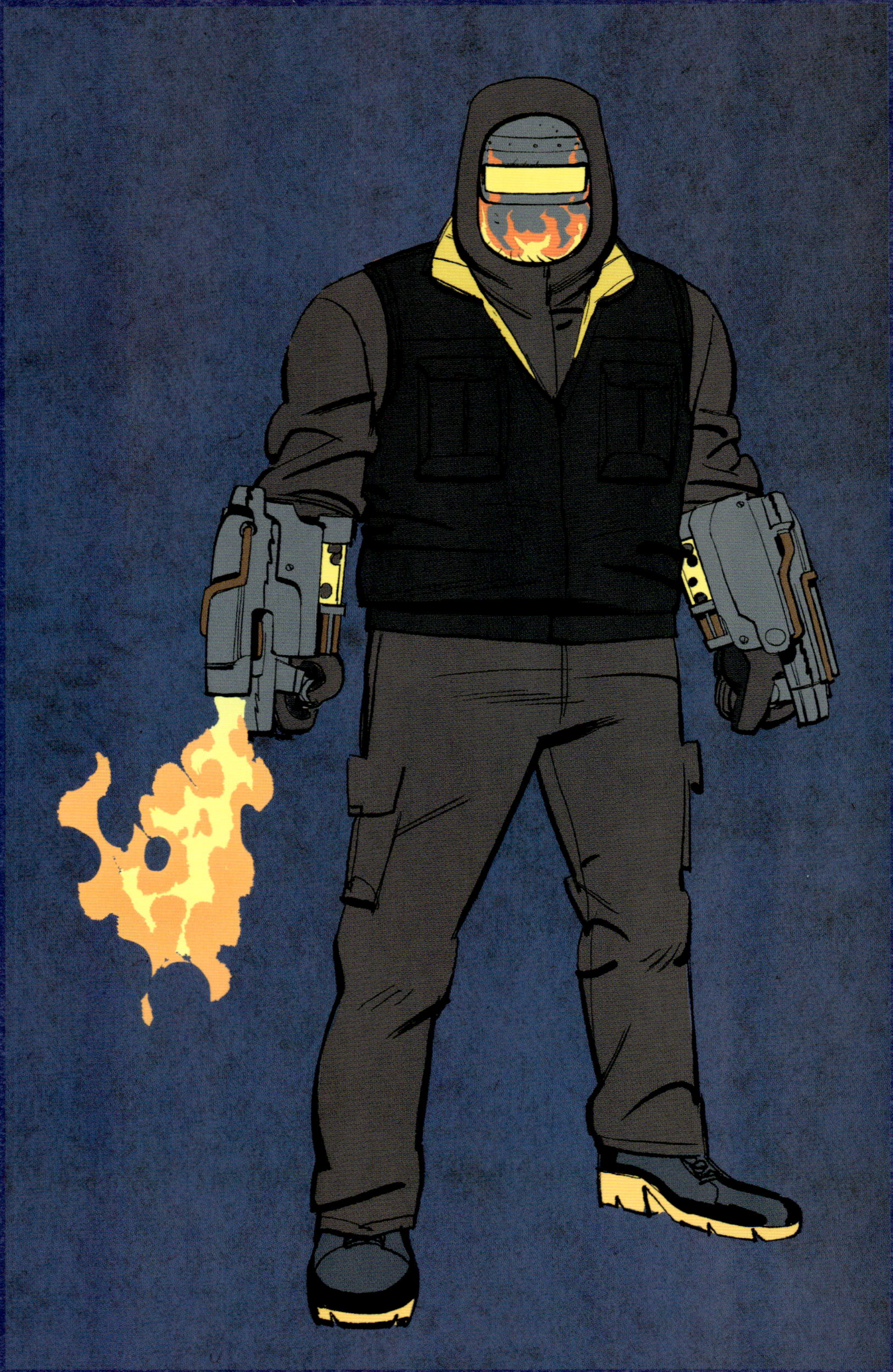

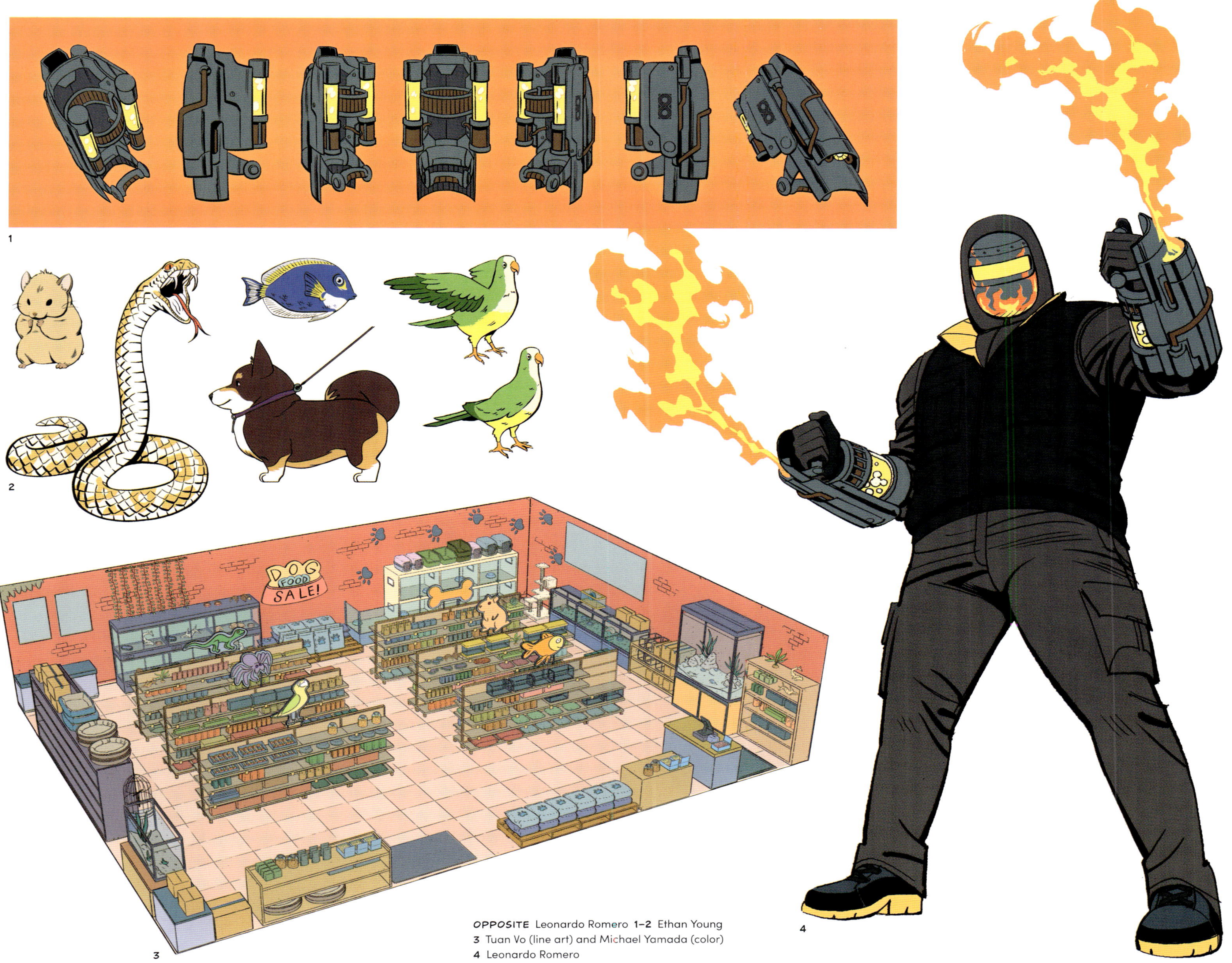

OPPOSITE Leonardo Romero **1–2** Ethan Young
3 Tuan Vo (line art) and Michael Yamada (color)
4 Leonardo Romero

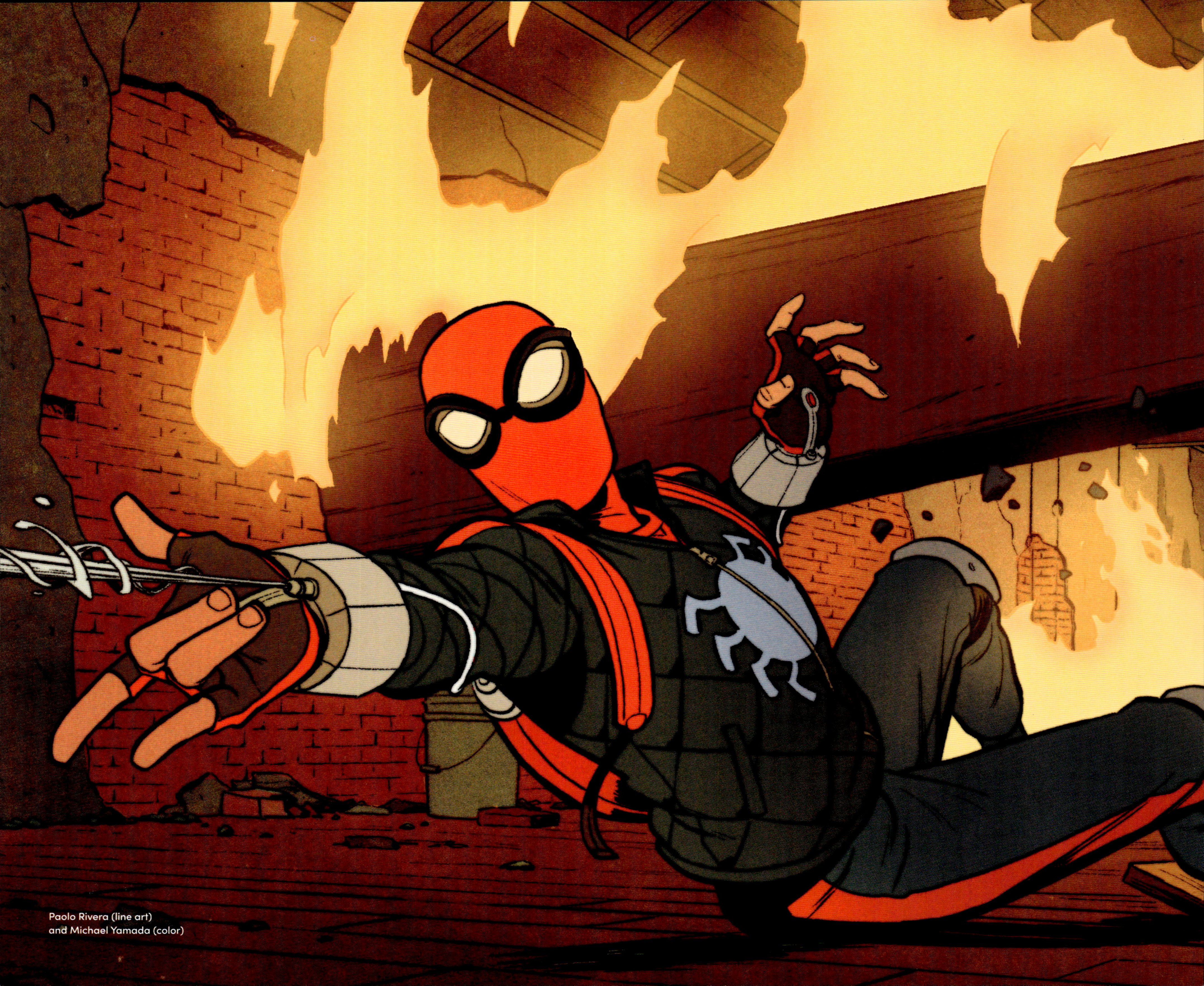

Paolo Rivera (line art)
and Michael Yamada (color)

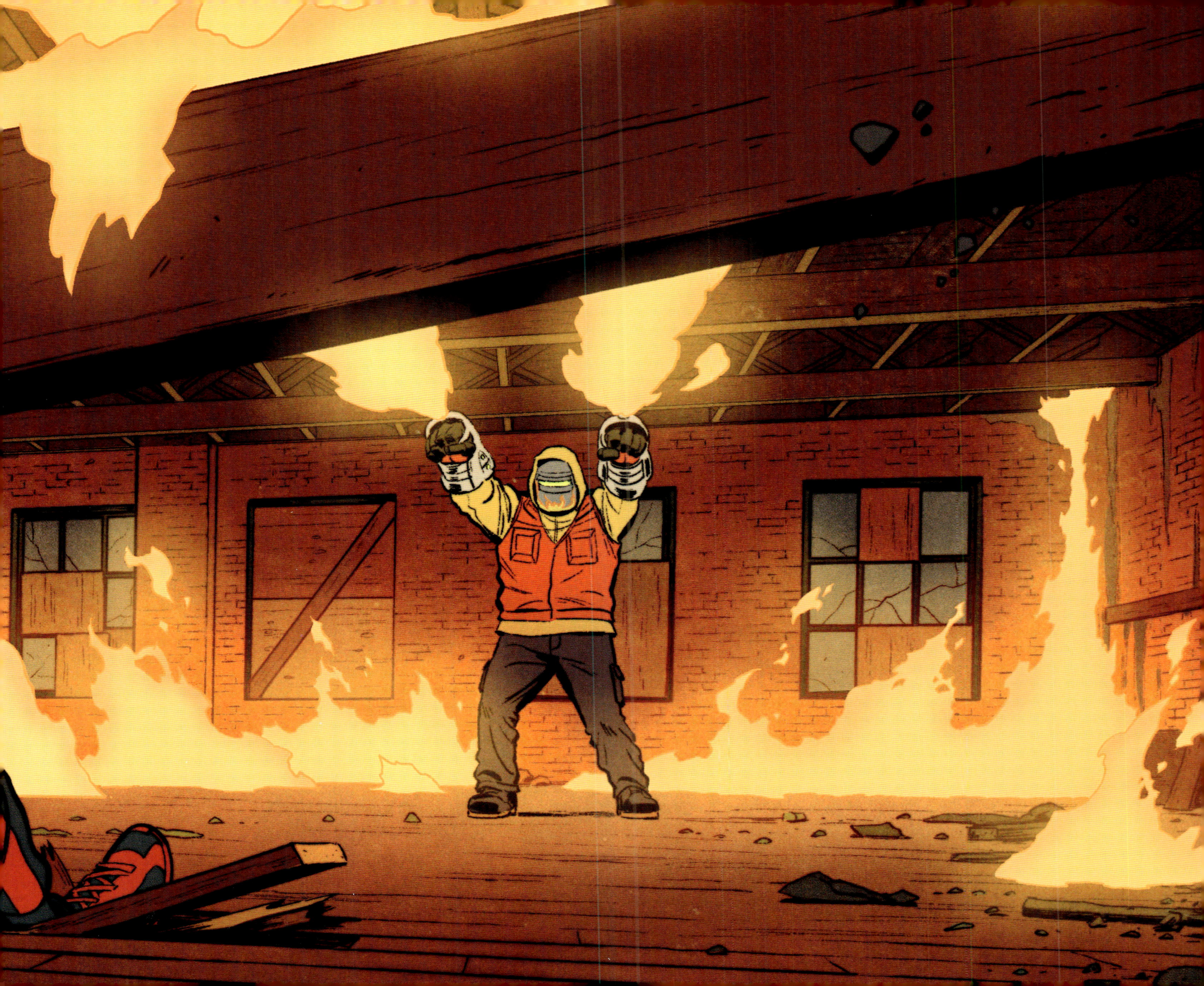

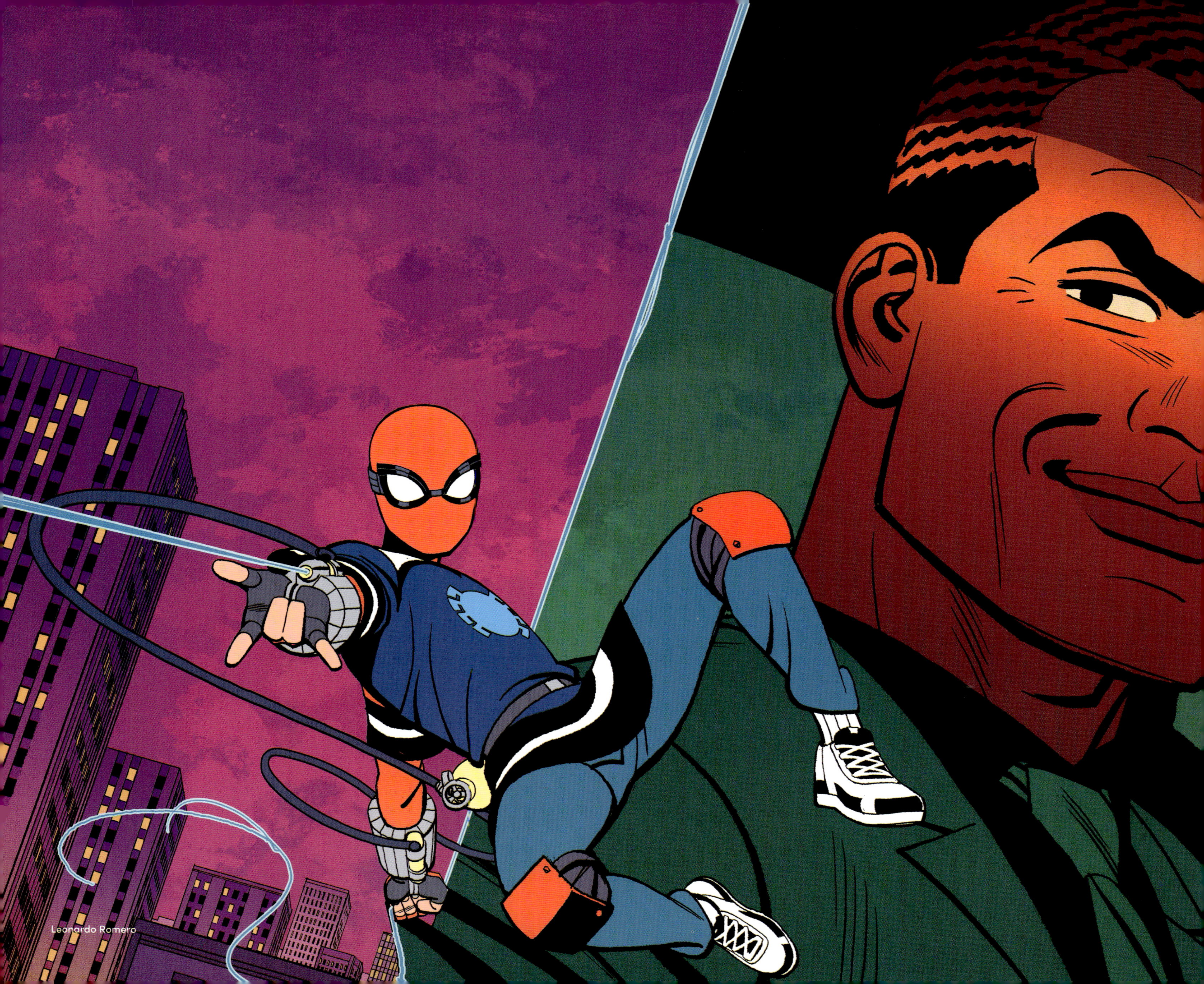
Leonardo Romero

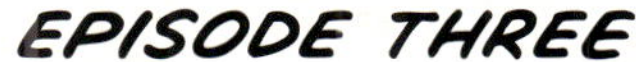

EPISODE THREE

SECRET IDENTITY CRISIS

THE PETER/NORMAN POWER DYNAMIC GETS MORE COMPLICATED AS NORMAN REVEALS HE BECAME INTERESTED IN DISCOVERING SPIDER-MAN'S IDENTITY AFTER THE RESCUE OF HIS SON, HARRY. IN THE THIRD EPISODE OF THE SHOW, PETER INITIALLY TURNS DOWN NORMAN'S OFFER OF PARTNERSHIP BUT CONTINUES HIS INTERNSHIP TO HELP AUNT MAY WITH HER BILLS. MEANWHILE, LONNIE LINCOLN'S YOUNGER BROTHER, ANDRE, HAS JOINED THE 110TH STREET GANG. LONNIE GOES TO THEIR HEADQUARTERS TO CHANGE ANDRE'S MIND AND IS ULTIMATELY FORCED TO JOIN THE GANG HIMSELF IN HIS BROTHER'S PLACE BY THEIR LEADER, BIG DONOVAN. THIS EPISODE ALSO INTRODUCES THE PETTY CRIMINALS MARIA VASQUEZ AND JAMES SANDERS, WHO ROB A JEWELRY STORE WITH THE AID OF SOME NIFTY HIGH-TECH GLOVES AND BOOTS, COURTESY OF A MYSTERIOUS BENEFACTOR.

"WE'RE OFF TO THE RACES HERE," says Executive Producer/Showrunner Jeff Trammell. "We get to meet James and Maria and realize what Peter can and can't do when he doesn't have someone watching his back. We also want the audience to begin questioning whether Norman has some sort of ulterior motive. There's also the fact that Peter *did* save Norman's son's life, so we feel like, of course, he wouldn't want to hurt the one who came to his son's aid."

The episode also takes viewers deeper into Lonnie's home life. "Lonnie is put in a position that we all know is not going to end well for him," says Trammell. "It's a big episode about partnerships, and we're seeing both Peter and Lonnie make decisions that will lead them down roads that may not pan out in the best possible way. There's also a bit of hopefulness for Peter as he begins his partnership with Norman Osborn. We get to see Norman's process to help Peter become a better Spider-Man."

"Secret Identity Crisis" director Stu Livingston says he was especially pleased with the street fight in the episode. "The mechanics of Spider-Man laying out the giant trip wire that makes James trip over and collide into Maria wasn't really developed on the page, so I came up with those details," he recalls. "That was an idea that I shaped in the storyboard, and it made it to the final stage almost one-for-one. I was just making things up, and Jeff went for it. The toughest part of the episode was coordinating all the moving parts of that big fight. You have all these characters involved, and Spider-Man's over there in the middle of the action, so the trick is to make everything work technically but also feel very, very exciting. I think that was how I got my action chops on a CG-animated show for the first time."

Livingston goes on to mention that he also enjoyed the dynamic between bumbling villains Maria Vasquez and James Sanders in this episode. "They are this terribly toxic couple," he says with a laugh. "I think all of us on the show kind of missed them after this episode and hope they show up again in the future."

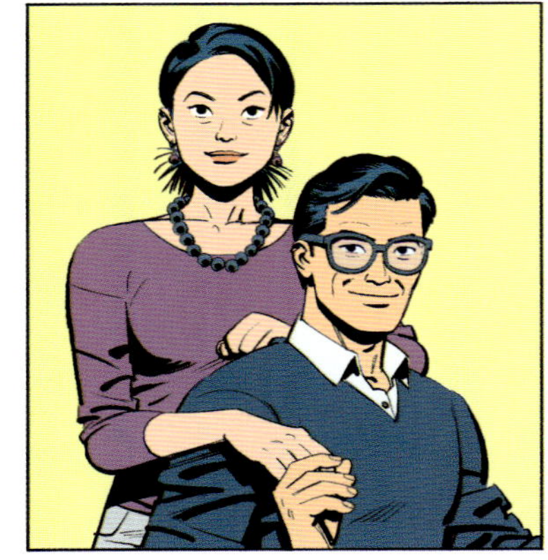

1

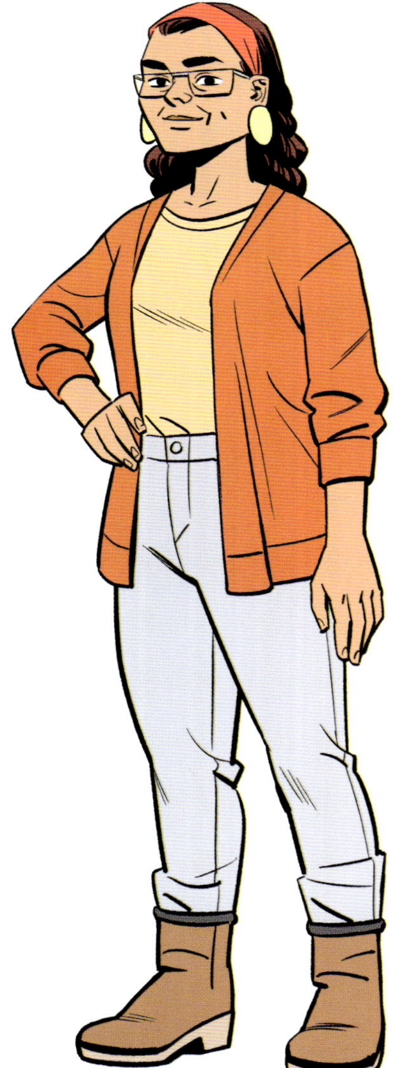

2

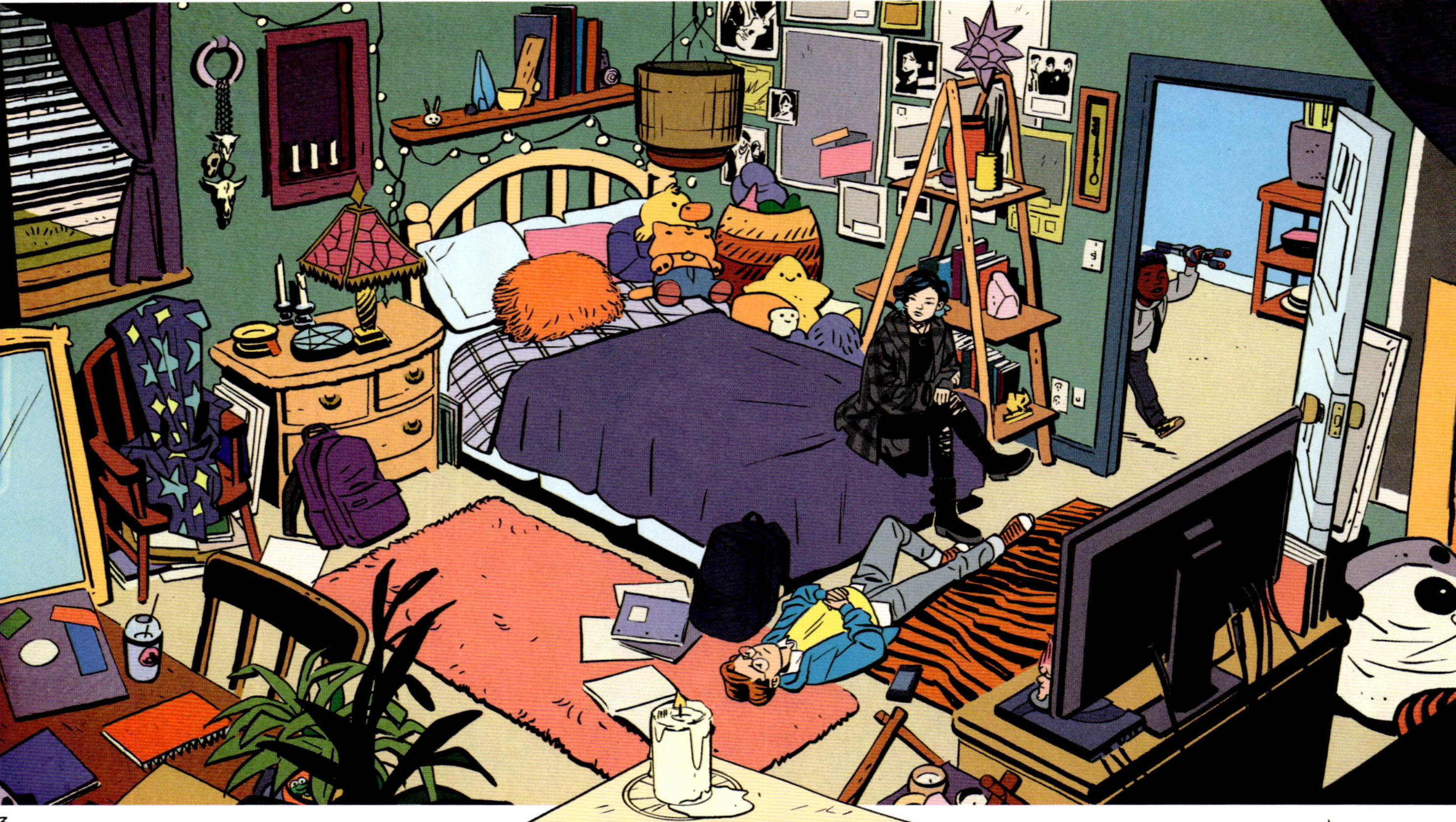

3

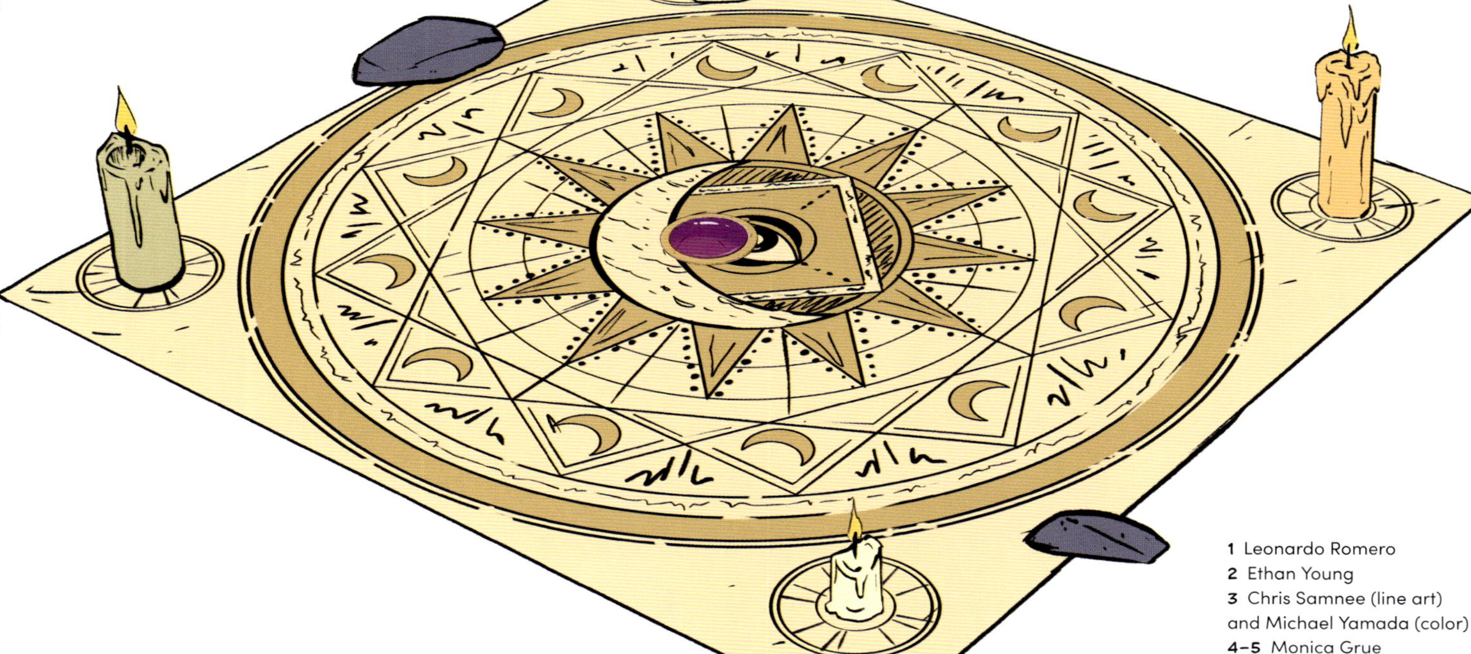

4

1 Leonardo Romero
2 Ethan Young
3 Chris Samnee (line art) and Michael Yamada (color)
4–5 Monica Grue
6 Paolo Rivera (line art) and Michael Yamada (color)

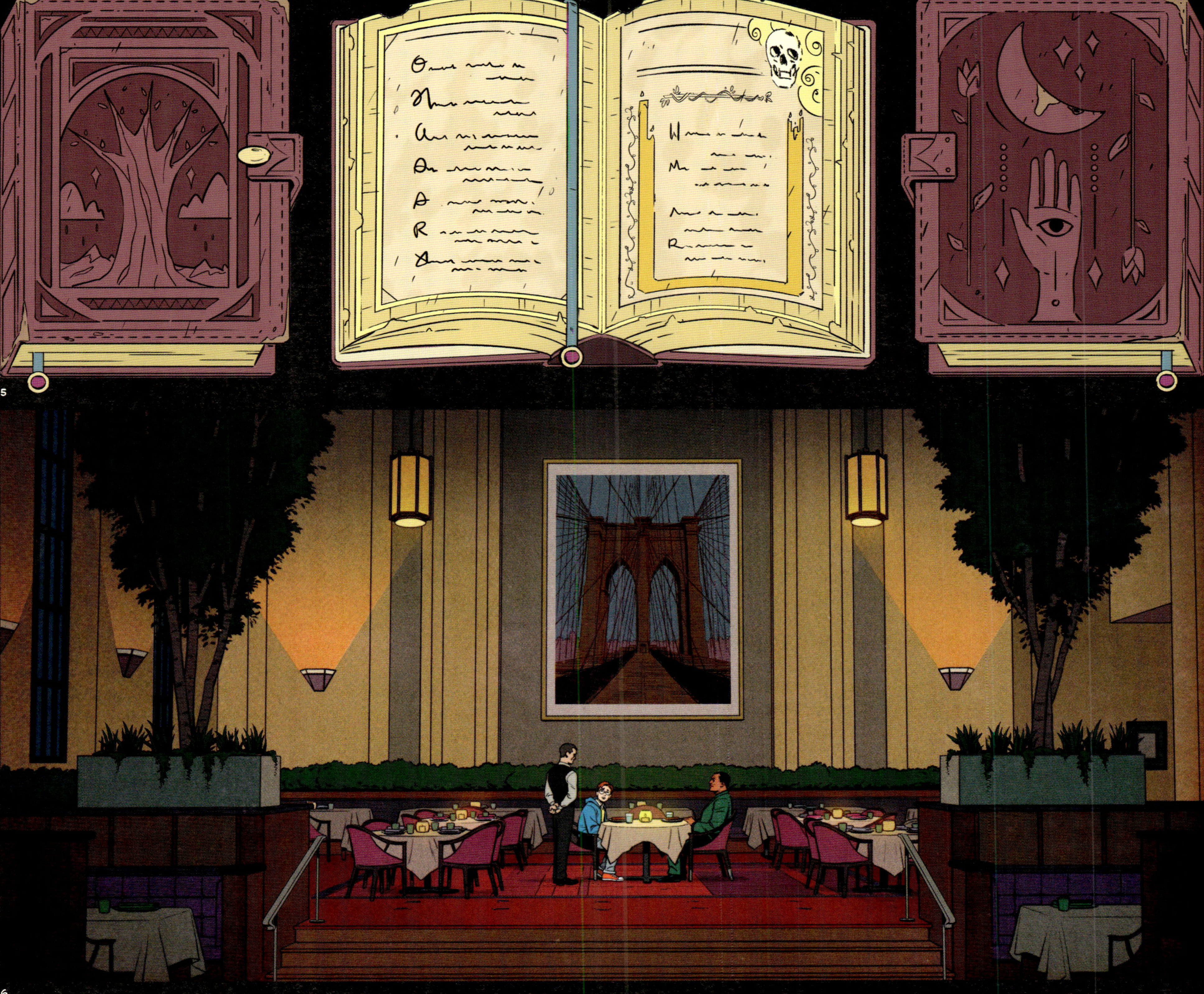

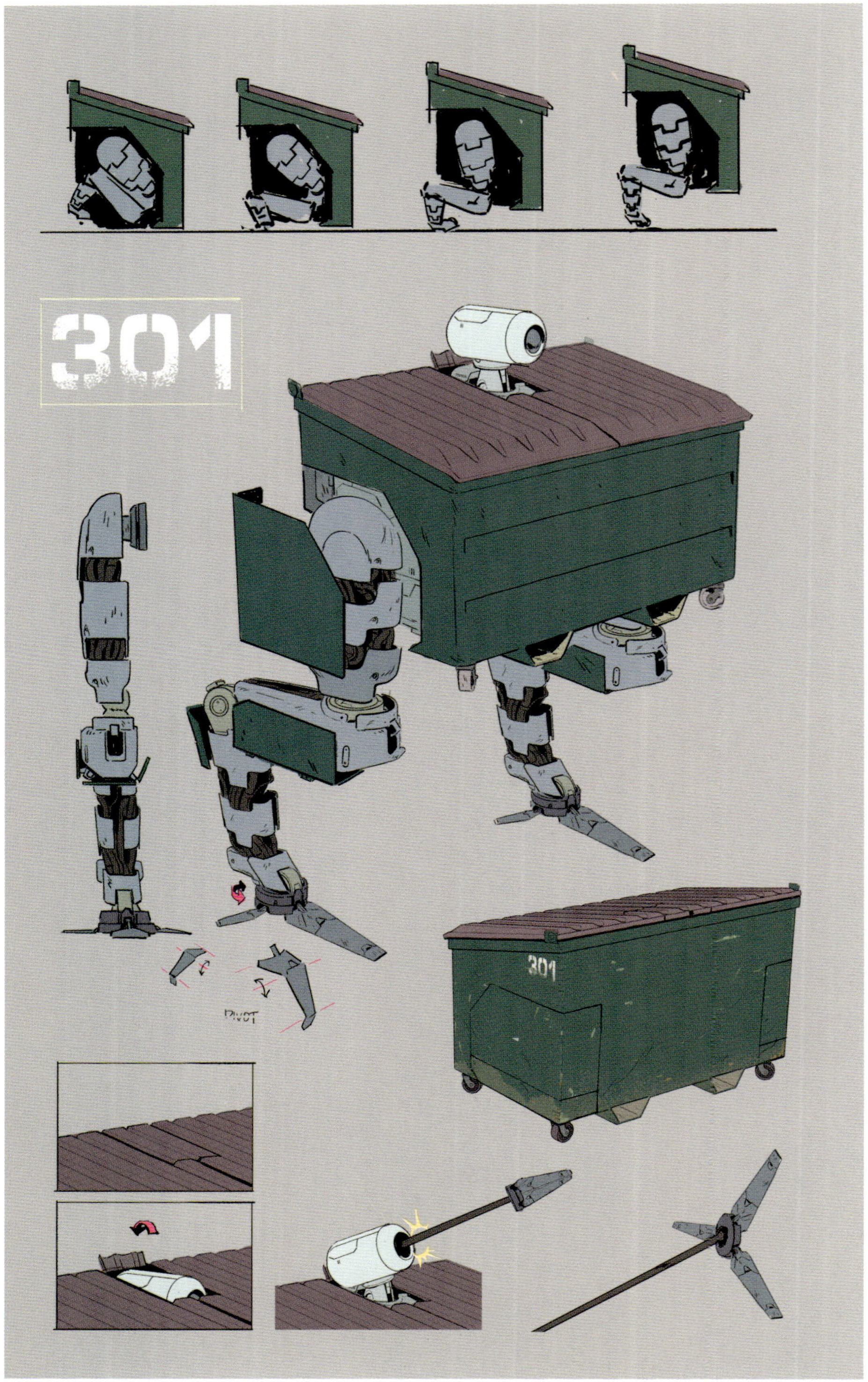

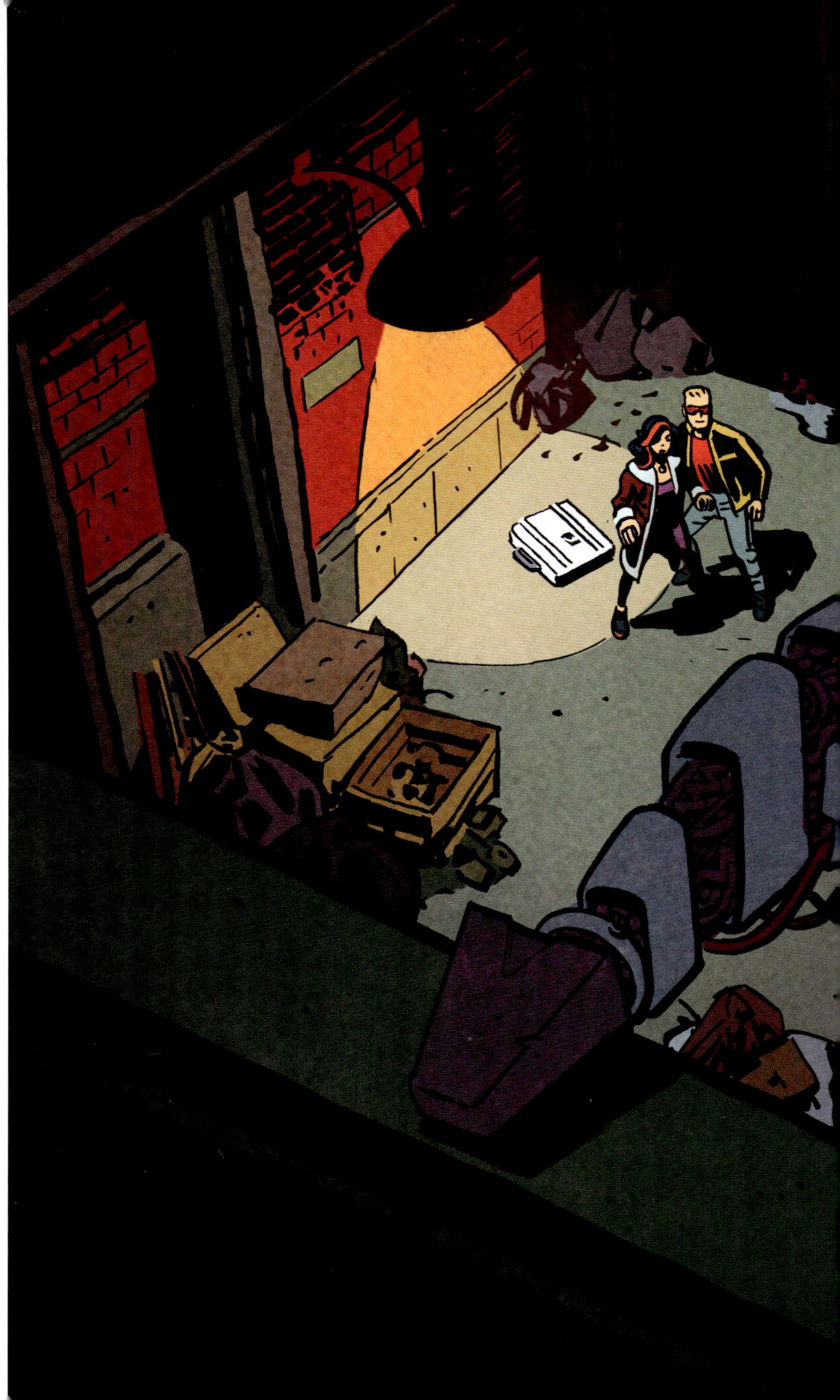

ABOVE Victor Calleja **RIGHT** Chris Samnee (line art) and Michael Yamada (color)

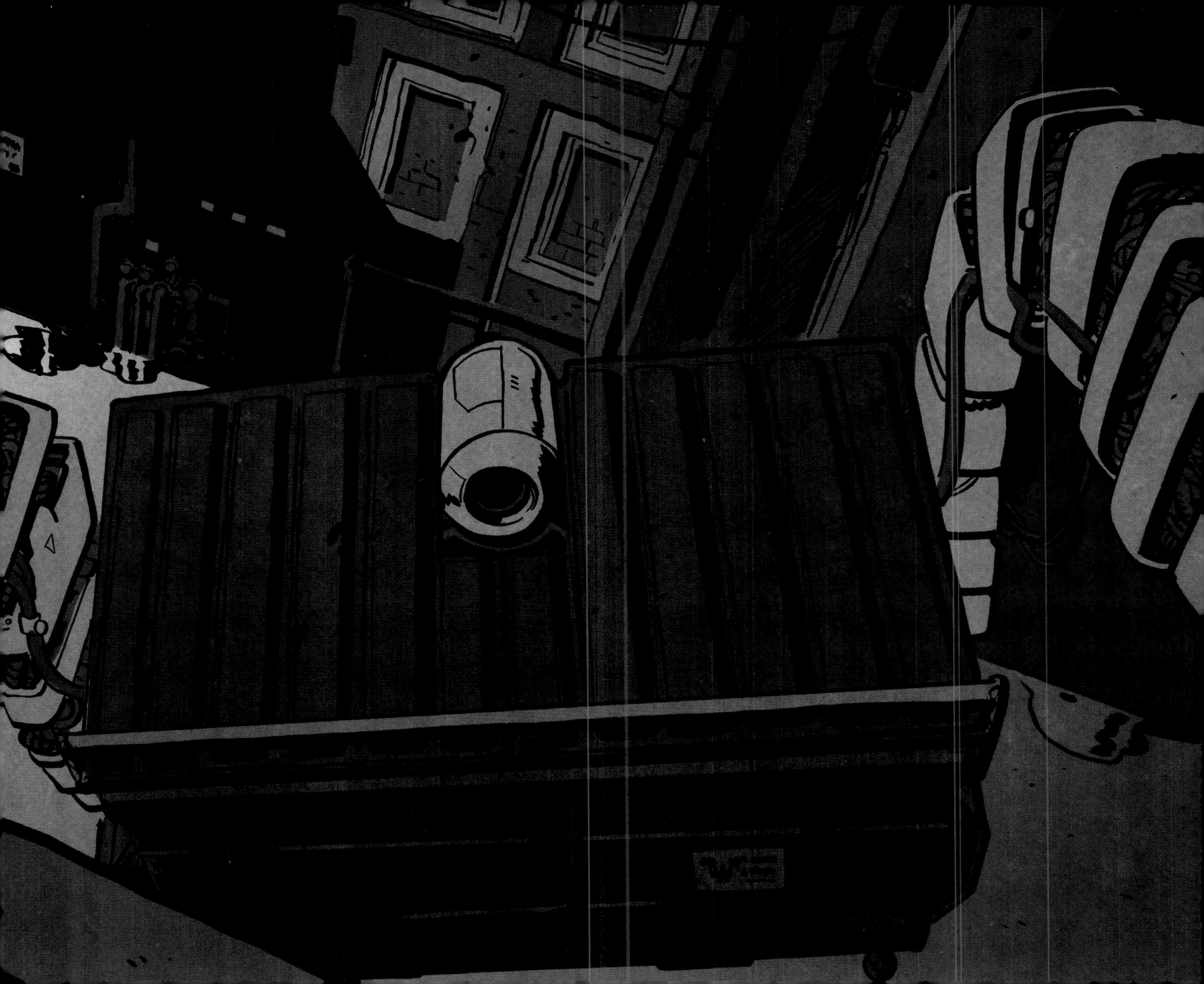

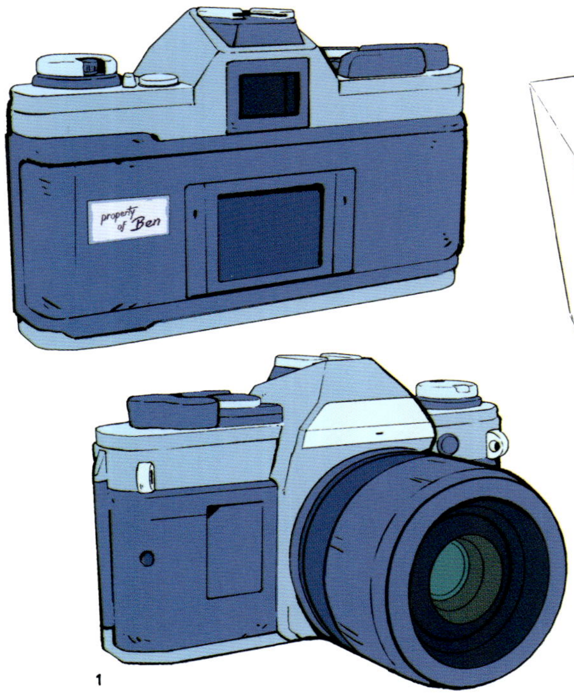

1

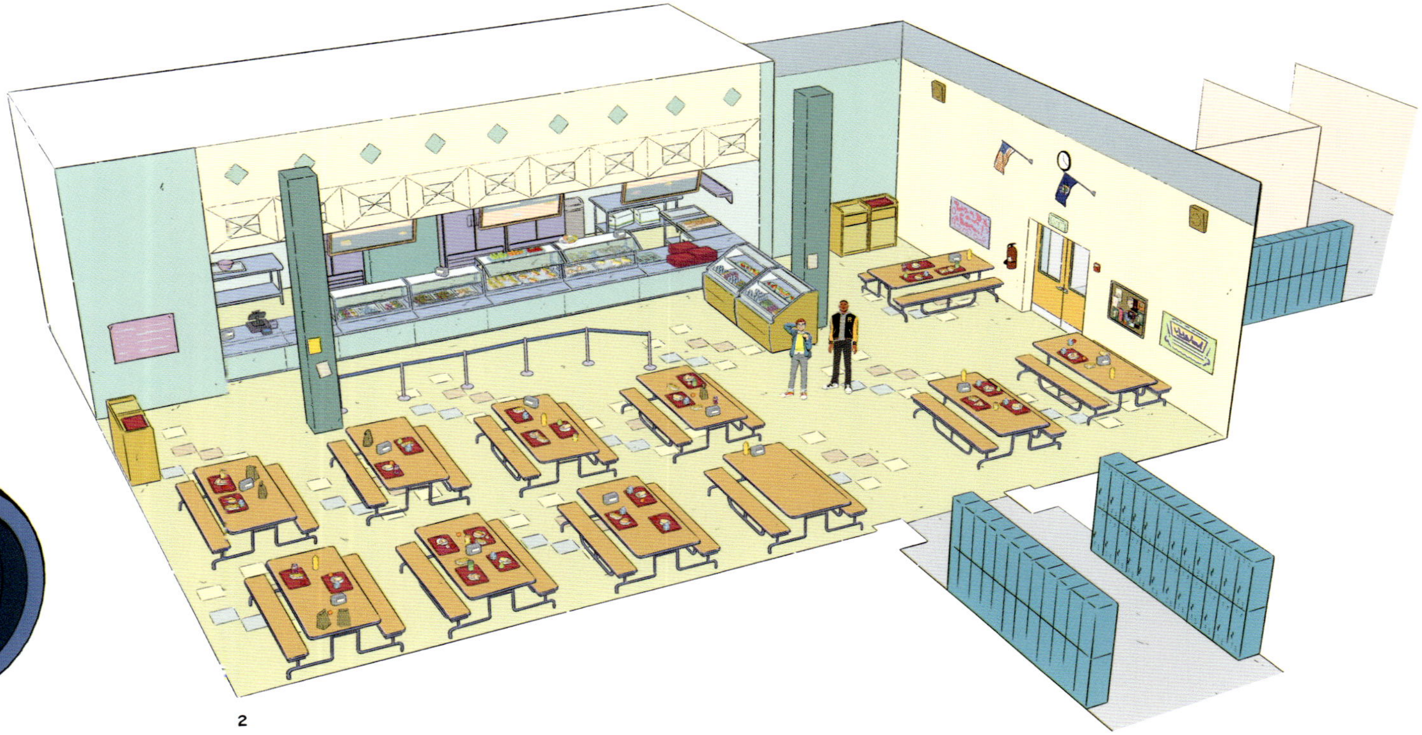

2

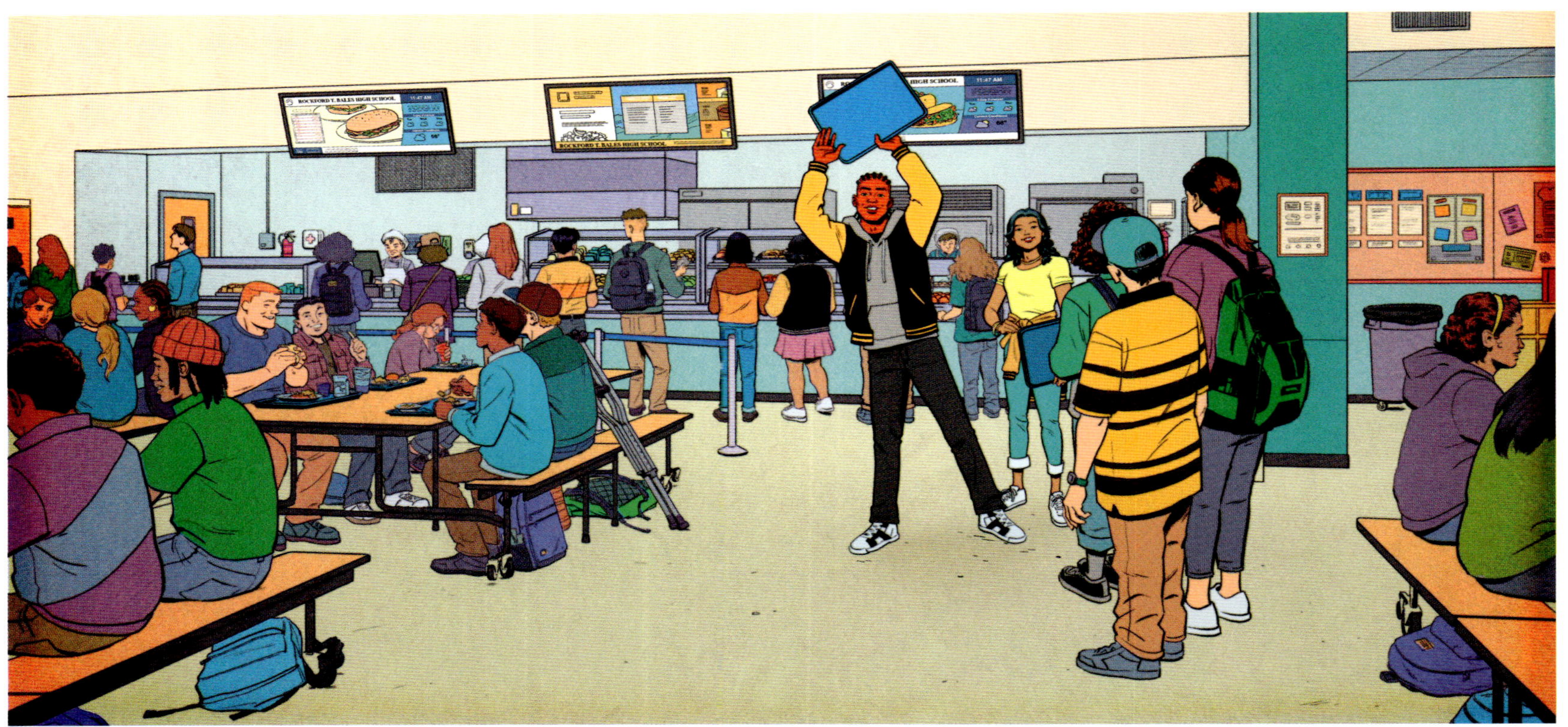

3

1 Victor Calleja 2 Tuan Vo
3 Paolo Rivera (line art) and Michael Yamada (color)
4 Leonardo Romero

LONNIE LINCOLN "TOMBSTONE"

Created by Gerry Conway and Alex Saviuk, Lonnie Lincoln made his debut in March 1988 in *Web of Spider-Man* and became a regular super villain in *The Spectacular Spider-Man*. The creators of *Your Friendly Neighborhood Spider-Man* put a new spin on the backstory of this complex character, voiced by Eugene Byrd.

Executive Producer/Showrunner Jeff Trammel says Lonnie is one of his favorite characters in the show. "It was really important to me that he wasn't a prototypical jock," he says. "We wanted him to be a good and kind person, and his journey was going to be very parallel to Peter's. I believe a lot of fans knew that Lonnie was going to become Tombstone, so it was important to show how his life was before he fell into a life of crime. I never wanted it to feel like he was a bad guy just for the sake of being bad. So, we see him change and get tested, just as we see Peter grow and make important decisions. Lonnie gets the chance to do the same things, although they take different roads, and we see their paths intertwine."

Lonnie also happens to be Brad Winderbaum's favorite character. "He has the most dynamic arc," says the executive producer. "If you've read the comics, you know that he's destined for tragedy, and because he is a good person, he has empathy and tries to make the right decisions. His tragedy is the fact that fate works against him, and that plays on your hopes and fears. You know from the mythology that he's going to become Tombstone sooner or later. You see that in the design of the character too. We don't just jump into the different versions of Tombstone in the comics or the 1990s animated series. We are choosing to show a more protracted version of his look."

When Lead Character Designer Leonardo Romero first started working on Lonnie, he wasn't aware the character was going to evolve throughout the first season. "The look was very different in the beginning," he recalls. "We didn't know about the story, so we were going by the comic book references. We thought he was just going to be a bad guy, so that's how I started to draw him, as just a jock or a villain. Then we got the notes that he doesn't start out as a bad guy, so I began to envision him as a good-hearted, kind character. I believe you won't really see the full evolution of his look until the next season."

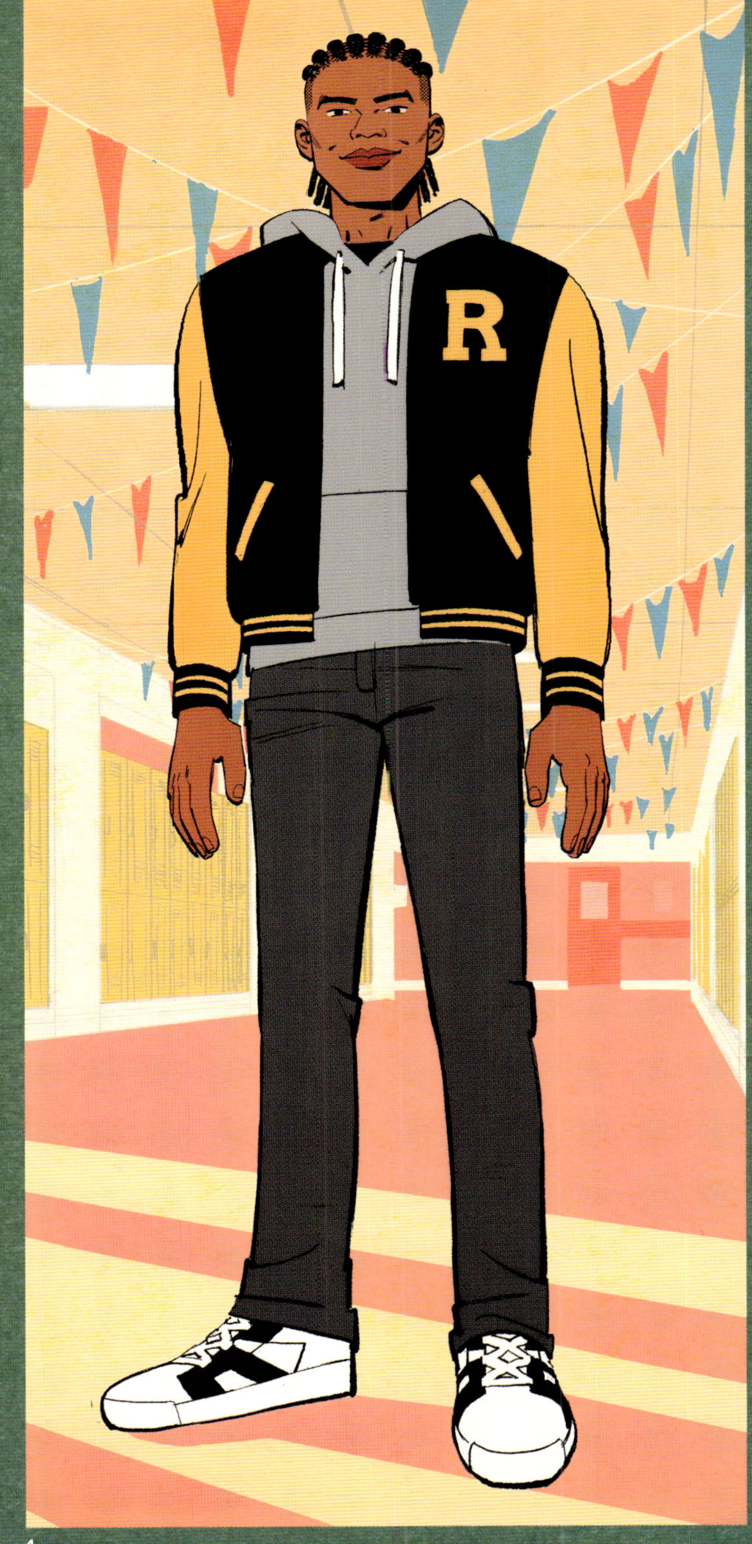

4

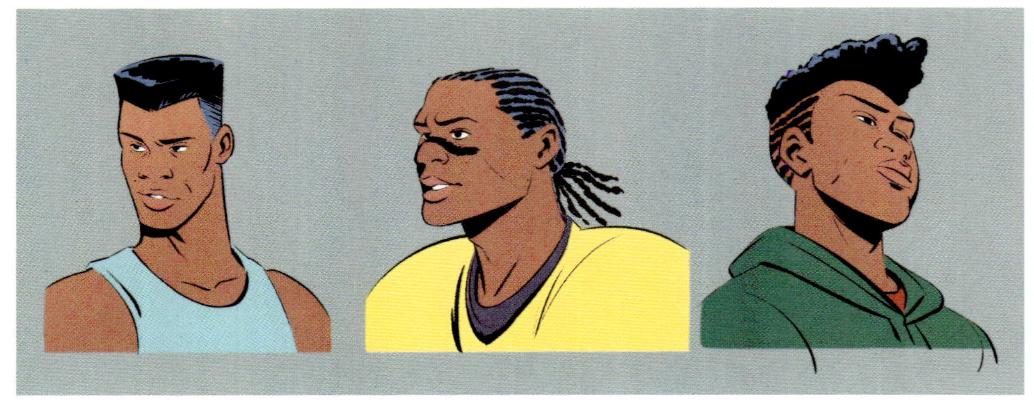

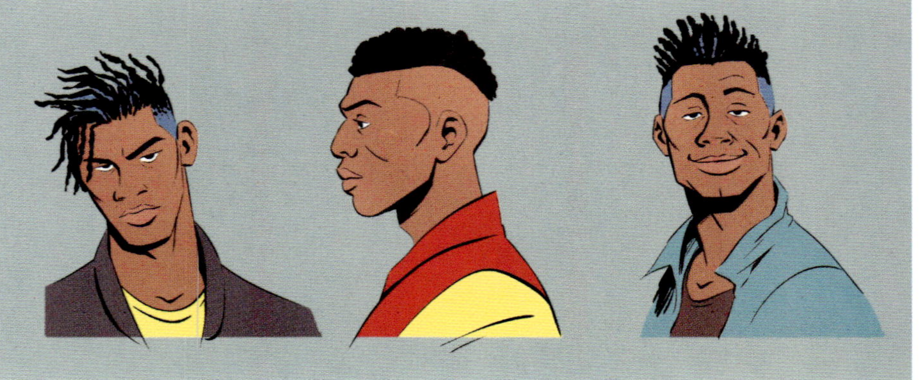

1

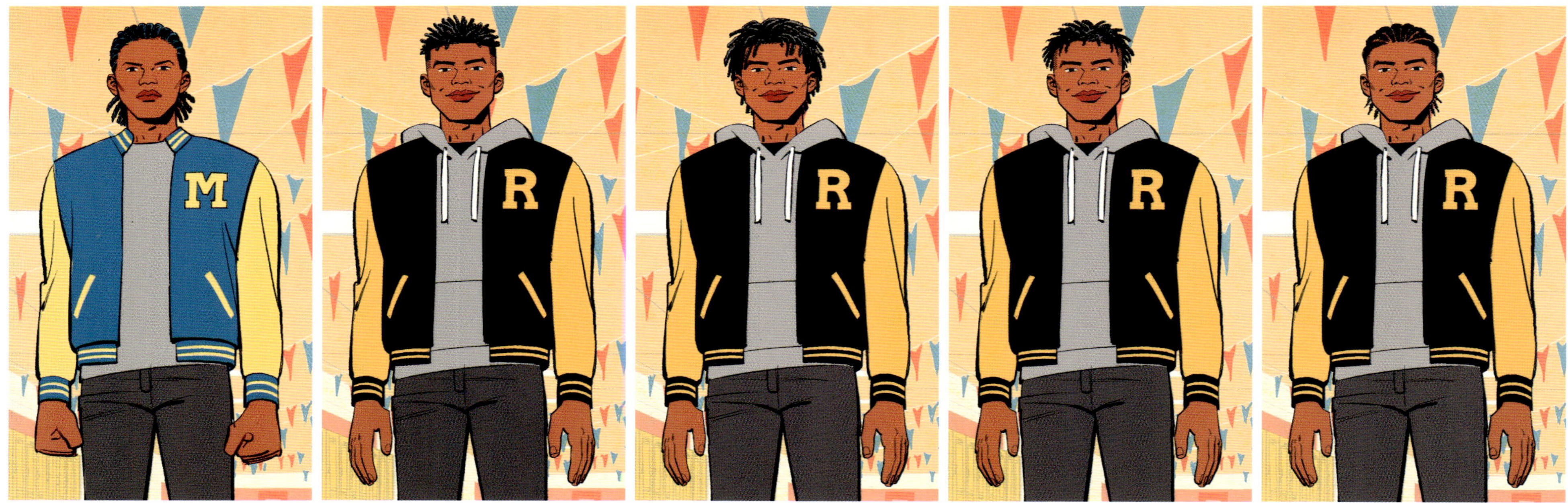

2

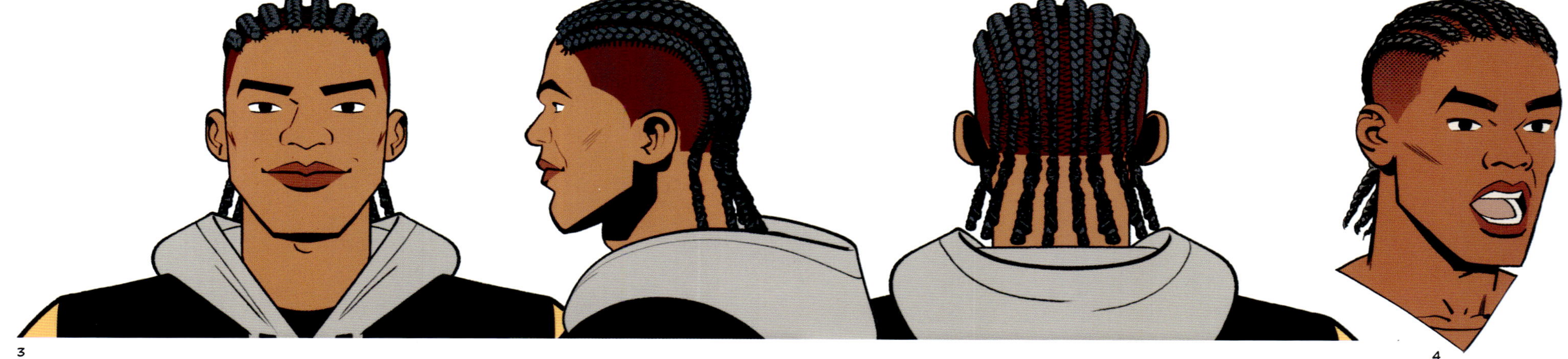

3

4

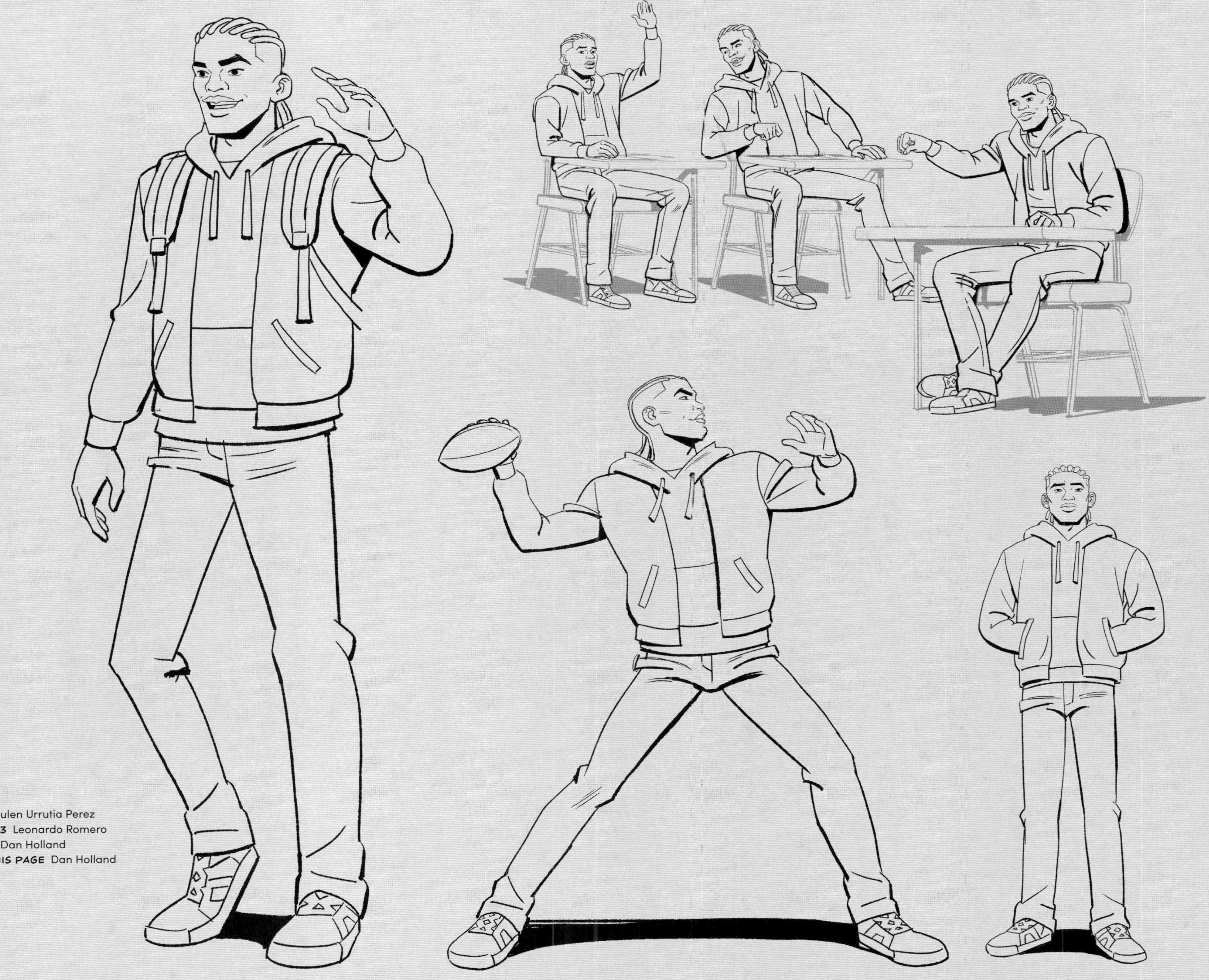

1 Julen Urrutia Perez
2–3 Leonardo Romero
4 Dan Holland
THIS PAGE Dan Holland

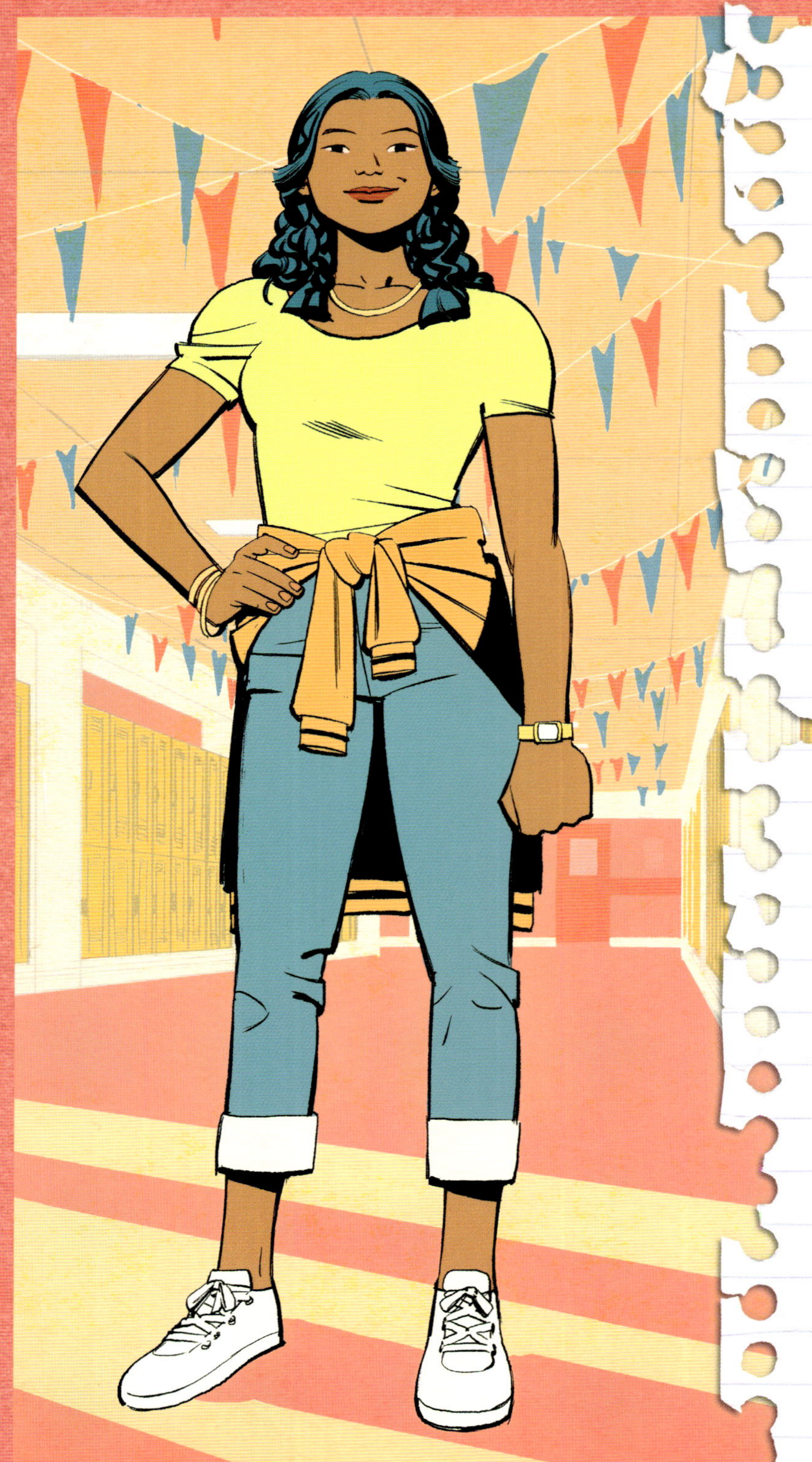

PEARL PANGAN

The object of Peter Parker's crush in the series, Pearl Pangan is three years older than him and used to babysit him when he was younger. Voiced by Cathy Ang, she's Lonnie's girlfriend who must make some tough decisions when he falls in with the wrong crowd. In the Marvel comics, Pearl is also known as Wave, a Filipina member of the Agents of Atlas who has hydrokinetic powers.

Executive Producer/Showrunner Jeff Trammell is a huge fan of the character in the comic books, so he thought it would be a fun way to bring her to Spidey's neighborhood. "One of my goals for the show was to make sure it's a good representation of modern New York City," he says. "I wanted a real melting pot with different races and creeds; I thought this would be a prime place to include a character like Pearl. We decided to bring her in as an upperclassman who has a history with Peter and Lonnie. I think it was the right spot for her to help [fill out our world]. What I like about her is that she's kind and bubbly and reminds me a bit of Aunt May. She is very likable, and I think that's one of the reasons Peter has also taken a liking to her. She's also very smart and patient. One thing that we'll get to explore is that there's a bit of a veil around who Pearl is. She's doing her best to help everyone, but sometimes, she fails to take care of herself. I look forward to hopefully revealing more about her in the future."

Lead Character Designer Leonardo Romero says he wasn't familiar with the character's alternative history in the comic books, but he did his research. "I took a look at the comic books that featured her as Wave just to gain some insights into her physical description," he says. "Initially, I imagined she was smaller, skinny, and around Peter's age. But as the descriptions for the character evolved, the design changed as well. Now she is older than Peter and has a very athletic body because she's a swimmer."

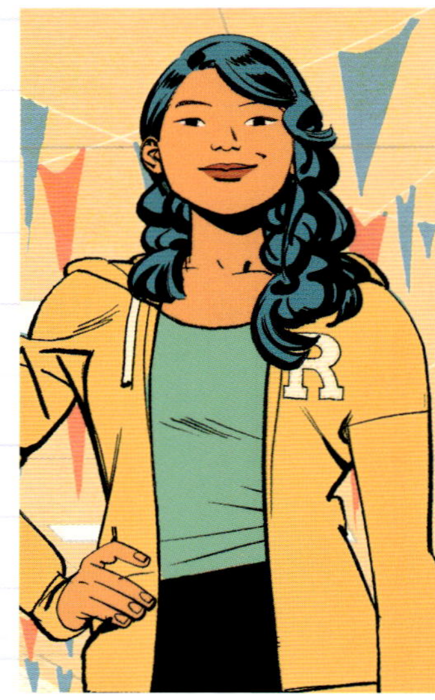

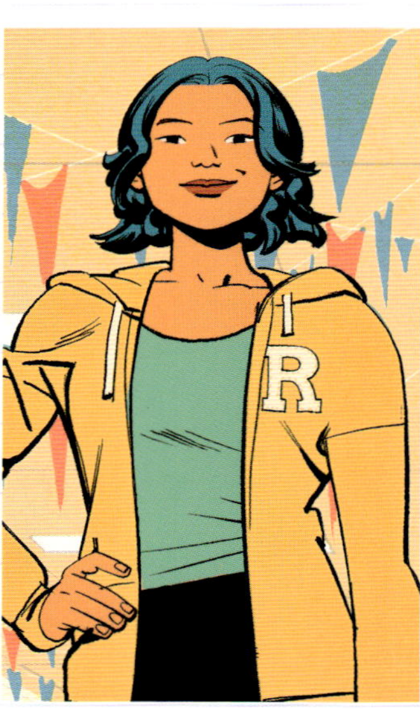

THIS PAGE Leonardo Romero
1 Paolo Rivera **2** Mauricio Leone
3–5 Joneale Emmanuel

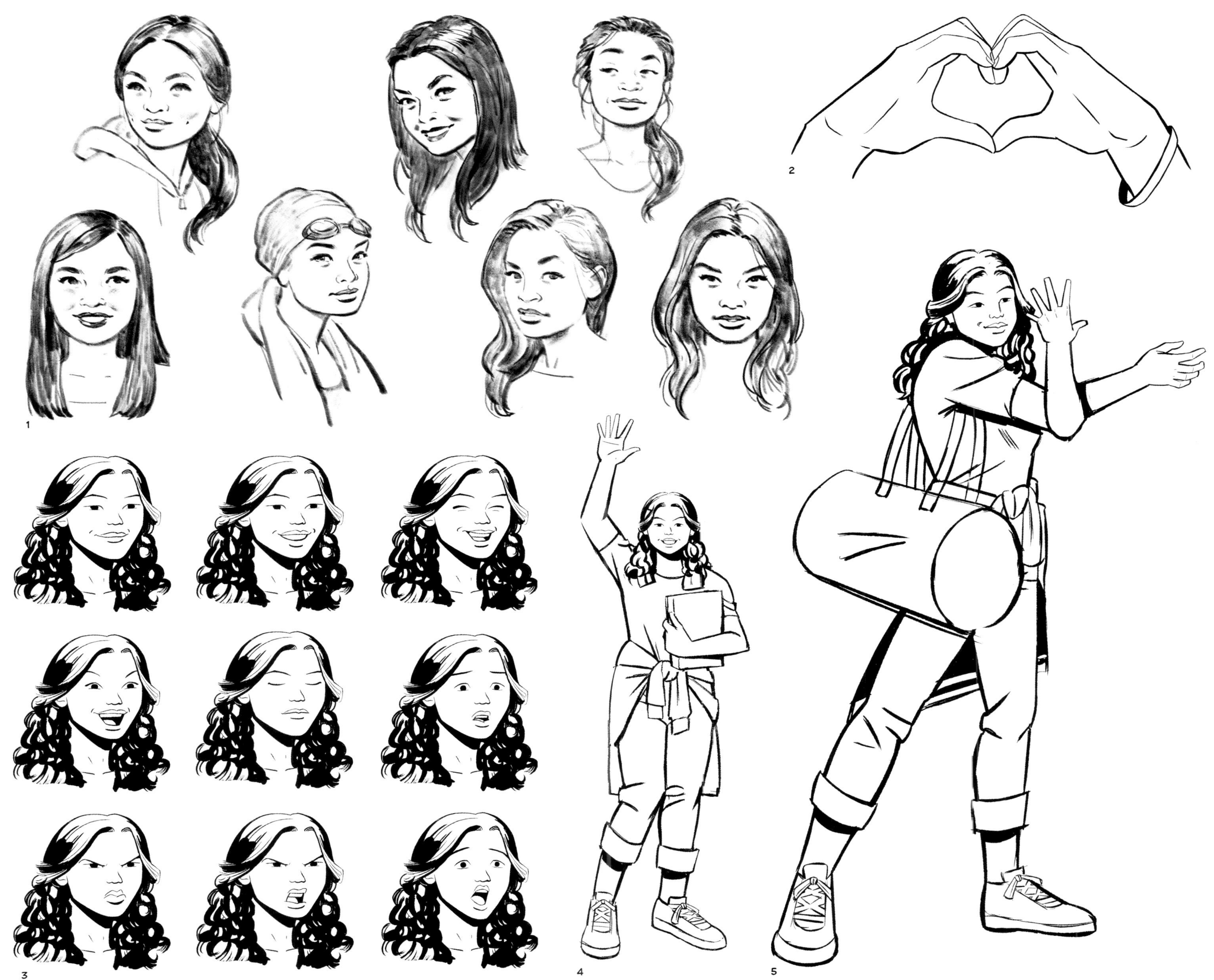

1
2
3
4
5

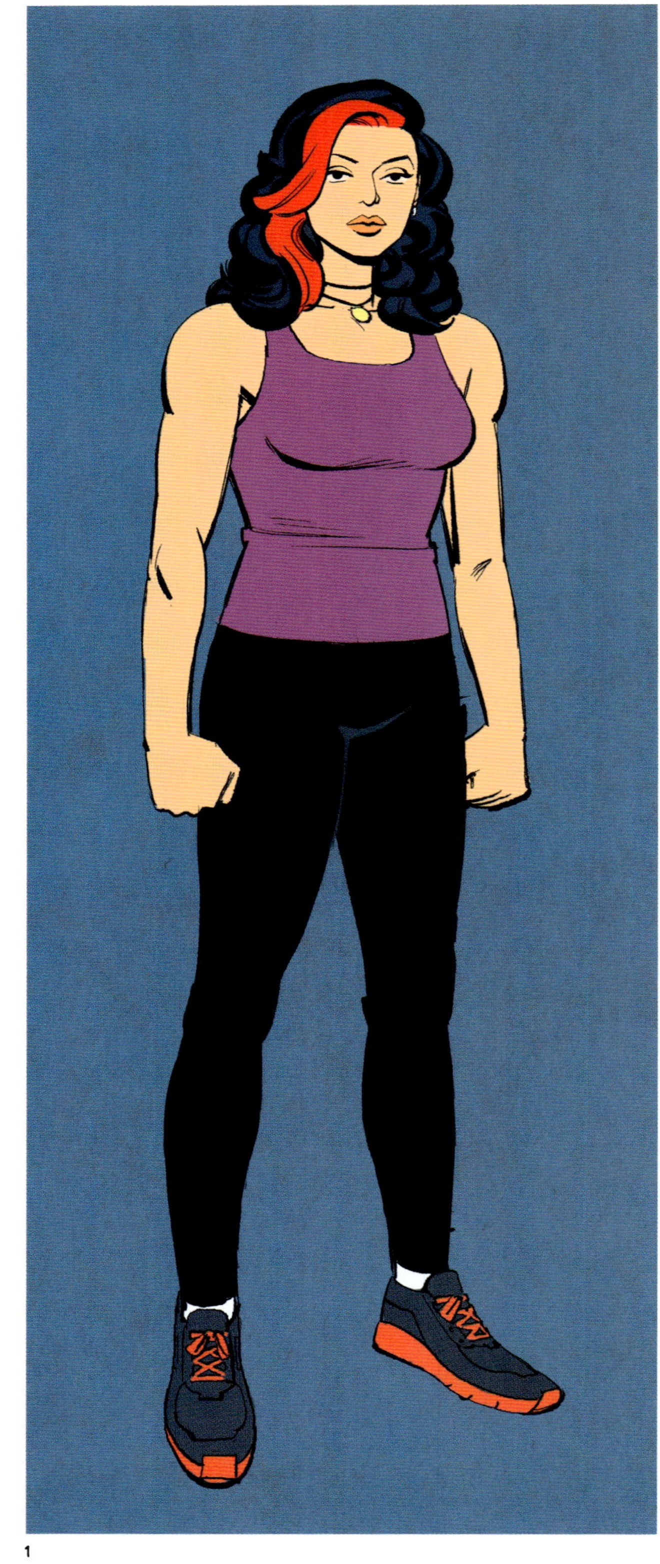

1

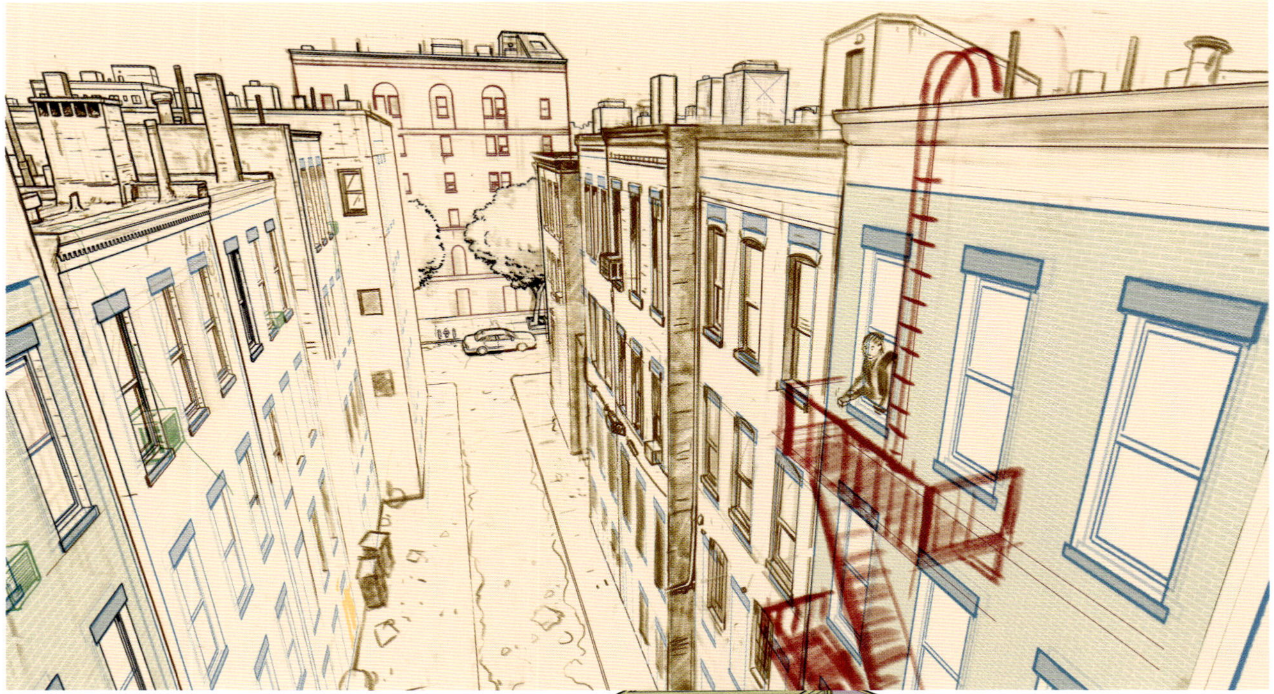

2

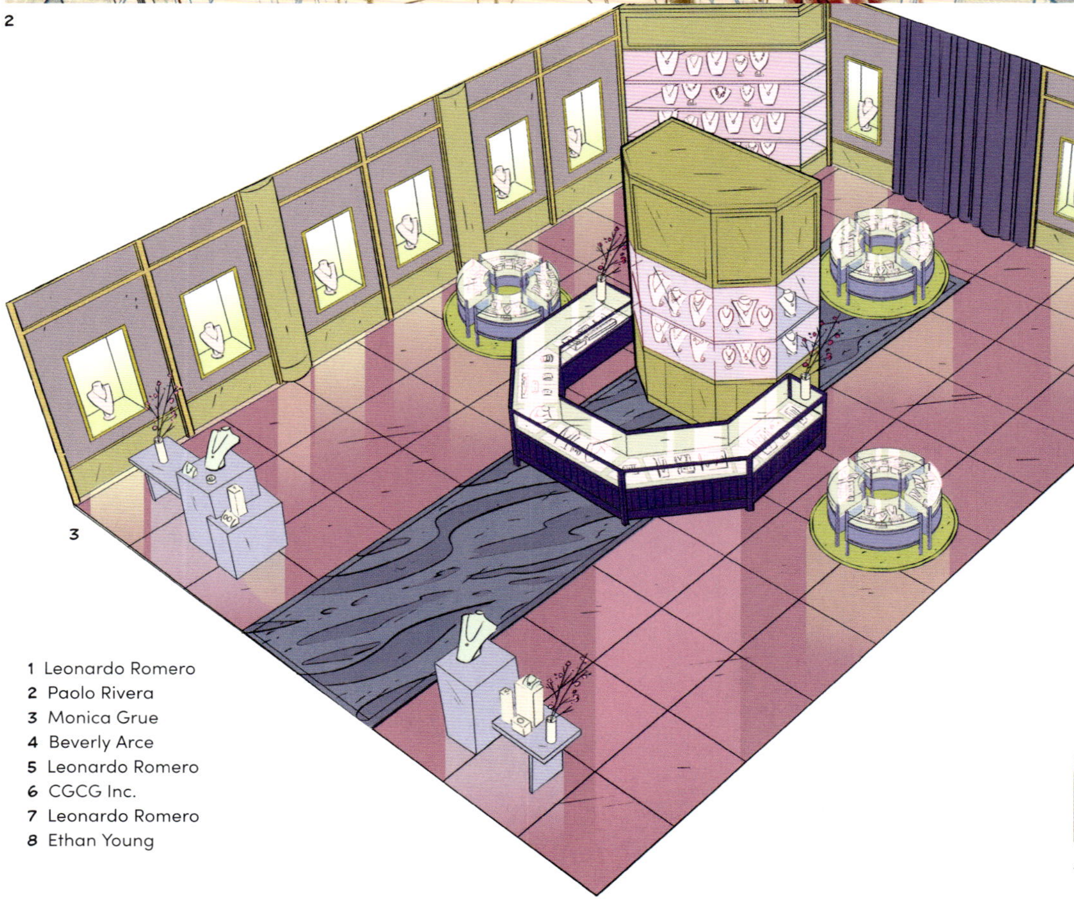

3

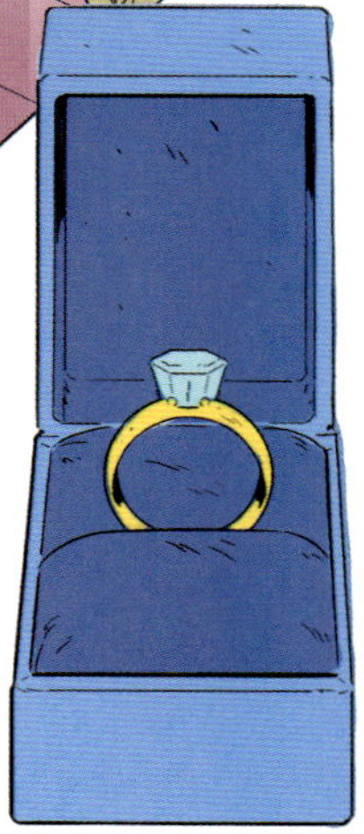

4

1 Leonardo Romero
2 Paolo Rivera
3 Monica Grue
4 Beverly Arce
5 Leonardo Romero
6 CGCG Inc.
7 Leonardo Romero
8 Ethan Young

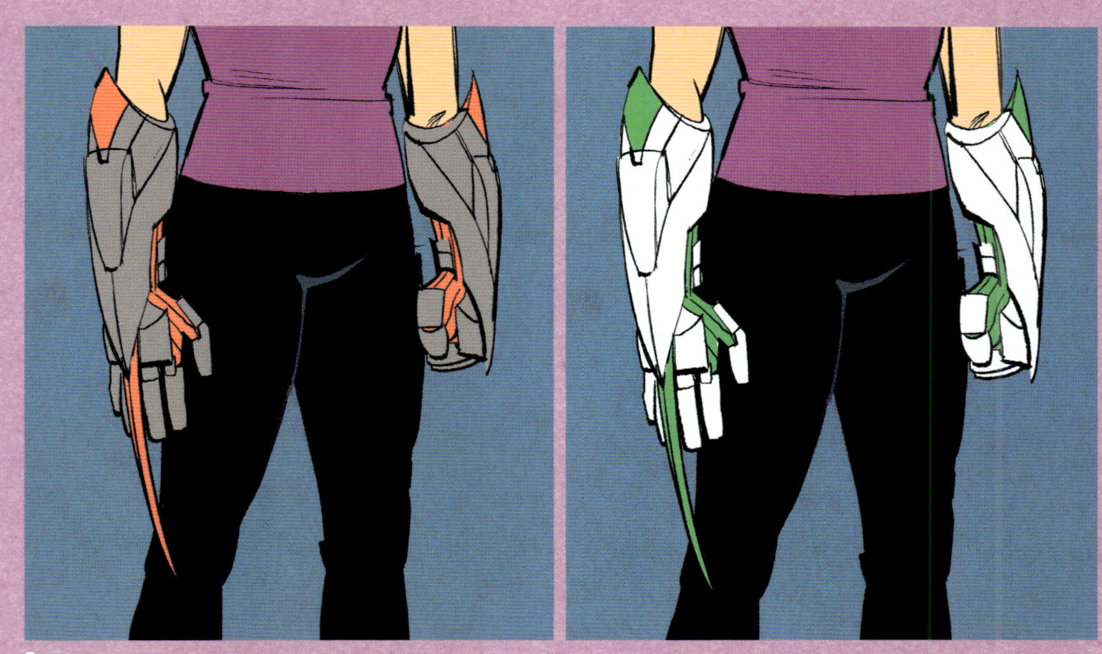

5

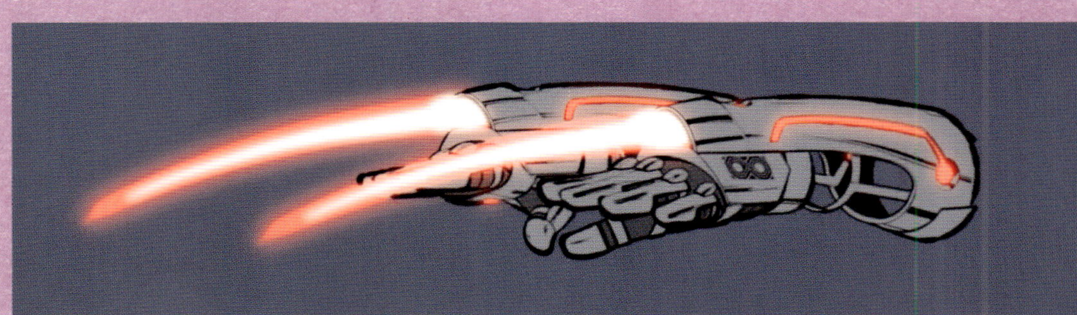

6

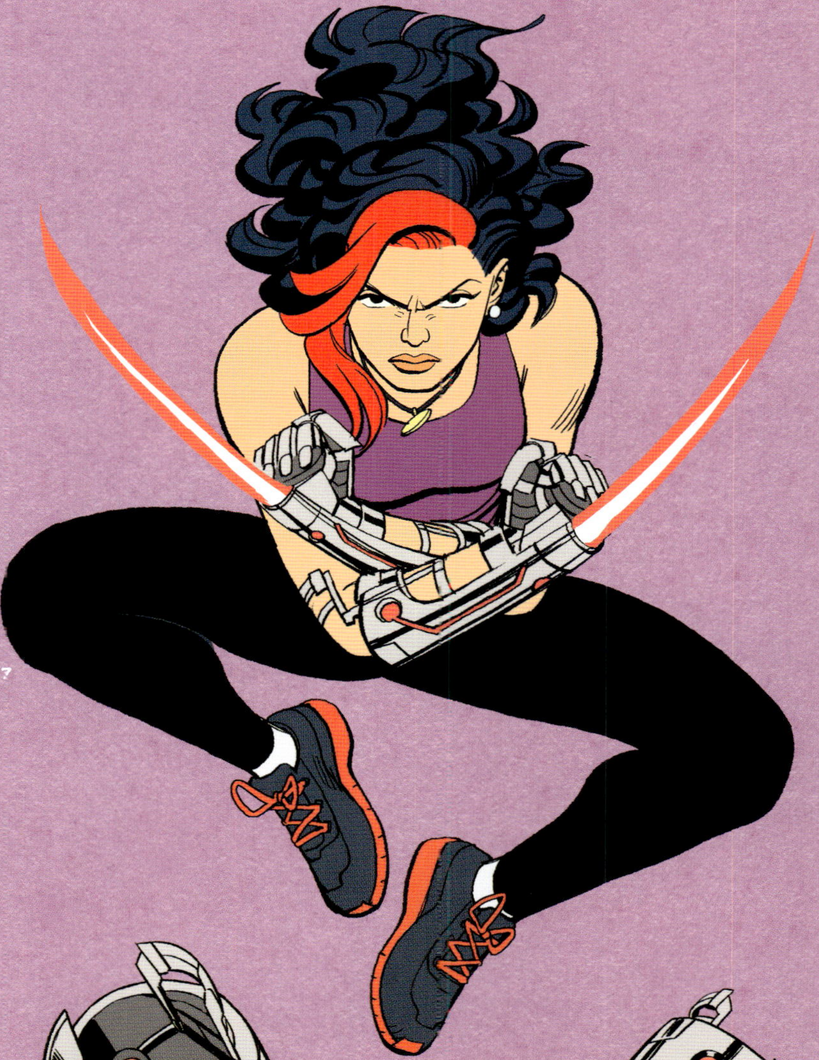

7

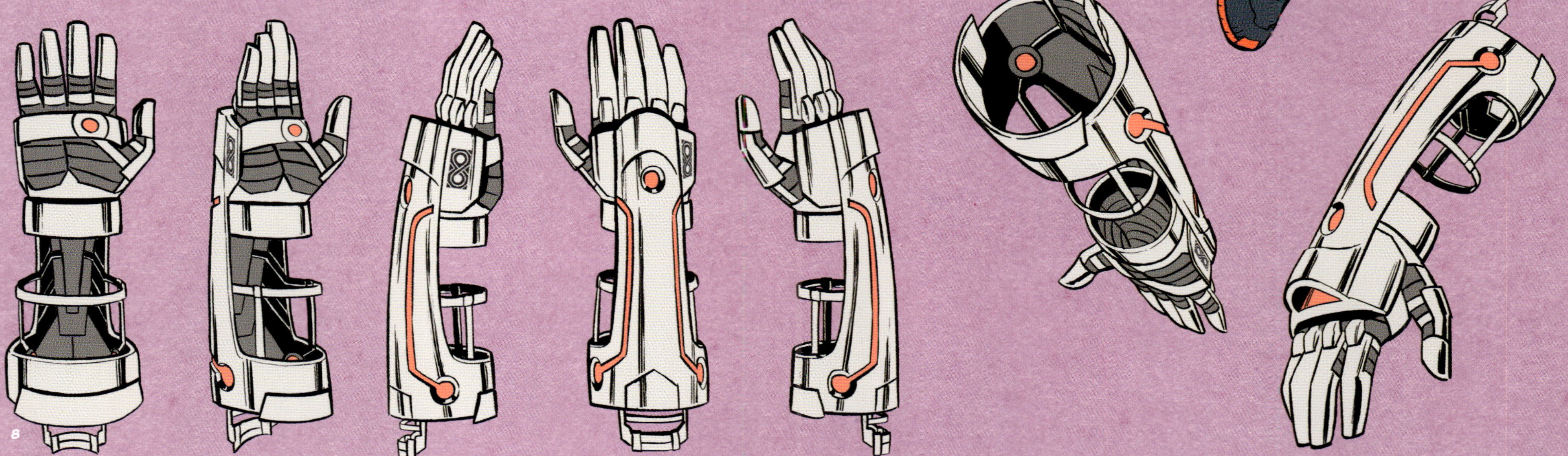

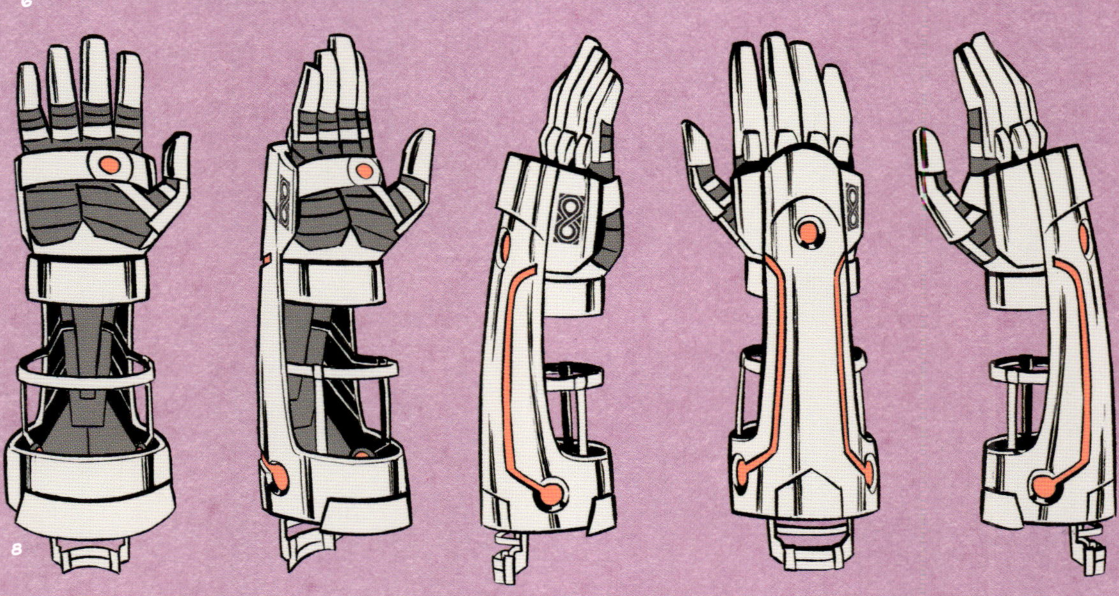

8

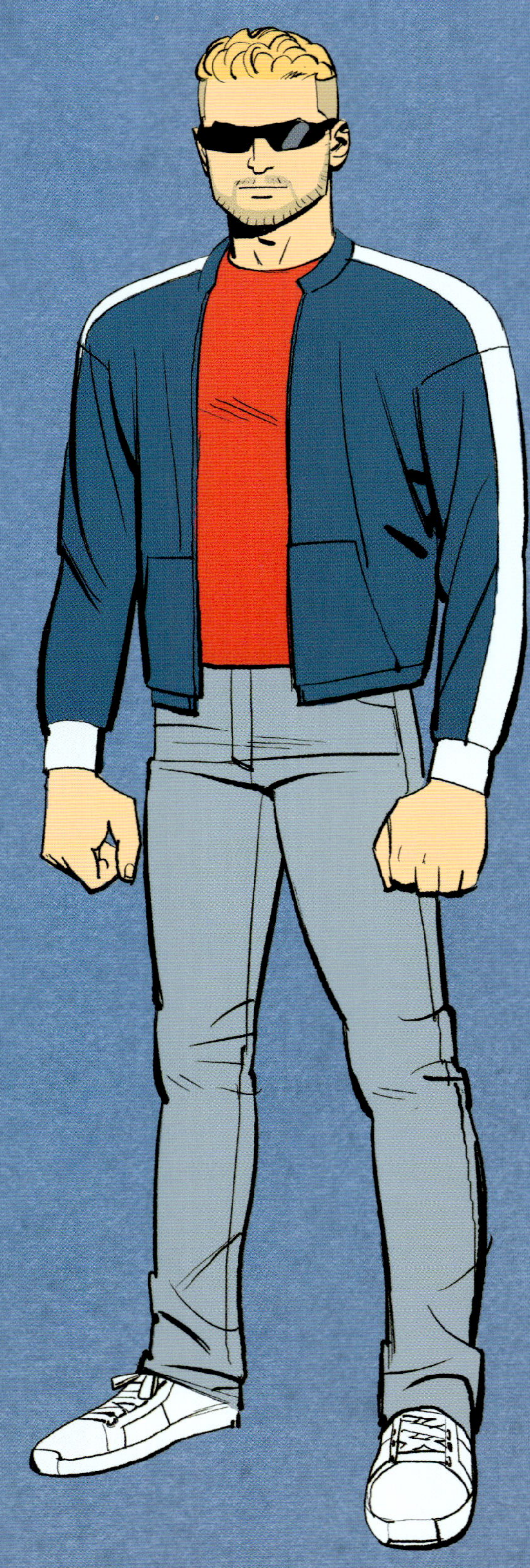

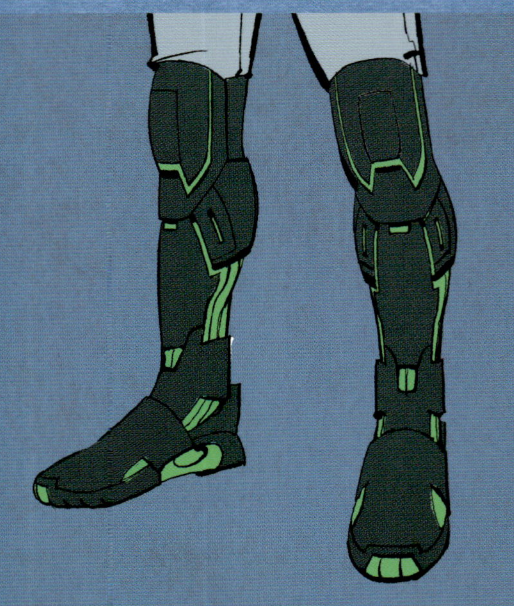

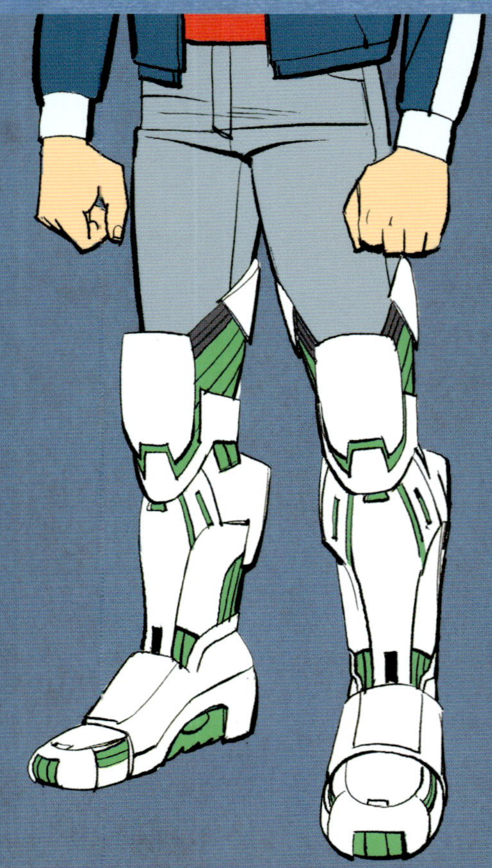

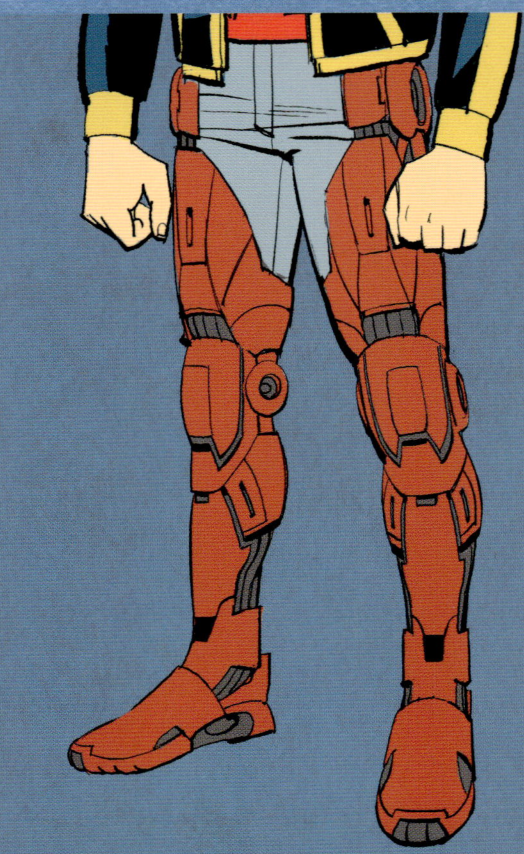

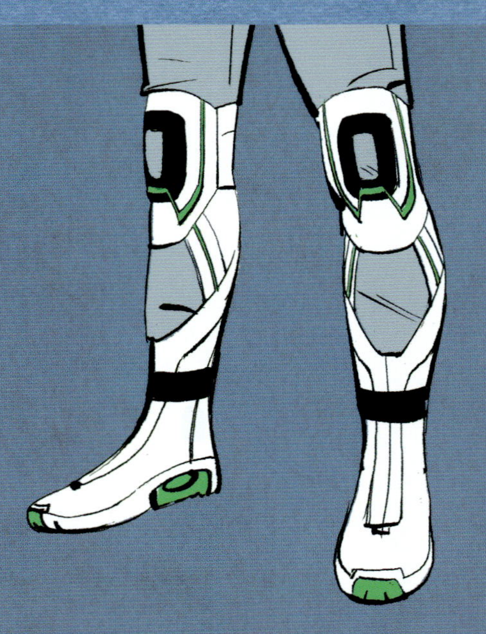

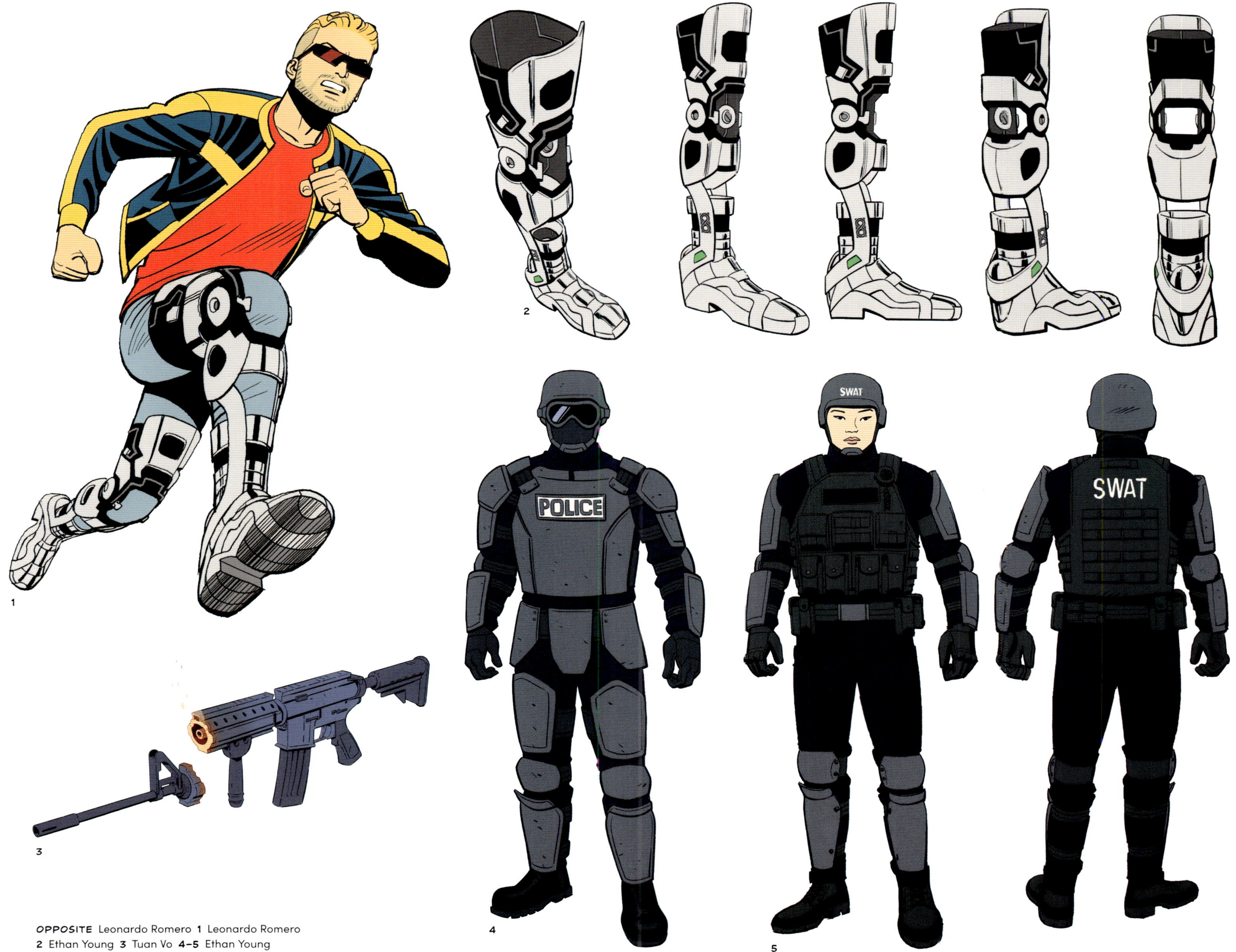

OPPOSITE Leonardo Romero **1** Leonardo Romero
2 Ethan Young **3** Tuan Vo **4–5** Ethan Young

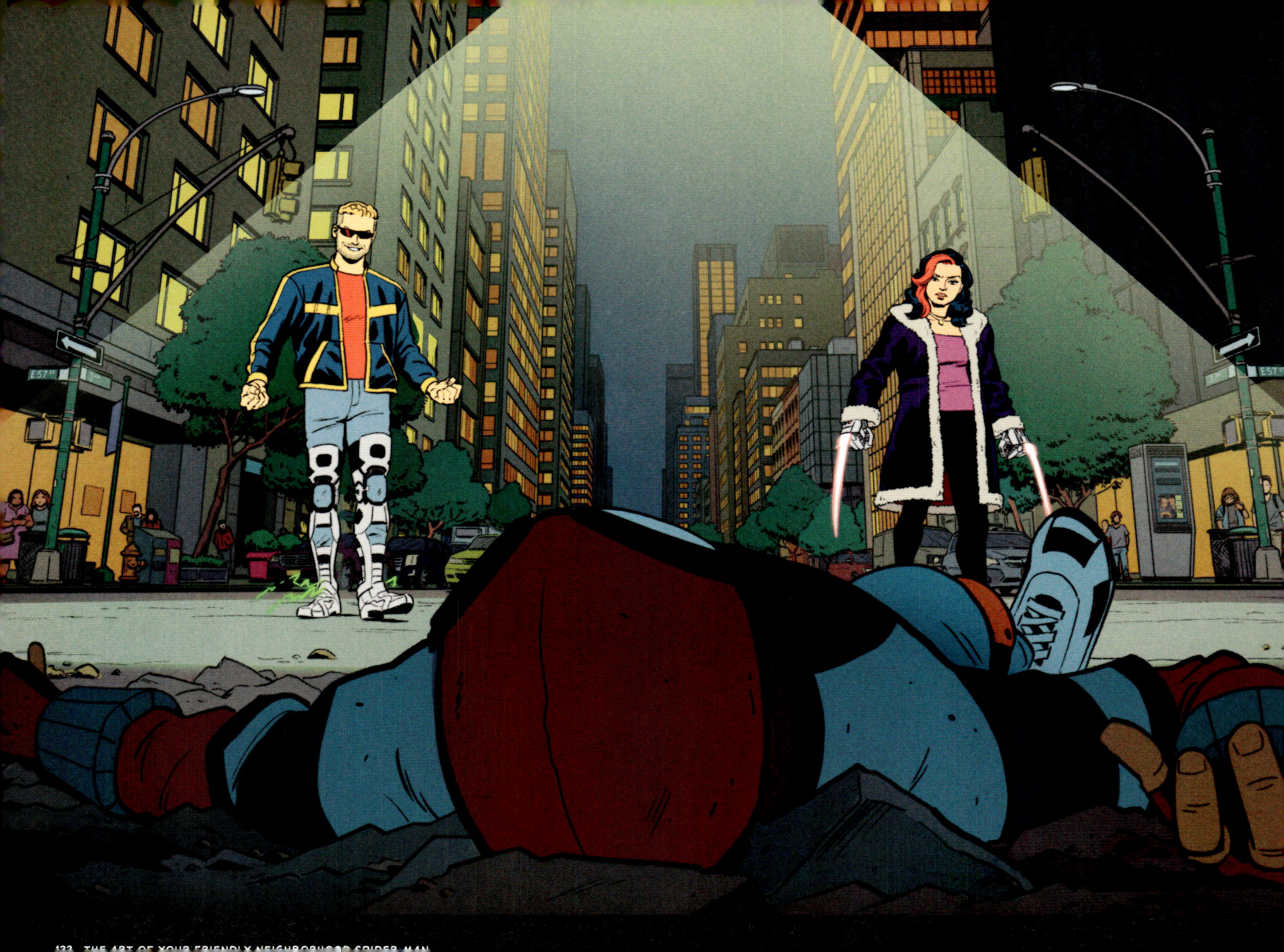

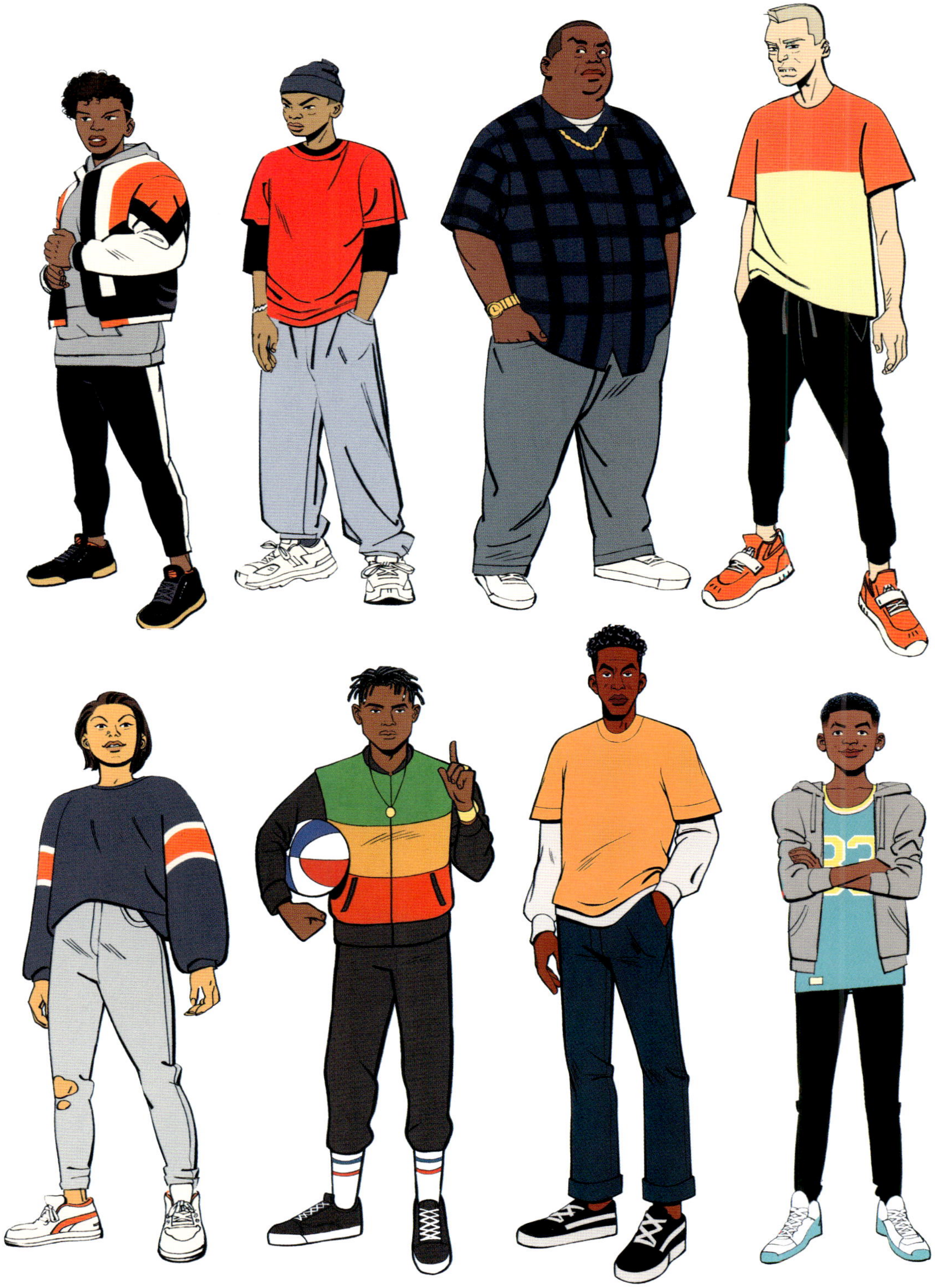

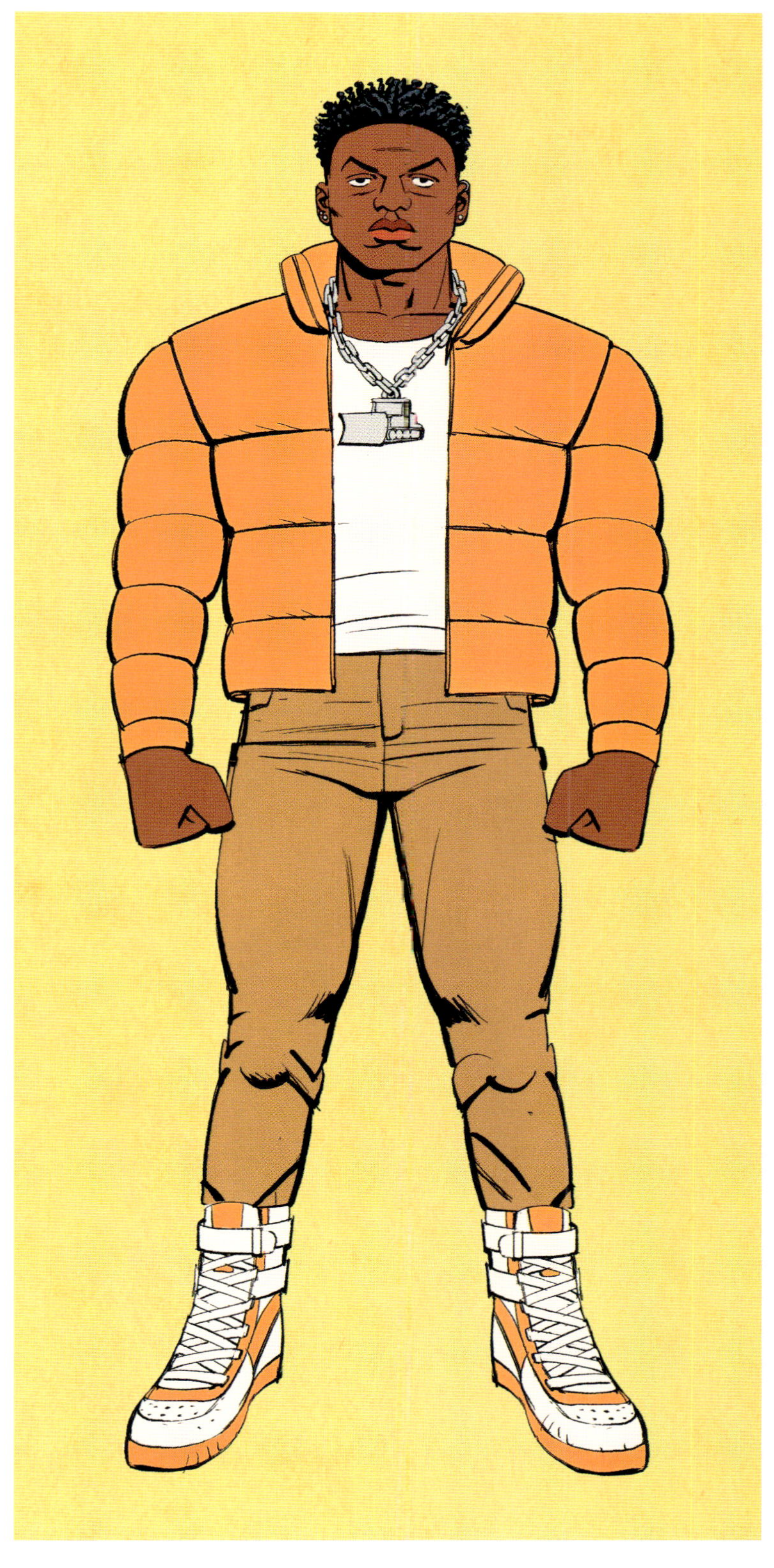

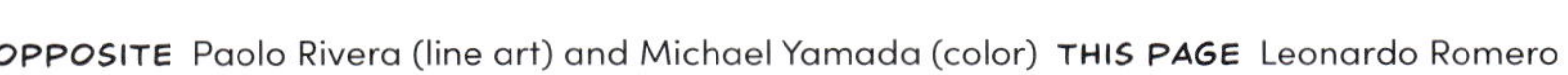

OPPOSITE Paolo Rivera (line art) and Michael Yamada (color) **THIS PAGE** Leonardo Romero

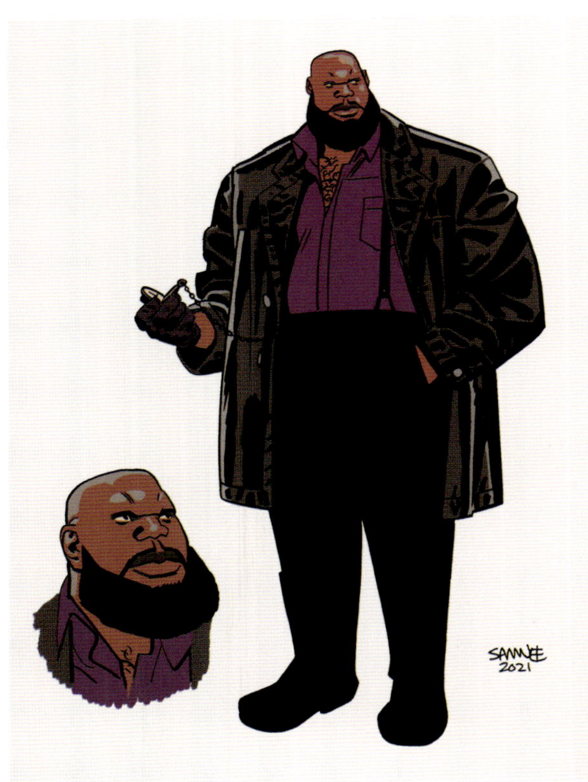

1

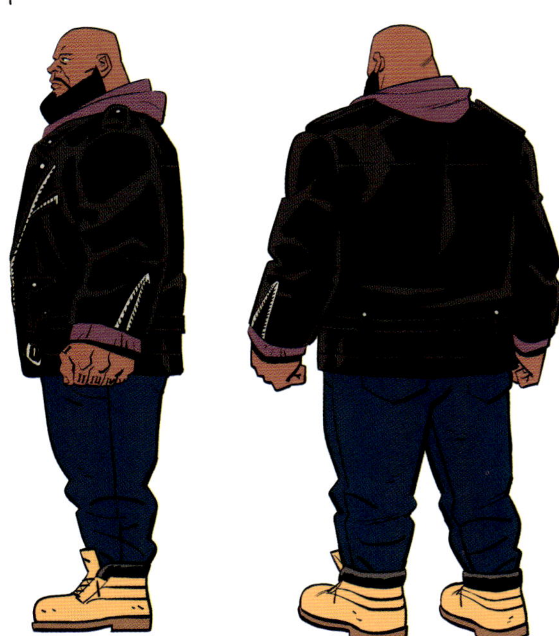

2

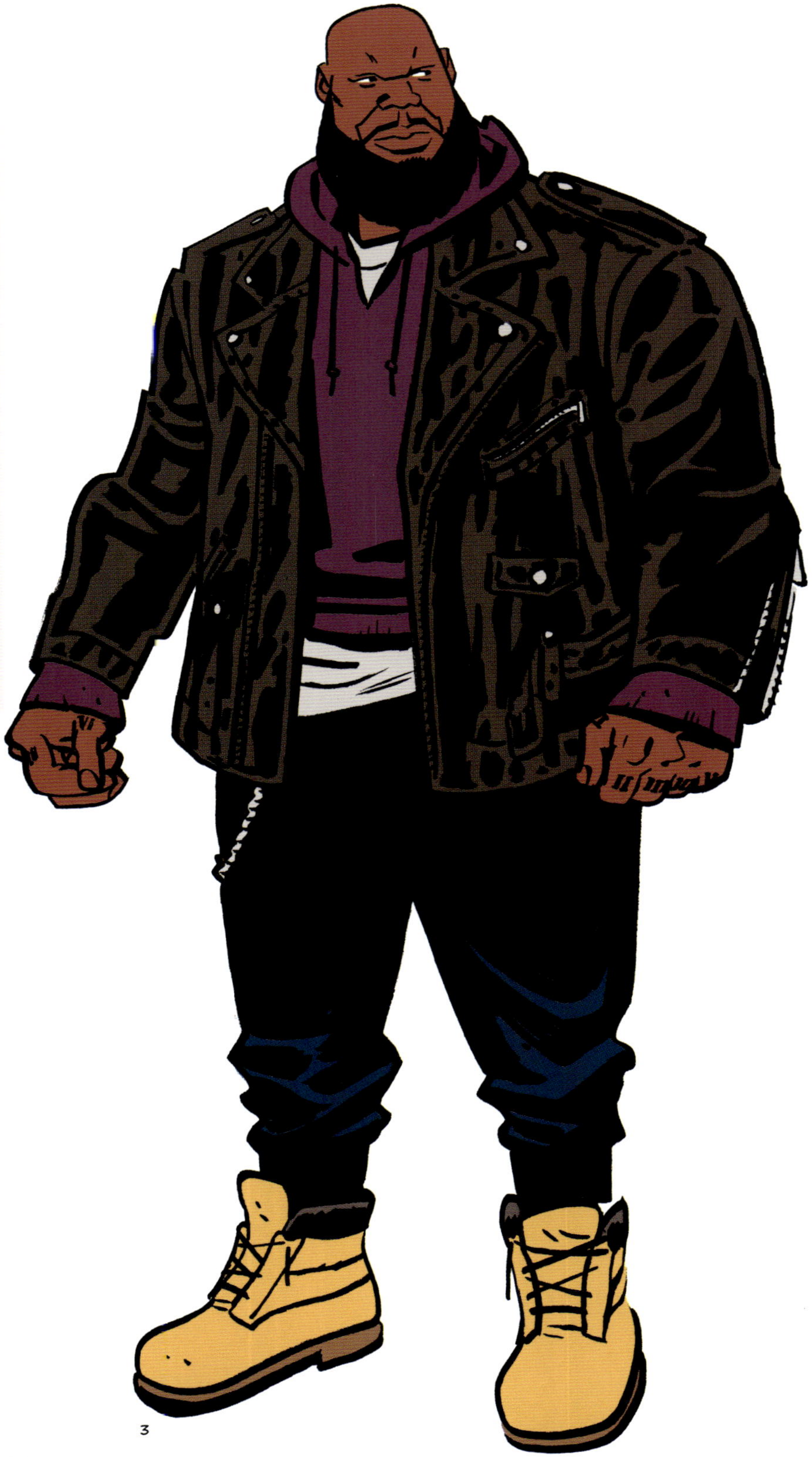

3

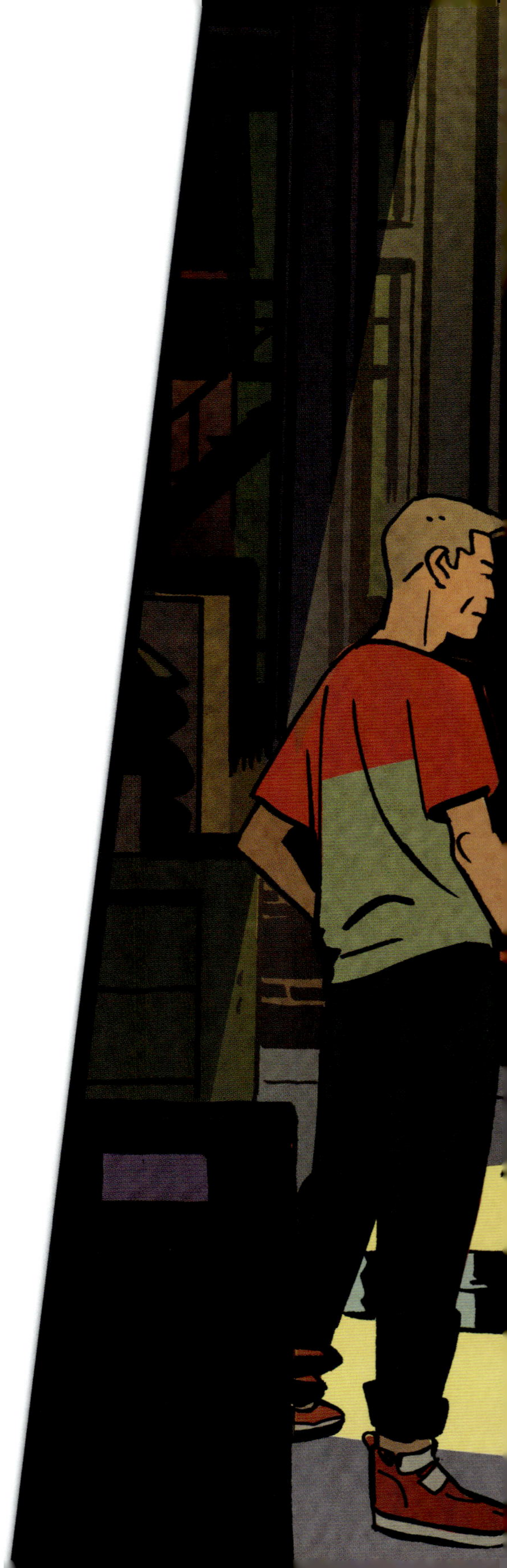

1 Chris Samnee **2** Ethan Young **3** Chris Samnee
RIGHT Chris Samnee (line art) and Michael Yamada (color)

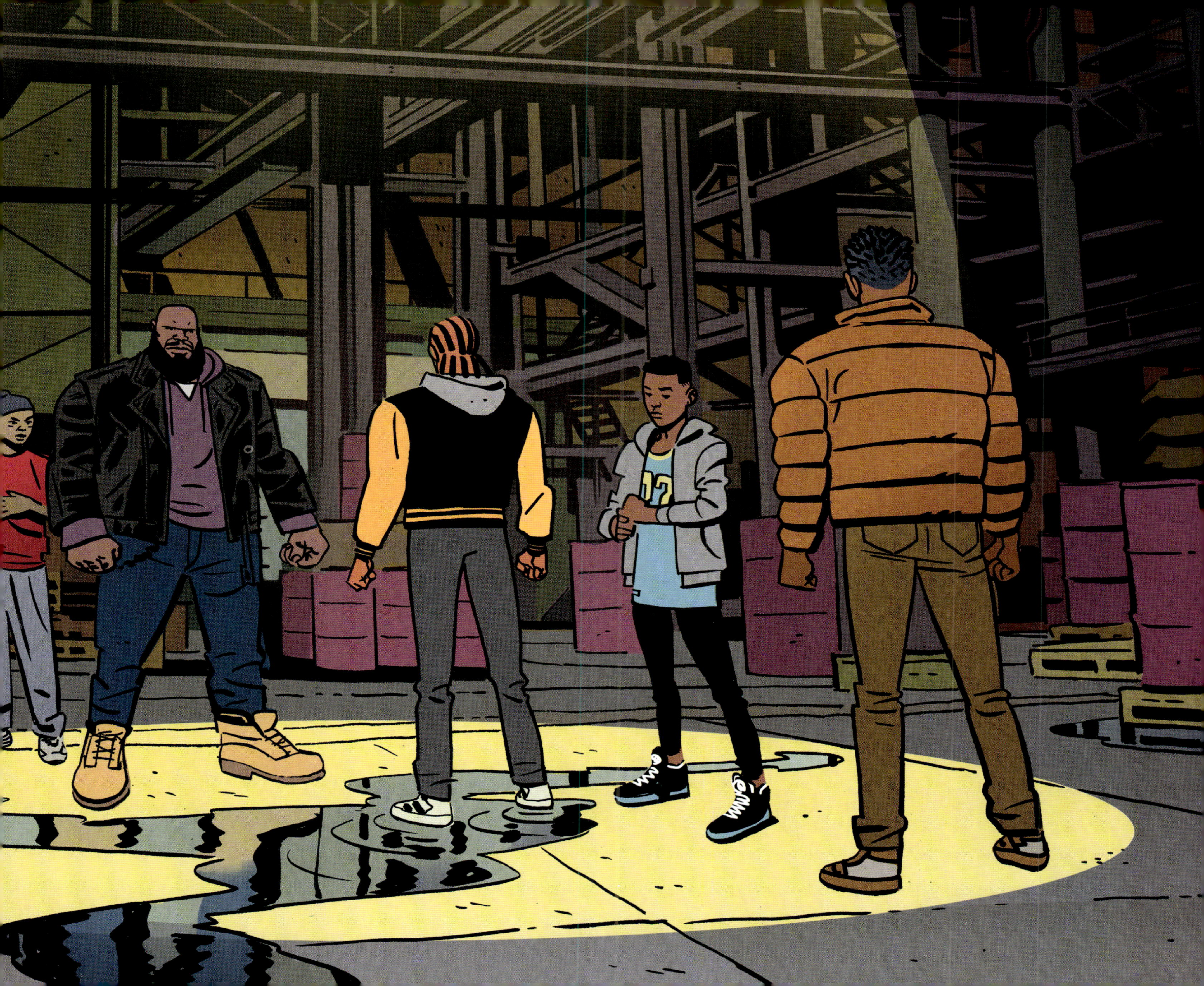

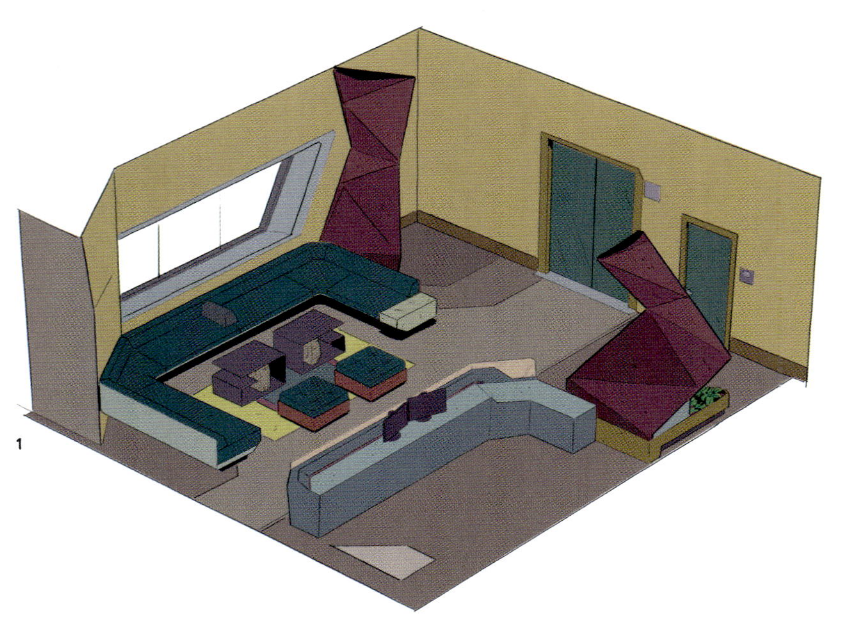

1

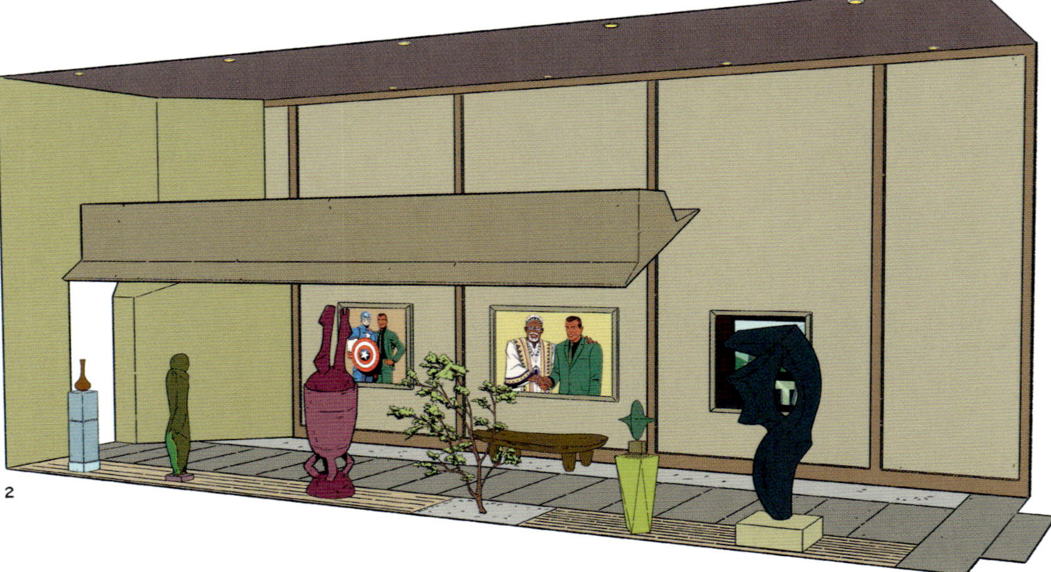

2

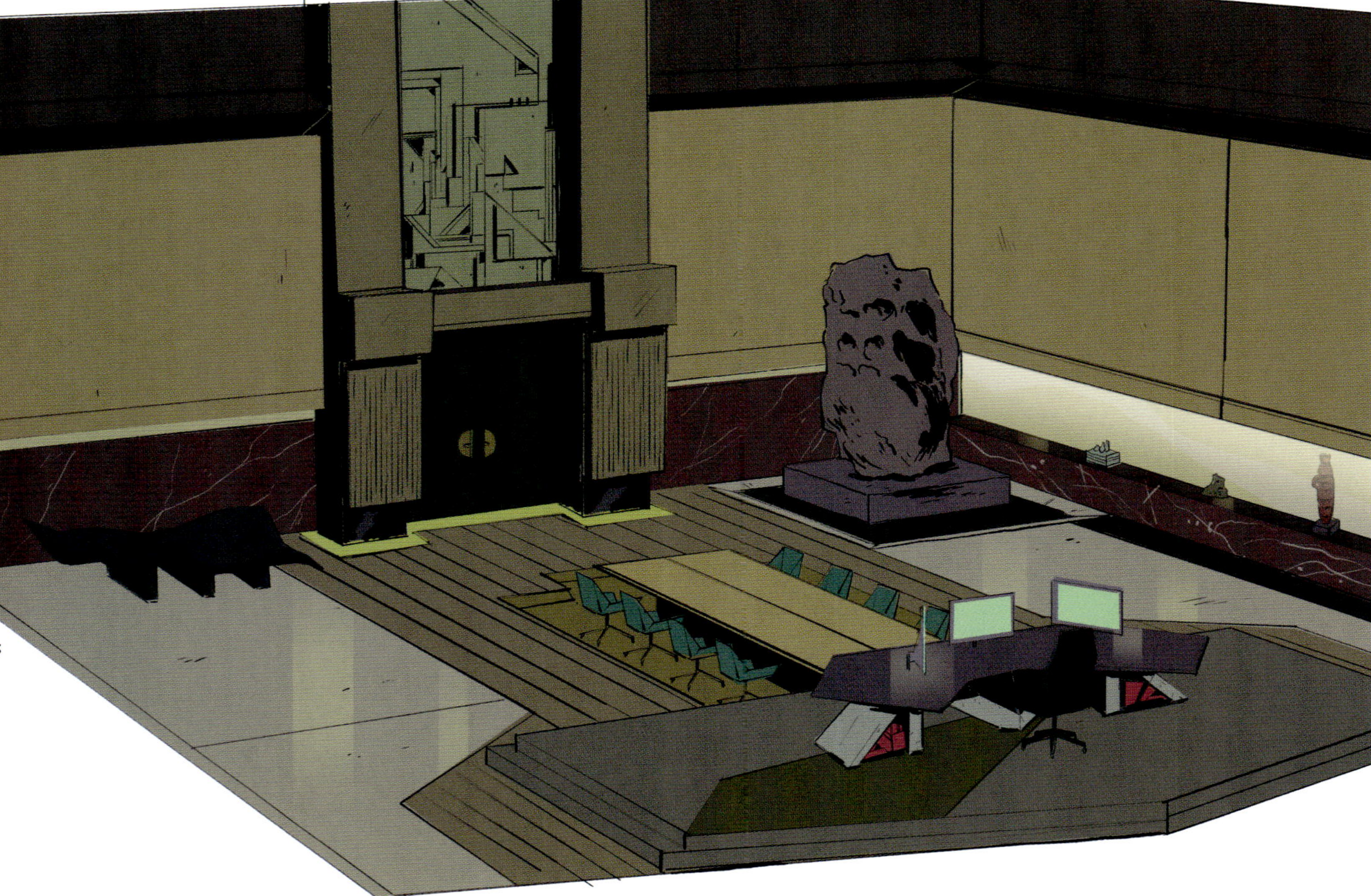

3

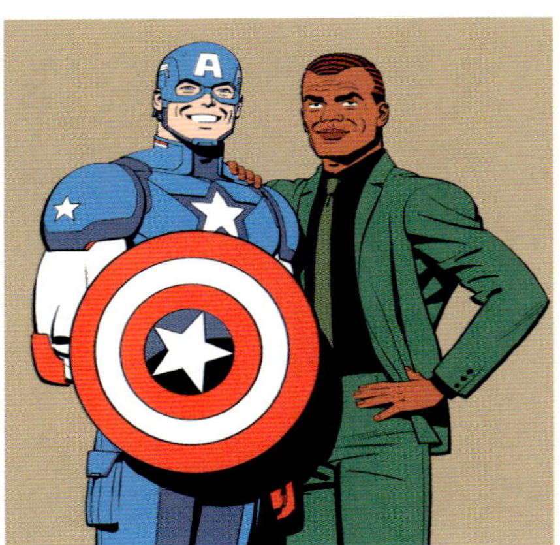

4

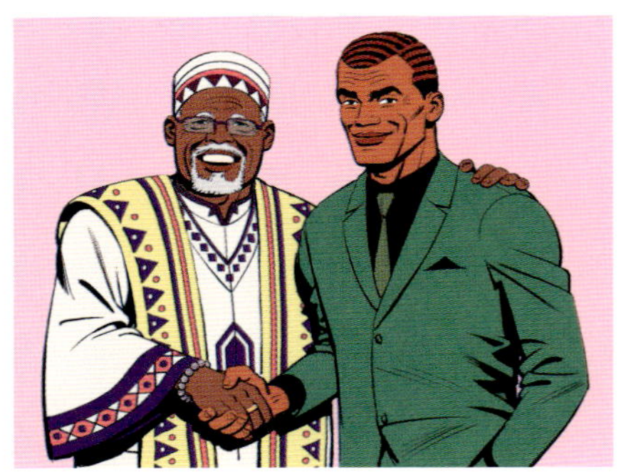

5

1 Michael Yamada **2** Tuan Vo **3** Sylvia Liu
4–5 Leonardo Romero ***OPPOSITE*** Paolo Rivera

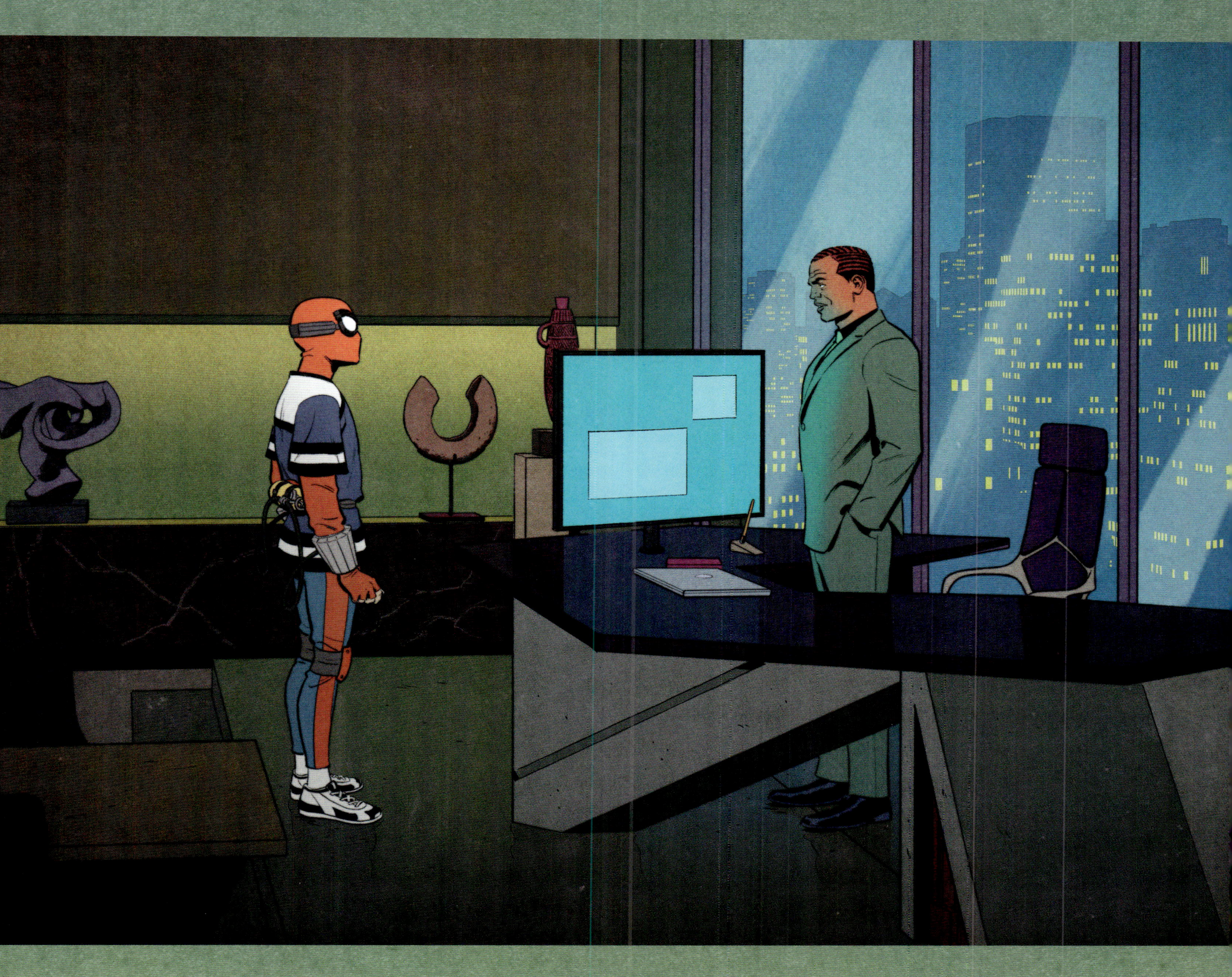

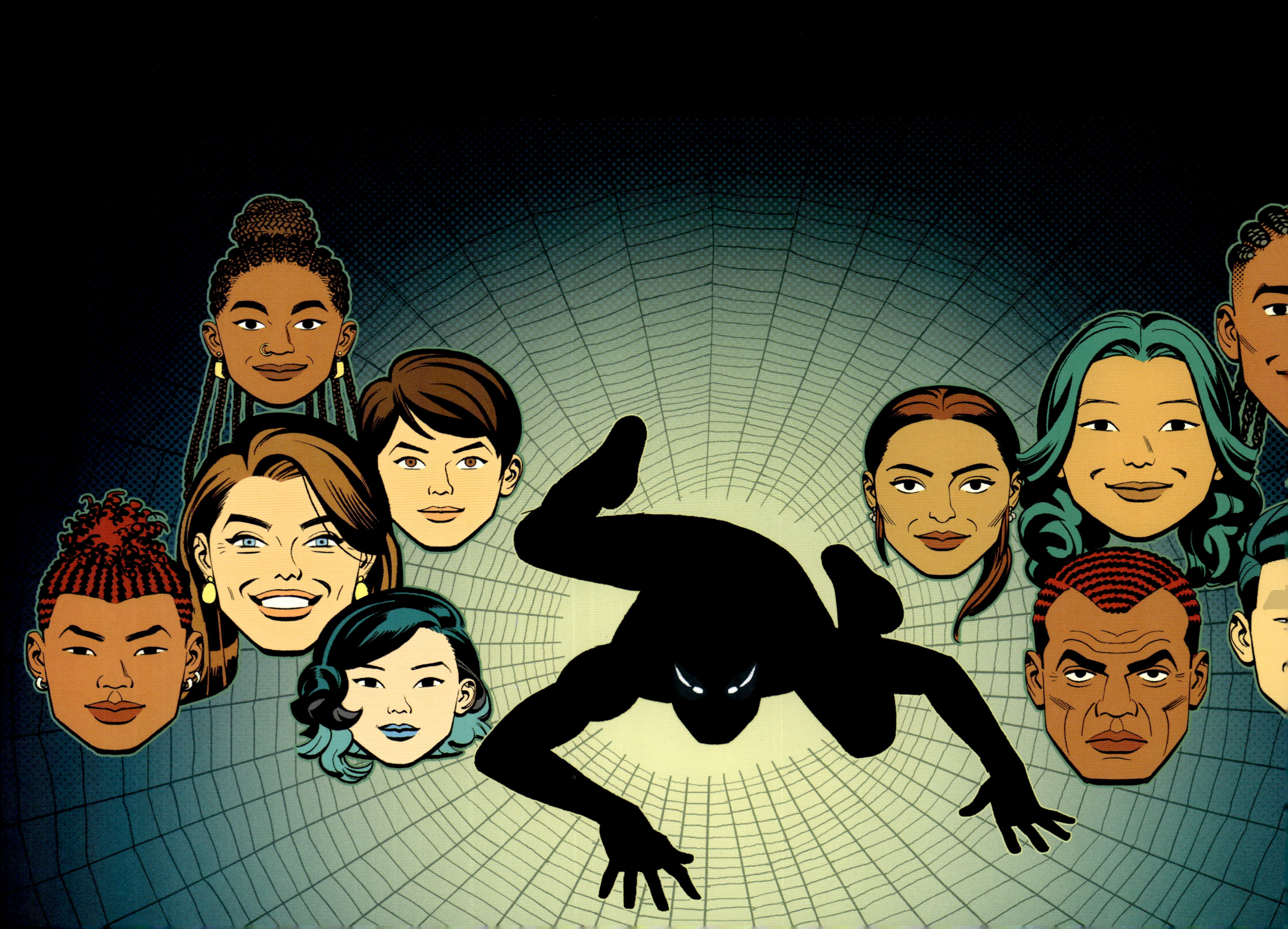

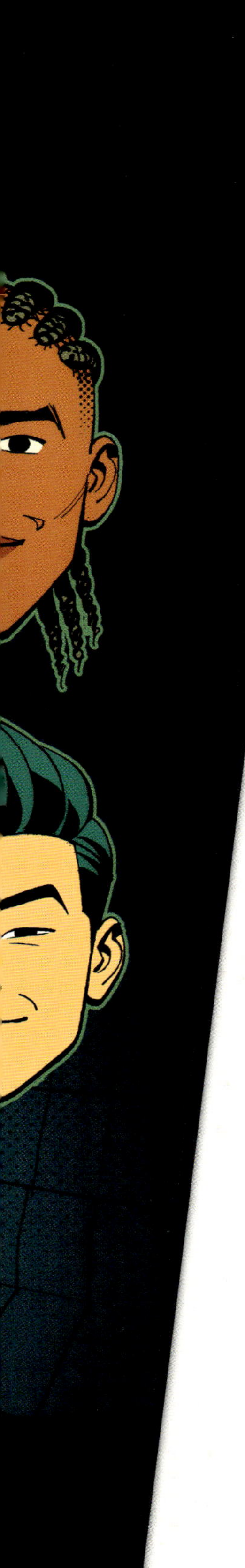

EPISODE FOUR

HITTING THE BIG TIME

THE PLOT THICKENS IN THE FOURTH EPISODE AS NORMAN OSBORN PROMISES PETER HE'LL TAKE CARE OF ANY ISSUES RELATED TO THE SOKOVIA ACCORDS (DOCUMENTS ESTABLISHED BY THE UNITED NATIONS TO CONTROL AND REGULATE THE ACTIVITIES OF SUPER HEROES, FIRST MENTIONED IN *CAPTAIN AMERICA: CIVIL WAR*) AND SHOWS OFF SEVERAL FAR-FROM-PERFECT COSTUMES CREATED WITH OSCORP TECH. LONNIE RUNS HIS FIRST BIG JOB FOR BIG DONOVAN, AND WE ALSO LEARN ABOUT CARMILLA BLACK AND THE VICIOUS VILLAIN KNOWN AS MAC GARGAN (SCORPION). SPIDEY FINDS HIMSELF UP AGAINST A RUSSIAN GANG (CHAMELEON, RHINO, THE UNICORN, AND ROXANNA VOLKOV) AND ENDS THE EPISODE BY ACCIDENTALLY UNMASKING HIMSELF IN FRONT OF HARRY. IT'S ALSO REVEALED THAT NONE OTHER THAN DR. OTTO OCTAVIUS (HUGH DANCY) IS THE INVENTOR SUPPLYING CRIMINALS ACROSS THE CITY WITH HIGH-TECH WEAPONS.

"THIS IS THE EPISODE where we get to see Norman's process for helping Peter become a better Spider-Man," notes Executive Producer/Showrunner Jeff Trammell. "I wanted to show that while Norman has great ideas and wants to help Peter, he isn't fully aware who Spider-Man is just yet. Peter must learn to speak up for himself: He can't just sit back and accept everything. He needs to say, 'This is why I'm a hero, and this is who I have to be.'"

Trammell says this episode also marks the first time Peter runs into Octavius since the season opener. "The one thing that I really wanted to do in this episode is to build a rhythm of Peter trying on costumes and taking off his mask so that by the time he forgets someone else is in the room, it's believable. We also have a reference to the 'Secret Identity' *Slingers* storyline from the 1998 comic books with the suits he tries on. I wanted to pay homage to that in this episode."

As Co-Executive Producer/Supervising Director Mel Zwyer explains, "We introduced the new suits Peter tries on, and that goes back to a mini-storyline where Spider-Man creates four different secret identities—Prodigy, Ricochet, Red Hornet, and Dusk—when Osborn makes him look like a killer. So, we have these suits, as well as the main Oscorp white suit. That was fun because we wanted something cool but sterile-looking. That's how we point out the difference between Norman and Peter, who's a fan of Captain America."

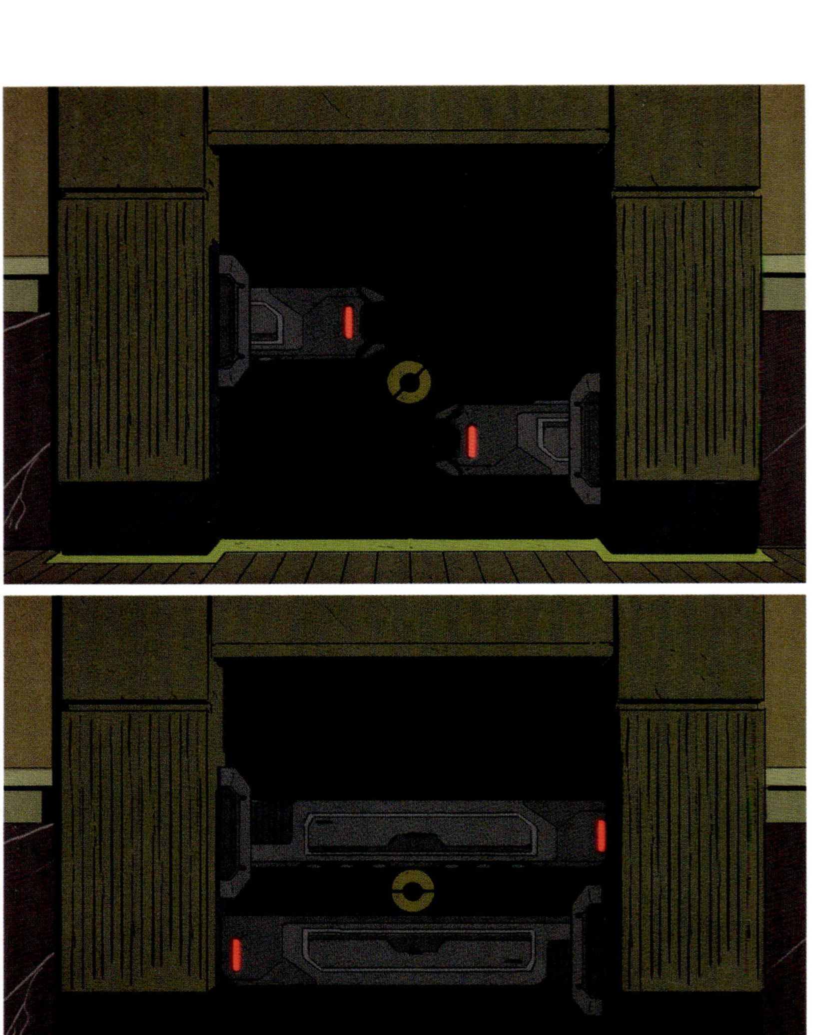
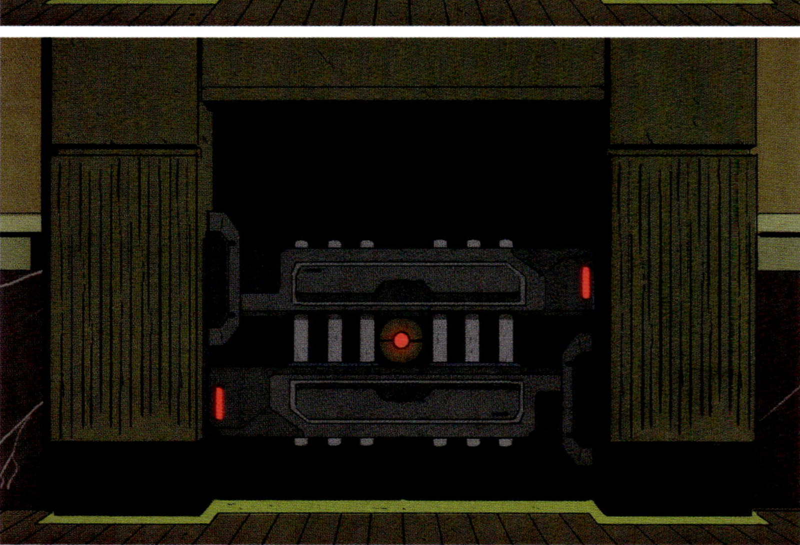
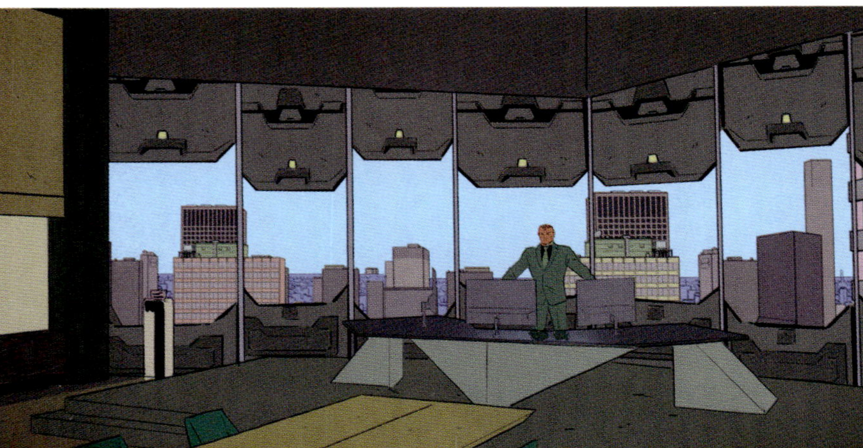
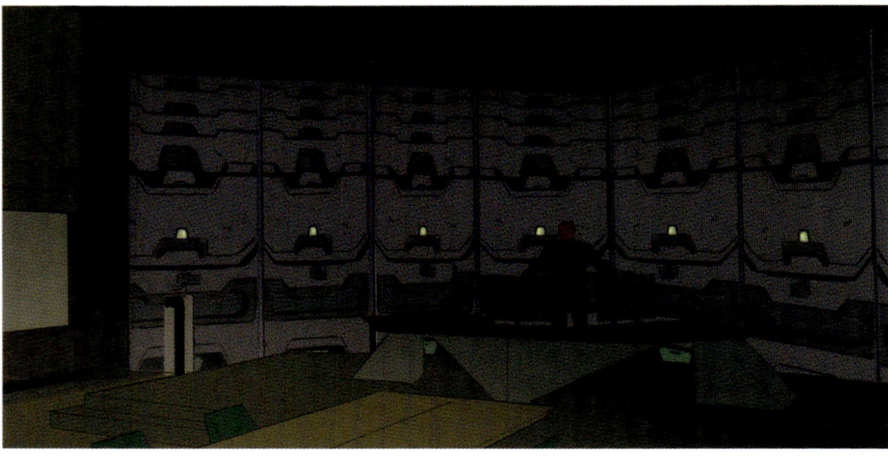
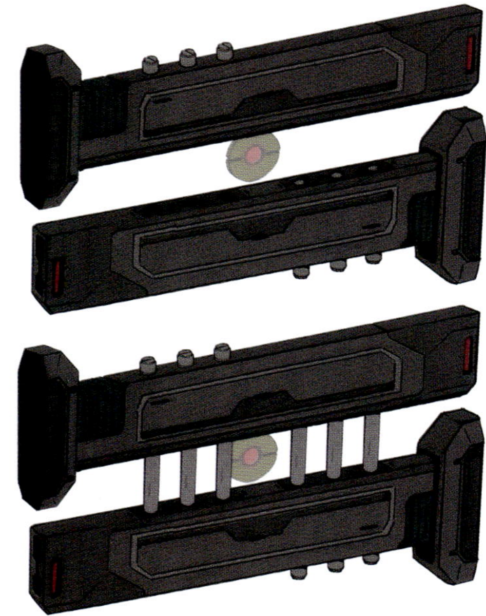
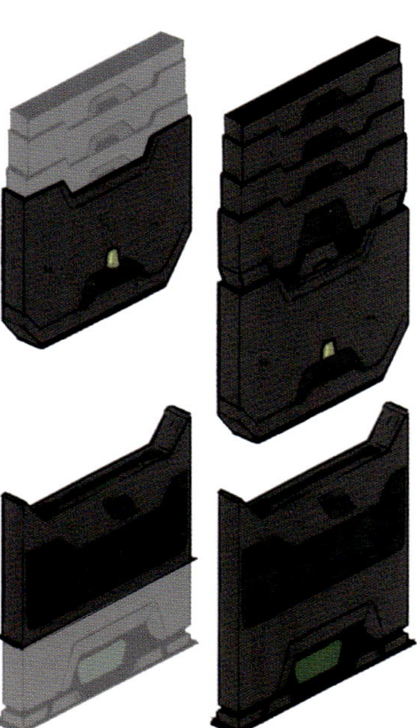

NORMAN OSBORN

Norman Osborn—a.k.a. Spider-Man's archnemesis, Green Goblin—was introduced back in Stan Lee and Steve Ditko's *The Amazing Spider-Man* comic (#14) in July 1964. In *Your Friendly Neighborhood Spider-Man*, Norman is a seemingly benevolent billionaire who hand-selects Peter Parker for an internship in the scientific research lab at Oscorp after he saves his son Harry's life in the first episode of the show.

"Colman Domingo is just one of the best actors working today, and we're so grateful that he voices Norman," says Executive Producer/Showrunner Jeff Trammell. "In our show, he becomes a mentor to Peter in the same way that Tony Stark was his mentor in the movies and Uncle Ben was in the comics. He doesn't always offer Peter the best advice, and he also creates a new kind of conflict for him. As the audience, we just hope that Peter does the right thing despite Norman's poor advice."

Trammell says Norman is an ego-driven character who wants to win at all costs. "He has earned every dollar he's made, and he has built an empire. His biggest conflict, however, is with his own son, Harry, because he never will have to go through the struggles he has had to go through," he says. "He builds false expectations for Harry that are likely to challenge him, but that never works out because his son grew up with money, and that becomes the core of their conflict."

He continues, "However, Norman sees himself in Peter, someone from a lower economic bracket, and he thinks he can mold him. When we first introduce Norman in the series, we want to allow the audience to reinterpret their thoughts about him. Maybe you think, 'Well, maybe he isn't a bad guy.' This isn't the Norman Osborn we know. This is a completely different universe. He has never looked or sounded like this. Just like Peter and Lonnie, he can be tested and tempted. Maybe he has good intentions, and perhaps they get twisted. He is looking out for Peter Parker as a hero, but perhaps he isn't offering the lessons that a hero really needs to learn."

Although Norman Osborn's design wasn't the easiest one to conjure, it was one of the first to get approved, according to Lead Character Designer Leonardo Romero. "I think I did one character sheet of him, and it got approved very quickly," he recalls. "Of course, the Green Goblin is my favorite Spider-Man villain, so I really wanted to do a good job. I tried to capture as much of the original, classic Norman in the design while modernizing it at the same time. Initially, we were trying to come up with a very imposing figure—someone like Gus Fring, the character played by actor Giancarlo Esposito in *Breaking Bad*. I remembered how he stole all the scenes he was in on that show. We needed a powerful face like that, someone who controls everything else around him, and I think it turned out well."

OPPOSITE Victor Calleja **1** Paolo Rivera **2** Mel Milton **3** Julen Urrutia Perez

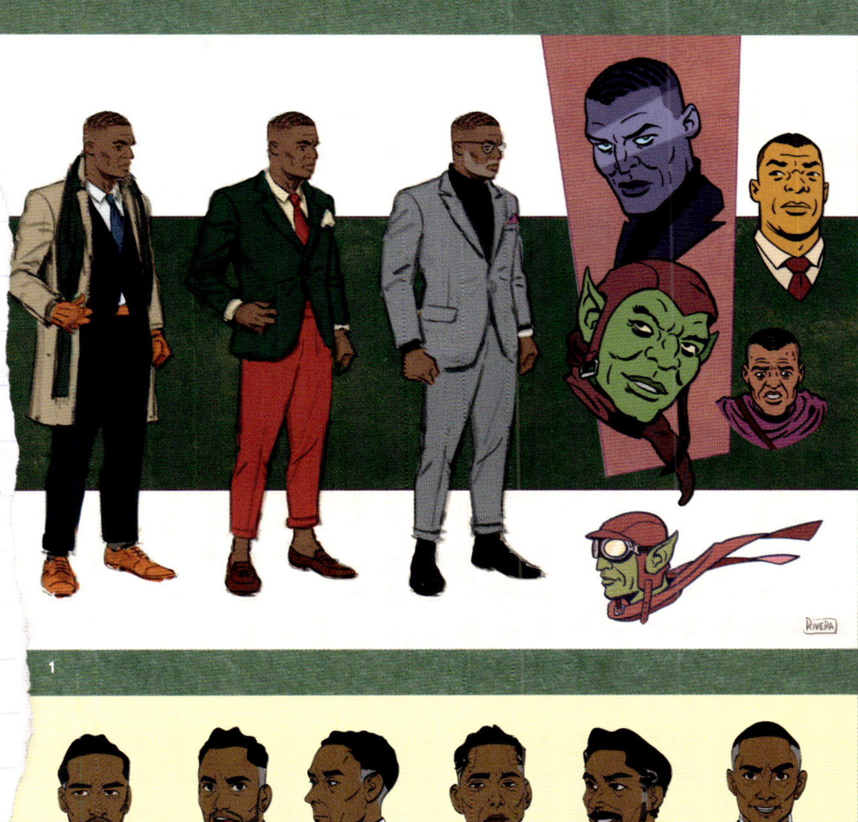

1

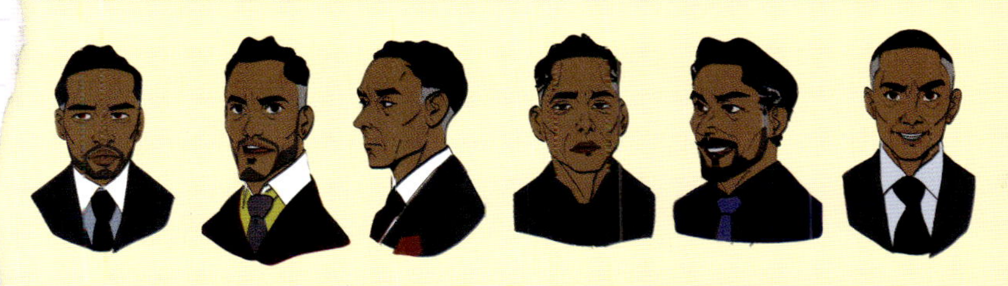

2

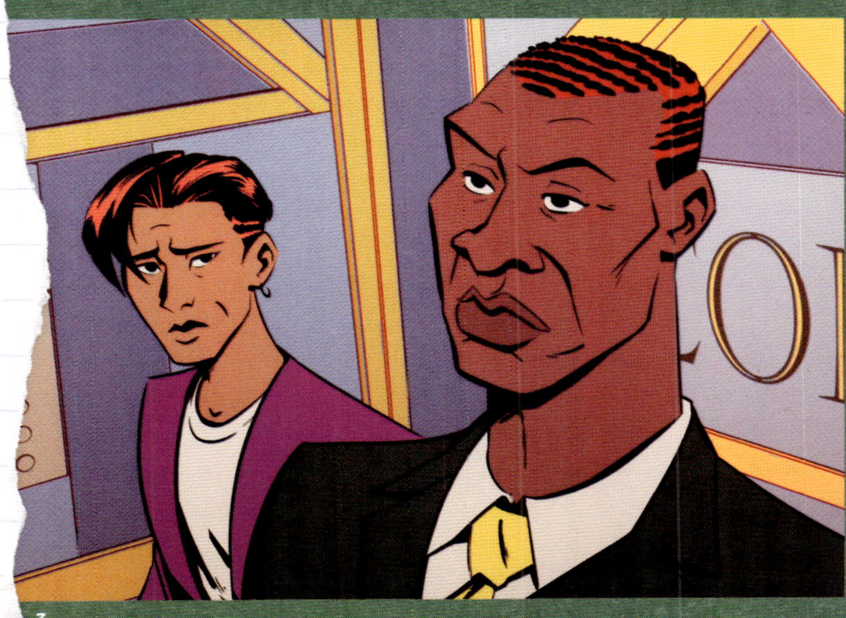

3

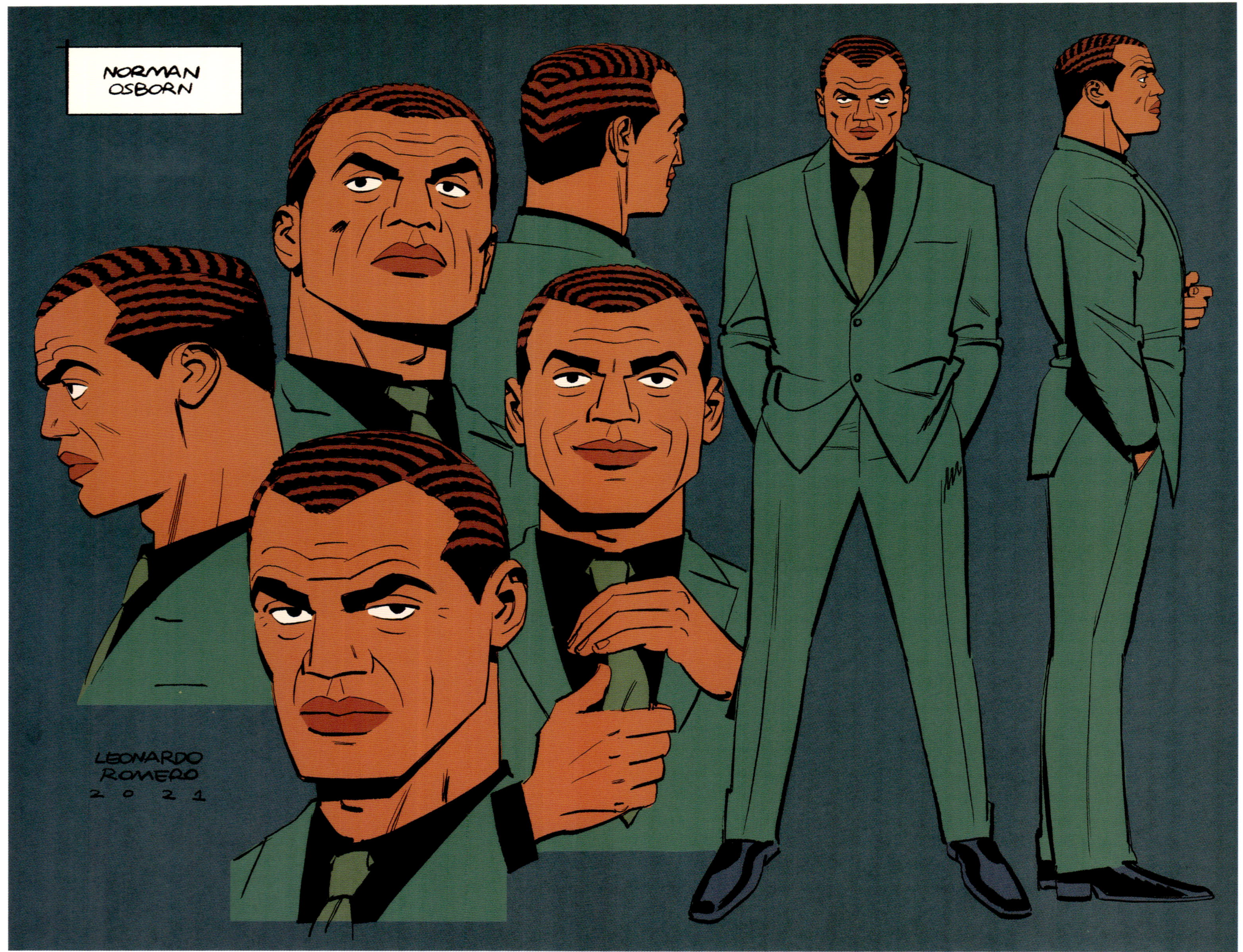
NORMAN
OSBORN
LEONARDO
ROMERO
2021

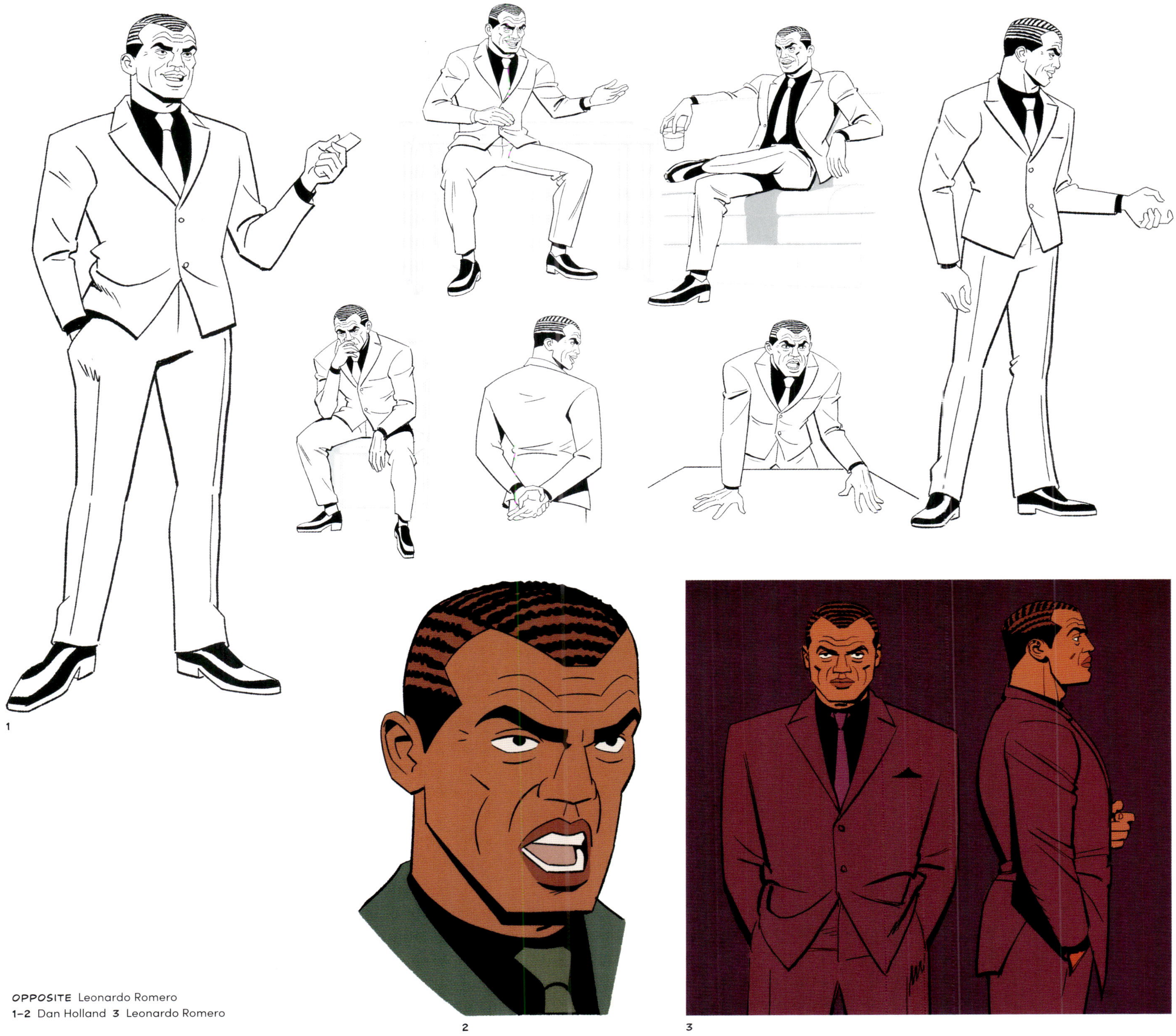

1

2

3

OPPOSITE Leonardo Romero
1–2 Dan Holland **3** Leonardo Romero

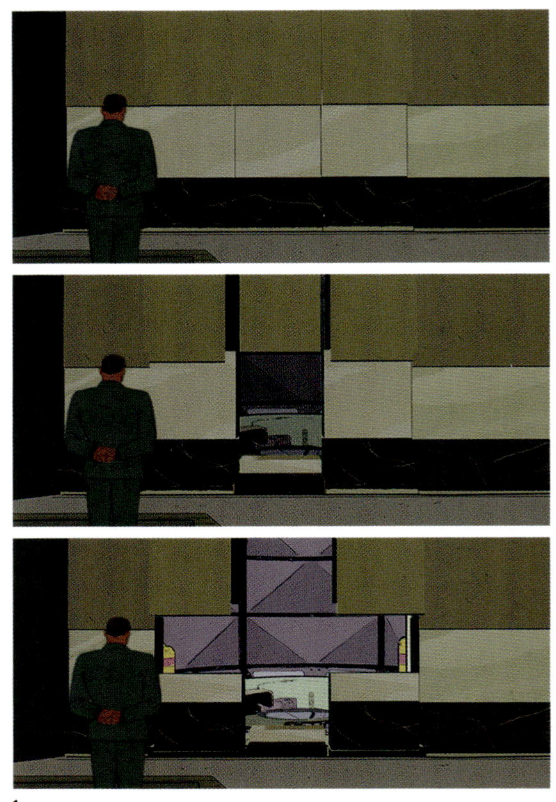

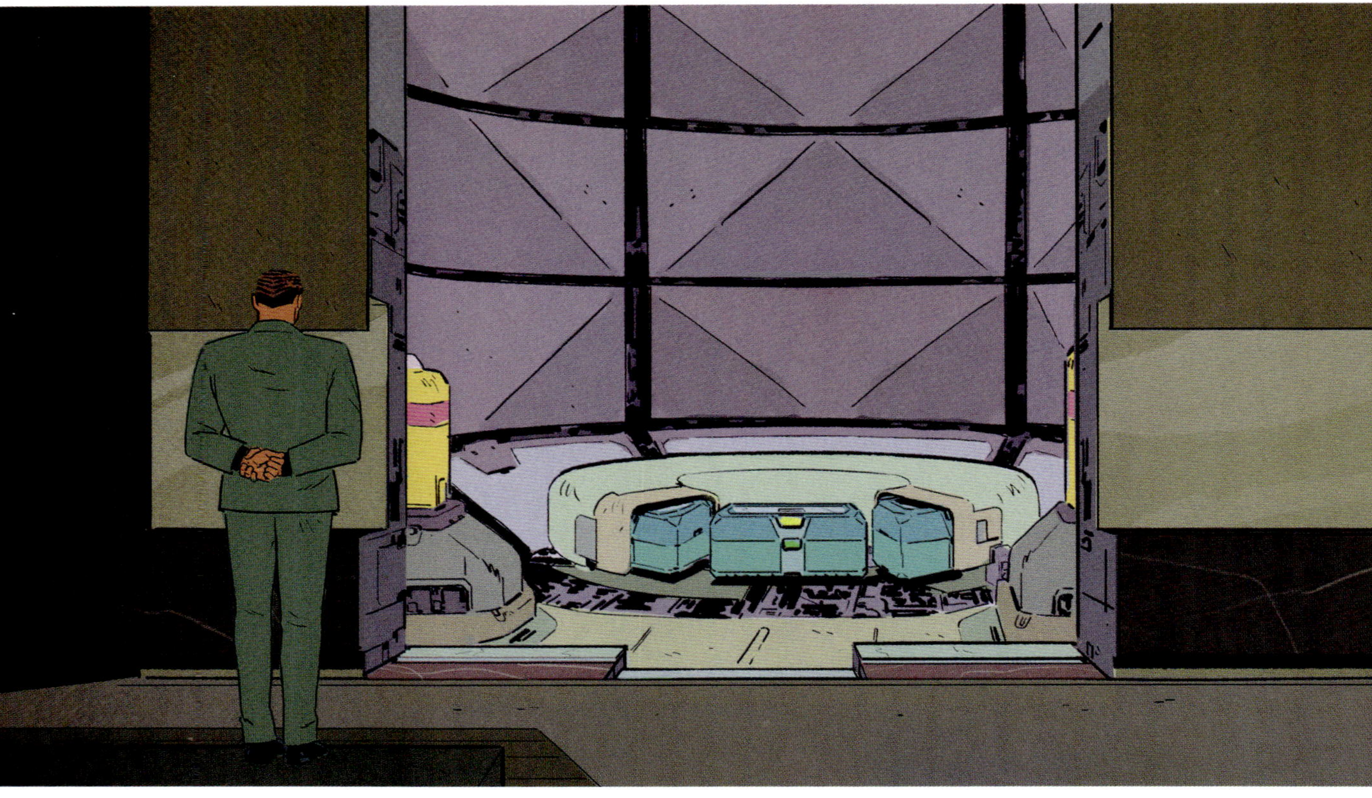

1

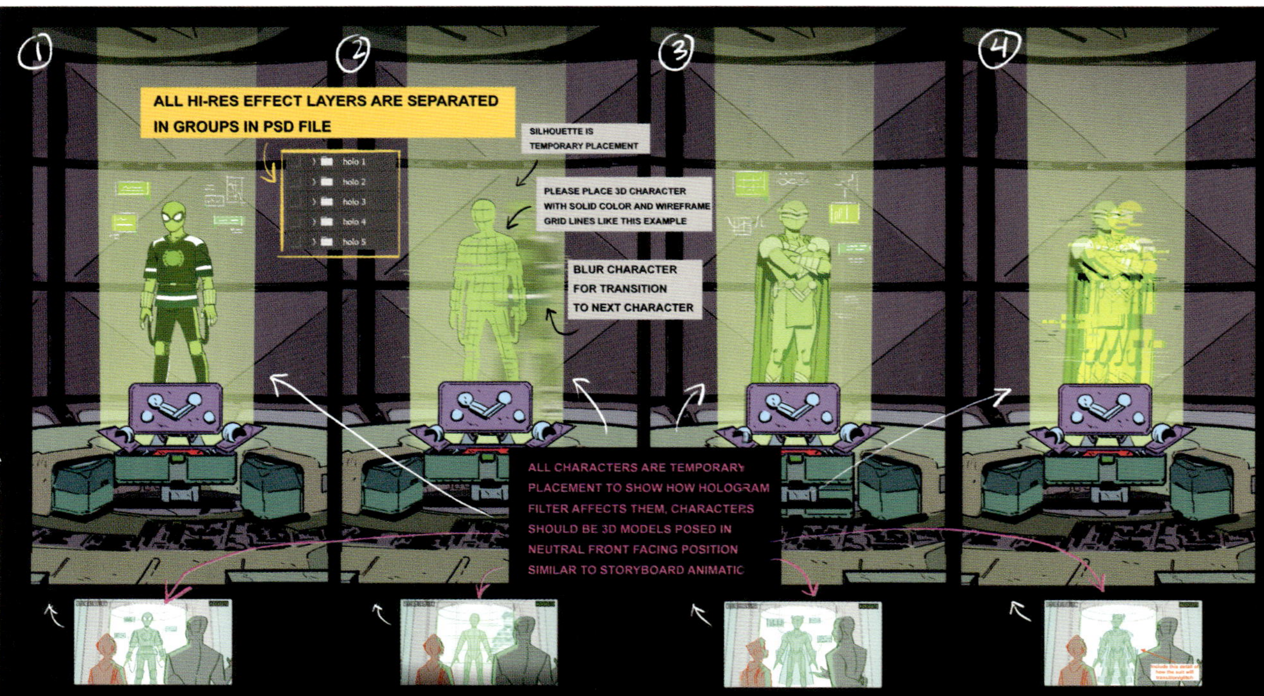

2

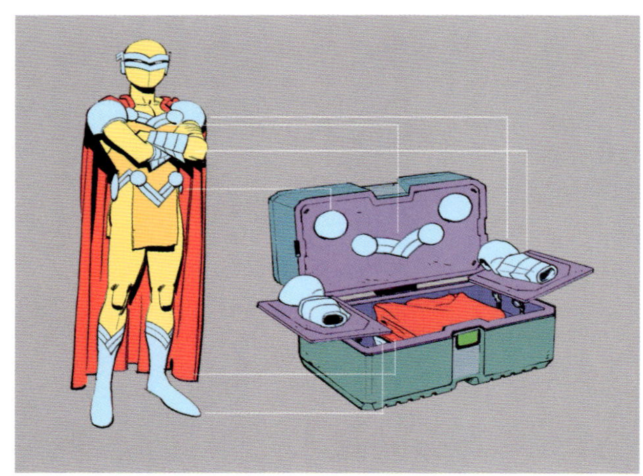

3

1 Victor Calleja **2** Sylvia Liu **3** Victor Calleja
4 Julen Urrutia Perez **5** Paolo Rivera **6** Mauricio Leone
7 Ethan Young **8** Leonardo Romero

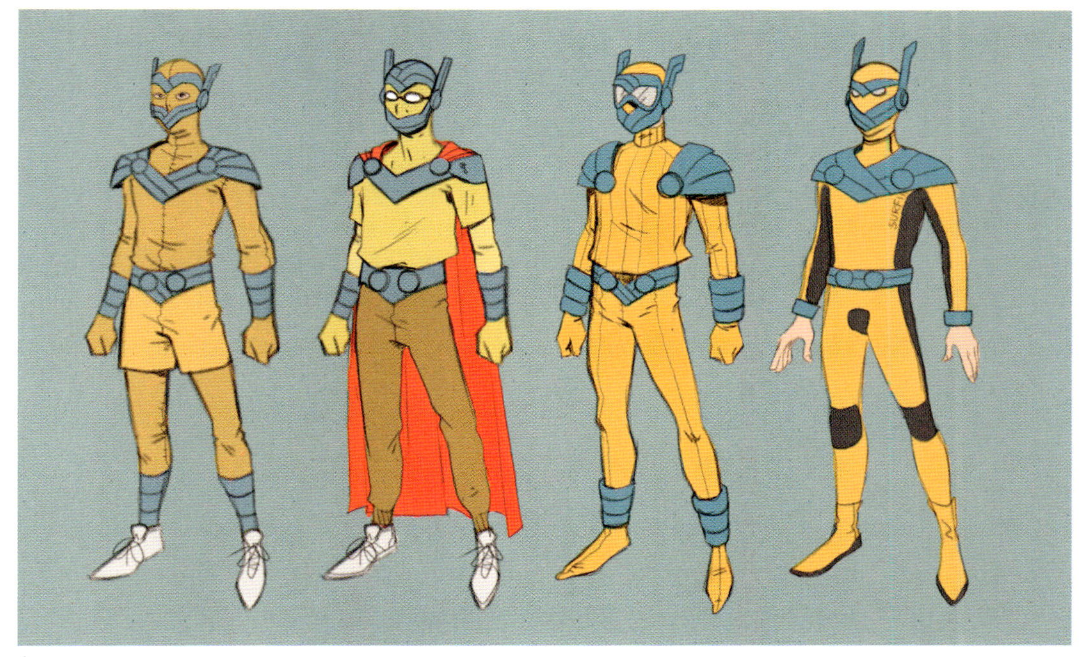

4

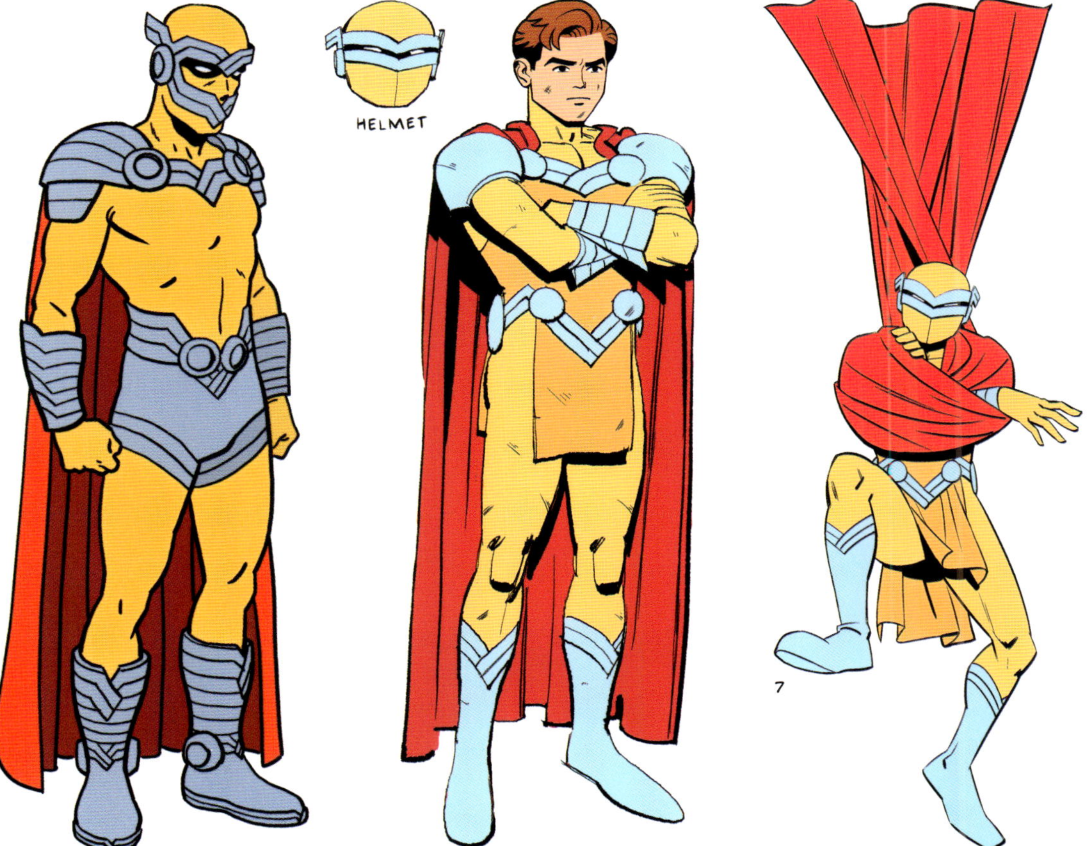

5

6

7

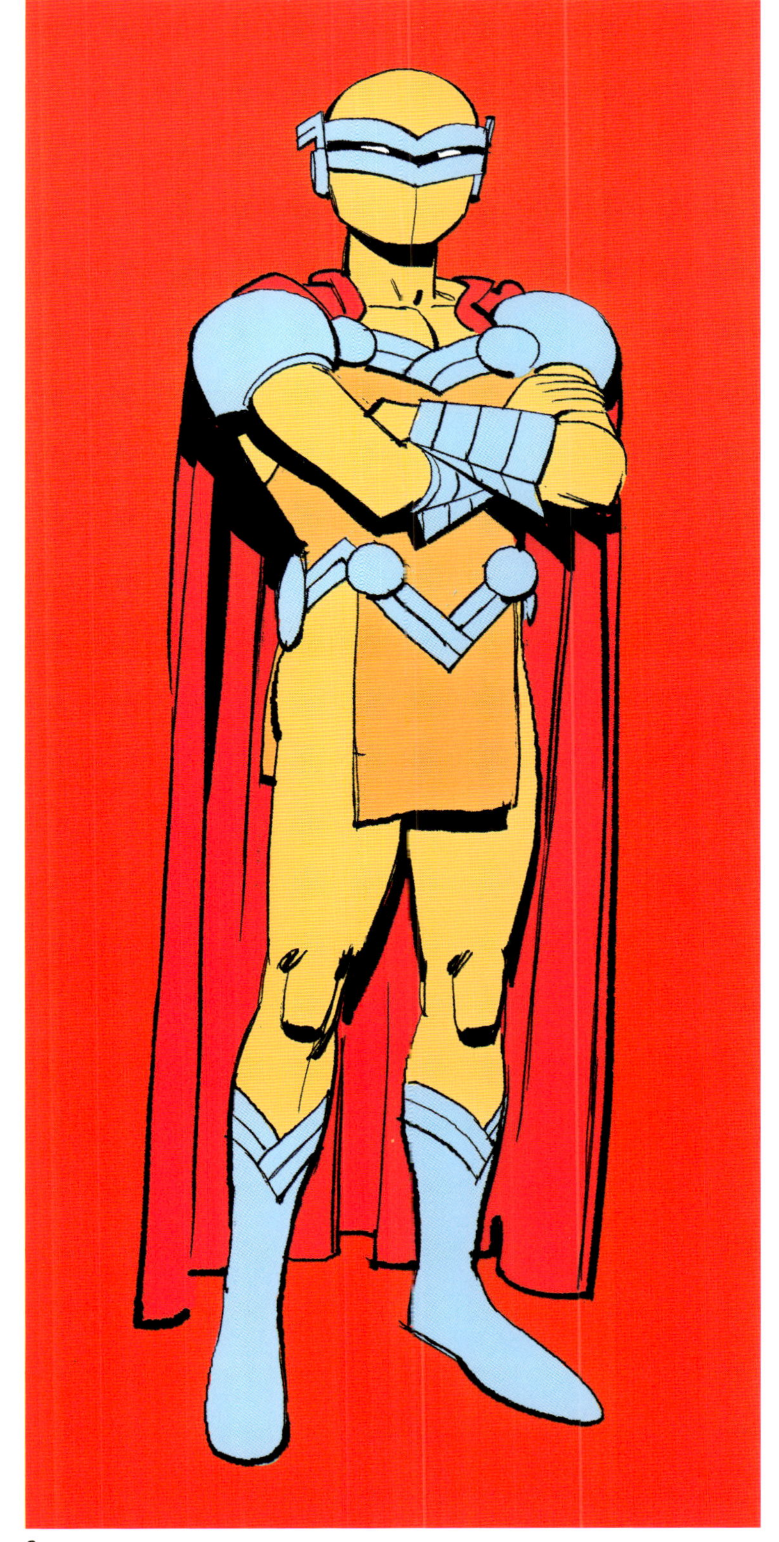

8

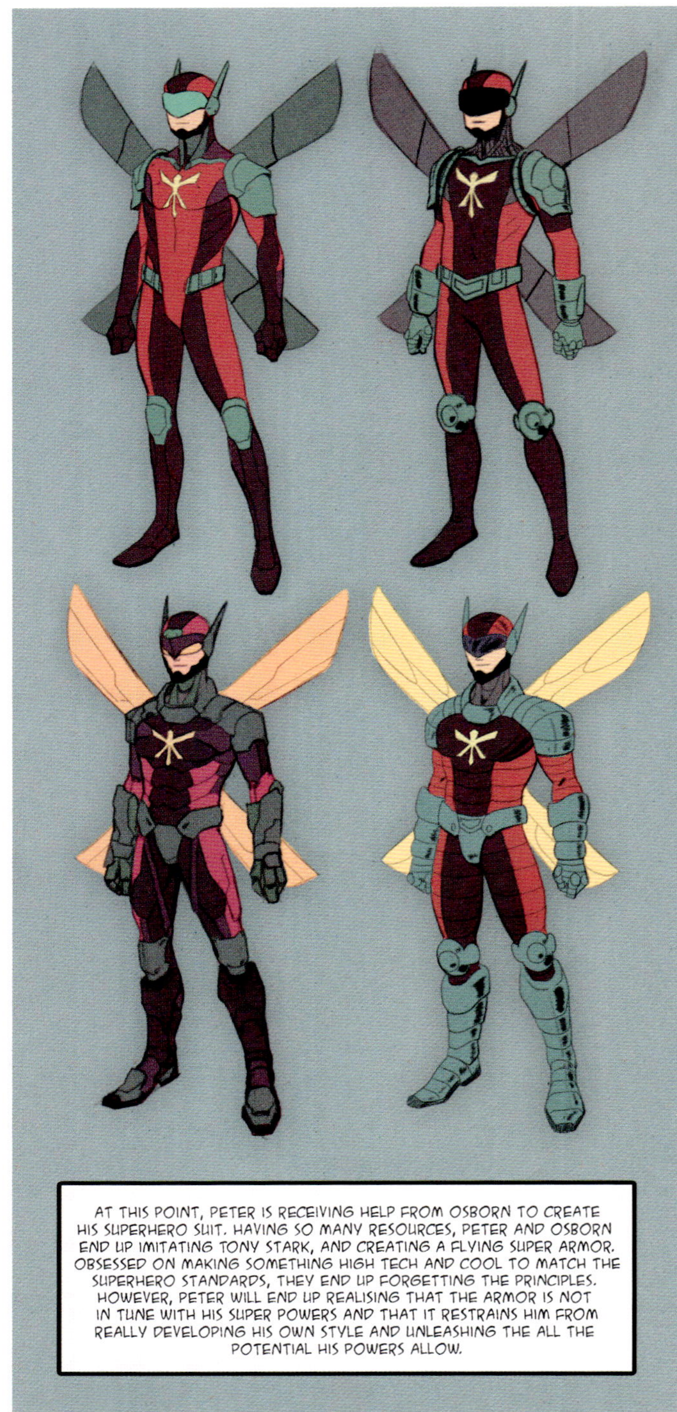

1

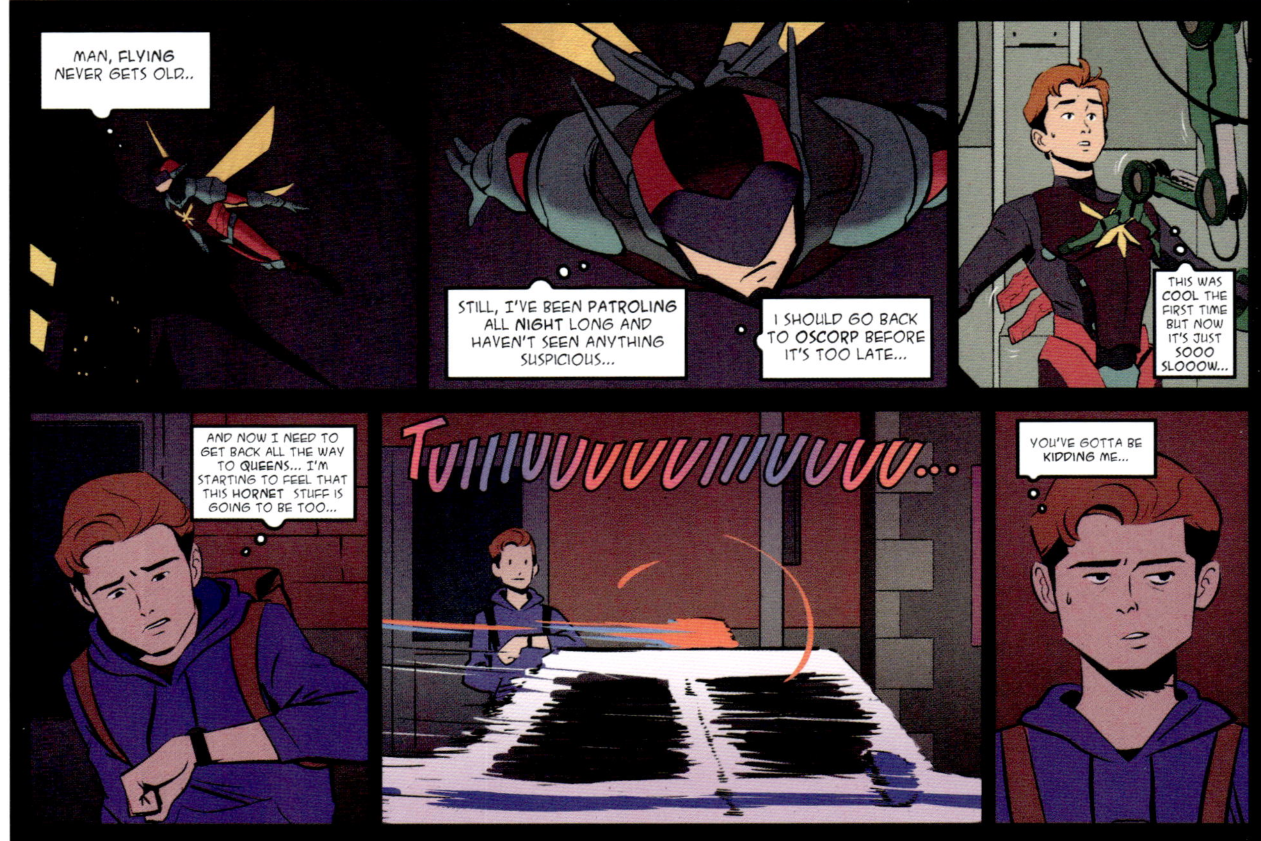

2

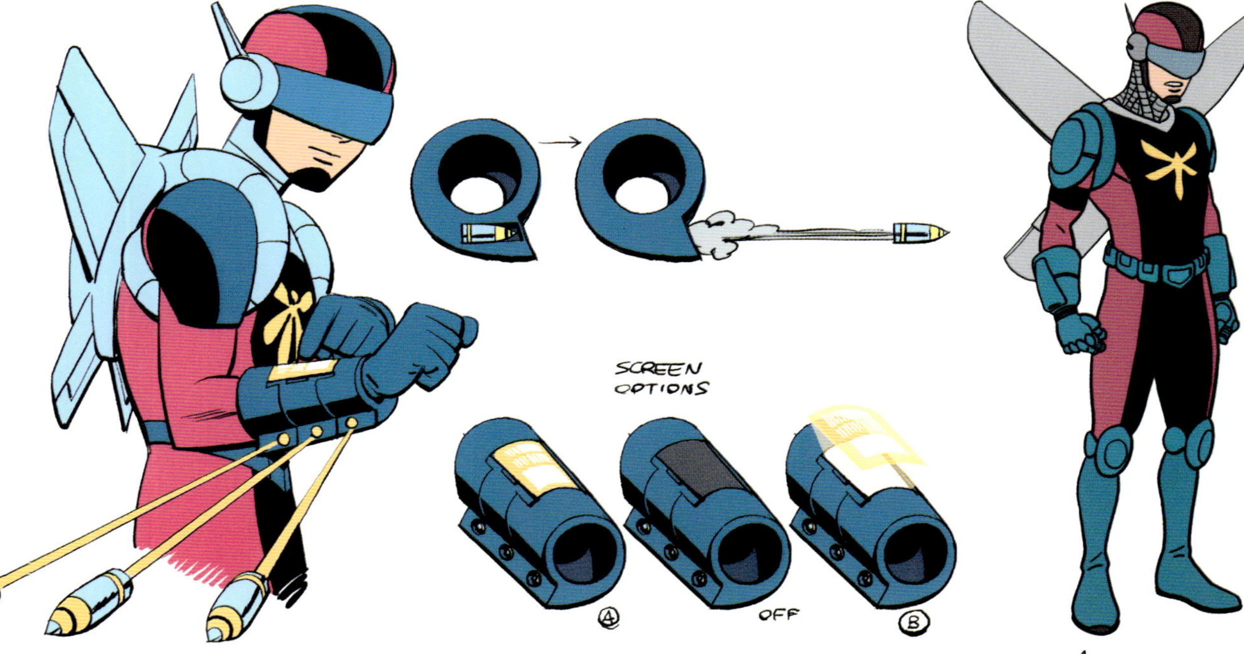

3

4

1–2 Julen Urrutia Perez **3** Leonardo Romero **4** Paolo Rivera **5–6** Leonardo Romero **7** Chris Samnee (line art) and Michael Yamada (color) **8** Leonardo Romero

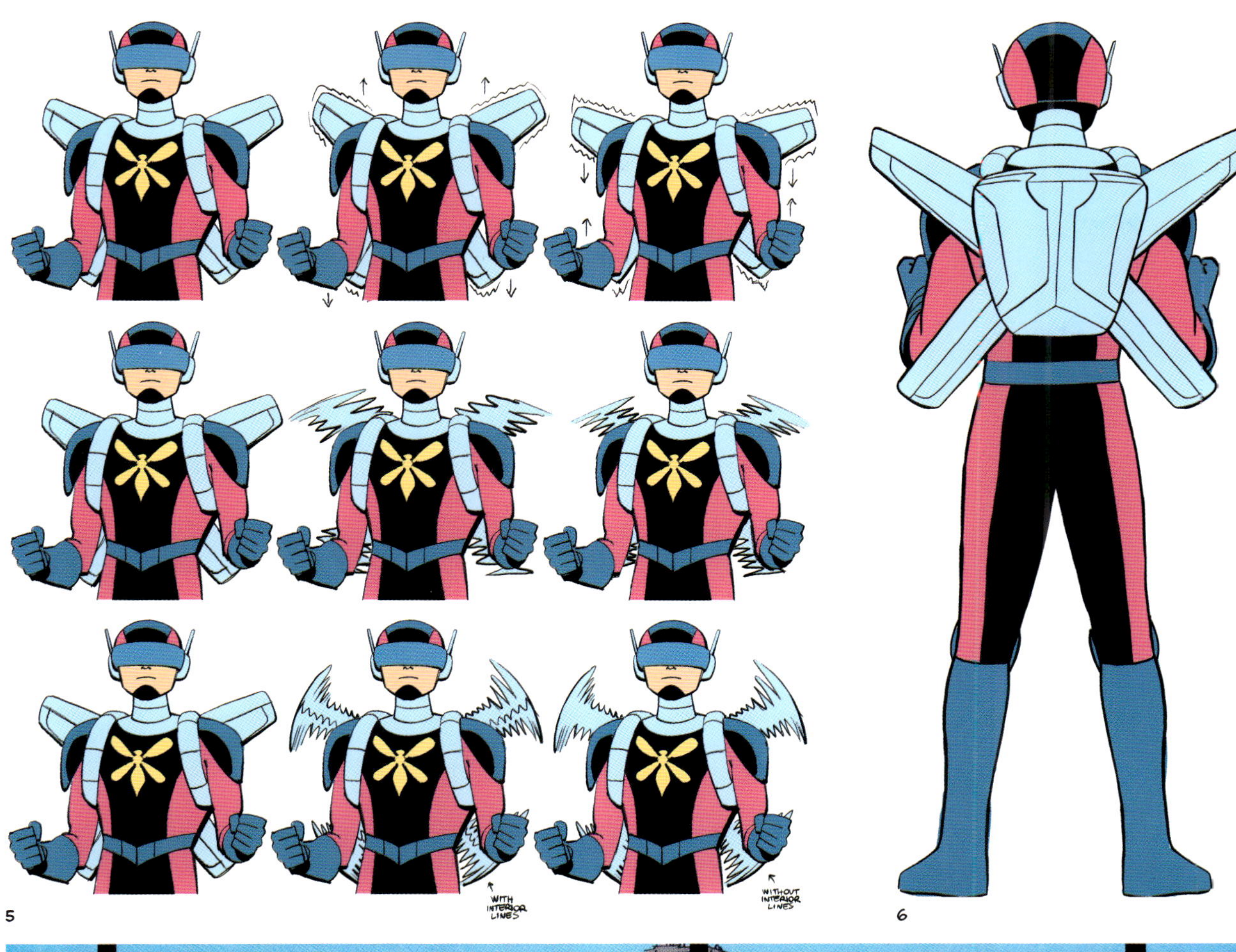

5

6

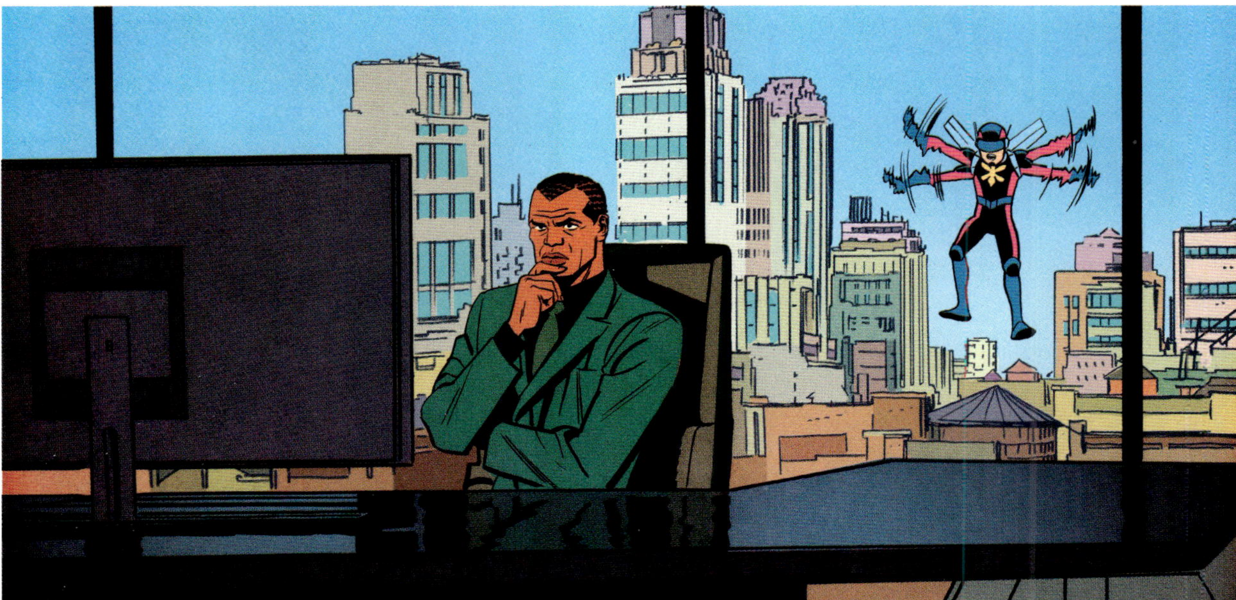

7

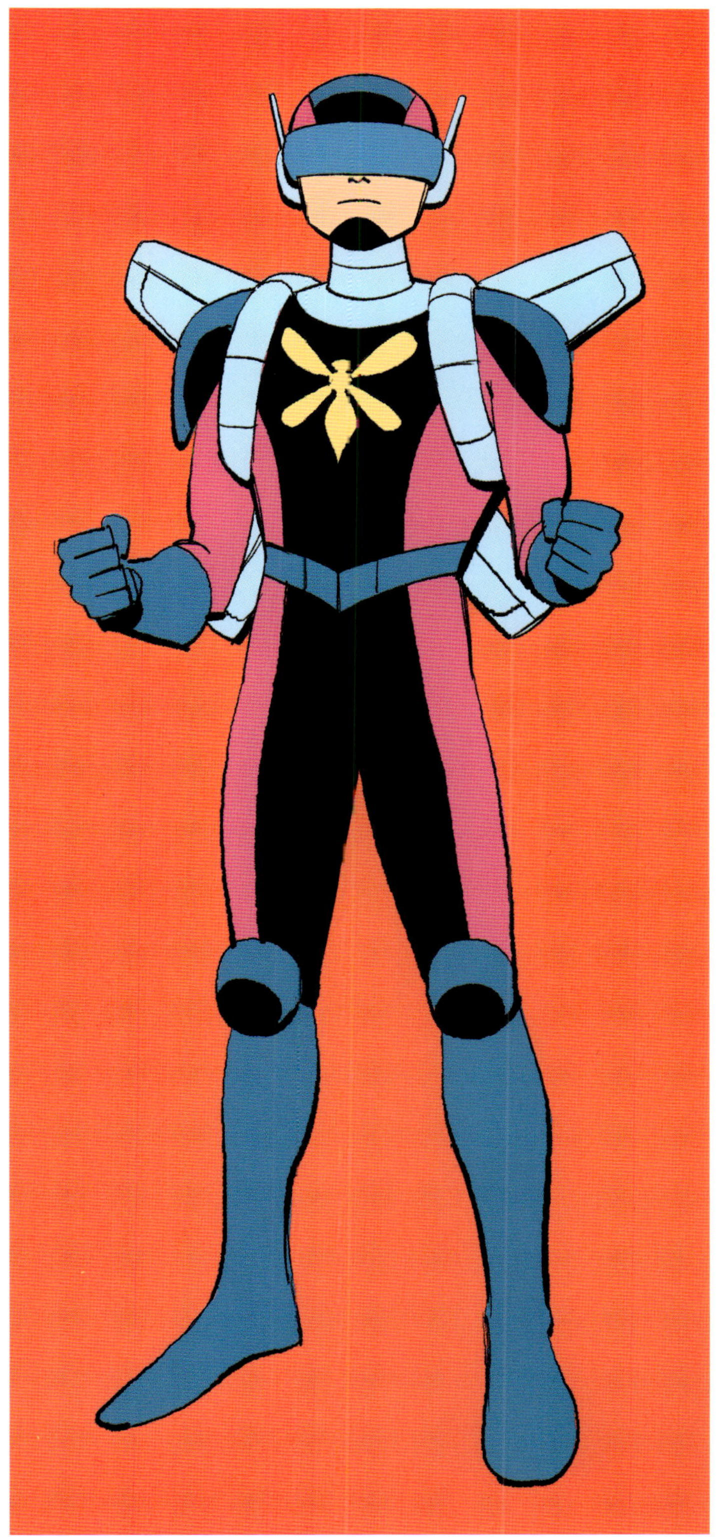

8

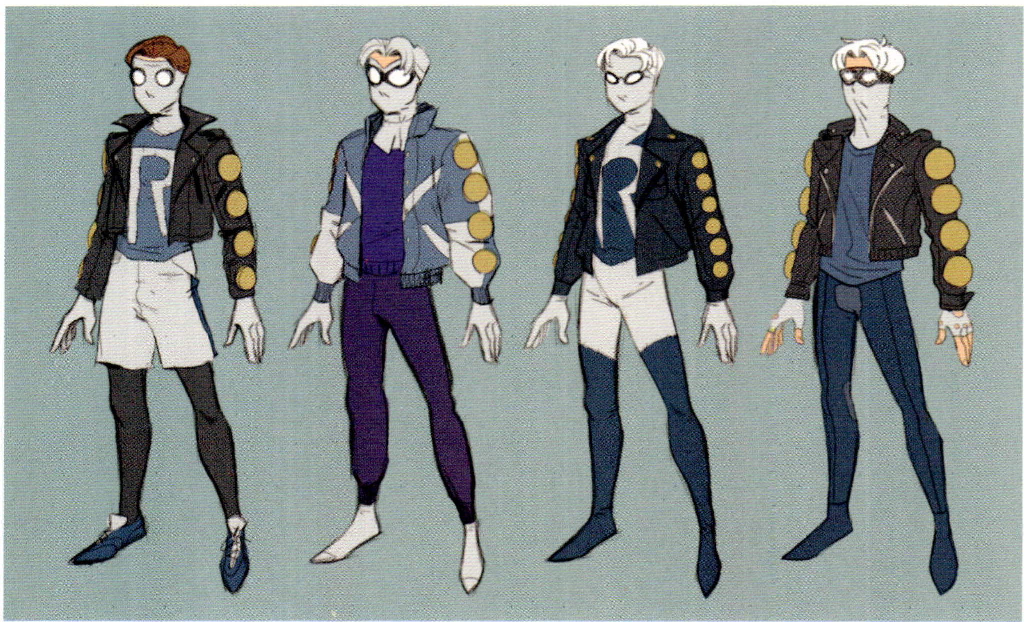

1

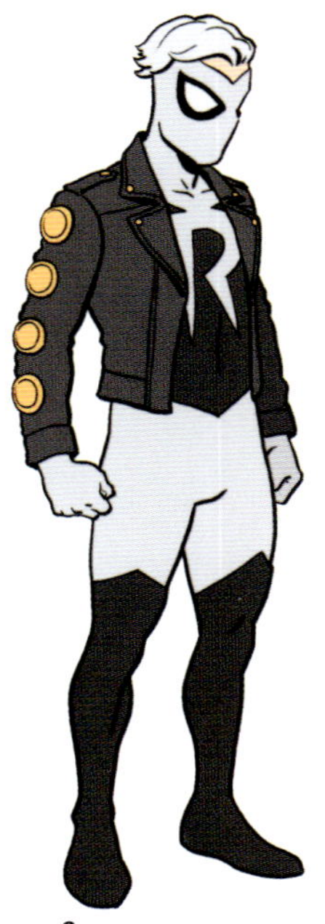

2

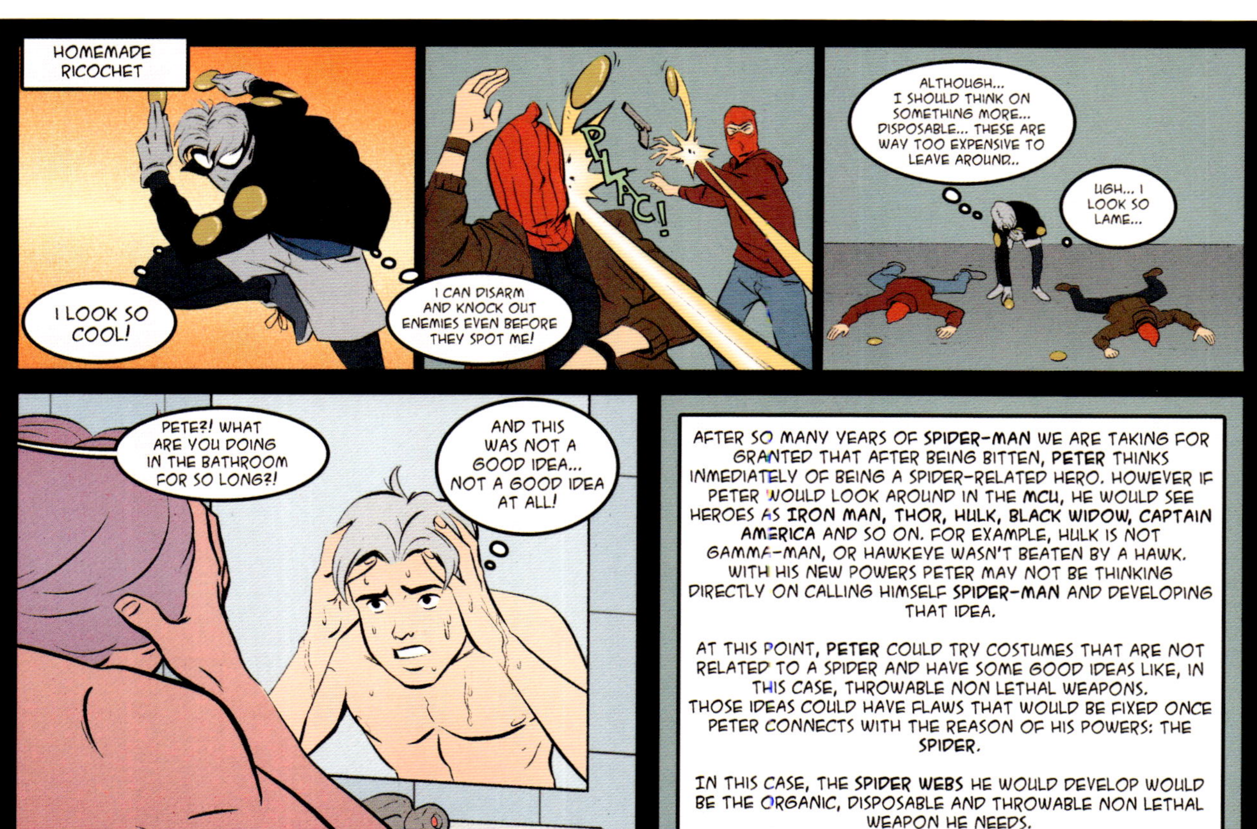

3

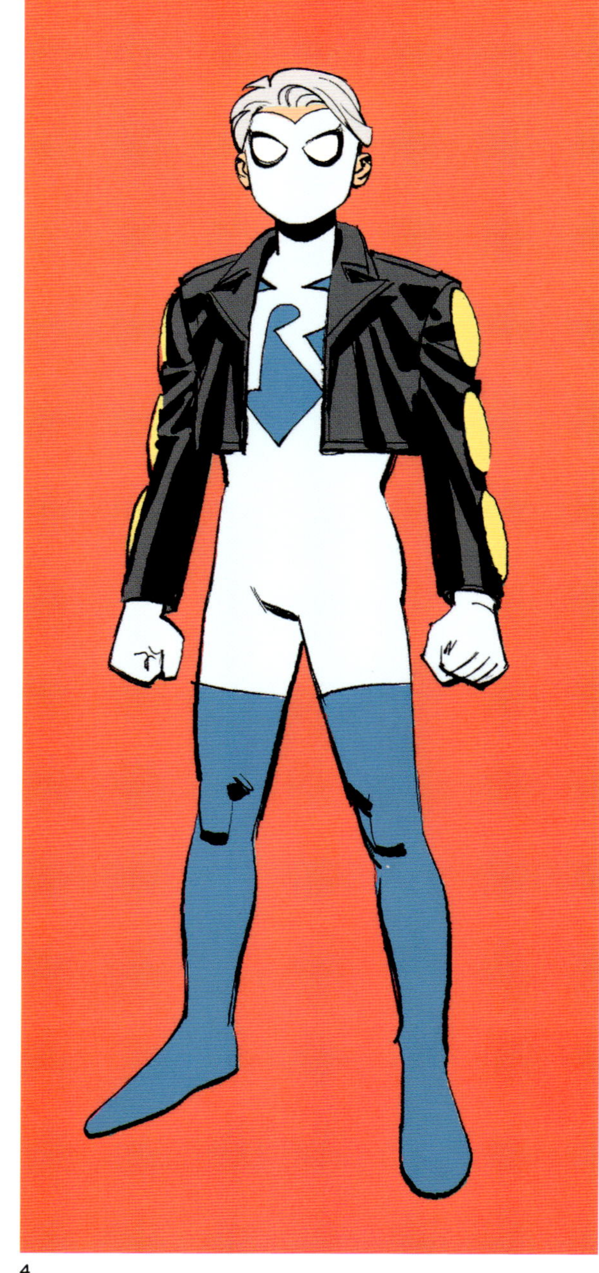

4

1 Julen Urrutia Perez **2** Paolo Rivera
3 Julen Urrutia Perez **4** Leonardo Romero
5 Julen Urrutia Perez **6** Paolo Rivera
7 Mel Zwyer **8–9** Leonardo Romero

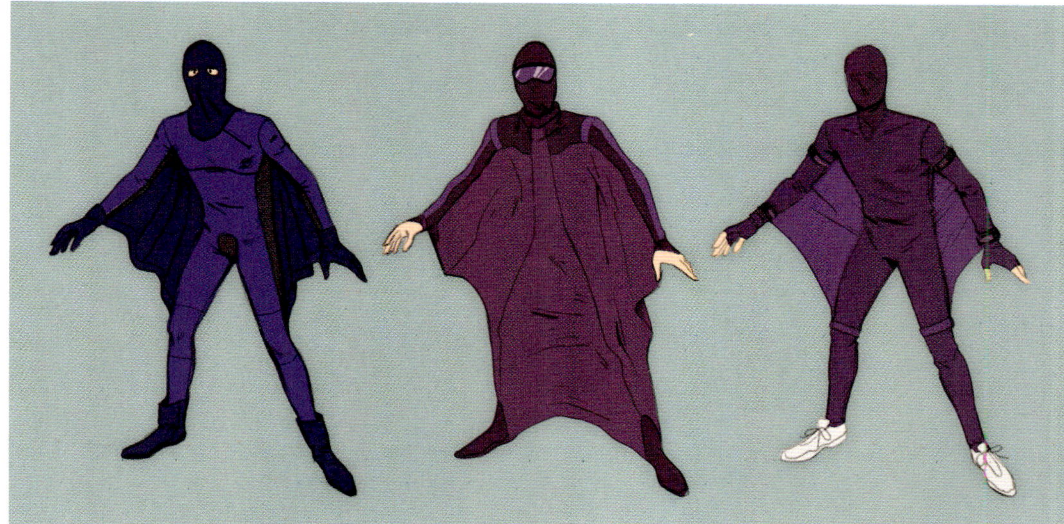

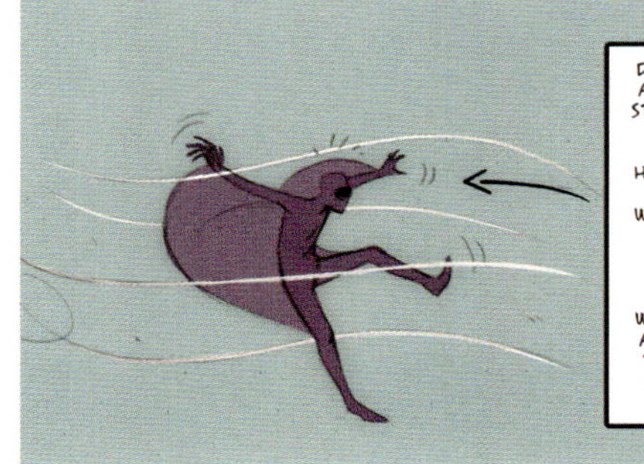

DRESSING AS **DUSK**, PETER WAS ABLE TO JUMP WITH HIS SUPER STRENGH AND USE IT TO COVER LONG **DISTANCES**.

HOWEVER, **WIND** COULD GET IN HIS WAY AT ANY MOMENT WHEN IT WAS **UNDESIRED** TOO.

THIS WOULD BE LATER **CORRECTED** AND **INCORPORATED** AS THE **WEBBING FLYSUIT** THAT CAN BE ACTIVATED AT WILL, DESIGNED TO BE USED WHERE HE CAN'T USE THE **WEBSHOOTERS** TO SWING.

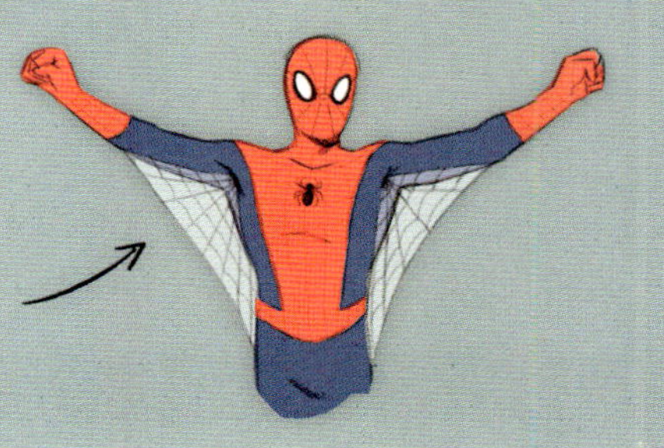

5

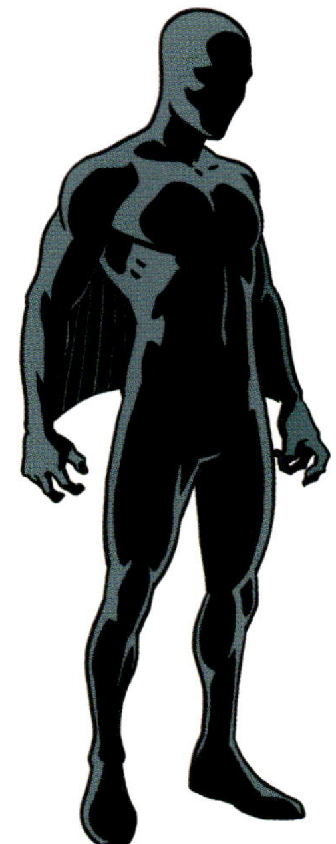

6

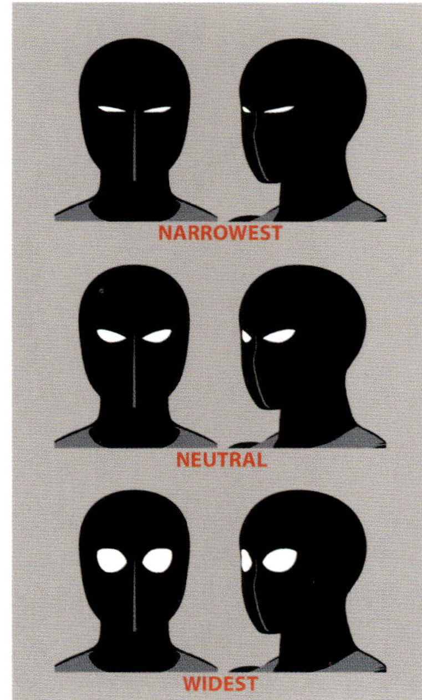

7

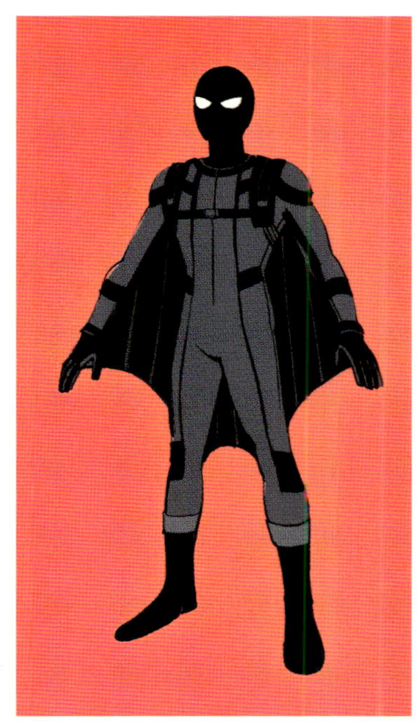

8

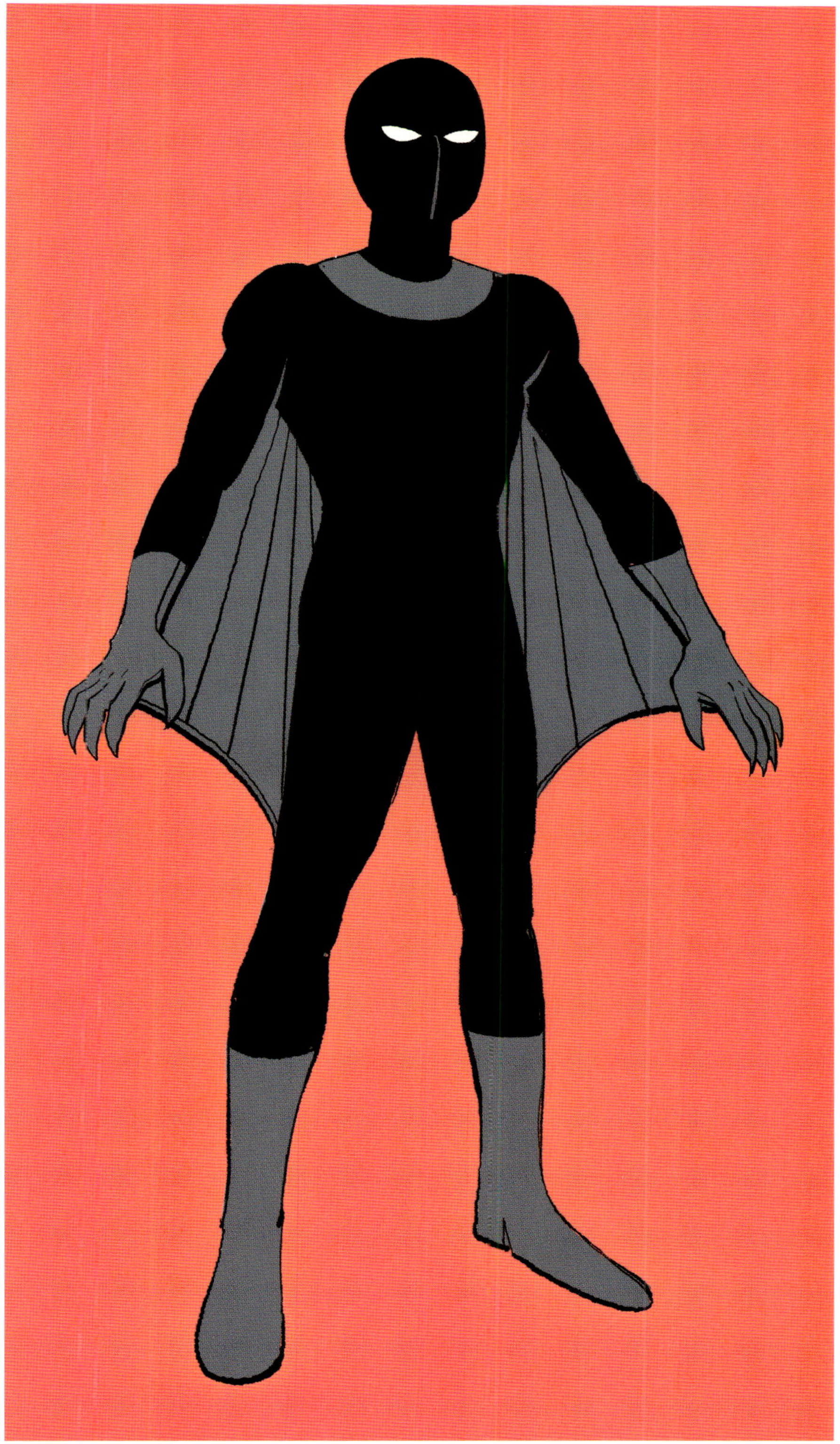

9

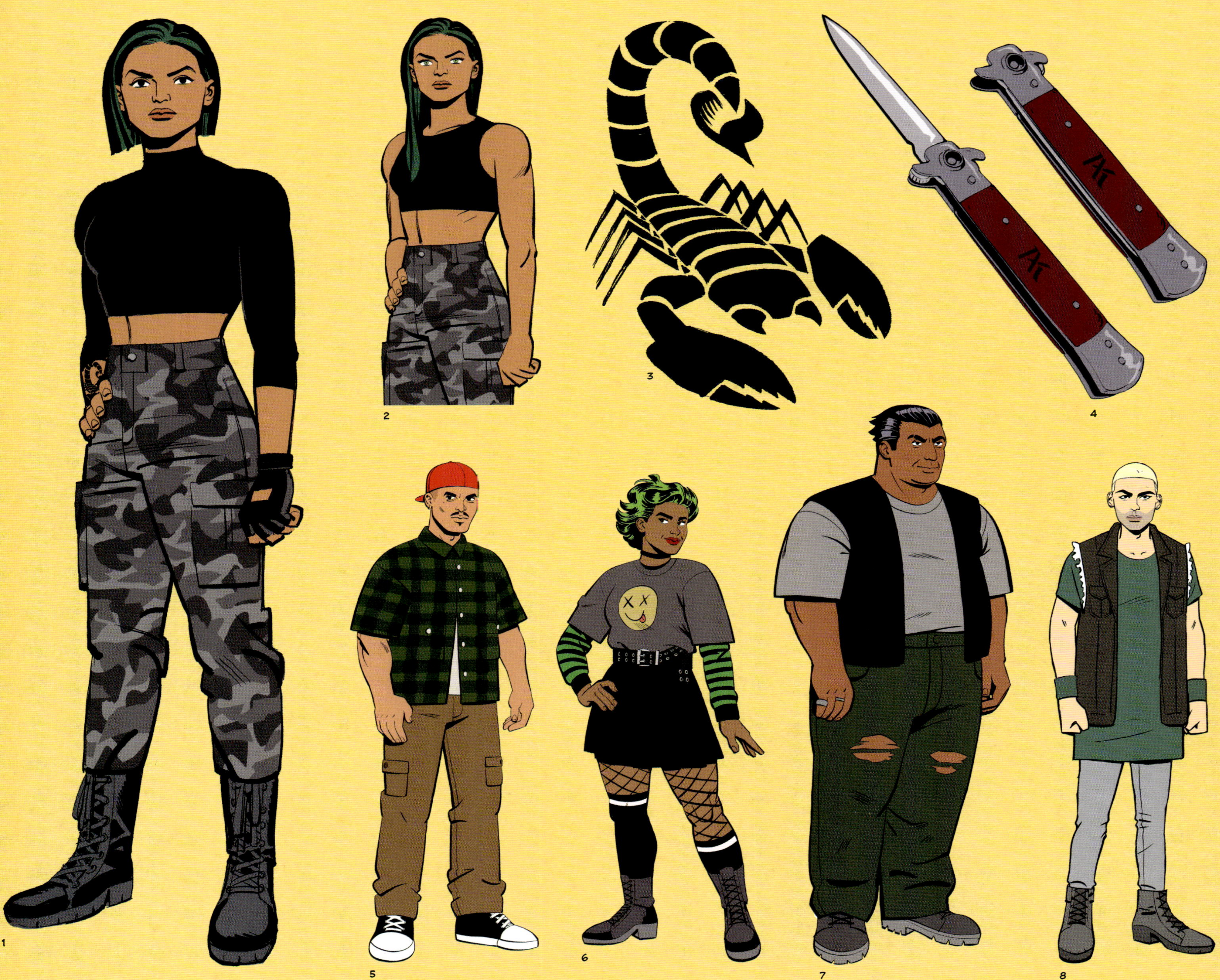
1
2
3
4
5
6
7
8

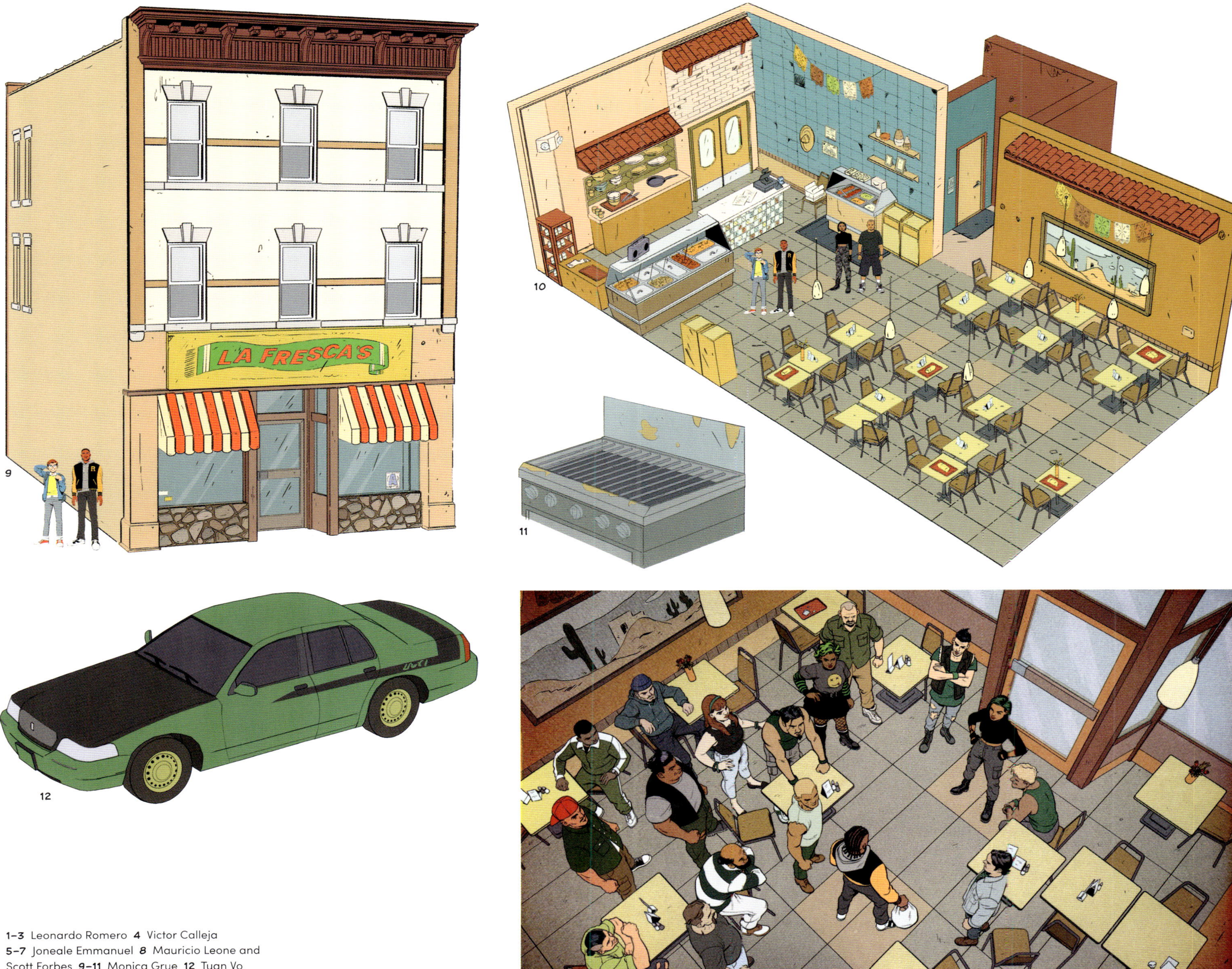

9
10
11
12
13

1–3 Leonardo Romero **4** Victor Calleja
5–7 Joneale Emmanuel **8** Mauricio Leone and
Scott Forbes **9–11** Monica Grue **12** Tuan Vo
13 Paolo Rivera (line art) and Michael Yamada (color)

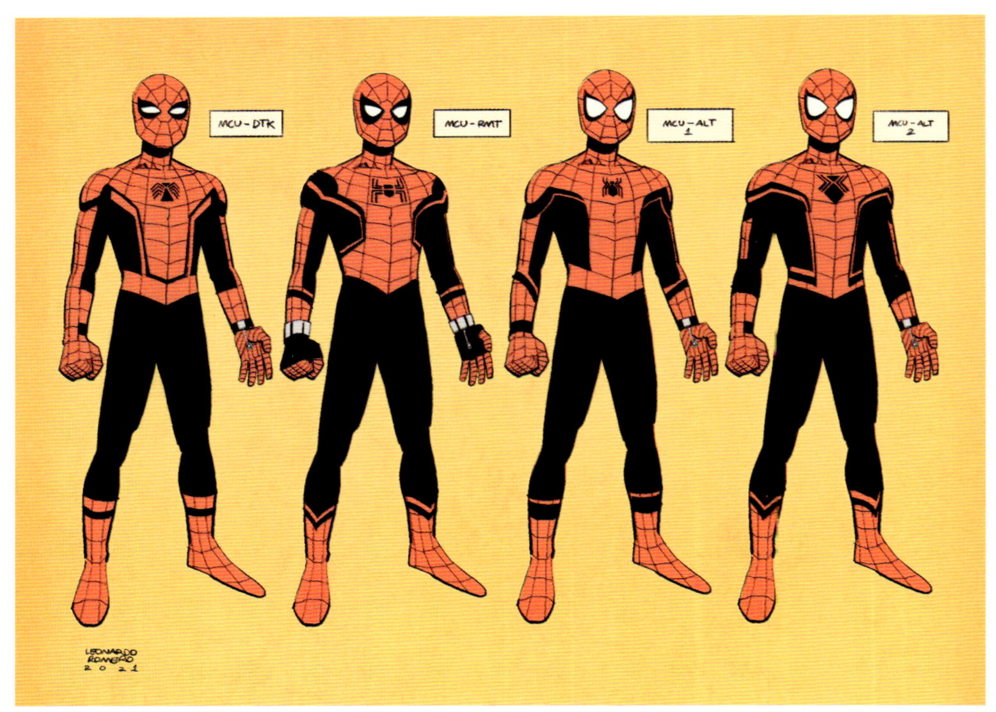
MCU - DTK
MCU - RMT
MCU - ALT 1
MCU - ALT 2
LEONARDO ROMERO 2021

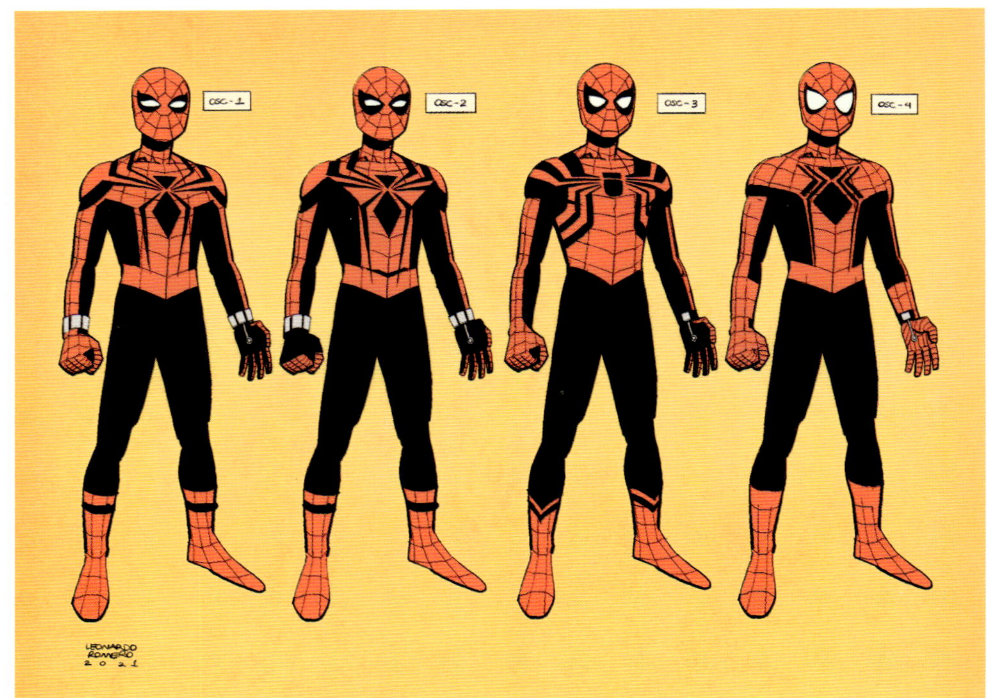
OSC - 1
OSC - 2
OSC - 3
OSC - 4
LEONARDO ROMERO 2021

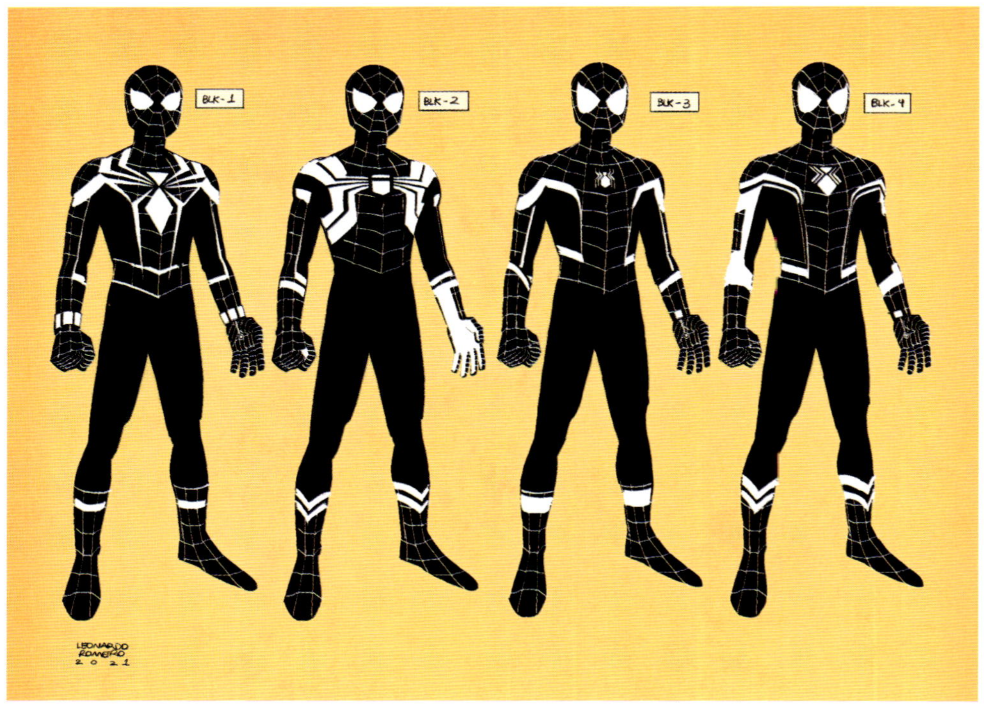
BLK - 1
BLK - 2
BLK - 3
BLK - 4
LEONARDO ROMERO 2021

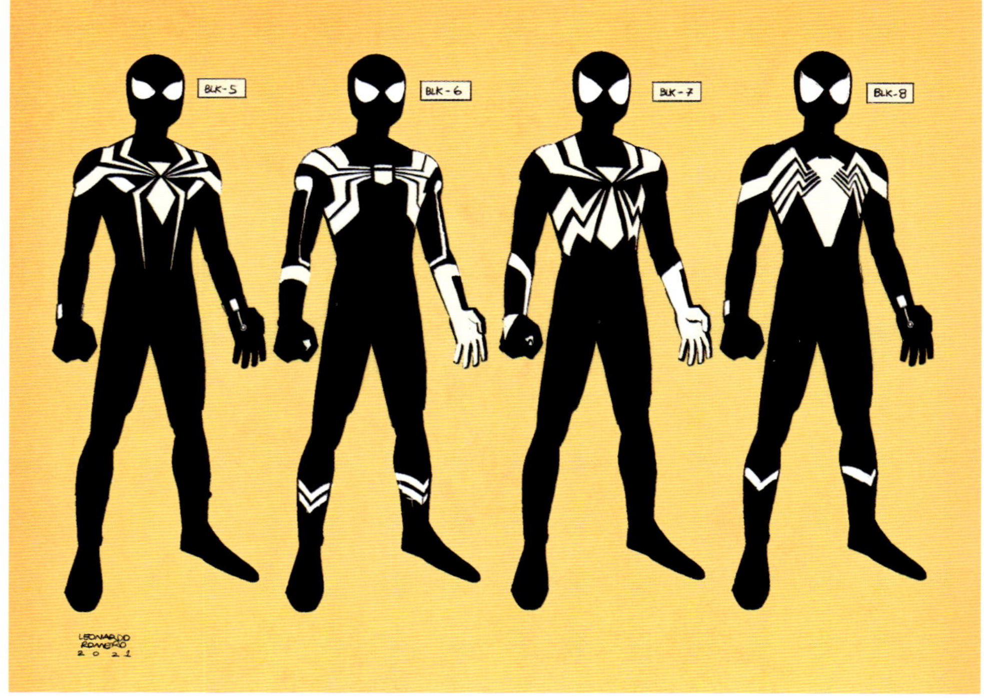
BLK - 5
BLK - 6
BLK - 7
BLK - 8
LEONARDO ROMERO 2021

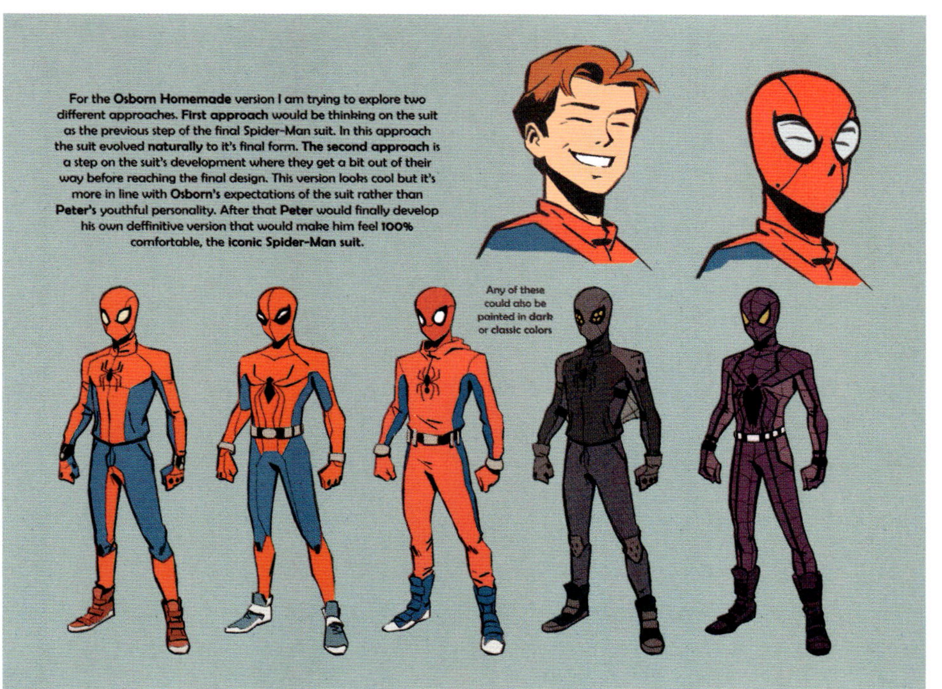

1

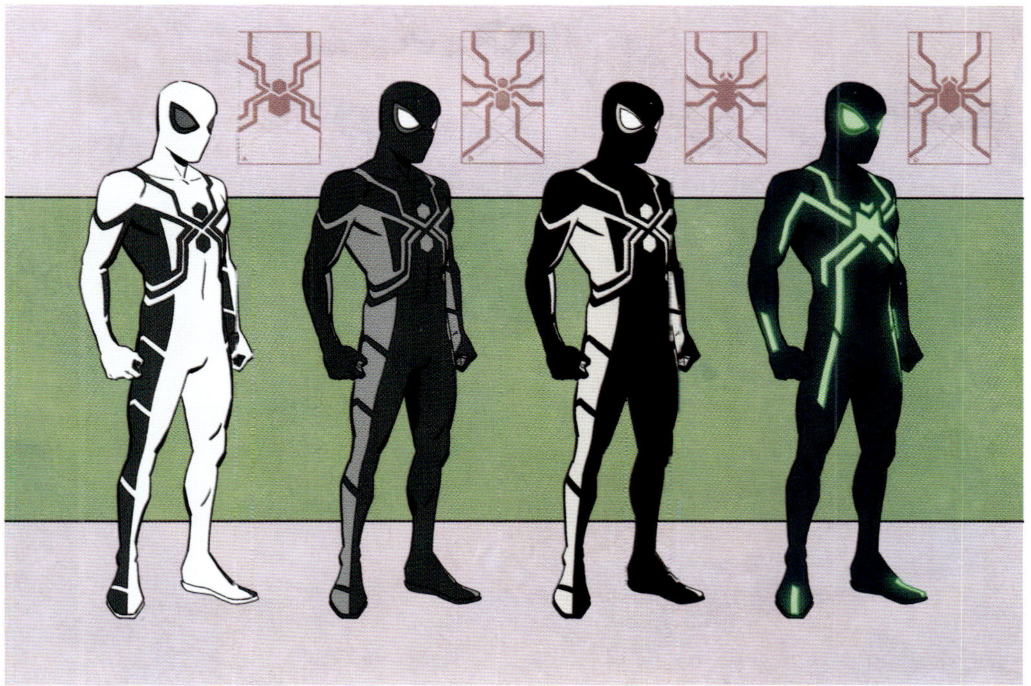

2

3

OPPOSITE
Leonardo Romero
1 Julen Urrutia Perez
2 Paolo Rivera
3 Joey Vazquez

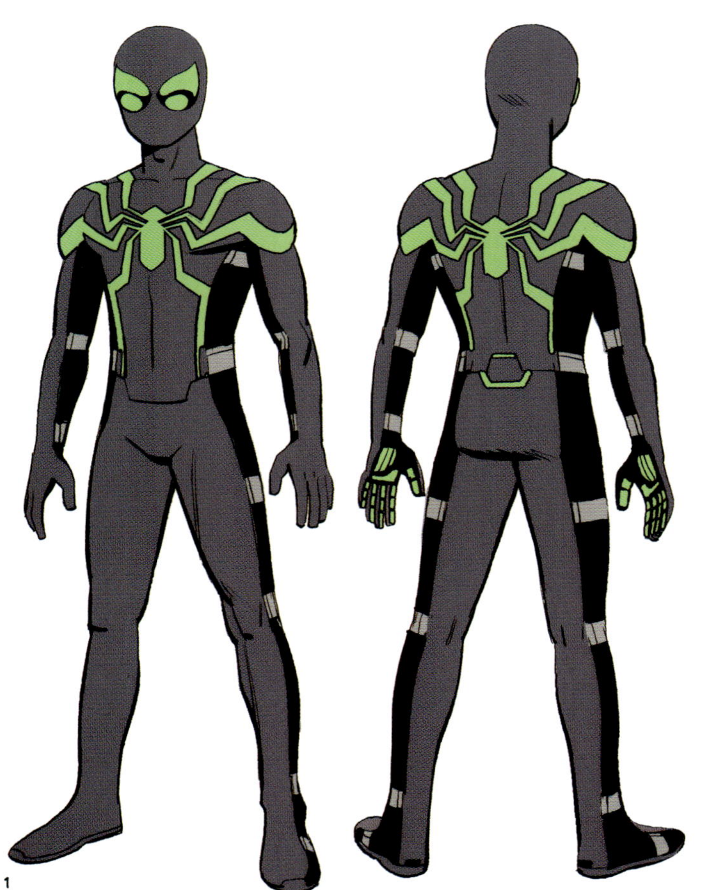

1

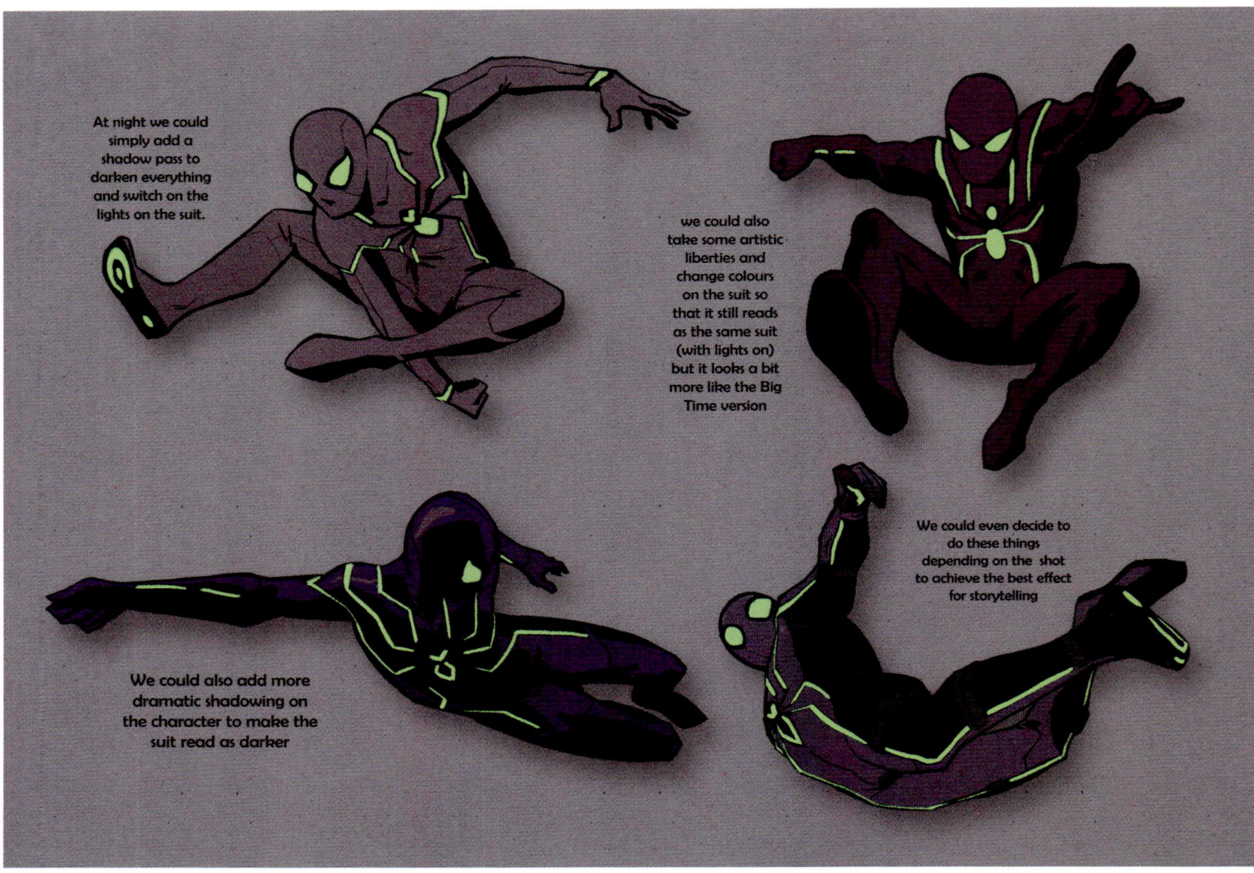
At night we could simply add a shadow pass to darken everything and switch on the lights on the suit.
we could also take some artistic liberties and change colours on the suit so that it still reads as the same suit (with lights on) but it looks a bit more like the Big Time version
We could also add more dramatic shadowing on the character to make the suit read as darker
We could even decide to do these things depending on the shot to achieve the best effect for storytelling

2

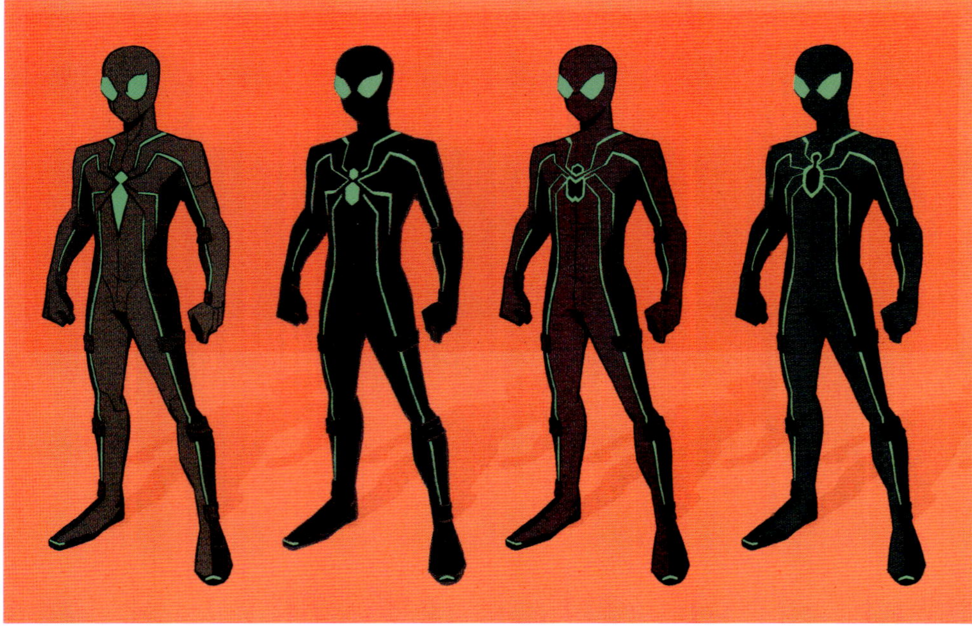

3

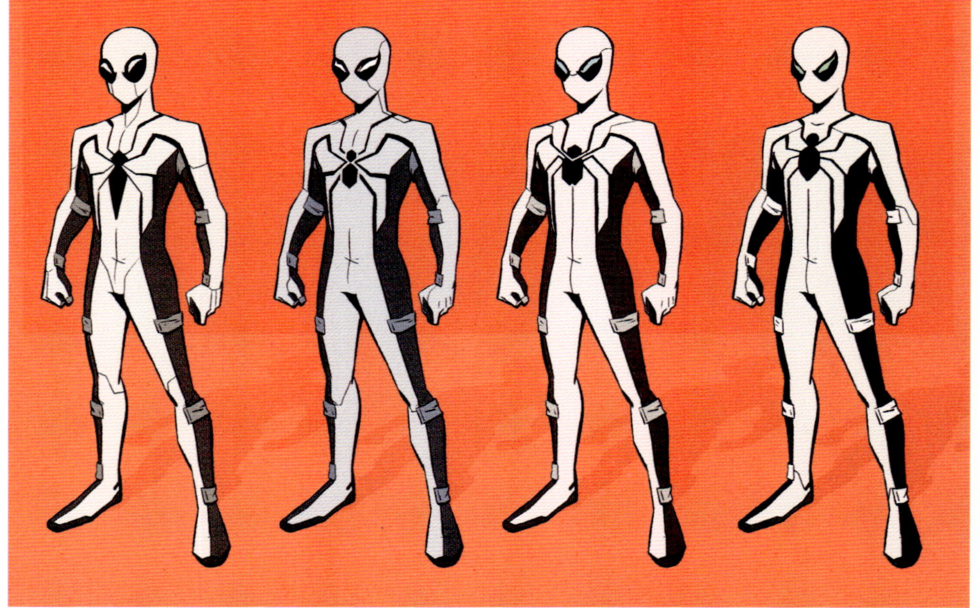

4

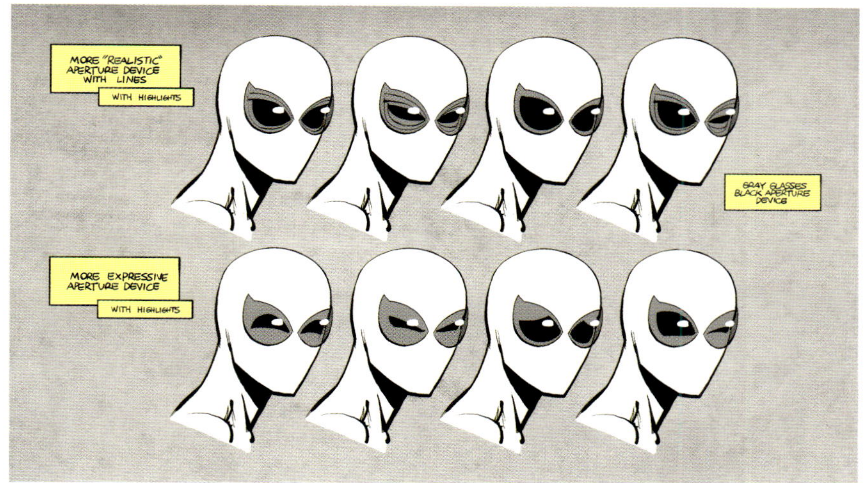

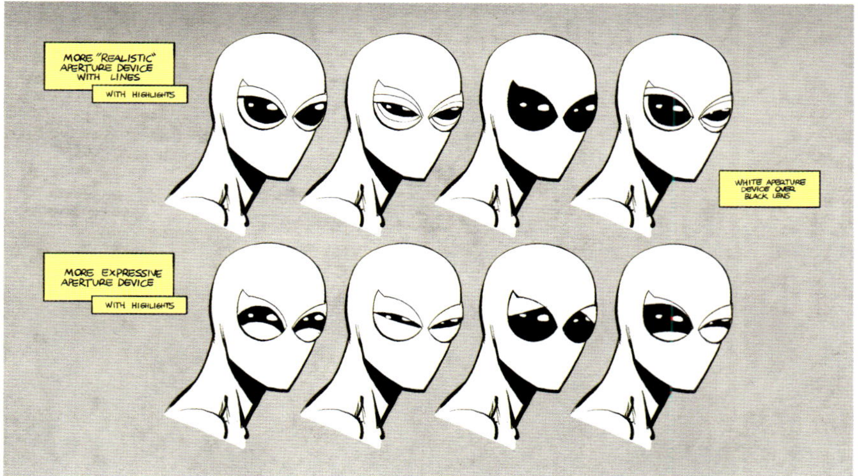

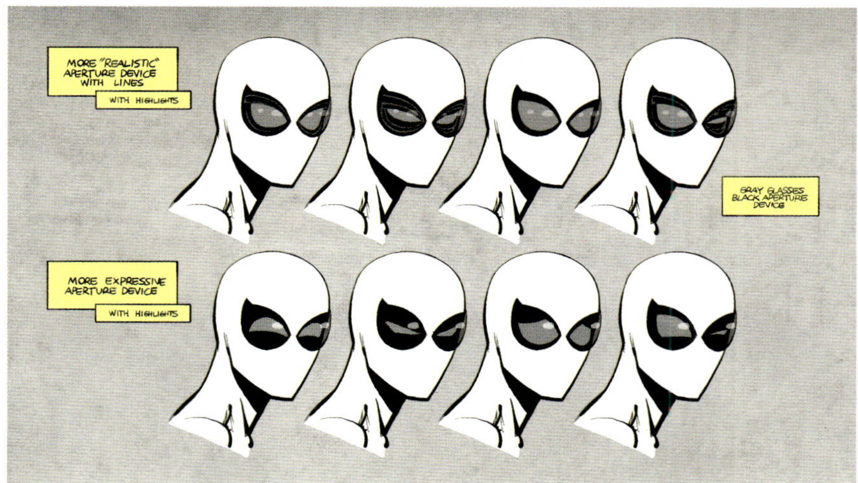

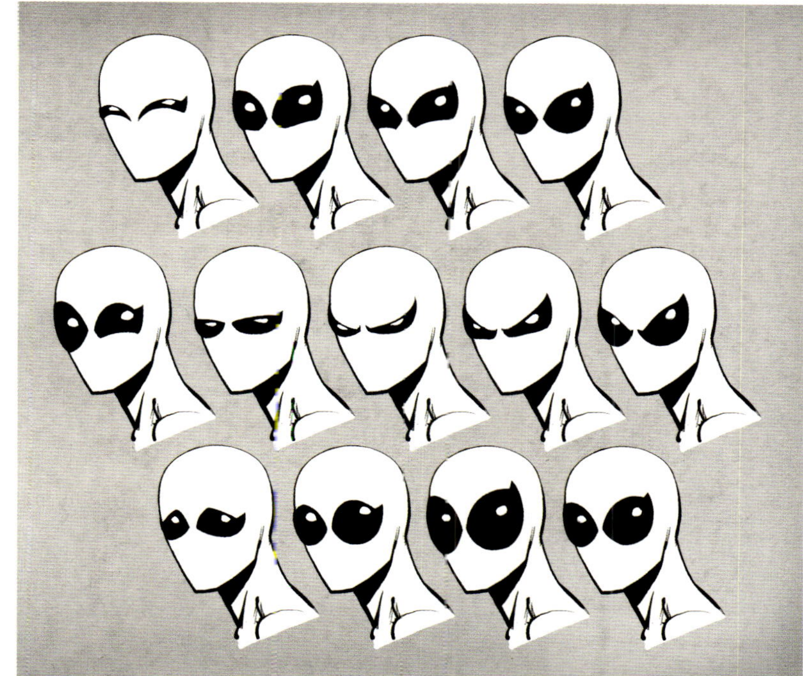

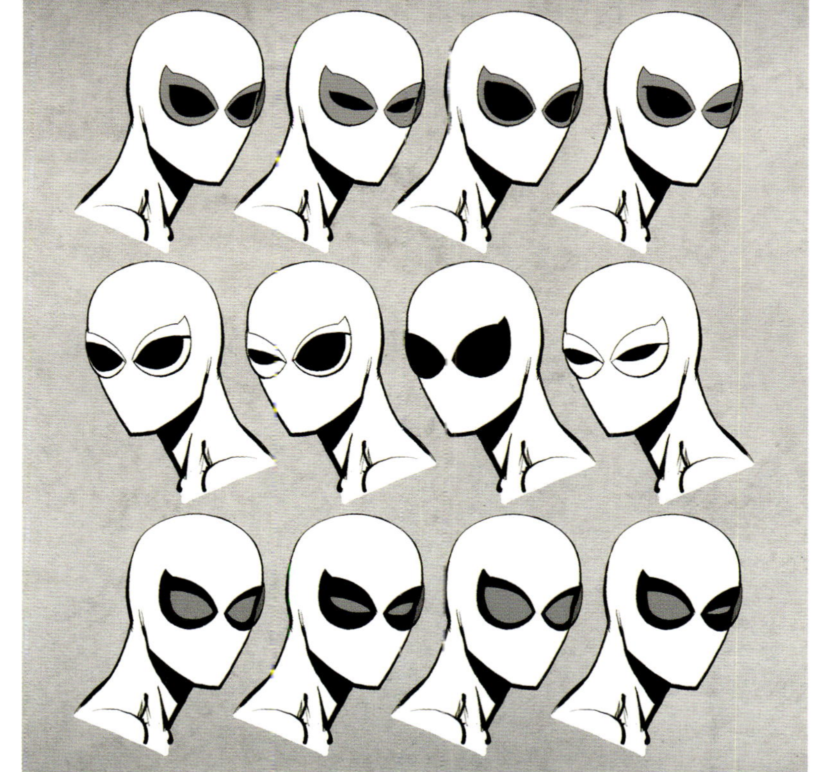

1 Leonardo Romero
2–4 Julen Urrutia Perez
THIS PAGE
Leonardo Romero

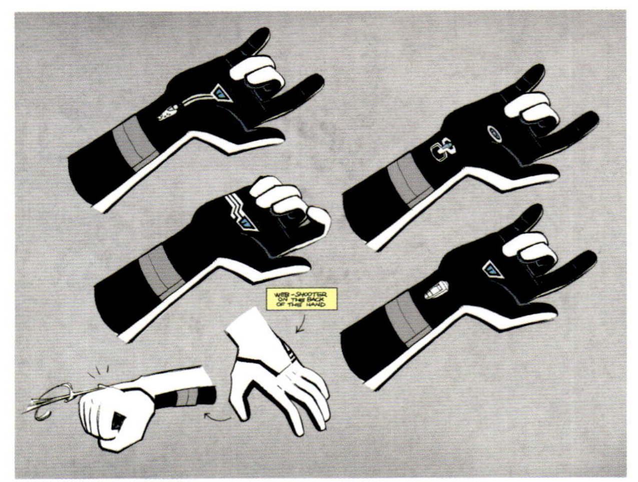
WEB-SHOOTER ON THE BACK OF THE HAND

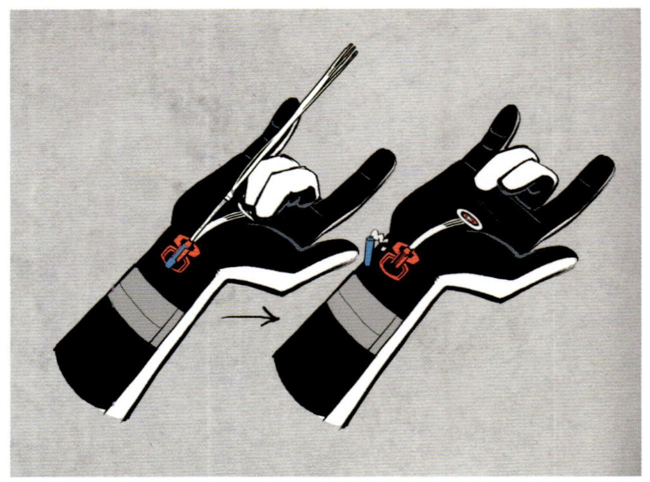

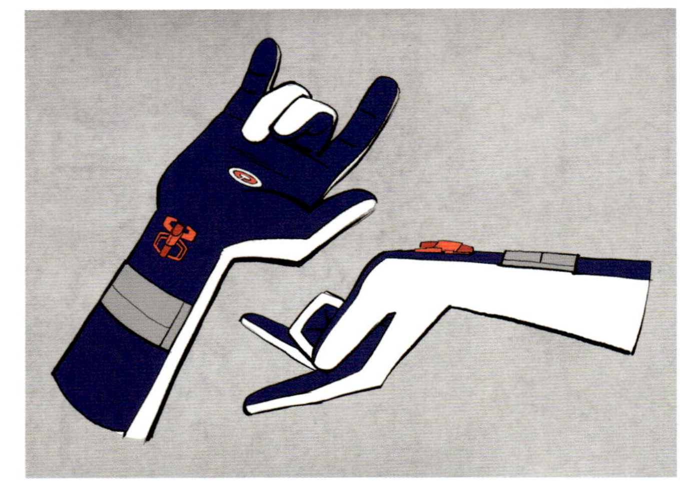

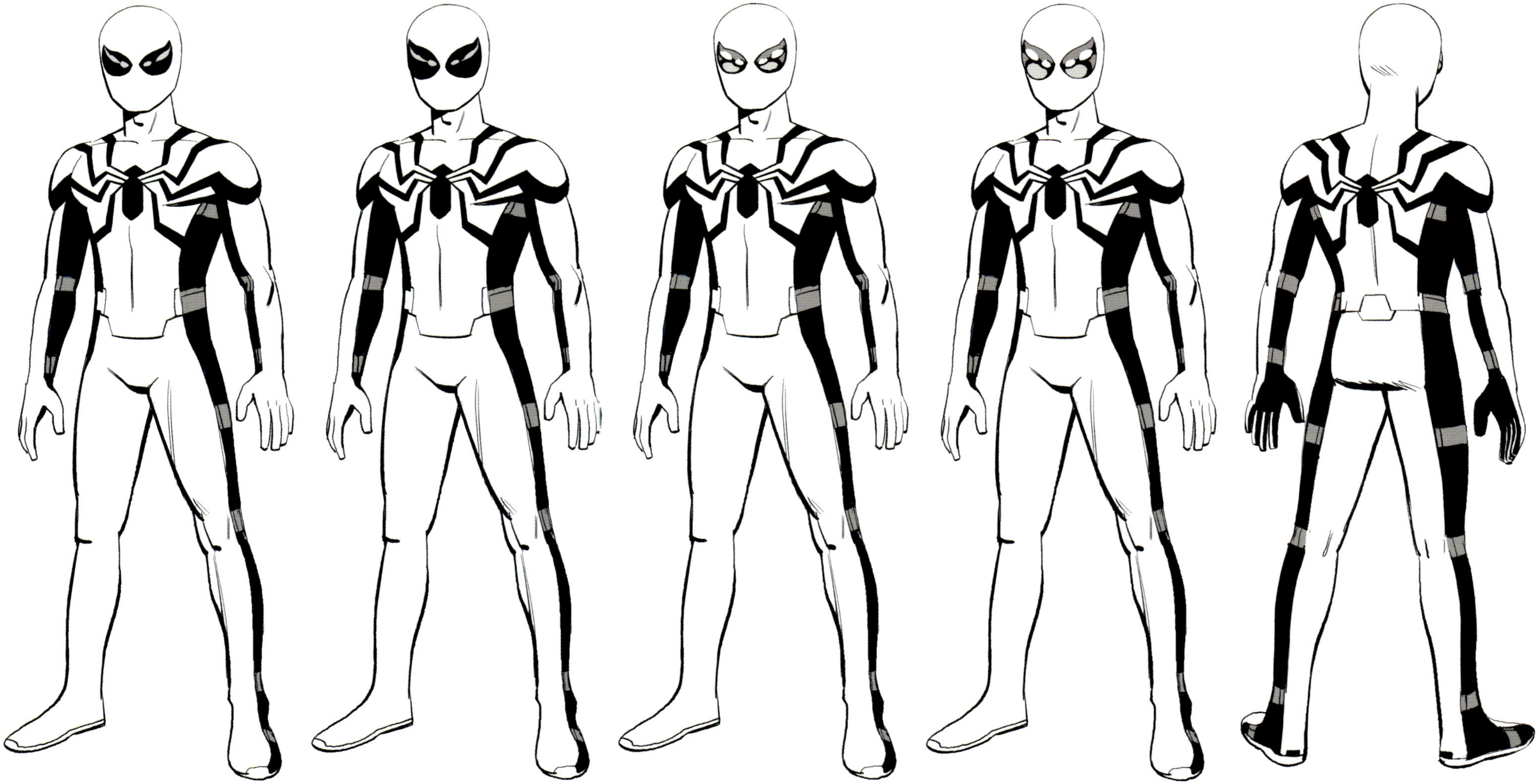

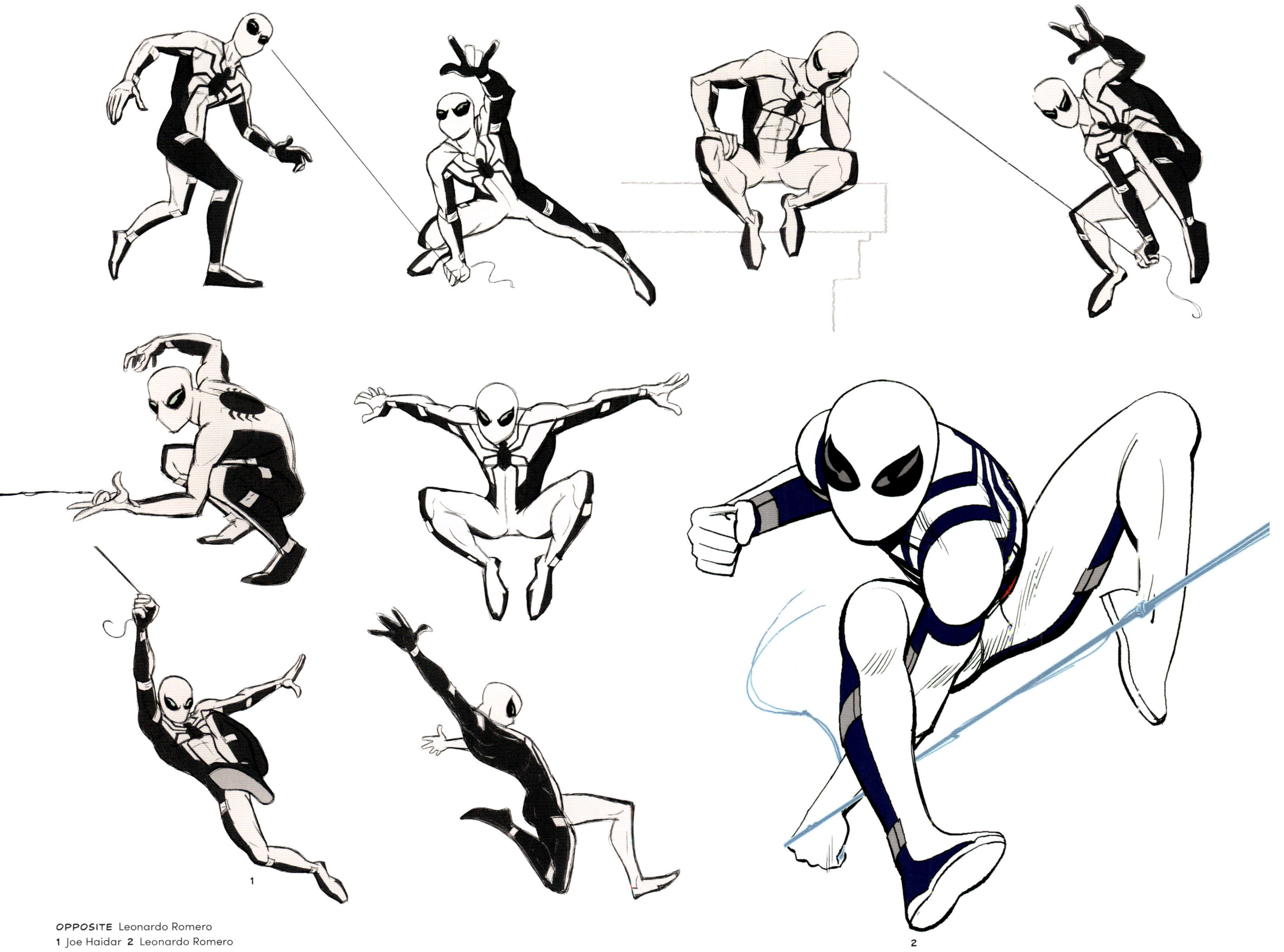

1

2

OPPOSITE Leonardo Romero
1 Joe Haidar **2** Leonardo Romero

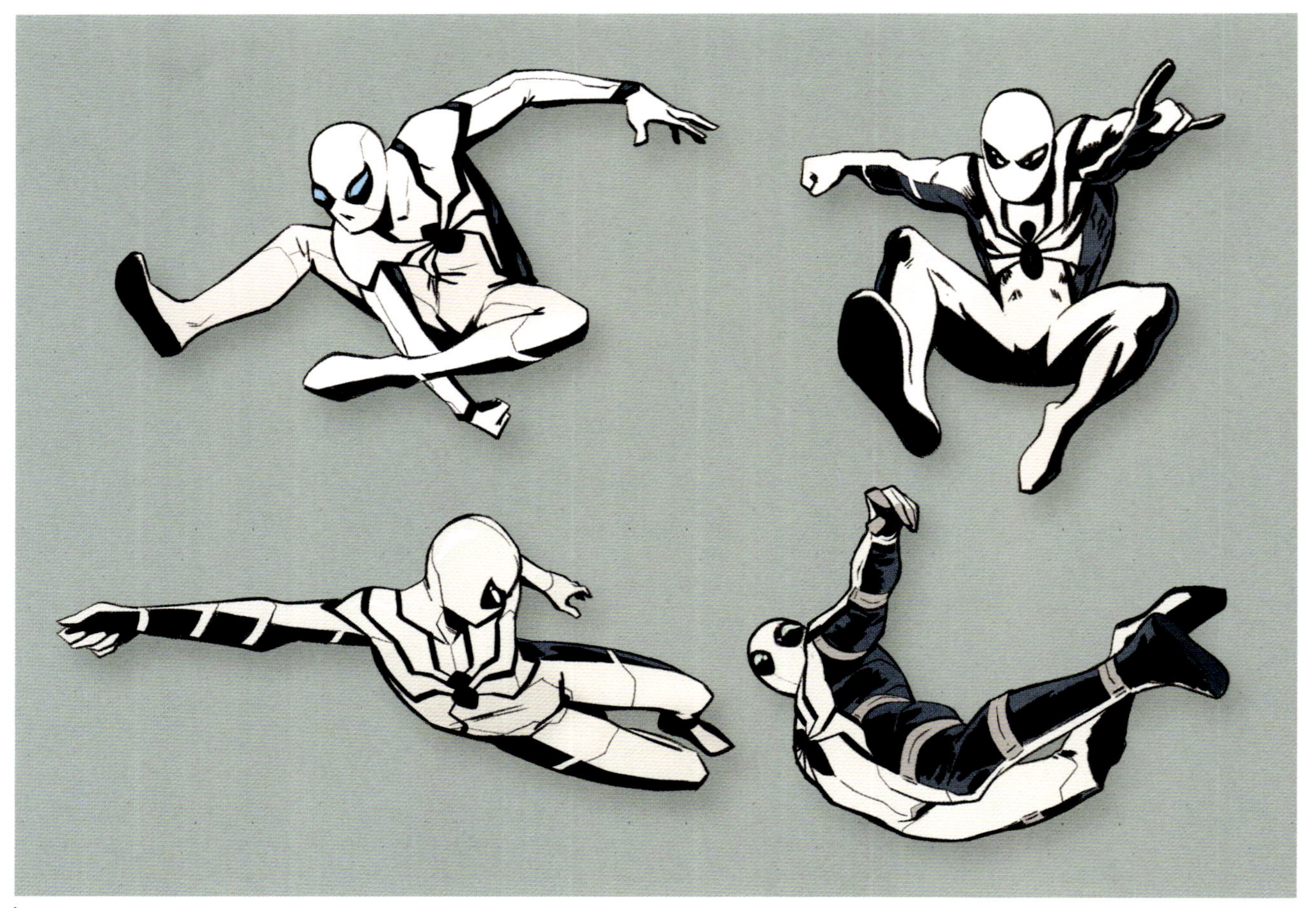

1

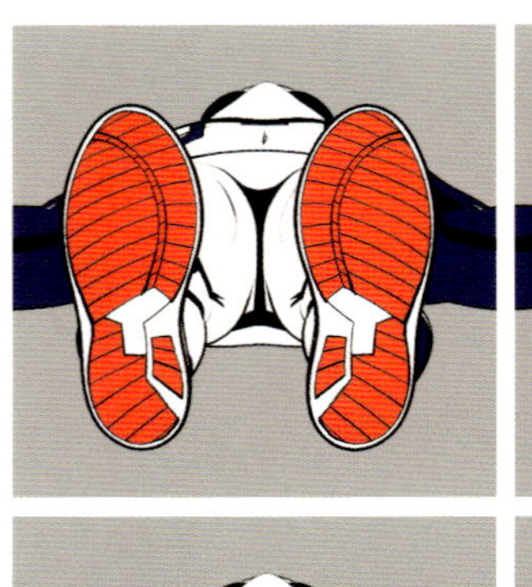

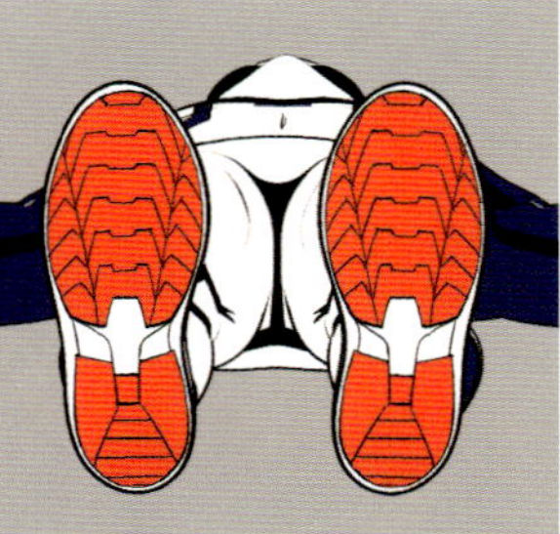

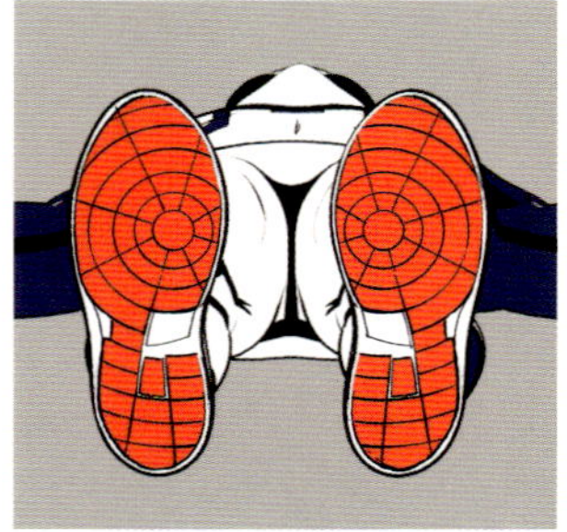

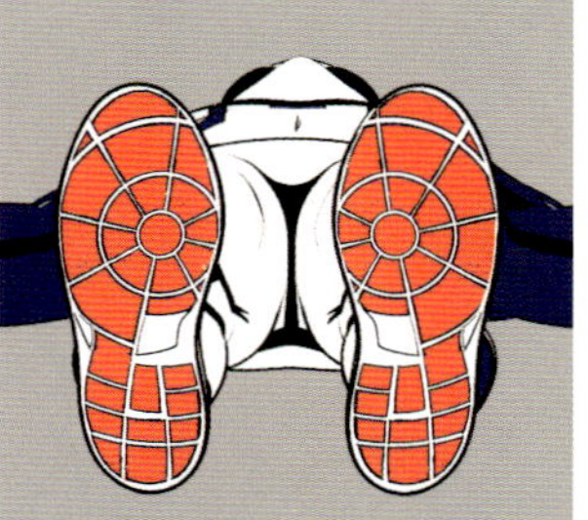

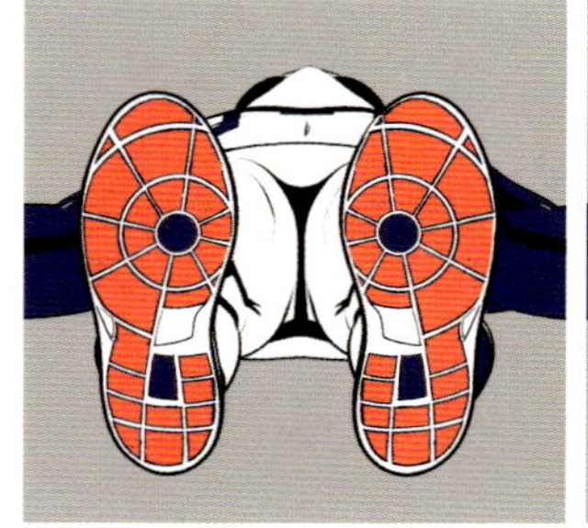

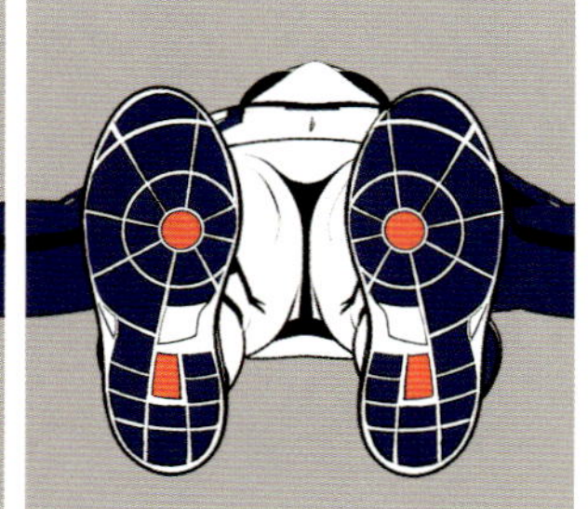

2

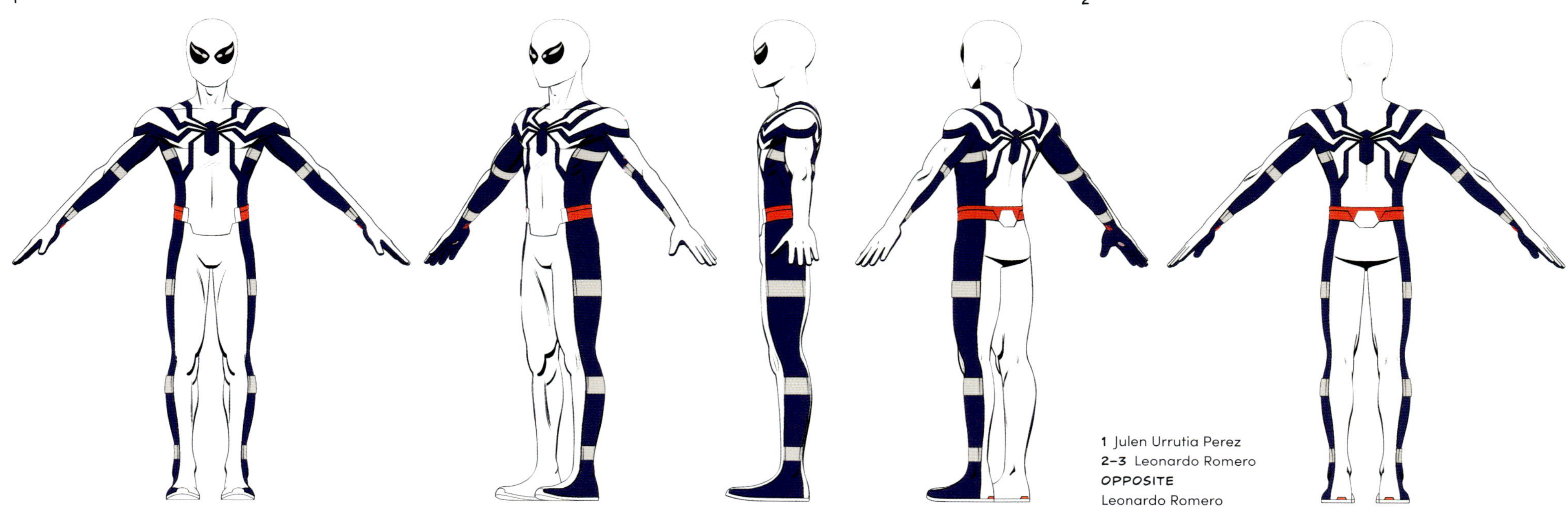

3

1 Julen Urrutia Perez
2–3 Leonardo Romero
OPPOSITE
Leonardo Romero

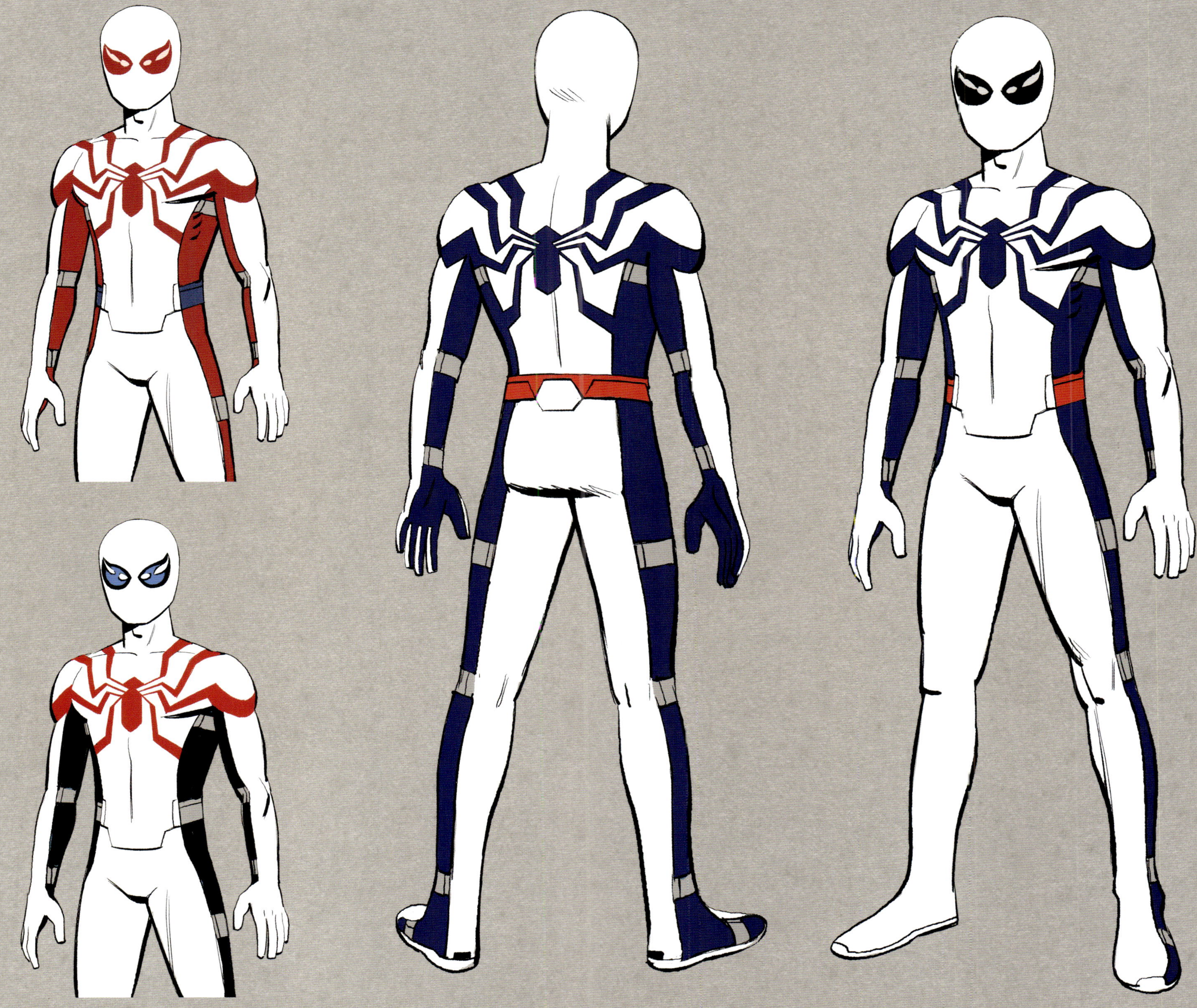

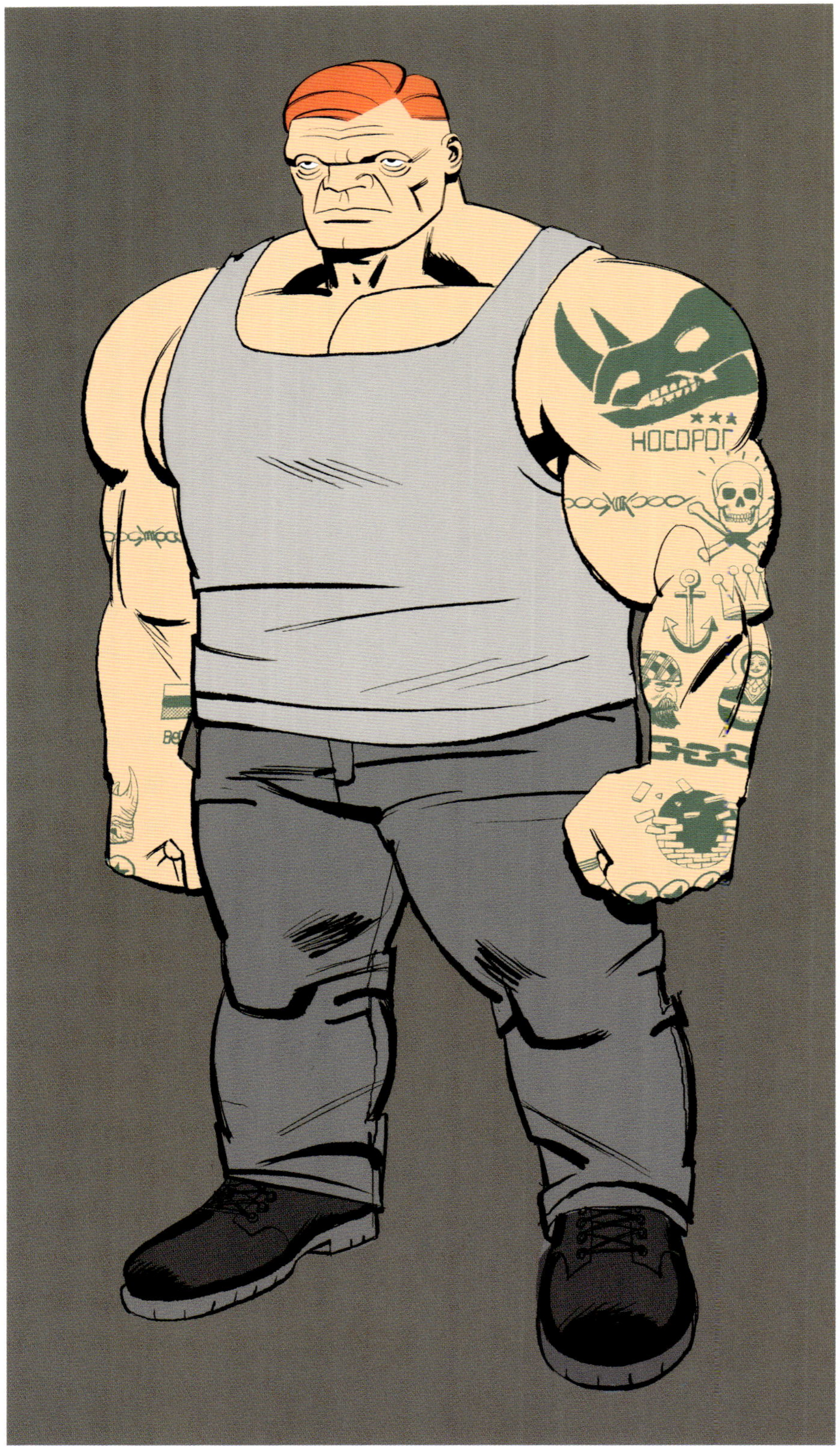

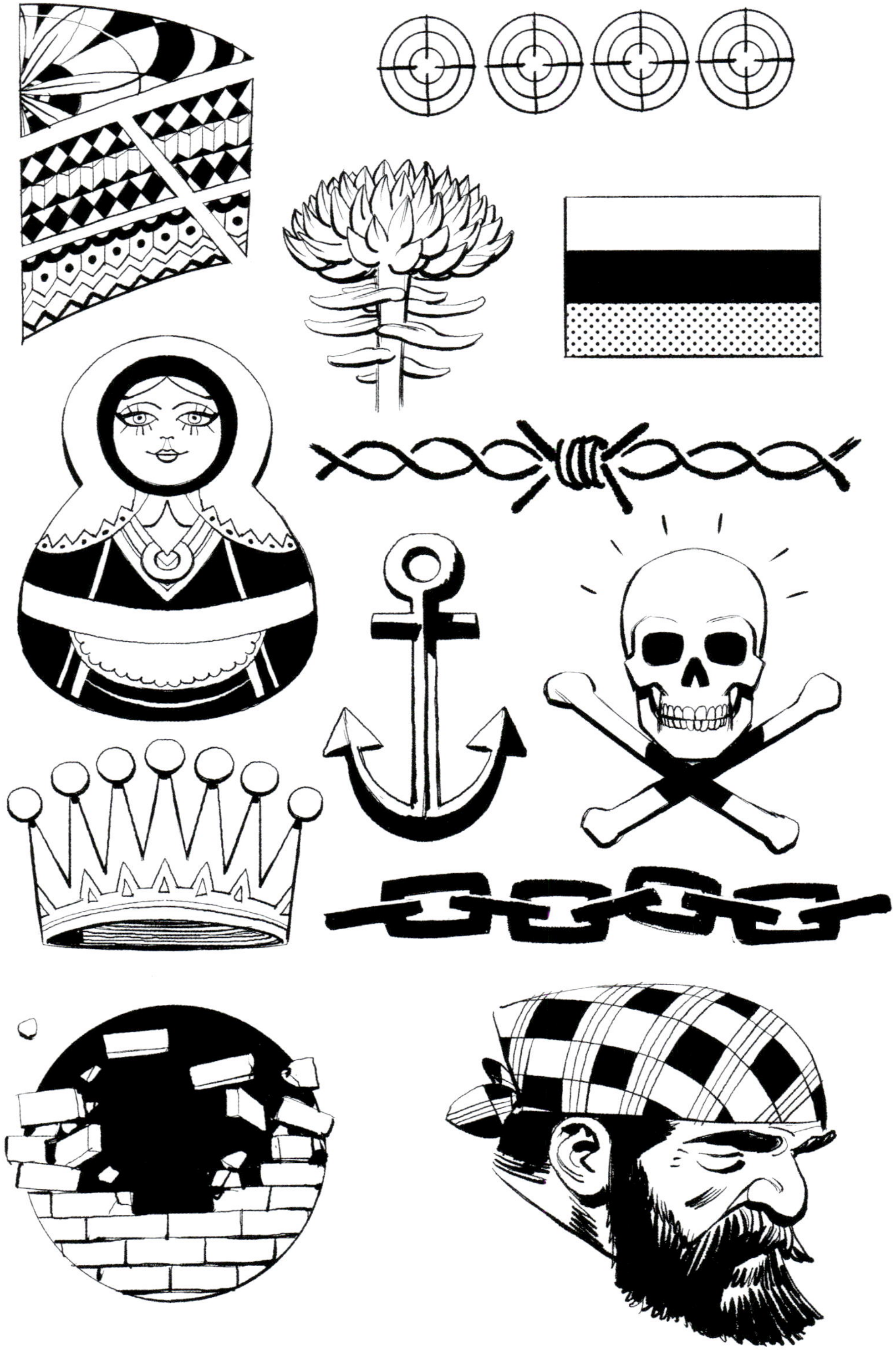

THIS SPREAD Leonardo Romero

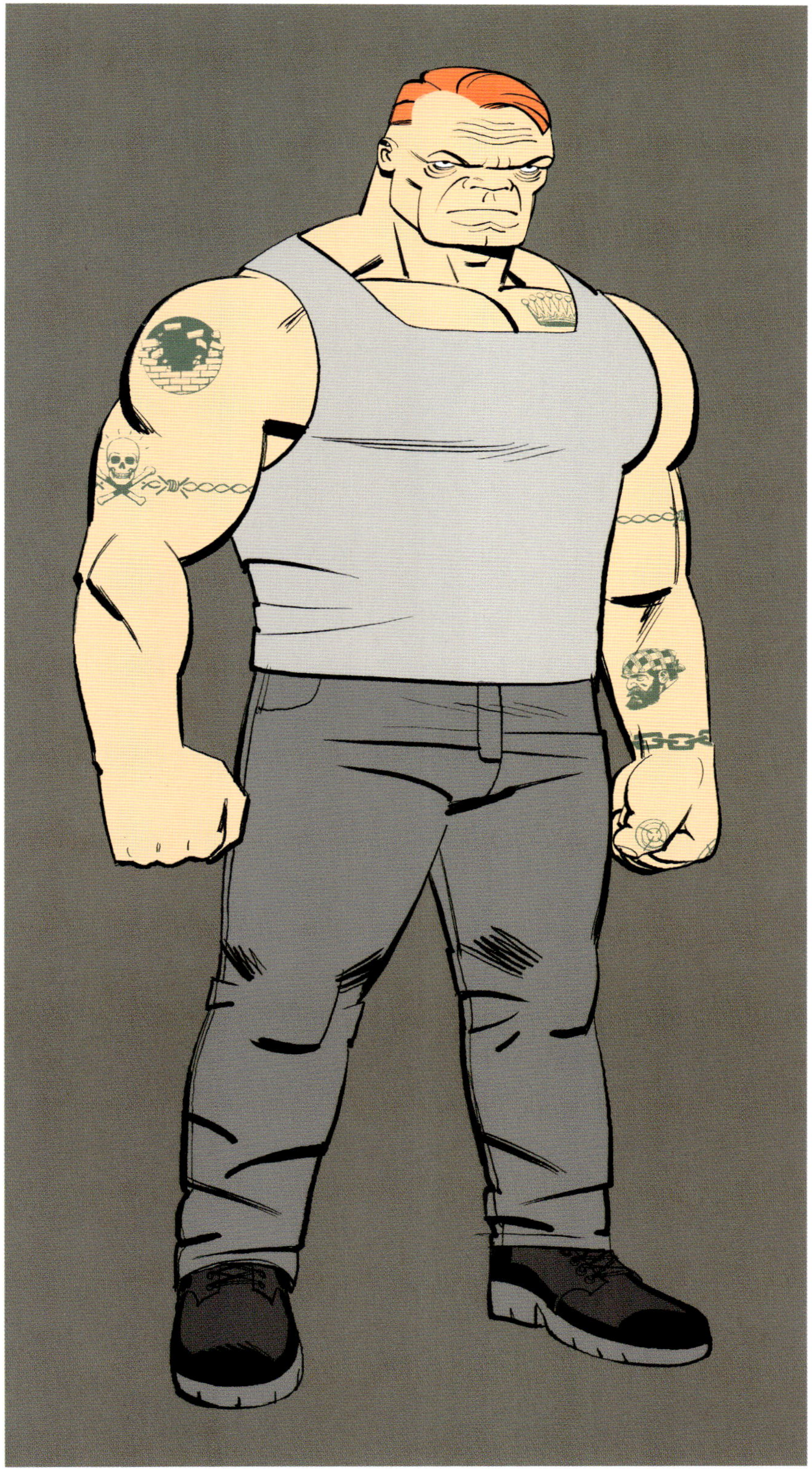

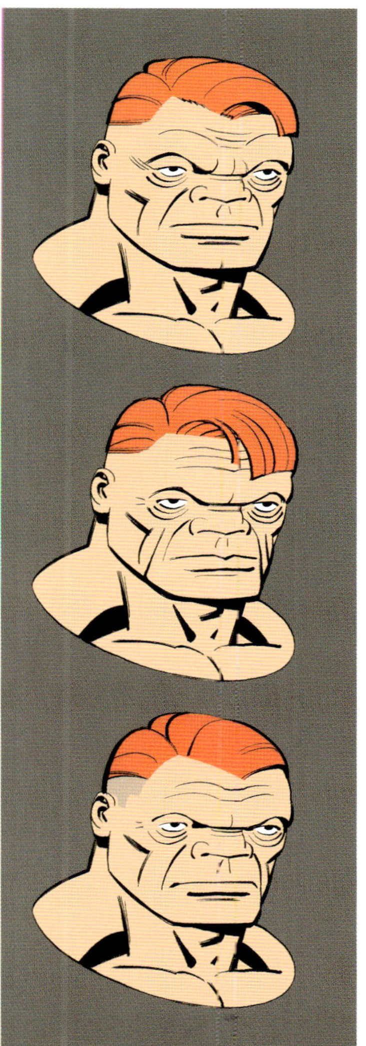

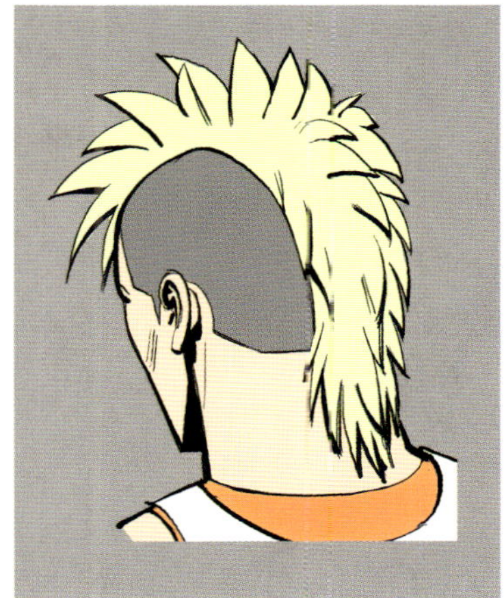

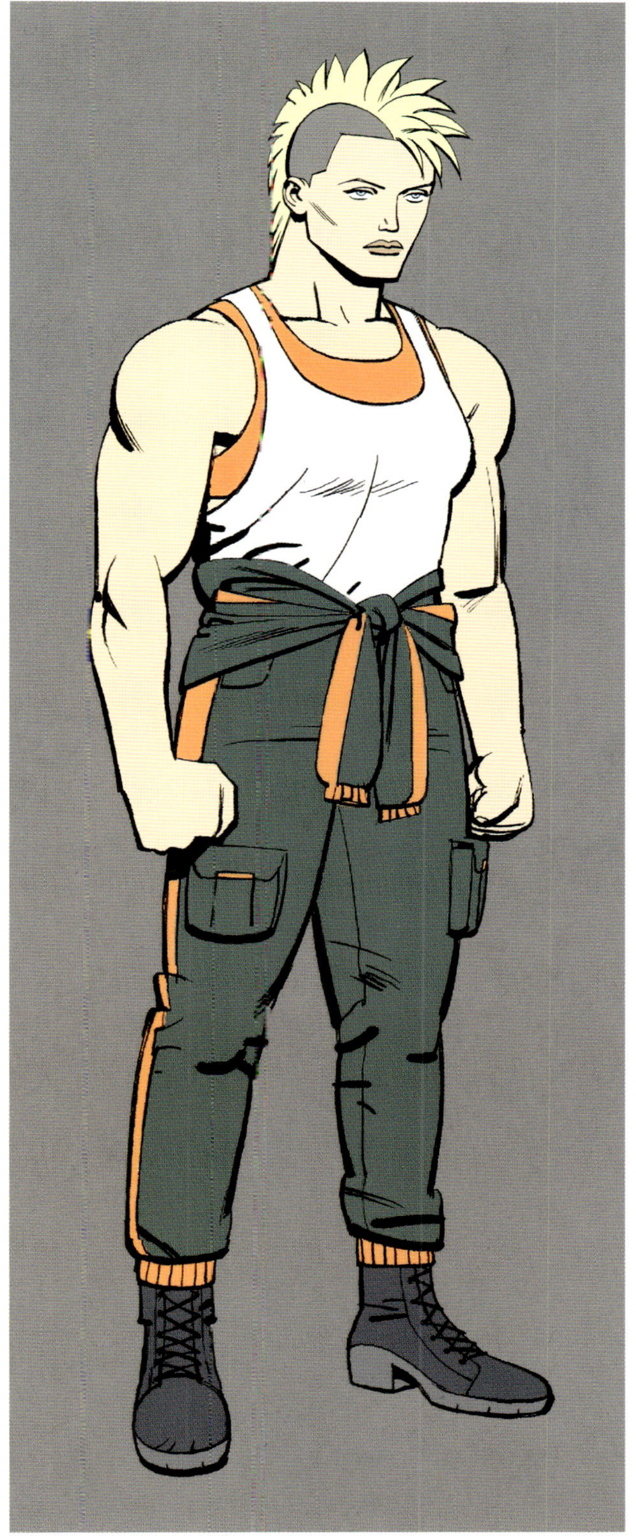

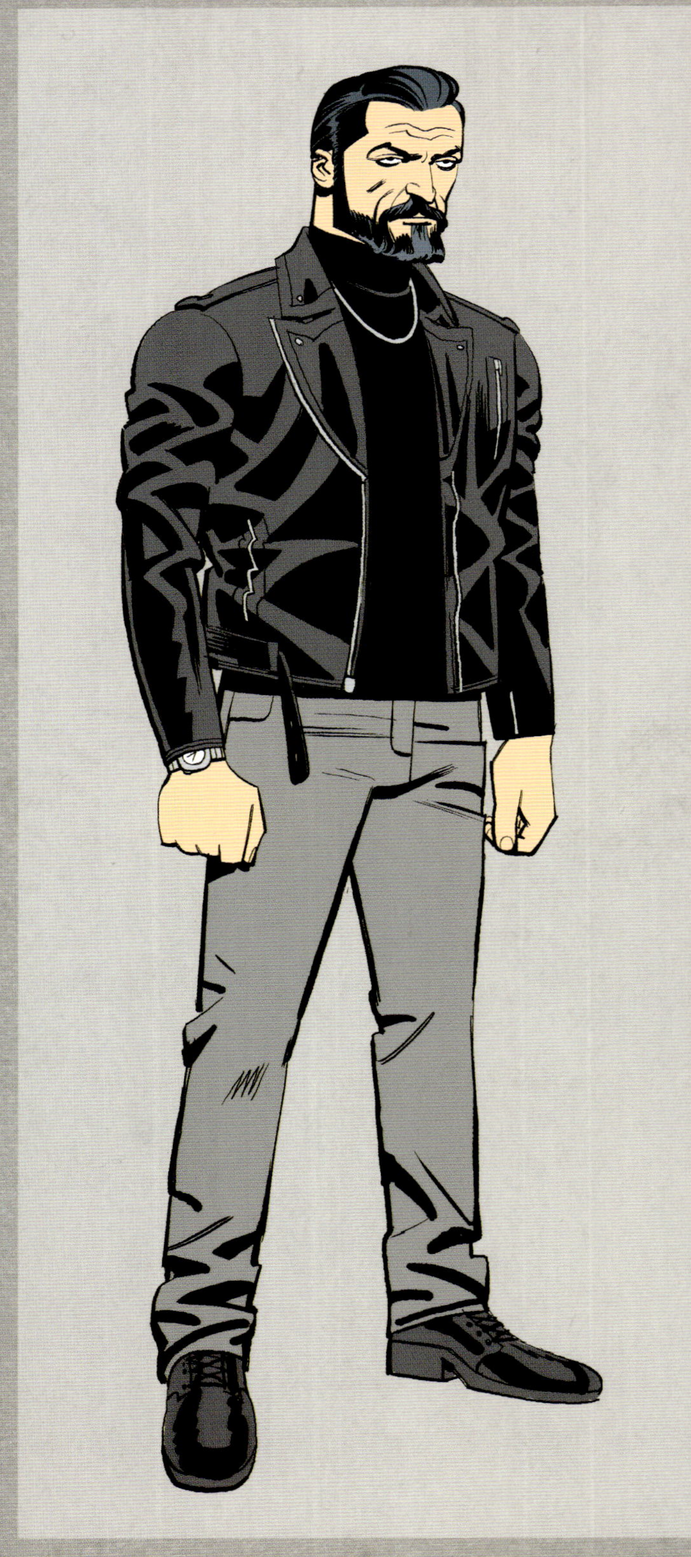

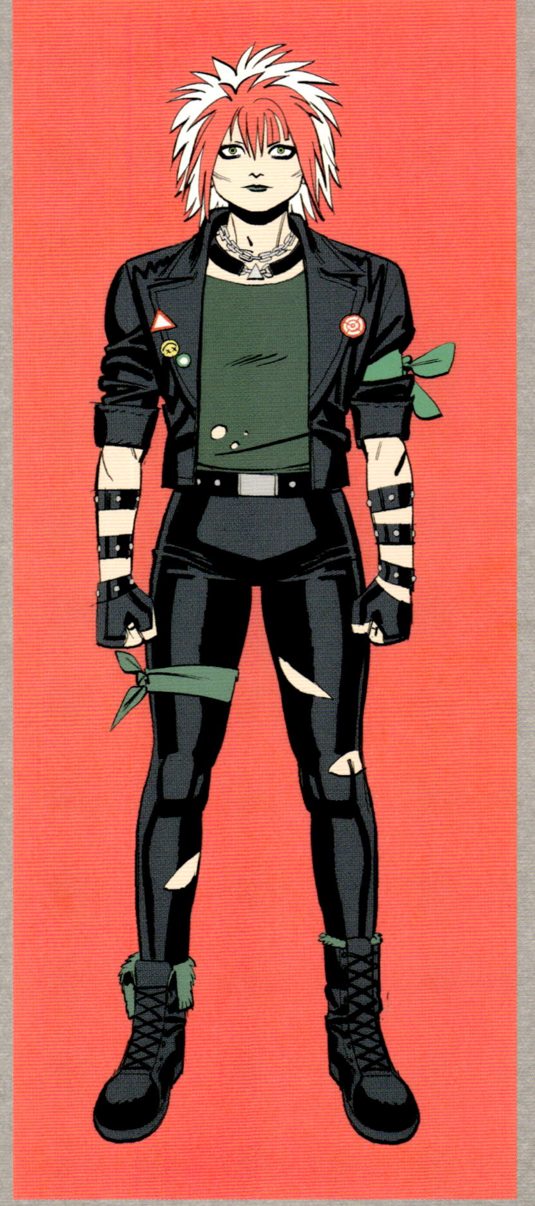

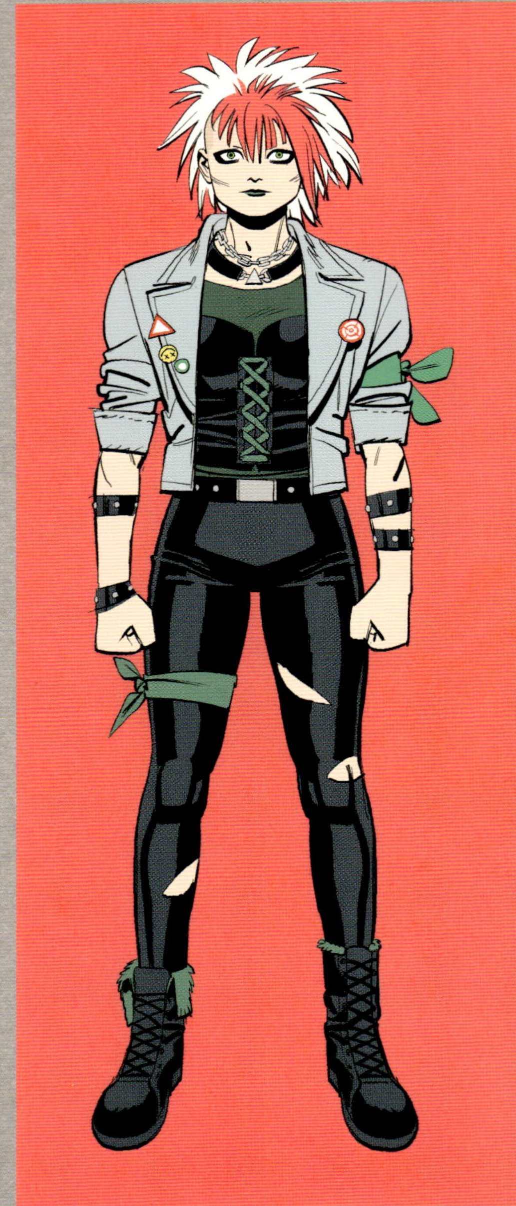

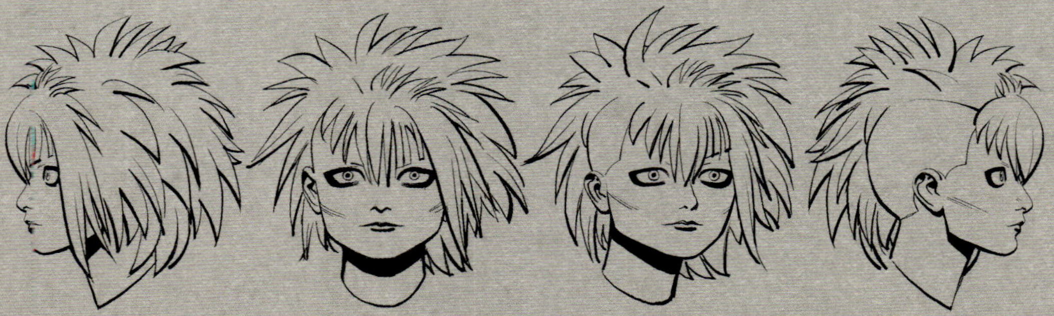

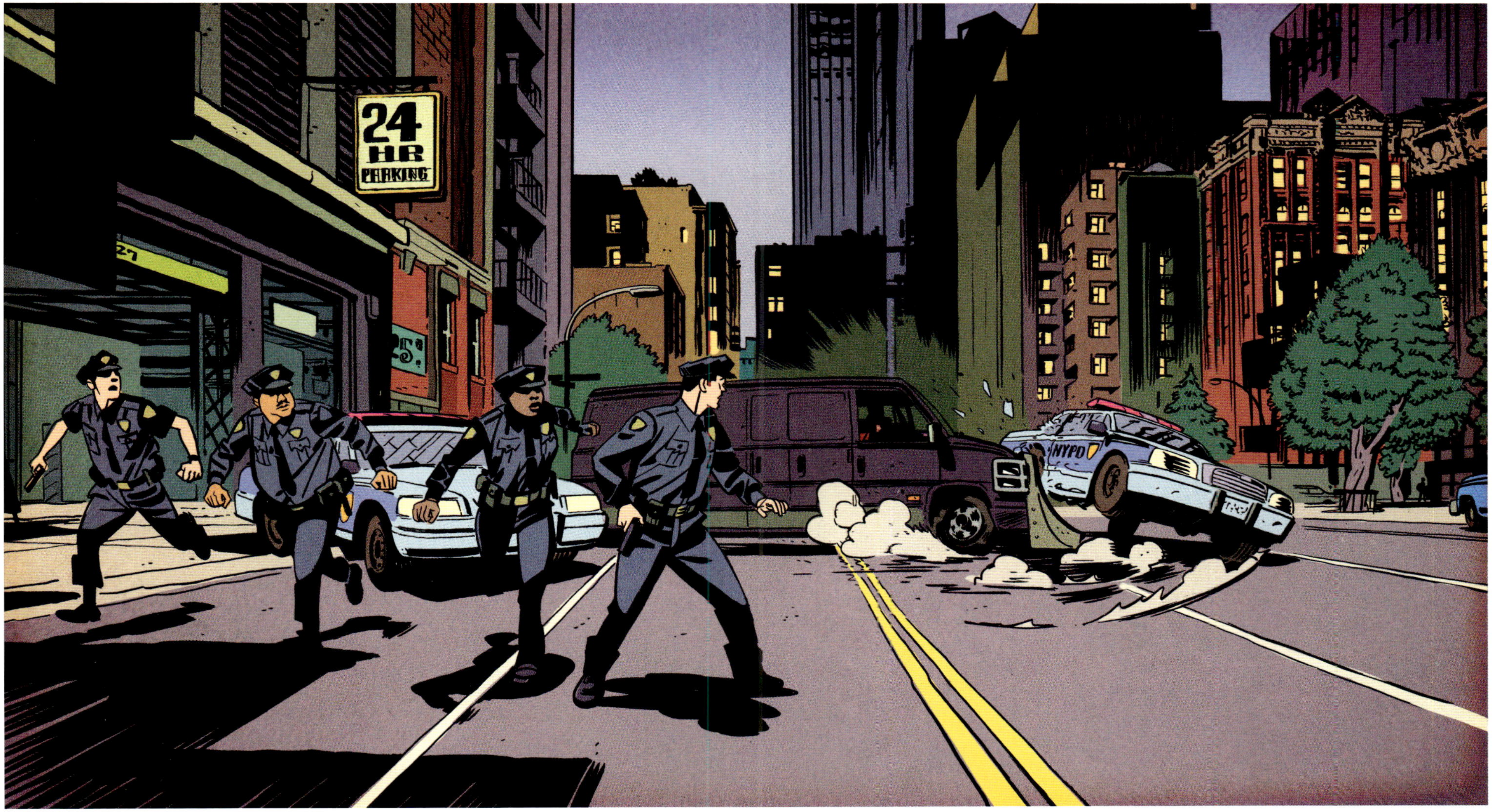

1

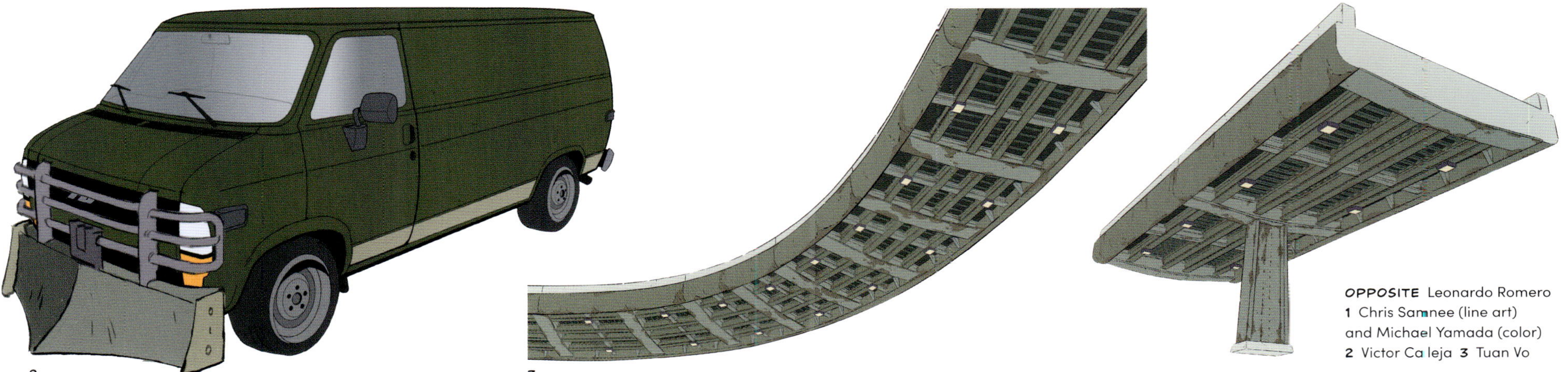

2 3

OPPOSITE Leonardo Romero
1 Chris Samnee (line art)
and Michael Yamada (color)
2 Victor Calleja **3** Tuan Vo

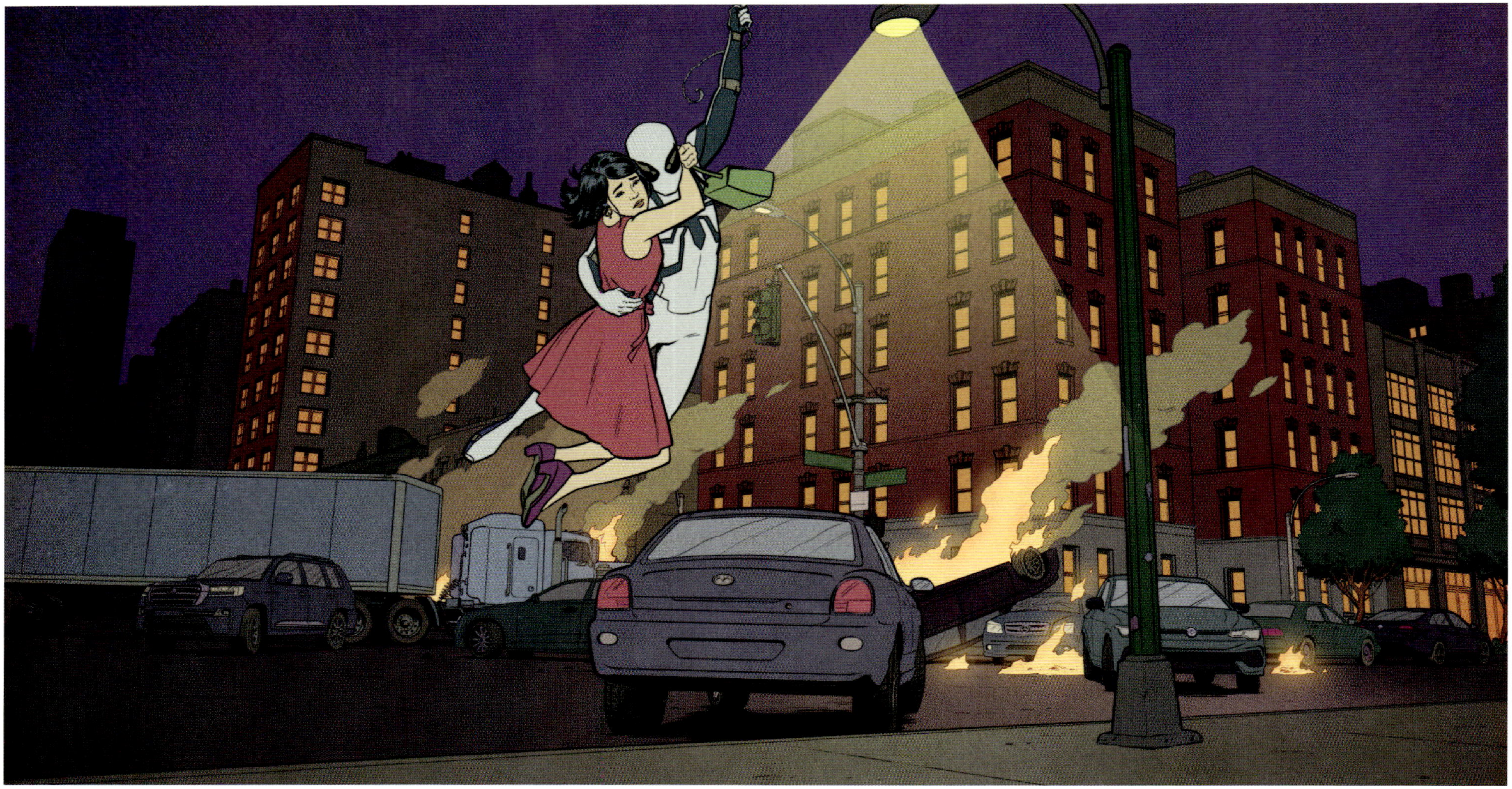

1

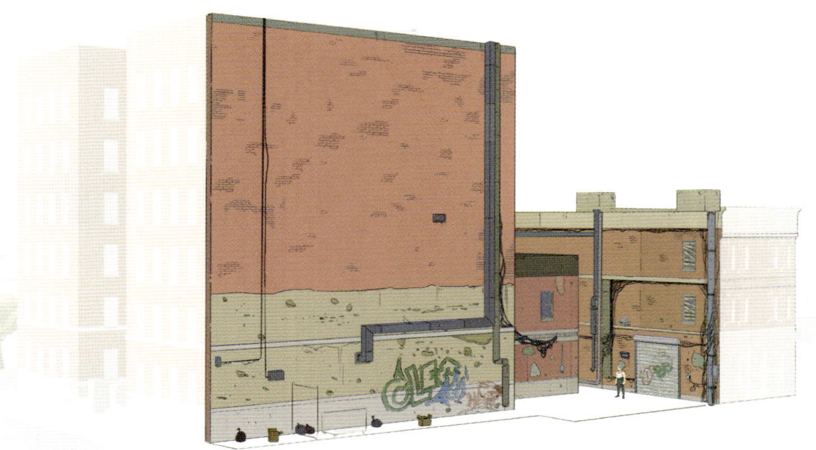

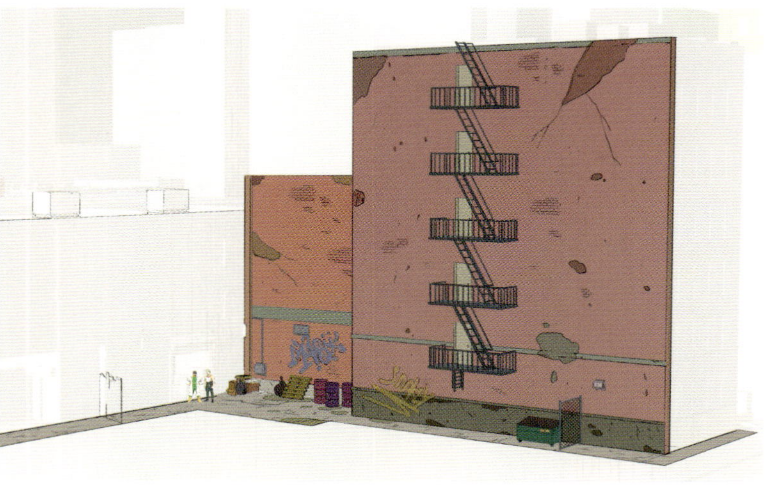

2

1 Paolo Rivera (line art) and Michael Yamada (color) **2** Monica Grue **OPPOSITE** Chris Samnee (line art) and Michael Yamada (color)

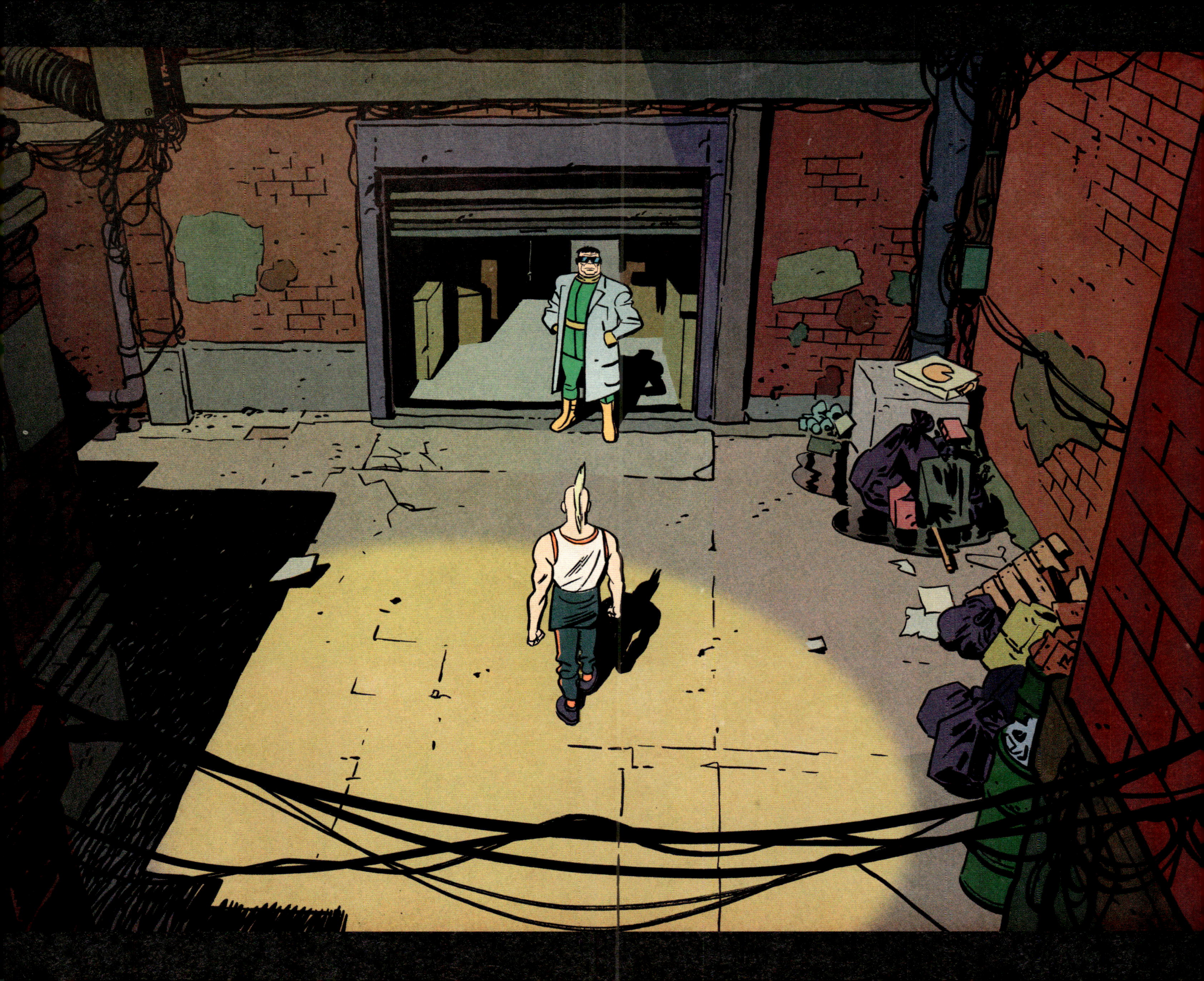

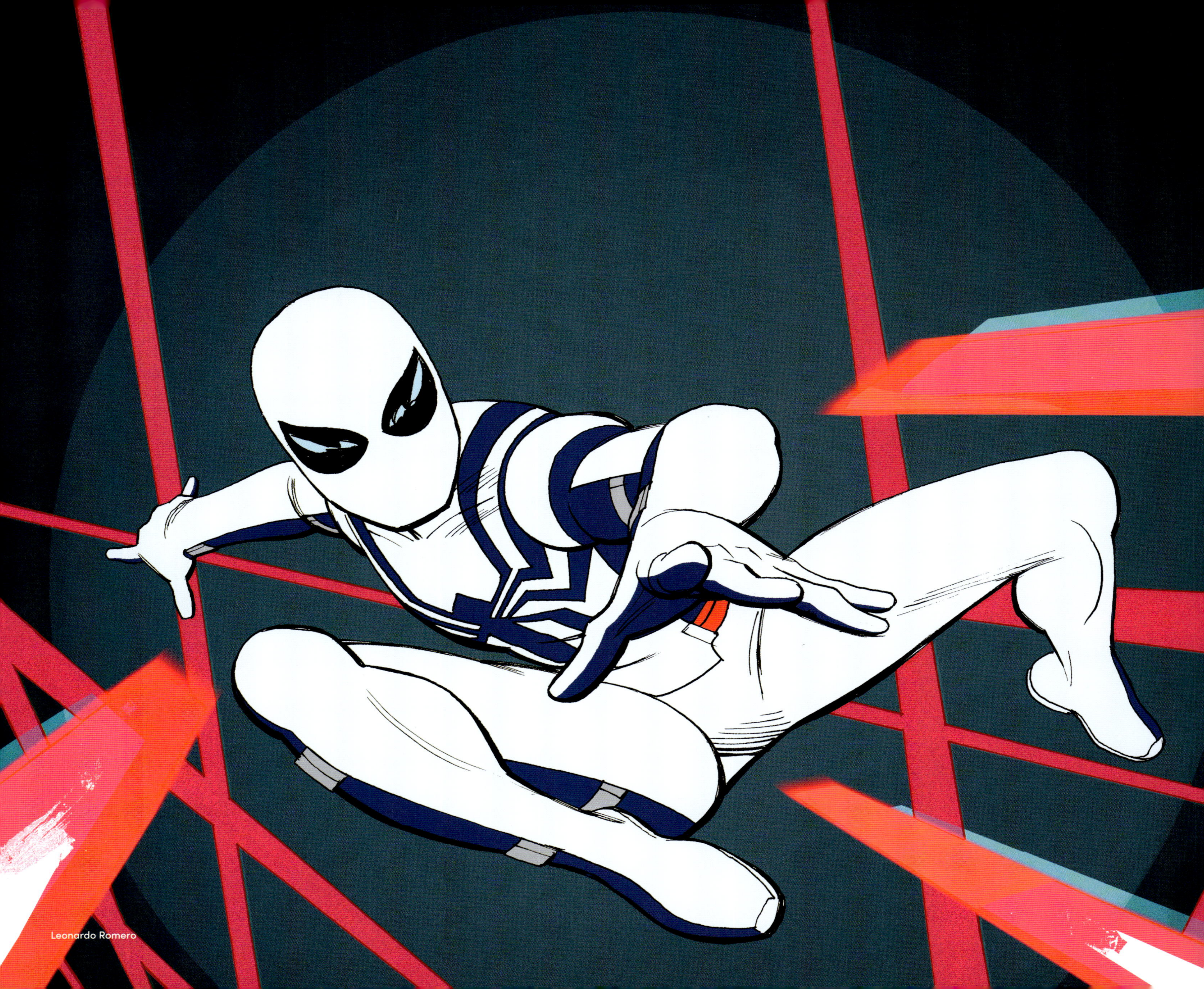

Leonardo Romero

EPISODE FIVE

THE UNICORN UNLEASHED!

AFTER LEARNING PETER'S SECRET IDENTITY, HARRY OSBORN JOINS THE SPIDEY TEAM, WHILE NICO WORRIES SHE MIGHT BE LOSING HER GOOD FRIEND TO THE WEALTHY INFLUENCER. ACROSS TOWN, THE UNICORN USES HER NEW POWERS TO BREAK HER FELLOW RUSSIAN CRIMINALS (CHAMELEON, RHINO, AND ROXANNA VOLKOV) OUT OF PRISON. WHEN SPIDER-MAN ARRIVES ON THE SCENE, SHE TRIES TO SHOOT HER LASER AT HIM, BUT RHINO PREVENTS HER FROM DELIVERING A KILLING BLOW. THE ACTION RAMPS UP AS SCORPION AND BIG DONOVAN FACE OFF IN A HUGE BRAWL. IN THE ENSUING MELEE, LONNIE GETS STABBED IN THE ARM, EARNING HIM THE NICKNAME TOMBSTONE.

THIS IS THE FIRST episode where viewers meet Dr. Otto Octavius and learn a bit about his past.

"There's an inkling that he has some history with Norman Osborn that we build to throughout the rest of the season, but also we get to see Peter, who is now working with Harry," says Executive Producer/Showrunner Jeff Trammell. "Here we have two guys who don't really know anything about each other, that are thrust together by Norman. Peter's still trying to make things right with Nico after missing her at the concert. But because he has brought a new addition to the friend group, that starts to ruffle Nico's feathers, especially at the end of the episode."

One of the goals of this episode is to show how Lonnie is becoming more and more involved in gang life. "We introduced the Scorpions in the previous episode," says Trammell. "Now we meet their leader, Mac Gargan (Jonathan Medina), who is unhinged, scary, and violent. Everything is screaming that Lonnie does not need to be here. Yet, at the end of the day, Lonnie's great personality and loyalty win out, and he endears himself to the group. When he gets the name Tombstone is a crucial moment in the arc of his character."

The episode's director, Stu Livingston, adds, "I'm really proud of the gang fight toward the end of this episode. My storyboard artist, Erwin Osias, who is always incredibly reliable, basically shaped that whole sequence. I remember when I first saw it, I thought it was amazing and perfect. The episode also has a lot of great action and drama with Mila, a.k.a. The Unicorn, and Spidey."

DR. OTTO OCTAVIUS

First introduced in *The Amazing Spider-Man* comic (#3) in July 1963, Doc Ock is one of Spider-Man's best-known nemeses (alongside Green Goblin and Venom). The brilliant mad scientist, whose four metal appendages resemble the tentacles of an octopus, is voiced by Hugh Dancy on the show and is introduced in the fourth episode as the man behind the high-tech gear created for the show's first batch of criminals.

"He works in the shadows and is responsible for 90 percent of the villains Peter crosses paths with in the season," explains Executive Producer/Showrunner Jeff Trammell. "But we never see them meet, even though Otto is one of Spider-Man's biggest enemies. Just as we witness Peter shining throughout the season, we also see Doc Ock's journey, and in some ways, they are similar, as they both work/worked for Norman Osborn. I like digging into his journey and exploring his personality, especially given his vindictive nature. The moment he and Spider-Man do meet will hopefully feel like a big, well-earned moment."

Lead Character Designer Leonardo Romero says Doc Ock was one of the first characters he worked on for the show. "In some of the variations, he resembled character actor Peter Lorre or the character Dwight (portrayed by Rainn Wilson) in *The Office*," he notes. "Once we learned which direction the creative team wanted to take the show, I tried to make it lean on the classic look as much as possible. We tried a lot of different shapes of glasses for him: We were trying to figure out whether we wanted rounder ones or triangle-shaped ones. He eventually ended up with the big, slick-looking black ones, which looked really good on the 3D model and the final animation."

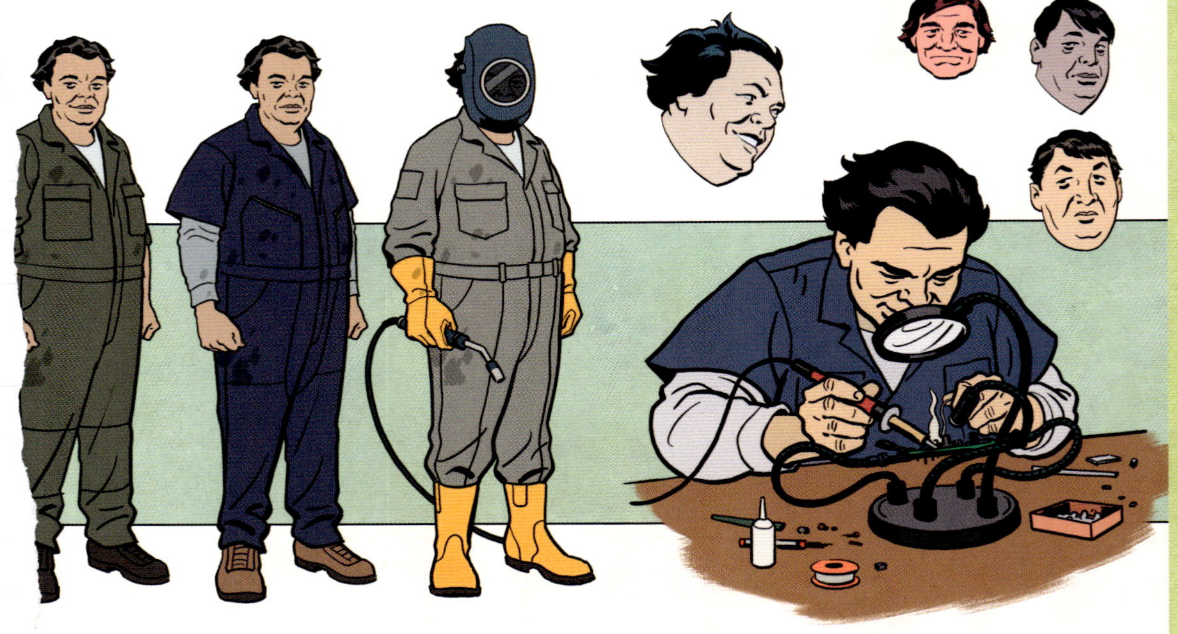

1

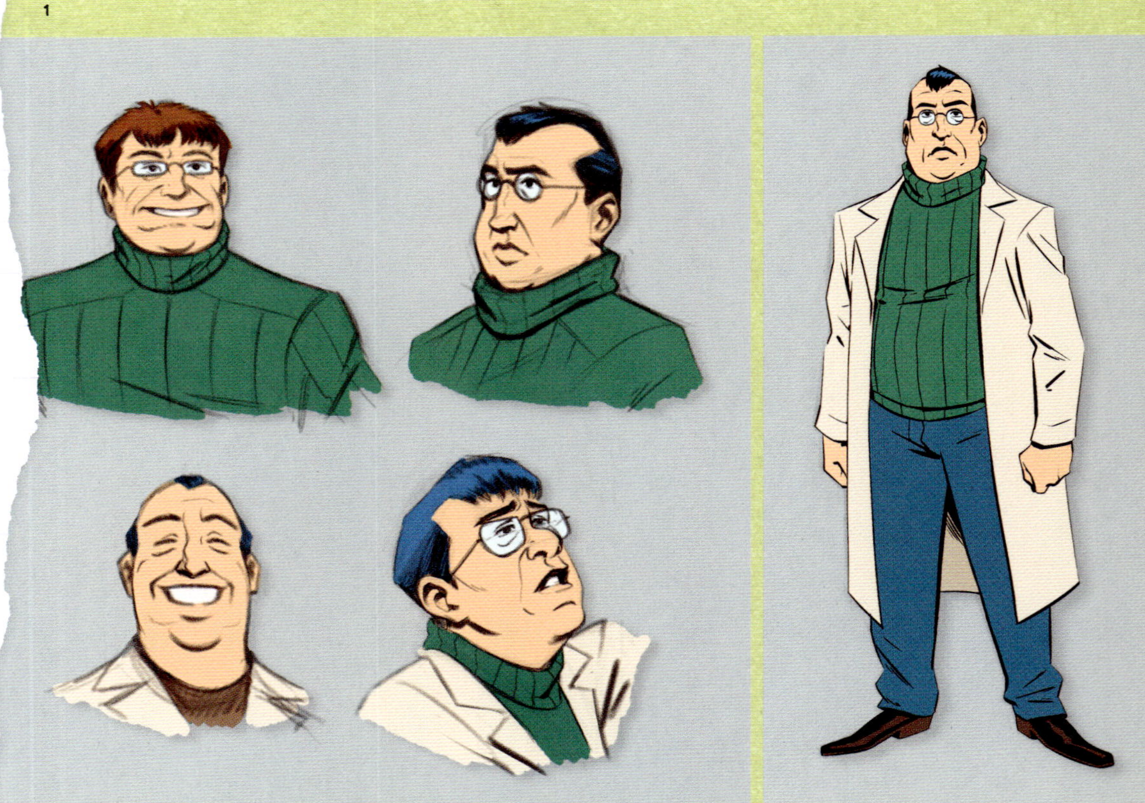

2

1 Paolo Rivera **2** Julen Urrutia Perez
OPPOSITE Leonardo Romero

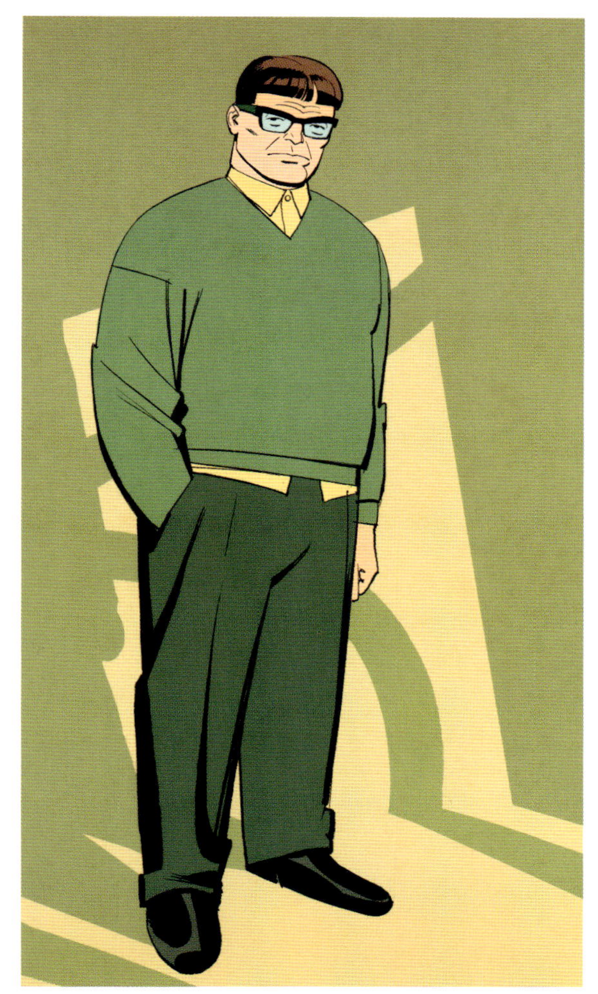

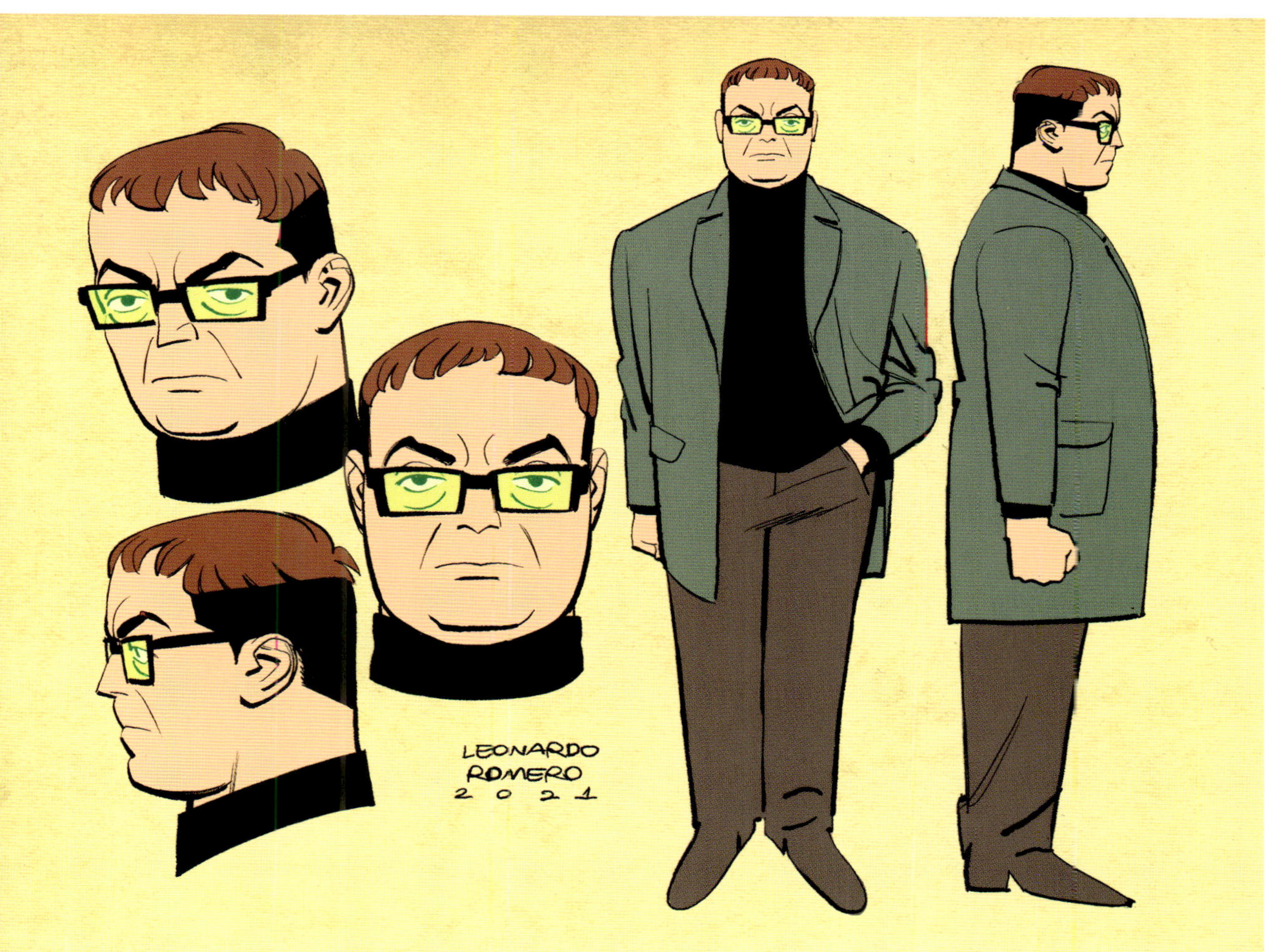
LEONARDO
ROMERO
2021

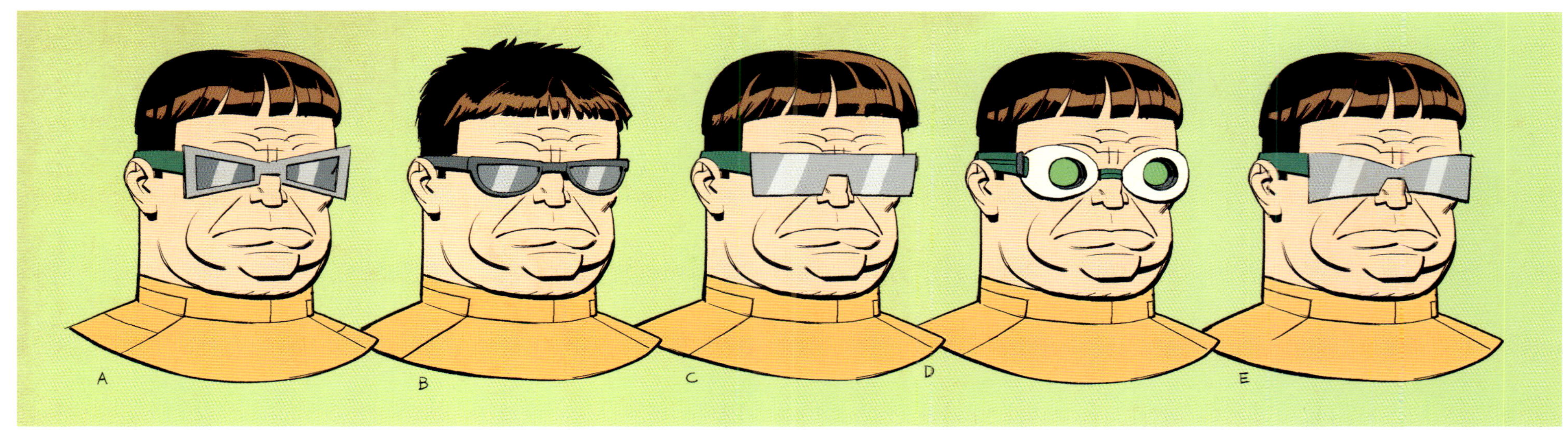
A
B
C
D
E

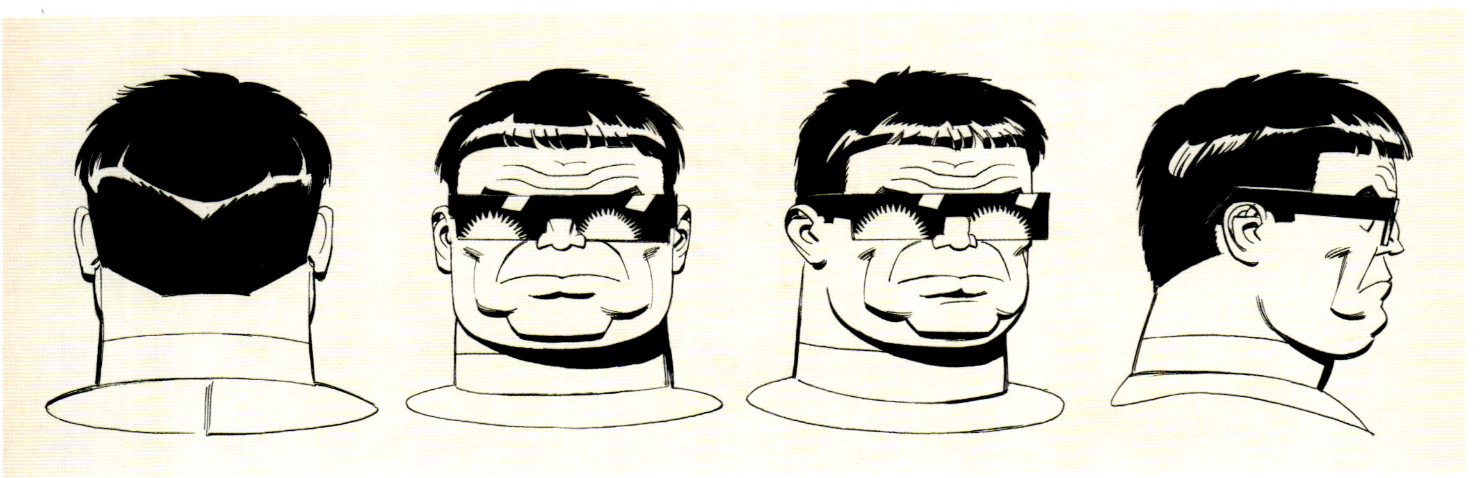

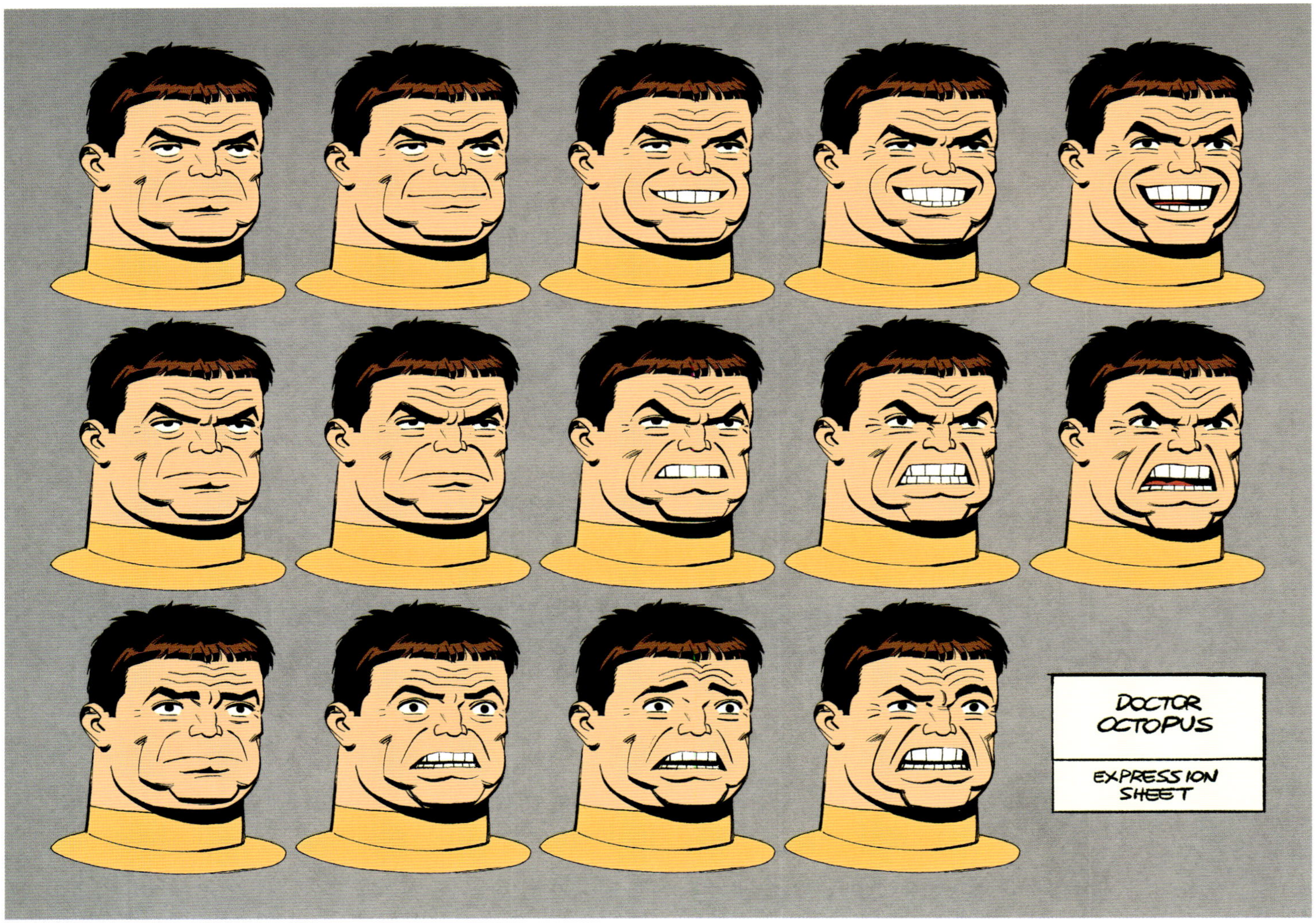

DOCTOR OCTOPUS

EXPRESSION SHEET

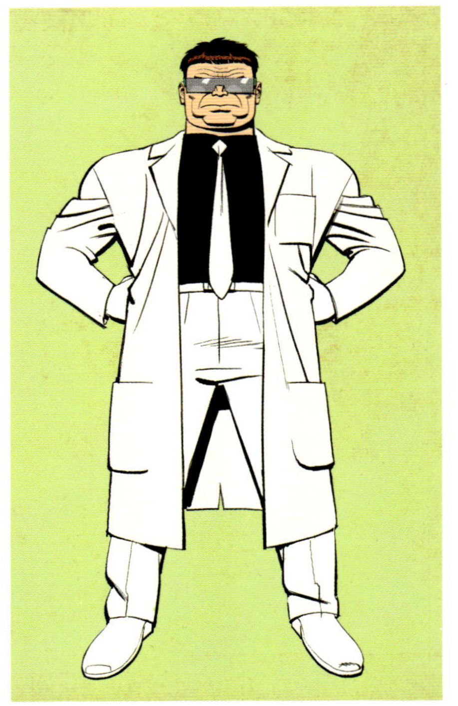

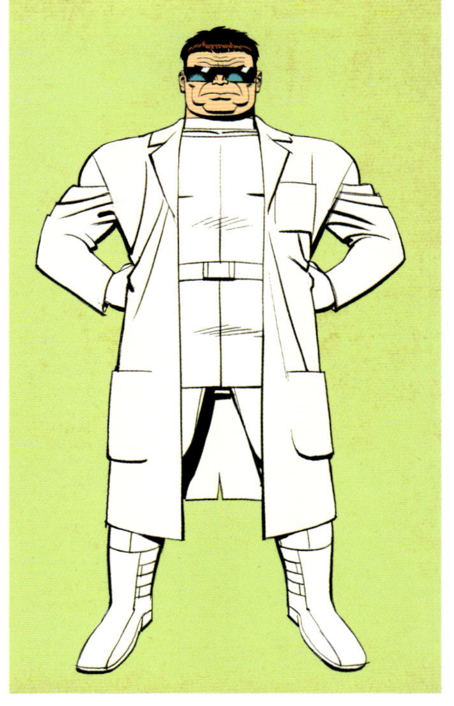

THIS SPREAD Leonardo Romero

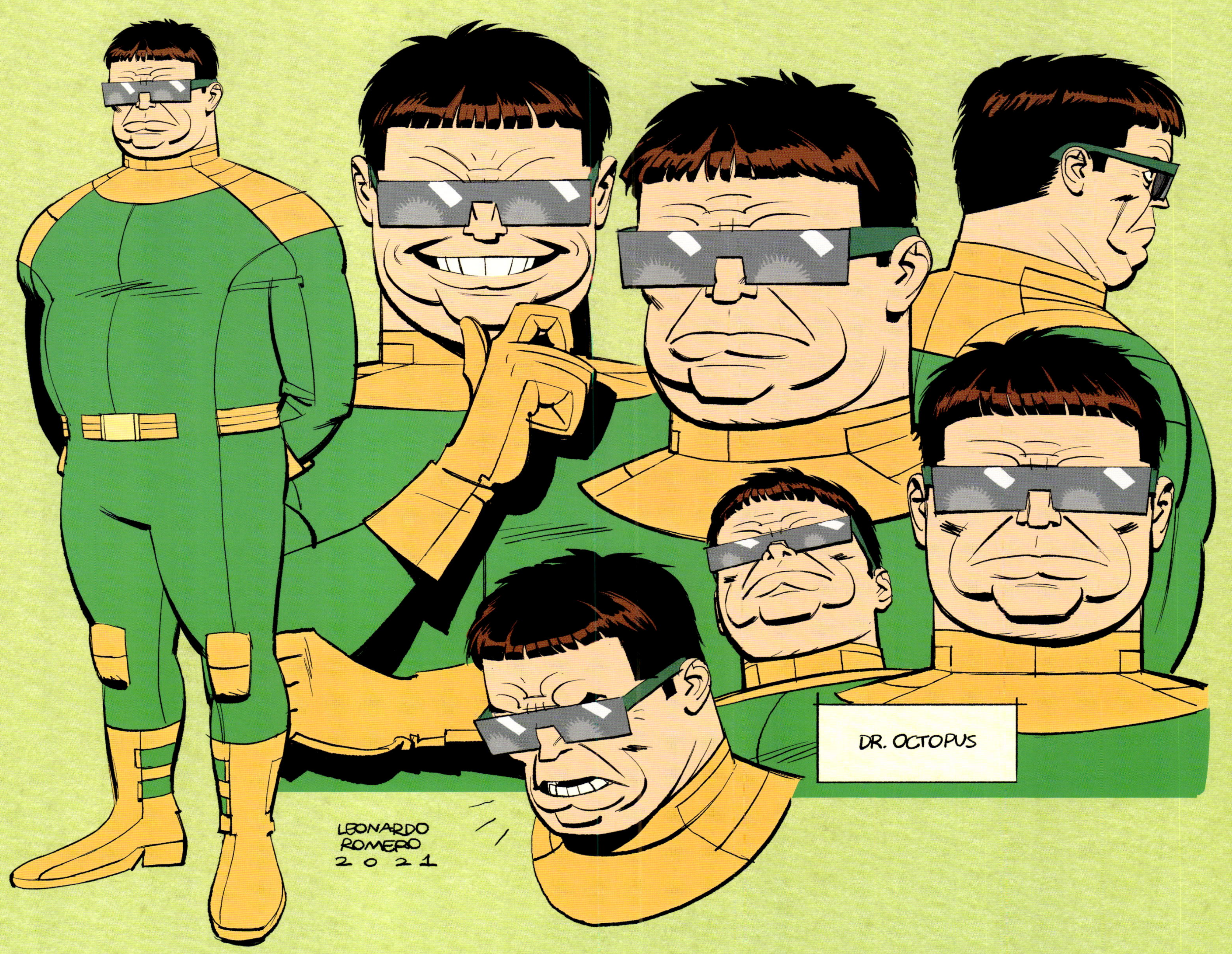
DR. OCTOPUS
LEONARDO
ROMERO
2021

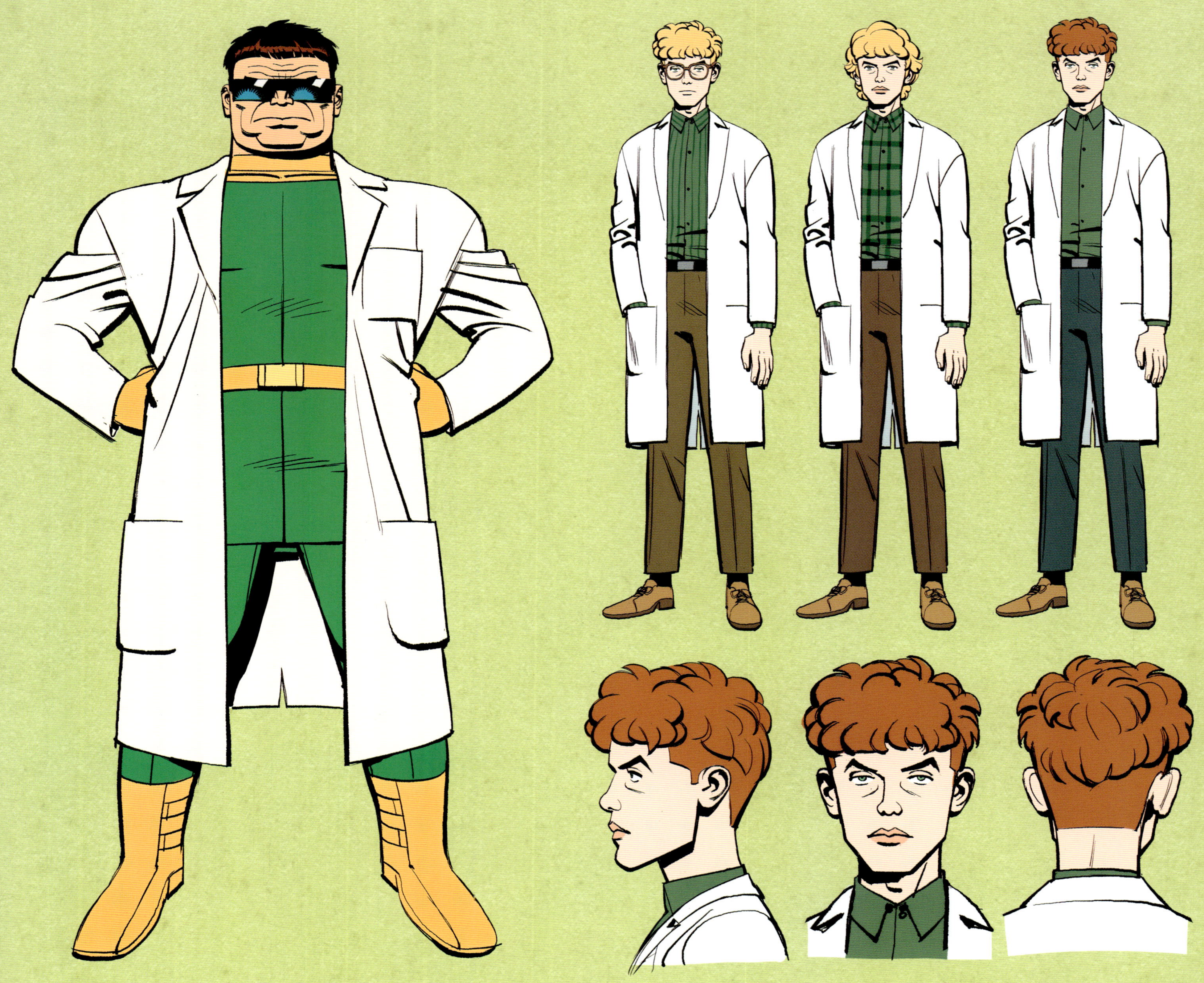

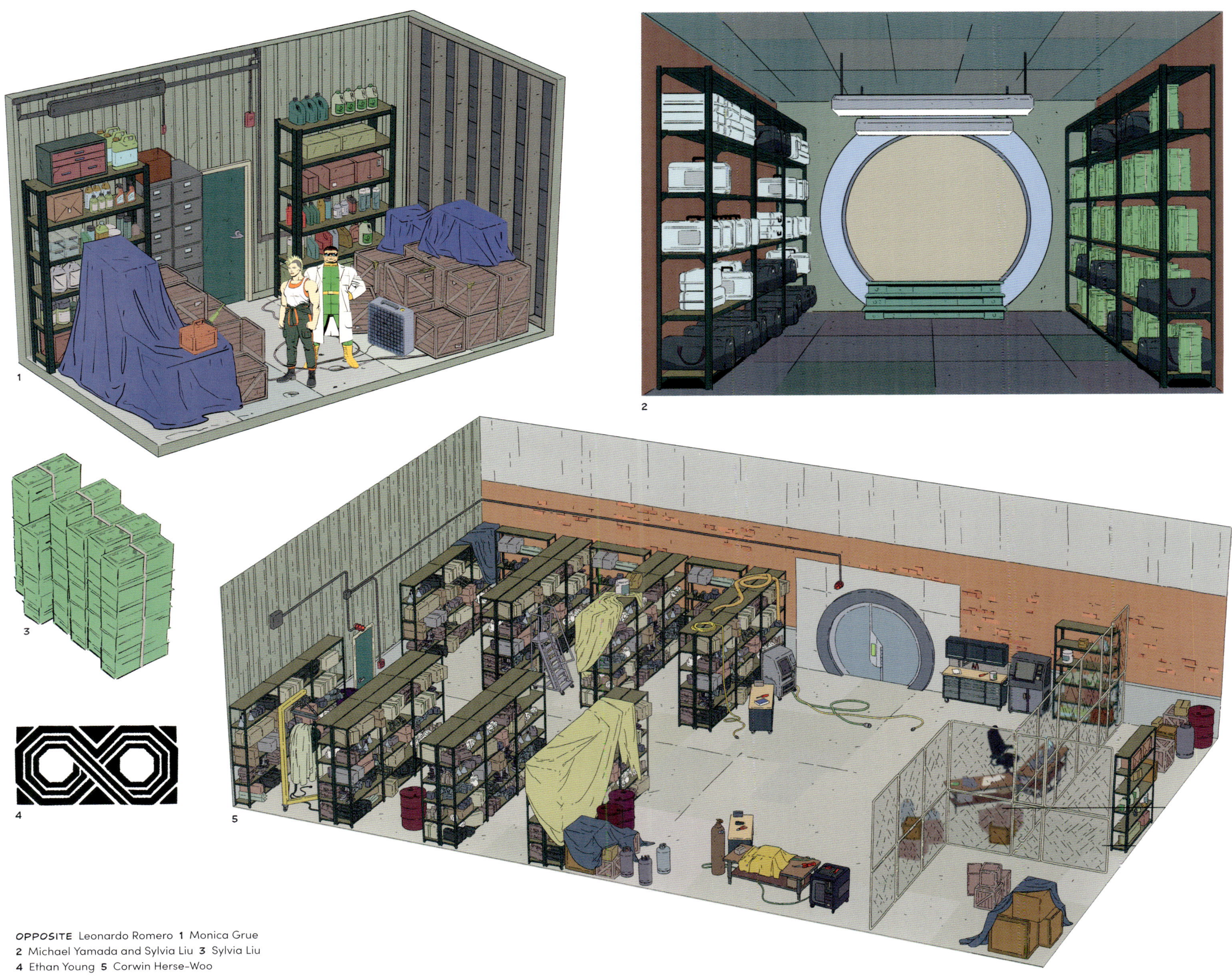

1

2

3

4

5

OPPOSITE Leonardo Romero **1** Monica Grue
2 Michael Yamada and Sylvia Liu **3** Sylvia Liu
4 Ethan Young **5** Corwin Herse-Woo

1

2

3

01:02:02:02
AEB0200
CAMERA 08
00:14:23.84
03/16/2022
AEB-0200-0003-v4.jpg

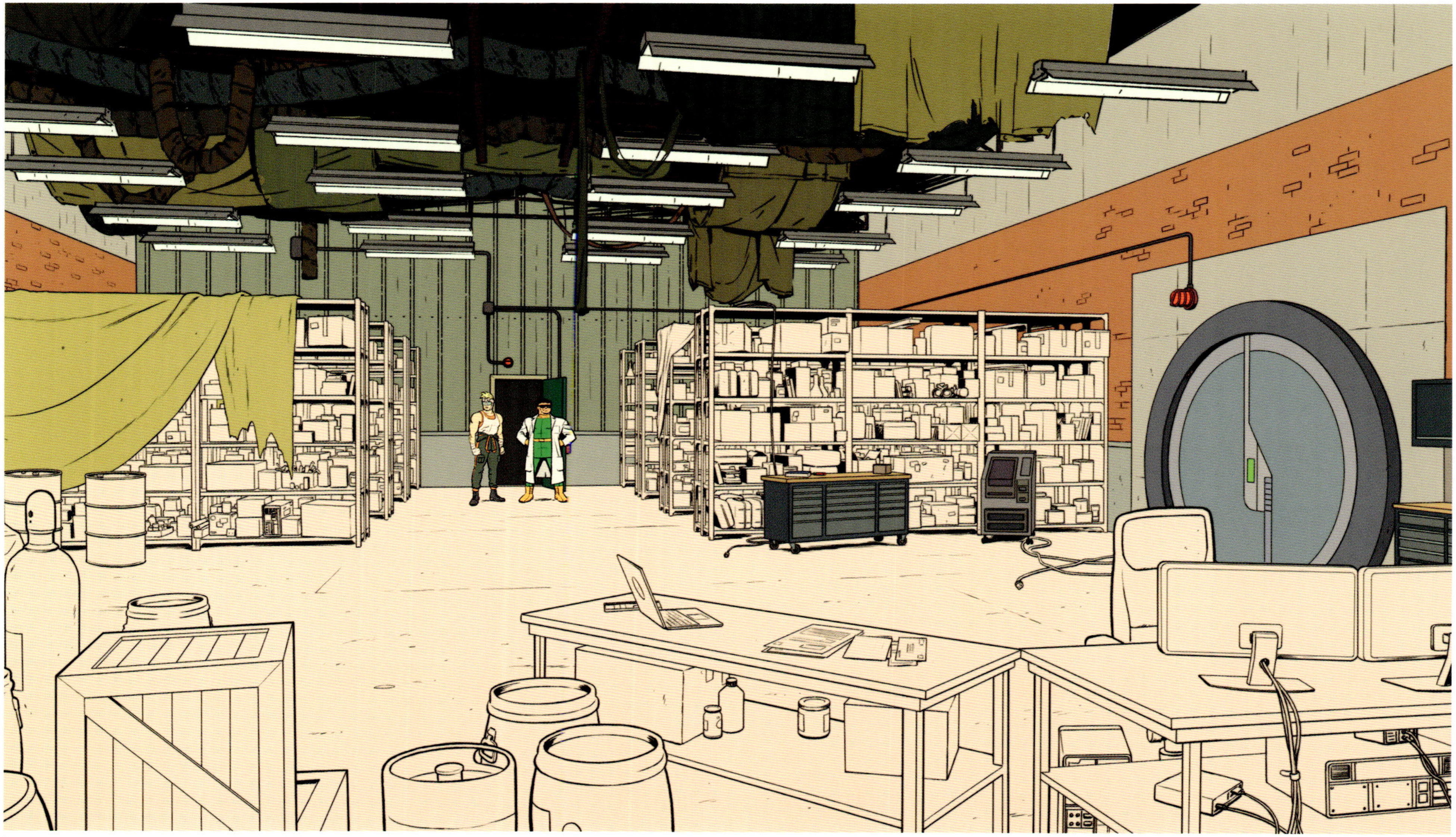

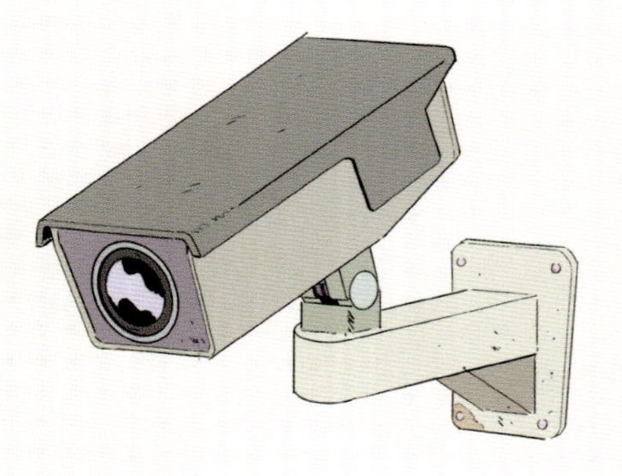

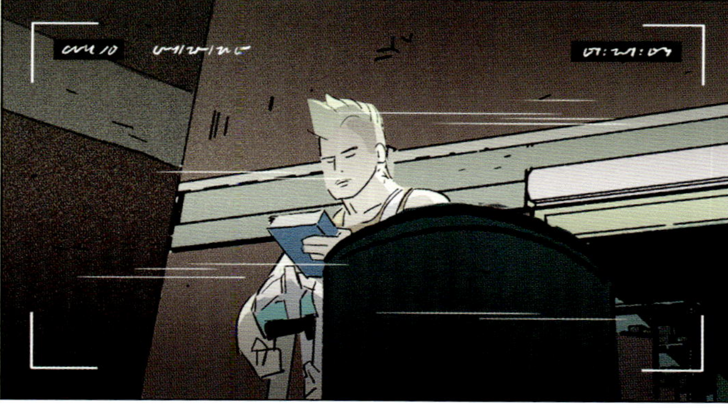

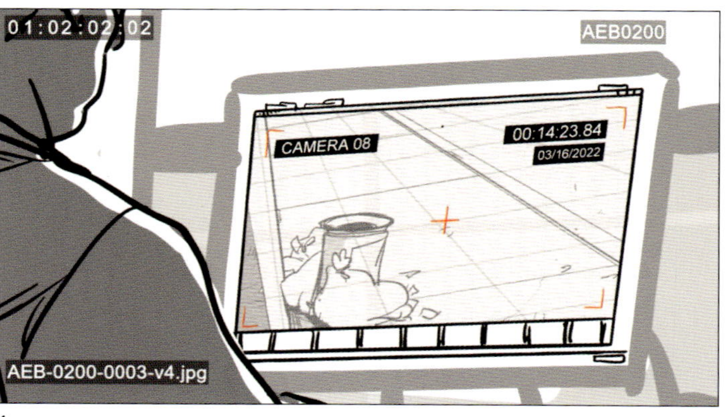

4

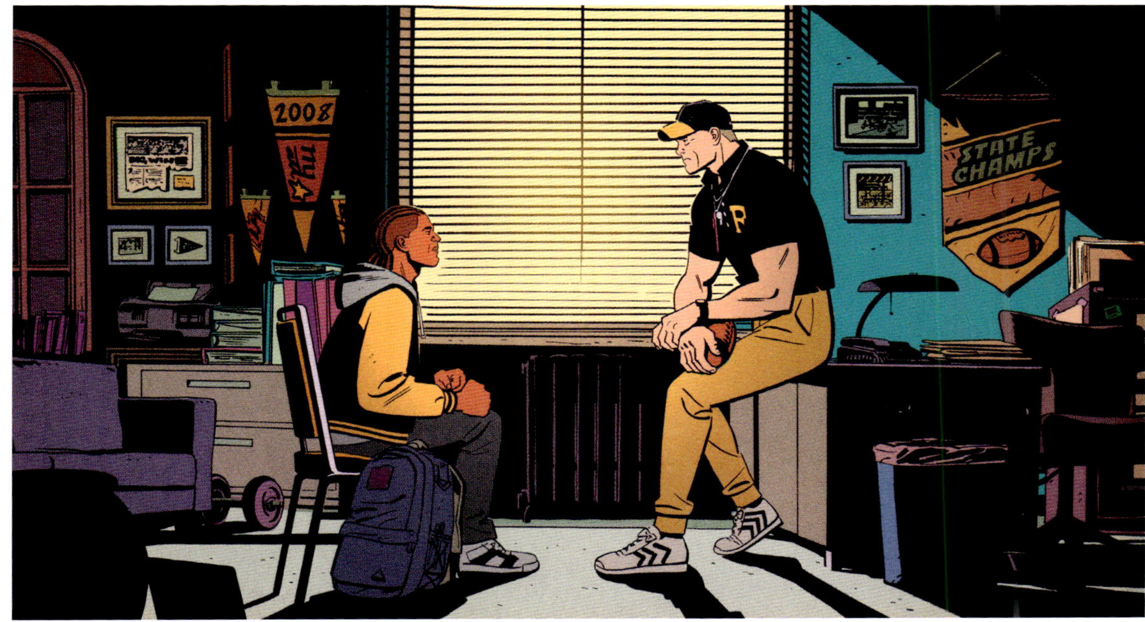

5

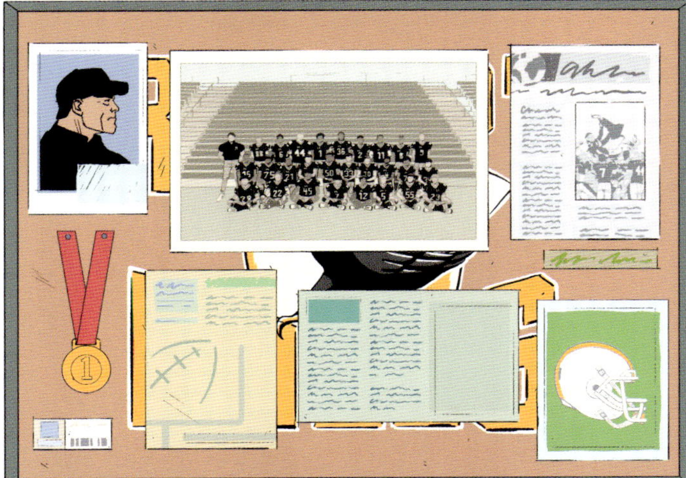

6

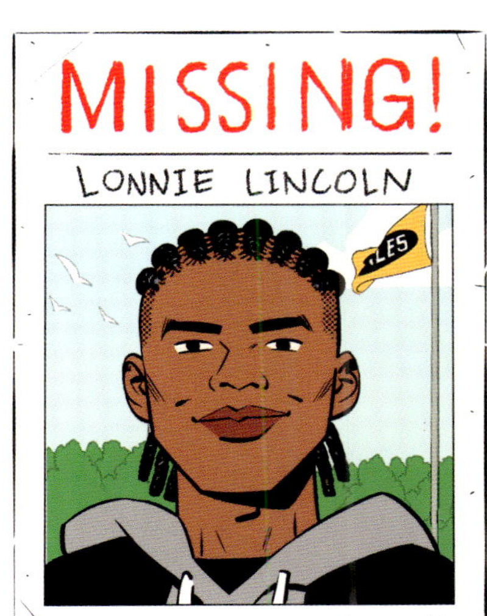

7

1 Paolo Rivera
2–3 Beverly Arce
4 Meg Syverud
5 Chris Samnee (line art) and Michael Yamada (color) **6** Kelsey Roland
7 Beverly Arce
8–9 Leonardo Romero

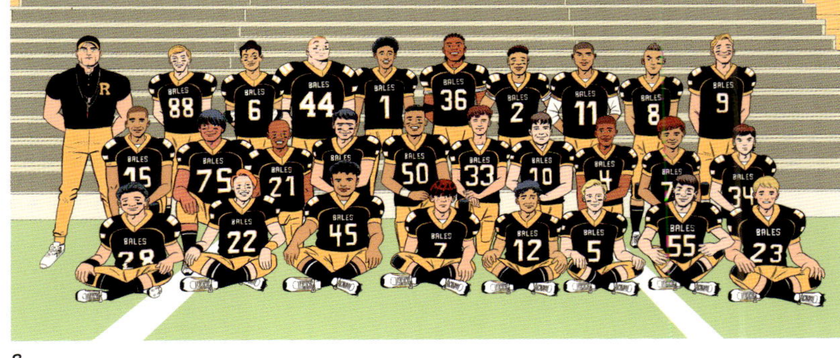

8

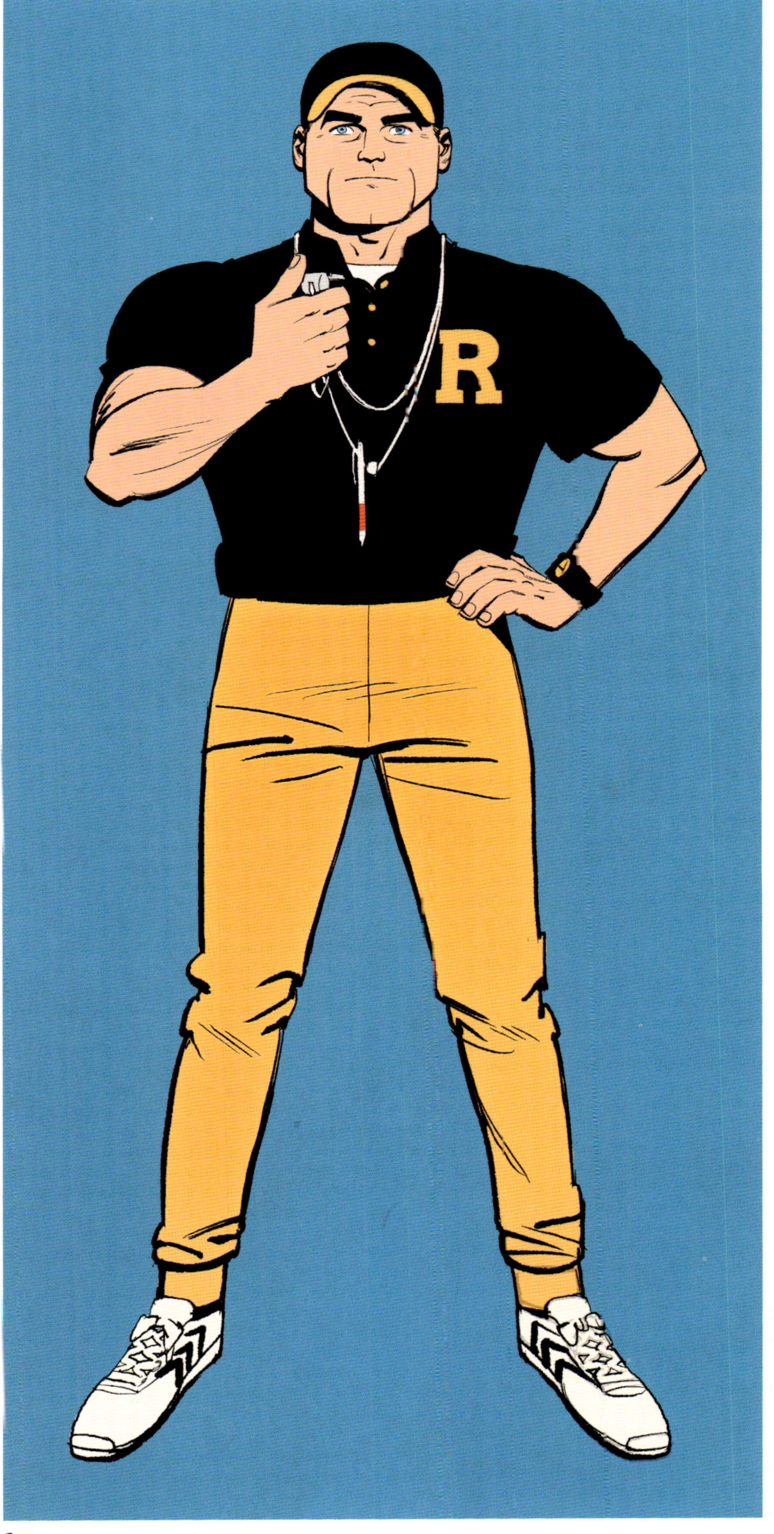

9

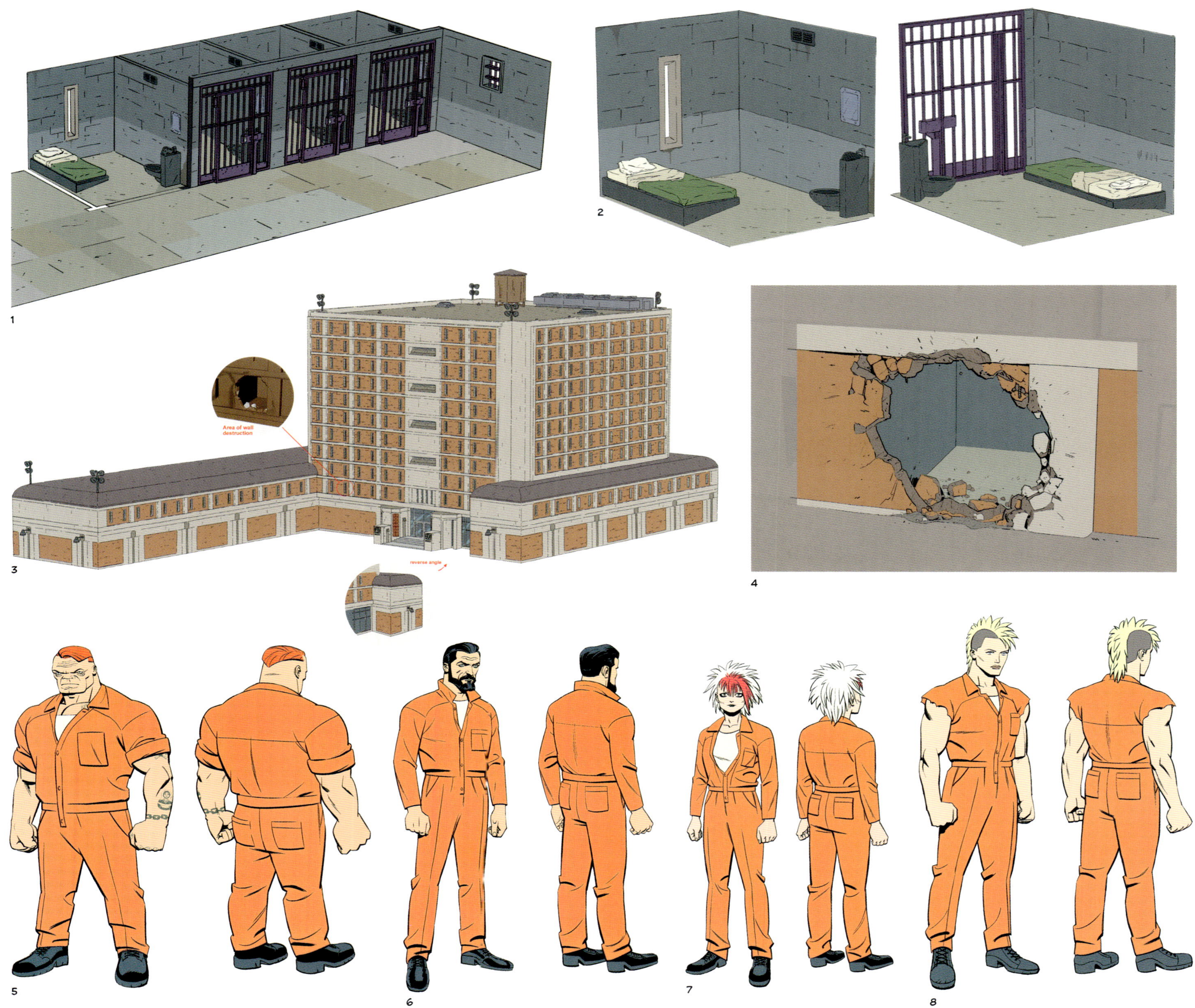

1
2
Area of wall destruction
3
reverse angle
4
5
6
7
8

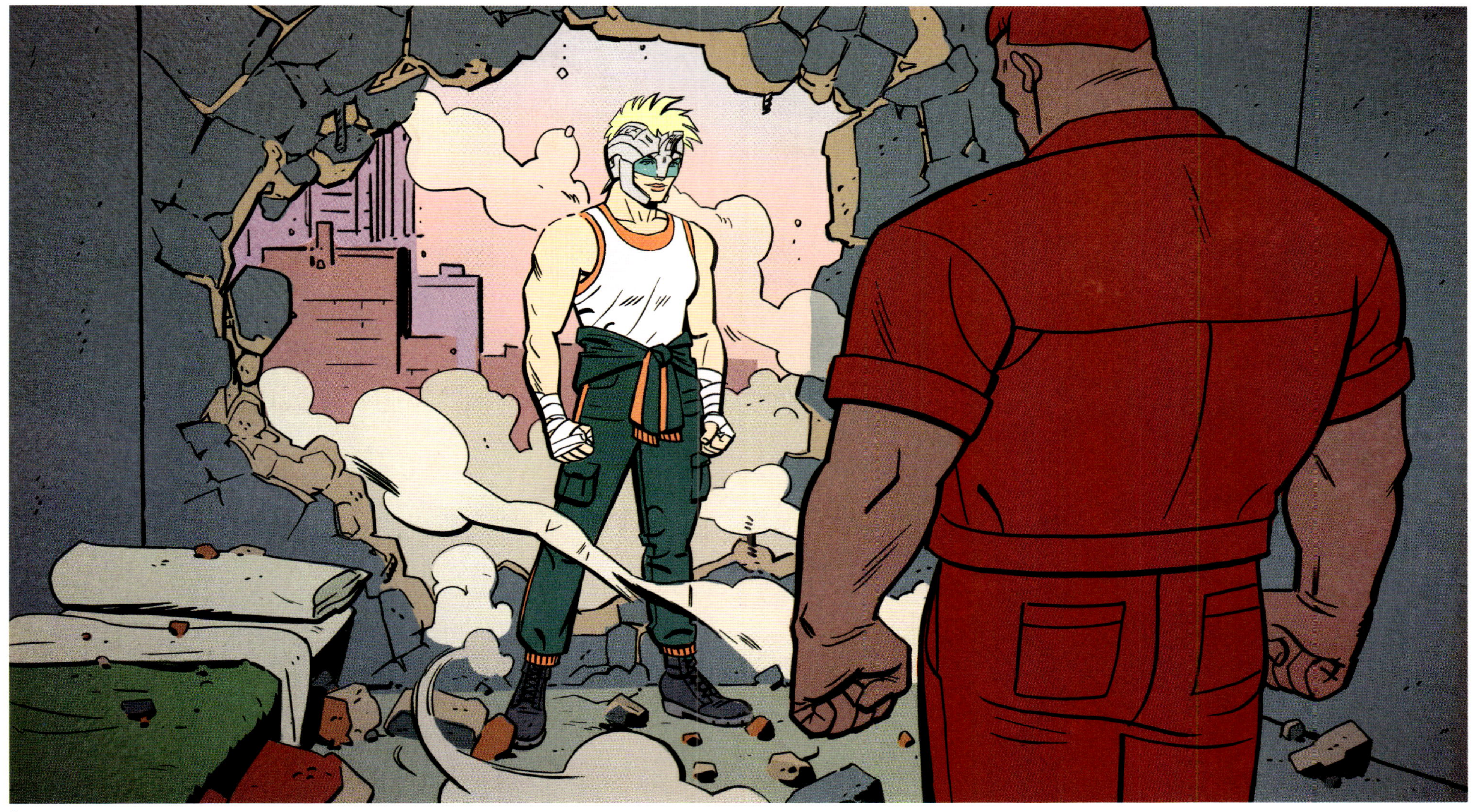

9

10

1–3 Corwin Herse-Woo
4 Junyi Wu
5–8 Ethan Young
9 Chris Samnee (line art) and Michael Yamada (color)
10 Ethan Young

USE THESE STAGES FOR THE BEGINNING BUILD UP BEFORE LASER BEAM FIRES

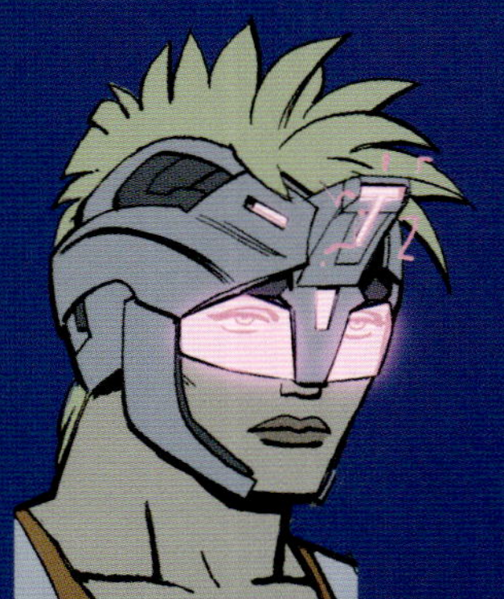

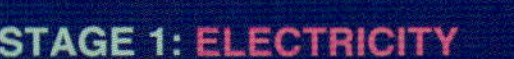

STAGE 1: ELECTRICITY

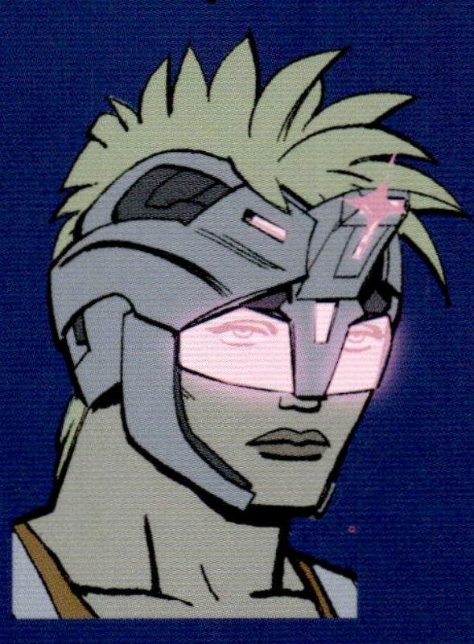

STAGE 2: STAR BUILD UP

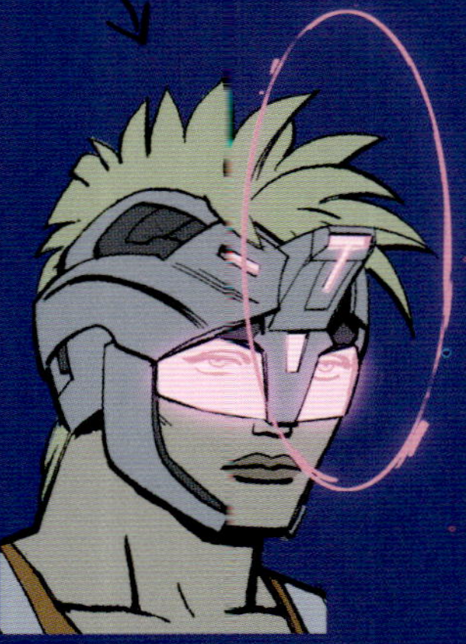

STAGE 3: RING

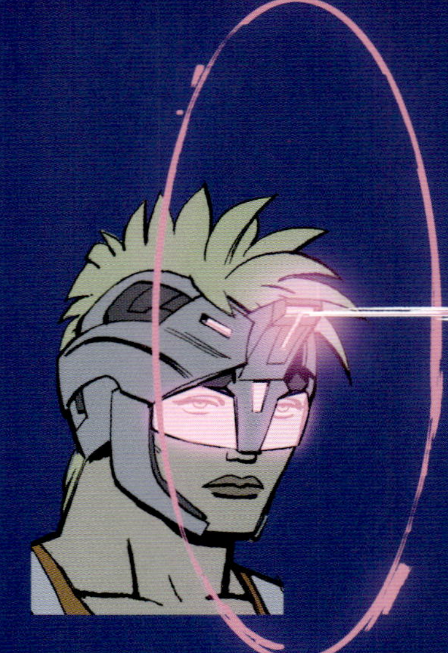

SMALL LASER BEAM

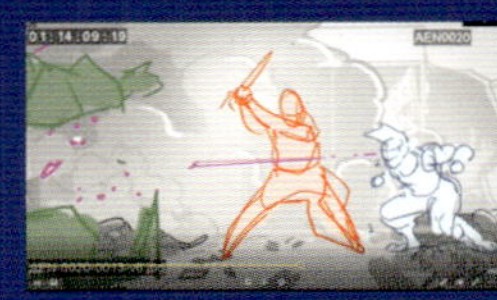

RING DISSIPATES AS SOON AS LASER SHOOTS

STAGE 1: LASER WITH RING SHOOTS OUT

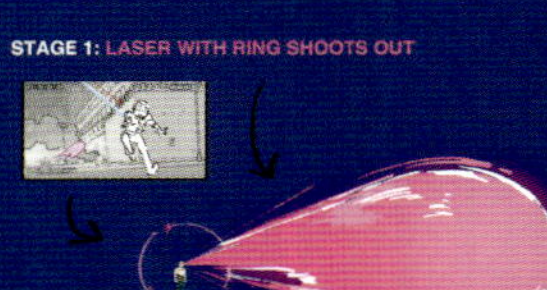

STAGE 2: RING STARTS TO DISSIPATE AND DISAPPEAR AS LASER BEAM IS SHOOTING MID FIRE

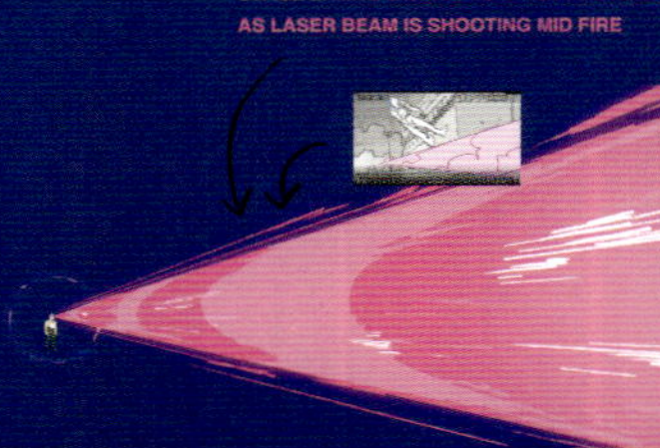

STAGE 3: BRIGHT GLOW FILLS SCREEN WHEN LASER BEAM CLOSER TO CAMERA

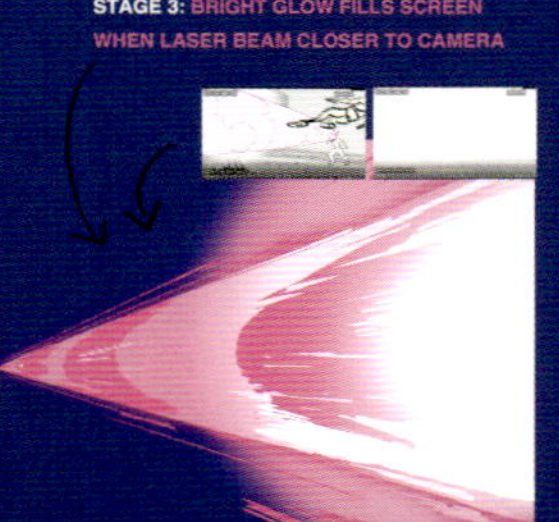

SIDE VIEW OF LASER BEAM

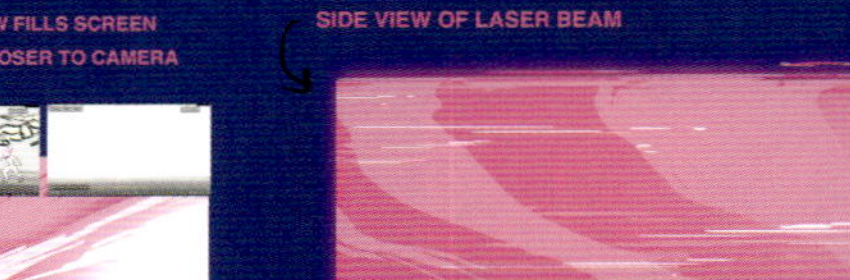

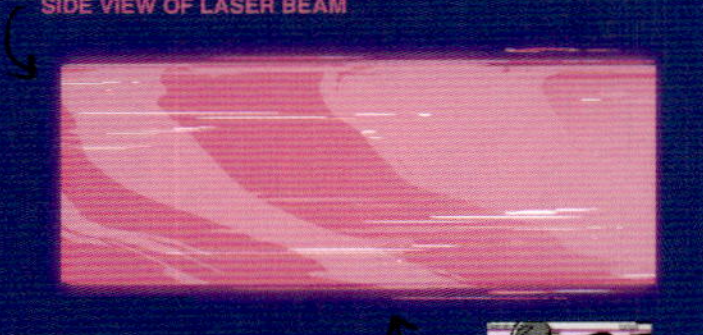

IMPACT OF LASER BEAM

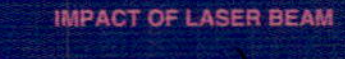

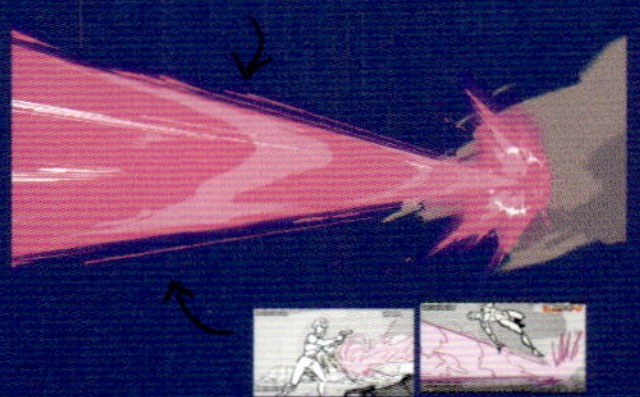

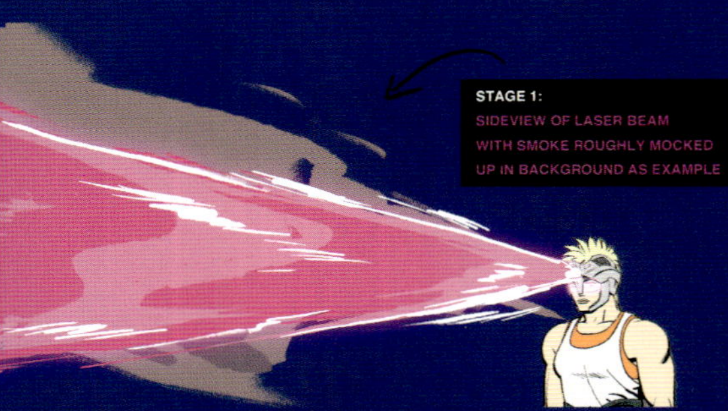

STAGE 1:
SIDEVIEW OF LASER BEAM WITH SMOKE ROUGHLY MOCKED UP IN BACKGROUND AS EXAMPLE

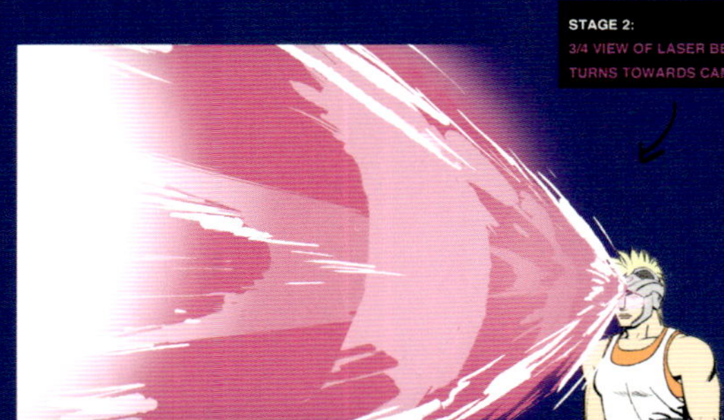

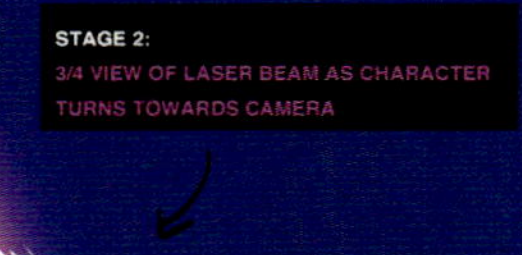

STAGE 2:
3/4 VIEW OF LASER BEAM AS CHARACTER TURNS TOWARDS CAMERA

STAGE 3:
FULL VIEW OF LASER BEAM FACES CAMERA, EFFECT COVERS ENTIRE SCREEN

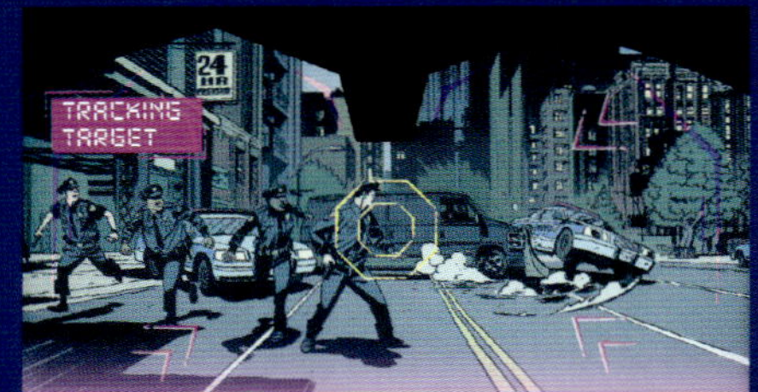

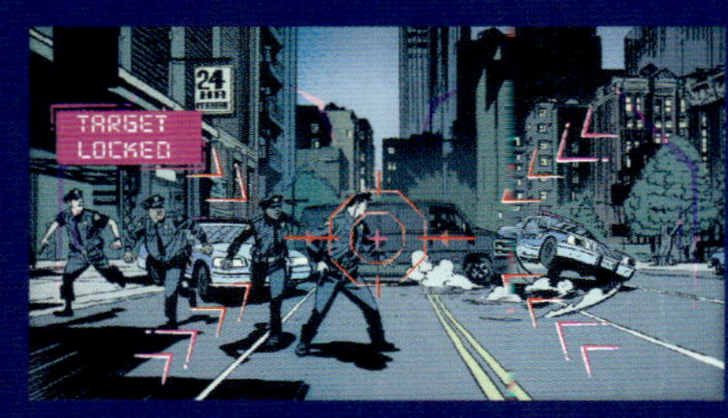

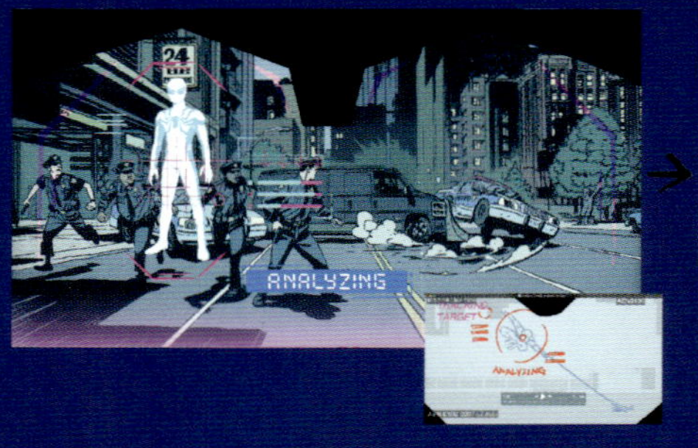

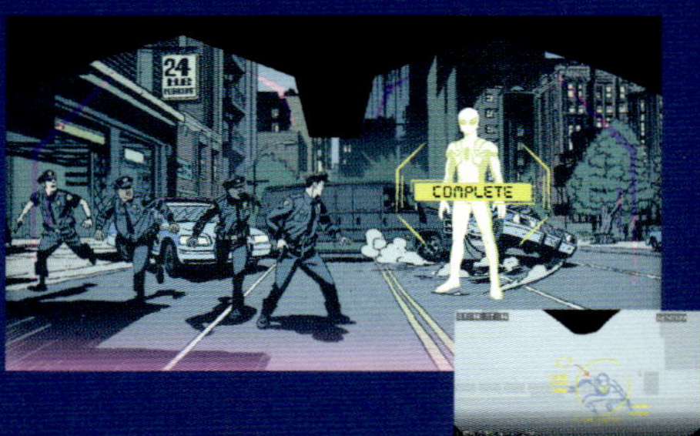

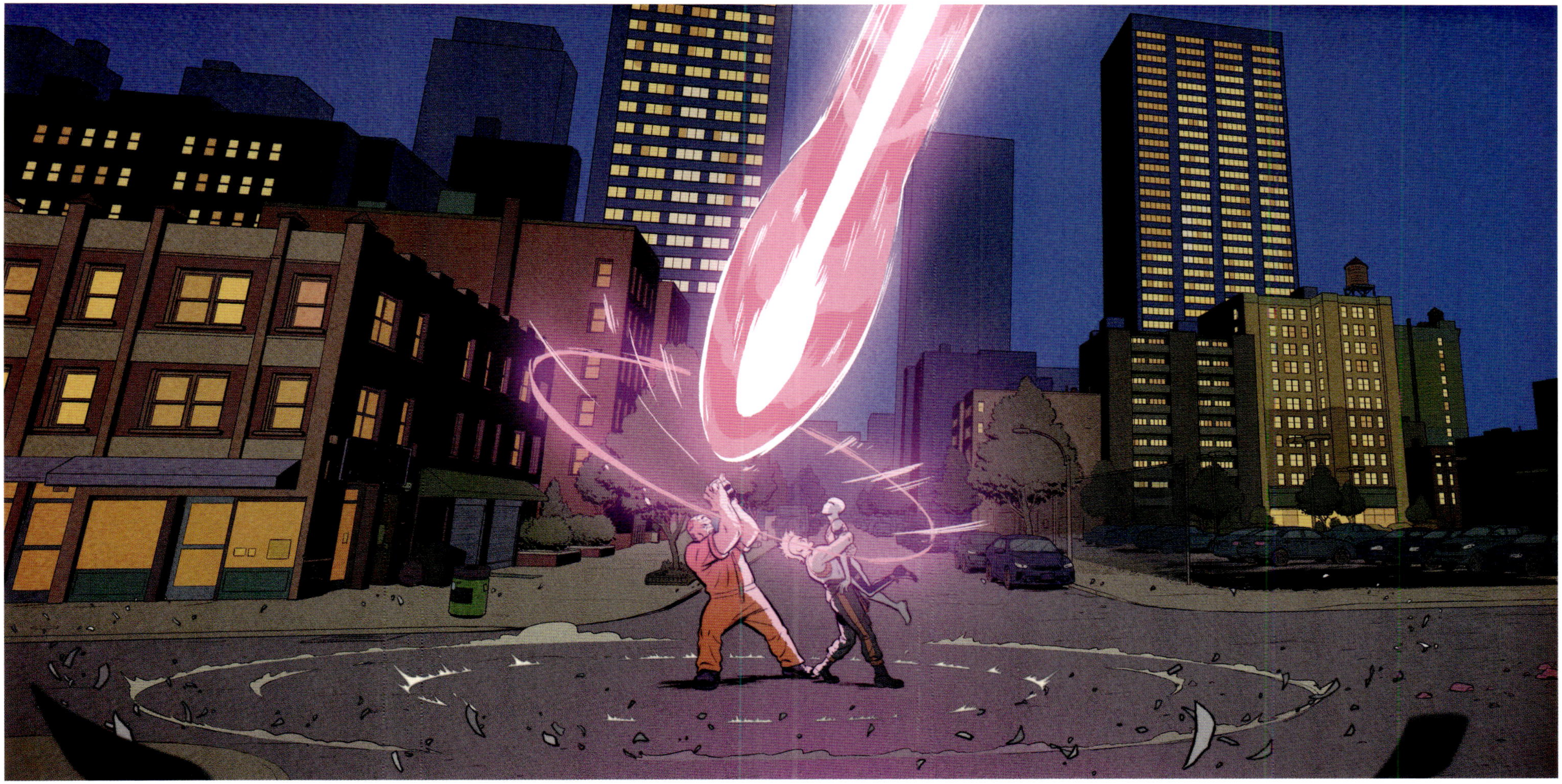

1

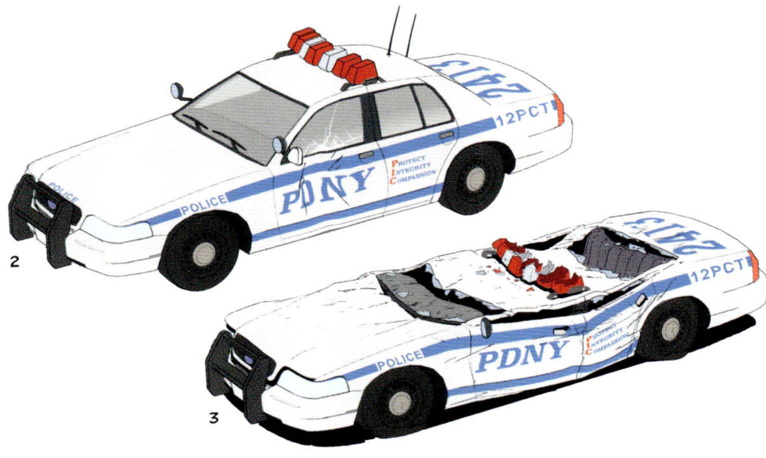

2

3

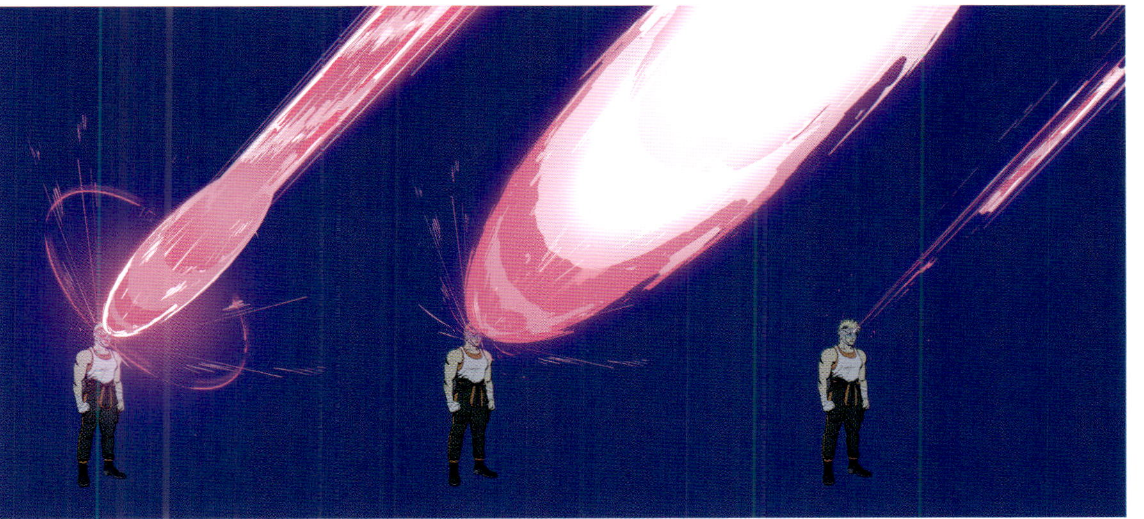

4

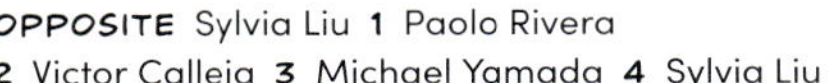

OPPOSITE Sylvia Liu **1** Paolo Rivera
2 Victor Calleja **3** Michael Yamada **4** Sylvia Liu

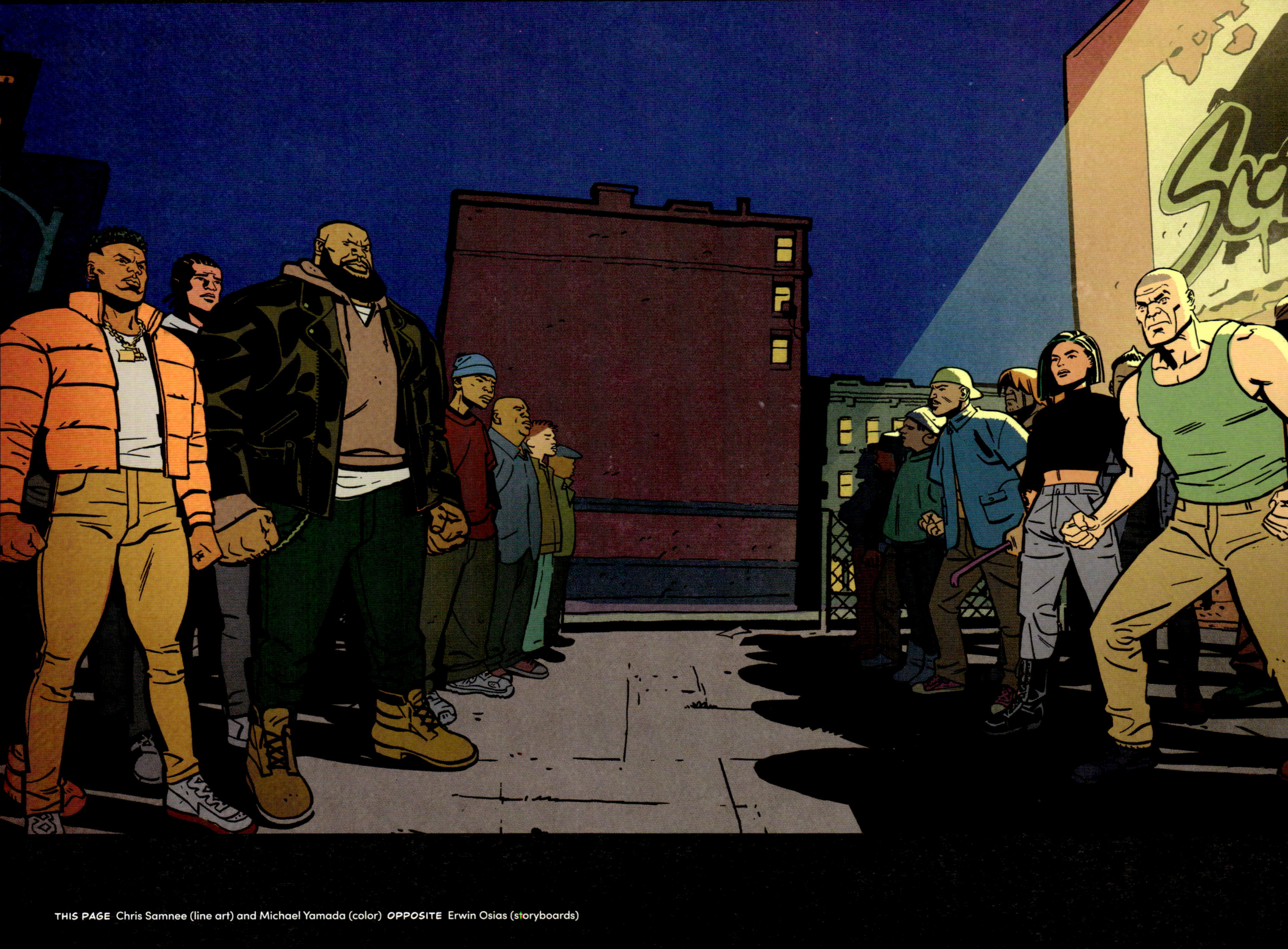

THIS PAGE Chris Samnee (line art) and Michael Yamada (color) OPPOSITE Erwin Osias (storyboards)

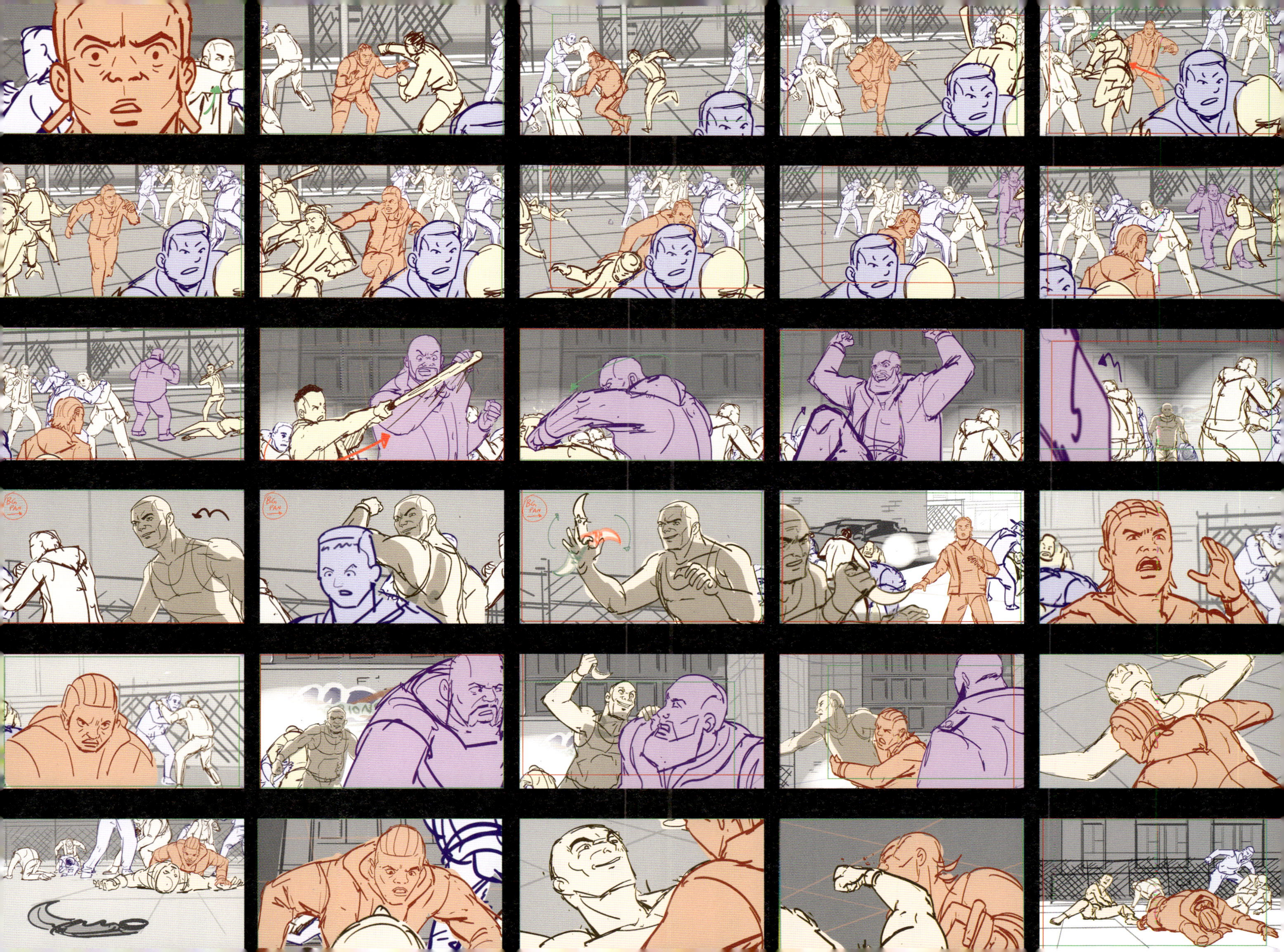

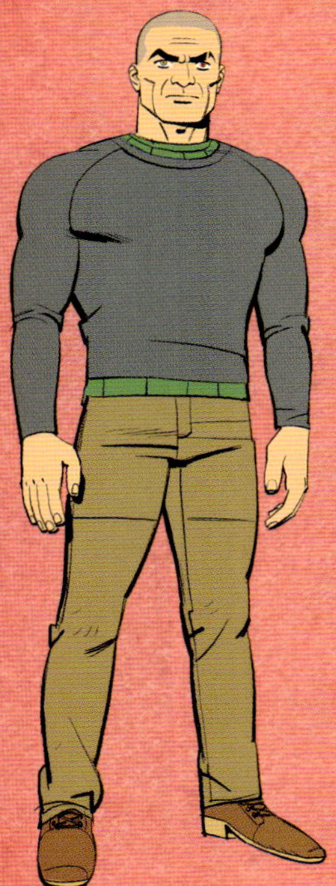

1

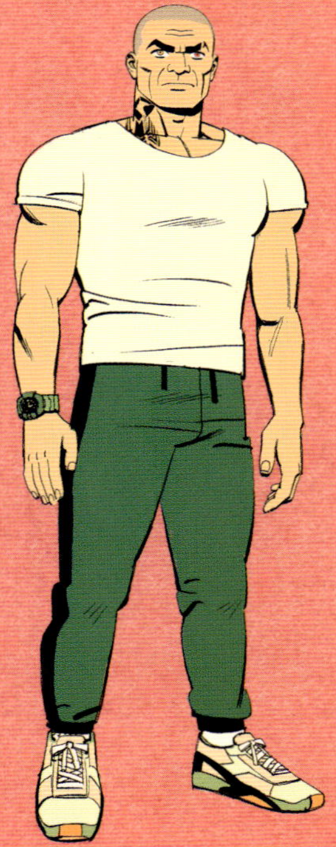

2

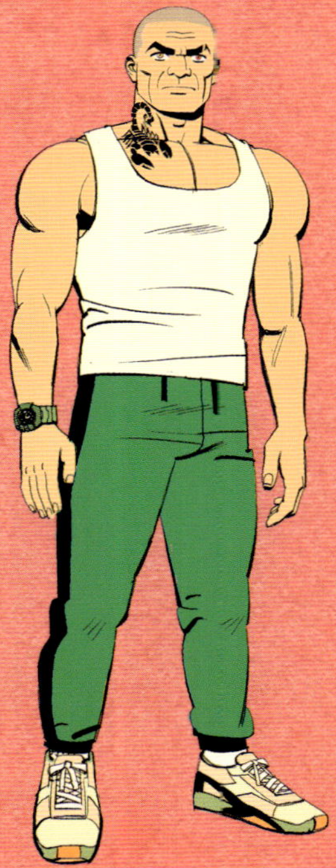

3

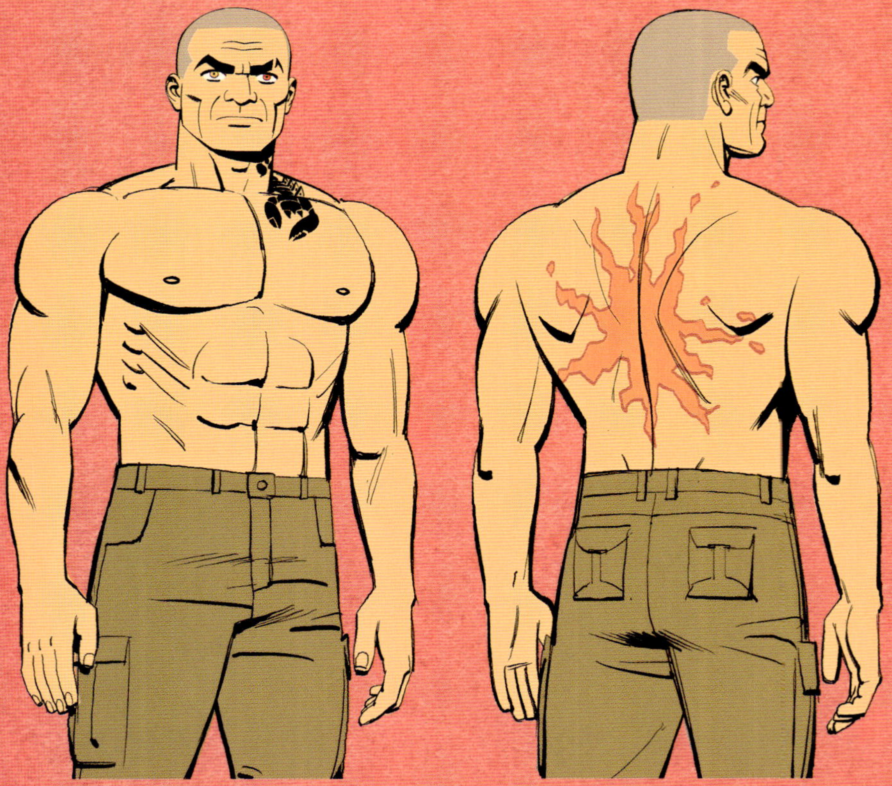

4

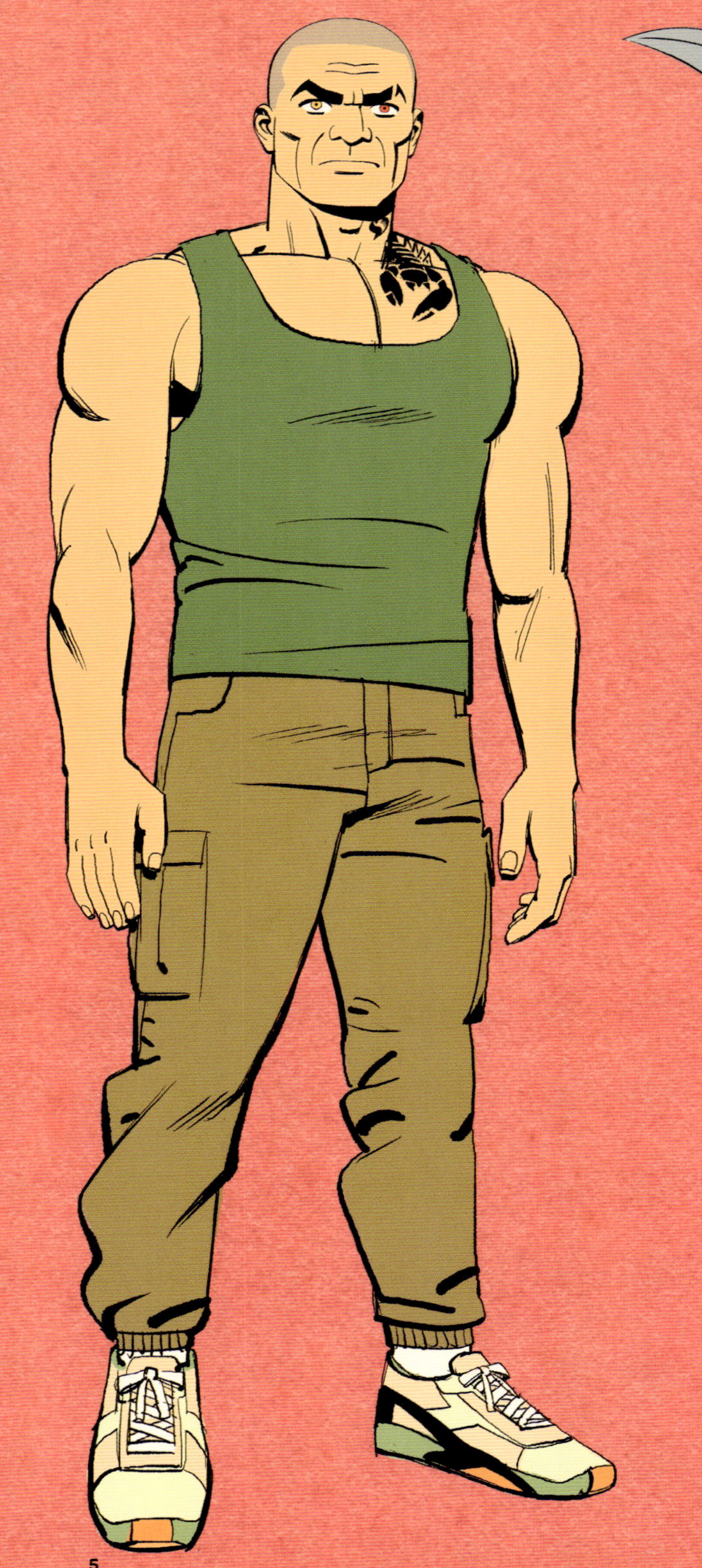

5

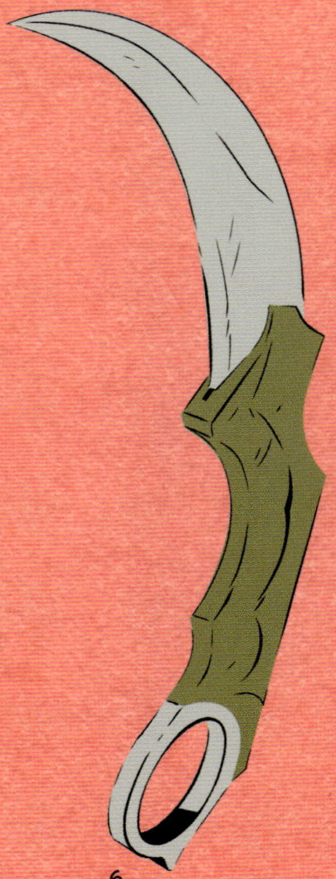

6

1–5 Leonardo Romero
6 Junyi Wu 7 Chris Samnee (line art) and Michael Yamada (color) 8–9 Kelsey Roland

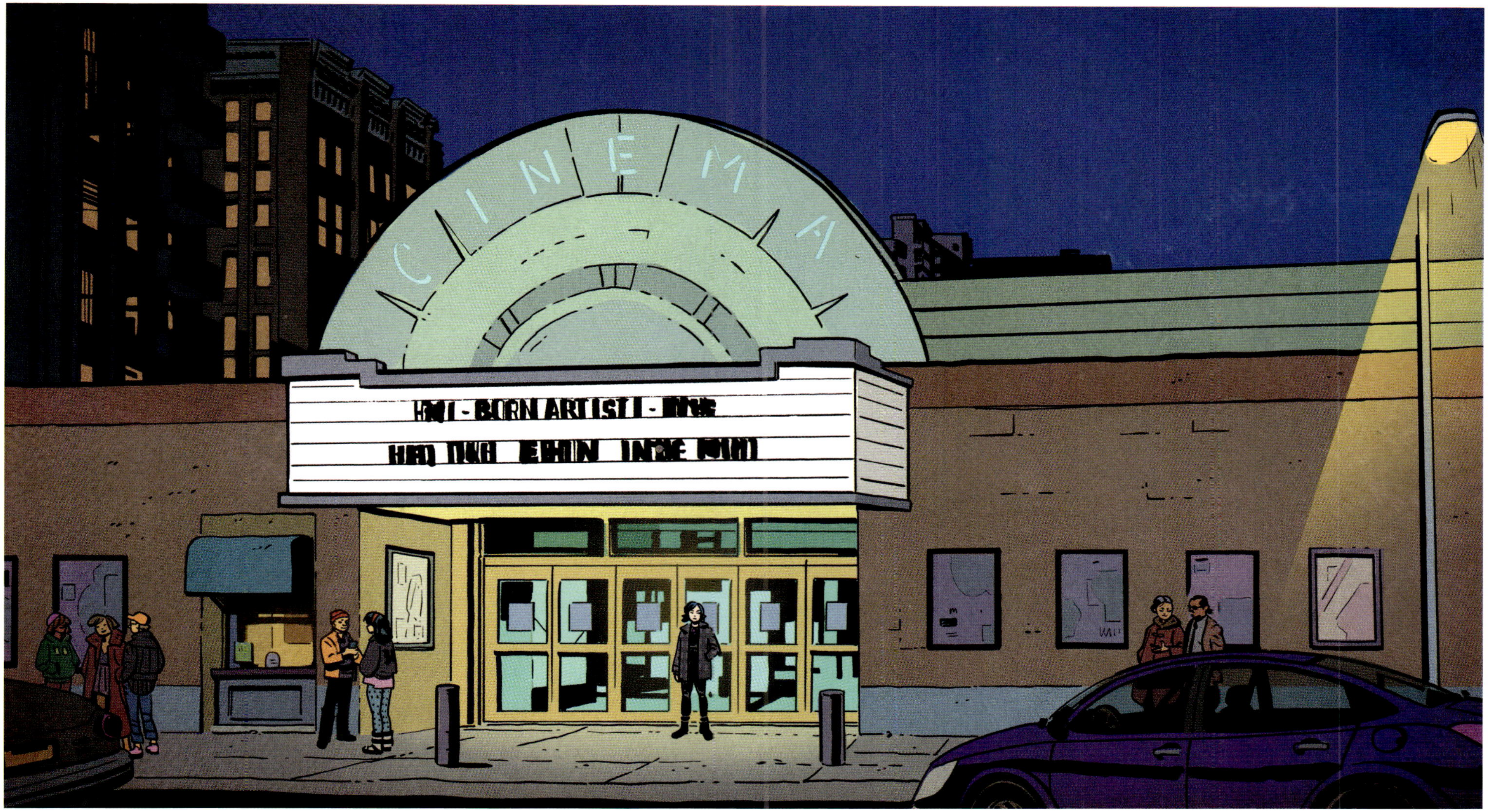

7

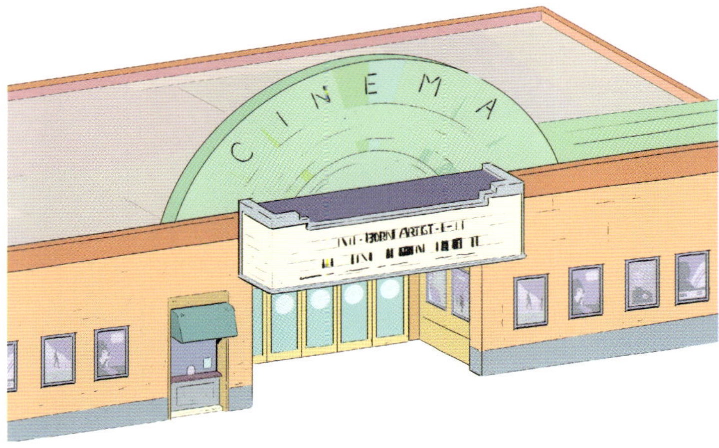

8

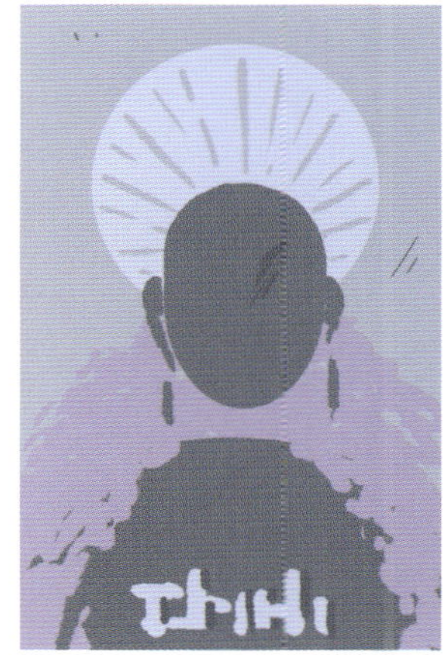

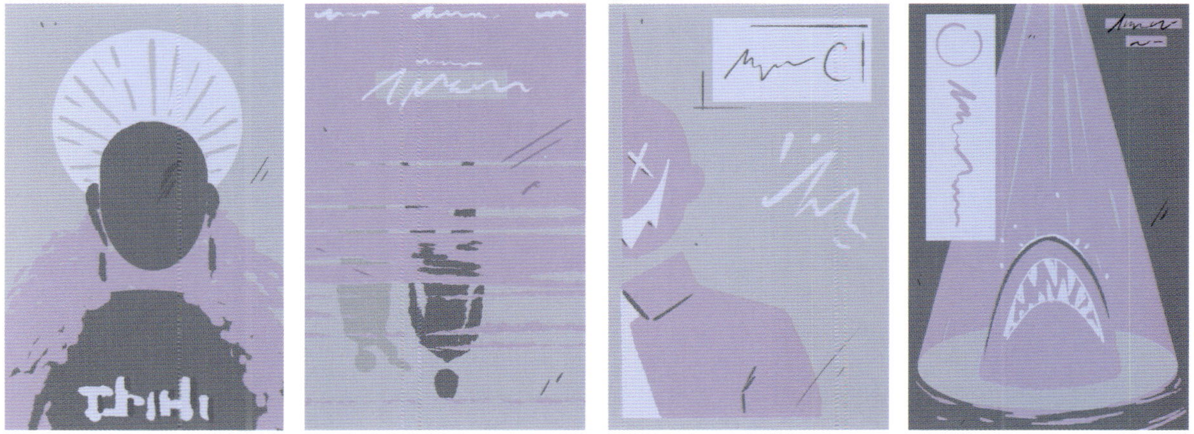

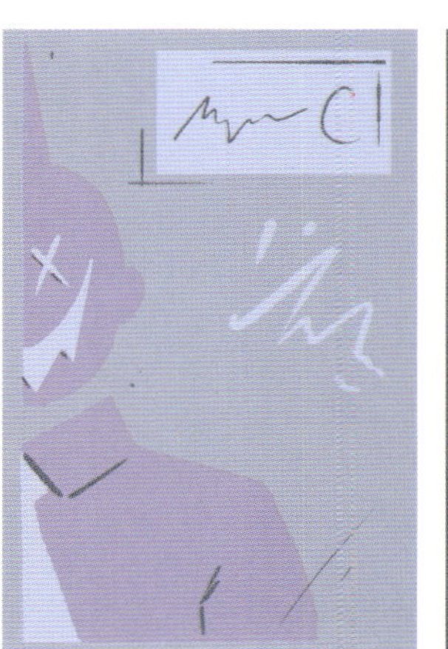

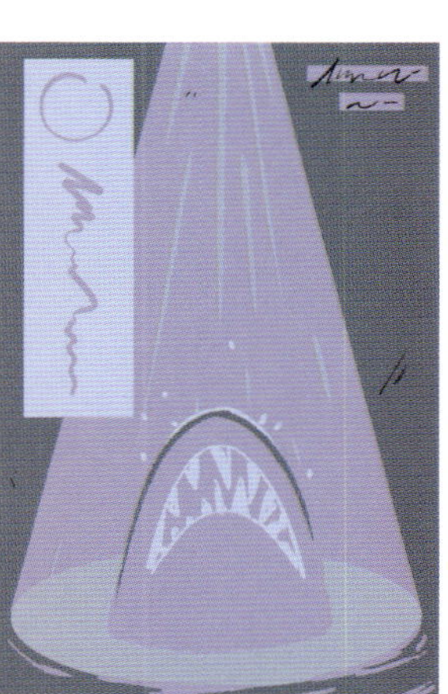

9

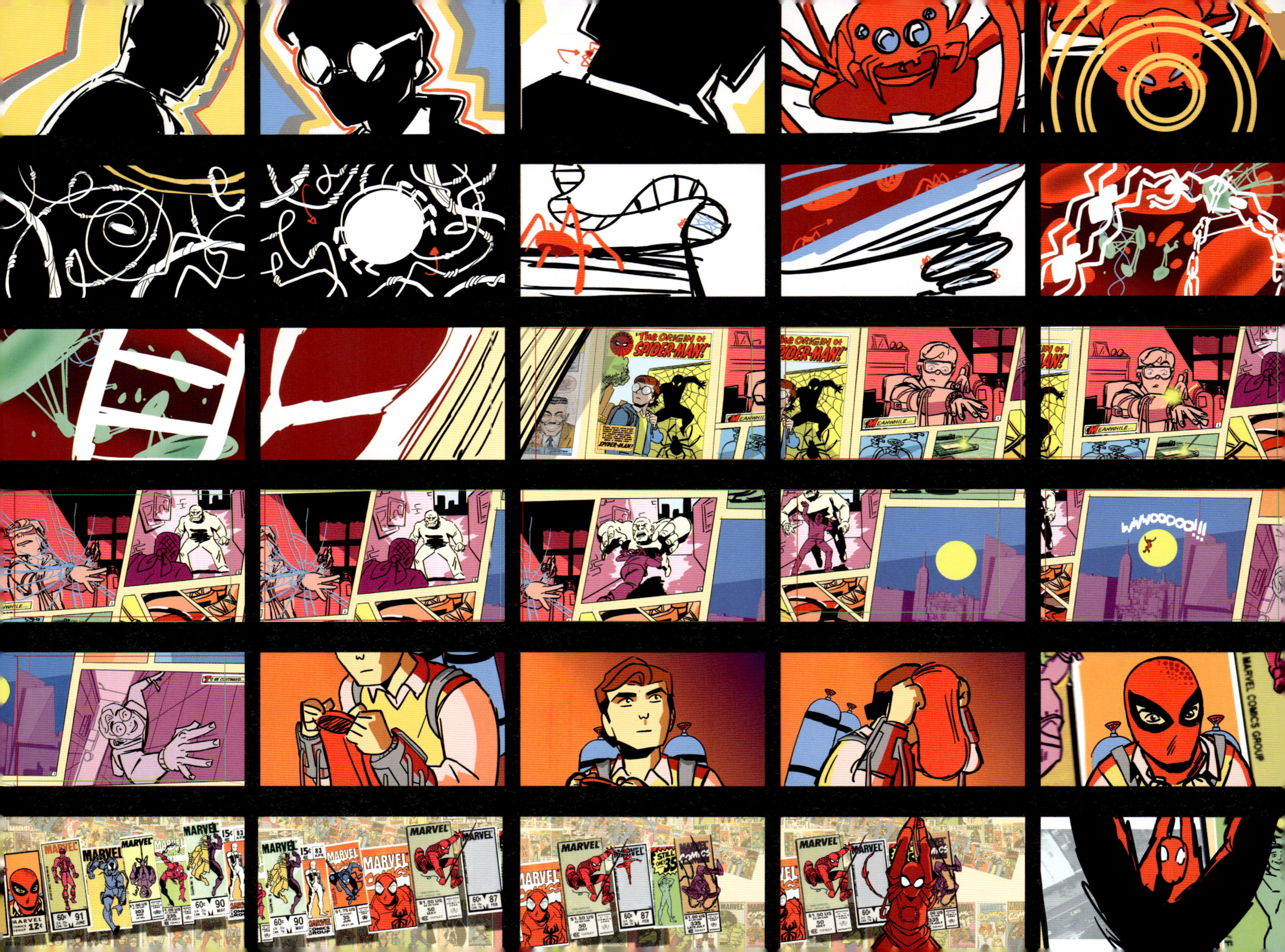

The ORIGIN of SPIDER-MAN!
MEANWHILE...
MARVEL COMICS GROUP
MARVEL

INTERLUDE

OPENING CREDITS AND THEME SONG

SPIDER-MAN'S catchy theme song from the 1967 animated series has been part of the long-lasting legacy of the property for years, and Marvel Animation's *Your Friendly Neighborhood Spider-Man* pays homage to Paul Francis Webster and Bob Harris's iconic composition. Executive Producer/Showrunner Jeff Trammell says incorporating the classic song was part of the original plans for the show.

"We thought it would be cool to use it, but I didn't know what the chances were of us being able to incorporate it," he recalls. "But then, Kevin Feige [President of Marvel Studios] said we should do it, so it happened. So much of our show is about paying homage to the past while also modernizing it. I was wondering how we could achieve that, but I told [theme song collaborators] Relaye and Melo Makes Music, 'I trust that you'll find the perfect way.' Then The Math Club came along, and they made this incredible song. You immediately recognize the old song, and then it pumps up the adrenaline with these raps that come in. I remember the first time I heard it, I thought it was very cool, and then this earworm of a song got stuck in my head for weeks!"

"I've watched so many videos of fans watching the show and singing and rapping along with the theme song," says Associate Producer Alex Scharf (*What If...?*, *X-Men '97*). "There's even an extended version of the song on Spotify, where there's a whole other verse, which is very cool. We were lucky to be able to get the rights for the original song. Every generation has their own version of Spider-Man that they grew up with, but everyone seems to know the 'Here comes the Spider-Man' song. It really ties the web of all the Spider-Men together. There are few characters who have an iconic song associated with them, and I'm so glad we were able to feature it with our credits too."

Co-Executive Producer/Supervising Director Mel Zwyer put a lot of effort into pulling the opening credits together, according to Scharf. "The credits sequence totally sells the show, with the way it overlays the colors on objects," he points out. "There's one part where you see Peter Parker walking through a crosswalk, and if you pay attention to the water puddle, there's a reflection of Spider-Man wearing his homemade suit. That detail also changes depending on the suit he wears through each specific episode. The title cards also pay homage to the classic comics, thanks to the art created by Leo Romero."

To help design the credit sequence, the production reached out to Storyboard Artist Steve Walker, who has an incredibly deep knowledge of everyone's favorite wall-crawler. "It was a dream come true because I've never had the privilege to design an opening of a TV show, let alone for something as iconic as Spider-Man, but I had great direction from Mel Zwyer and Jeff Trammell," he says. "I think my lifelong love of comics, the character, and the opportunity to design it really shaped it in the end."

Narrative-wise, the big goal was to sum up Peter's early days. "Everyone's familiar with Spider-Man's origin by now, and the show employs a big time skip after he gets bitten by the spider, so it was important to show those iconic images in some capacity," Walker says. "My ultimate and personal goal was to create

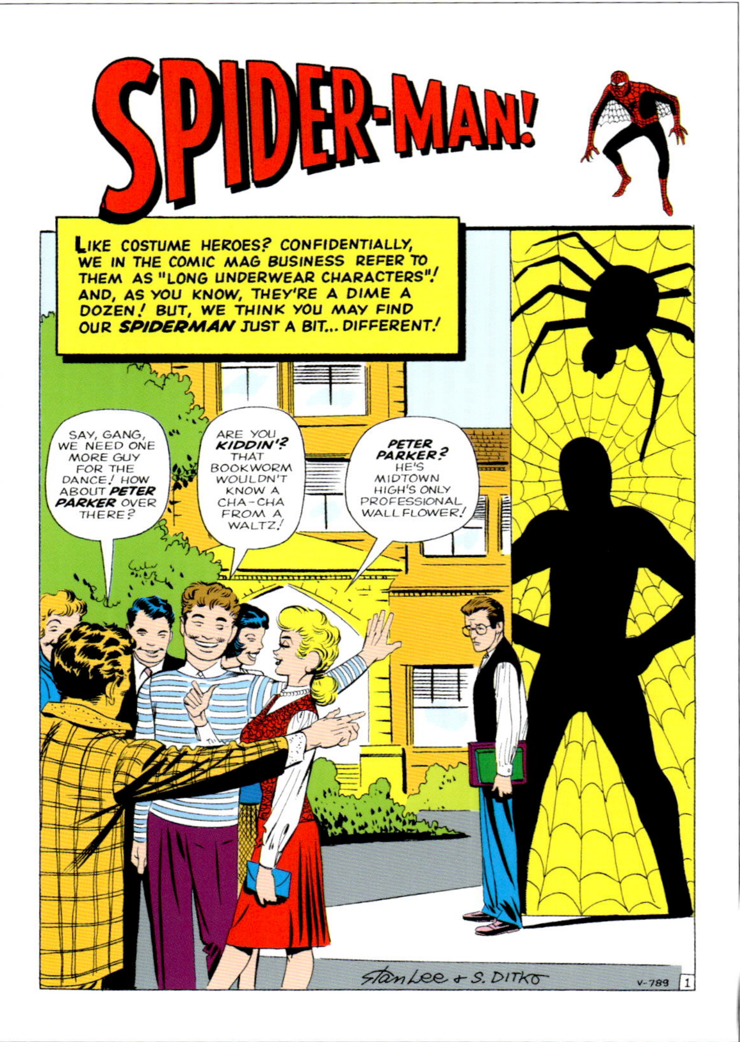

1

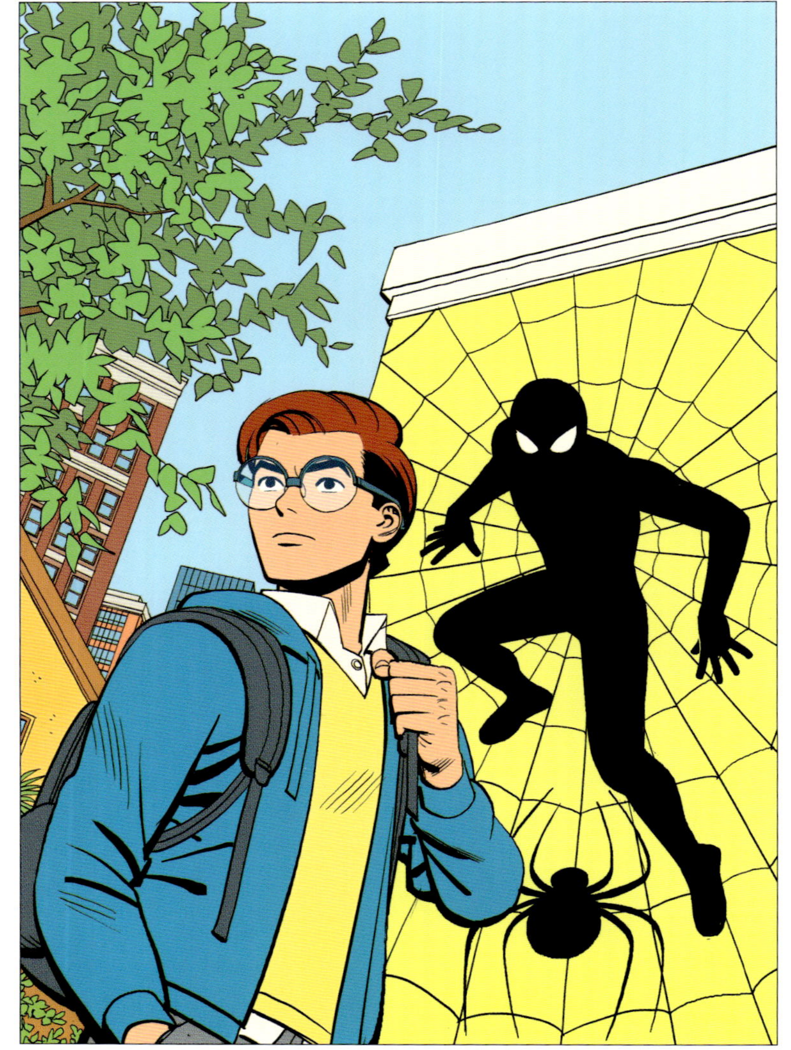

2

something that lived up to the character and what's come before, [while making] something people enjoyed and didn't just skip in the streaming era."

Walker says he challenged himself to work in a very graphic style on the storyboards. "That included everything from the big sound effect lettering [to] how each scene translates to one another, all the vibrant color, and all [the] the fun, retro, halftone dot effects throughout," he points out. "I was absolutely floored with how good it looked; seeing the final product was the greatest thing ever, humongous thanks to the 3D team that nailed it! I also loved the page-turn and comic panels laying out Spider-Man's origin sequence. I was super happy with the corner box art section as well; [that's] kind of a lost art in modern comics, but I feel everyone loves it when that pops up again. Most of all, I think the big stand-out is how every episode got an original comic cover title card, done masterfully by Leo Romero. The idea felt like such a novel addition to such an already bold art style of a show."

Walker mentions that he was inspired by every artist who has worked on the character in the last sixty years. "I'd like to hope you can see shades of every great Spider-Man artist in the show," he concludes. "The most notable inspiration was from the legends Steve Ditko and John Romita Sr.; we tried to pull all we could from Peter's younger early years, notably the mid-century printing color palette and the vibe of the era. I made a very intentional nod to Ditko in the comic page section: Peter, with Spider-Man's shadow behind him. Now that's such an iconic image!"

1 *Amazing Fantasy* (1962) #15. Steve Ditko (pencils and inks) and Stan Goldberg (colors) **2** Homage to *Amazing Fantasy* #15 in the show's credit sequence. Leonardo Romero **3** *Amazing Fantasy* (1962) #15. Steve Ditko (pencils and inks) and Stan Goldberg (colors) **4** Leonardo Romero **5** *The Amazing Spider-Man Annual* (2018) #1 (Dennis Chan Video Game Variant). Garry Brown (pencils) **6** Leonardo Romero

AMAZING FANTASY
12¢
15 AUG.
APPROVED BY THE COMICS CODE AUTHORITY
INTRODUCING SPIDER MAN
THOUGH THE WORLD MAY MOCK PETER PARKER, THE TIMID TEEN-AGER...
...IT WILL SOON MARVEL AT THE AWESOME MIGHT OF... SPIDER-MAN!
ALSO IN THIS ISSUE: AN IMPORTANT MESSAGE TO YOU, FROM THE EDITOR--ABOUT THE NEW AMAZING!

3

15¢
90 MAR
MARVEL COMICS GROUP
YOUR FRIENDLY NEIGHBORHOOD
SPIDER-MAN
WRITTEN BY
JEFF TRAMMELL
DIRECTED BY
MEL ZWYER

4

the AMAZING SPIDER-MAN
OSCORP
Just the Facts
with J. Jonah Jameson
MARVEL
SPIDER-MAN

5

15¢
90 MAR
MARVEL COMICS GROUP
YOUR FRIENDLY NEIGHBORHOOD
SPIDER-MAN
Oscorp
WRITTEN BY
CHARLIE NEUNER
DIRECTED BY
LIZA SINGER

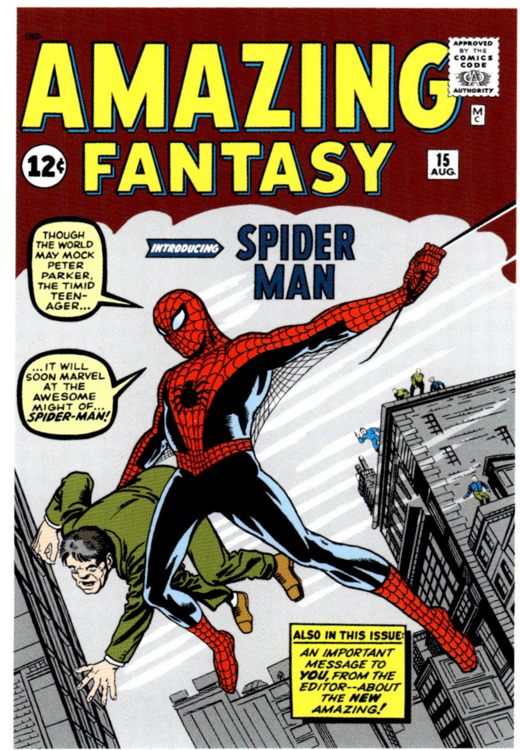

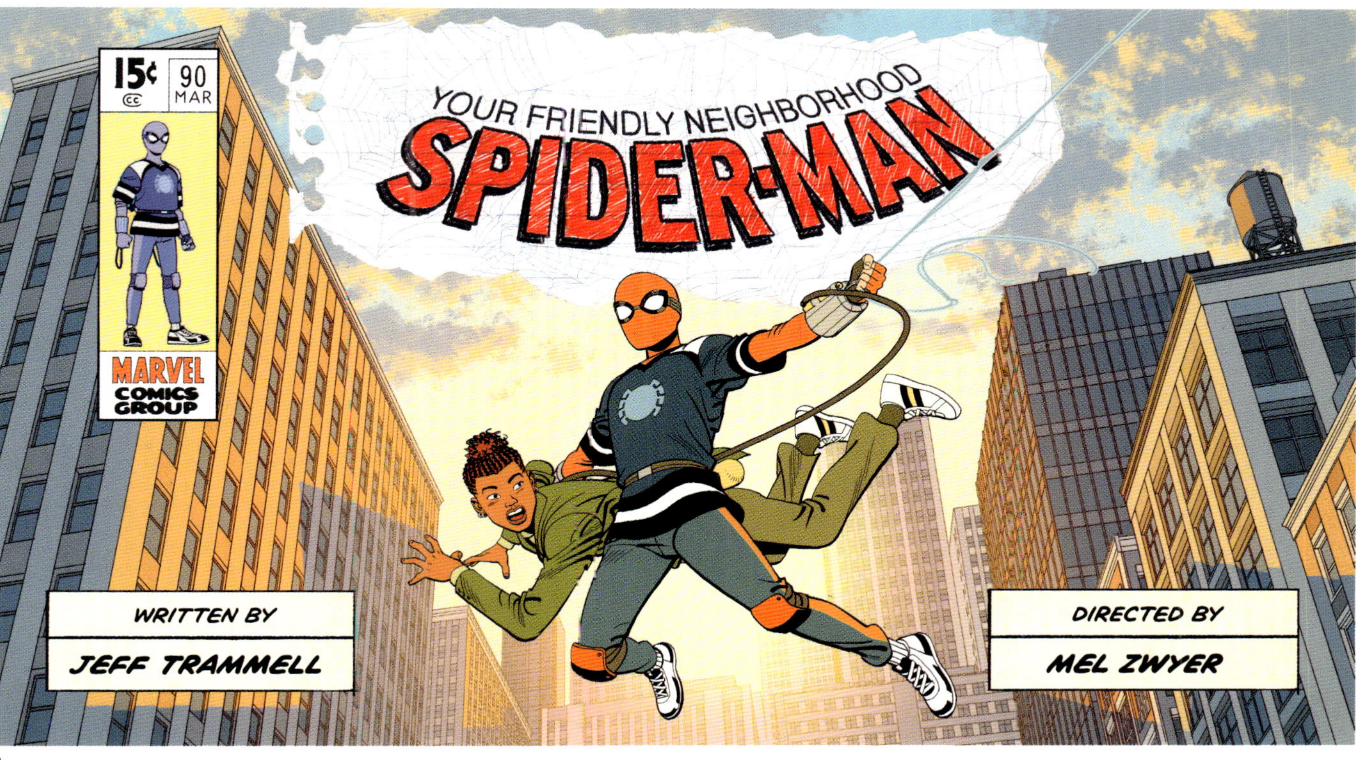

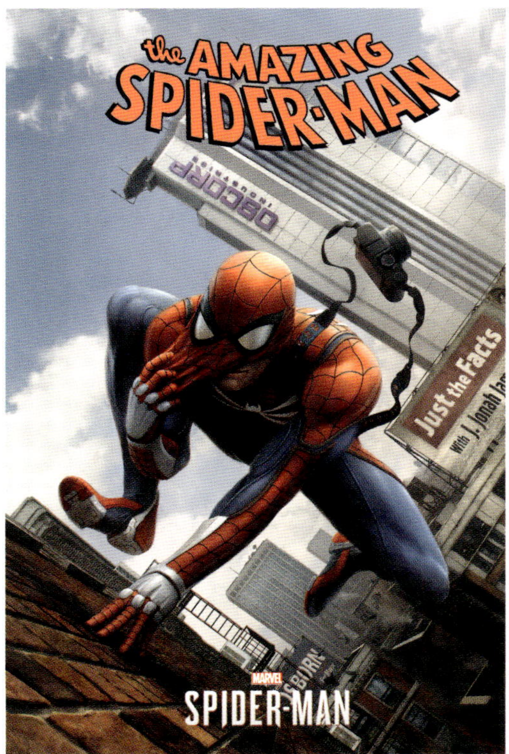

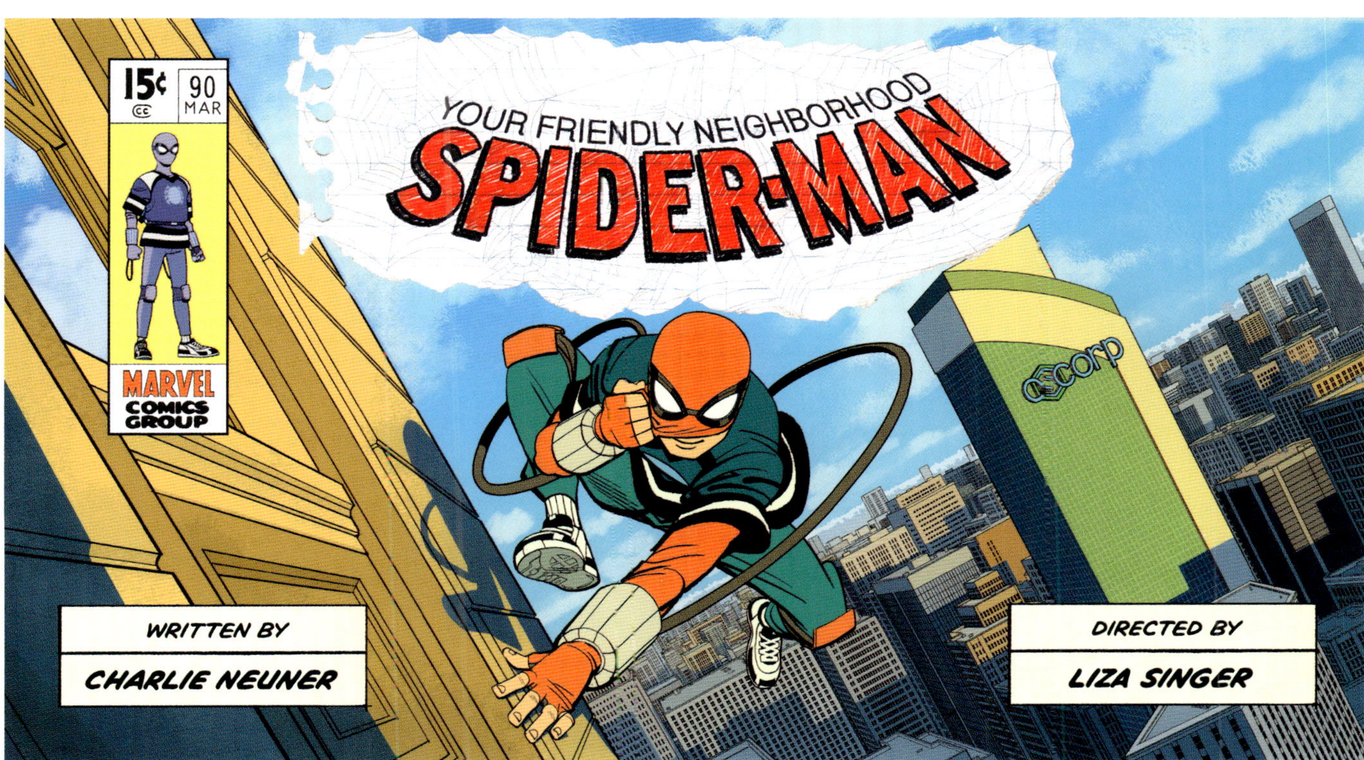

6

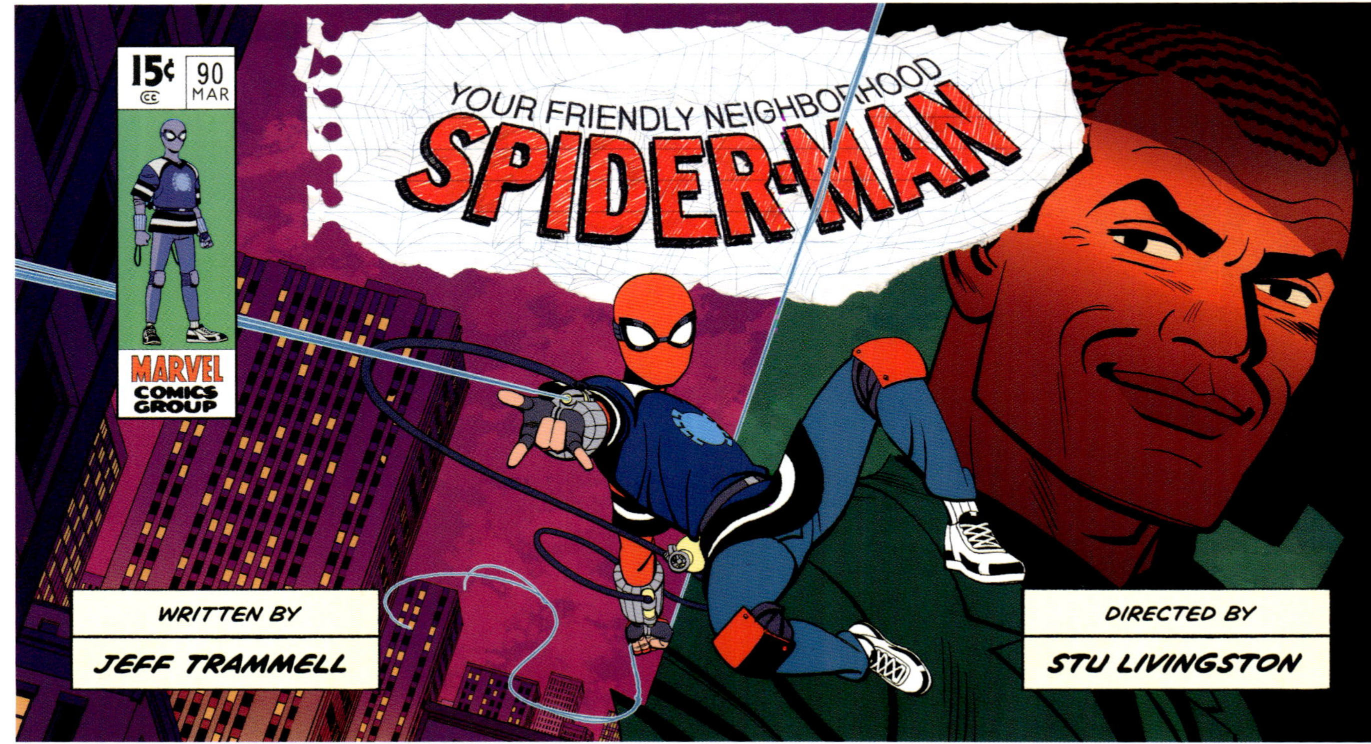

1

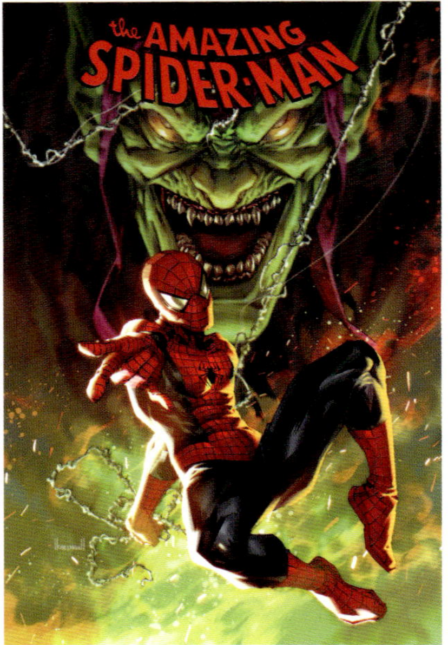

2

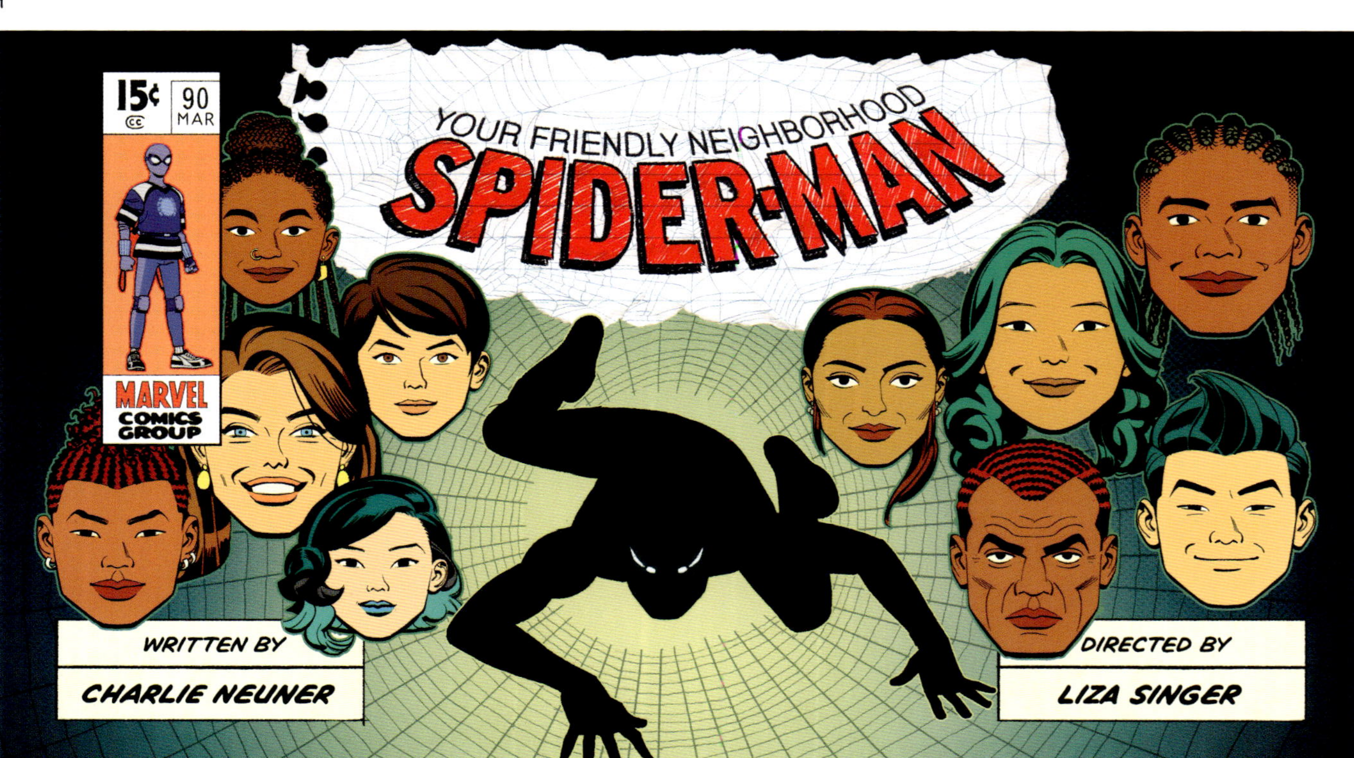

3

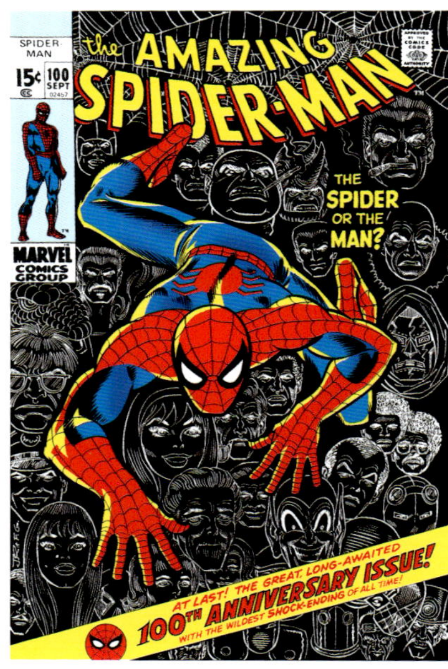

4

1 Leonardo Romero **2** *The Amazing Spider-Man* (2018) #49 (Kael Ngu Exclusive Trade Variant). Chris Bachalo, Mark Bagley, Aaron Kuder, Tradd Moore, Ryan Ottley, and Humberto Ramos (pencils) **3** Leonardo Romero **4** *The Amazing Spider-Man* (1963) #100. Gil Kane (pencils)

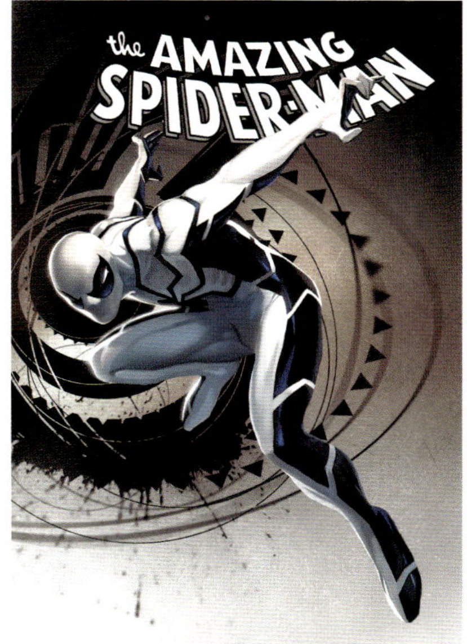

5

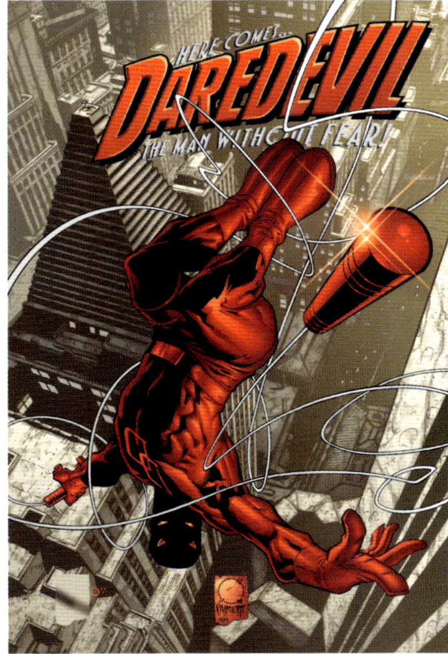

7

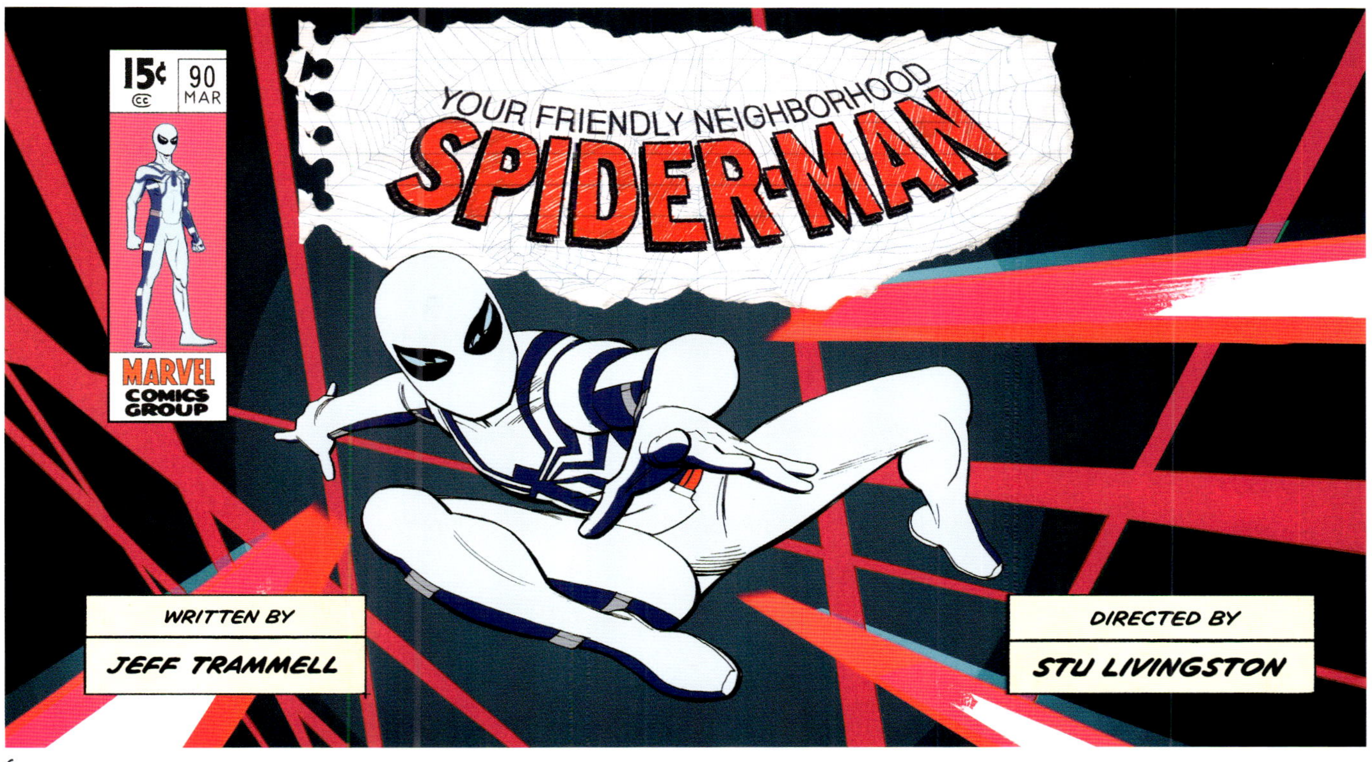

6

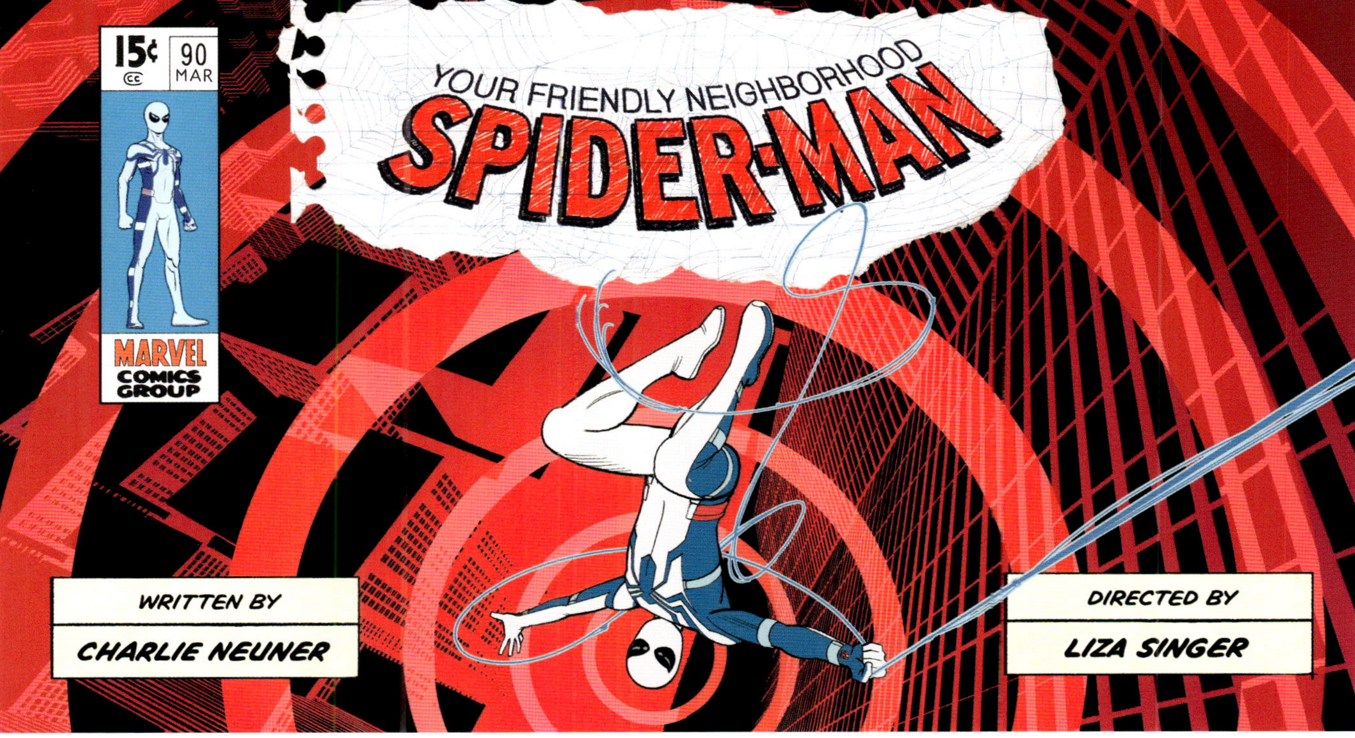

8

5 *The Amazing Spider-Man* (1999) #658. Lee Garbett and Javier Pulido (pencils), Javier Pulido and Alejandro Sicat (inks), and Fabio D'Auria, Javier Rodríguez, and Muntsa Vicente (colors) **6** Leonardo Romero **7** *Daredevil* (1998) #1. Joe Quesada (pencils), Jimmy Palmiotti (inks), and Dan Kemp (colors) **8** Leonardo Romero

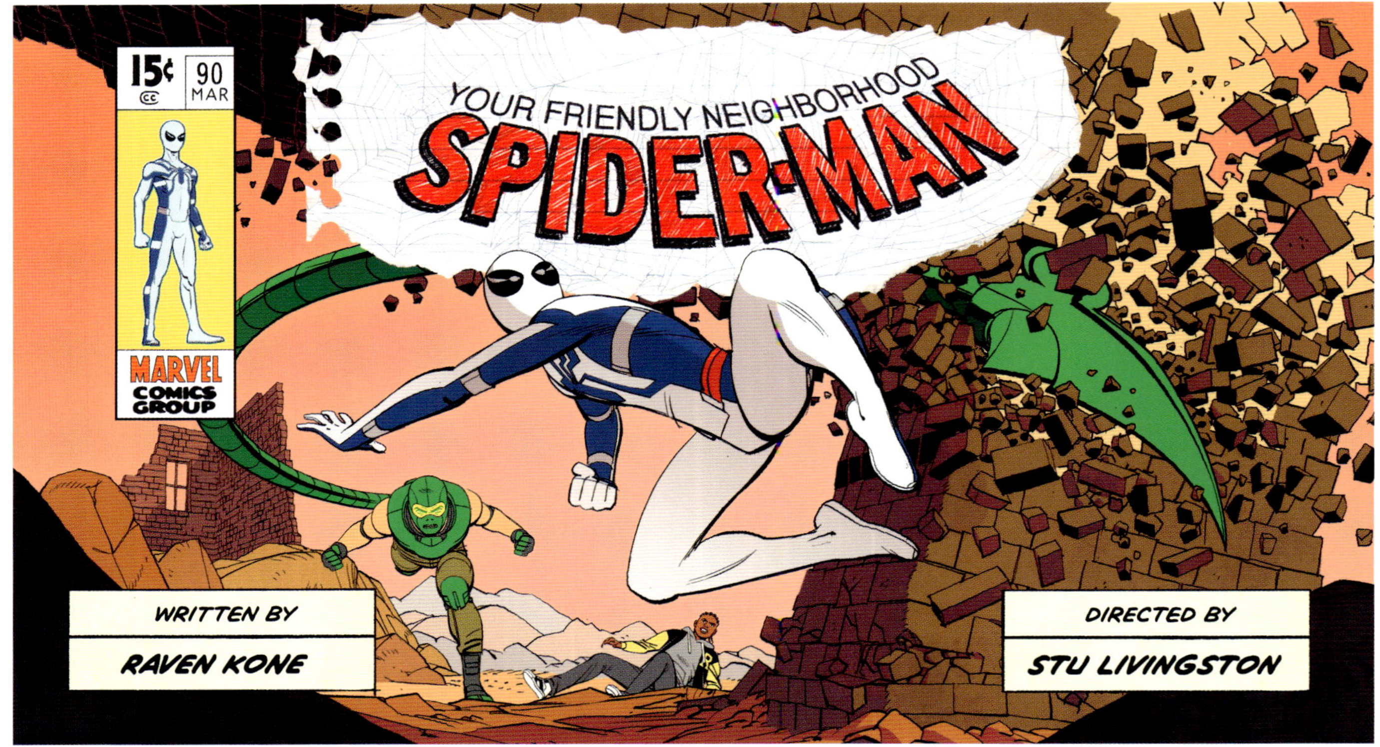

1

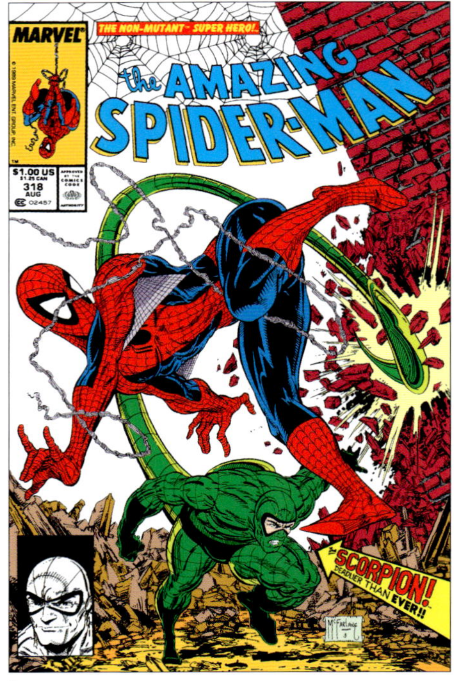

2

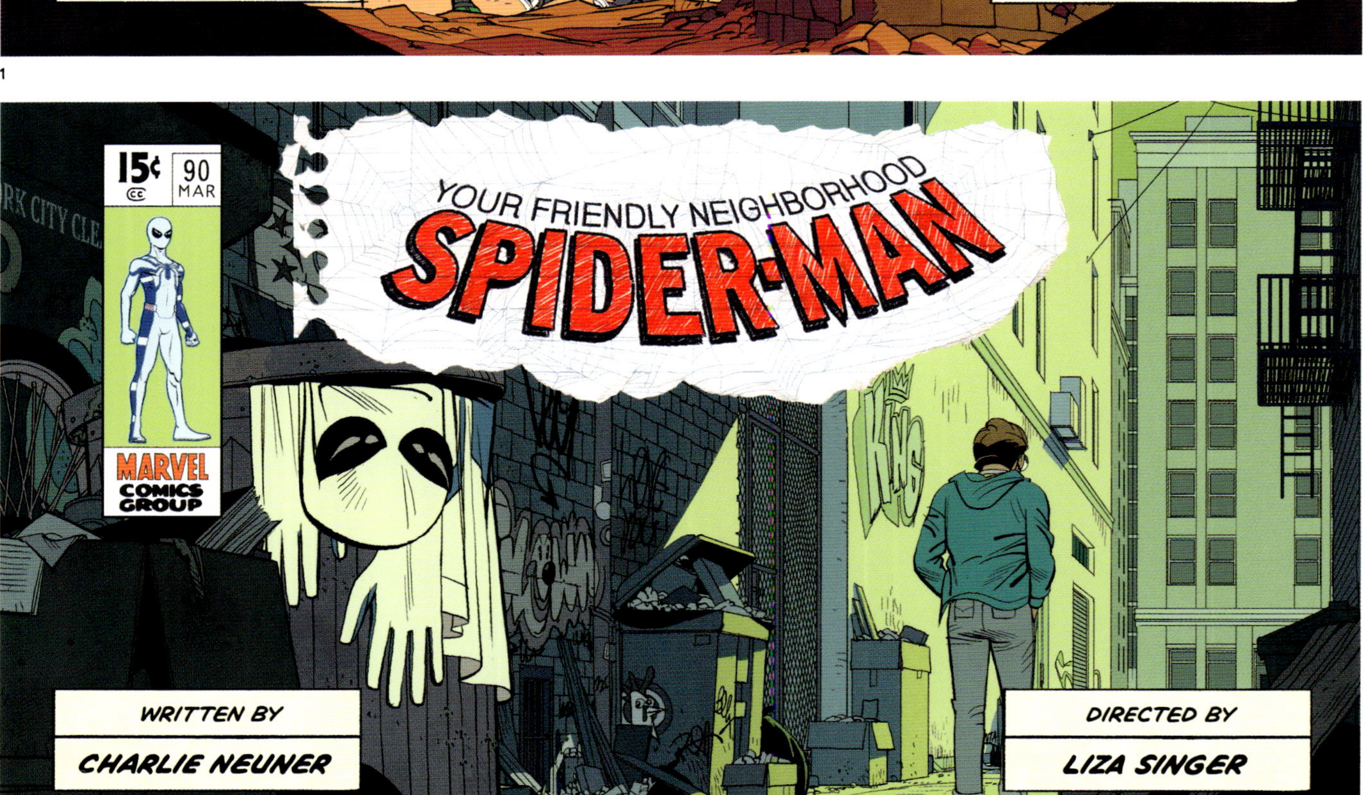

3

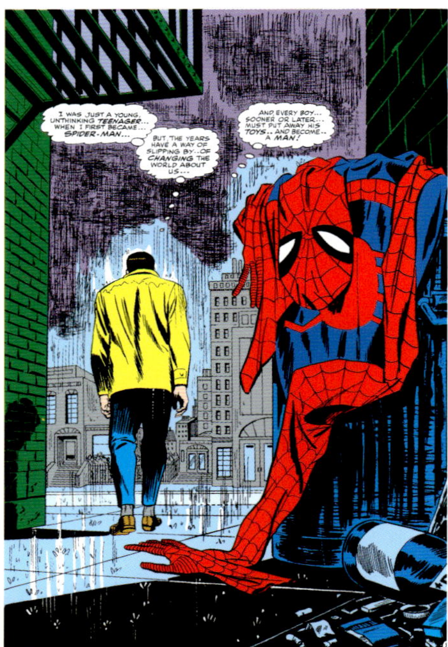

4

1 Leonardo Romero **2** *The Amazing Spider-Man* (1963) #318. Todd McFarlane (pencils and inks) **3** Leonardo Romero **4** *The Amazing Spider-Man* (1963) #50. John Romita Sr. (pencils) and Mike Esposito (inks)

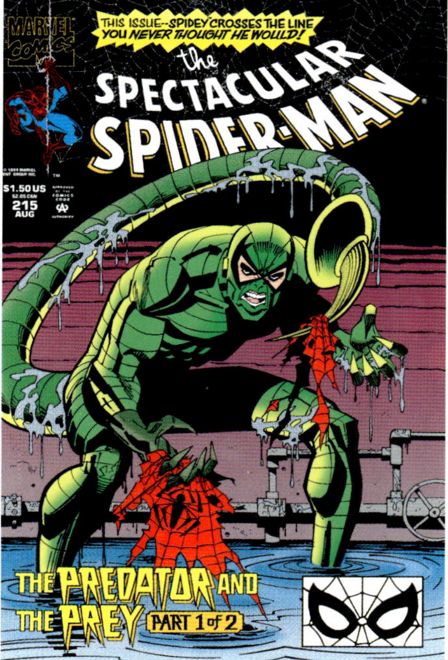

5

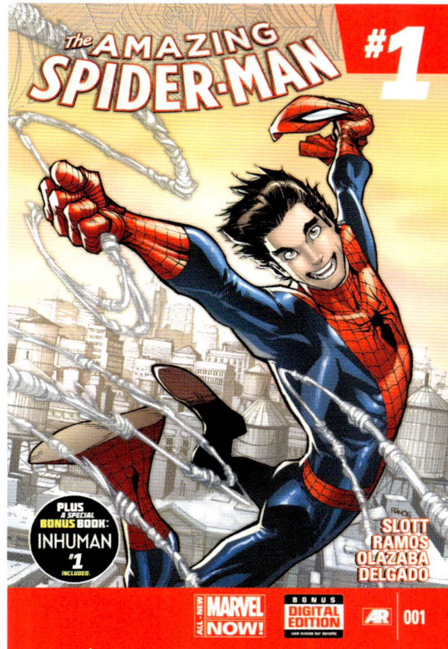

7

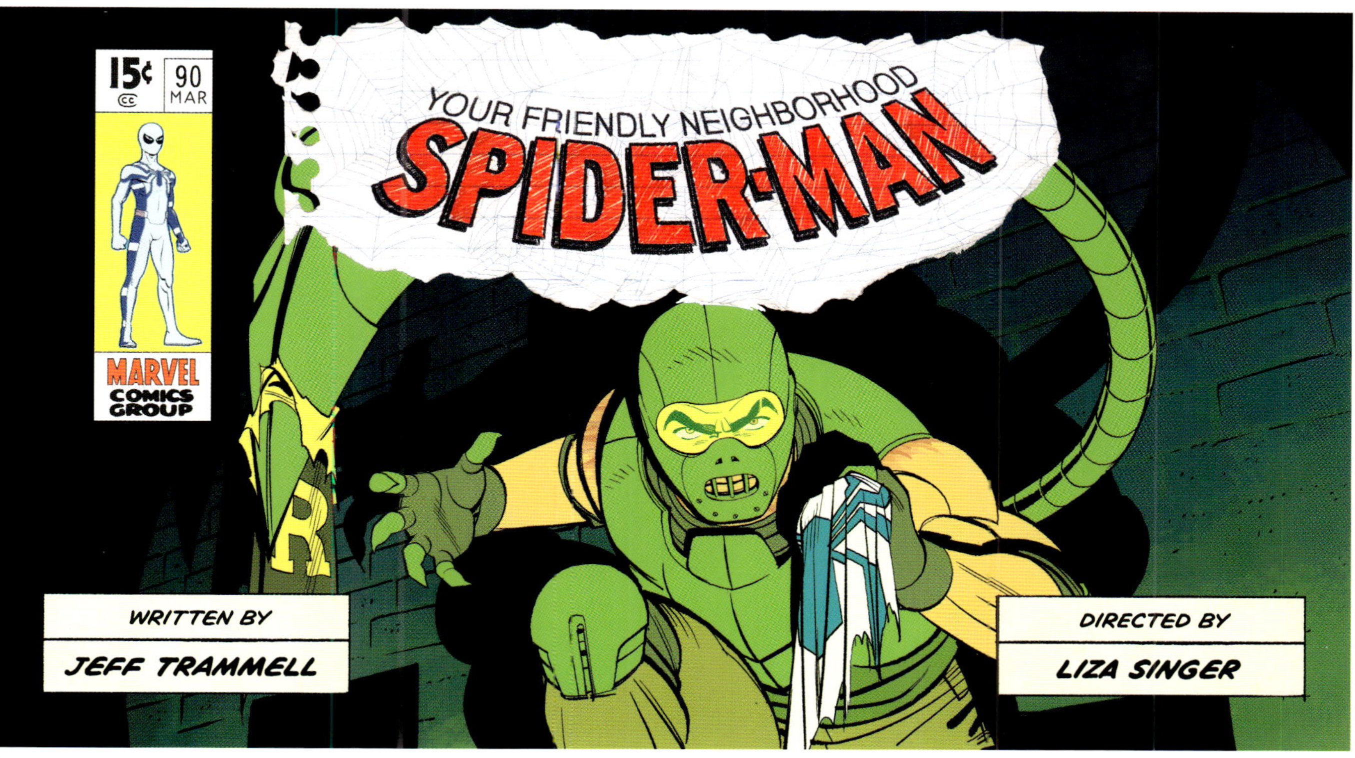

6

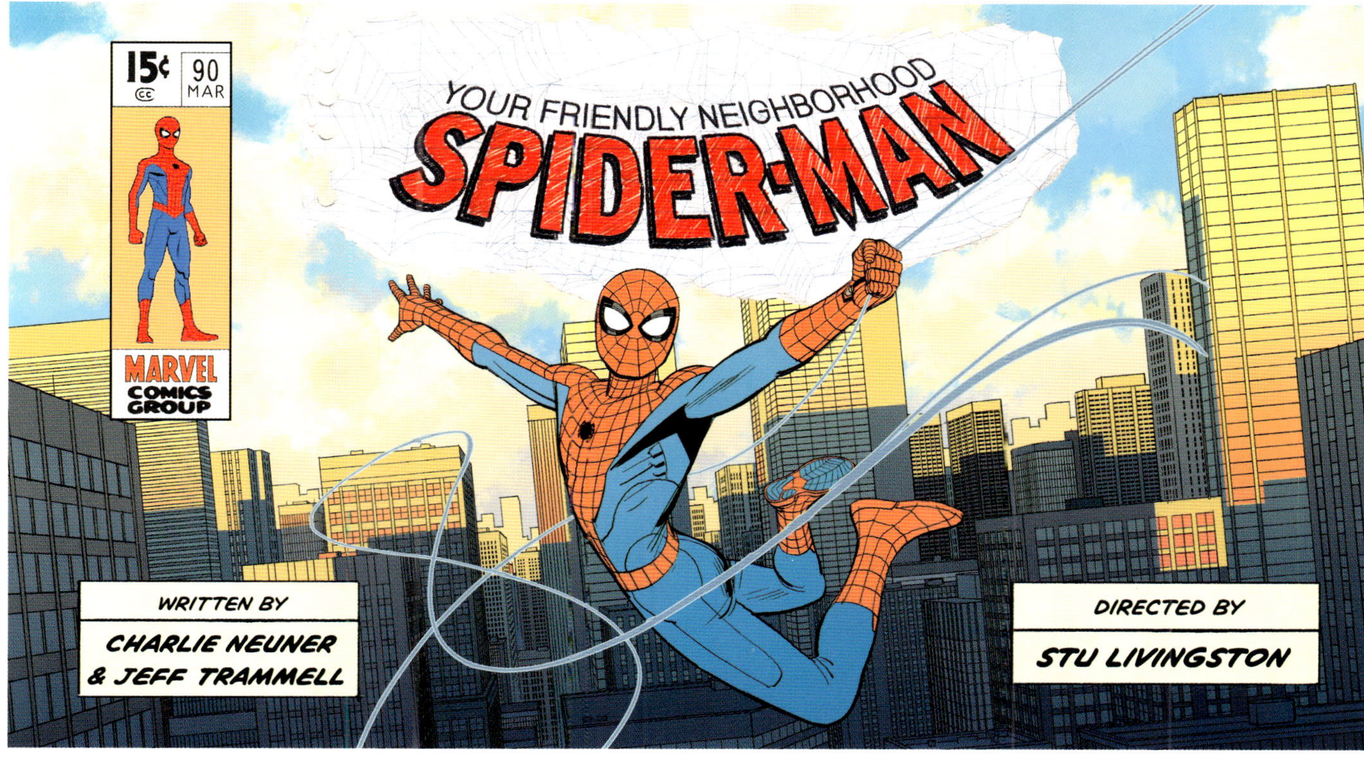

8

5 *The Spectacular Spider-Man* (1976) #215. Sal Buscema (pencils and inks) and Glynis Oliver (colors) **6** Leonardo Romero **7** *The Amazing Spider-Man* (2014) #1. Humberto Ramos (pencils) **8** Leonardo Romero

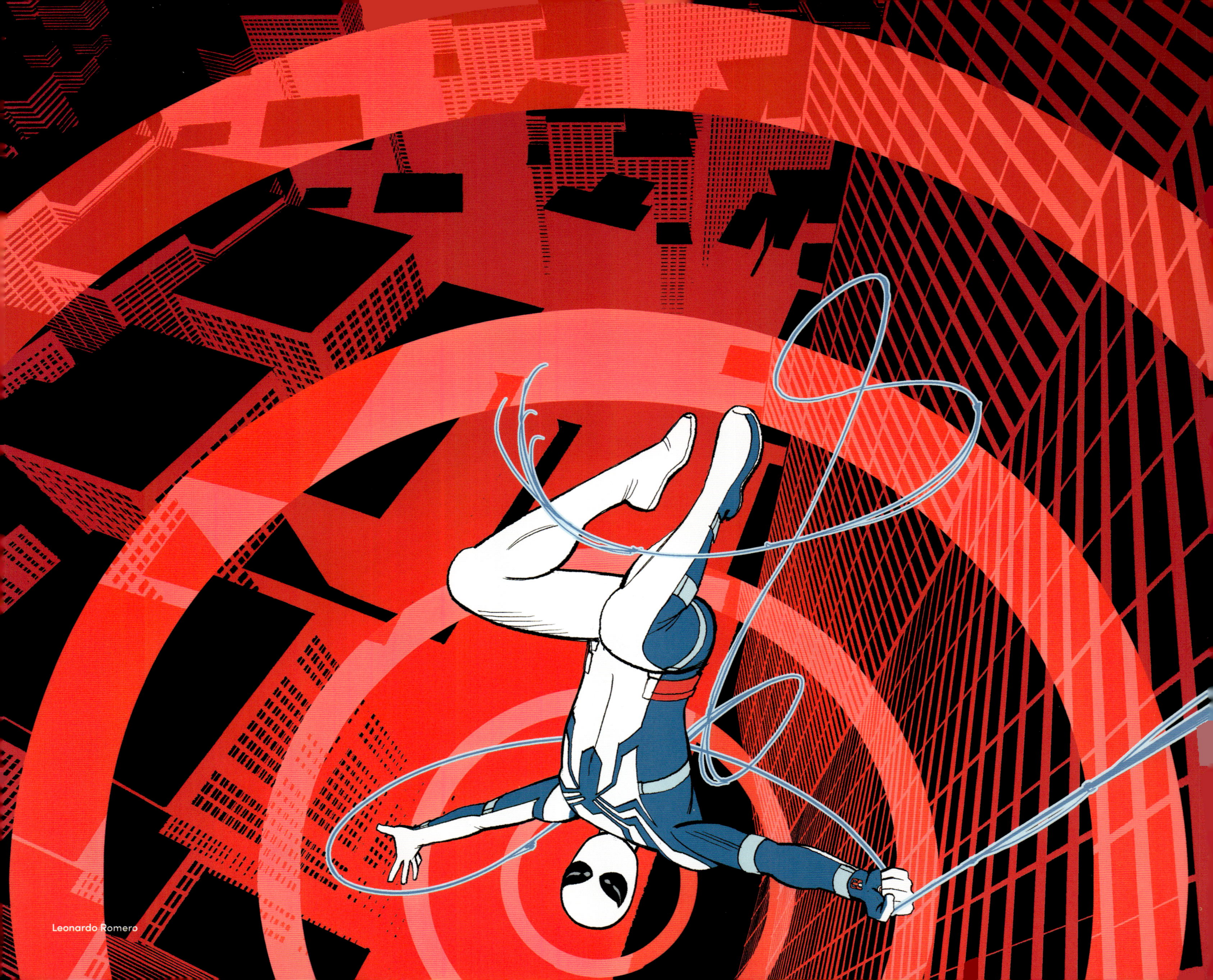
Leonardo Romero

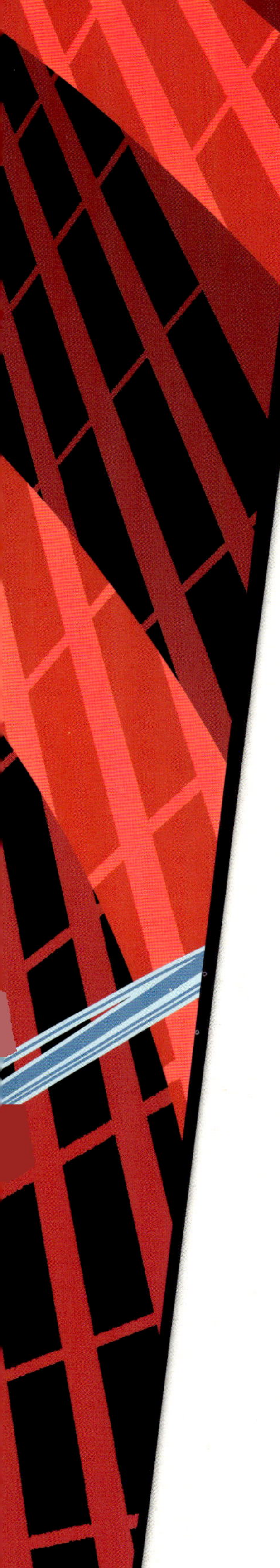

EPISODE SIX

DUEL WITH THE DEVIL

IN THIS PIVOTAL EPISODE, PETER MEETS ANOTHER FAMOUS—AND AT THIS POINT IN HIS CRIME-FIGHTING CAREER, MORE ESTABLISHED—MARVEL SUPER HERO, DAREDEVIL (VOICED BY CHARLIE COX, RETURNING TO THE ROLE ONCE AGAIN AFTER MAKING CAMEO APPEARANCES AS MATT MURDOCK IN *SHE-HULK*, *ECHO*, AND *SPIDER-MAN: NO WAY HOME*), WHO IS INVESTIGATING OSCORP AND BELIEVES NORMAN IS KEEPING A DARK SECRET. DAREDEVIL AND SPIDER-MAN ENGAGE IN A ROOFTOP BATTLE, AND PETER IS KNOCKED OUT BY A FLYING BILLY CLUB. WHEN HE COMES TO, NORMAN EXPLAINS THAT OCTAVIUS IS BEHIND THE INVENTIONS USED BY THE CRIMINALS WREAKING HAVOC IN THE CITY. HE ALSO BELIEVES THAT OCTAVIUS IS ALIGNED WITH DAREDEVIL TO STEAL TECH FROM OSCORP. AT HOME, TENSIONS INCREASE BETWEEN NICO AND PETER WHEN SHE LEARNS FROM HARRY THAT PETER IS SPIDER-MAN AND THAT HE'S BEEN KEEPING THIS SECRET FROM HER.

"THIS EPISODE SHOWS US Peter, Nico, and Harry all hanging out," says Executive Producer/Showrunner Jeff Trammell. "I wanted to make the viewer feel the awkward and tense moments that we all experience when our friends don't get along. When Peter is pulled away to fight Daredevil, and Nico and Harry are stuck together, you feel the tension and uneasiness between them. Nico is very guarded, and Harry kind of failed to endear himself, which, of course, leads to him making a mistake and leading to Peter's secret being revealed."

Trammell says it was important to show that Daredevil was always a player in this world. "The reason we didn't know about him was because Peter didn't know," he explains. "So, the rule is that there are things that have happened that are kind of beyond our scope. I think that's nice because we get to focus on Peter's world and then introduce the characters instead of being aware of everyone around him."

One of the interesting moments in this episode is when we see Jeanne Foucault going up to the top floor of Oscorp, scoping out the area, and then quickly leaving. "That might feel weird in the moment, but I don't know that a lot of people will connect it with the fact that Daredevil appears there later," explains Trammell. "We knew where we were going with the character later, as we reveal that she is Finesse, his sidekick. So, she was just gathering information for Matt to use later. We also introduce Secretary Ross in the gala that Norman goes to, so we see the relationship that will pay off in episode eight."

Co-Executive Producer/Supervising Director Mel Zwyer adds, "Fans have been wanting to see Spider-Man face Daredevil/Matt Murdock for a long time. We saw a little glimpse of it in *Spider-Man: No Way Home* with the introduction of Matt Murdock the lawyer, but this is the first time we see Spider-Man interact with Daredevil, and that was a lot of fun for us to include in this episode."

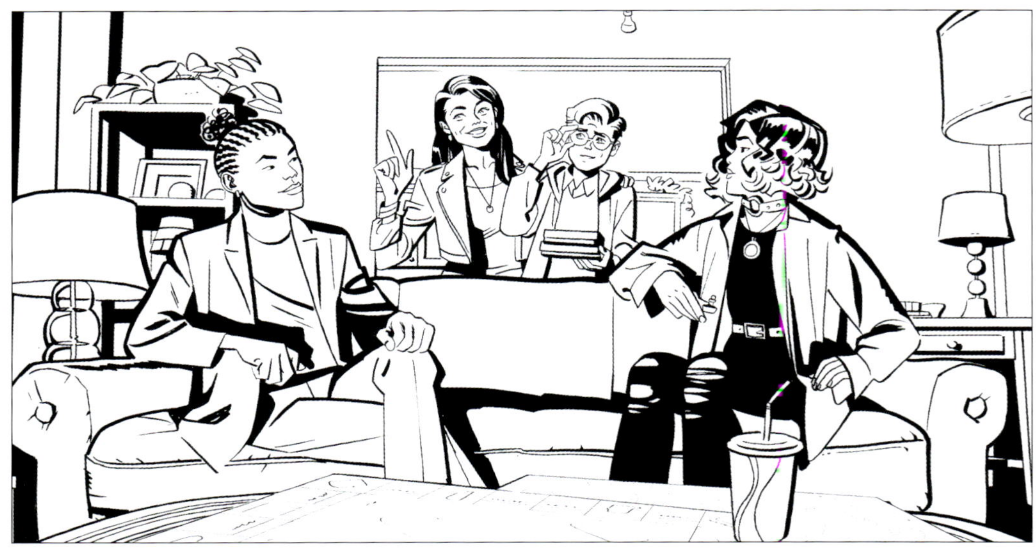

1

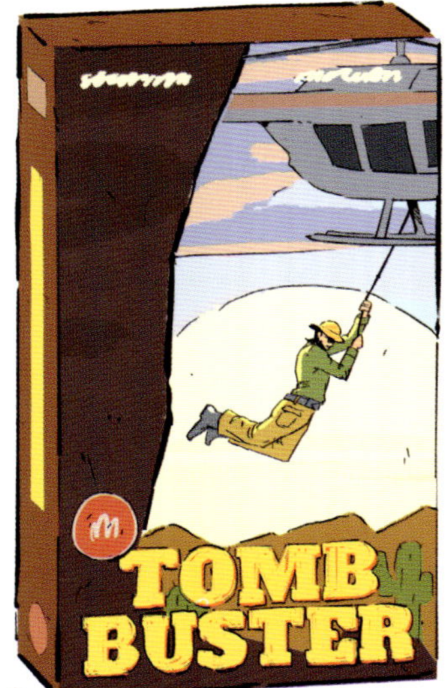

2

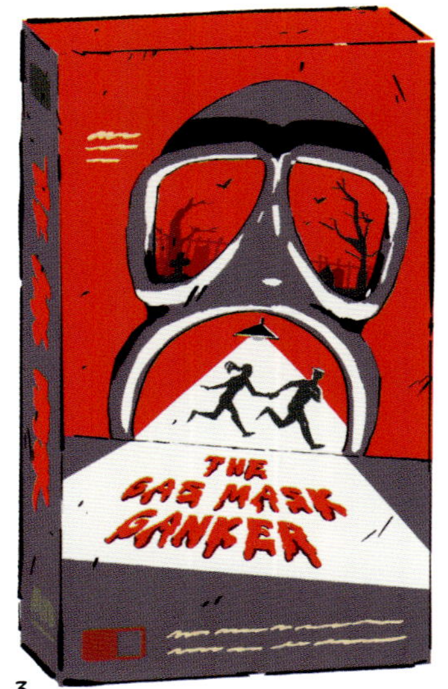

3

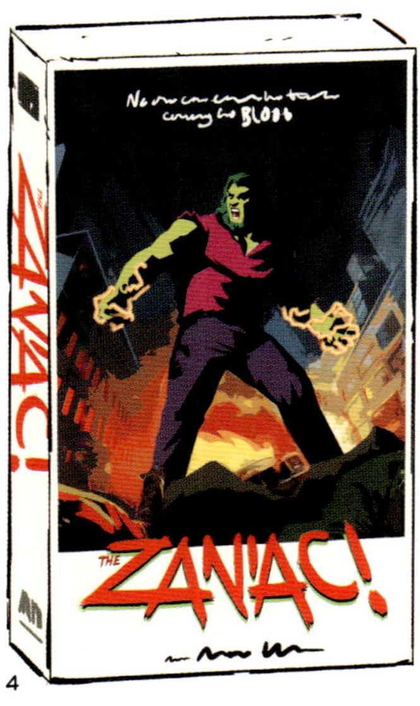

4

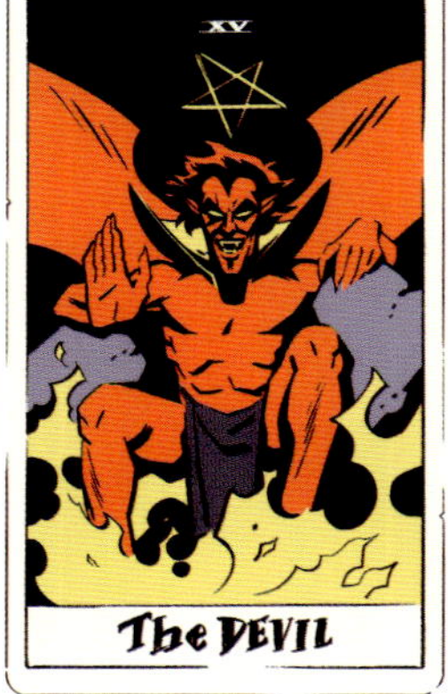

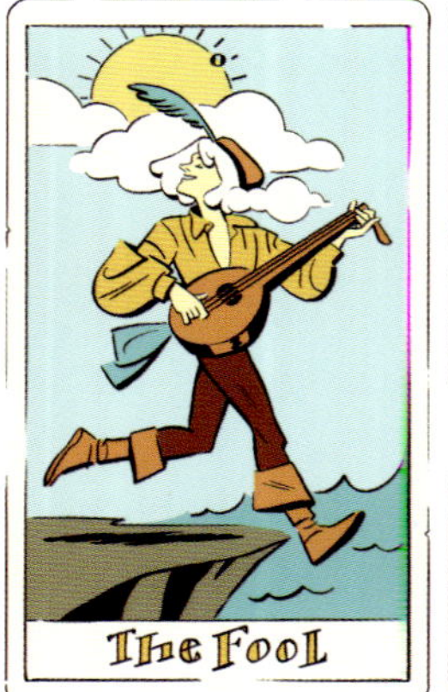

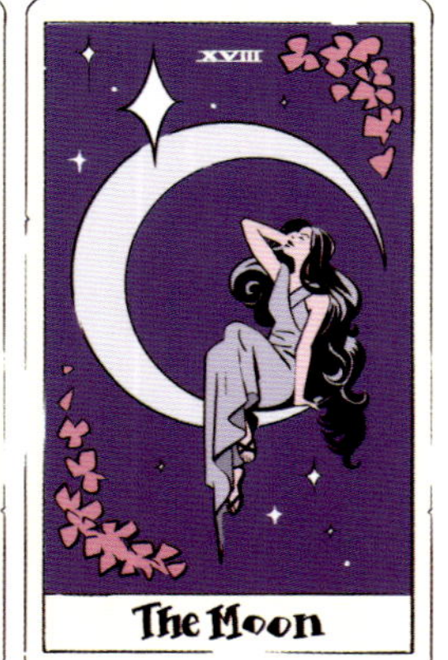

6

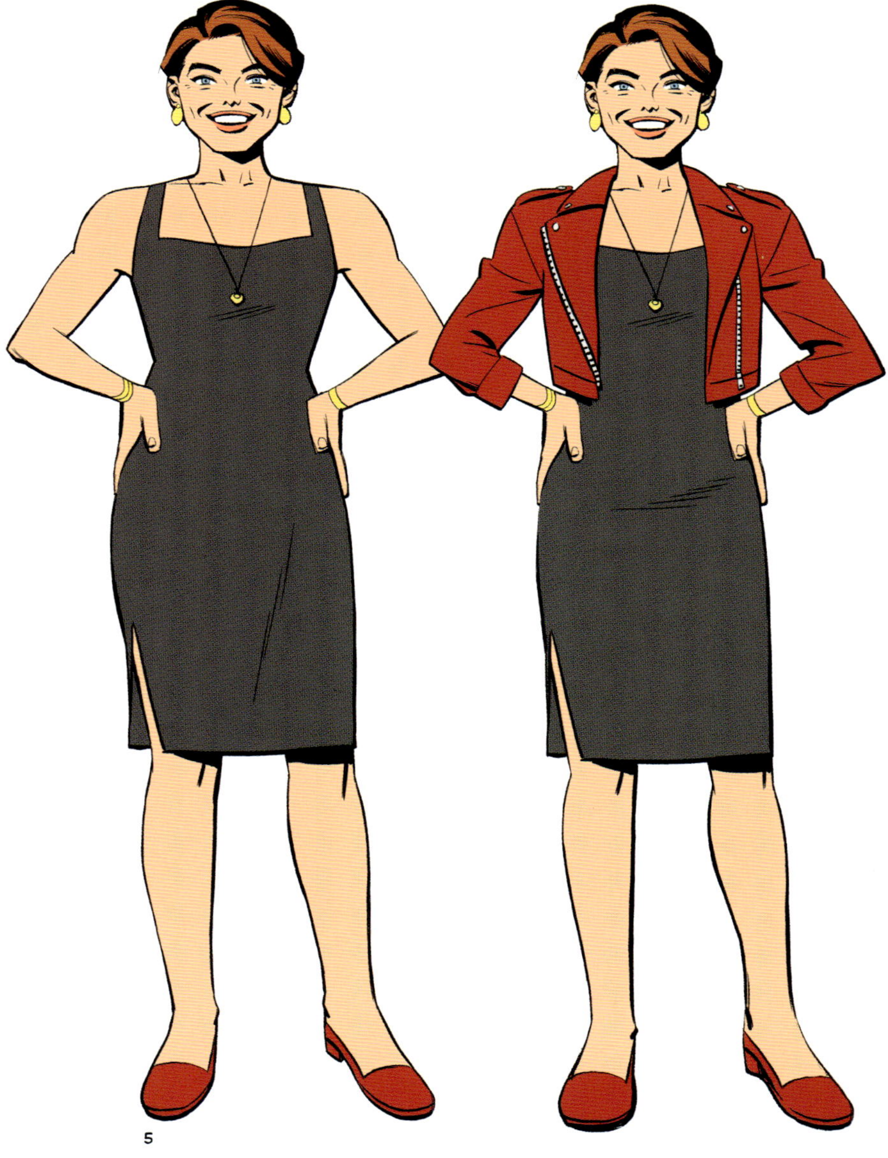

5

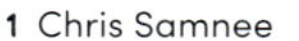

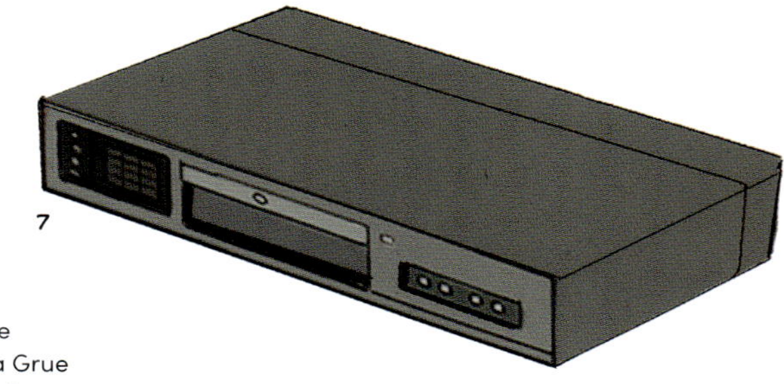

7

1 Chris Samnee
2–3 Elizabeth Chee
4 W. Scott Forbes
5 Ethan Young
6 Chris Samnee (line art) and Junyi Wu (color)
7 Kelsey Roland 8 Monica Grue
9 Leonardo Romero 10 Monica Grue
11 Elizabeth Chee 12 Leonardo Romero

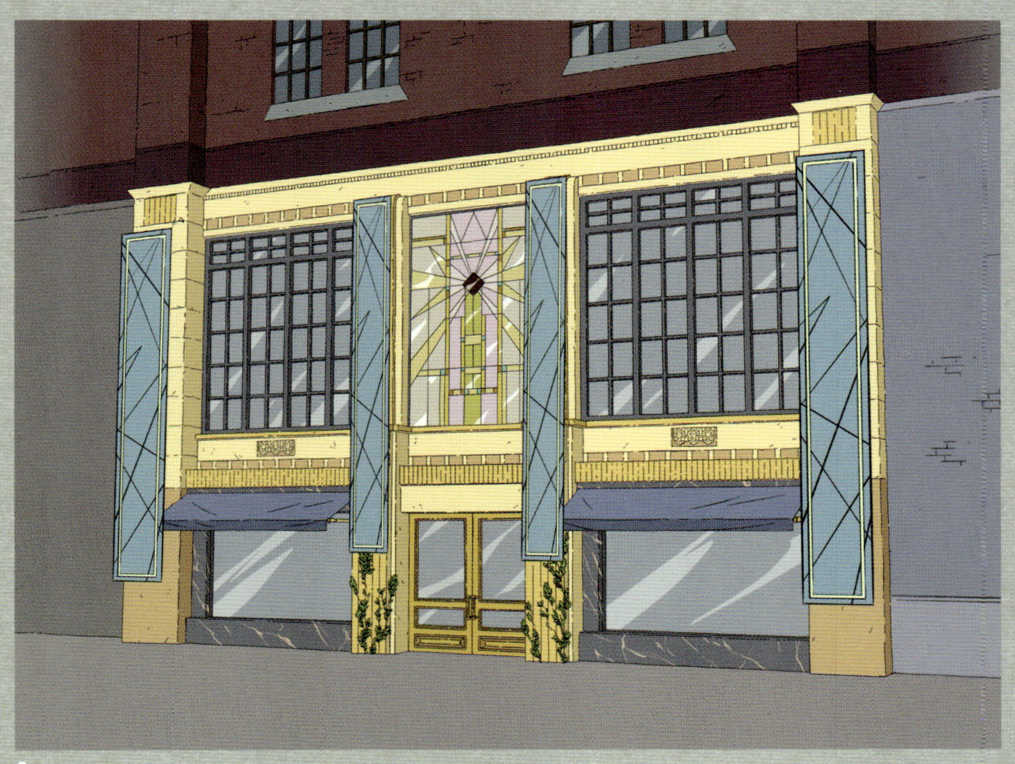

8

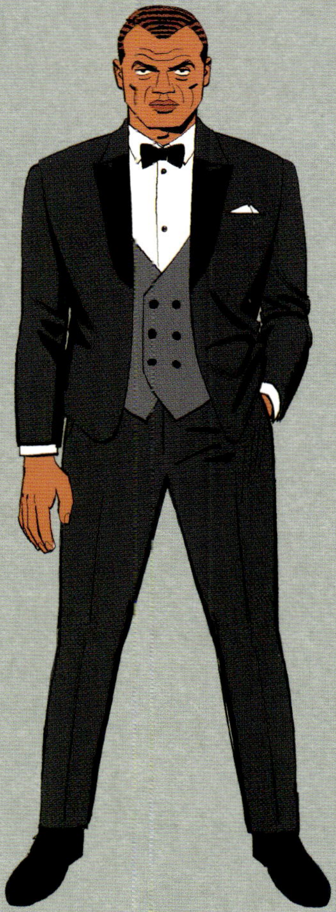

9

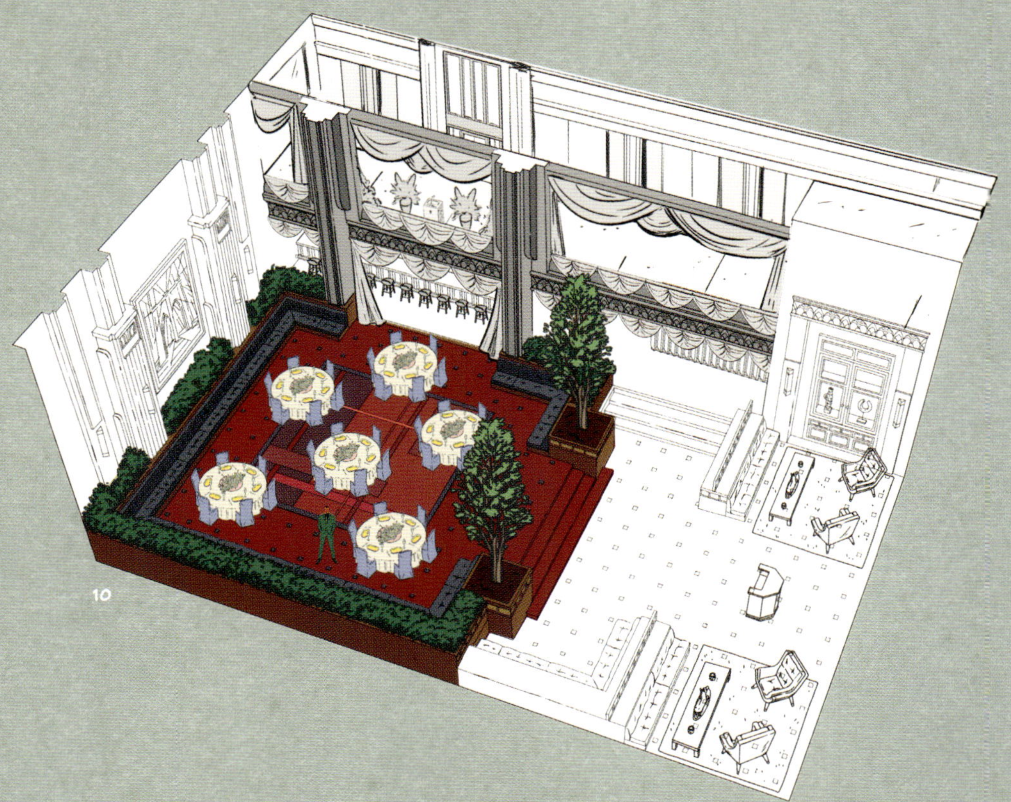

10

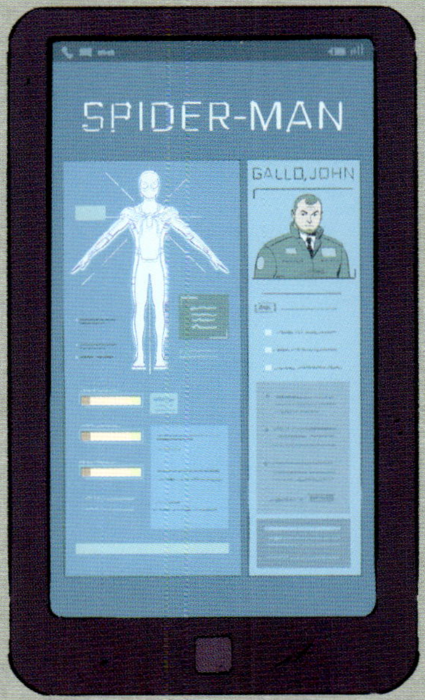

11

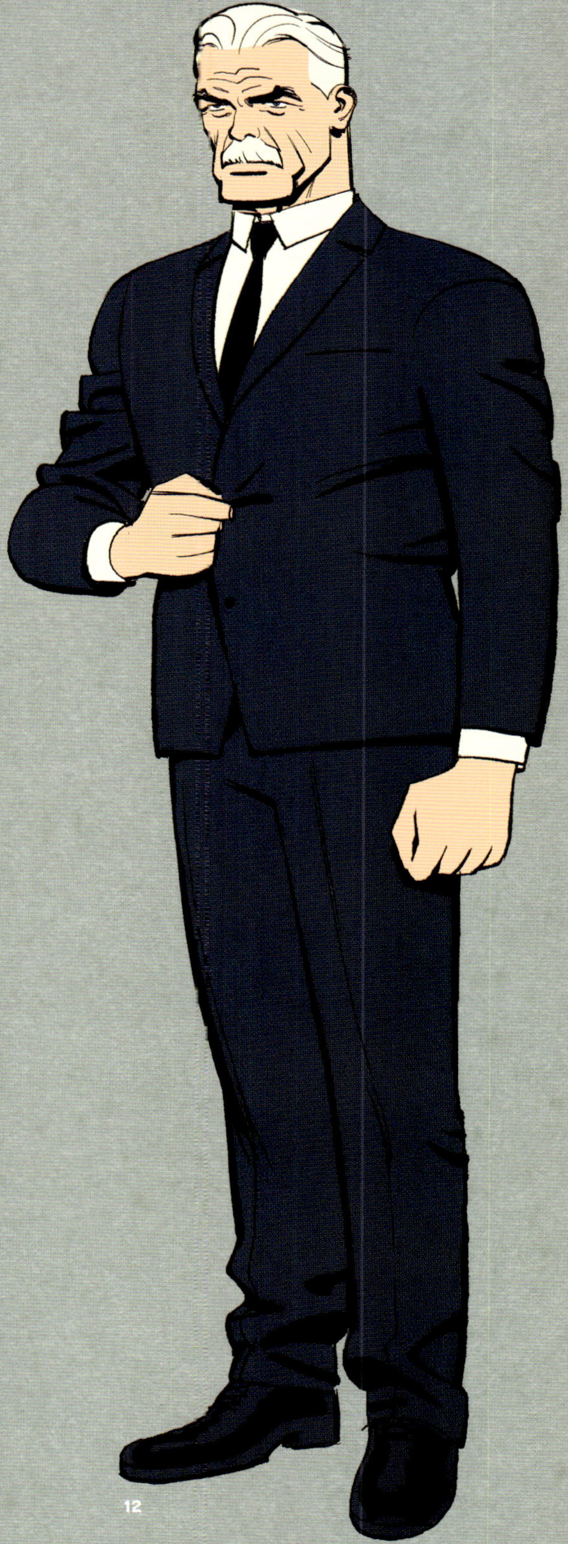

12

MATT MURDOCK/ DAREDEVIL

Daredevil is another famous Marvel crimefighter who crosses paths with Spider-Man in the series. Blind lawyer Matt Murdock, alter ego of the horn-headed vigilante, grew up in New York City's Hell's Kitchen, so it makes sense that he'd pop up in Peter's world. Charlie Cox, who also portrays Murdock in Netflix's *Daredevil* (2015–2018), *Spider-Man: No Way Home* (2021), and the Disney+ series *Daredevil: Born Again* (2025), returns to voice the character.

"I remember pitching the idea and thinking that we were going to get a little pushback because we weren't sure what the future of the character was at that point," says Executive Producer/Showrunner Jeff Trammell. "So, when they said you can use him, and we can even get Charlie Cox to voice the character, I thought to myself, 'This is the coolest job ever!' One of the things that I really wanted to convey was that Daredevil is, in many ways, everything Peter hopes to be. He's polished, knowledgeable, and the prototypical hero. Also, the Daredevil of Hell's Kitchen is kind of a myth in our world, and no one is sure that he's real. I wanted to use him as a street-level version of Spider-Man's heroic values—someone that he can aspire to be. I also wanted to have them face off the first time they meet. He's kind of a litmus test because, despite how good Spidey is as a hero, he's still got a long way to go until he's as good as Daredevil."

1

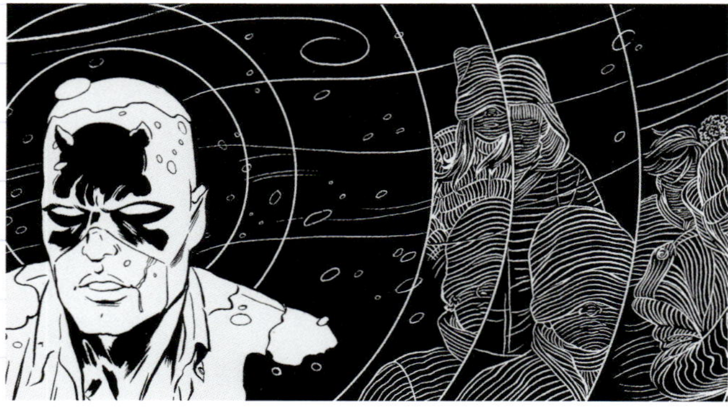

2

1 Leonardo Romero 2 Paolo Rivera
3 Joey Vazquez 4–5 Paolo Rivera

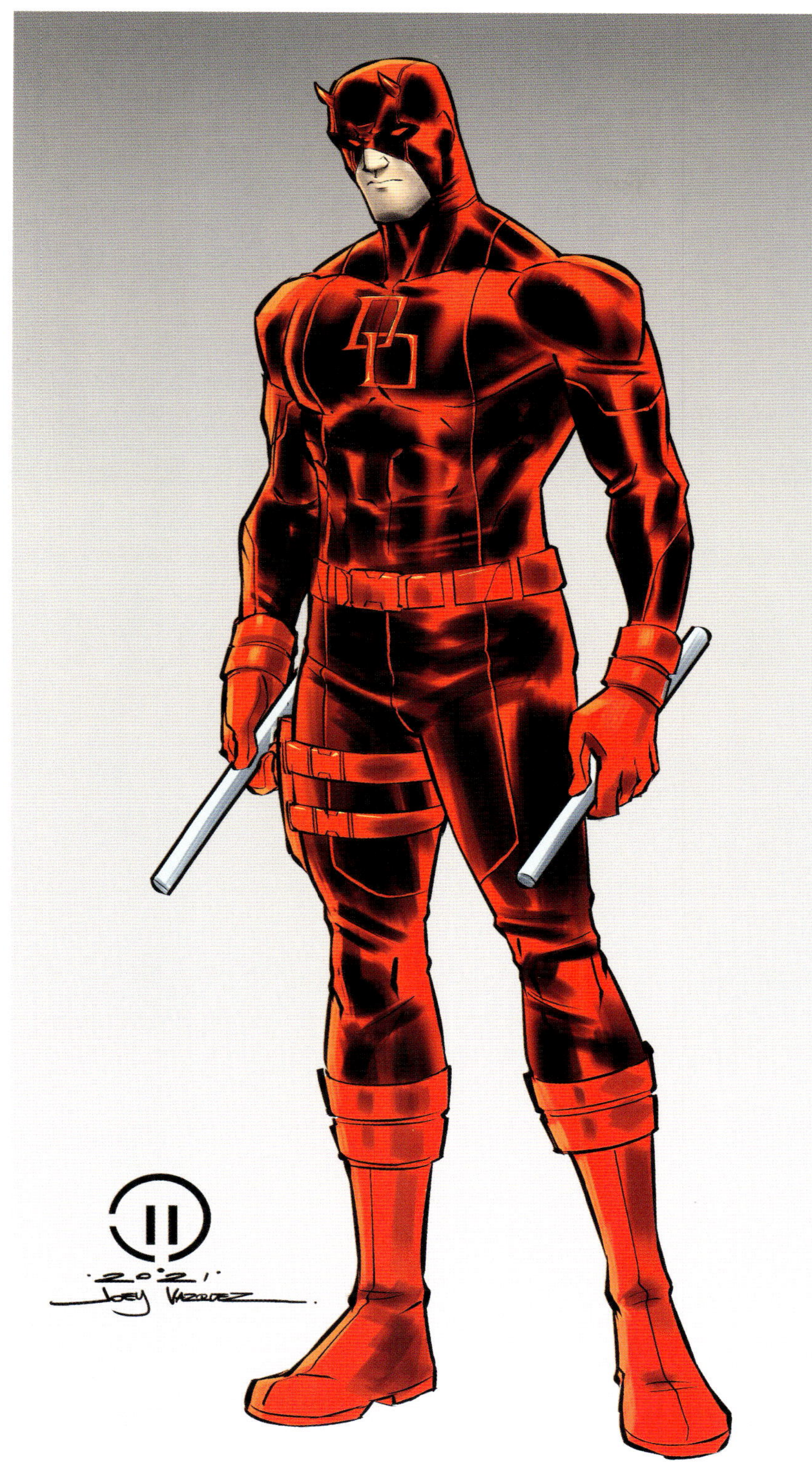

3

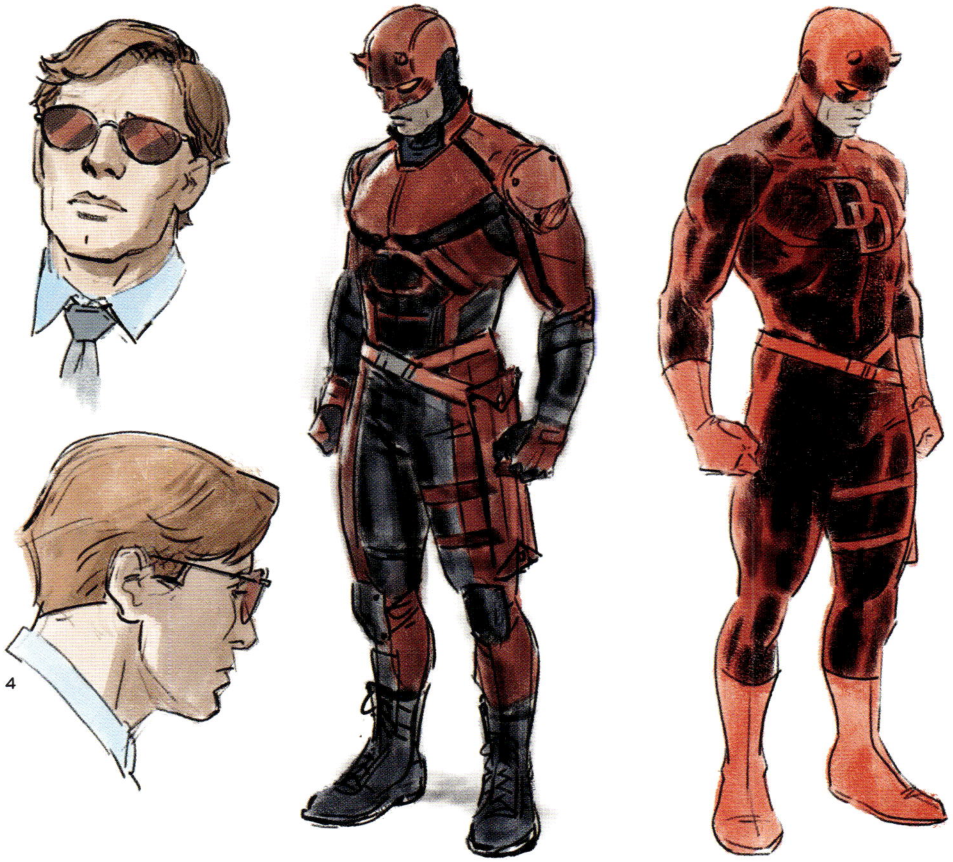

4

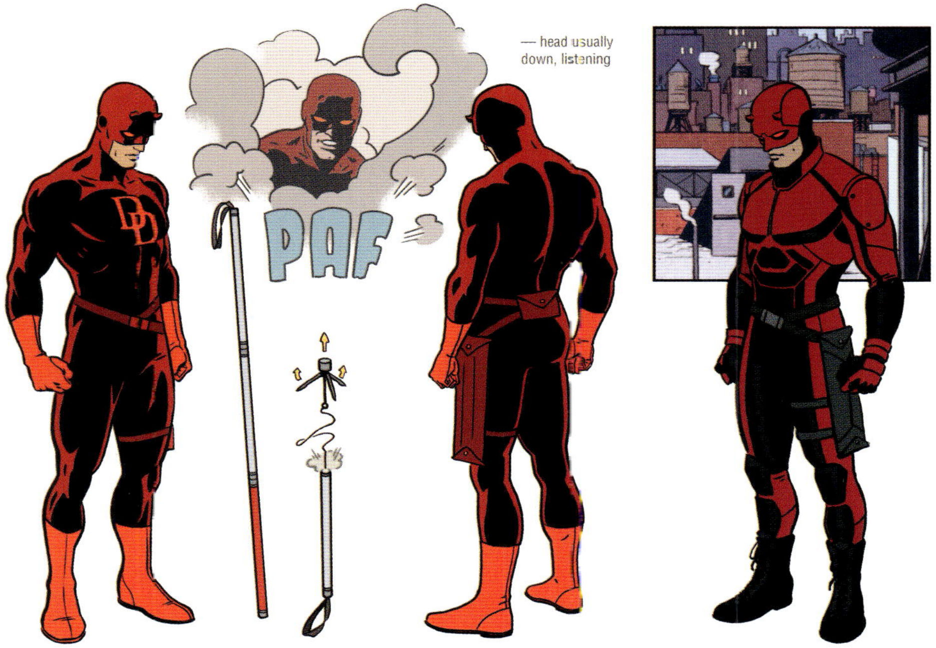

— head usually down, listening

PAF

5

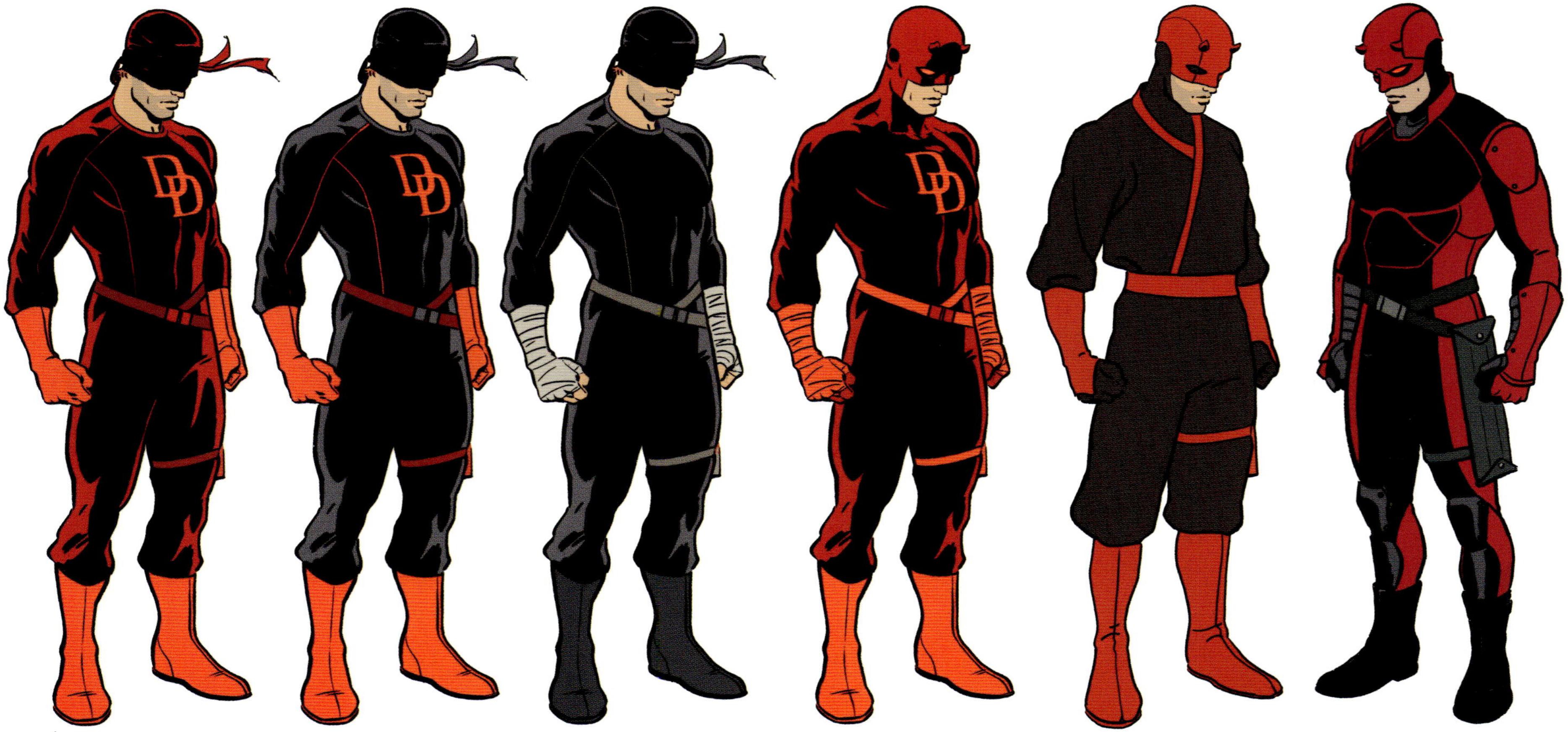

1

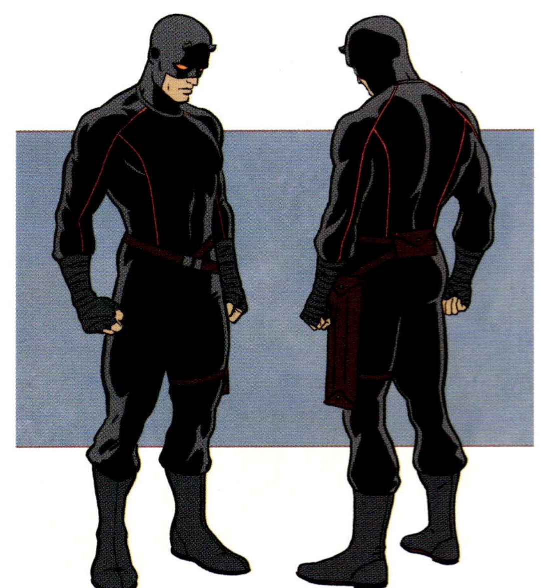

2

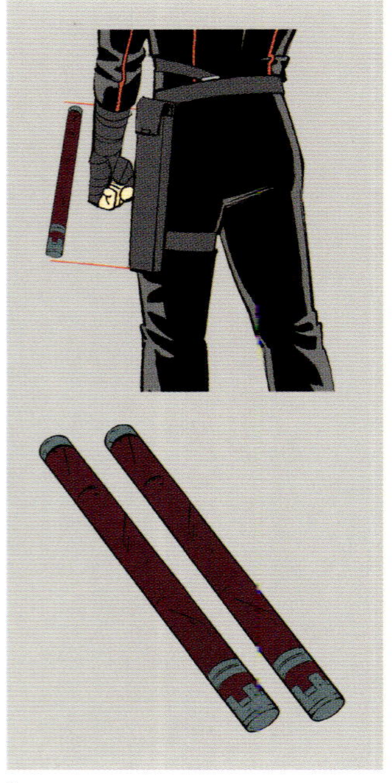

3

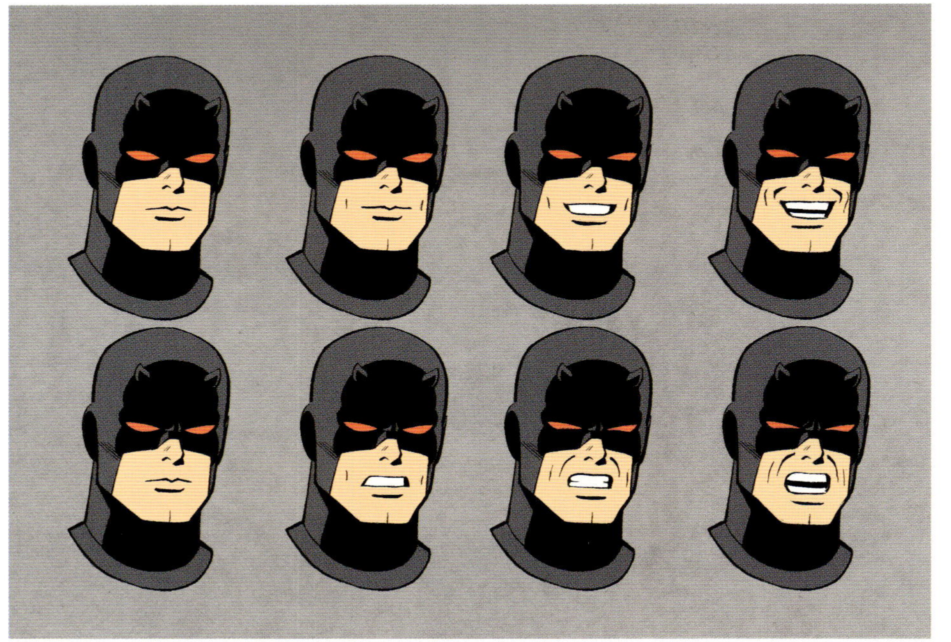

4

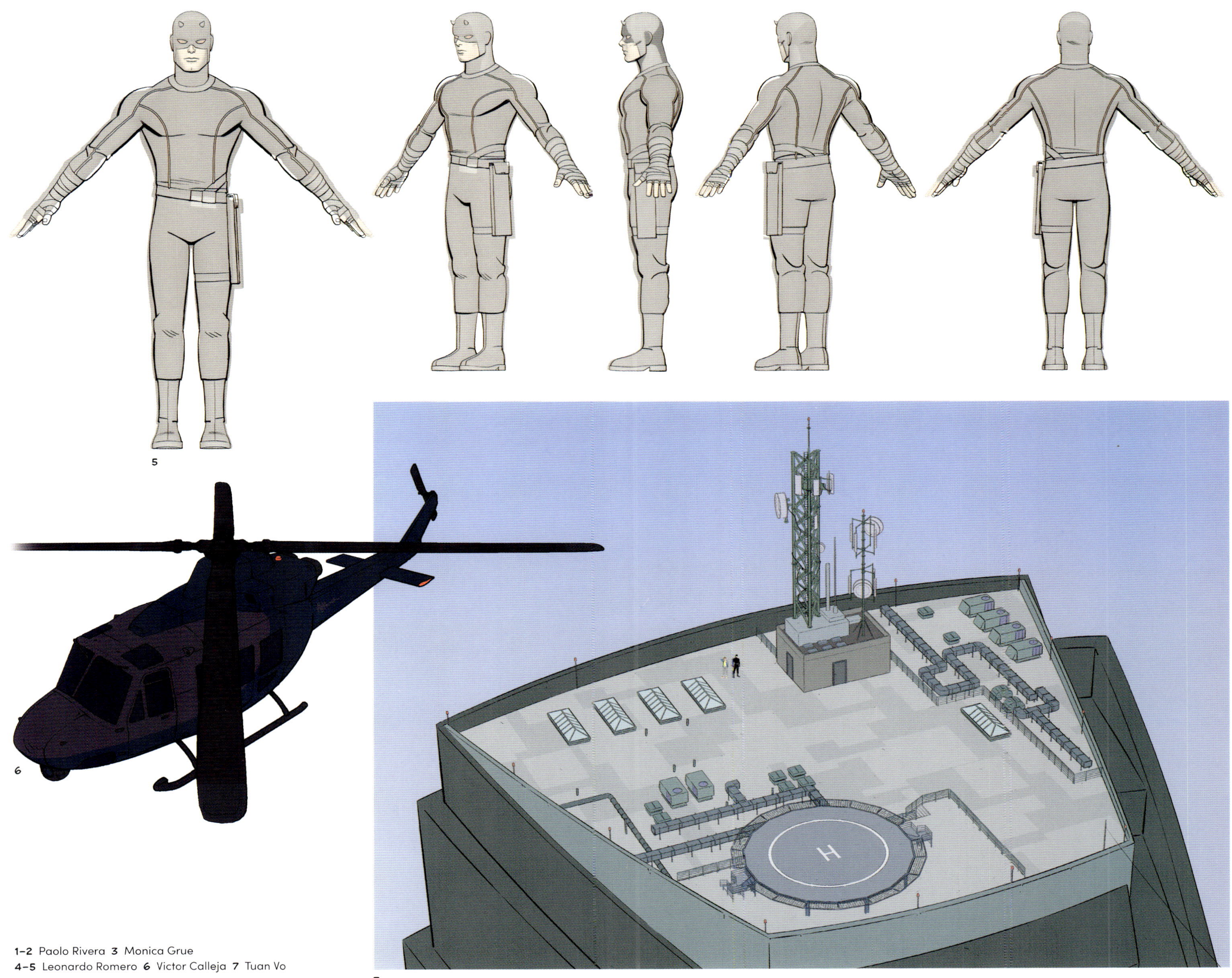

5

6

7

1–2 Paolo Rivera 3 Monica Grue
4–5 Leonardo Romero 6 Victor Calleja 7 Tuan Vo

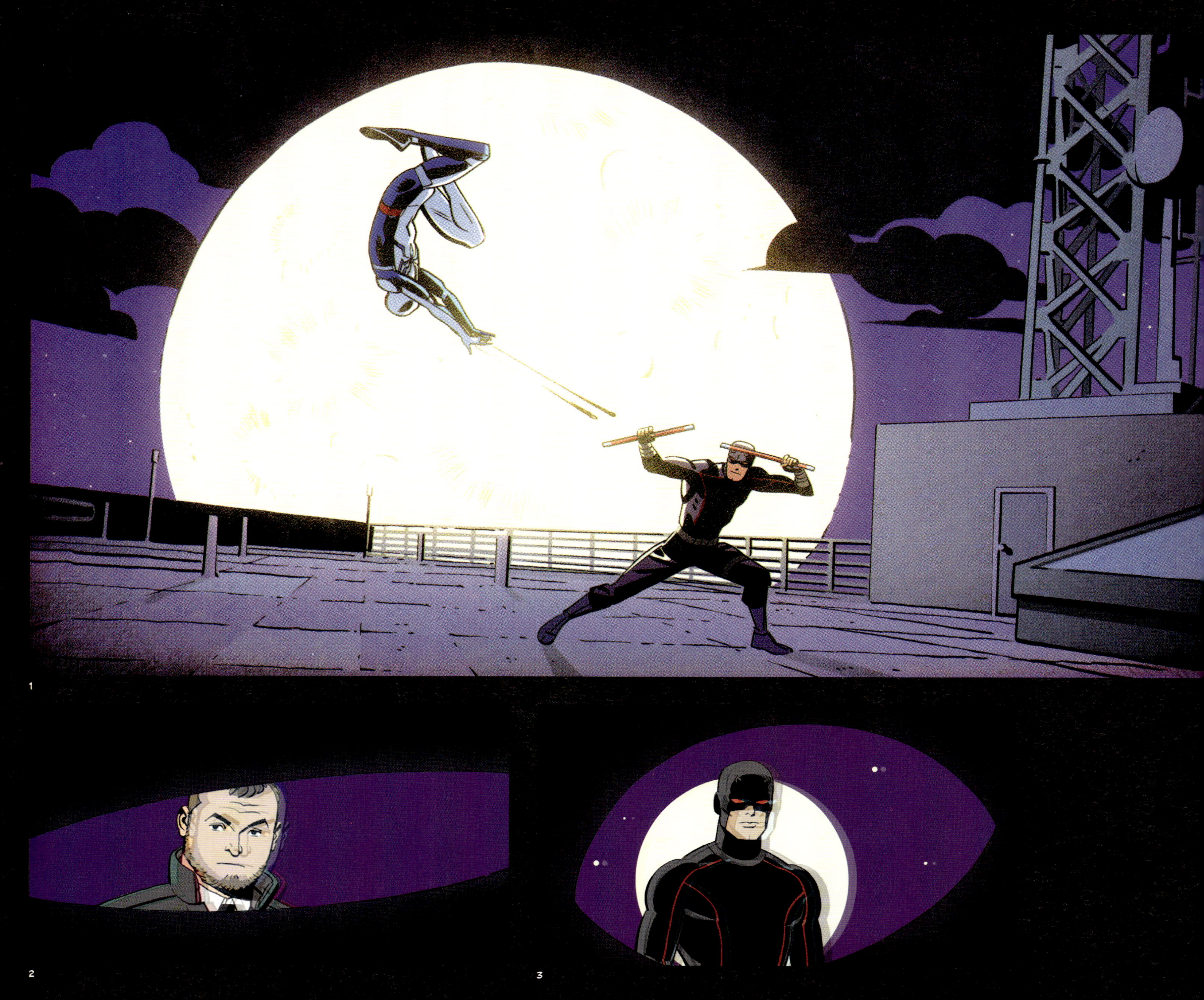
1
2
3

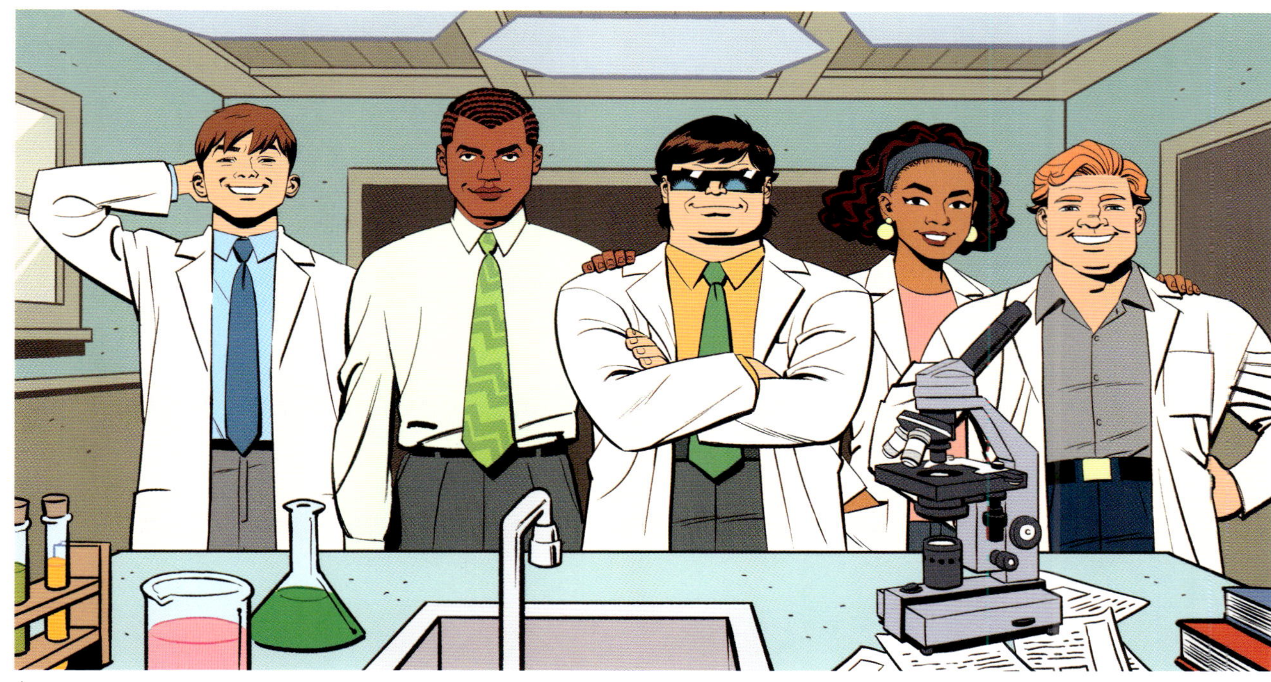

4

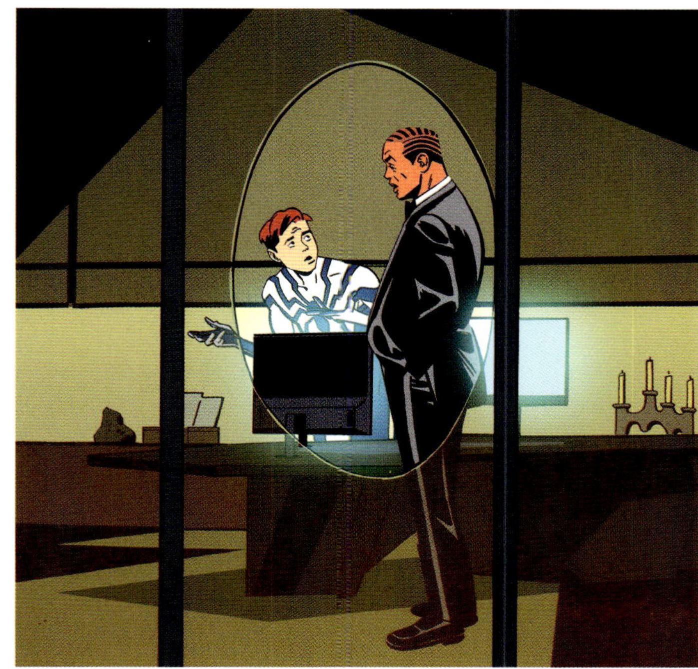

5

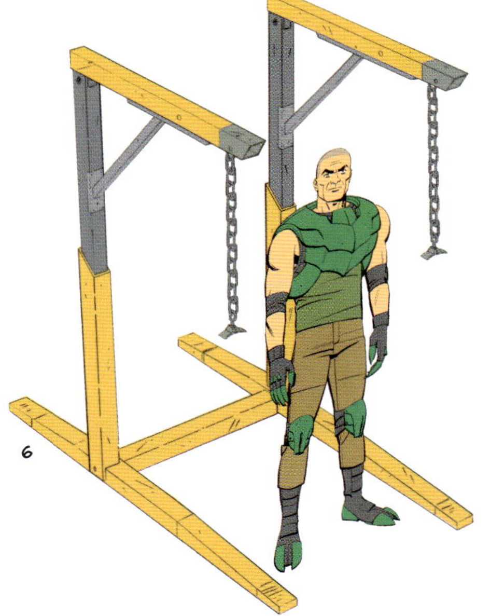

6

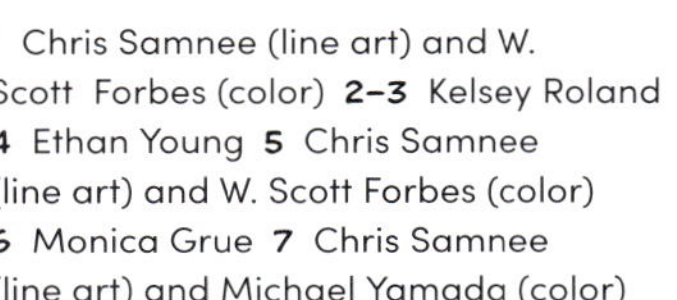

1 Chris Samnee (line art) and W. Scott Forbes (color) **2–3** Kelsey Roland **4** Ethan Young **5** Chris Samnee (line art) and W. Scott Forbes (color) **6** Monica Grue **7** Chris Samnee (line art) and Michael Yamada (color)

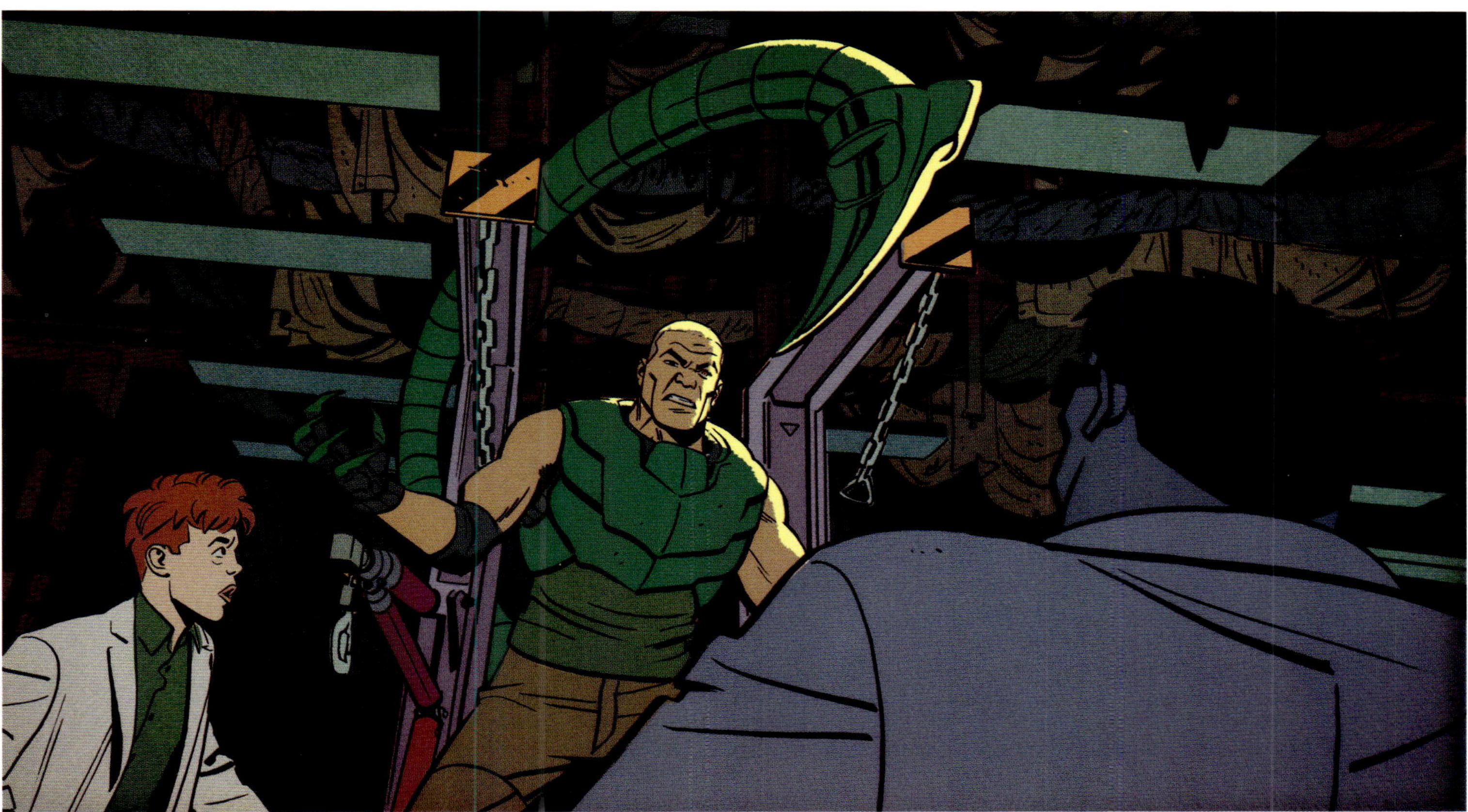

7

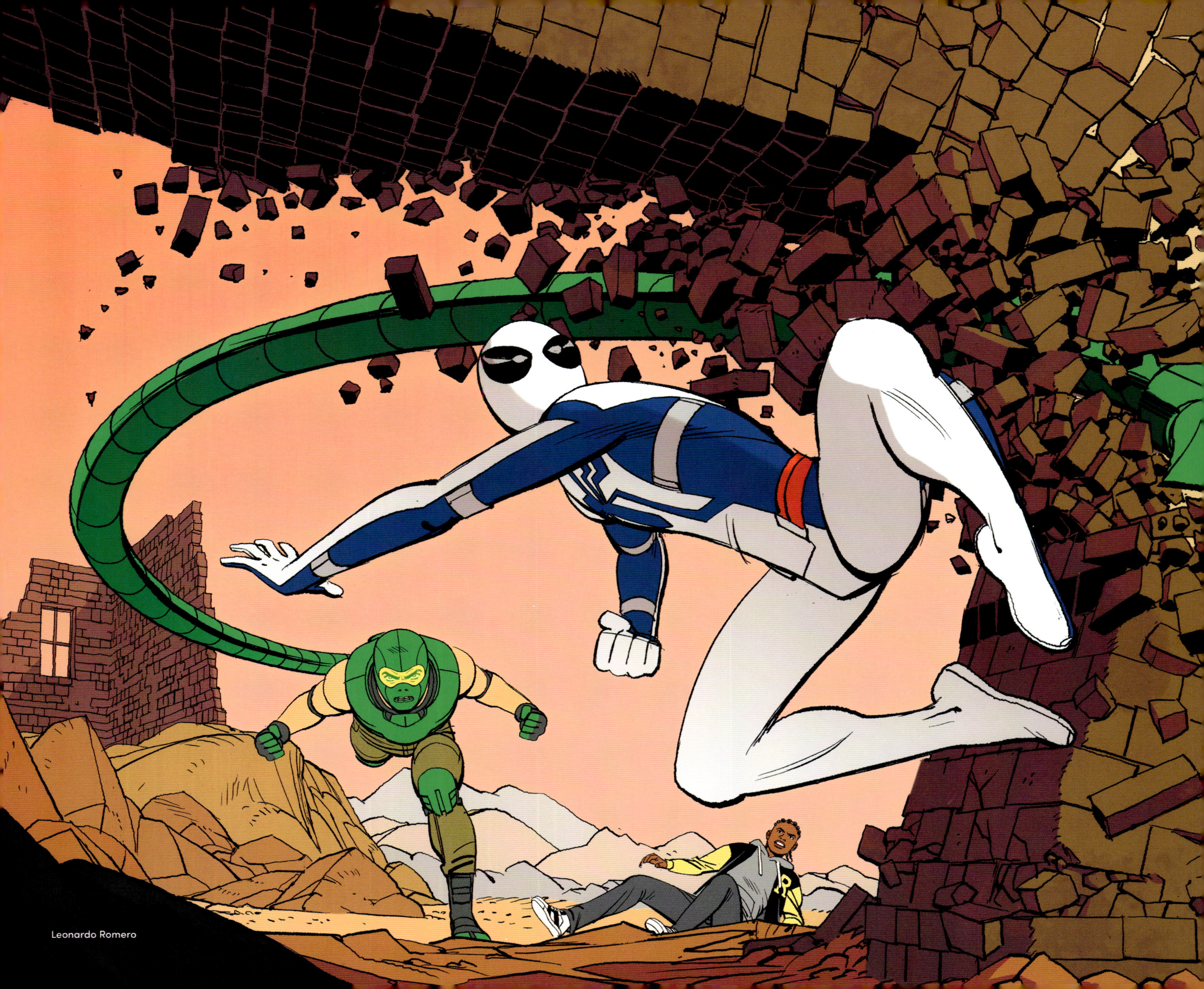

Leonardo Romero

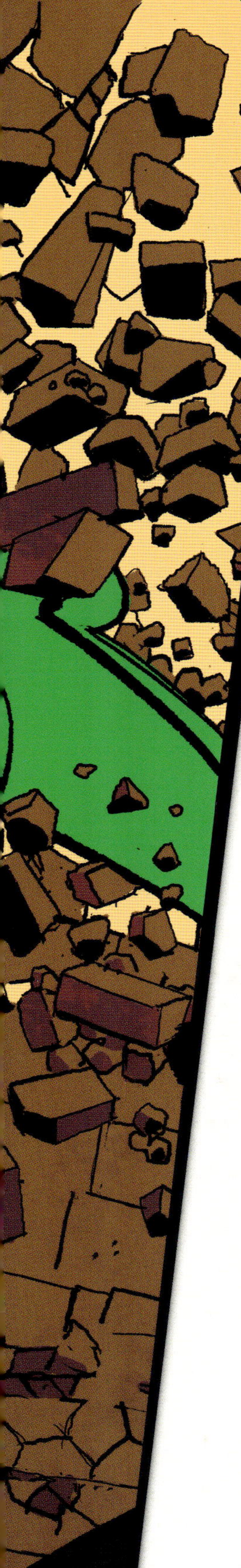

EPISODE SEVEN

SCORPION RISING

THE DYNAMIC BETWEEN PETER AND NICO SLOWLY GETS BACK TO NORMAL AFTER HARRY TELLS HER THAT PETER KEPT HIS SECRET IDENTITY ONLY TO PROTECT HER. MEANWHILE, PEARL CONFRONTS LONNIE ABOUT HIS GANG INVOLVEMENT AT THE 110TH STREET GANG HIDEOUT AND IS CAUGHT IN THE MIDDLE OF AN ATTACK BY GARGAN, NOW KNOWN AS SCORPION. PETER COMES TO SAVE PEARL AND LONNIE AND IS SEVERELY HURT IN HIS CLASH WITH SCORPION. FROM THE OSCORP OFFICES, NORMAN TRACKS OCTAVIUS USING GAMMA RADIATION WHILE ALSO MONITORING PETER'S MOVEMENTS AND SENDS A GLIDER TO SAVE HIM FROM CERTAIN DEATH.

"THE BIG THING at play in episode seven is relationships," notes Executive Producer/Showrunner Jeff Trammell. "Pearl learns that Lonnie is doing some dangerous things, and I wanted to make sure that she tries to get through to him. I never wanted to feel like Lonnie's fully set in this gang world, and there was a chance that maybe he could be swayed. Showing Lonnie that she cares for him was a big moment, but it also endangers her, especially with Gargan showing up. Pearl will give him an ultimatum in the next episode after she has seen firsthand how dangerous his life is."

Trammell also wanted to explore the Nico/Harry dynamic as both feel like Peter is the one who understands them. "Nico is thinking that Peter has met a new friend who's more positive and fun and richer, and he will leave her behind. So, they both worry that they are losing the other one. But this bond brings Nico and Harry together in their big street race scene. At the end of the day, Nico is still a bit mad at Peter because he kept his secret from her."

Episode director Stu Livingston says it was probably his favorite of the first season. "It had a tremendous amount of emotional weight in every single scene," he recalls. "I was a shy kid and felt these intense crushes, so I identified with Peter a lot. We have the scene where Peter is reassuring Pearl on the steps of the school in the beginning of the episode, and then, the longer storyline with Harry and Nico, which culminated in the scene with them on the steps of her home. It was fun to direct these intense dialogue scenes, which have a lot of things that are left unsaid. You just want to save them both so badly."

Livingston also storyboarded most of the fight scene with Scorpion, where Spidey gets stabbed in the back and nearly dies. "I think even on the page, it felt like a downturn for Spider-Man," he says. "I really wanted to push the emotion and show how painful, desperate, and horrible it was for him. I will just click back through the storyboard a million times because I'm so proud of it, and the reaction to that particular scene was very strong."

"Lastly, we also dig into the relationship between Peter and Norman," says Trammell. "Norman is withholding information from Peter, and toward the end of the episode, he gets so absorbed in

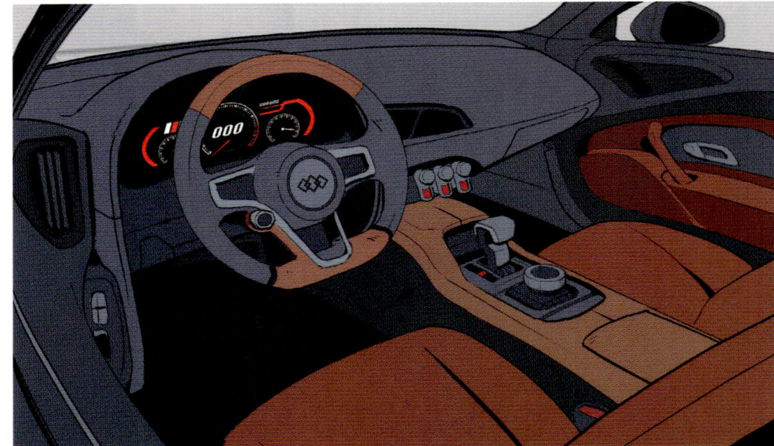

1

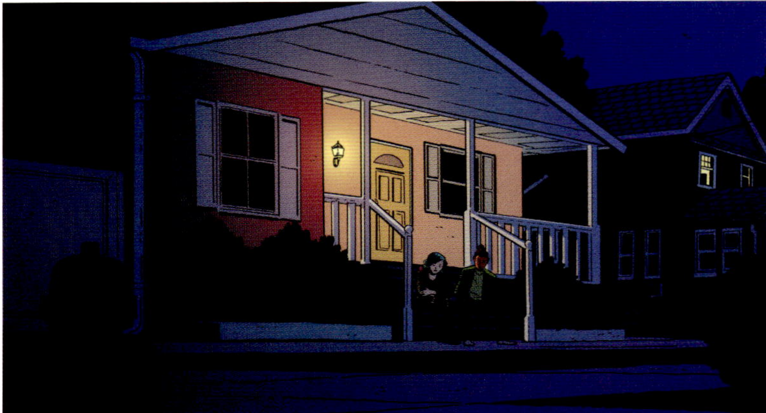

2

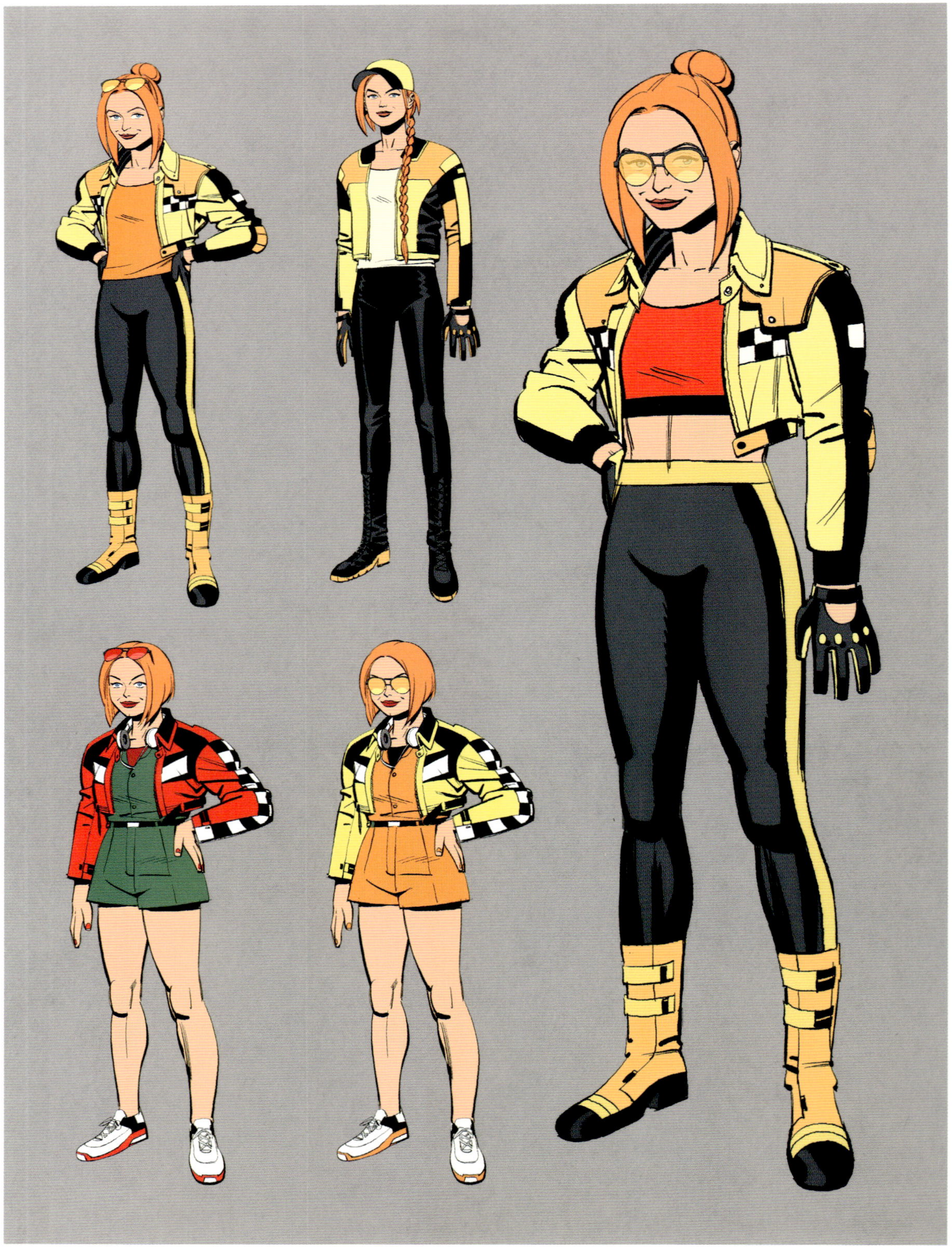

trying to find Otto, he ignores Peter and endangers his life. This was one of the moments on the show that Peter was outmatched. You do remember that he is just a kid after all, and he probably shouldn't be there. So, we see him get roughed up by Scorpion and barely make it out by the skin of his teeth. I think that's a shocking moment for the series because I don't think anyone expected us to go there."

Co-Executive Producer/Supervising Director Mel Zwyer believes this episode was probably the darkest of the season. "When Spider-Man intervenes in the fight at the gang warehouse, Scorpion nearly kills him. Osborn comes to the rescue, not by himself but with the Goblin Glider, which is another great Easter egg that hints at what's ahead."

1 Victor Calleja **2** Chris Samnee (line art) and W. Scott Forbes (color) **3** Leonardo Romero **4** Paolo Rivera (line art) and W. Scott Forbes (color) **5–6** Victor Calleja

3

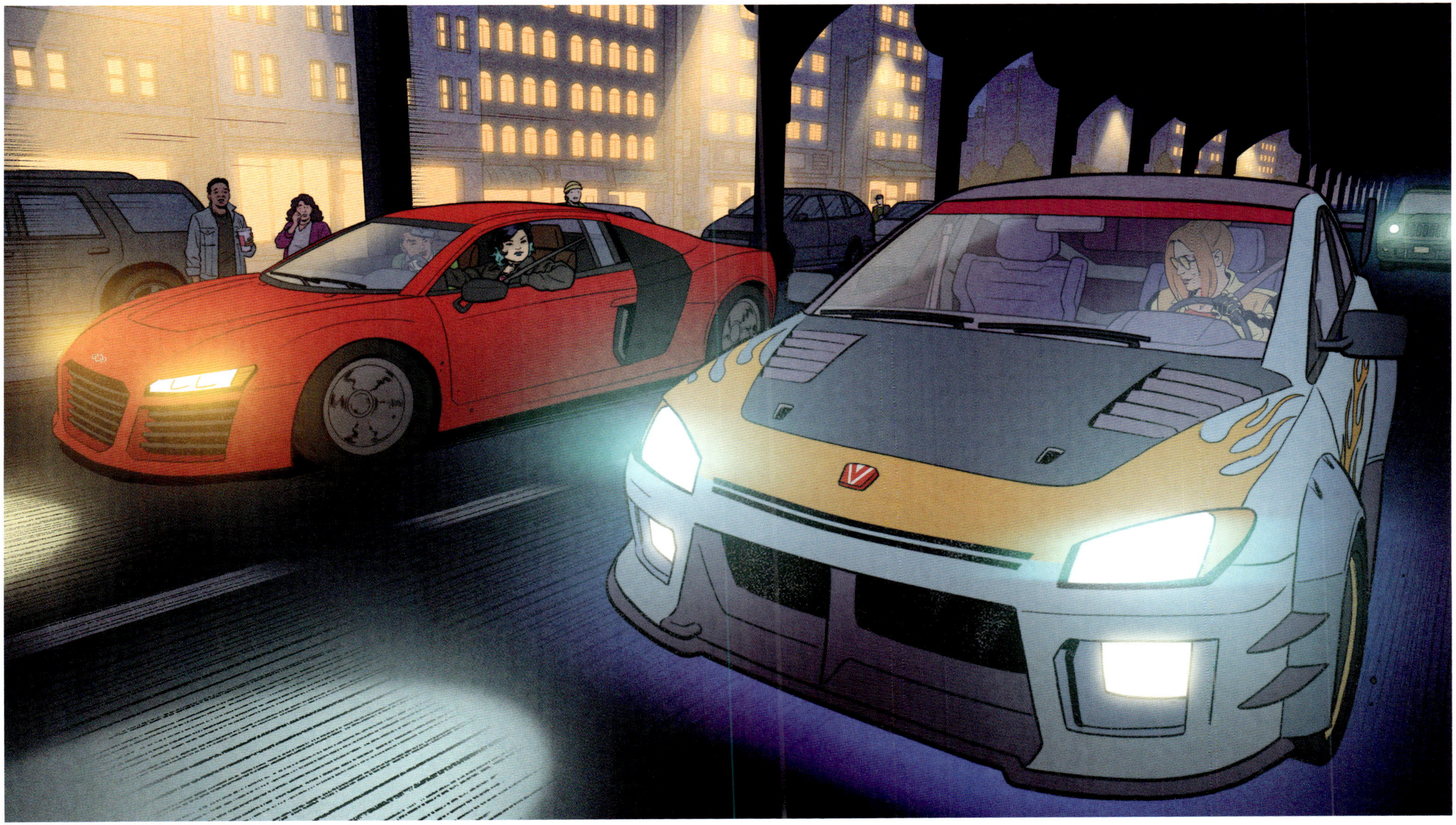

4

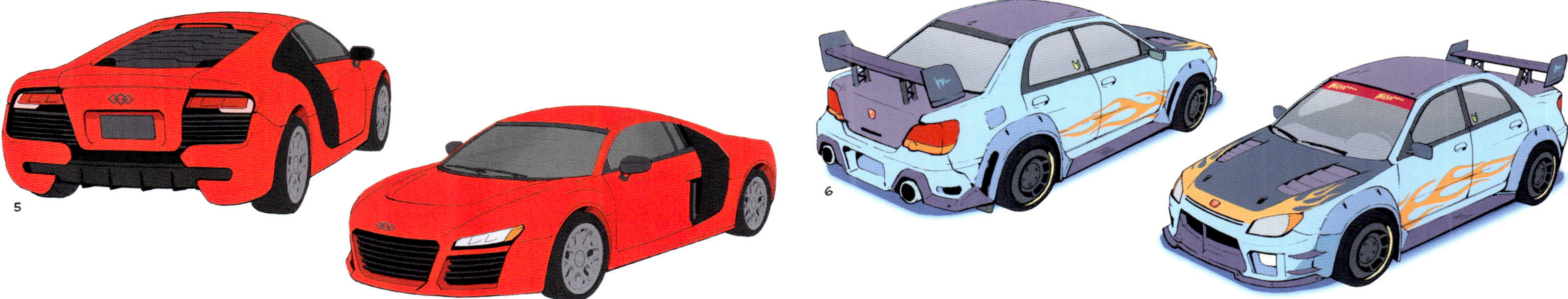

5

6

MAC GARGAN/SCORPION

Mac Gargan, the dangerous and super-violent criminal, also has a long and complicated history in the Spider-Man oeuvre. The character, who debuted in December 1964 in Stan Lee and Steve Ditko's *The Amazing Spider-Man* (#20), first appears in the show as the leader of the Scorpions gang. Voiced by Jonathan Medina, he wears armor equipped with a mechanical scorpion-like tail.

"I was very excited to be able to include Scorpion in this show because he's one of my favorite villains," notes Executive Producer/Showrunner Jeff Trammell. "He's so unhinged, dangerous, and scary—especially in the comics. We wanted our world of Spider-Man to be big and bright, but I didn't want anyone to forget that, ultimately, Peter is just a kid in a mask and a suit. When he tries to protect this city, he will definitely run into very dangerous characters. Mac is a brutal, no-nonsense kind of villain. I believe that for Spider-Man, the bigger the opposition is, the bigger his wins or failures are going to be. Someone like Scorpion is not someone who will quietly go into the shadows. If he returns, he will come back more dangerous and scarier than ever. Of course, he's a natural predator to our spider—because he's a scorpion."

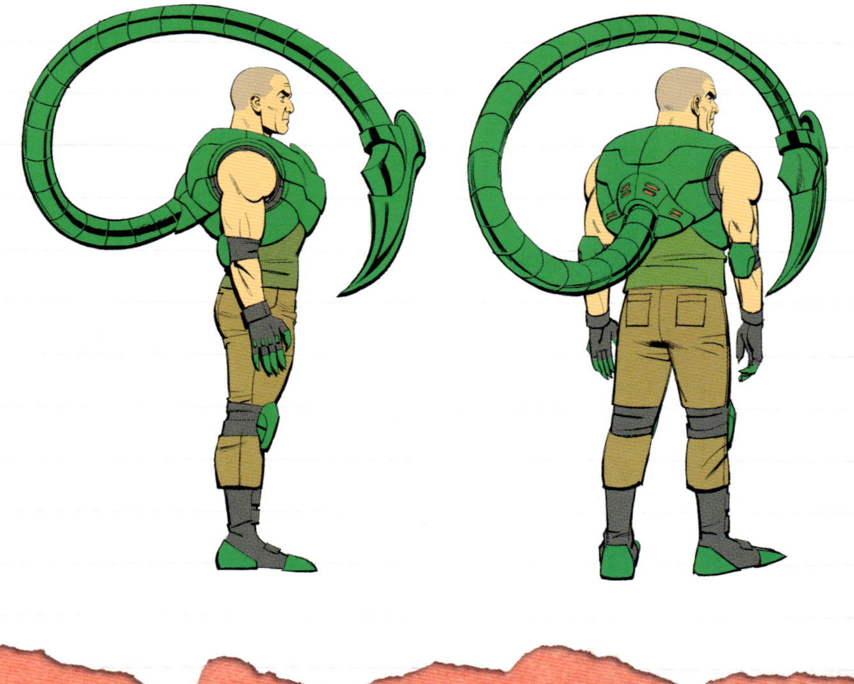

THIS PAGE Leonardo Romero
1–2 Leonardo Romero **3** Julen Urrutia Perez

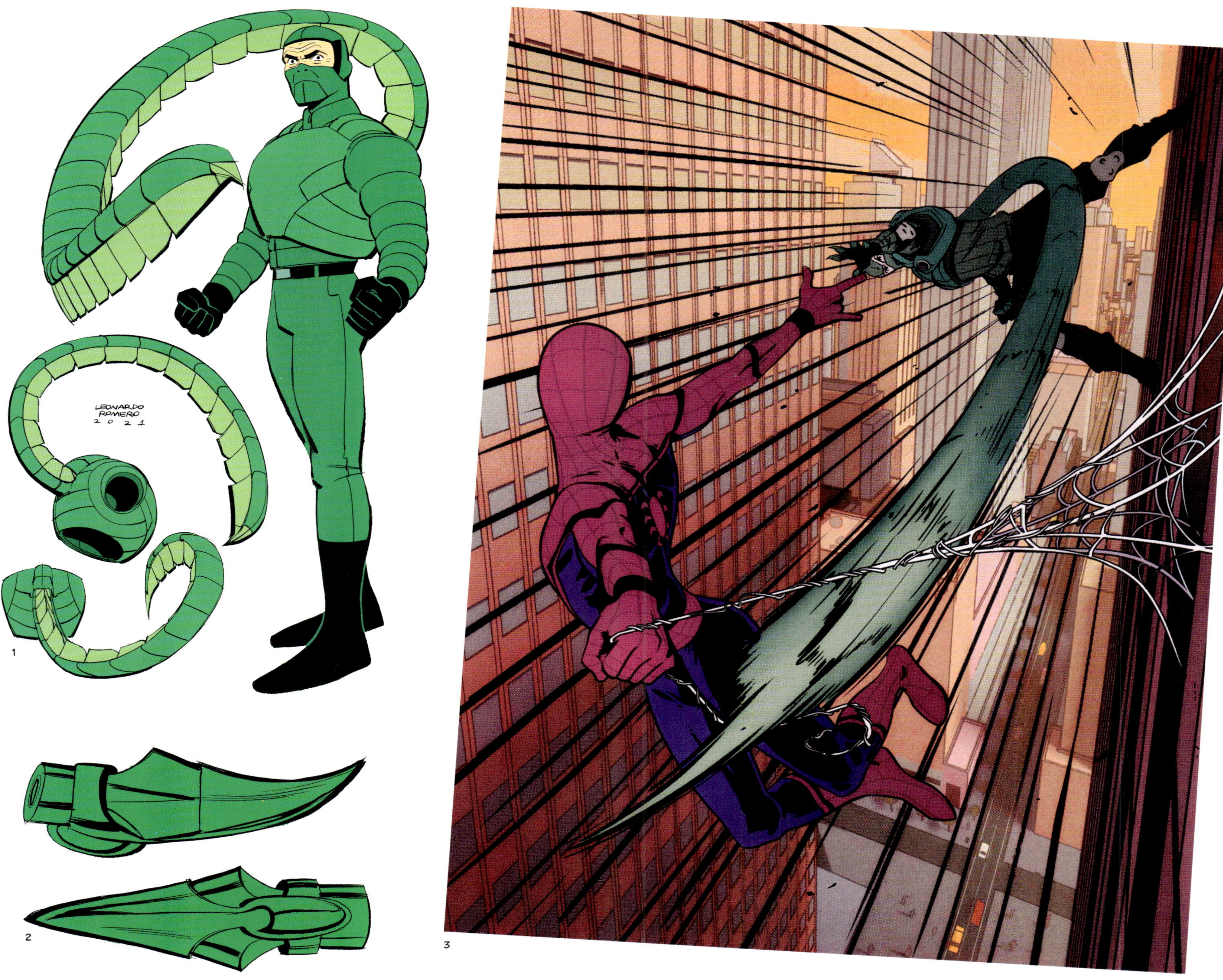
LEONARDO
ROMERO
2021
1
2
3

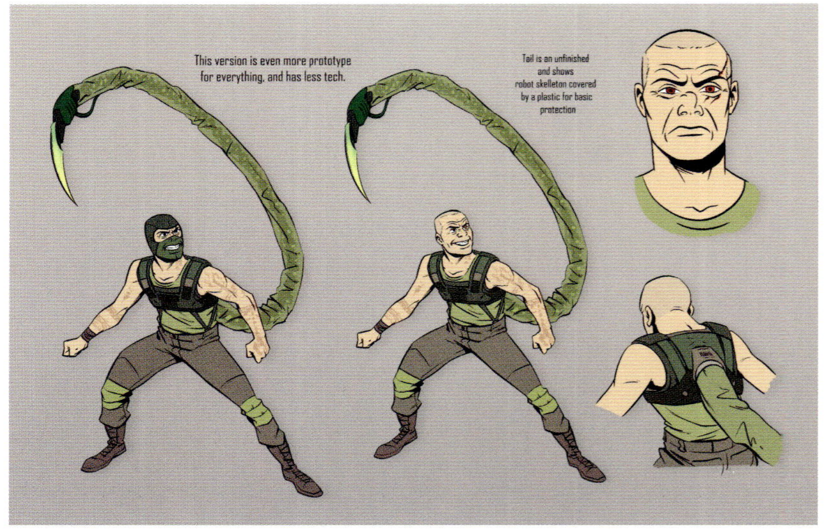

1

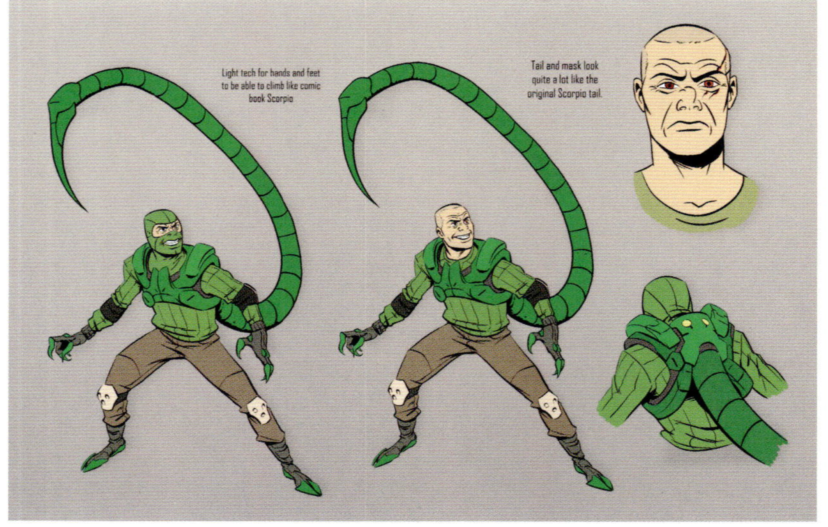

2

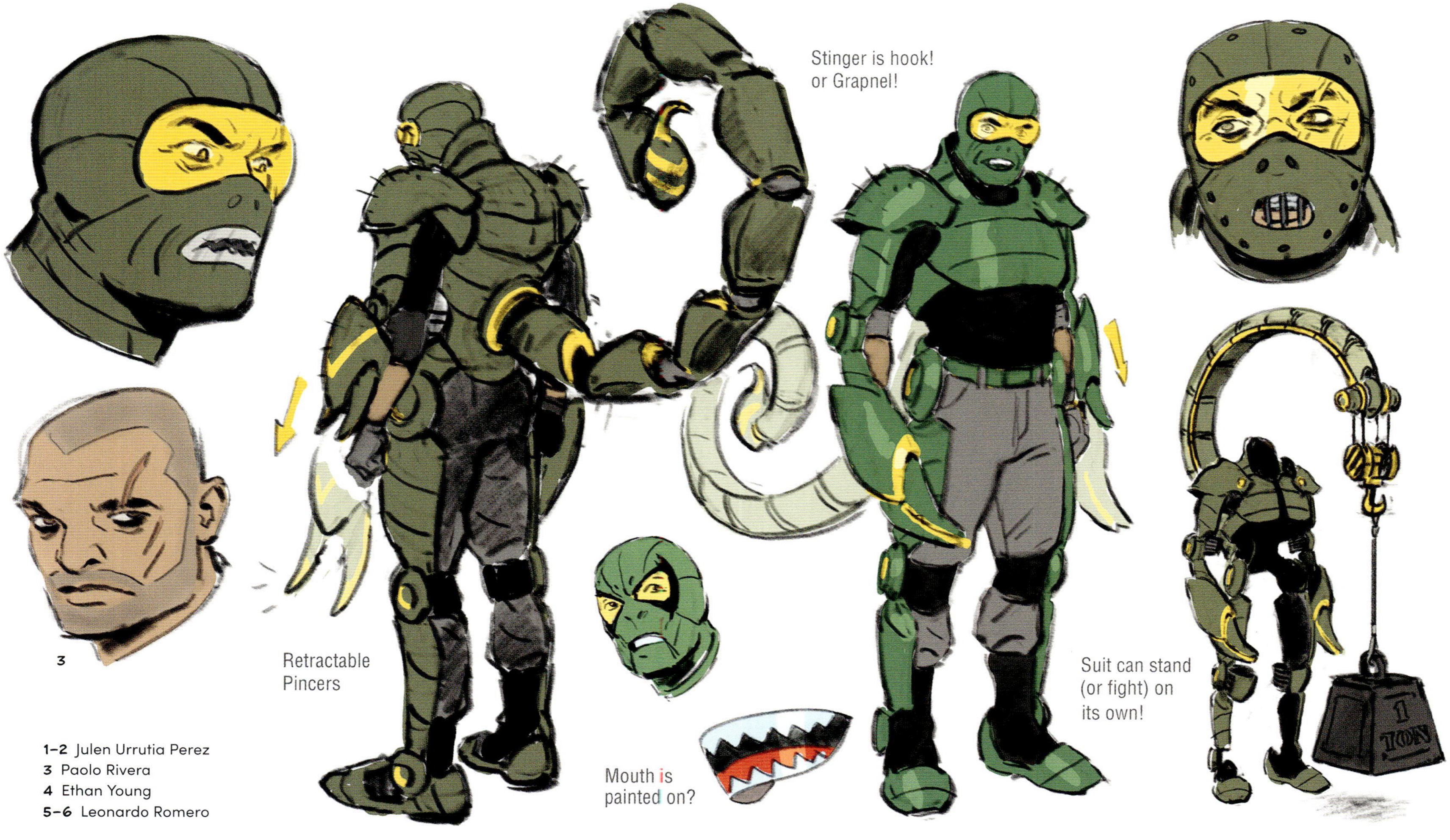

3

1–2 Julen Urrutia Perez
3 Paolo Rivera
4 Ethan Young
5–6 Leonardo Romero

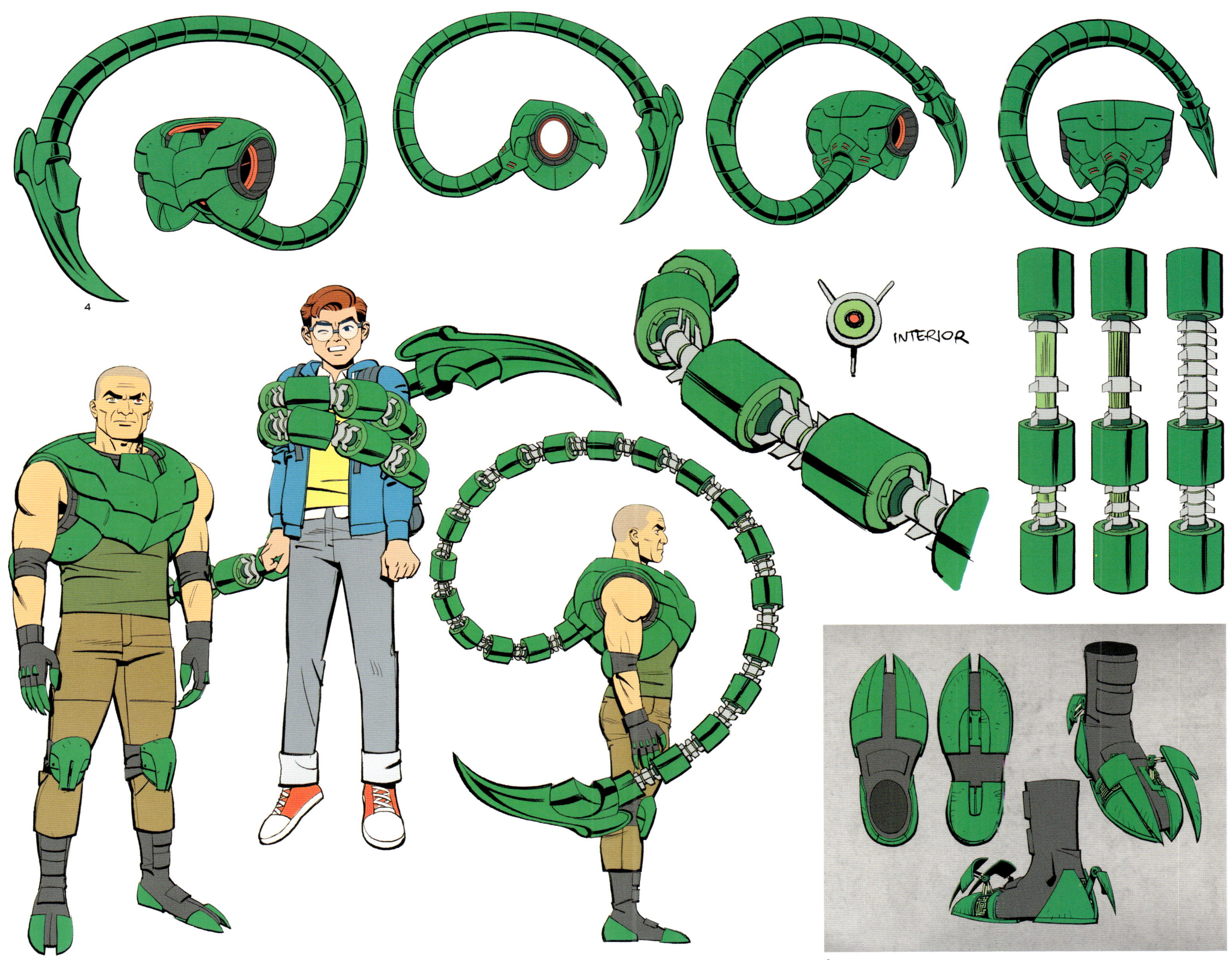

4

5

6

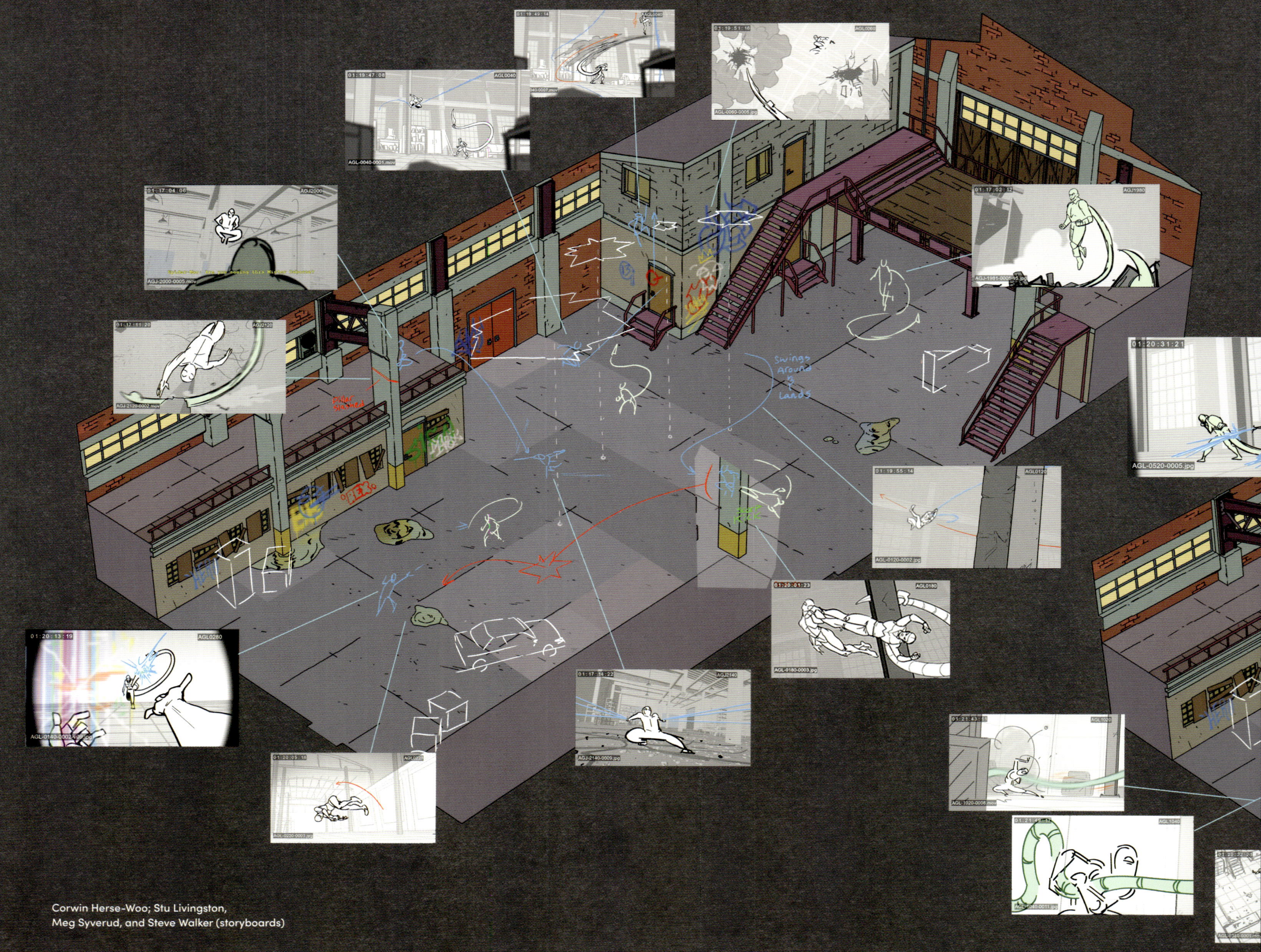

Corwin Herse-Woo; Stu Livingston,
Meg Syverud, and Steve Walker (storyboards)

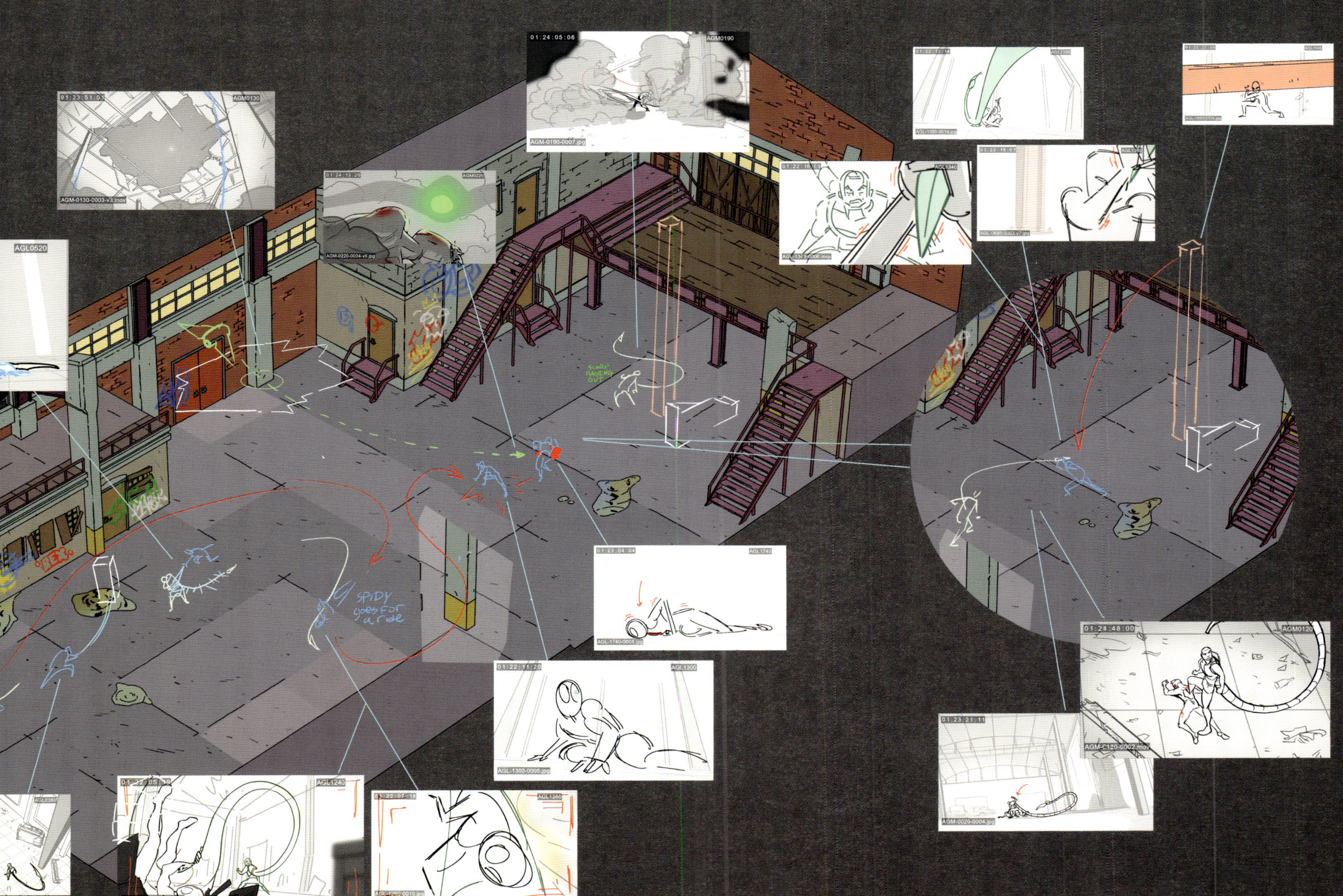
AGM0130
AGL0520
AGM0190
01:24:05:06
AGL1740
AGL1300
AGL1240
AGM0120
01:23:48:00
spidy goes for a ride

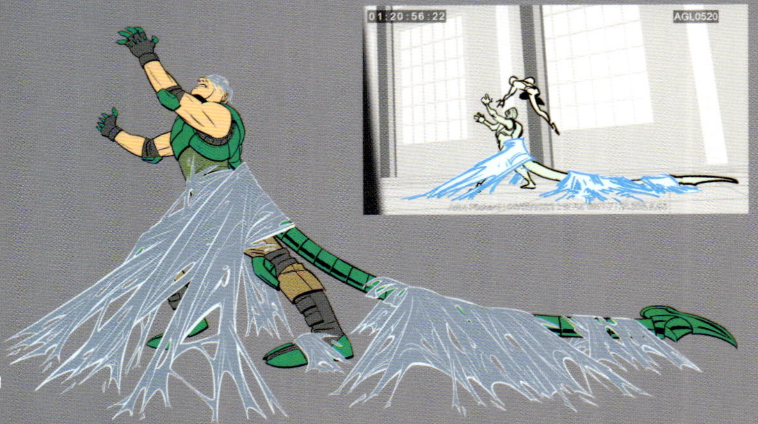

1

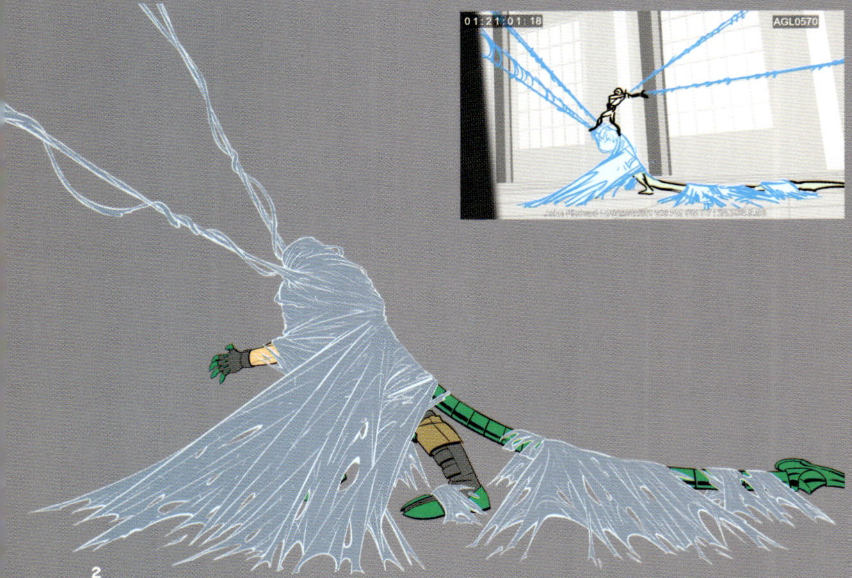

2

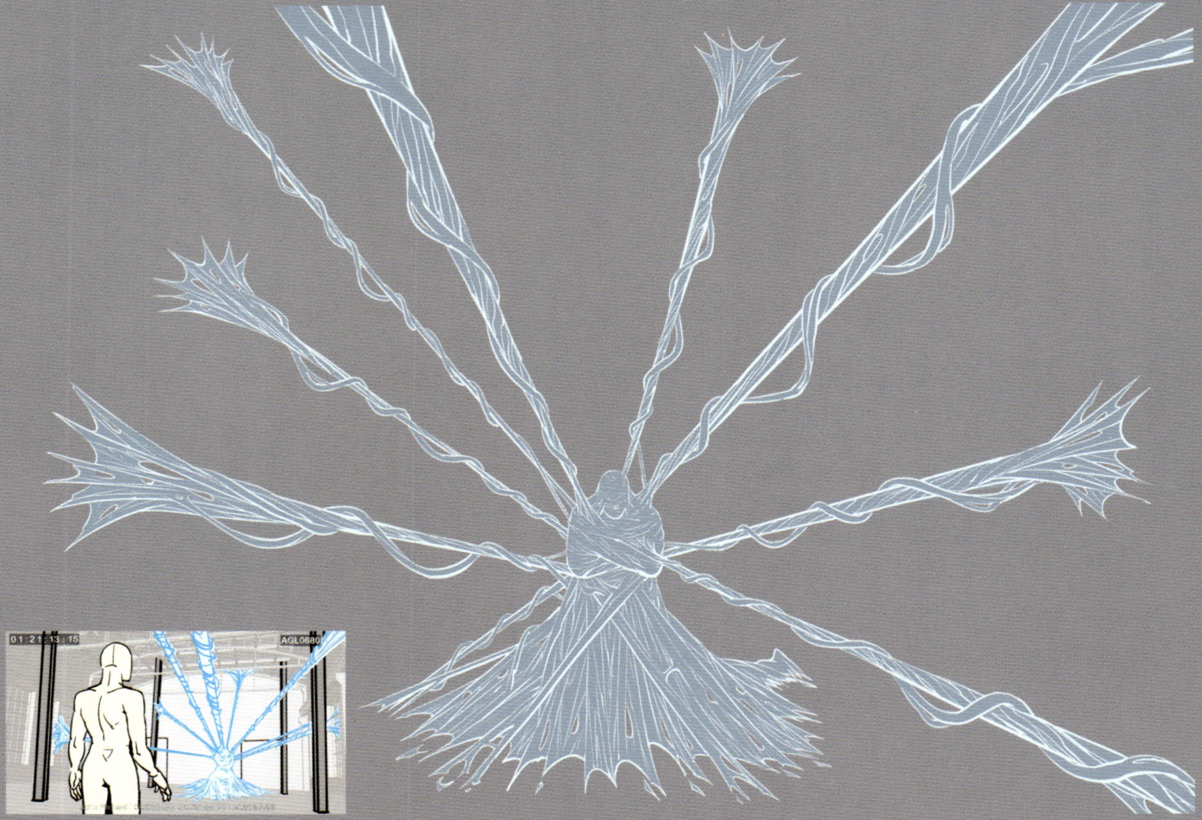

3

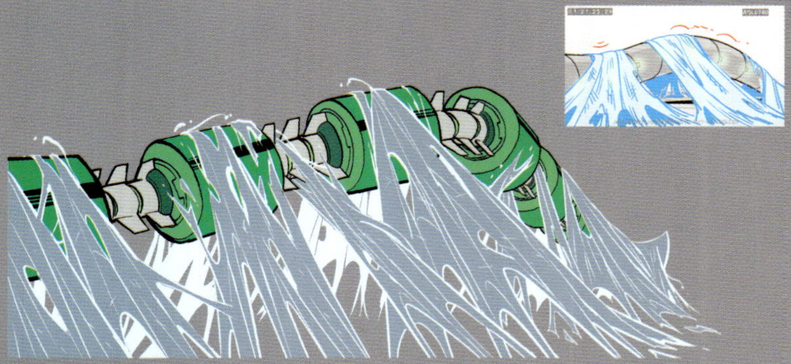

4

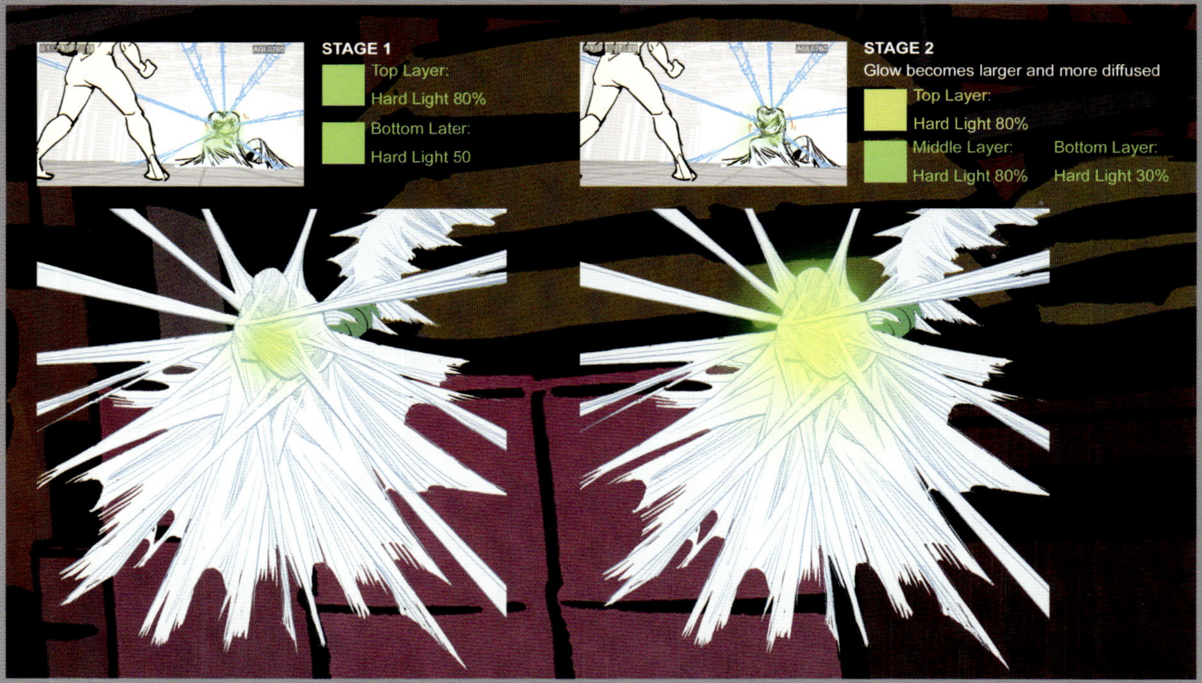

STAGE 1
Top Layer:
Hard Light 80%
Bottom Later:
Hard Light 50

STAGE 2
Glow becomes larger and more diffused
Top Layer:
Hard Light 80%
Middle Layer:
Hard Light 80%
Bottom Layer:
Hard Light 30%

5

1–4 Ethan Young 5 Junyi Wu 6–7 Ethan Young
8 Junyi Wu 9–10 Ethan Young; Meg Syverud (storyboards)

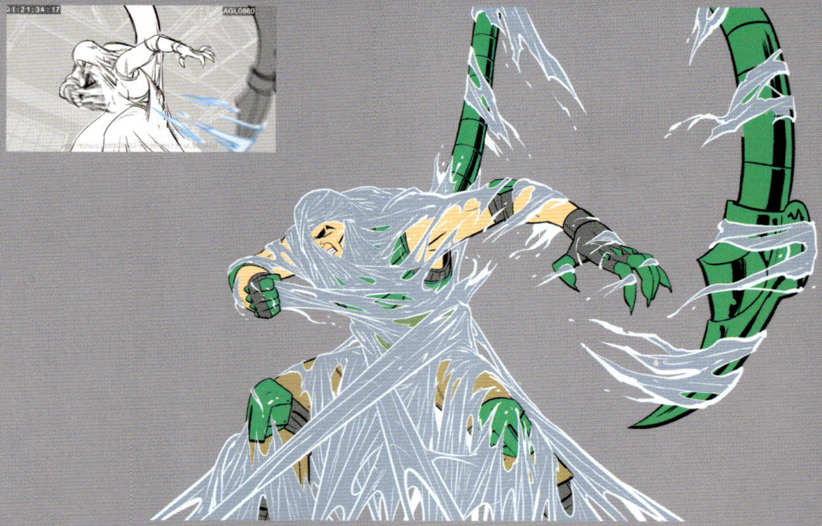

6

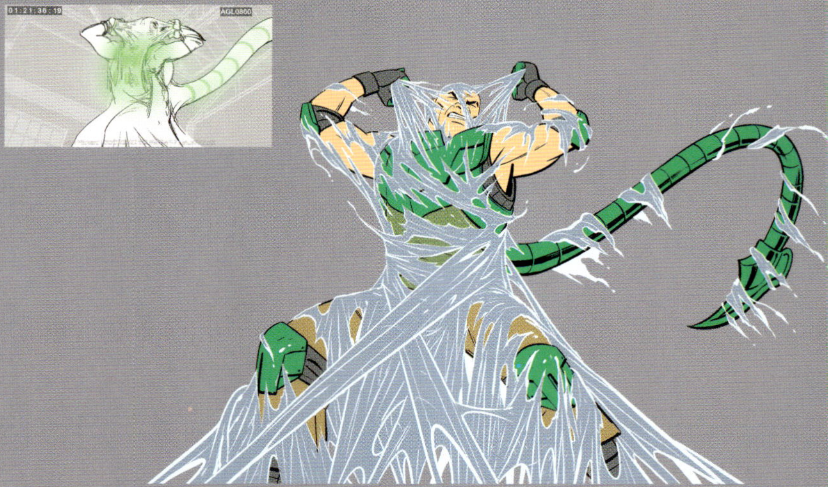

7

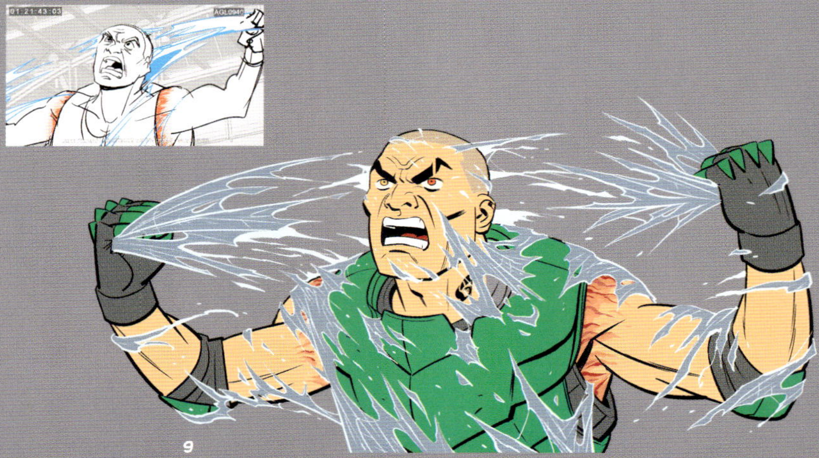

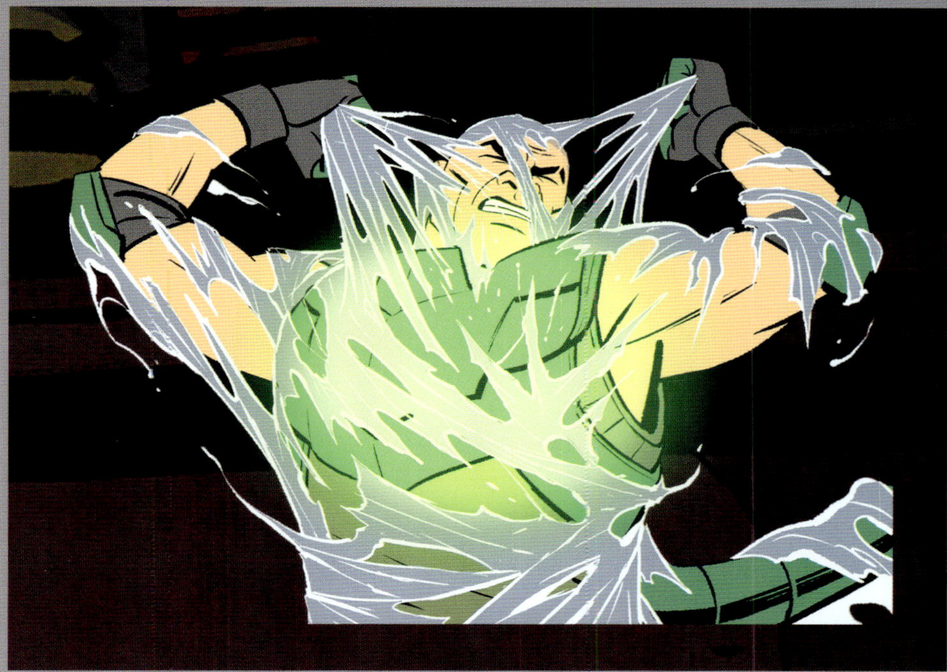

8

9

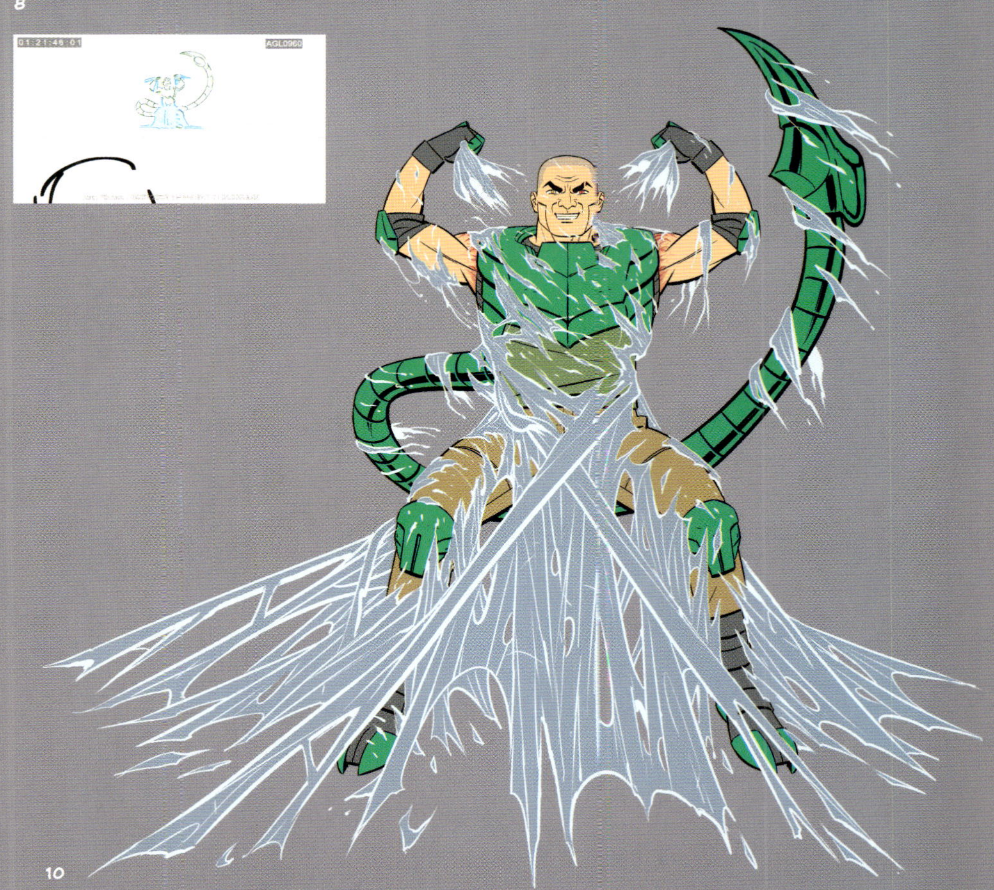

10

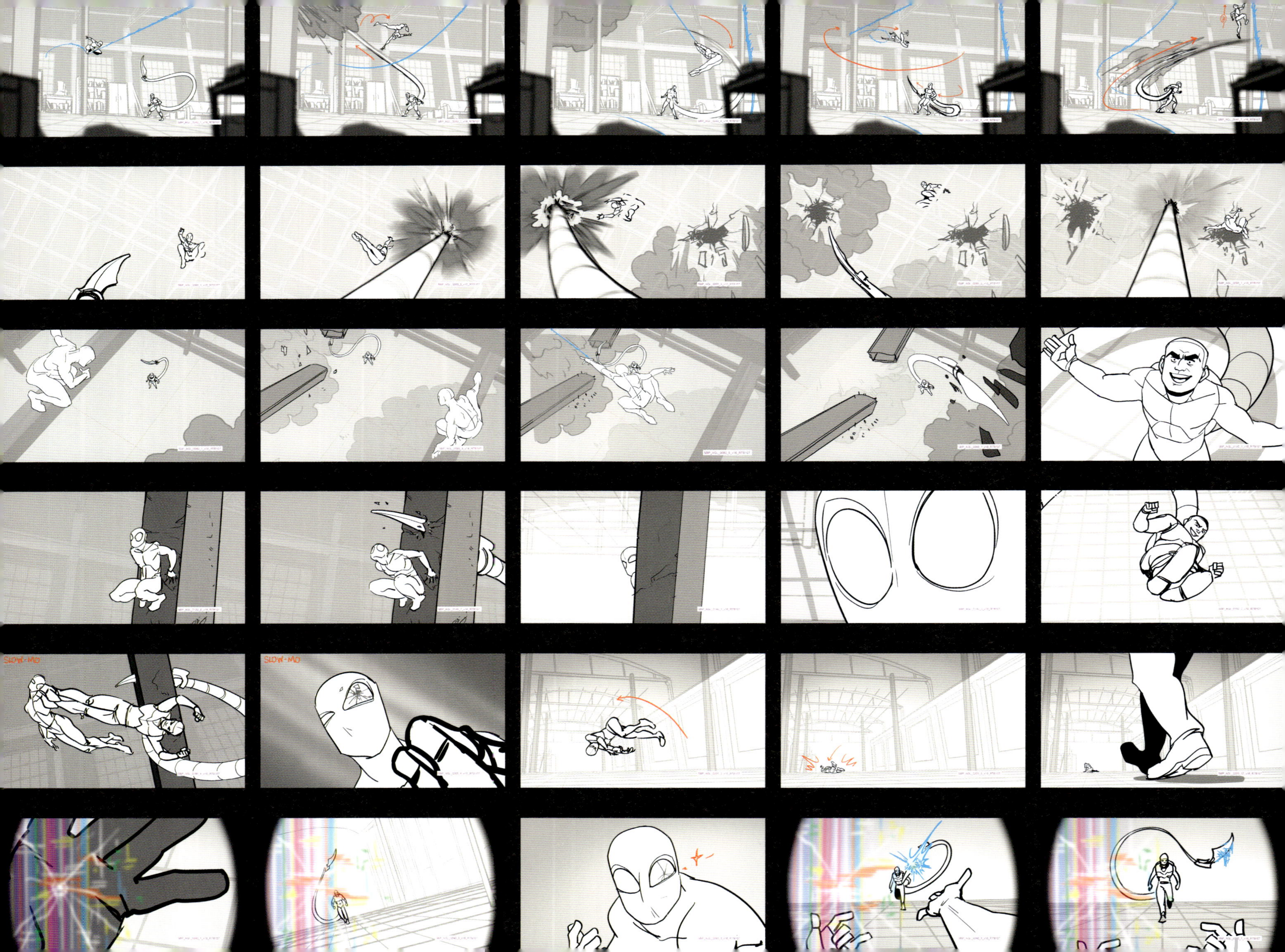
SLOW-MO
SLOW-MO

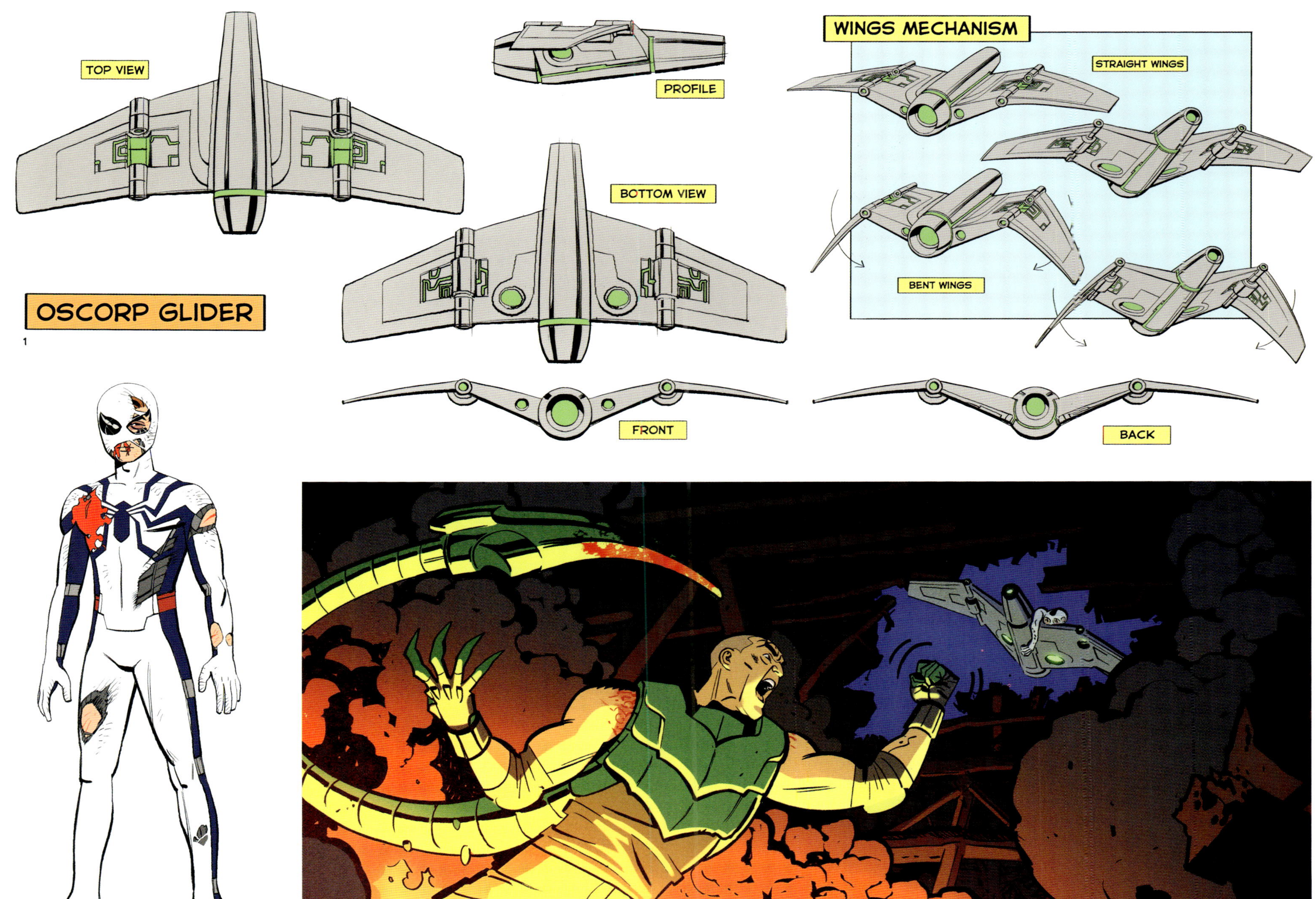

1

2

3

OPPOSITE Stu Livingston and Meg Syverud **1–2** Leonardo Romero **3** Chris Samnee (line art) and W. Scott Forbes (color)

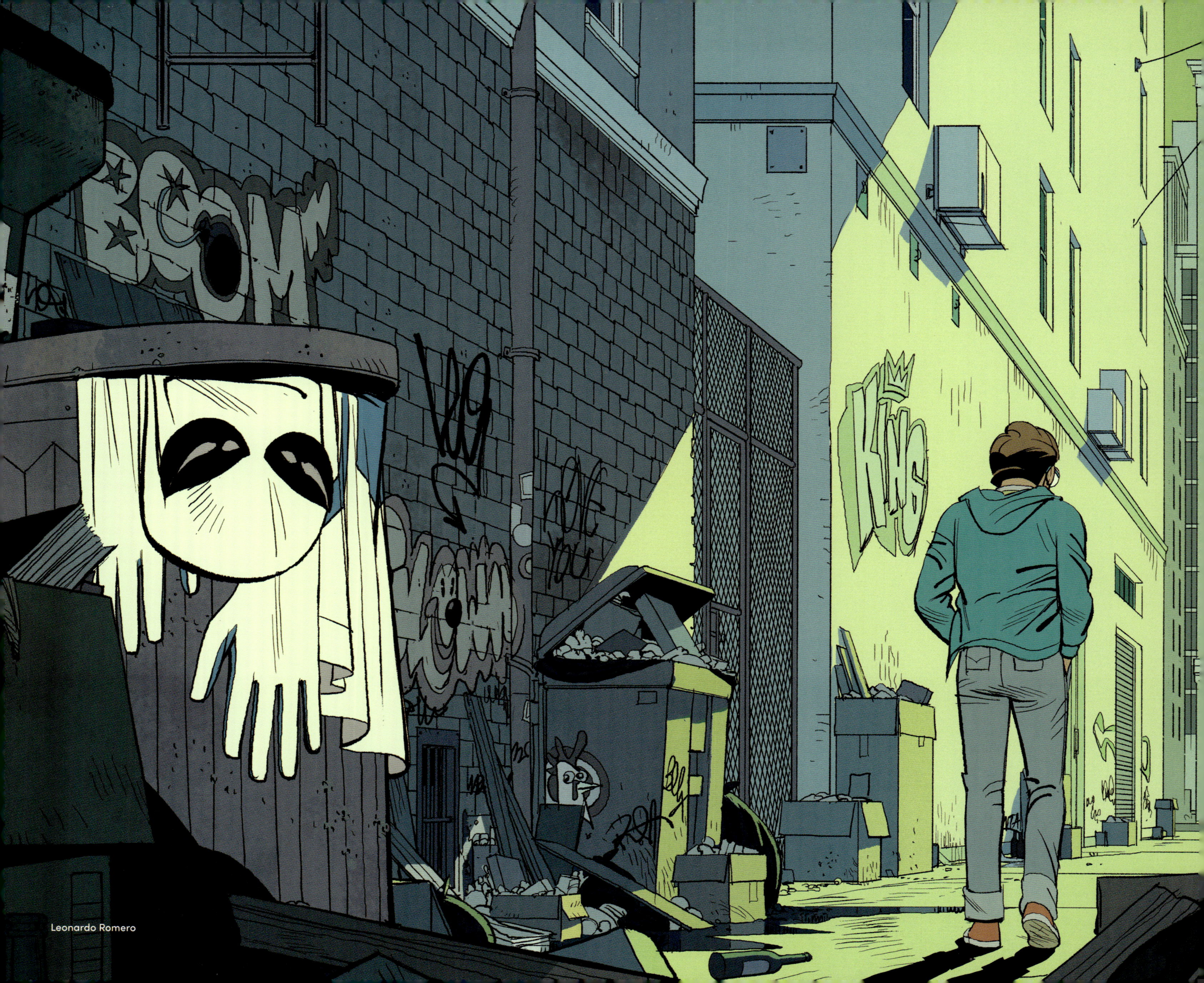

Leonardo Romero

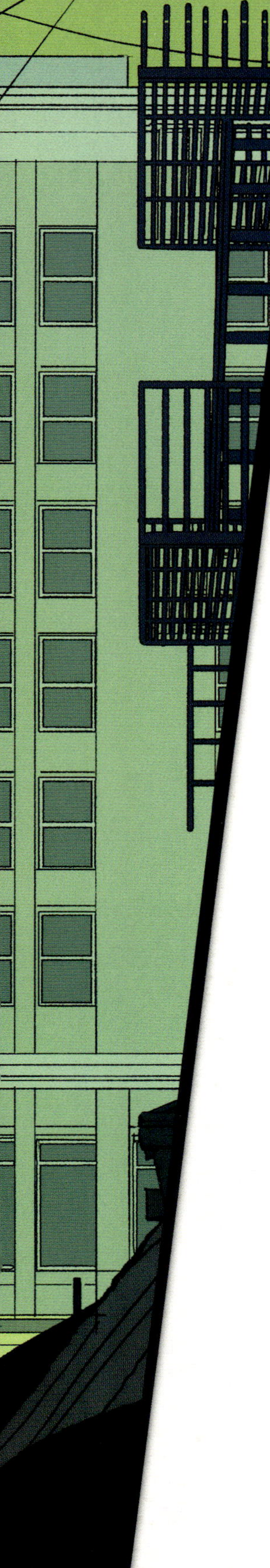

EPISODE EIGHT

TANGLED WEB

AFTER PETER RECOVERS FROM HIS FIGHT WITH SCORPION, NORMAN TELLS HIM HE NEEDS TO FURTHER DEVELOP HIS SKILLS AND LEVEL UP HIS AMBITIONS AS SPIDER-MAN. NORMAN ALSO SHARES OCTAVIUS'S WHEREABOUTS WITH SECRETARY ROSS, WHO, WITH A LITTLE HELP FROM IRON MAN, HAS THE CREATOR OF THE GAMMA-POWERED WEAPONS THAT HAVE PROLIFERATED ACROSS THE CITY ARRESTED FOR VIOLATING THE SOKOVIA ACCORDS. UPTOWN, PEARL BREAKS UP WITH LONNIE AFTER HE REFUSES TO LEAVE THE 110TH STREET GANG, AND BIG DONOVAN PAYS CHAMELEON TO REVEAL THE LOCATION OF OCTAVIUS'S ABANDONED WAREHOUSE SO THE GANG CAN GET THEIR HANDS ON WEAPONS POWERFUL ENOUGH TO TAKE ON SCORPION. AS THE EPISODE CLOSES, HARRY GIVES PETER A NEW RED AND BLUE SPIDEY SUIT DEVELOPED BY OSCORP SCIENTISTS.

THIS EPISODE builds up to the culmination of Lonnie and Pearl's relationship. "After losing his leadership of the football team, Lonnie found respect in the gang as Tombstone, and there's a part of him that doesn't want to give that up," says Executive Producer/Showrunner Jeff Trammell. "Pearl gives him an ultimatum, and he chooses the gang over her. I don't think Pearl expected that to happen, so I think that was a very tough moment for both characters. It really showed Lonnie's headspace at this moment and how this gang experience changed the person that we met in the first episode of the show."

The eighth episode also zeros in on the psychological damage inflicted on Peter because of the savage attack by Scorpion. "He feels that everyone that gets hurt is because of him," says Trammell. "It's that classic Spider-Man burden of putting everything on his own shoulders. I wanted that moment that he shares with May to feel like he might just break down and tell her his secret. We have another mention of Ben here and how his absence has affected both of them. It's a sweet exchange, but it's also heartbreaking."

As Peter looks for somebody to fill Ben's absence, it's natural that he would gravitate toward Norman. "We all realize that Norman is not the mentor that Peter needs when he tells him, 'With great power comes great *respect*,'" Trammell points out. Audiences were of course expecting "responsibility"—the version of this advice that Uncle Ben has given to Peter in many other iterations, and what May told him in *Spider-Man: No Way Home*. "In a way, this is the moment that the series has been building toward. Every Spider-Man fan knows how wrong that is. You feel like, 'Wait, is he going to say that?' and then he breaks it!

"He turns this important phrase into something that it shouldn't be. It's the last thing Peter needs to hear at the worst possible time. The way audiences interpreted this scene meant a lot to me."

Otto Octavius also has his moment in the spotlight in this episode. "That was a lot of fun because we get to see these crazy arms and then the raid in the warehouse," says Trammell. "It was important for me to show Otto go down fighting. Initially, we had Otto walk into that alley and be surrounded by officers. As we were working through the scene, I remember Brad [Winderbaum] told us, 'What if Iron Man shows up and catches Otto?' and I was like, 'You're a genius!' It's a great way to show that Iron Man is in our world, especially because we know from the movies that Peter and Tony have this bond. That was a nice homage to all of that history."

Co-Executive Producer/Supervising Director Mel Zwyer believes the episode stands out because it's mostly about Peter Parker, not Spider-Man. "It's the first time we get a glimpse of Uncle Ben in that picture on the fridge," he notes. "Peter starts questioning his own fitness to be Spider-Man, and we're still wondering whether Norman is a good guy or a bad one. When Peter realizes that his Oscorp suit is totally ruined, he thinks he's done being Spider-Man. Harry shows that he is a very good friend to him because he's the only one that actually listens to Peter. Harry uses his connection with his dad, makes him a new suit, and we get a little teaser at the very end with the reflection of the suit."

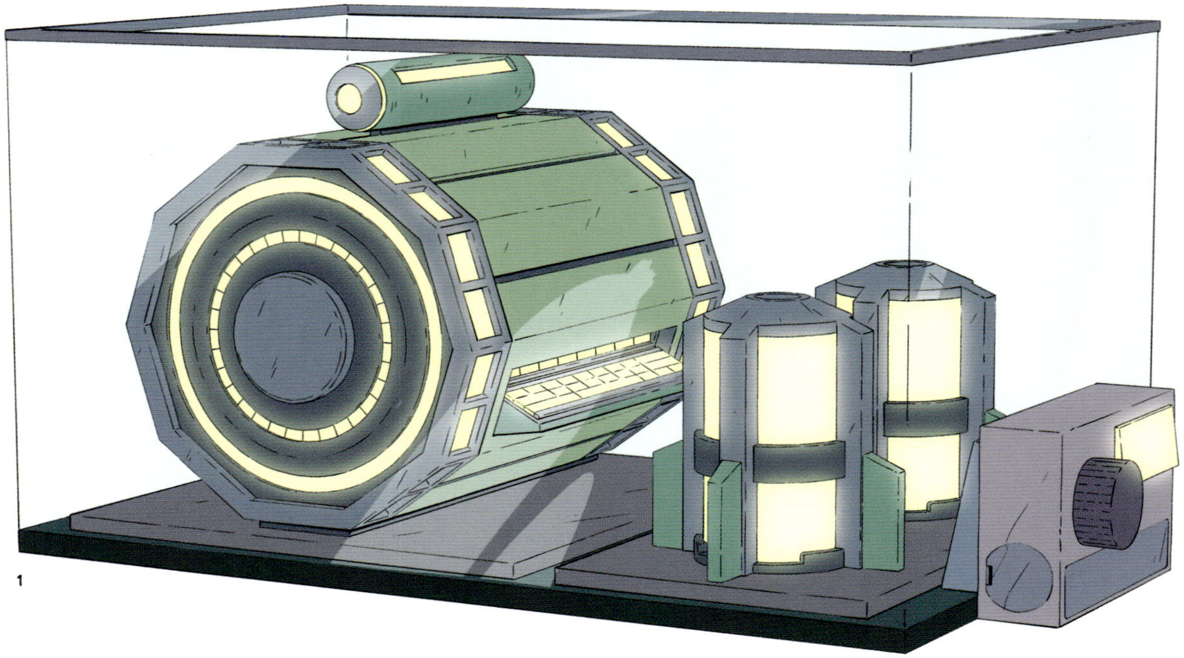

1

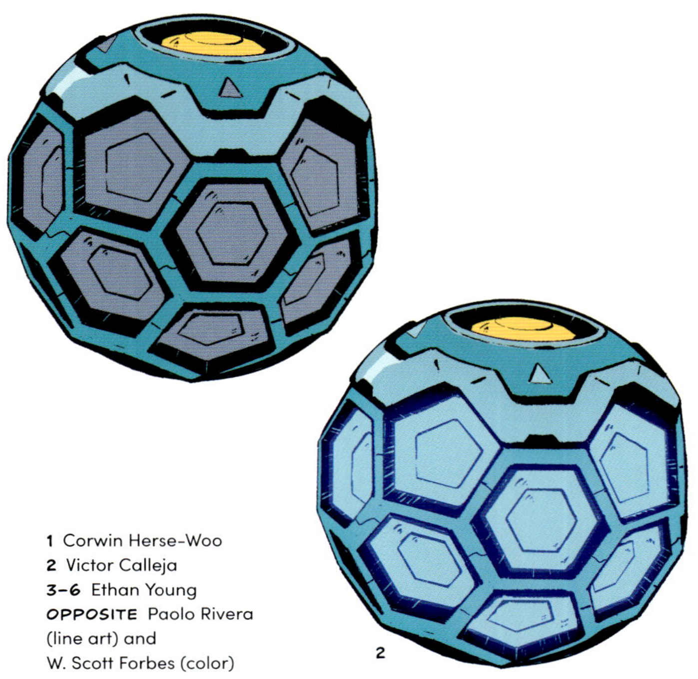

2

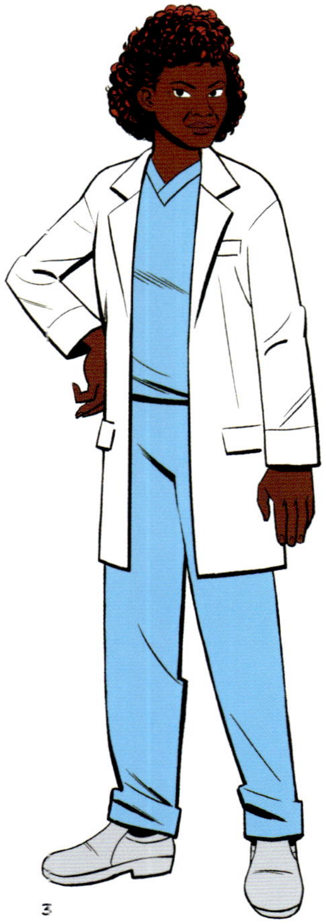

3 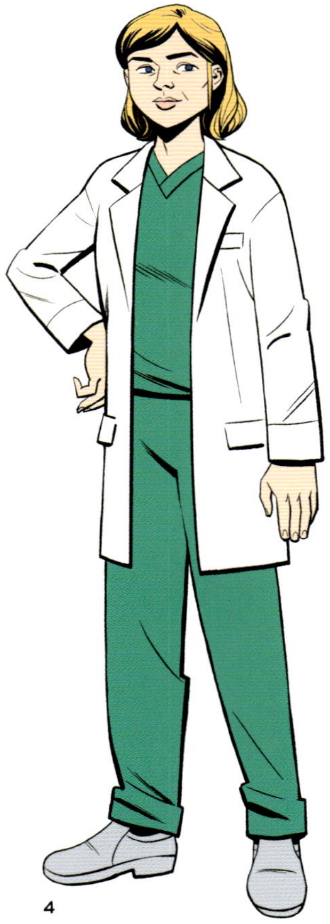 4 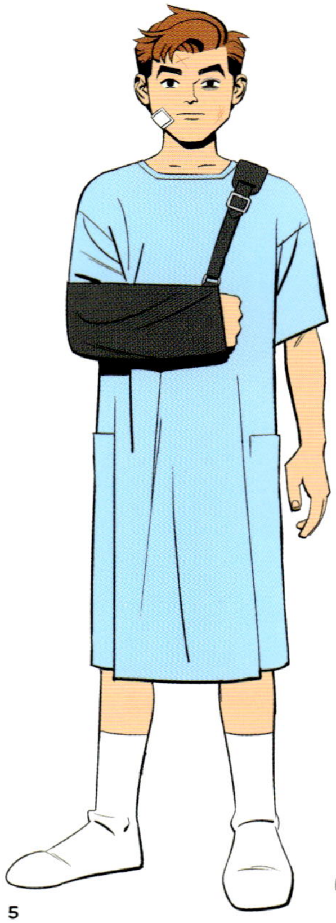 5 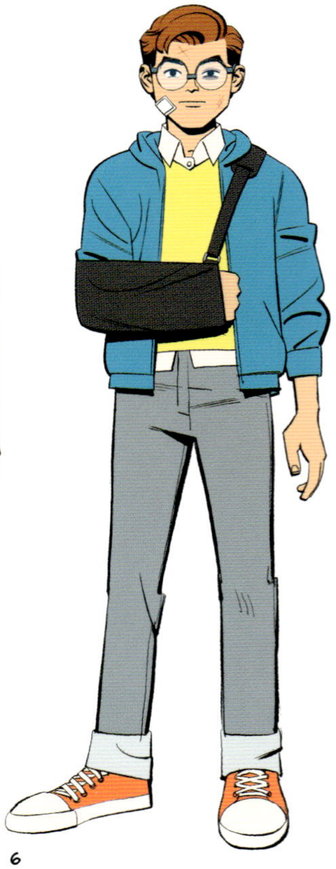 6

1 Corwin Herse-Woo
2 Victor Calleja
3–6 Ethan Young
OPPOSITE Paolo Rivera (line art) and W. Scott Forbes (color)

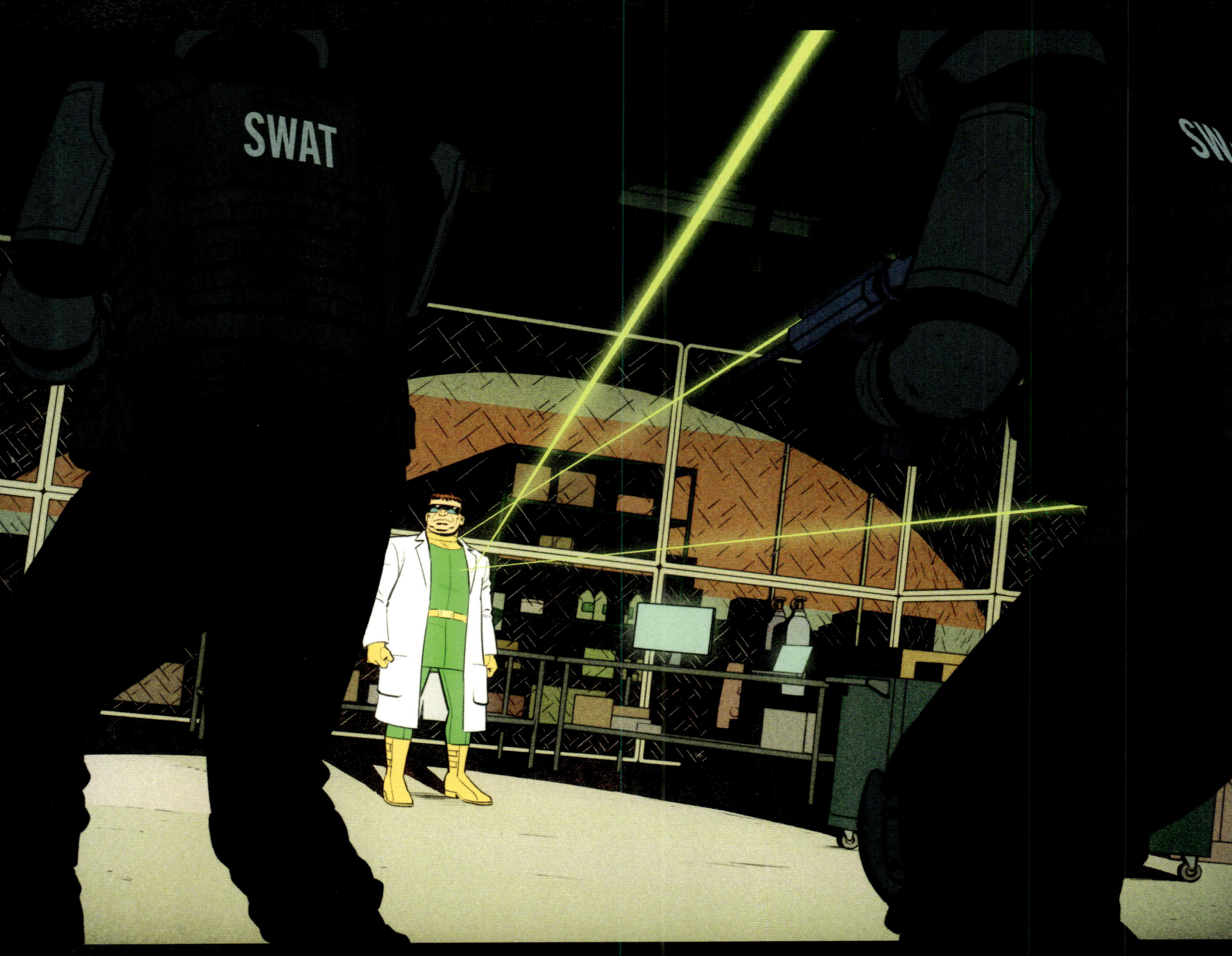
SWAT

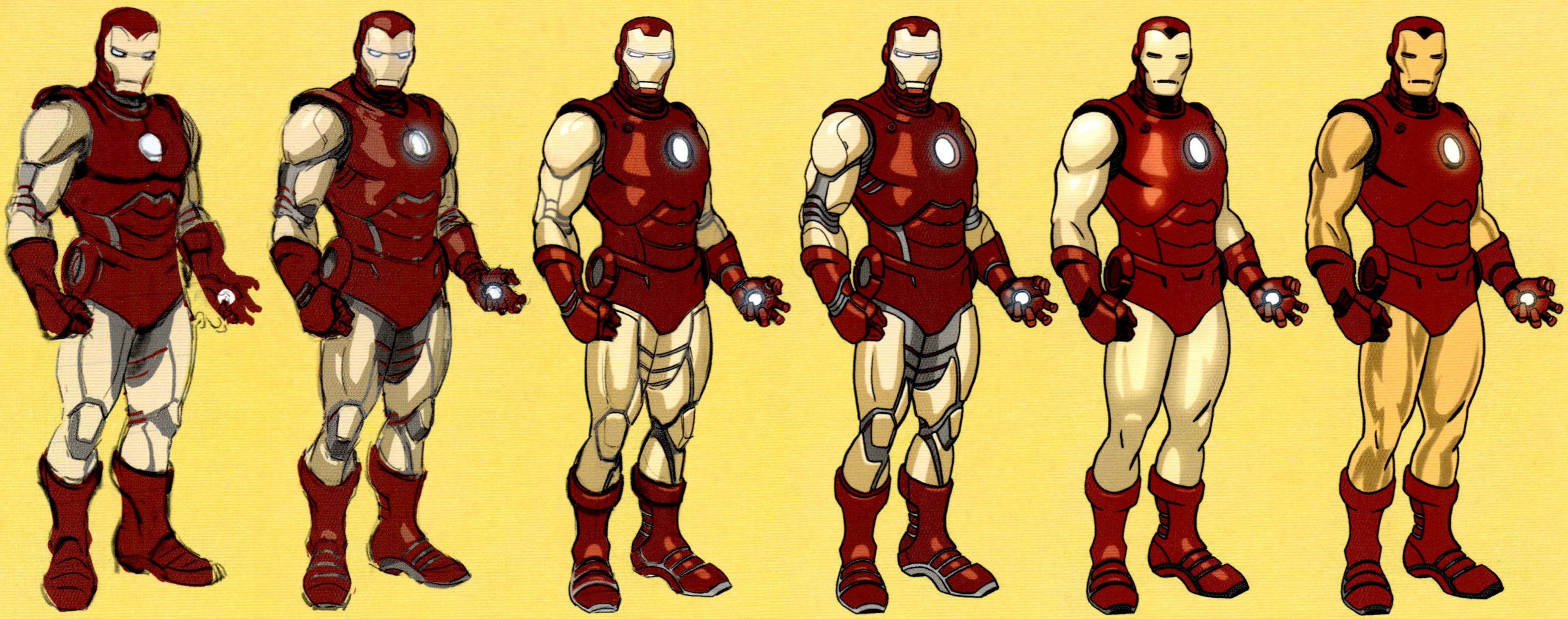

1

TONY STARK/IRON MAN

Since Peter Parker and Tony Stark have had an interesting relationship in the comic books and the MCU movies, it was inevitable that the charming CEO of Stark Industries would pop up in the neighborhood as well. Voiced by Mick Wingert (Marvel Animation's *What If...?*, Marvel's *Avengers Assemble*), the character makes his appearance in the eighth episode, helping in the arrest of Otto Octavius.

Lead Character Designer Leonardo Romero said that in the early stages of the show's development, he wasn't sure which direction the art was going to go, so he looked at both the MCU versions of Iron Man and the classic comic books. "I did one version that was inspired by his classic look, but with very small tweaks, and it seemed that a lot of people really liked it," he recalls. "It's one of the things that I am very proud of. We kept the classic Tony Stark look with the small mustache."

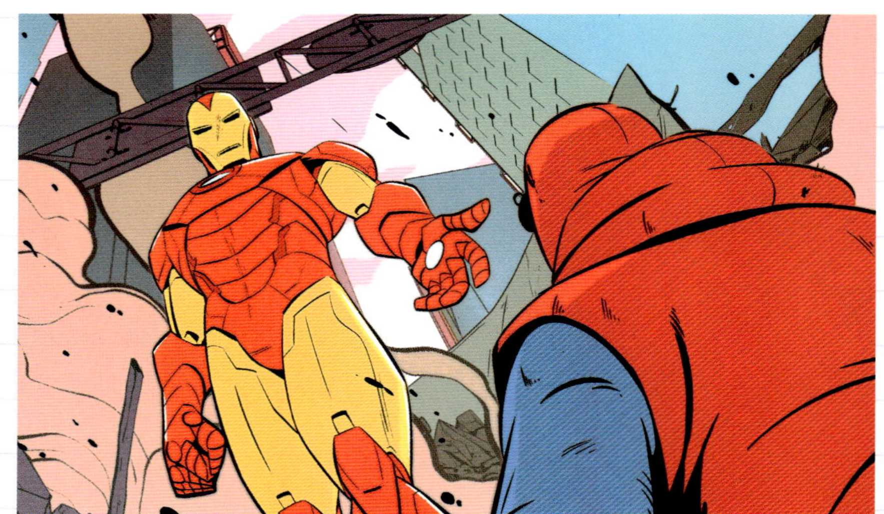

2

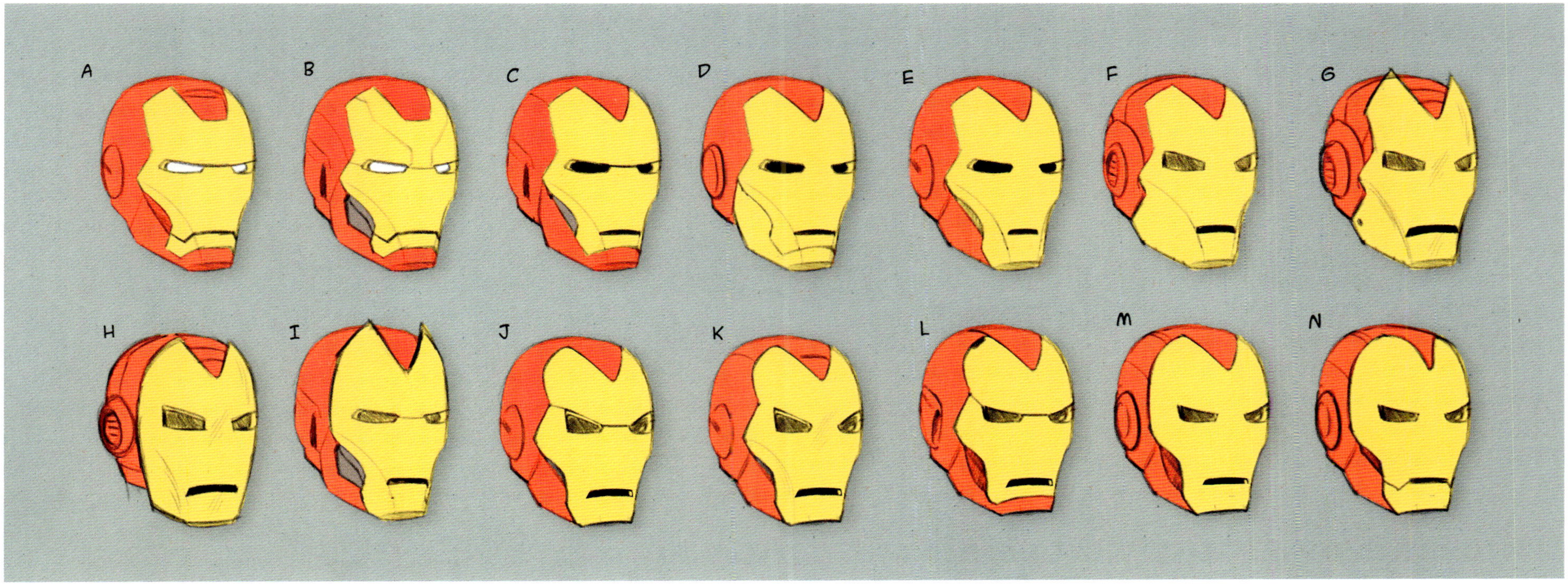

3

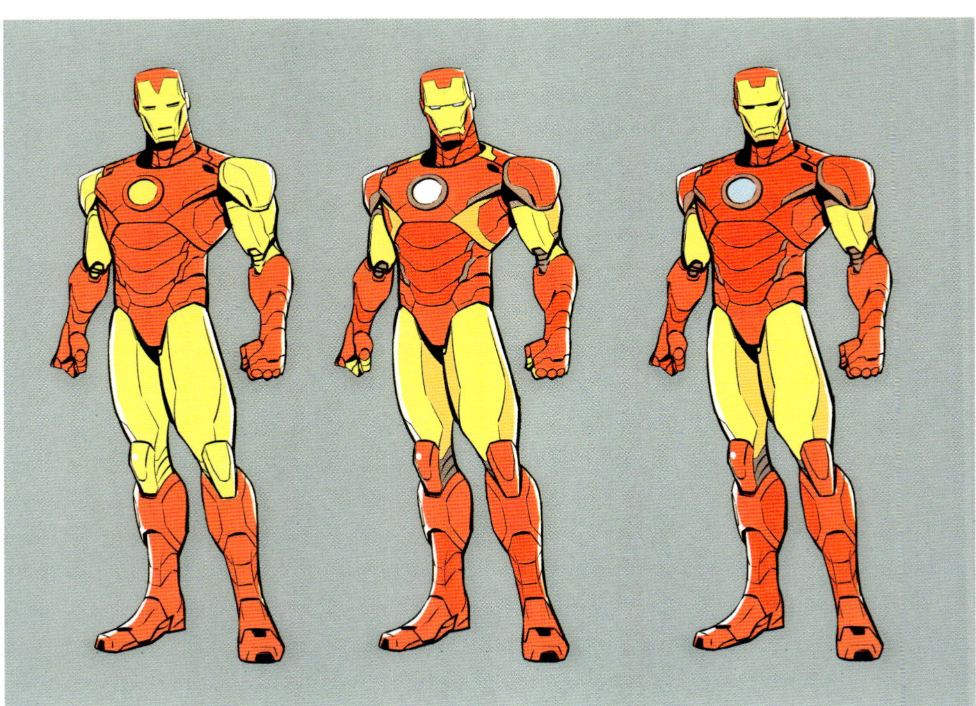

4

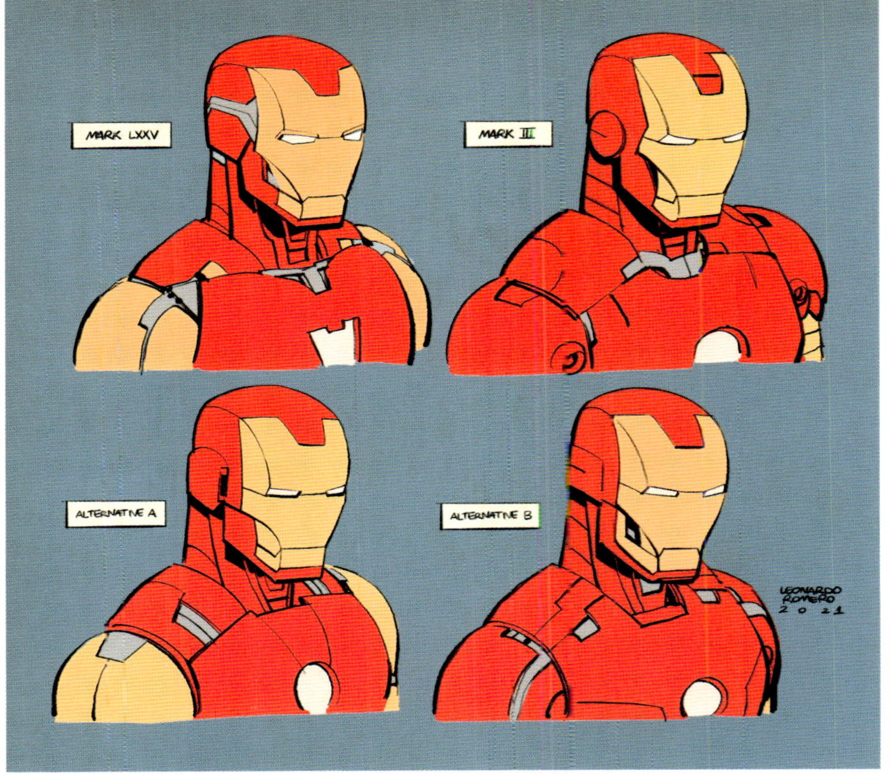

5

1 Paolo Rivera **2–4** Julen Urrutia Perez **5** Leonardo Romero

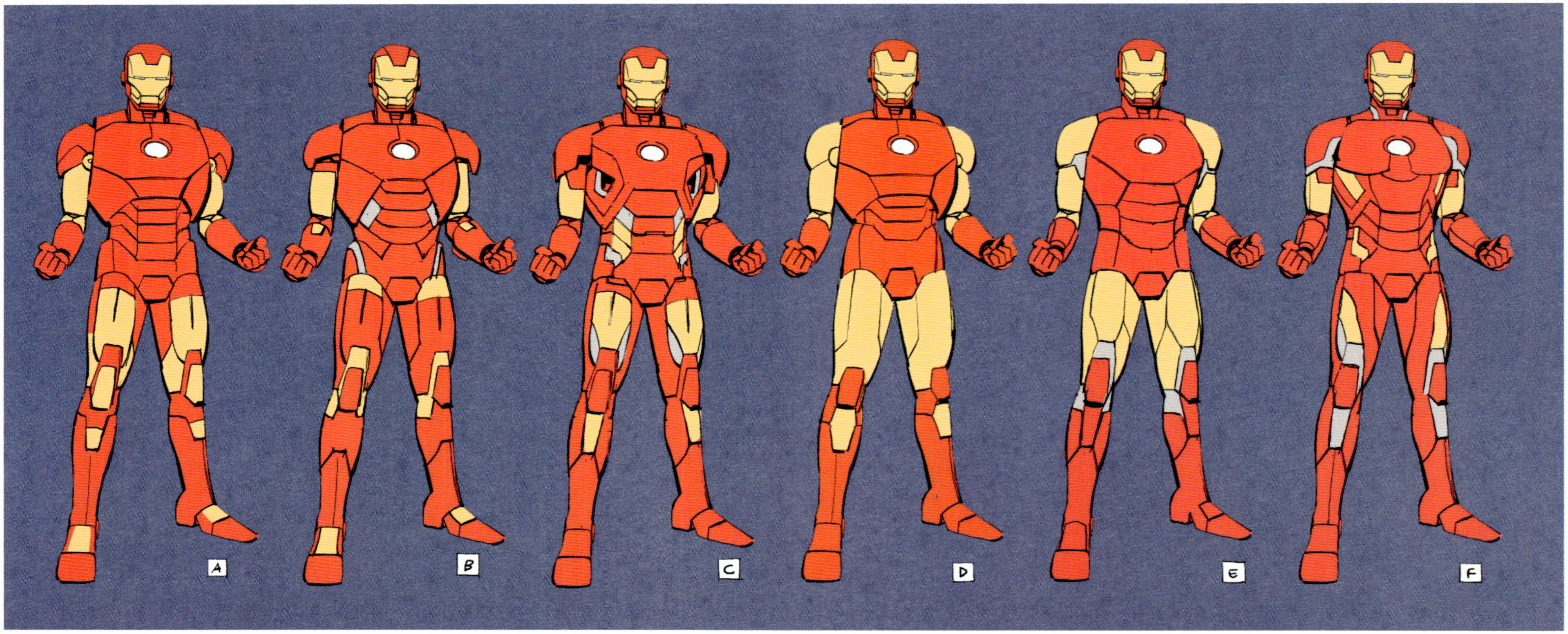

A B C D E F

1

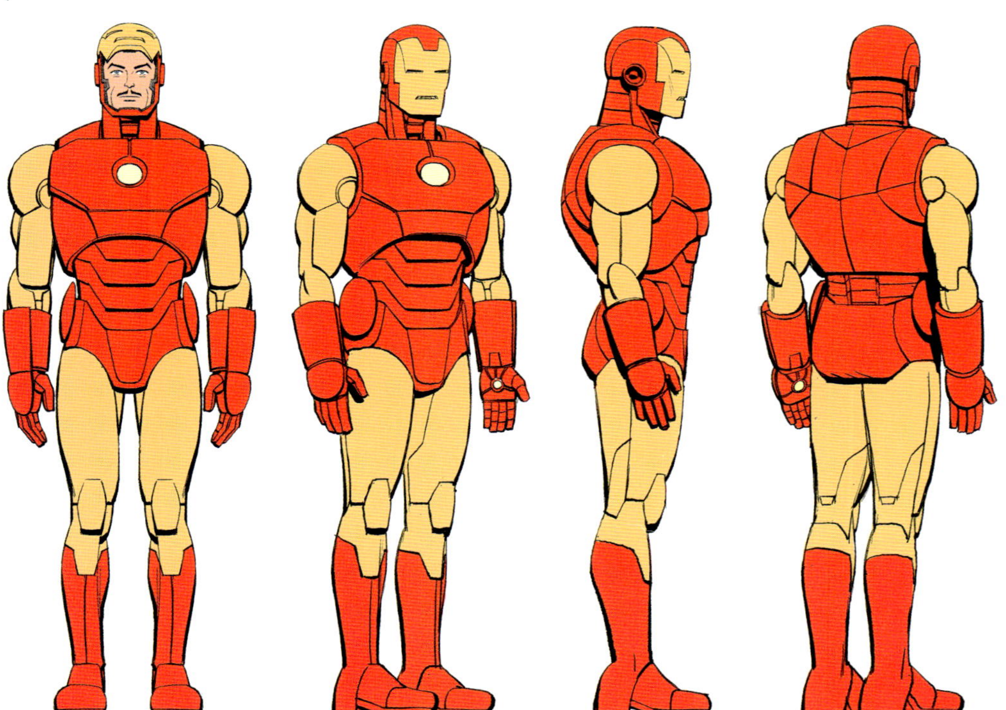

2

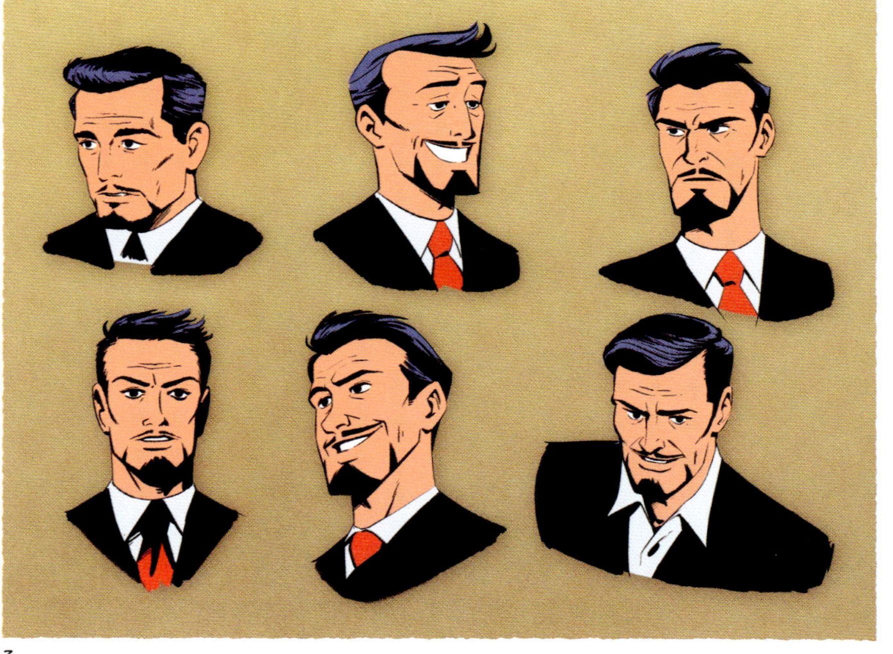

3

1–2 Leonardo Romero **3** Julen Urrutia Perez **OPPOSITE** Leonardo Romero

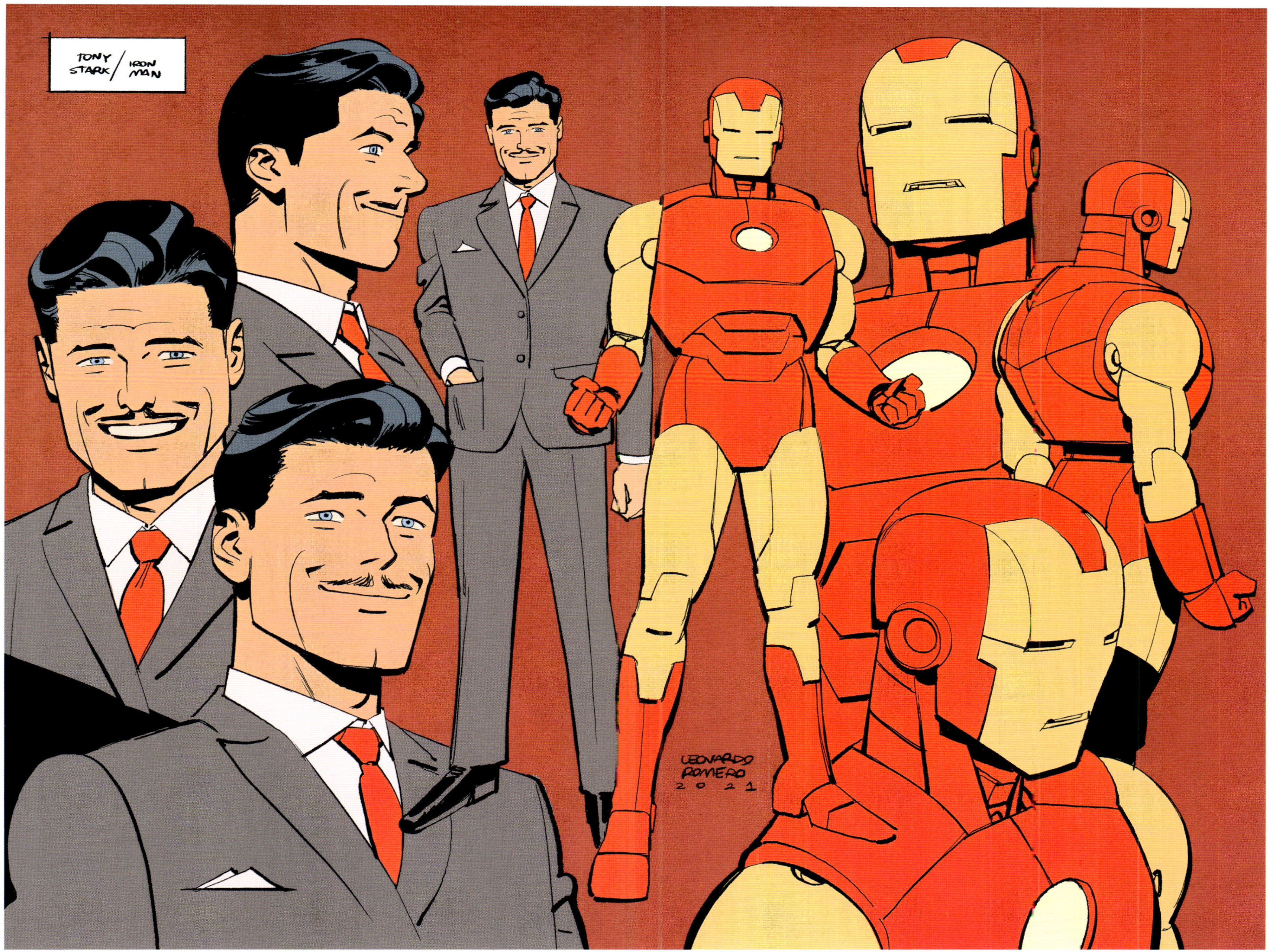
TONY STARK / IRON MAN
LEONARDO ROMERO 2021

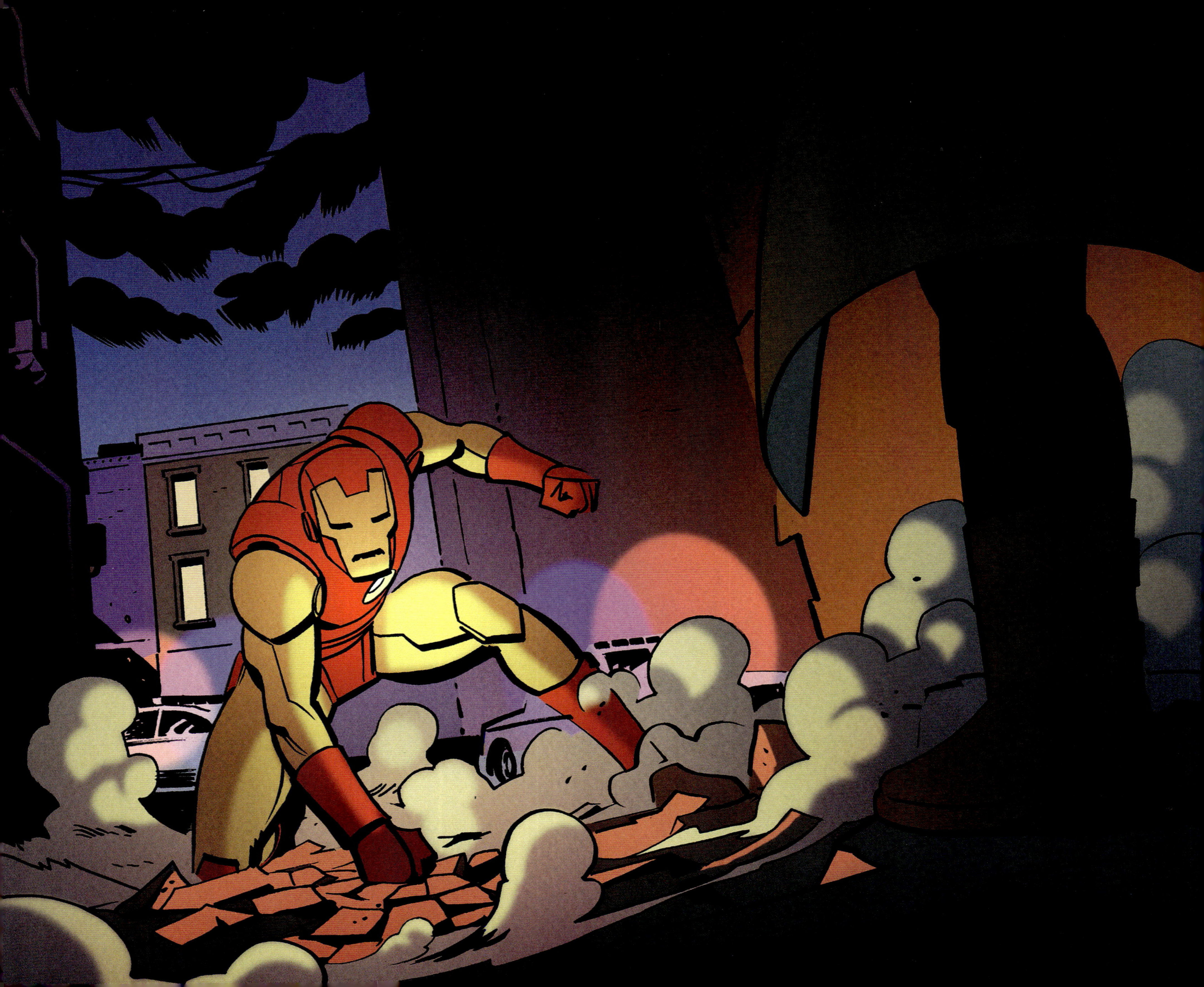

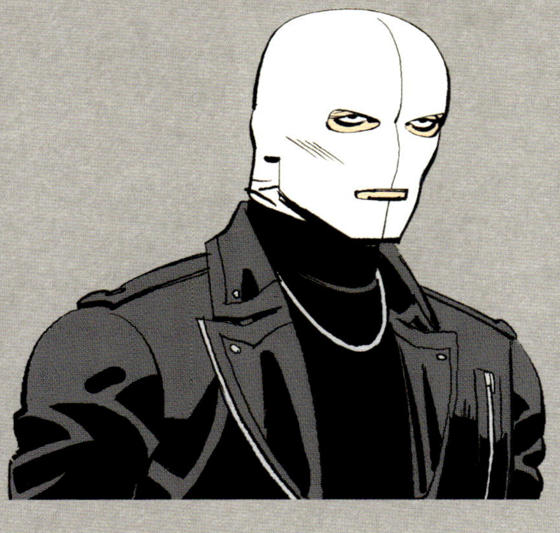

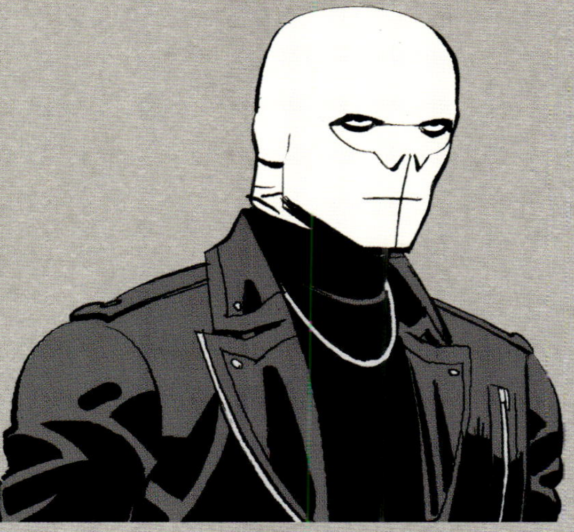

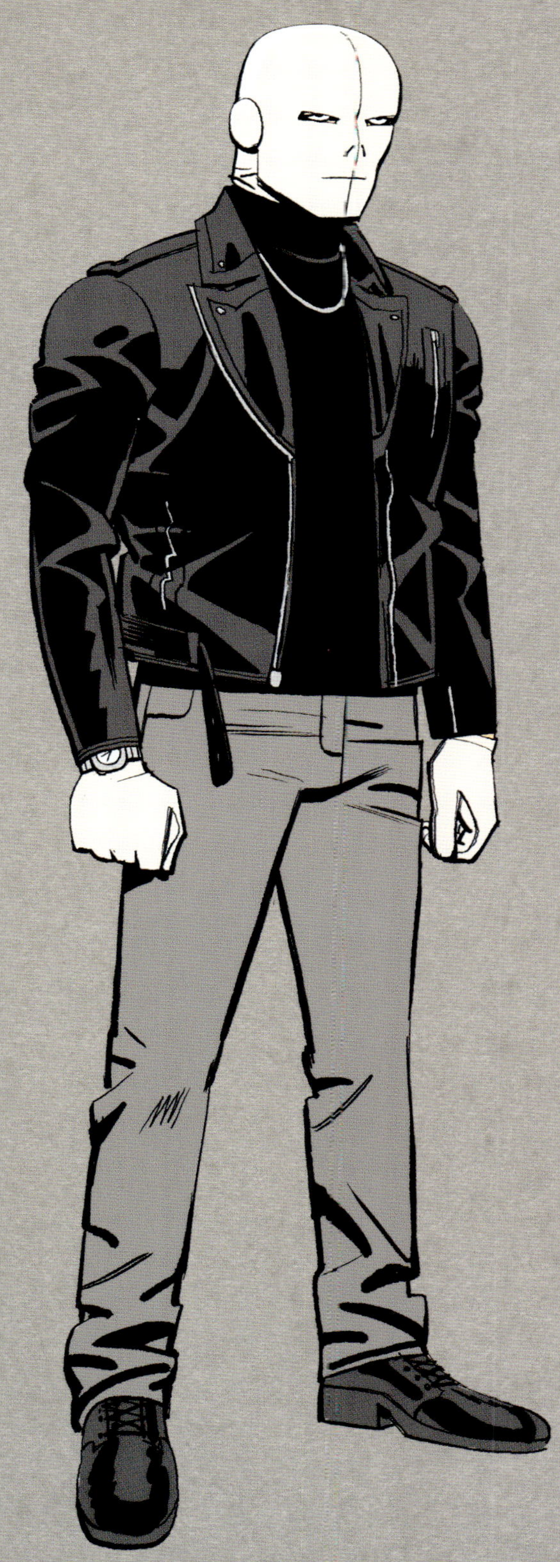

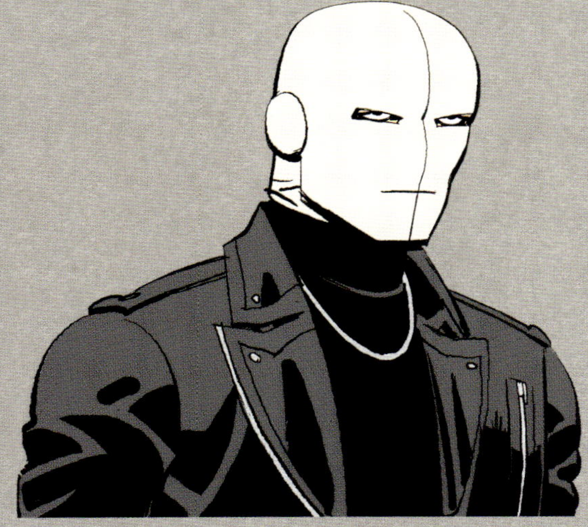

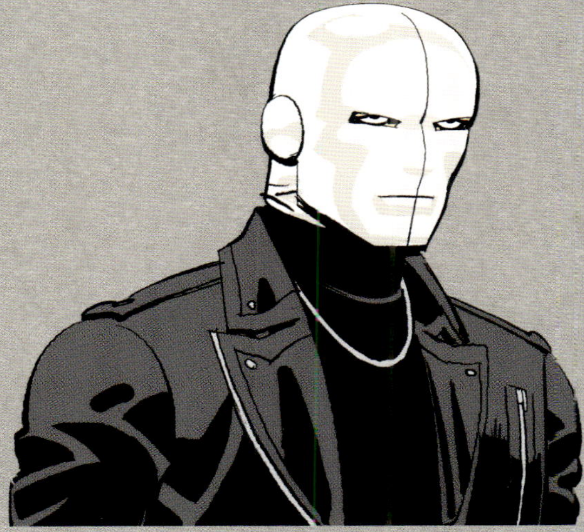

OPPOSITE Chris Samnee (line art) and W. Scott Forbes (color)
THIS PAGE Leonardo Romero

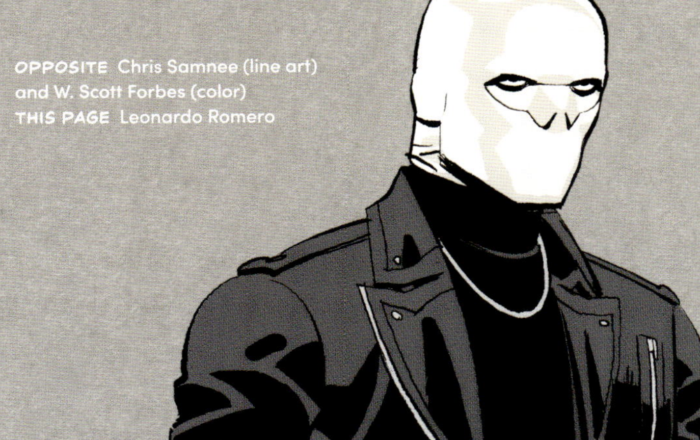

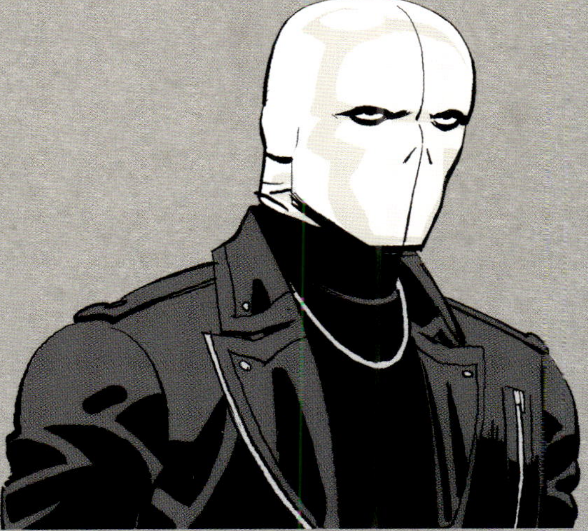

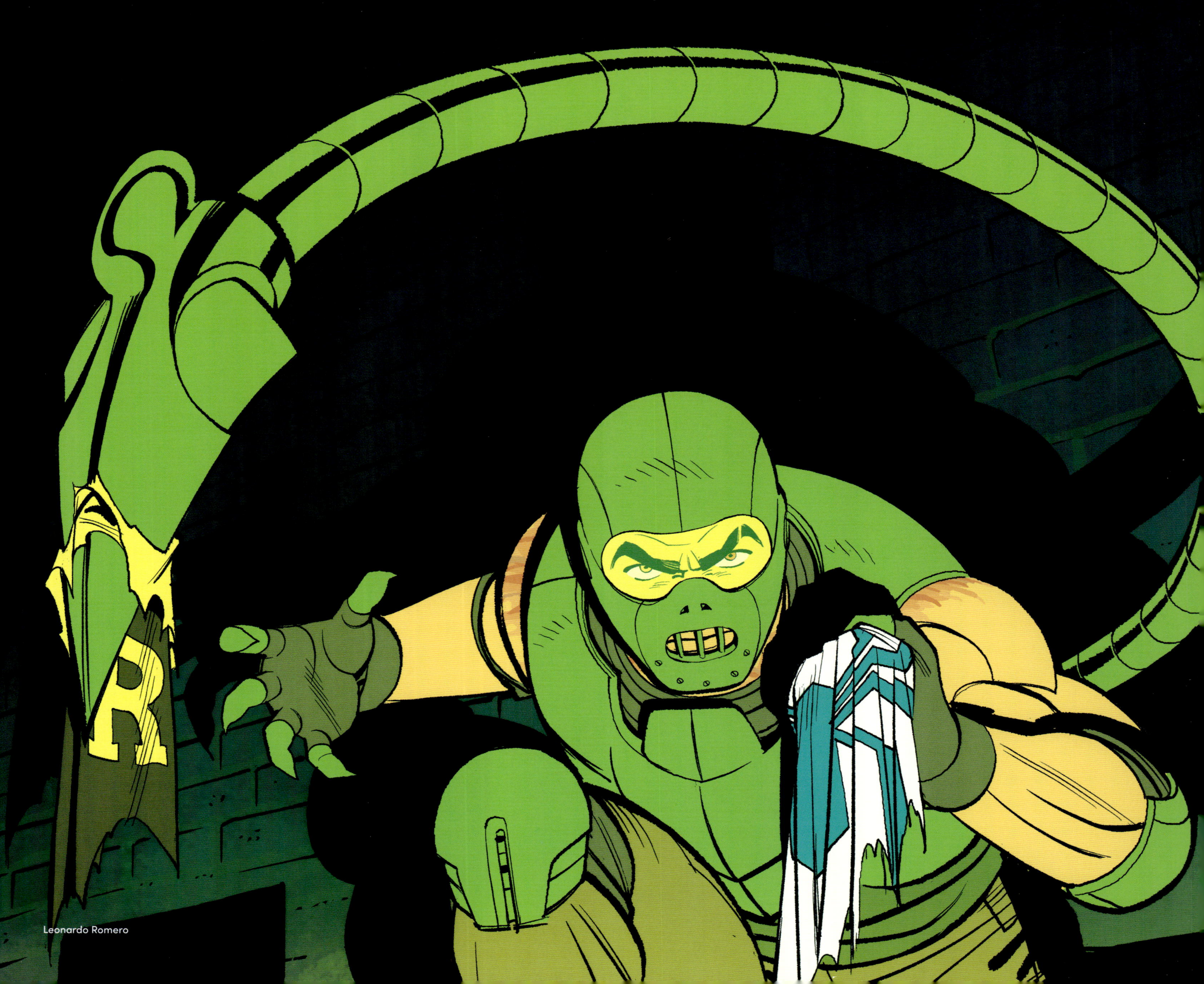
Leonardo Romero

EPISODE NINE

HERO OR MENACE

IN THE AFTERMATH OF DR. OCTAVIUS'S ARREST AND IMPRISONMENT, NORMAN TELLS HIM THE TECHNOLOGY HE DEVELOPED WILL NOW BE THE PROPERTY OF OSCORP. MEANWHILE, PETER STOPS THE 110TH STREET GANG'S ATTEMPT TO STEAL THAT TECH AS IT'S BEING TRANSPORTED, AND LONNIE IS EXPOSED TO A MYSTERIOUS GAS DEVELOPED BY OCTAVIUS. HE EMERGES FROM THE CLOUD OF GAS WITH NEWFOUND SUPER-POWERS, WHICH HE USES TO HELP PETER FIGHT SCORPION. THE VILLAIN GETS THE UPPER HAND ON LONNIE AND TRIES TO BURY HIM UNDER RUBBLE, BUT PETER STEPS IN. IN THE HEAT OF BATTLE, PETER NEARLY KILLS SCORPION, BUT LONNIE PERSUADES HIM NOT TO GO TOO FAR. BACK AT OSCORP, SCIENTISTS ARE TRYING TO DUPLICATE SPIDER-MAN'S SUPER-POWERS BY INJECTING A SPIDER WITH PETER'S BLOOD . . .

IN MANY WAYS, the first season's penultimate episode could be the finale, says Executive Producer/Showrunner Jeff Trammell. "There's so much happening, and there are so many character payoffs here," he notes. "One of the key things in this episode is seeing Peter and Nico rekindle their friendship, not just because Peter apologizes to her but also because Nico now understands why Peter didn't tell her his secret. I didn't want it to feel like Nico was upset because she felt entitled as a friend to know this secret. Getting to hear her side of it was very important to me."

The episode is also another big one for Scorpion because it's the first time he's seen with his helmet on. "Some may not have caught that the reason he's wearing it is because he got hit in the face," Trammell shares. "We also see that he still has radiation burns from episode seven. Each time we see him, he has changed a little bit more."

Trammell also points out that this is the first time we see Peter wearing the famous red and blue suit. "I wanted this moment to feel earned," he says. "This is the first time he is having a big save moment, and I don't think there would be a better time to debut this classic suit in our series."

Lonnie is carrying a lot on his shoulders in the ninth episode, as well. "He gets his Tombstone powers thanks to the gang's raid on Doc Ock's warehouse," Trammel says. "We finally get Peter teaming up with him against Gargan, just like when they fist-bumped in episode one. I still get chills watching that fight because so much work went into making sure that everything felt congruent. When you hear that music by Leo Birenberg and Zach Robinson, and you watch these two characters team up, [it's] one of my favorite moments. We also see Lonnie becoming the captain of his new team, essentially when Big Don abandons the 110th."

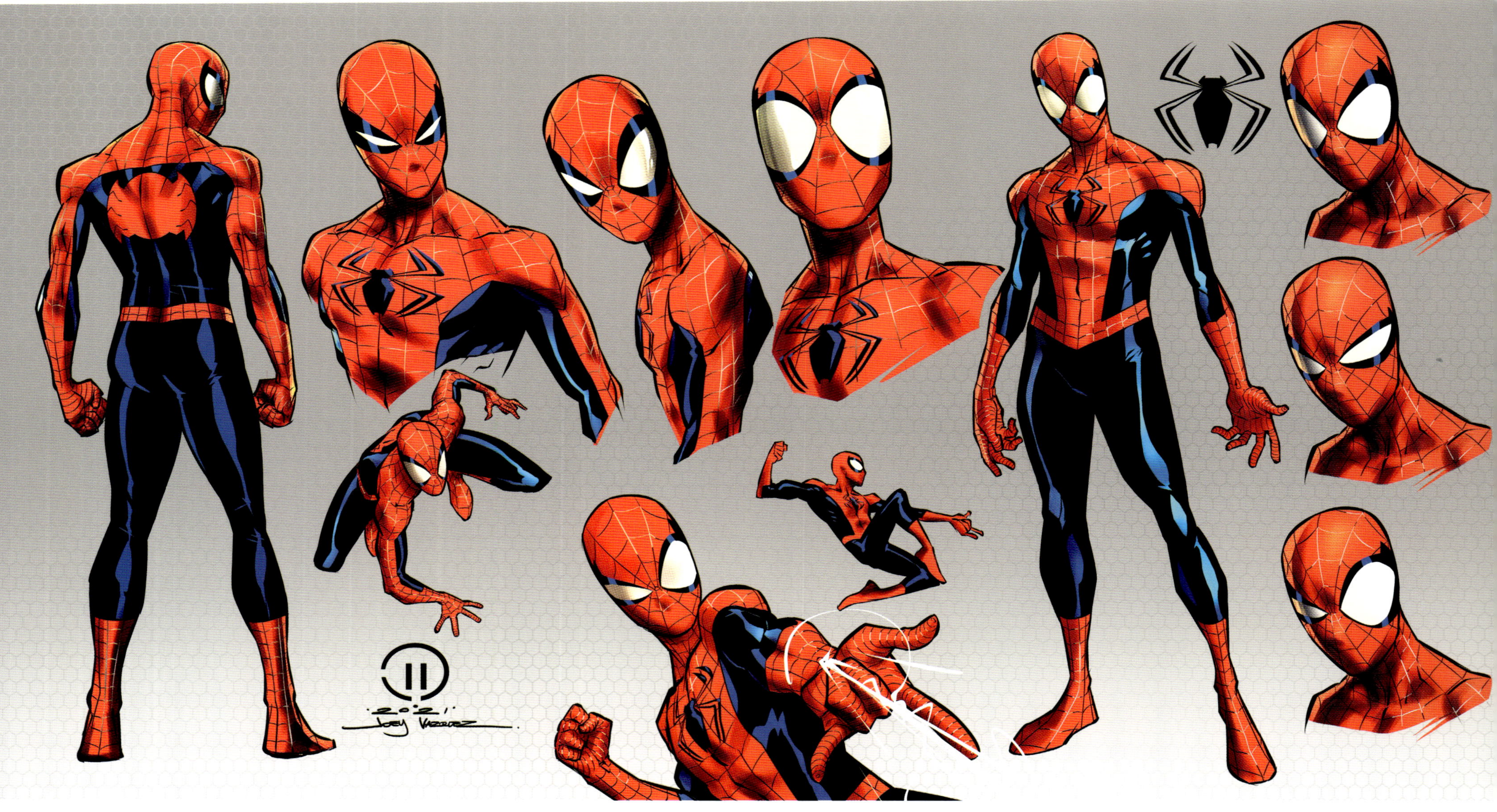

Trammell reveals that seeing Lonnie take the moral high ground to stop Spider-Man from killing Scorpion was quite a big moment in the show. "The thinking is always 'No one is perfect, and anyone can falter,'" he explains. "Spider-Man could easily go down the wrong path, and Tombstone could easily do the right thing. Despite everything that Gargan has done to Lonnie and his friends, he [Lonnie] stands up and stops Spider-Man from making a huge mistake, which was very important for me."

Liza Singer, who directed this key episode, also believes that the ninth episode did a great job putting a bow on the Lonnie and Peter story arc. "It culminated with the Scorpion storyline," she adds. "I had a lot of fun with the final sequence. We all really tried to make it feel rewarding and a payoff to the adventure we've seen unfold throughout the season. It was also one of the toughest ones because of all the tracking we had to do for all the characters and figuring out their positions as they go back and forth. All the artists were giving us their input and worked a lot on that scene to figure out this puzzle. And things will get even more complicated next season!"

ABOVE Joey Vazquez
OPPOSITE Leonardo Romero

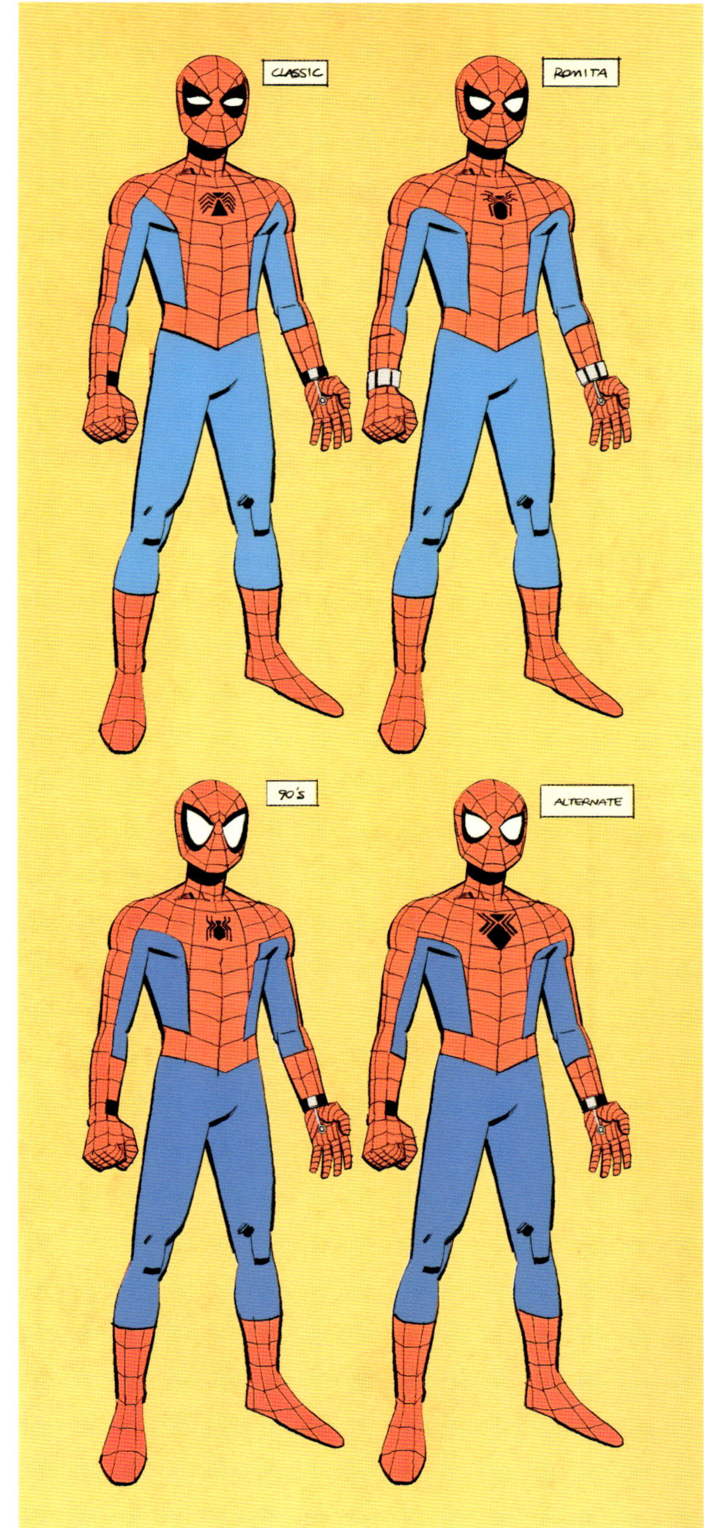
CLASSIC
ROMITA
90's
ALTERNATE

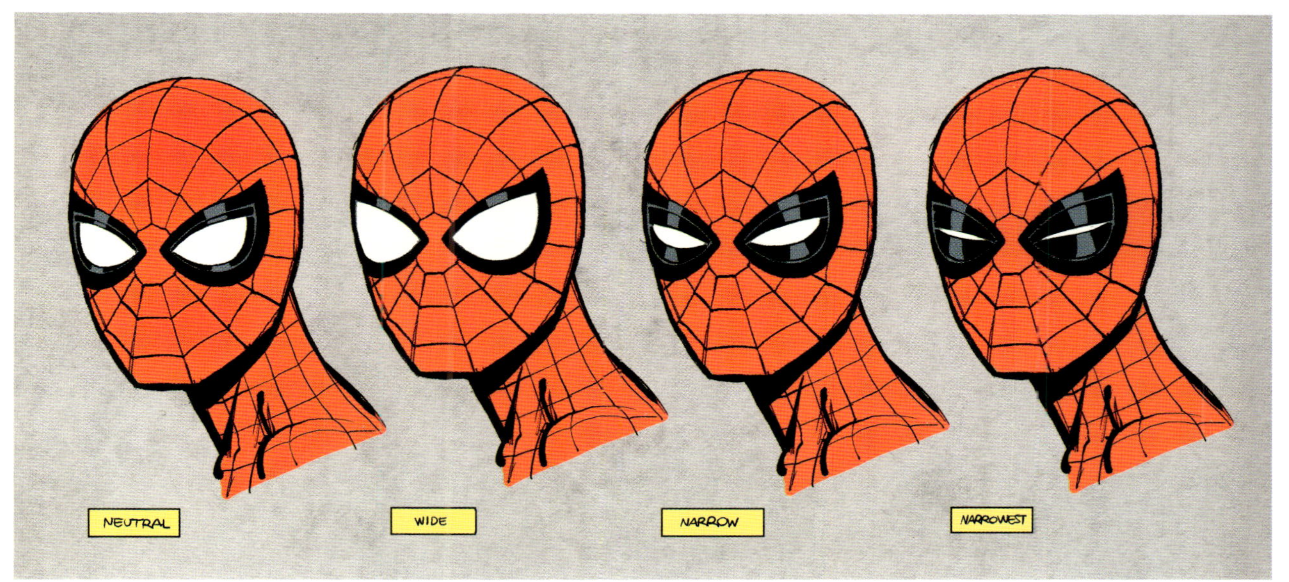
NEUTRAL
WIDE
NARROW
NARROWEST

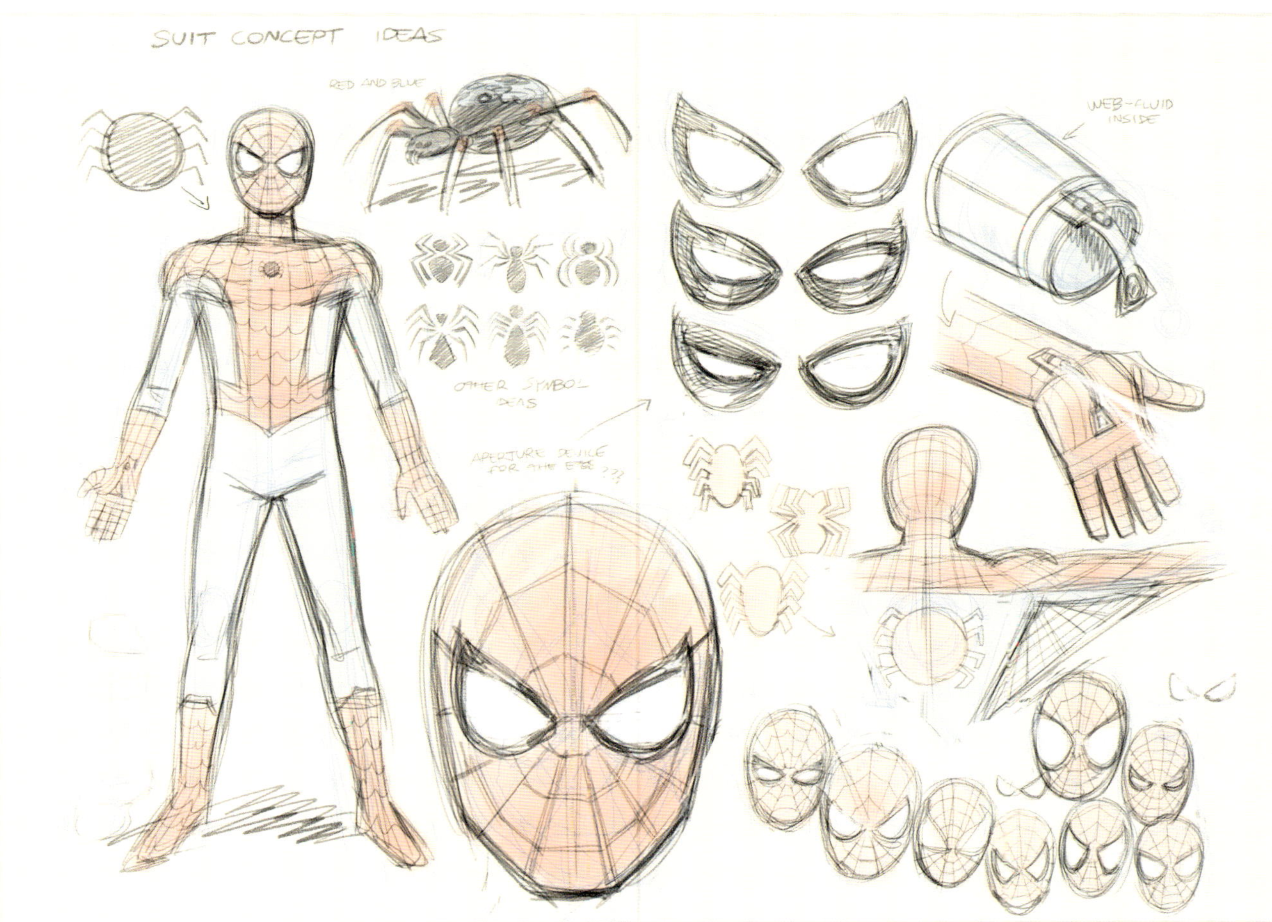
SUIT CONCEPT IDEAS
RED AND BLUE
WEB-FLUID INSIDE
OTHER SYMBOL IDEAS
APERTURE DEVICE FOR THE EYE???

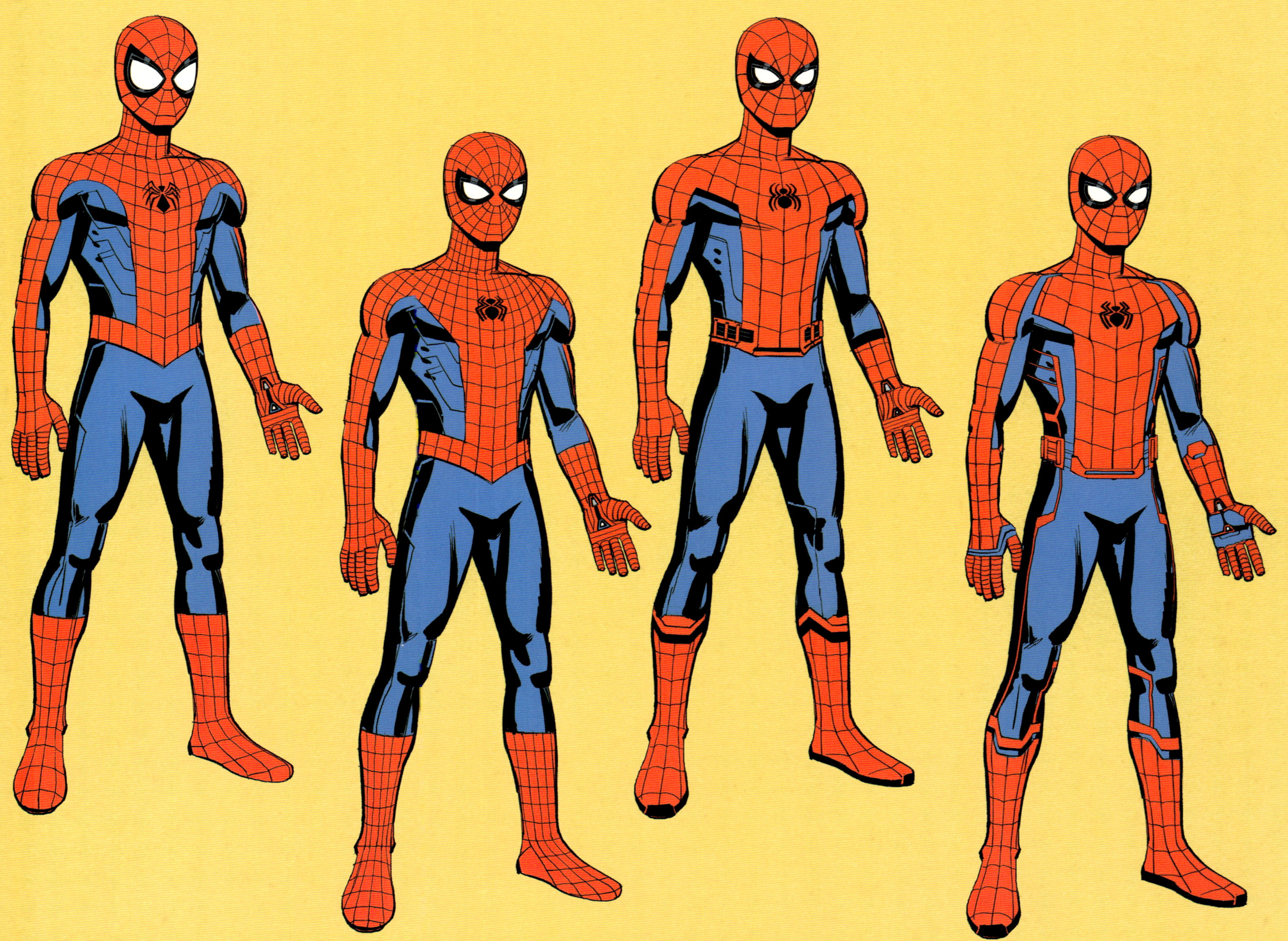

Leonardo Romero

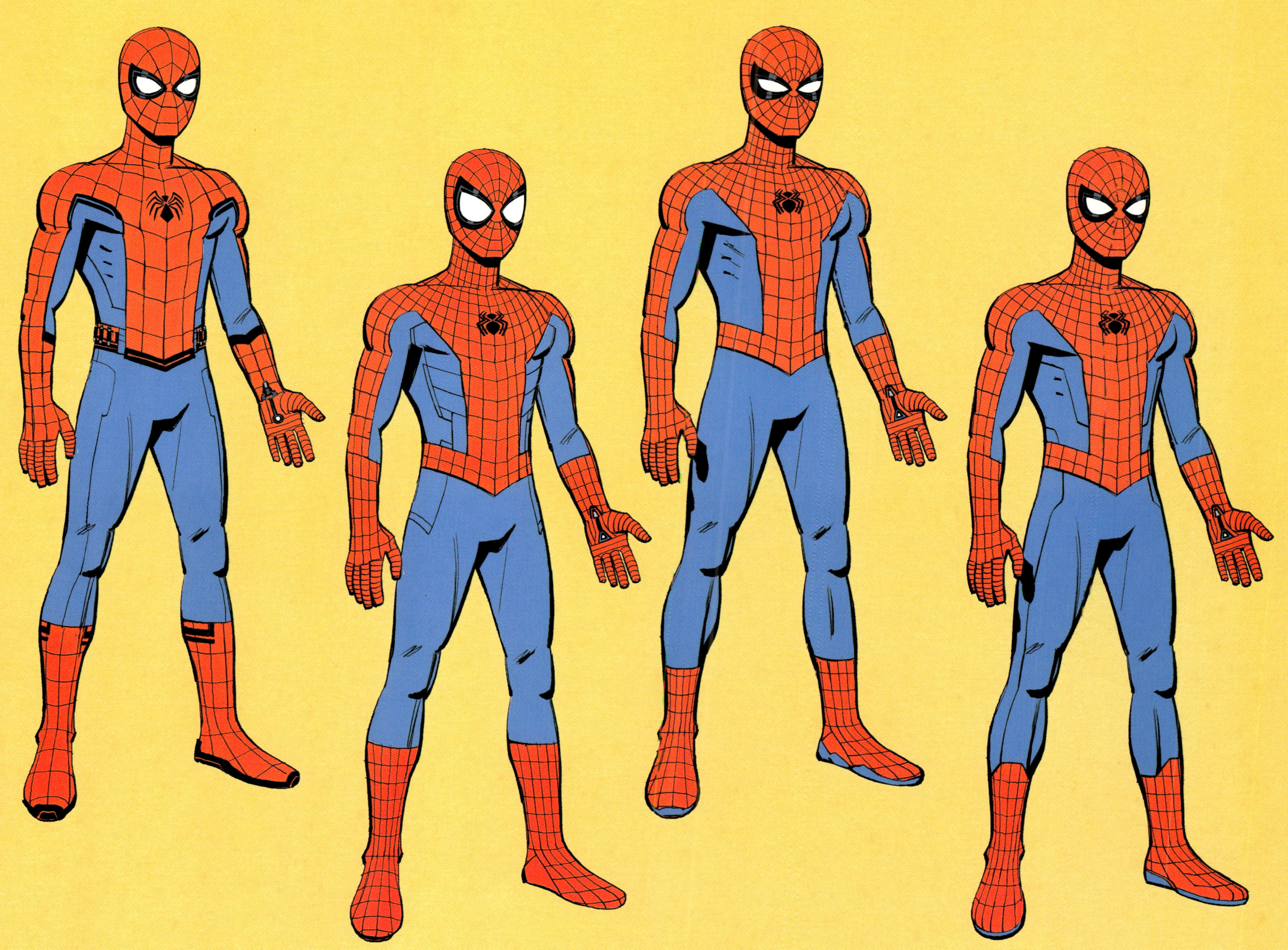

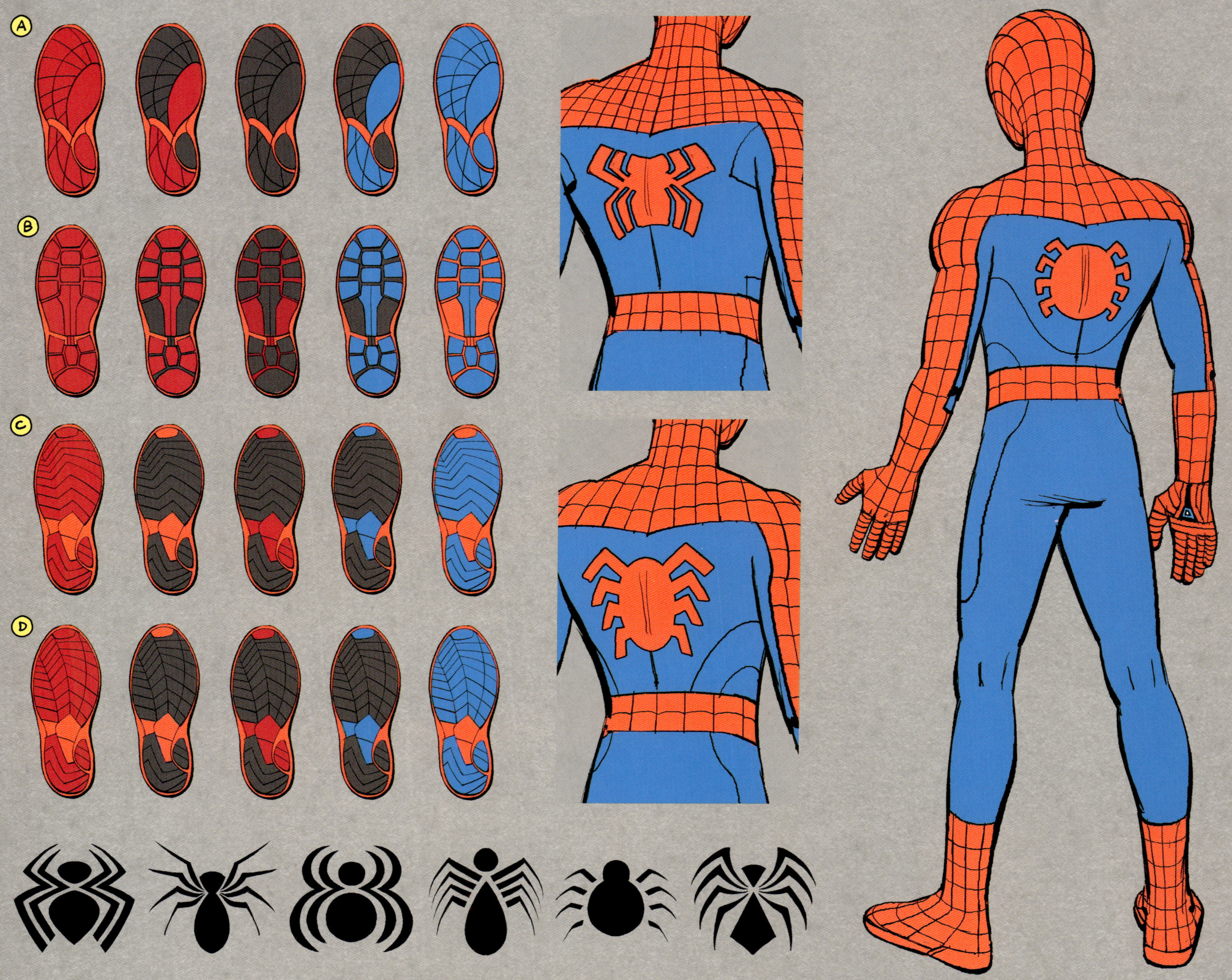
A
B
C
D

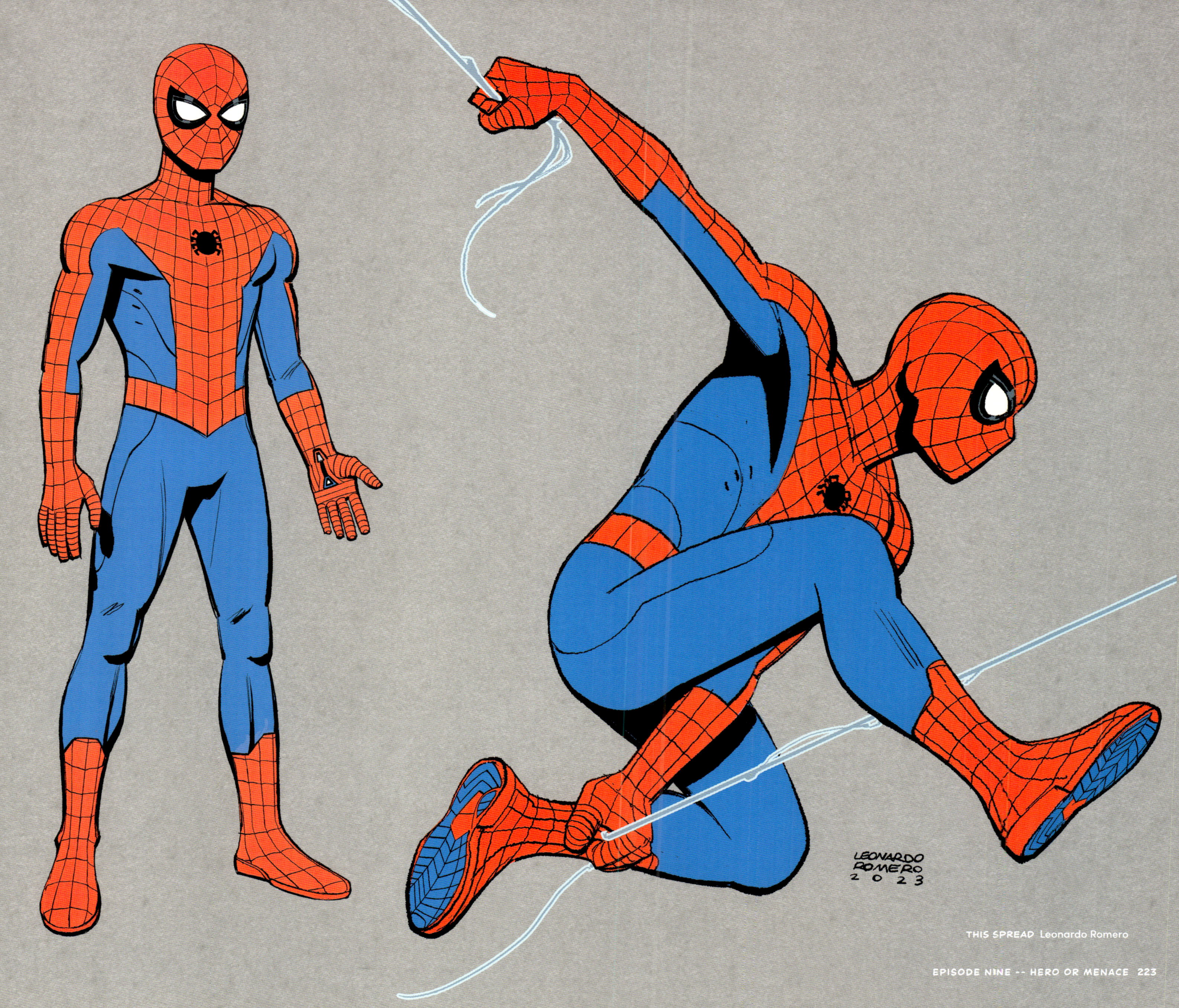

THIS SPREAD Leonardo Romero

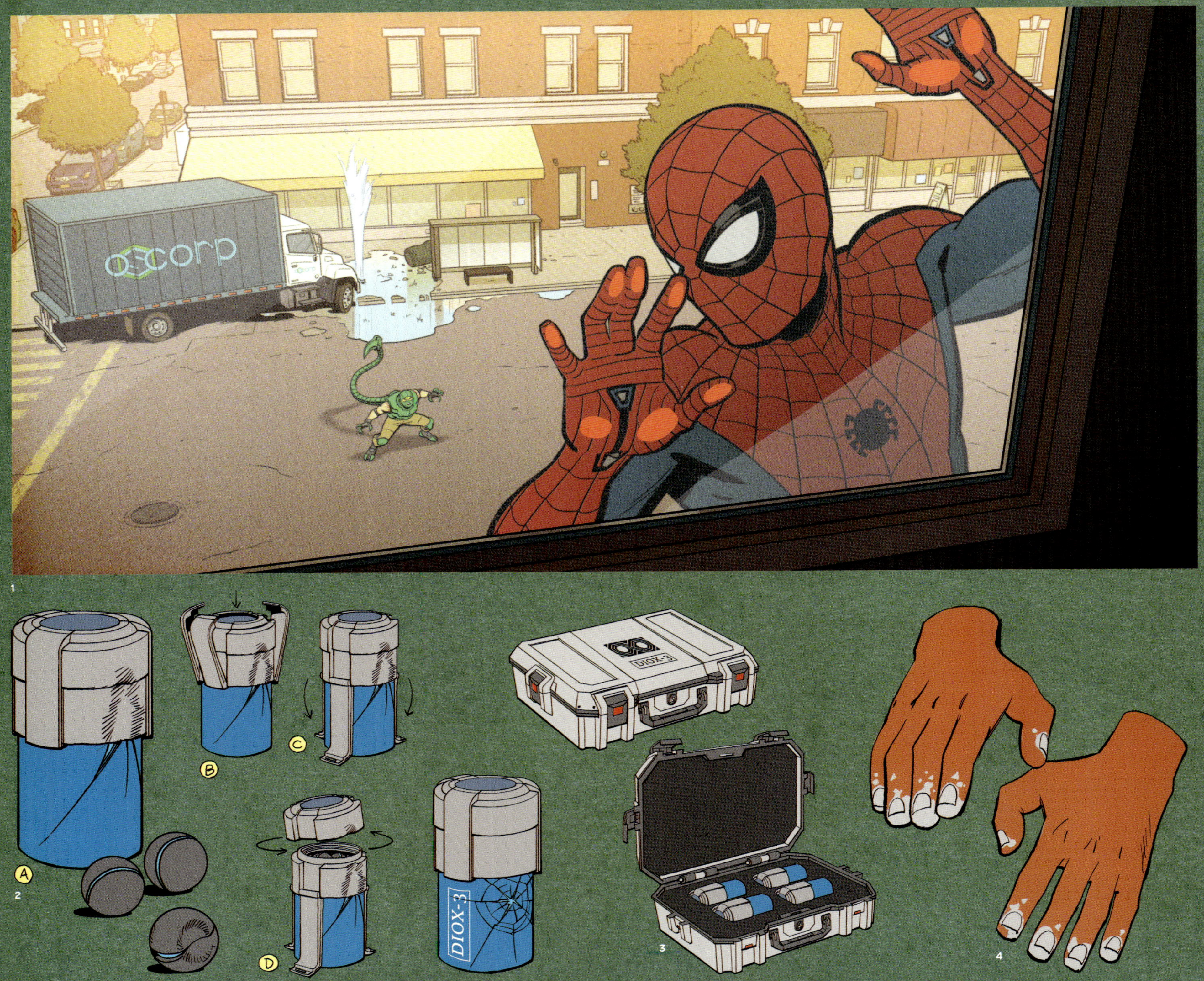

1

2

3

4

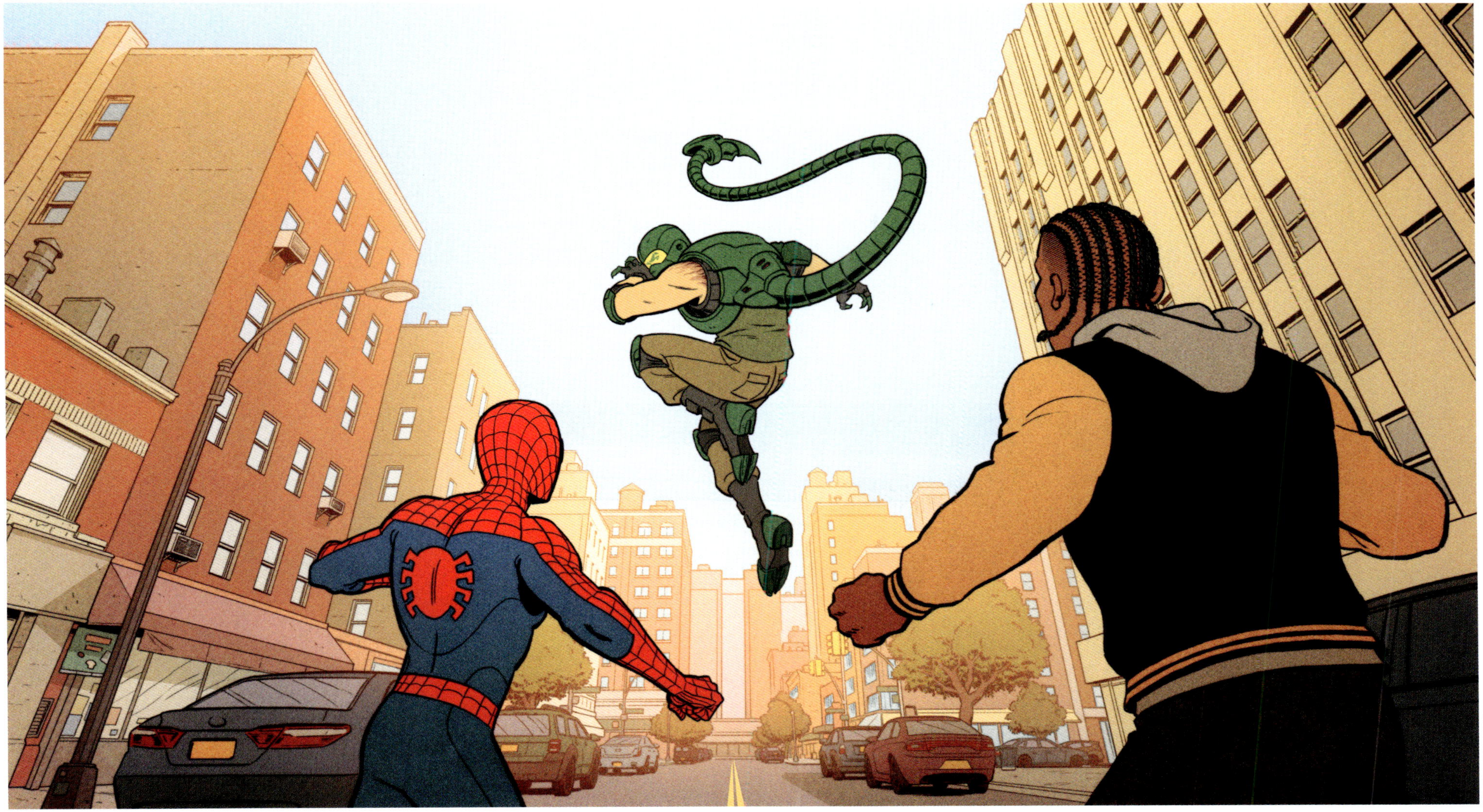

5

1 Paolo Rivera (line art) and W. Scott Forbes (color)
2–4 Leonardo Romero
5 Paolo Rivera (line art) and W. Scott Forbes (color)
6–7 Leonardo Romero

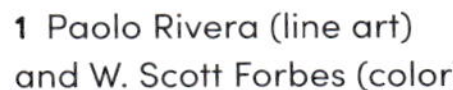

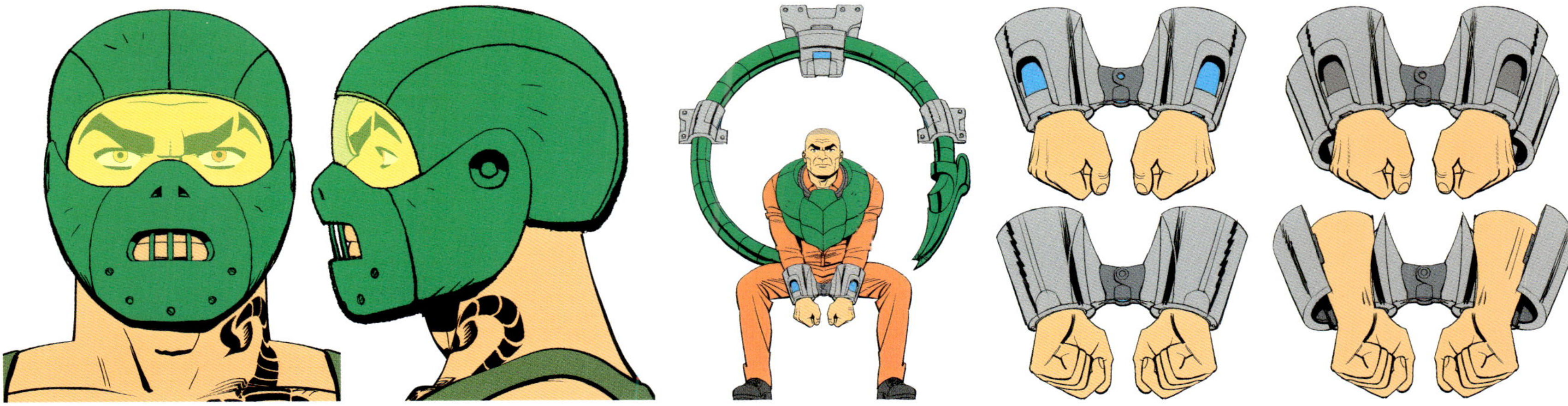

6

7

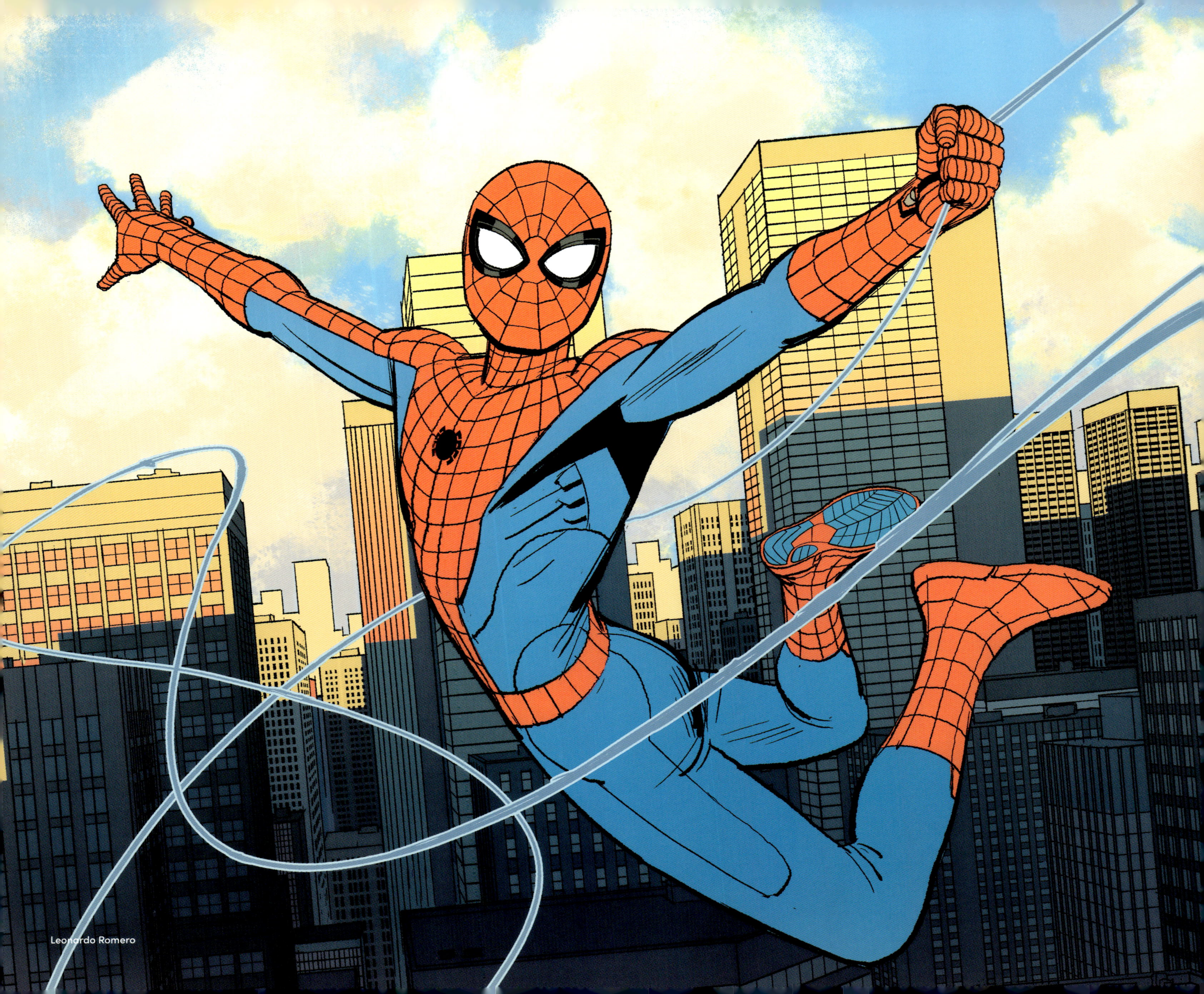

Leonardo Romero

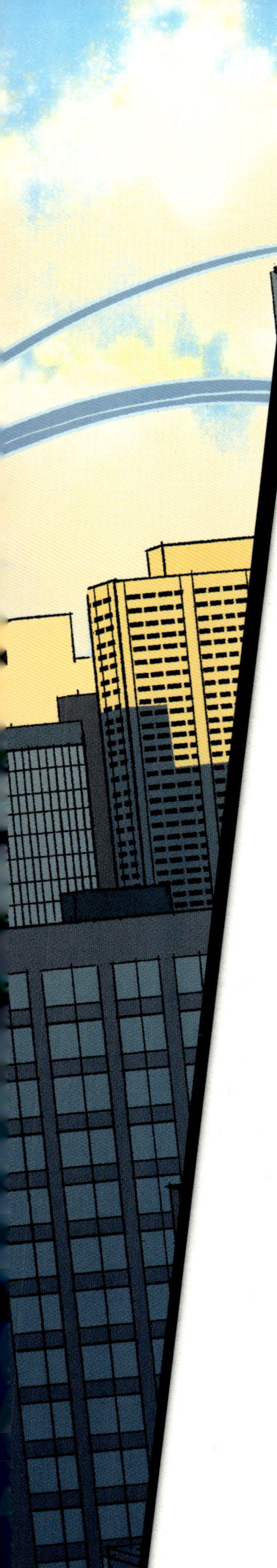

EPISODE TEN

IF THIS BE MY DESTINY...

TIME TRAVEL FANS HAVE A LOT TO CHEW ON IN THIS EPISODE, AS NORMAN REVEALS THAT PROJECT MONOLITH IS CREATING A GATEWAY TO SPACE, WHICH LEADS TO DOCTOR STRANGE POPPING IN TO STOP IT. WHEN THE SYMBIOTIC ALIEN EMERGES FROM THE OPEN GATEWAY, STRANGE CREATES A PORTAL THAT TAKES HIM AND THE CREATURE BACK TO PETER'S FIRST DAY AT MIDTOWN HIGH SCHOOL. THINGS GET COMPLICATED WHEN ONE OF THE SPIDERS INJECTED WITH PETER'S BLOOD ESCAPES THROUGH THE PORTAL AND BITES THE YOUNGER PETER. AFTER PETER SENDS THE ALIEN BACK, PART OF THE SYMBIOTE REMAINS AND IS DISCOVERED BY NORMAN. HARRY CREATES HIS OWN COMPANY TO SUPPORT YOUNG GENIUSES AND INVITES AMADEUS CHO (WHO REJECTS AN OFFER TO WORK FOR OSCORP), JEANNE (A.K.A. FINESSE), AND LONNIE TO JOIN HIM.

"WE GET TO SEE OUR FAVORITE TRIO of Peter, Nico, and Harry all on the same page and working together for the first time in this episode," says Executive Producer/Showrunner Jeff Trammell. "Peter has also endeared himself to Pearl, and he's no longer a needy, younger boy in her eyes. Then, as we go to Oscorp, we learn that everything that Peter has been doing throughout the entire season has essentially been in service of something that he didn't know about. Norman has been lying to him all along. I thought it was nice that we were building everything up to lead to the big Einstein-Rosen bridge portal to anywhere in the universe."

Knowing that Doctor Strange and the Symbiote will go back in time to the first few minutes of the opening episode colors how we see the final episode. "We were able to build the fight scene so that Strange is taking some big hits because he is worn out and that allows him to make slight mistakes, as well as seeing the Symbiote activate the Time Stone right before they go through the portal," explains Trammell. "I always thought that was a fun shift from the way Spider-Man [was] first created—because he gets bitten by a spider that has his own blood. It's a great instance of the bootstrap paradox." (In theoretical physics, the bootstrap paradox occurs when an object or piece of information is sent back in time and becomes trapped in a loop where there is no discernible origin point.)

The final scene of the season reveals Peter's dad is alive and in prison. "A lot of people may not pick up on this, but in the sixth episode, Peter, Nico, and Harry are talking about their parents, and Harry says, 'Your mom is an excellent cook!' Peter says, 'May is actually my aunt. My mom passed away a while back.' We specifically made him say 'my mom' and not 'my parents.' So, yes, Richard Parker has always been there, and I'm really excited to dig into that story. There are so many instances of Peter's life that we don't know about, and they have had big impacts on him."

Finale director Stu Livingston says the big portal fight scene was one of the most memorable parts of the half hour for him. "The scene was largely storyboarded by Steve Walker. We were crafting our spaces, and design would then follow us. For the final scenes in the episode, I was using a lot of camera movements and wipes to bring a lot of momentum to it. Even when May is talking to Richard, I'm holding the shot on her to show her discomfort and to build up to the fact that it's Richard she's visiting in prison. That final image, too, where we see Spidey flying straight at the camera, has to be one of the top five most gratifying experiences of my whole career."

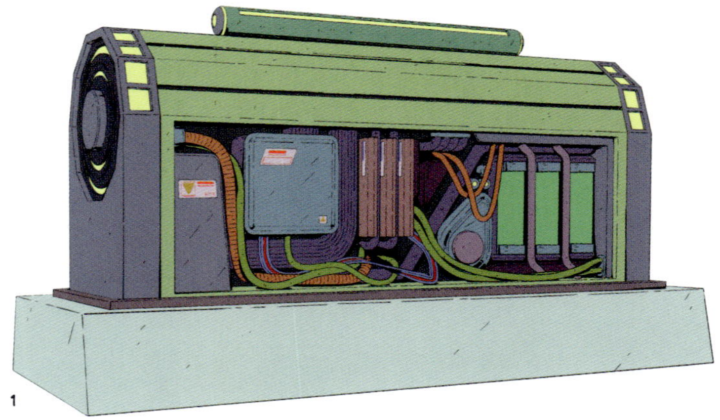

1

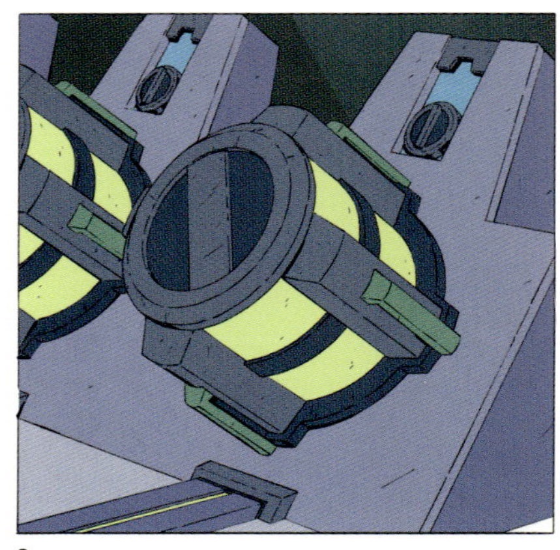

2

3

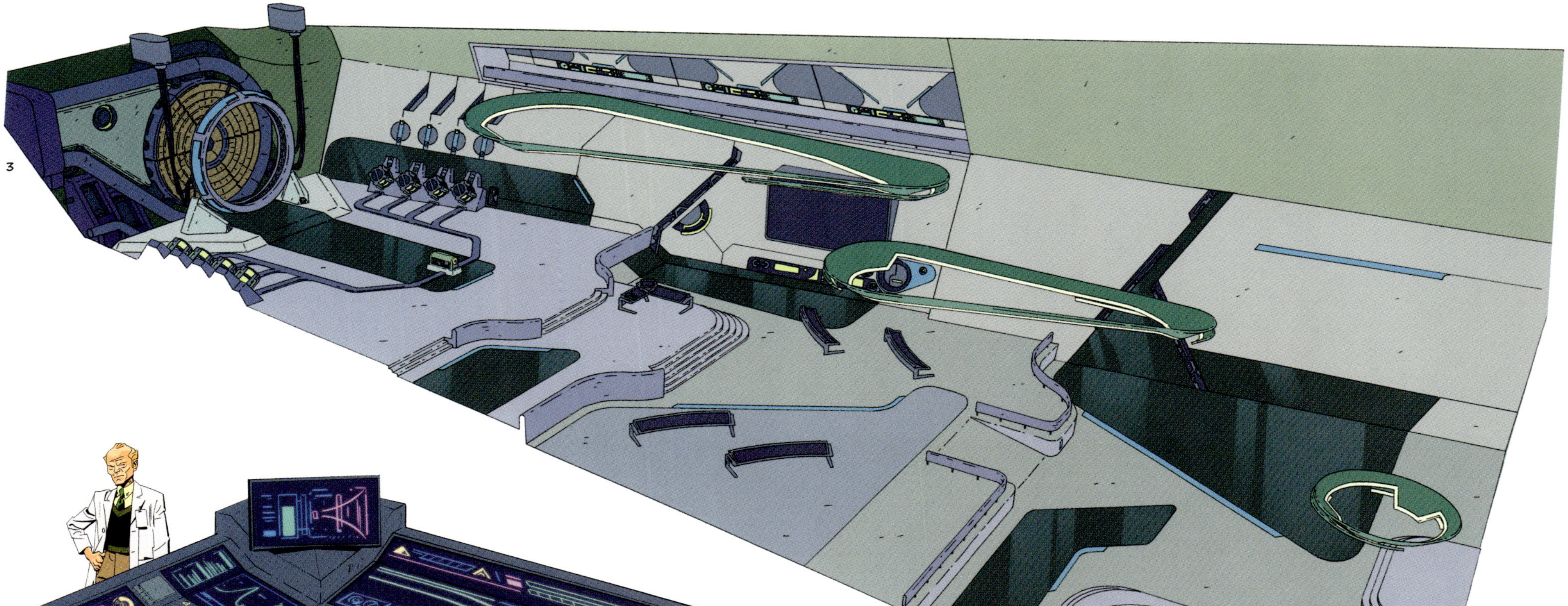

4

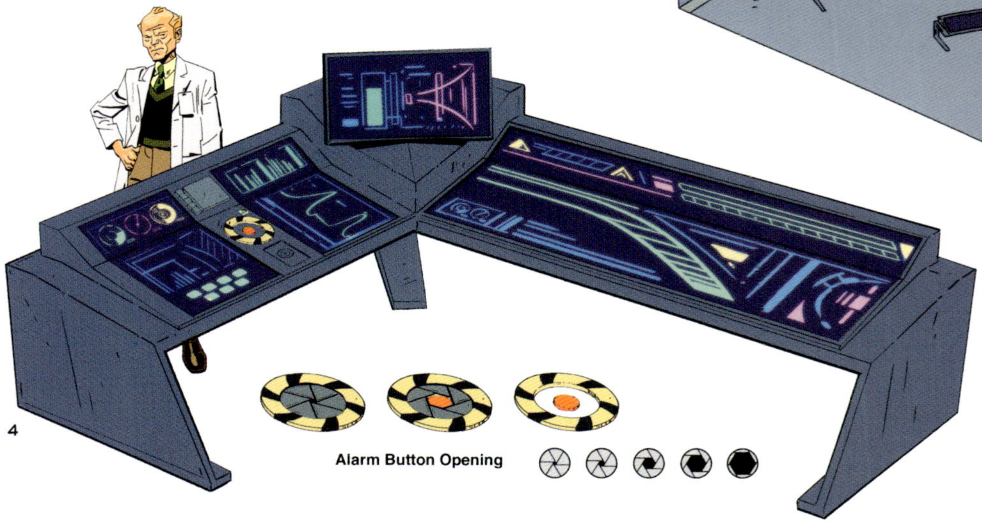

Alarm Button Opening

1–3 Corwin Herse-Woo
4 Monica Grue **5** Mel Zwyer
6 Paolo Rivera (line art) and W. Scott Forbes (color) **7** Sylvia Liu **8** Polygon Pictures

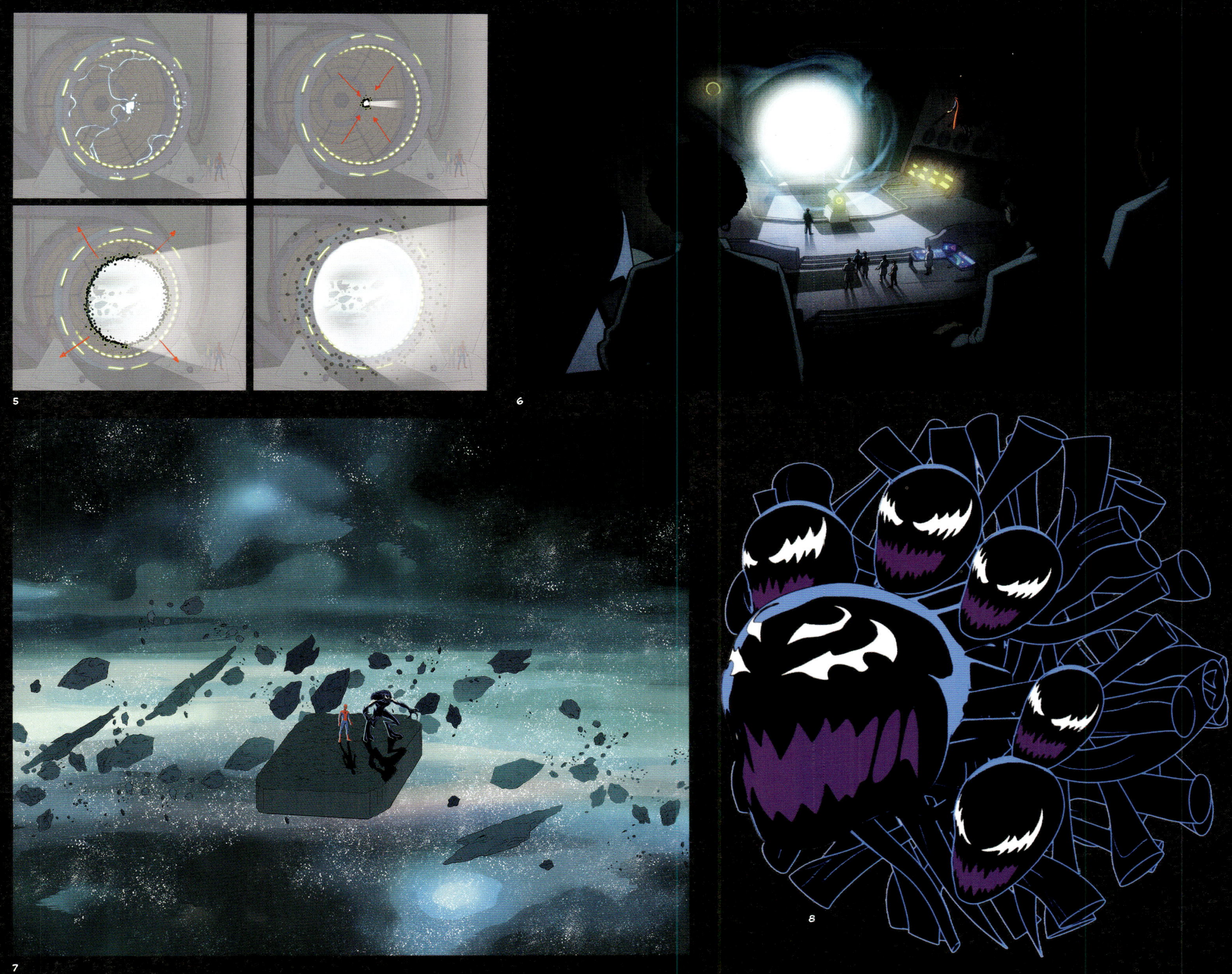

5

6

7

8

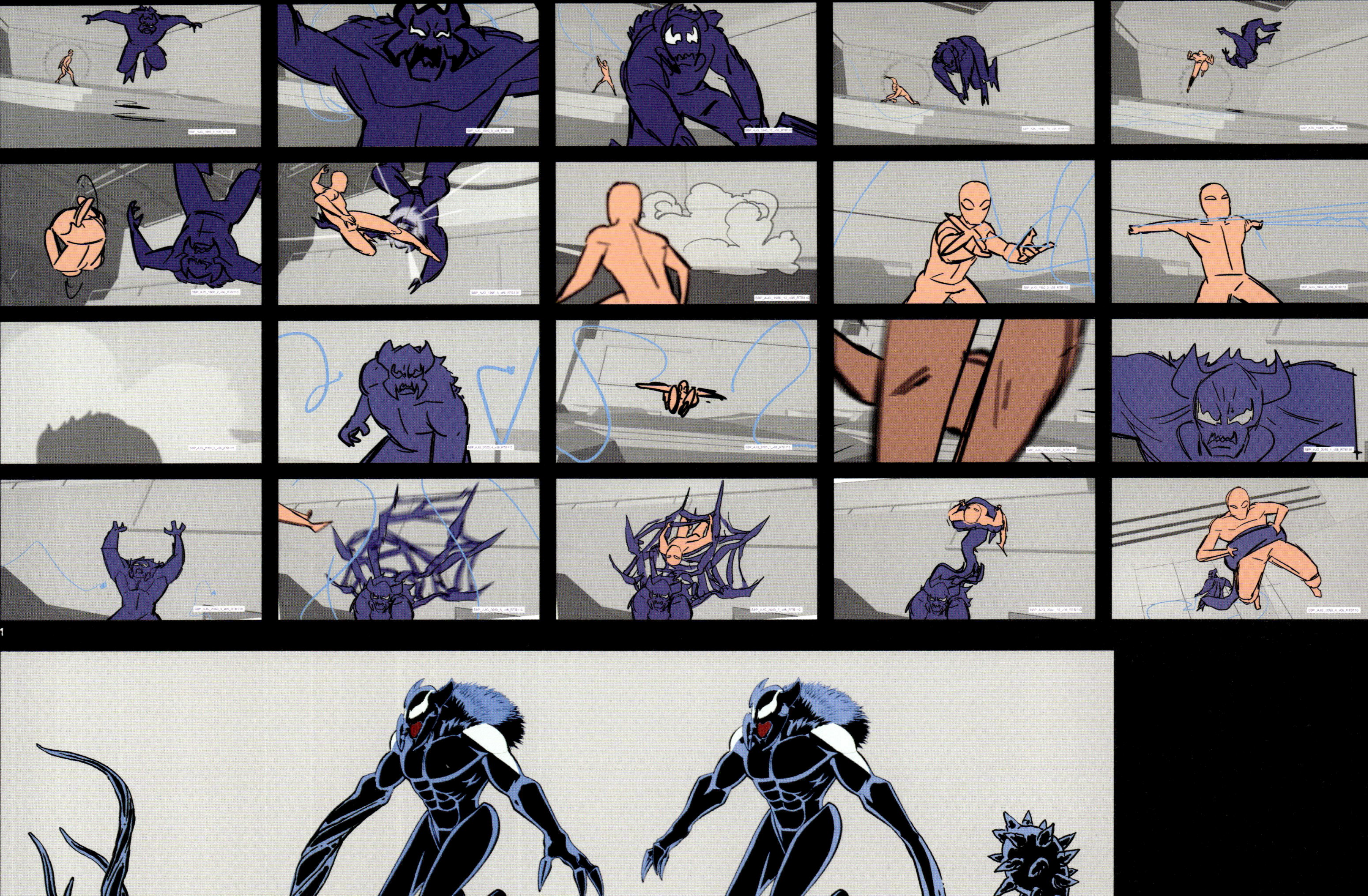

1

2

1 Steve Walker
2 Mel Zwyer
OPPOSITE Mel Zwyer

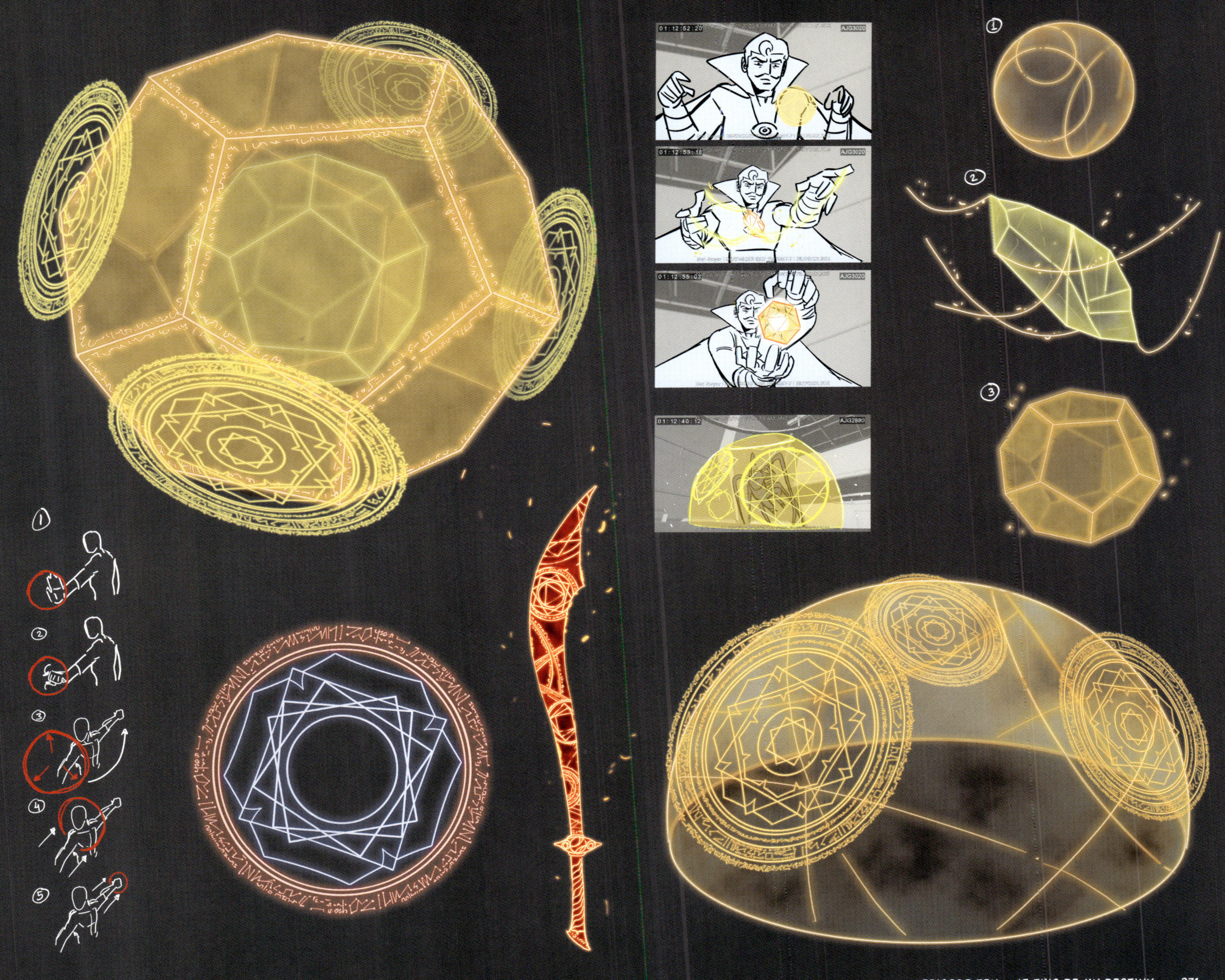

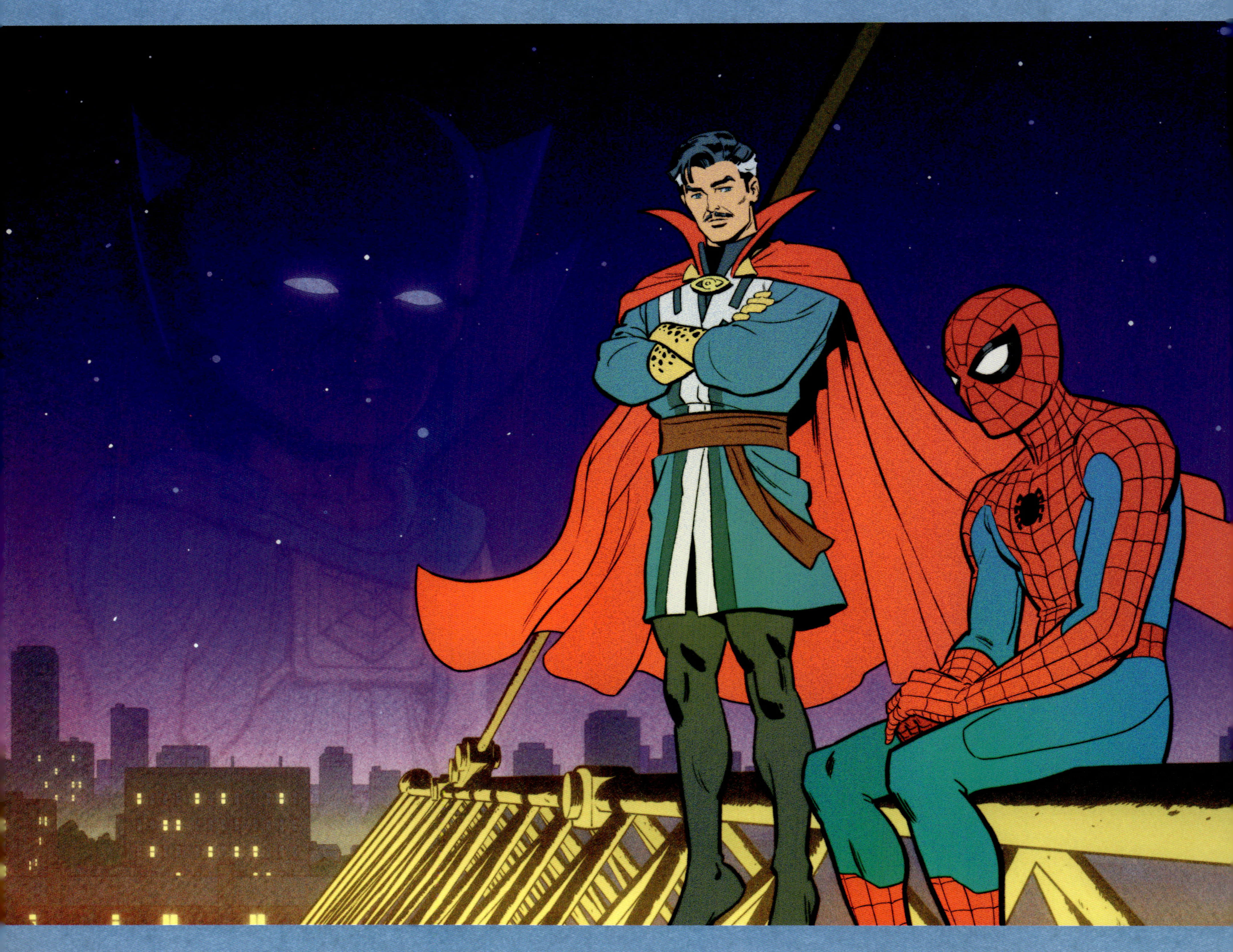

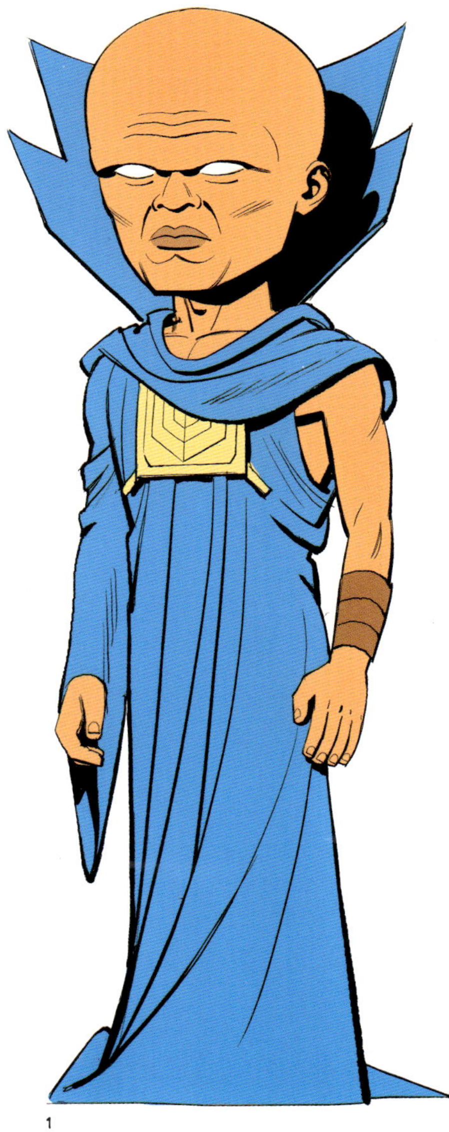

1

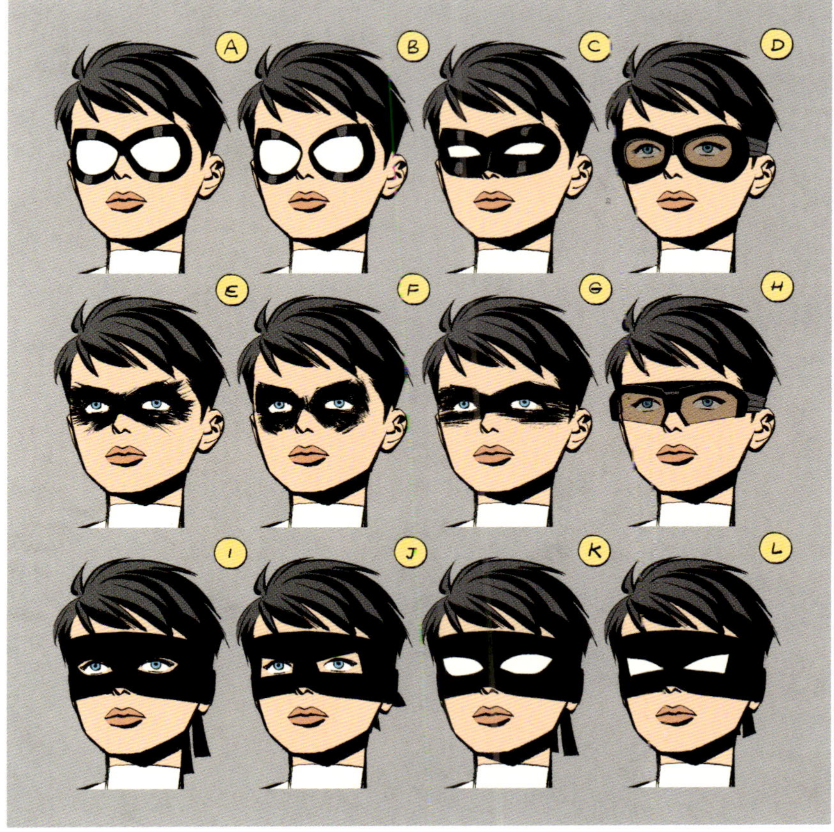

2

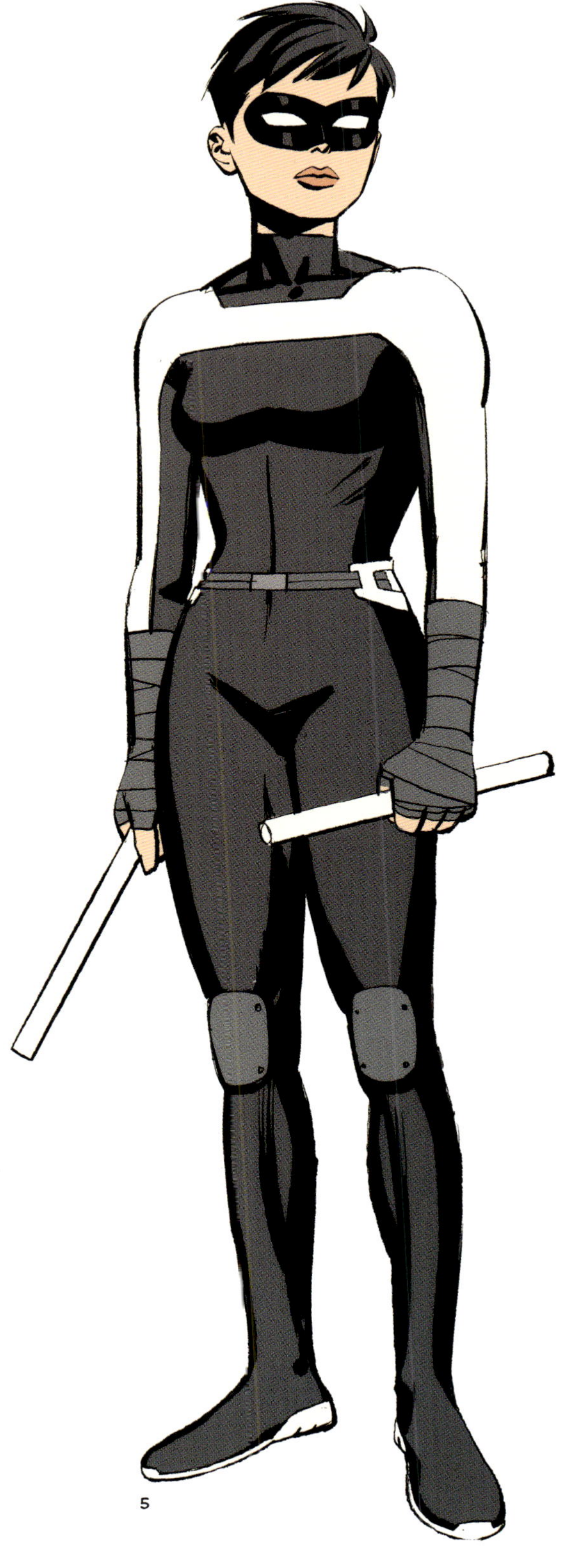

5

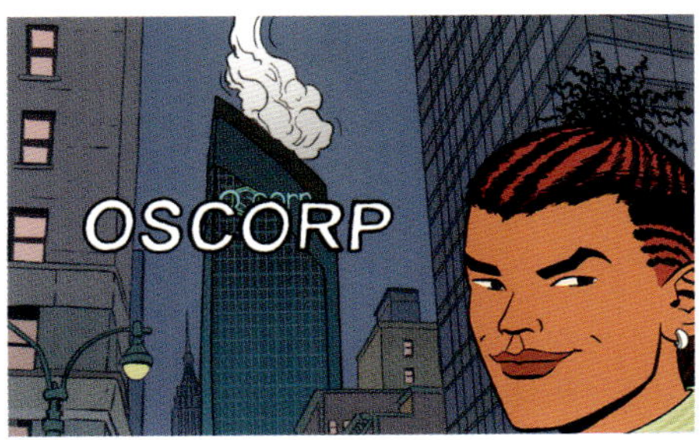

3

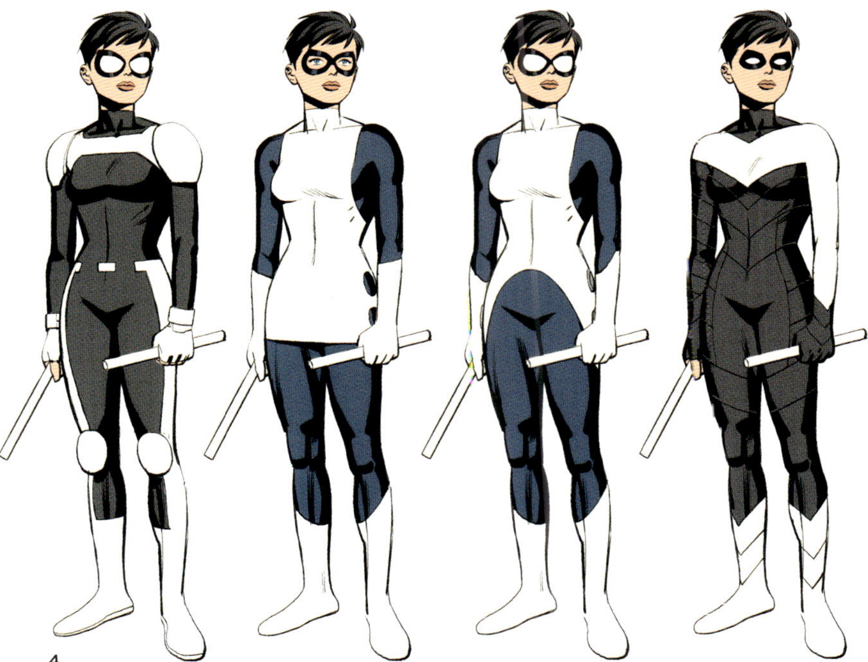

4

OPPOSITE Paolo Rivera (line art) and W. Scott Forbes (color) **1–2** Leonardo Romero **3** Mauricio Leone **4–5** Leonardo Romero

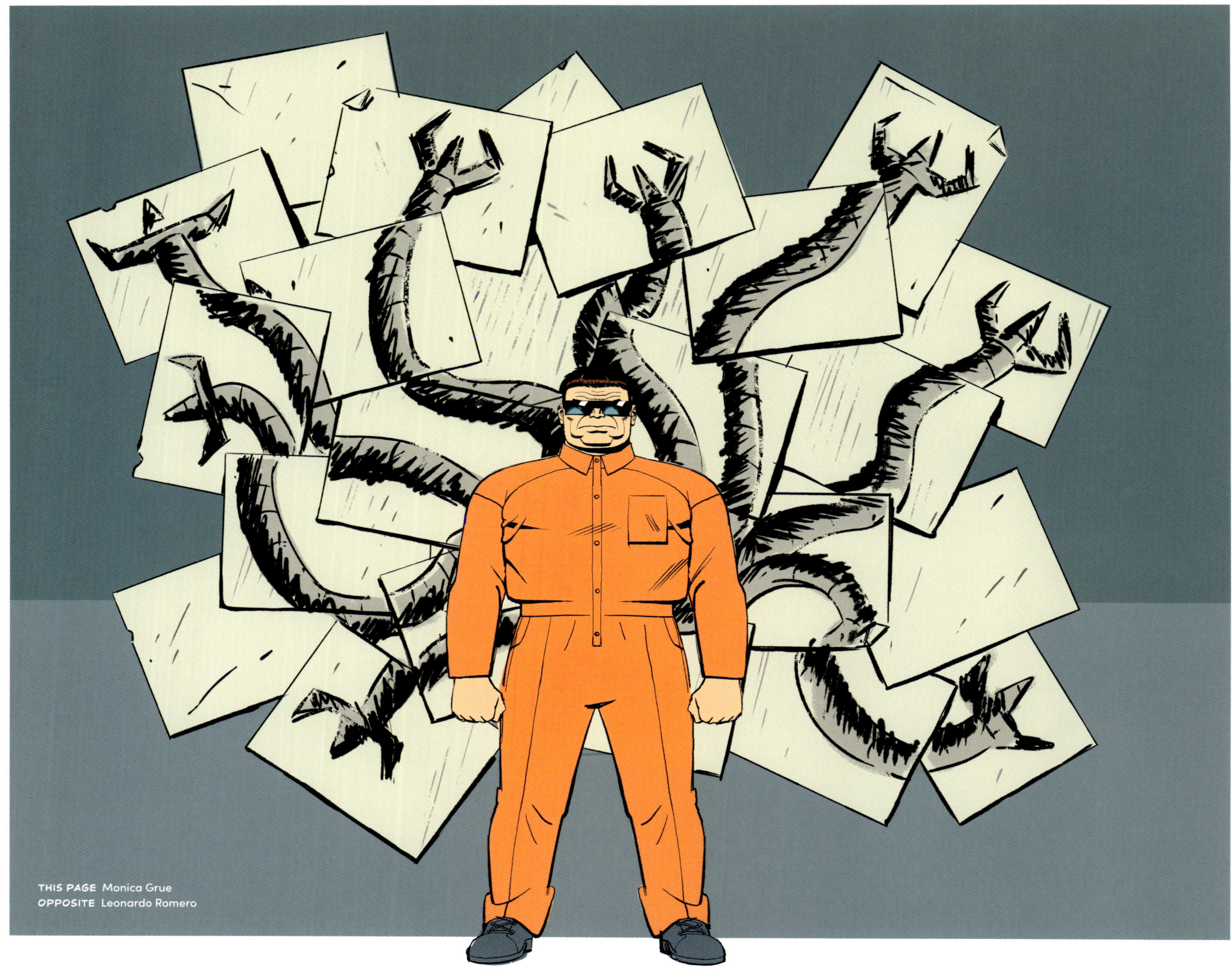

THIS PAGE Monica Grue
OPPOSITE Leonardo Romero

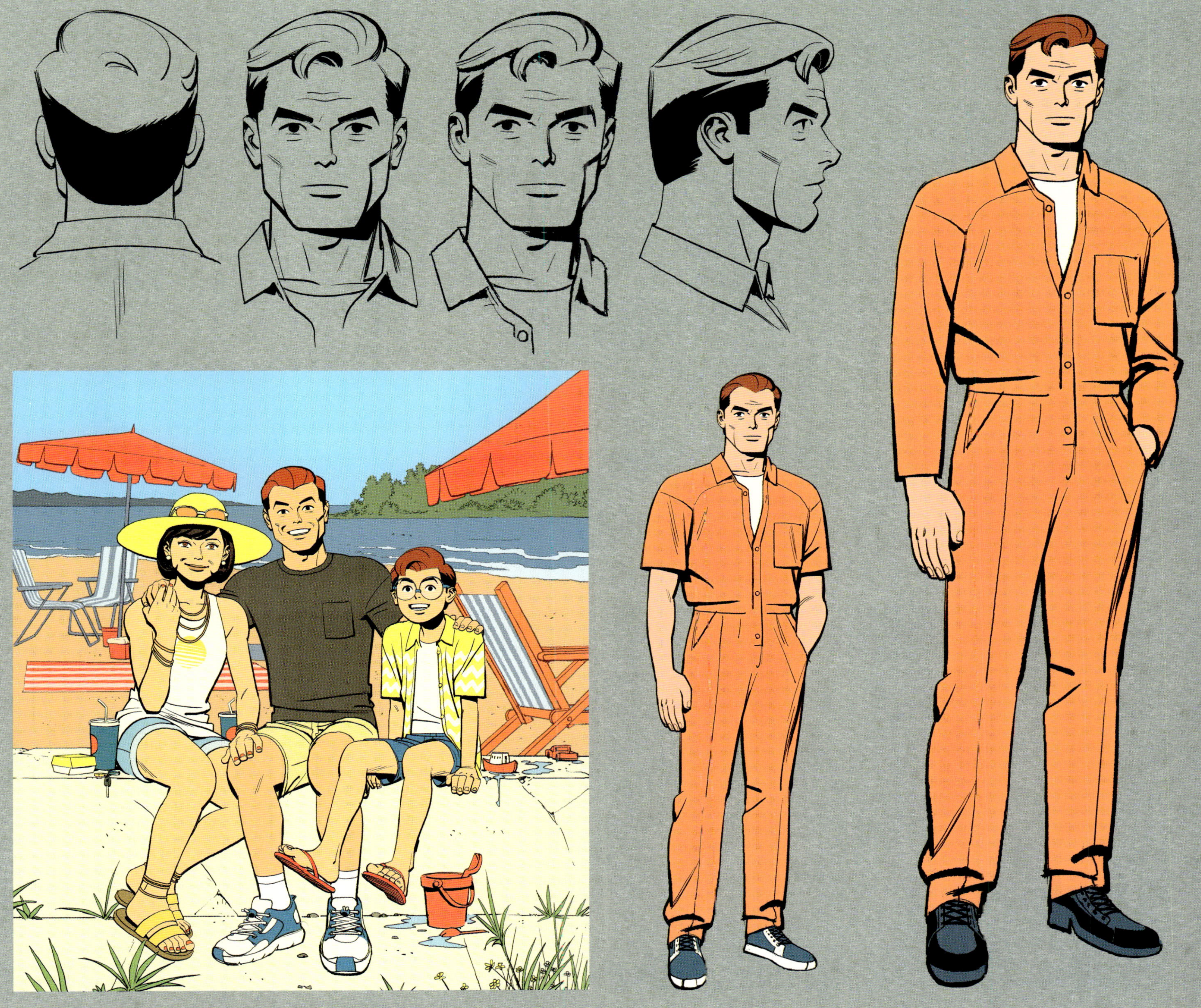

A BRIEF HISTORY OF ANIMATED SPIDER-MAN TV SHOWS

SEPTEMBER 9, 1967

SPIDER-MAN

The first animated series adaptation, *Spider-Man* (1967–1970), debuts on ABC and runs for three seasons (fifty-two episodes). The first season is executive produced by Robert L. Lawrence (Grantray-Lawrence Animation), and the second and third are executive produced by Ralph Bakshi (Krantz Films). Paul Soles voices Peter Parker.

SEPTEMBER 12, 1981

SPIDER-MAN

The second animated *Spider-Man* cartoon arrives in syndication. Executive produced by David H. DePatie and Lee Gunther (Marvel Productions), it runs for only one season (twenty-six episodes). Ted Schwartz voices Peter Parker.

SEPTEMBER 12, 1981

SPIDER-MAN AND HIS AMAZING FRIENDS

The crossover series *Spider-Man and His Amazing Friends* chronicles the adventures of Spider-Man, Iceman, and Firestar. Like *Spider-Man* (1981), it is executive produced by David H. DePatie and Lee Gunther (Marvel Productions). The show airs on NBC and in syndication and runs for three seasons (twenty-four episodes). In the second and third seasons, it is paired with *The Incredible Hulk*, an animated series starring the Hulk. Peter Parker is voiced by Daniel Gilvezan.

NOVEMBER 19, 1994

SPIDER-MAN: THE ANIMATED SERIES

Spider-Man: The Animated Series swings to Fox Kids Network. The show is executive produced by Avi Arad and Stan Lee, with John Semper as producer and story editor. Produced by Marvel Studios, TMS Entertainment, and Saban Entertainment, it runs for five seasons (sixty-five episodes). The series finale introduces the Spider-Verse storyline. Christopher Daniel Barnes voices Peter Parker.

OCTOBER 2, 1999

SPIDER-MAN UNLIMITED

Spider-Man Unlimited, Marvel Studios and Saban's cyberpunk show runs for one season (thirteen episodes) on Fox Kids Network. It is executive produced by Avi Arad and Eric S. Rollman. Rino Romano voices Peter Parker.

JULY 11, 2003

SPIDER-MAN: THE NEW ANIMATED SERIES

Spider-Man: The New Animated Series is another one-season wonder, running for thirteen episodes on MTV. The series is produced by Mainframe Entertainment and Sony Pictures Television. Avi Arad, Rick Ungar, Stan Lee, and Morgan Gendel are executive producers. Neil Patrick Harris (Peter Parker), Lisa Loeb (Mary Jane Watson), Ian Ziering (Harry Osborn), and Keith Carradine (J. Jonah Jameson) are part of the voice cast.

MARCH 8, 2008

THE SPECTACULAR SPIDER-MAN

The Spectacular Spider-Man premieres on The CW. Executive produced by Stan Lee, Craig Kyle, and Eric S. Rollman and produced by Adelaide Productions, Culver Entertainment, and Marvel Studios, the show runs for two seasons (twenty-six episodes) on The CW and Disney XD. Josh Keaton voices Peter Parker.

APRIL 1, 2012

ULTIMATE SPIDER-MAN

Ultimate Spider-Man is executive produced by Alan Fine, Dan Buckley, Joe Quesada, Jeph Loeb, Cort Lane, and Stephen Wacker. Produced by Marvel Animation and Film Roman, it premieres on Disney XD and lasts for four seasons (104 episodes). The third season is subtitled *Web-Warriors* and the fourth season is retitled *Ultimate Spider-Man vs. the Sinister 6*. Peter Parker is voiced by Drake Bell.

AUGUST 19, 2017

SPIDER-MAN

Spidey gets a new animated show simply titled *Spider-Man*, produced by Marvel Animation and executive produced by Alan Fine, Dan Buckley, Joe Quesada, Jeph Loeb, Cort Lane, and Eric Radomski. The show airs for three seasons (fifty-eight episodes) on Disney XD and is subtitled *Maximum Venom* for its final season. Peter Parker is voiced by Robbie Daymond.

AUGUST 6, 2021

SPIDEY AND HIS AMAZING FRIENDS

Targeting preschool audiences, *Spidey and His Amazing Friends* lands on Disney Jr. The show is executive produced by Harrison Wilcox, Bart Jennett, and Chris Moreno, and it has run for four seasons (ninety-one episodes), with a fifth greenlit. Marvel Studios Animation and Atomic Cartoons produce the animation. Benjamin Valic voiced the pint-sized version of Peter Parker for two seasons, followed by Alkaio Thiele for seasons three and four.

JANUARY 29, 2025

YOUR FRIENDLY NEIGHBORHOOD SPIDER-MAN

Marvel Studios Animation's *Your Friendly Neighborhood Spider-Man* premieres on Disney+. The show is executive produced by Kevin Feige, Louis D'Esposito, Jeff Trammell, Dana Vasquez-Eberhardt, and Brad Winderbaum. The first season consists of ten episodes, and the show has already been greenlit for two more seasons. Polygon Pictures and CGCG are animation production vendors. Hudson Thames voices Peter Parker.

1 Marketing materials for the series **2** *Your Friendly Neighborhood Spider-Man* (2024) #1–#5. Leonardo Romero

MARVEL ANIMATION
YOUR FRIENDLY NEIGHBORHOOD
SPIDER-MAN
MEET THE NEW HERO ON THE BLOCK
ALL-NEW SERIES
January 29
Disney+

Peter Parker
MARVEL ANIMATION
YOUR FRIENDLY NEIGHBORHOOD
SPIDER-MAN
This is not a test.
ALL-NEW SERIES
January 29
Disney+

MARVEL ANIMATION
YOUR FRIENDLY NEIGHBORHOOD
SPIDER-MAN
WITH GREAT POWER...
...COMES EXTRA HOMEWORK
ALL-NEW SERIES
Now streaming
Disney+

MARVEL ANIMATION
YOUR FRIENDLY NEIGHBORHOOD
SPIDER-MAN
ALL EPISODES
Now streaming
Disney+

1

MARVEL
1
GAGE
GAPSTUR
CAMPBELL
MARVEL ANIMATION
YOUR FRIENDLY NEIGHBORHOOD
SPIDER-MAN
OFFICIAL PREQUEL TO THE UPCOMING DISNEY+ SERIES!

MARVEL
2
GAGE
GAPSTUR
CAMPBELL
MARVEL ANIMATION
YOUR FRIENDLY NEIGHBORHOOD
SPIDER-MAN

MARVEL
3
GAGE
GAPSTUR
CAMPBELL
MARVEL ANIMATION
YOUR FRIENDLY NEIGHBORHOOD
SPIDER-MAN

MARVEL ANIMATION
YOUR FRIENDLY NEIGHBORHOOD
SPIDER-MAN
MARVEL
4
GAGE
CAPSTUR
CAMPBELL

MARVEL ANIMATION
YOUR FRIENDLY NEIGHBORHOOD
SPIDER-MAN
MARVEL
5

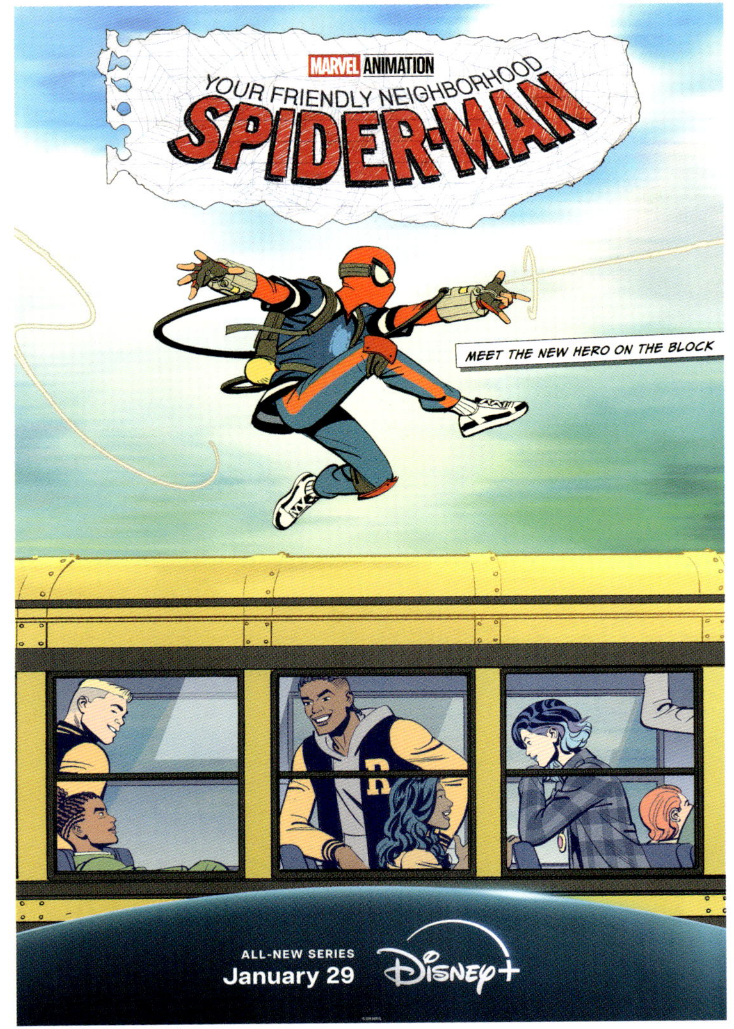

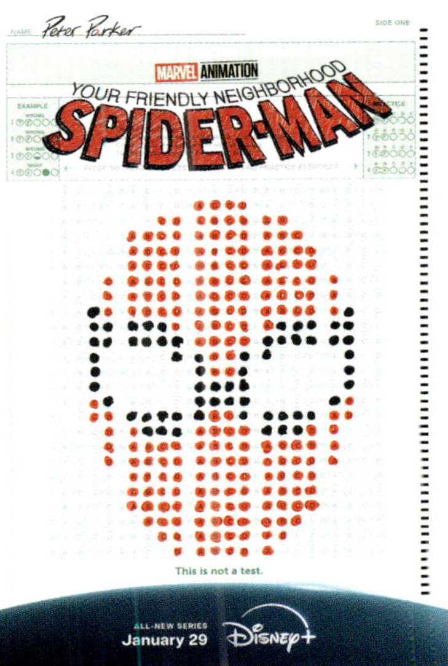

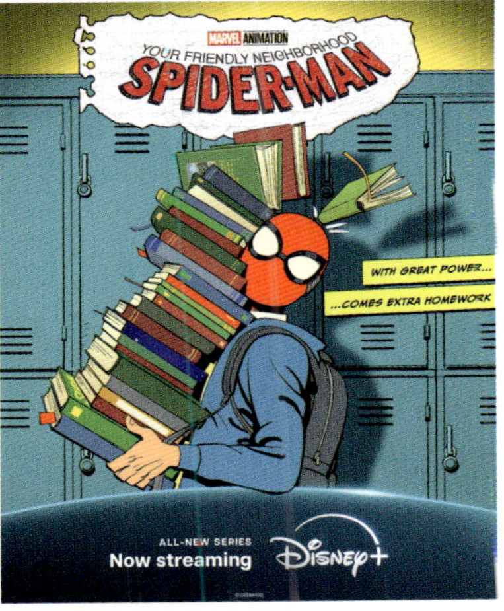

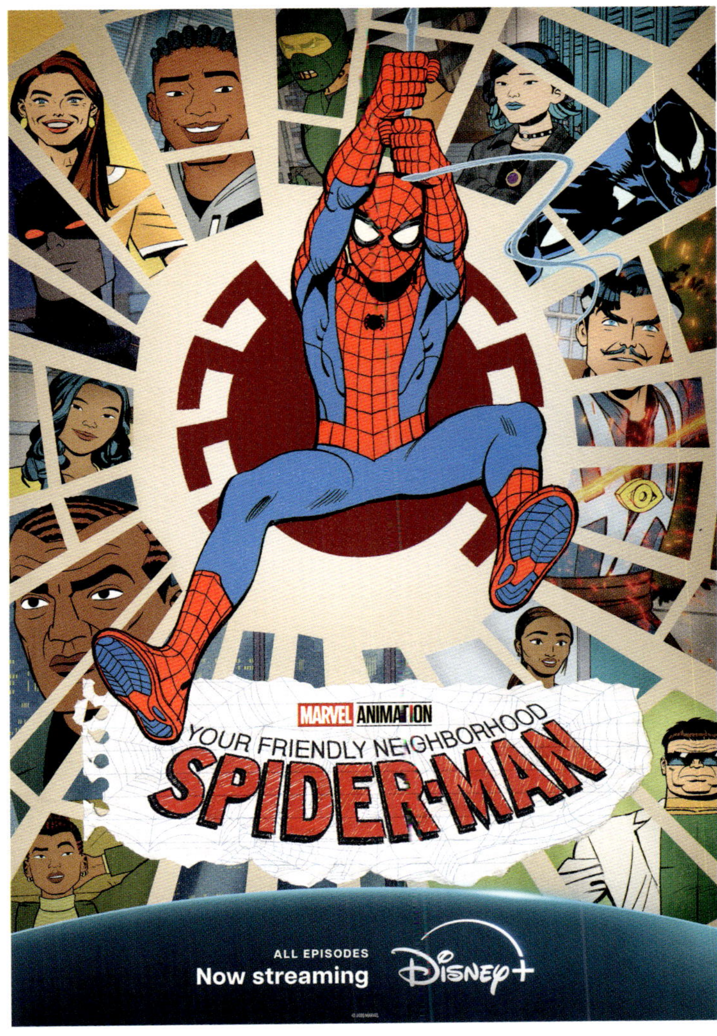

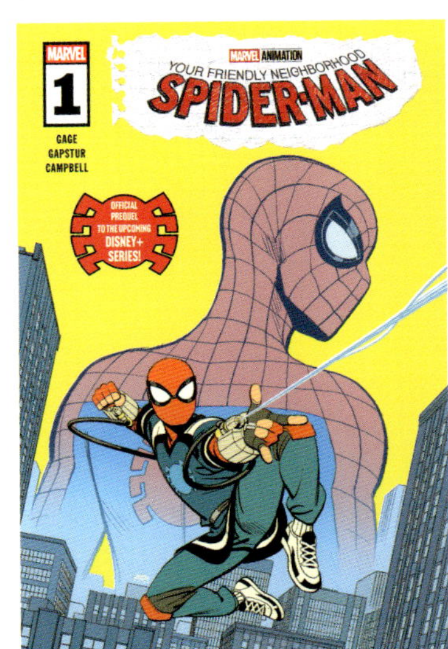

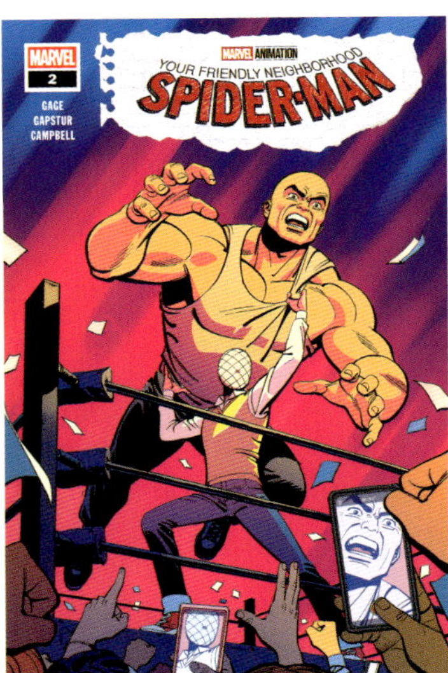

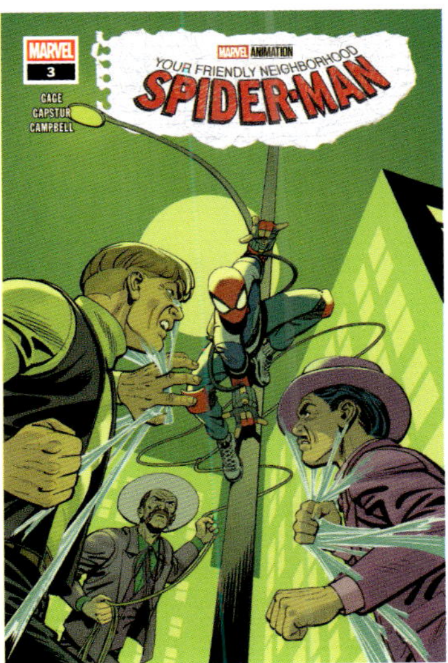

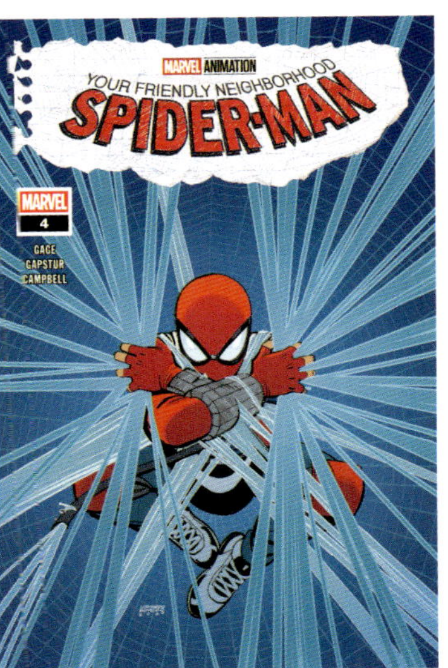

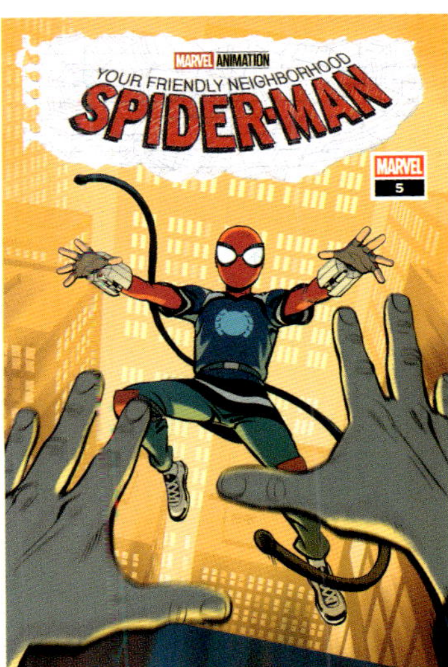

2

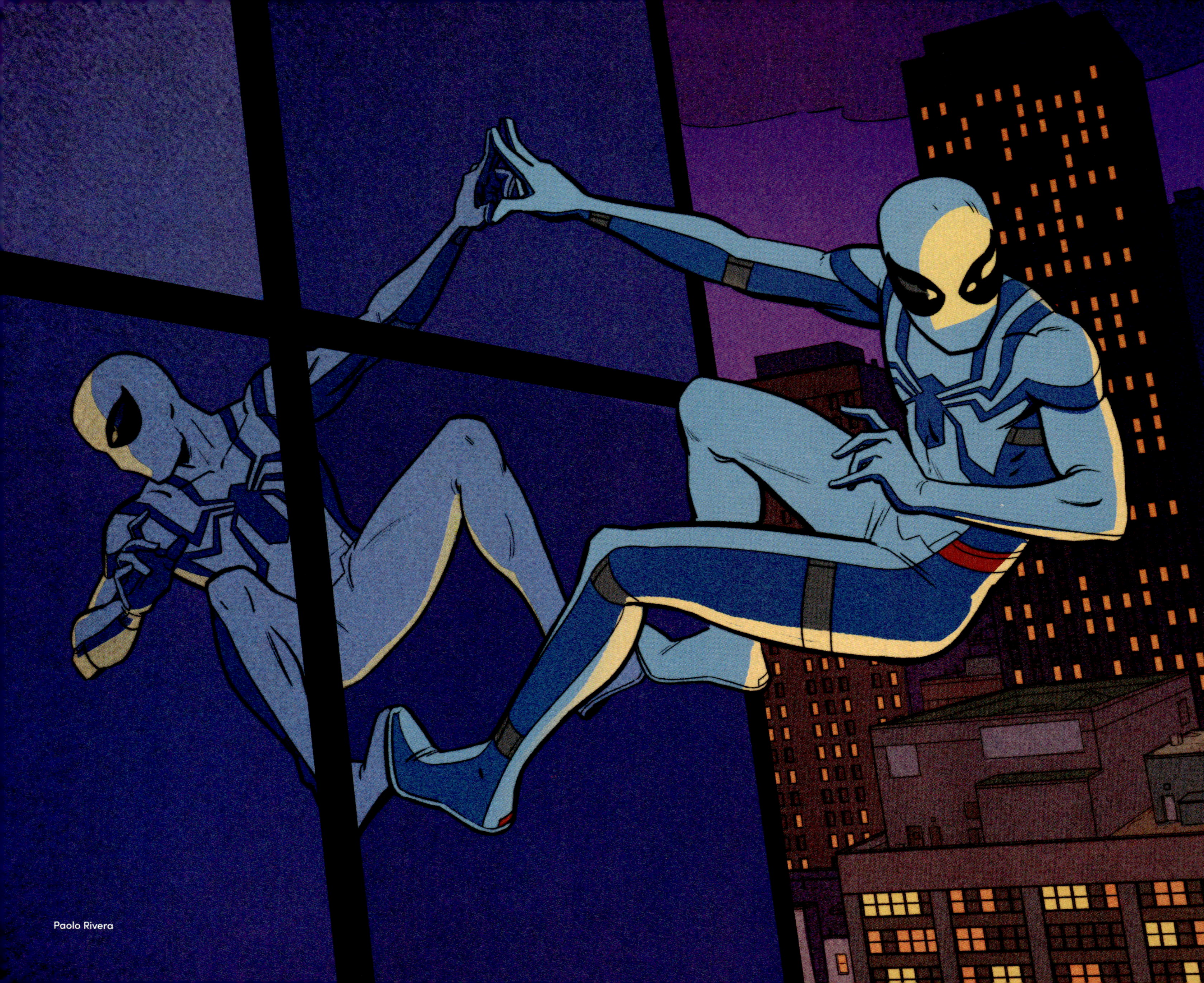

Paolo Rivera

AFTERWORD BY

MEL ZWYER

ONE OF MY EARLIEST MEMORIES was watching the classic '60s *Spider-Man* cartoon series that my father introduced to me. This was accompanied by one of my favorite action figures (Mego Pocket Super Heroes) that I carried everywhere with me. Then came the '80s comics, and *Spider-Man and His Amazing Friends* cartoons, which I watched religiously. And let's not forget those Secret Wars action figures! Spider-Man was always my favorite, and the black suit version was my holy grail figure (that I sadly never attained). I never quite realized that Spider-Man, in some form or another, has always been part of my daily life until it came down to writing this afterword. With every animation project I've worked on, the one constant you'll find is a Spider-Man action figure sitting at my desk to help out with drawing poses. My other cherished Spider-Man memory was drawing him. I loved to draw. And I LOVED drawing Spider-Man.

Flash forward twenty-six years later and here I am, drawing Spider-Man for a living. Man, what a trip. When I came aboard the show, the one visual note that was established was: We're going for a retro, Silver-Age comic book look. Exciting! With so many great Spider-Man projects done in the past, making *Your Friendly Neighborhood Spider-Man* stand out was no easy task. Leading the charge for character designs is the uber talented Leo Romero. His design language was the perfect fit for the look the studio was going for. Very stylized, very old school, very 2D. "These designs are great! But there's no way they'll work in 3D!" I thought. I have never been happier to be proven wrong. The moment I saw the first 3D character-turn, I knew Marvel Animation had pulled off the impossible.

The next part of the puzzle was fitting these characters into a comic book environment. That job went to our very talented Production Designer Michael Yamada and our animation partners (Polygon Pictures Inc. in Tokyo and CGCG in Taipei). Figuring this out was an even tougher nut to crack since everything in our world had to have an outline (just like in the comic books). How do we fit characters with outlines into a world where everything has an outline and not lose them into the backgrounds? With a ton of R&D and good old trial and error. That's how. It took a lot of tests and fine-tuning before we found the right balance of line thickness, detail drop-out, and textures where our characters can thrive in a "line-forward" environment.

Great! With the look nailed down, it was time to start the show! As Co-Executive Producer/Supervising Director for this show, I could not have asked for a better Showrunner/Executive Producer than the great Jeff Trammell. Anyone who works in the industry knows that when you get paired up with someone you've never worked with before, it's always a crapshoot. I've seen productions fail and crumble due to the incompatibility of its leaders. This was the opposite. Jeff and I are almost always on the same wavelength, and that helped tremendously when it came to hiring the rest of the crew. Every crew member on this show shares one common trait: a love for Spider-Man that truly shows with each episode being completed. It was clear from the earliest drafts of the scripts all the way down to the final storyboard animatic. Every crew member poured so much love into this project. This show has been truly blessed with the greatest crew that I have ever worked with, and all this is thanks to our amazing Producer, Tim Pauer.

I would be remiss if I didn't take this chance to thank the wonderful leaders at Marvel Studios for trusting us with the handling of (what many consider to be the greatest IP in the world) Spider-Man. Under the guidance of Dana Vasquez-Eberhardt (VP of Marvel Animation) and Brad Winderbaum (Head of Marvel Television and Marvel Animation), *Your Friendly Neighborhood Spider-Man* wouldn't be nearly as strong as it is today. I have learned so much from them as a director here at Marvel. I also want to thank Laura Barbara and Danielle Costa for their constant support of our show. A huge shout-out to Ryan Meinerding and Joshua Shaw for their input on Spider-Man's visual language. It's truly an honor to have some of the live-action MCU artists help out on our animated series.

MEL ZWYER,
Co-Executive Producer/Supervising Director

MARVEL PUBLISHING

VP, PRODUCTION AND SPECIAL PROJECTS Jeff Youngquist
EDITOR, SPECIAL PROJECTS Sarah Singer
MANAGER, LICENSED PUBLISHING Jeremy West
VP, BUSINESS DEVELOPMENT AND LICENSED PUBLISHING Sven Larsen
VP, COMIC SALES AND CONTENT PLANNING David Gabriel
EDITOR IN CHIEF C. B. Cebulski

ABRAMS BOOKS

EDITOR Connor Leonard
DESIGNER Liam Flanagan
MANAGING EDITOR Nate Lee
PRODUCTION MANAGER Katie Gaffney

A Library of Congress Control Number has been applied for

ISBN: 978-1-4197-8775-1

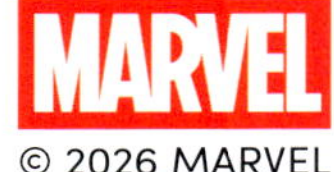

Published in 2026 by Abrams, an imprint of ABRAMS.

Printed and bound in China
10 9 8 7 6 5 4 3 2 1

Abrams books are available at special discounts when purchased in quantity for premiums and promotions as well as fundraising or educational use. Special editions can also be created to specification. For details, contact specialsales@abramsbooks.com or the address below.

Abrams® is a registered trademark of Harry N. Abrams, Inc.

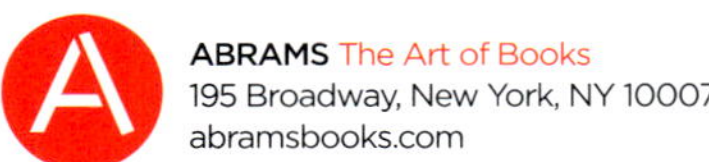

ABRAMS The Art of Books
195 Broadway, New York, NY 10007
abramsbooks.com

ABRAMS is represented in the UK and Europe by Abrams & Chronicle Books, 22-24 Ely Place, London EC1N 6TE and Média-Participations, 57 rue Gaston Tessier, 75166 Paris, France.

MARVEL STUDIOS

PRESIDENT Kevin Feige
CO-PRESIDENT Louis D'Esposito
HEAD OF TELEVISION, STREAMING & ANIMATION Brad Winderbaum
HEAD OF VISUAL DEVELOPMENT Ryan Meinerding
EXECUTIVE, PRODUCTION & DEVELOPMENT Dana Vasquez-Eberhardt
VISUAL DEVELOPMENT SUPERVISOR Bill Perkins
MANAGER, VISUAL DEVELOPMENT Samantha Ballard
CHARACTER DESIGN SUPERVISOR Joshua James Shaw
MANAGERS, PRODUCTION & DEVELOPMENT Alex Scharf & Lynsey Brown
FRANCHISE STORY MANAGER Jacqueline Ryan-Rudolph
FRANCHISE STORY COORDINATOR Kandon Haynes
ASSOCIATE PRINCIPAL COUNSEL Nigel Goodwin & Danny Sturm
SENIOR PARALEGAL Matthew Gilbert
DIRECTOR, CLEARANCES Erika Denton
MANAGER, CLEARANCES Jennifer Wojnar
DIRECTOR CREDITS & ADMINISTRATION Jeff Willis
MANAGER, CREDITS Jennifer Giandalone
MANAGER, DIGITAL ASSETS Eli Holmes
DIGITAL ASSET COORDINATORS Jacinda Dolwick & Aly Girling

EXECUTIVE PRODUCER/HEAD WRITER Jeff Trammell
CO-EXECUTIVE PRODUCER/SUPERVISING DIRECTOR Mel Zwyer
PRODUCER Tim Pauer
LEAD CHARACTER DESIGNER Leonardo Romero
CHARACTER DESIGNERS Joneale Emmanuel, Dan Holland, Mauricio Leone, Chris Samnee, Paolo Rivera, and Ethan Young
PRODUCTION DESIGNER Michael Yamada
ART DIRECTOR Sylvia Liu
EPISODIC DIRECTORS Liza Singer, Stu Livingston
ANIMATION SUPERVISOR Rick Glenn
VISUAL DEVELOPMENT ARTISTS Kal Athannassov, Ryan Lang, Adam Liepins, Mel Milton, Julen Urrutia Perez, Joey Vazquez
STORYBOARD ARTISTS Chris Pianka, Lydia Anslow, Meg Syverud, Erwin Osias, Olga Ulanova, Steve Walker, Elsa Garagarza, Jessica Traugott, Wade Turner, Micah Lewis, Cole Harrington, Li Cree, Armando Atencio
ART DEPARTMENT ARTISTS Beverly Arce, Victor Calleja, Elizabeth Chee, W. Scott Forbes, Nic Gregory, Monica Grue, Corwin Herse-Woo, Christine Jung, Kelsey Roland, Youa Vang, Tuan Vo, Junyi Wu
3D LAYOUT SUPERVISOR Huan Phan
3D ARTISTS Jennifer Van Horn, Melissa Murphy, Luis Vega Hernandez, Kyle Lopez, Michelle Del Rosario, Amy Vatanakul, Long-Hai Pham, Ken Lee
3D MODEL LEAD Isaac Gelman
3D MODELERS Habini Bae, Paul Deasy, Cole Decker, Joe Dela Torre, Craig Dowsett, Alexandria Federico, Emmanuel Marenco, Mariano Tazzioli, Daniel Zeni

SPECIAL THANKS TO Kristy Amornkul, Sarah Beers, Craig Elliot, Emily Matsunami, Randy McGowan, Julio Palacol, Bryan Parker, Lauren Perez, Ryan Potter, Ariel Shasteen, Angela Shaw, Amit Kumar, Kerynne Tejada, and John Terranova.

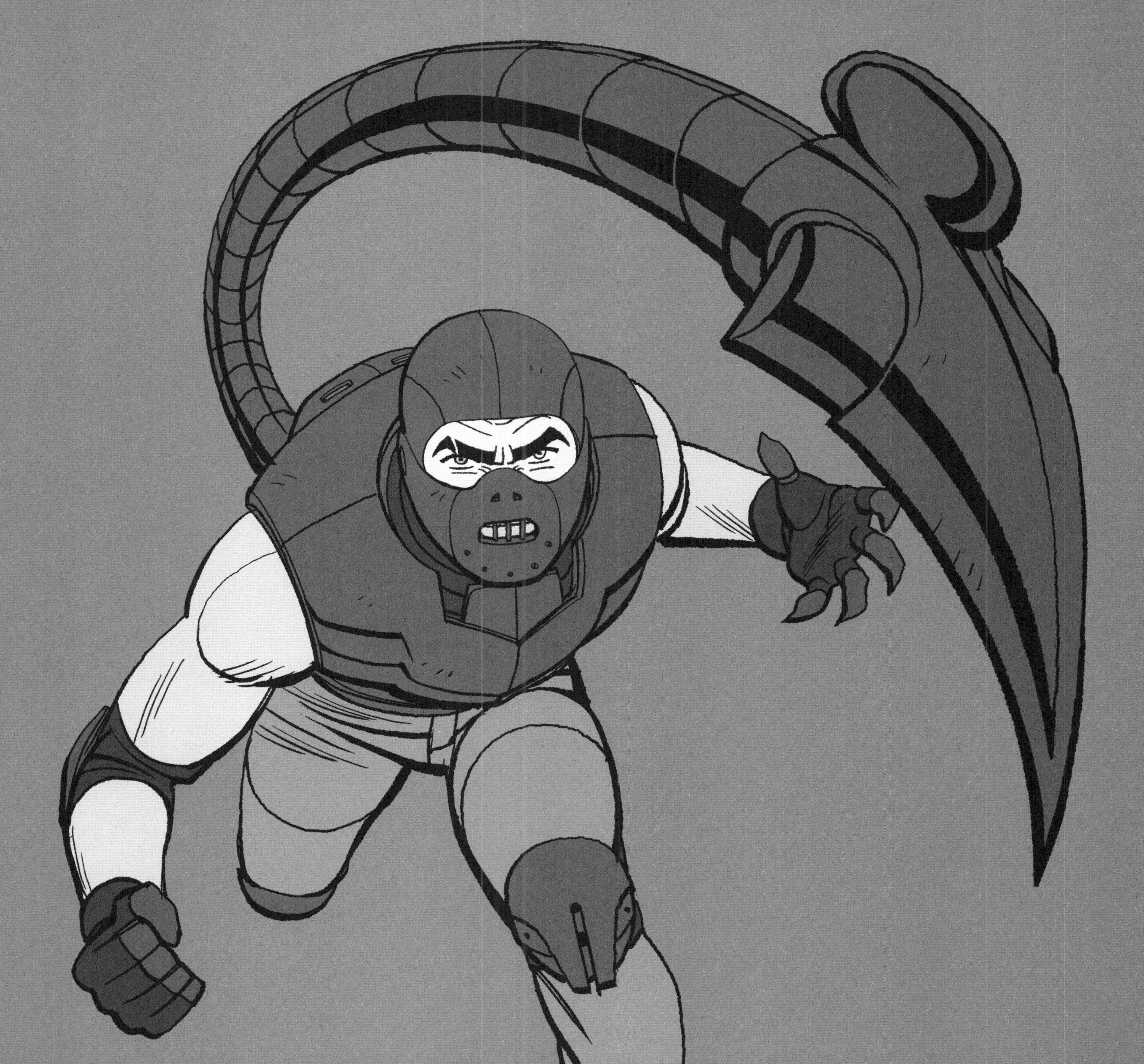

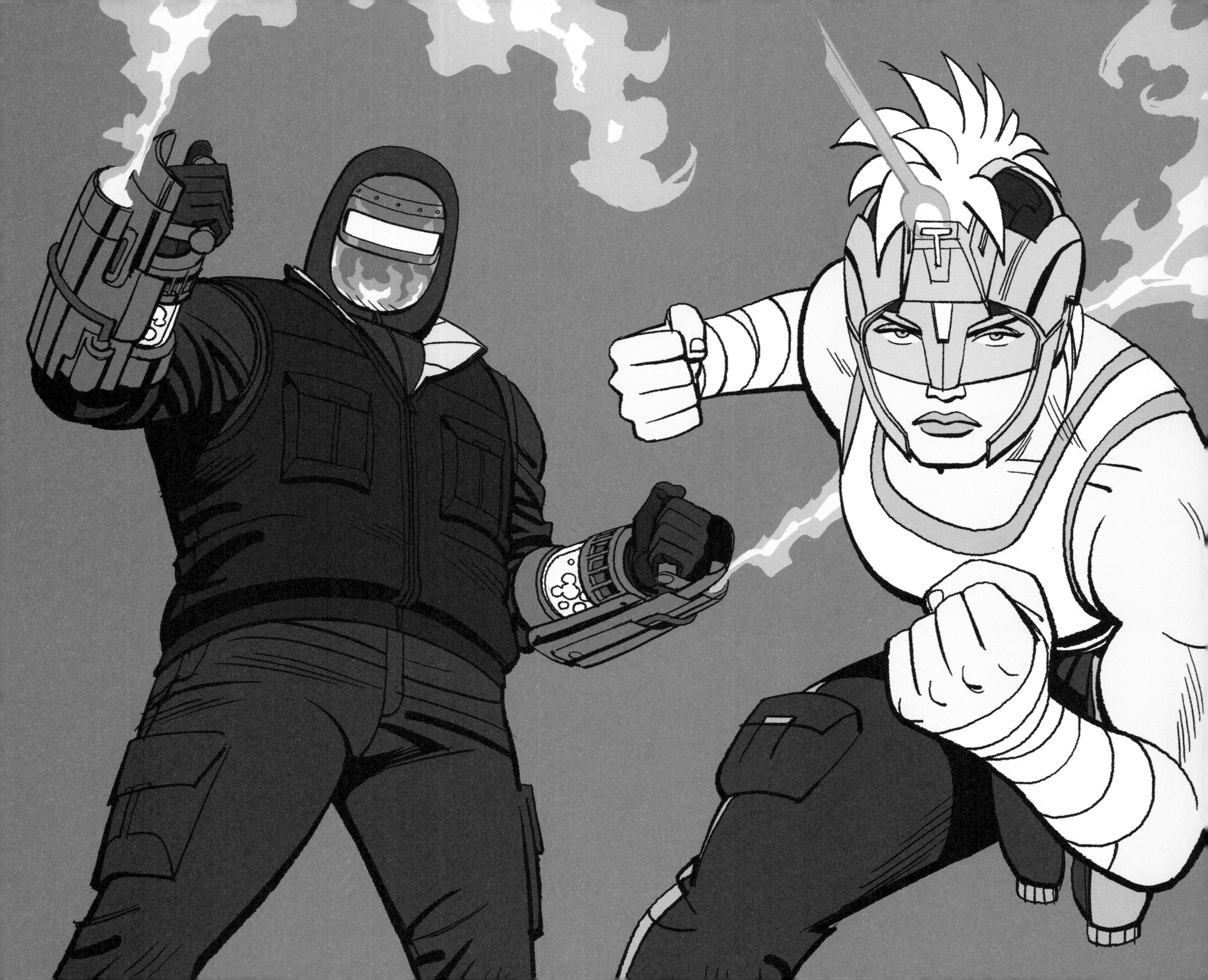